TCP/IP Clearly Explained

FOURTH EDITION

Pete Loshin
Internet-Standard.com

MORGAN KAUFMANN PUBLISHERS

AN IMPRINT OF ELSEVIER SCIENCE

AMSTERDAM BOSTON LONDON NEW YORK OXFORD
PARIS SAN DIEGO SAN FRANCISCO SINGAPORE
SYDNEY TOKYO

Senior Editor	*Rick Adams*
Publishing Services Manager	*Diane Grossman*
Developmental Editor	*Karyn Johnson*
Project Manager	*Nancy Zachor*
Cover Design Management	*Elisabeth Beller*
Cover Designer	*Laurie Anderson*
Cover Image	*Digital Vision/Getty Images*
Composition	*Cepha Imaging PVT LTD*
Text Design	*Graphic World*
Copyeditor	*Laura Healy*
Proofreader	*Graphic World*
Indexer	*Edwin Durbin*
Printer	*The Maple-Vail Manufacturing Group*

Morgan Kaufmann Publishers
an imprint of Elsevier Science
340 Pine Street, Sixth Floor
San Francisco, California 94104-3205
www.mkp.com

Copyright 2003, Elsevier Science (USA)
All rights reserved.
Printed in the United States of America

07 06 05 04 03   5 4 3 2 1

Library of Congress Control Number: 2002113772
ISBN: 1-55860-782-X

This book is printed on acid-free paper. ∞

Contents

0.1

Preface

When I began writing the first edition in 1994, there were only a handful of books about TCP/IP networking. Most of those were largely inaccessible to readers with no formal computer science background. The objective then was to provide such a book to anyone who needed or wanted to understand TCP/IP, but needed it in plain language.

The objective for this edition is roughly the same, but as of early 2002, there were hundreds of books written about TCP/IP networking, with many hundreds (if not thousands) more that include one or more chapters about TCP/IP.

Most of those books follow roughly the same blueprint for explaining how TCP/IP works. Virtually every one of these books and chapters start out by pointing to research funded in the 1960s by the US Department of Defense as the birthplace of the internet and its TCP/IP protocol suite. (A *protocol* is a set of rules that define how data is communicated. We'll define the term in much greater detail in Part One.) Those books introduce the OSI 7-layer protocol stack model and the Internet 4-layer protocol stack model with more or less detailed definitions of what the different layers represent.

Then, the authors introduce the various TCP/IP protocols in order: some, from lower layers to higher; others, from higher to lower.

Virtually every book and chapter about TCP/IP networking covers IP addressing, basics of IP headers, the UDP and TCP transport layer protocols, internet application protocols such as HTTP and FTP, IP routing, and the Domain Name System (DNS). Other topics typically covered include multicast, SNMP, IPv6, SSL, IPsec, and various application protocols.

Longer books cover more protocols, and may cover topics that are not strictly speaking part of IP networking: they may be obsolete (IP network classes and Privacy Enhanced Mail), or peripherally related (digital commerce, system administration, HTML). Additional length can be garnered by including lists of RFC numbers and titles, lists of well-known ports, glossaries, exhaustive lists of URLs and other Internet resources, and much more filler.

This edition of *TCP/IP Clearly Explained* has been substantially updated to better introduce the topic of TCP/IP networking to a broad audience. Rather than attempt to be exhaustive in describing (in detail) as many protocols as possible, this edition first introduces the fundamental concepts of TCP/IP internetworking and then shows how the TCP/IP protocols build on these concepts to provide a global internet.

The changes are significant: many topics that may have been useful five years ago have been dropped, while new topics have been added. These changes include:

- A top-down approach to the TCP/IP protocol stack, starting with application protocols and working our way down the protocol stack. This approach provides a more accessible path to understanding, starting as it does from applications most readers will be familiar with and then moving to the underlying protocols that make those applications possible.
- Addition of key new protocols, including the Stream Control Transmission Protocol (SCTP), the Blocks architecture for application protocols, and the Transport Layer Security (TLS) protocol.
- An overview to the "life" of an internet packet. In Chapter 7, "Meet Joe's Packets", before covering the details of any

protocols we follow the path of TCP/IP packets as they move
through systems and networks.

This book explains in clear language the core protocols of TCP/IP and how
they make the global internet possible. And if many of the terms used in
the preceding paragraphs are unfamiliar, rest assured they will be defined
and explained throughout this book.

0.2

Audience

The first edition of this book was intended as a guidebook to anyone who needed to understand how TCP/IP works. And this edition is also intended as a guidebook to anyone who needs to understand how TCP/IP works. That is not to say that we are targeting the same audience now that was being targeted in 1994. Back then, almost any task—even the most trivial, such as doing file transfers or configuring a PC to connect to an IP network—could be done more easily with an understanding of the underlying protocols. Likewise, marketing and sales personnel in many high-tech firms needed to understand IP to understand how their own products worked. Network managers, technical support staff, power users who provided their own support, programmers and software developers and analysts, all had to get themselves up and running on IP quickly.

Certainly today there are many people in the same positions who still need to learn more about TCP/IP; however, most have already learned it or have learned to fake it. By far, the greatest number of people who need to understand IP networking today are students—whether or not they are studying full-time in high school or college, or they are studying part-time at night, studying in an elementary or middle school, or even studying on their own.

Our goal with this edition is to help the reader understand TCP/IP networking on a fundamental level. Simply knowing what the protocols do, or how to use an internet application, is not enough. When you understand why the protocols do what they do, and how applications can be extended, and how changes in the environment necessitate changes in the protocols, then you will understand TCP/IP networking.

0.3

Acknowledgments

Many people were involved in this and all the previous editions of this book. These include Karyn Johnson, Rick Adams, Ken Morton, Gabrielle Billeter, and many others over the years. Many readers have been kind enough to point out areas for improvement in previous editions.

If you have any questions or comments about this edition, please let me know at pete@loshin.com; your input is always invaluable.

. . .

Many thanks must go to the expert reviewers who were kind enough to look over the last edition and suggest improvements, including Bill Higgins, Unisoft; Bob Natale, ACE*COMM; Brent Baccala; Aaron Silverman, KBC Financial Products; Peter Samuelson, CAD/CAM Lab, Wichita State University; Tony Metke, Motorola; David Valiquette, Network Manager, Karl Storz Endovision; Marc Whinery, USA Sports; Thomas Nadeau, Cisco.

Many more thanks to Richard Nieporent, Ph.D., Senior Principal Engineer for the MITRE Corporation and senior adjunct faculty member in the Johns Hopkins University part-time graduate program in computer science, and Barry Margolin, Genuity, Inc., who generously reviewed the entire manuscript of this edition, as well as Chris Crane, Memorial University of Newfoundland; Timothy Walker and Bob Natale, ACE*COMM; who also offered their expertise during the technical review process.

Finally, thanks to the love of my life and soulmate, Lisa, and our children, Jacy and Zoom, for their support and indulgence during the writing of this book.

Part One

**Concepts and Fundamentals
of Networking**

Part Goals

- Understand basic networking and internetworking concepts
- Learn difference between packet-switched and circuit-based networks
- Understand what network protocols are and how they work
- Introduce the basic components of the internet and its protocols

1

Introduction: What is This Book About?

If you want to talk the TCP/IP talk, you need to know which words to say and what they mean. TCP/IP internetworking is neither rocket science nor brain surgery, but networking professionals have their own extensive and sometimes confusing language. Most of this book is devoted to teaching the reader how to speak the TCP/IP dialect of network-speak. It's not enough to know that TCP/IP is a compound acronym for "Transmission Control Protocol/Internet Protocol"; you've got to understand what makes TCP different from other transport layer protocol and how IP addresses are parsed for packet delivery.

Building on a general foundation, this book provides a primer for understanding the language of networking by understanding the specifics of TCP/IP.

Most discussions of internetworking sooner or later get around to comparing it to a postal delivery system. We'll do it right now:

When you send a letter, your envelope goes into a mail slot or box, is picked up by a postal worker, dumped into the system, and ultimately delivered by a letter carrier (after considerable sorting, moving, packaging, and handling). The postal worker who collects the mail from mailboxes needs to know nothing about where the mail came from or where the mail is destined, ultimately. He or she just collects mail from certain boxes at certain times, puts it in a vehicle, and delivers it to a local postal facility. Then, someone else takes over.

final ←

TCP/IP internetworks move data in much the same way the post is moved: network data moves from one point to another, is processed in some way by intermediate systems (if necessary) and moves around the network one step at a time.

The comparison between networking—the delivery of digital messages and packages—and postal service—the delivery of physical messages and packages— is appropriate for many reasons. The one that I'd like to point out first is that just as no part of the process of getting a letter from your hand to the hand of the addressee is terribly difficult or complex, so too, none of the fundamental principles of TCP/IP networking are beyond the grasp of the intelligent and interested reader.

The brilliance of the two—TCP/IP internetworking and mail delivery organizations—derives from each system's ability to deliver packages (digital or physical) from any point on the network to any other point on the network, with excellent reliability, efficiency, and speed.

1.1   Graphical Conventions Used in this Book

Diagrams always help understanding whenever networks and internetworks are being discussed. Network diagrams, particularly in this book, have their own language and conventions. Detailed definitions of most terms used in this section are provided in Part I, and Figure 1–1 illustrates what they look like. Here are the important terms to keep in mind throughout this text:

Cloud: The cloud represents some kind of system with its insides hidden from view. There may be systems to which we connect (or want

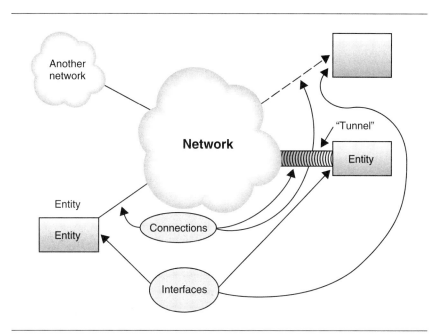

Figure 1–1: **Graphical conventions used to illustrate networks.**

to connect) inside the system, or those systems may actually be on the other side of the cloud. It doesn't matter, because we can know only what's going on outside the cloud. What is a blank cloud in one diagram may be represented in detail in another diagram; a large network cloud may contain within it other, smaller, networks represented as smaller clouds.

Connections: Connections between network entities are usually linked by simple black lines. The black line indicates there is some direct connection, even if there is no physical link (e.g., in wireless networks). In some cases, an entity may be connected indirectly but transparently through one or more intermediate systems to another entity. To observers at either of the endpoint entities, the connection appears to be direct, even though intermediate systems help enable the connection. In those cases, the direct links are shown as solid black lines while the indirect link (the one that endpoint observers view as correct) is represented with a dotted black line.

Entities: A network entity is usually represented as a labeled box. An entity ("a thing that does some function") can be a piece of single-purpose hardware or it can be a program running on a network node, in parallel with other programs, that does something. In this book, I've attempted to include in all diagrams descriptive labels on network entity boxes.

Interfaces: A node's network interface is usually implicit in a diagram unless the interface itself has some relevance. For example, a node may have more than one interface to the same network, or interfaces to more than one network (such nodes are known as "multi-homed hosts"). In cases where network interfaces are relevant, they are labeled with appropriate network addresses.

1.2 Notes on Style

As terms enter a language, they change, particularly words that begin life as proper names or as compound words. Consider *scuba*: originally an acronym (Self-Contained Underwater Breathing Apparatus), it is now properly spelled in lowercase characters.

In this book, I will be using styles for certain terms that may not yet (as of early 2002) be universally accepted but are likely to gain currency quite soon. The terms and justifications for the newer usages are as follows:

- *internet* rather than *Internet*: The addition of the terms *intranet* and *extranet* make the use of *internet* as a synonym for *internetwork* redundant. That means the word *internet* can unambiguously refer to the global network of networks formerly known as *The Internet*.
- *mail* rather than *electronic mail*, *e-mail*, or *email*: Specifications for internet mail use the term *mail* rather than any form of *electronic mail*; differentiating digitally delivered mail from physically delivered mail will be done using the back-formations *postal mail* or *snail mail*.
- *web* rather than *Web* or *World Wide Web*: The word *web* has long been used as an adjective (web server, web browser, web site, web page) as well as a noun. Again, in most contexts there is little or no ambiguity about which web is intended, so there is

no need to use a proper noun (*Web*) when a common one (*web*) will do.

These usages tend to clarify rather than confuse networking discusssions. Furthermore, they better reflect common usage, which tends to drive formal style sooner or later. Better to get used to it now than have to change everything later.

1.3   Overview

The first part of this book, Concepts and Fundamentals of Networking, provides the reader with a basic vocabulary of networking and introduces the fundamental concepts of networking and internetworking upon which the rest of the book is built.

Part II, Internet Applications, examines how people and other entities interact with each other across a network transport (in this case, the internet). By beginning at the top of the stack, looking at how applications interact with each other over the internet, we can see clearly how systems use networks to exchange information. Applications offer concrete examples of the types of data exchanged over networks, and chapters in this section provide an overview to the world of internet applications (Chapter 6), and an overview to the way application data flows through networks as well as up and down protocol stacks (Chapter 7). Specific protocols are examined in-depth, including the Domain Name System (Chapter 8), internet mail (Chapter 9), Telnet (Chapter 10), File Transfer Protocol (Chapter 11), and the world wide web protocols (Chapter 12). A third wave of new and still-developing internet applications is previewed (Chapter 13), and a brief discussion of how internet applications are evolving is presented (Chapter 14).

Part III, The Transport Layer, examines the protocols that mediate communication between processes. This is where internetworking can be said to begin, as each of these protocols treats the data it transports as a commodity—mere bits to be packaged and transmitted. Opening with a look at how and why processes would communicate (Chapter 15), other chapters examine the two original transport protocols, User Datagram Protocol (Chapter 16) and Transmission Control Protocol (Chapter 17). This section closes with a look at the newest internet transport protocol, the

Stream Control Transmission Protocol (SCTP) and other future transport protocols (Chapter 18).

Part IV, The Internet Layer and Below, digs into the processes by which different computers, with different operating systems, hardware architectures, different local area network mechanisms, all around the world, interoperate seamlessly. Starting with a description of the Internet Protocol (Chapter 19), other topics covered in this section include the Internet Control Message Protocol (ICMP) covered in Chapter 20, the interface between LAN and internet (Chapter 21), internet routing (Chapters 22 and 23), and IP multicast (Chapter 24).

Part V, Internet Infrastructure and Special Applications, addresses some of the pressing issues that continue to challenge the growth of the internet, including Quality of Service (Chapter 25), IP security (Chapter 26), and the next generation of IP (Chapter 27).

As demonstrated in Part VI, Practical Internetworking, there are practical applications of all the material in this book—as well as issues that arise from the implementation and administration of networks based on IP protocols. The first chapter in this section discusses how implementations of one application, FTP, evolved over the years (Chapter 28). Other topics covered include planning an IP network (Chapter 29), and a general discusssion of security (Chapter 30). The last chapter examines the Simple Network Management Protocol (SNMP), how it works, and why it is still relevant two decades after it was created.

1.3.1 APPENDICES

Appendices include information that is particularly relevant, but doesn't always fit into the rest of the book. Appendices included with this volume include:

- Appendix A: Internet and Standards Organizations. A summary of key organizations and groups that are involved in the process of defining and maintaining networking protocols
- Appendix B: Protocol Summaries. This appendix includes quick introductions to various internet protocols that have not been discussed at length in this text, including the basic header structures and protocol command summaries.

2

A Language of Networking

What is TCP/IP? What does "internet" really mean? What about "network" or "node" or "host" or "client" or "server"? You may know exactly what they mean, or perhaps you have a general understanding or even just a vague feeling about what those terms mean.

Everyone knows, viscerally, what a network is: a vague something that connects other, possibly many other, somethings by allowing those some-things to somehow exchange information with each other. A *computer network* can be defined more precisely as consisting of some number of systems that can transmit and receive data to and from each other.

Precision is important, as is accuracy when discussing networking terms. Precision is a matter of granularity. The value of 45 microns is a precise measurement. Accuracy is a measure of closeness to "truth." While precise, 45 microns is an inaccurate measure of the distance from London to Lima.

The previous paragraph uses several terms that could be better defined: network, computer network, computer, systems, transmit, receive, data. A *computer network* is easily handled: a network that links computers.

Not all networks link computers: there are telecommunications networks linking phones, social networks linking people, and just plain networks that link entities.

This may be obvious, but some of the basic assumptions we make about terms such as "network" do not always hold. The rest of this chapter is devoted to building definitions of networking and internetworking terms and concepts.

When defining network terms, a balance between accuracy and accessibility must be struck. Although it may be easier to think of a network node as being the same as thing as a network client, that characterization may be any of several things:

- Perfectly apt and appropriate
- Completely and dangerously wrong
- Slightly misleading
- Completely misleading but completely irrelevant

Knowing the terminology and understanding the nuances of the terminology offers one important avenue to understanding a topic. The language of networking can be difficult for the unitiated to understand, and for good reason. Internetworking terms have been created and used by many different individuals, from computer scientists, software engineers, hardware engineers, cyberneticists, physicians, historians, physicists, astronomers, mathematicians, marketing executives, business managers, personnel managers, linguists, programmers, and many others. As a result, words that seem logical to a mathematician may make less sense to a business manager; new terms often carry either too much or too little excess baggage of existing meaning.

Making matters more confusing, todays' internet derives from over 30 years of academic research as well as decades of corporate research, development, implementation and deployment of proprietary as well as standards-compliant systems, software, and networks. (*Standards-compliant* means conforming to a set of standards that allow the product to interoperate with products produced by other vendors. Until the mid-1980s, most vendors sold network applications products that would interoperate only with other products supporting the same proprietary systems.)

As a result, the same terms or phrases often meant different things depending upon who uttered them and what his or her affiliation was.

Throw in a brand of humor, heavily leavened with puns and other wordplay, shared by many of the people involved in creating (and naming) network technology, and network terms range from crystal-clear to confusing to whimsical, and just about everything in between.

This chapter introduces key terms, defining them generally as they apply to networking, as well as (where appropriate) defining them as they are used within the context of the internet. It would be nice to have a well-defined vocabulary of networking terms, with only one definition for each term, and with all terms and definitions universally accepted. Unfortunately, the languages of computing and networking can be precise and vague—at the same time. It helps to maintain a flexible state of mind and to use the context of the discussion of any new term to help understand its meaning.

One important set of standards applies to operating systems. *POSIX* is a standard that is usually associated with operating systems (OSes) like those based on some flavor of UNIX, Berkeley Software Distribution (BSD), or Linux. However, not all Linux distributions are necessarily POSIX-compliant, while Windows (or other OSes) not usually thought of as UNIX-like may be POSIX-compliant. UNIX is a registered trademark, and thus it is inappropriate to use the term to refer to the family of OSes that includes NetBSD, FreeBSD, BSDI, Linux, and others that are modeled on or work similarly to UNIX in some way. Instead, we'll use the term **nix* to indicate the family of operating systems that includes all commercial varieties of UNIX, commercial and open-source versions of BSD, Linux, and any other OS that is able to compile and run programs intended for UNIX and so on.

2.1 Network Terms

The internet is a network; so is a desktop Personal Computer (PC) connected directly to a laptop. Clearly, there are significant differences among different types of network. An internet is a network of networks. This section presents a vocabulary for talking about all types of network.

Networked systems are often considered to be connected with the implication of a physical connection, such as is provided by a cable linking systems together. The recent surge of deployed technologies for wireless voice and data networking shows that sharing a network requires only that systems share a mechanism by which they can communicate.

For the moment, we can assume that those systems use the same communication channel (whatever that is) and the same sets of rules (whatever
those are) to govern their transmissions and receptions. However, in any
particular network, we can also assume that there is only one channel and
one set of rules governing that channel. There will also be limits to how
much data can be transmitted on the channel and how many systems can
communicate through the same channel.

Before going further, some definitions are in order:

Entity: Some "thing" that does some "thing." Depending on context, an
entity can be a computer, or a person, or a program, or a device, or a
process. Or, perhaps something else. "Entity" may refer to something
that is about to be introduced.

System: Any entity with observable and reproduceable behaviors. Also
sometimes called a *black box*, a system may be a piece of hardware or a
process running on a piece of hardware. A system accepts inputs and
produces outputs; whatever happens inside (in particular, how those
inputs are processed to produce the outputs) is largely irrelevant as
long as the system behaves consistently. Inside a system may be one
or more other systems; discussing the outer system does not require
any knowledge of the internal systems.

Network: Some set of systems that share a common communication
medium (see below). Simply sharing the medium is not enough,
however, as the networked systems must share some set of rules
that govern communication across that medium, called *protocols*.
A network is also a system.

Protocol: A set of rules that define how systems interact.

Internet: A network of networks. Which makes it a network as well. An
internet may use a single physical medium, or may span different
physical media by using a virtual medium.

Media/medium: The physical thing(s) over or through which network signals are carried. In some cases, a network can be confidently seen
as bounded by its medium, as, for example, insulated metal wires
used for coaxial or twisted pair connections. These cables, plus any
required network devices, and attached systems define the full extent

of the network itself. Networks always require some kind of infra-structure to operate: a wireless network may depend on a network of signal repeaters; cabled networks on their connecting cables as well as (often) on systems called *hubs* or *switches* through which the cables can be connected.

A specific instance of a thing that carries signals is usually called the *medium*. For example, a cable carrying signals can be said to be the medium over which the signal is carried; likewise, a specific net-work can be said to use Ethernet as its medium. As may be gleaned from the context, Ethernet refers to a type of network. We will return to Ethernet throughout this book; it is the dominant form of LAN medium in business as well as many home settings.

When referring to more than one thing that carries signals, the term *media* is usually preferred. Thus, coaxial cable, unshielded twisted pair cable, and wireless are all network media. But at the same time, all the things that carry Ethernet signals in a network can also be referred to as the network media, including cabling, network interfaces, hubs, switches, and any other physical things that carry signals.

Interface: The point at which two entities make contact.

Node: Any entity connected to a network and capable of both creating and using network data.

Host: Any node that supports users and runs application software. Host and node are often used interchangeably (usually with no ill effect), but the two are distinct types of entity.

Client: A network entity that requests some network service from a server.

Server: A network entity that fulfills requests from clients.

LAN: Local Area Network; usually a network that connects nodes across a small distance using direct physical mechanisms with minimal use of infrastructure devices such as *routers* or *switches* to relay data. Most often the network a person uses to communicate with a sys-tem in the same room, floor, or building. Routers and switches are network devices that accept network traffic for proper delivery or forwarding. We will discuss these devices, especially routers, throughout the book.

WAN: Wide Area Network; usually a network that connects nodes across great distances. And a MAN, or Metropolitan Area Network, is a network linking nodes spread across a single metropolitan area. These terms are vague: a MAN might span only a few blocks or link nodes across distances measured in kilometers or tens of kilometers. There is undoubtedly some overlap between the largest MANs and the smallest WANs.

WANs may use dedicated telecommunications circuits to link remote nodes, or they may use networks offered by telecommunications vendors to make their connections.

Many things may be connected to a network, and each can be referred to by at least one name. For instance, the same personal computer might function simultaneously as a *client* and as a *server*. People speaking of *hosts* and *nodes*, *clients* and *servers* and *routers* and *gateways* frequently confuse the sometimes subtle differences. (A gateway is usually a device that forwards network data at the same time it translates that data from one protocol to another; routers typically don't translate network data.) The rest of this chapter explores the nuances of these, and other, network terms.

2.1.1 MORE ABOUT ENTITIES

If we define *entity* as a [thing] that does some [function], the term becomes useful in many contexts, including discussions of networks as well as discussions of network protocols. The network protocols we will discuss in this book cover communication between application-level entities—human and other users—as well as between processes, between internet nodes, and between nodes connected to the same physical network.

- Application-level entities are those "things" that do "things" related to applications. For example, a person can use a web browser to get information from a web server. The browser and server are applications, and they interact in a specific manner. The browser interprets, formats, and submits requests from the user to the server; the server interprets, formats, and responds to those requests.
- A process is an *instantiation* (or, specific instance) of a program actually executing on a computer. The program itself must be

executed on a computer before it can do anything; by running the program on a computer, it becomes instantiated. The program may be executed more than once on the same system, in which case there will be more than one process based on the same program.

Thus, Netscape Navigator is the name of a widely used program; each time a user runs Navigator on a PC, it is instantiated. There may be more than one instantiation of the same program, which means that protocols must have some way to uniquely identify processes. That allows two instances of a browser to maintain two separate browsing sessions with different web sites.

- Any entity on a physical network (e.g., it can communicate with other nodes using the same network medium) is a network node. If that network is connected to one or more other networks in an internet, then network nodes may also function as internet nodes. If a node is an internet node, it will also be a network node—but not all network nodes are necessarily internet nodes.

- Internet nodes interoperate with protocols that can pass across network boundaries. Within a local network, all nodes can be expected to be able to communicate directly, through their shared medium (see next bullet as well as next section). But when nodes are communicating across network boundaries, they've got to use a different set of protocols that don't care what protocols the local networks use.

- Network nodes communicate with each other using protocols that format and package data for transmission on a shared network medium. When nodes on the same network medium communicate, they already "know" how the data should be packaged, and they are able to assume more about the nature of the communicating nodes.

When nodes on an internet communicate, they apply simultaneously (or nearly so) protocols at different layers, as we'll see throughout this chapter.

2.2   Network Media and Interfaces

Marshall Macluhan notwithstanding, the network medium is not necessarily the message, although network messages do travel across a network medium. Three things must be present for any network to exist: something to carry messages, some things between which the messages are to be carried, and some points at which these things can connect. In other words, it requires a networking medium, entities to be connected across the networking medium, and interfaces through which different entities can pass messages.

2.2.1 MEDIA

A network medium is the physical thing or mechanism over or through which network signals are carried. In some cases, a network can be confidently seen as bounded by its medium, as, for example, insulated metal wires used for coaxial or twisted pair connections. The combination of these cables, plus any required network devices, plus attached systems, define the full extent of the network itself.

Although many if not most data networks still use cables to carry electronic signals over wire, this is not the only option. Fiberoptic strands carry data encoded as light, while wireless networks encode data as radio waves. These are not the only options, either. However, all systems connected to the same network require a set of rules (protocol) that govern how signals transmitted across the shared medium must be interpreted. Any system connected to an Ethernet must be able to differentiate line noise from actual data, as well as data to which it must respond from data it can safely ignore. Any system using a wireless medium must be able to transmit and receive data over the shared radio spectrum, and any system using an optical medium must be able to send and receive light signals over that medium.

The term *link* is often used to refer to the shared medium and the set of rules governing transmissions on that medium.

2.2.2 INTERFACES

An *interface* is the point at which two entities make contact. A network interface is the point at which an entity makes contact with any other entity. For example, consider the point of contact between a network node and a LAN. In this case, a *network interface card* (*NIC*) provides a point of contact between a PC and, for example, an Ethernet LAN. The NIC includes a plug into which an Ethernet cable can be attached.

In network terms, the node (PC) passes data intended for the network to the NIC. The NIC takes that data and, after putting it into an appropriate form for the network (usually an electronic signal), sends it out onto the cable. Network interfaces convert a node's data into electronic signals for transmission over a metal wire, or into signals appropriate for optical cable, for wireless radio transmission, or for any other mode of communication.

There are also interfaces between entities within a network entity. For now, it's enough to think about how letters being typed into a keyboard by a human using a PC to access a web site are converted into a form that the browser software running on that PC can understand, how that data is formatted for transmission over the Internet, and how that data is in its turn packaged so that the network interface can convert it for transmission on a local network.

To illustrate, the interface between system and medium is where the raw signals—whether radio waves, photons, or electrons—are translated into a digital form that a computer (or other attached system) can readily process. Although subtle, a distinction must be drawn between the data that computers send and receive over networks and the signals that carry that data over the network media. When the data is "in flight" across a wire (or wireless) link, it comprises pure signal; when the signal is received at a network interface, it is interpreted according to a set of common rules and it becomes data again.

People often assume that this intercommunication invariably occurs between nodes separated by some amount of network. However, that is not necessarily the case: there is no reason that an entire "network" communication can occur within the same system. For example, a web developer may use a server on her workstation to host content she is working on, and use her browser to access the data.

2.3   Nodes and Hosts

Any device connected to a network and capable of both creating network data and using network data is called a *node*.

A printer with a network interface is considered a node if it accepts and processes requests transmitted over the network and produces its own network data to return completion codes to whatever system requested printer services. A PC with a network interface, properly connected to a network and running networking software, is a node because it can transmit and receive data over the network. A LAN hub, however, is probably not a node: it does not create its own data but merely passes other nodes' data without responding to or making any changes in that data.

The term *host* is often used as a synonym for node, but this is not strictly correct. A node is any device that emits and absorbs data to and from a network, but a host is any node that supports one or more users and runs network application software.

A networked PC can be called a host if it is set up to allow one or more users to use network application software over the network. Most PCs these days qualify by virtue of having network applications such as a browser or mail client setup to permit access in from other nodes, but a PC configured to reject all inbound network sessions would likely be considered a node and not a host. A networked printer could be considered a host if it allowed users to log in and use some kind of application running on the printer. Printers that implement a web server to allow users to check print queue status are hosts.

Confusion over the two terms often arises because most nodes are given *hostnames* by which they can be more easily identified by humans (naming and addressing will be addressed in Chapter 3).

2.4   Clients and Servers

The terms *client* and *server* are throwbacks to the time when networking meant connecting clients (e.g., PCs or dumb terminals) to servers (e.g., mainframe or other multiuser computer systems). The client system acts as a client, using only specific mechanisms to access the server. Saying that a network consists of clients and servers is misleading when speaking of an IP-based network.

A client is any system requesting a network service; a server is a system that fulfills requests from clients. If this definition seems circular, it is. At times, a client may request that a server transmit data from the server to the client; at other times, the client may request that the server accept data from the client. The nature of the service often defines which node can be considered a client and which a server.

Cost, size, or location are not always good indicators of whether a system is a client or server. For example, a standard commercial, off-the-shelf (COTS) PC costing under $1,000 can be used as a file server, while a custom-built, multi-processor monster worth hundreds of thousands of dollars could just as easily use a network strictly to access, as a client, files stored on that PC server.

An IP node may behave as both a client and a server simultaneously for the same service, requesting a service from one node at the same time it is responding to a request for the same service from another node. This is, in fact, quite common. The Domain Name System (DNS) is a good example of such a service. And the same node may be acting in client and server roles for different services as well.

To reduce confusion, it is best not to think of a particular piece of hardware as a client or a server, but rather to attribute those roles to systems on the basis of what they are doing at any given moment.

2.5   LAN, MAN, WAN, SAN

Several terms have become common to differentiate networks that span larger areas than local area networks (LANs). A *metropolitan area network*, or *MAN*, may cover an area roughly equivalent to a town or city; a *wide area network*, or *WAN*, refers to a network linking nodes separated by as much as hundreds or even thousands of miles.

Although these terms carry little precision, LAN almost always refers to a network contained within a single location. Connections are almost always directly cabled or wired by the LAN user/operator and limited in the numbers of users linked. Although an organization may contract out all or part of the installation, support, and maintenance of a LAN, the organization in general owns or controls all of the LAN infrastructure.

In contrast, a WAN is far more likely to be created out of networks controlled by others. For example, an international organization might control LANs at its individual site while purchasing WAN connectivity among those sites through a global telecommunication company. WAN links may use fiberoptic cable, satellite, and other high-speed/high-capacity networking media that are shared among the network owners' customers. Furthermore, WANs are generally possible only with such facilities; it is not practical for most organizations to connect sites by stringing a coaxial cable across a continent or over an international border.

The MAN, then, is something in between the WAN and the LAN: it covers a smaller area than a WAN but larger than a LAN. It uses technologies that may be leased/shared, but they are not always out of the reach of all organizations. For example, line-of-site microwave or radio links may connect a company's branches within a metropolitan area; depending on the situation, the cost of such a link may be low enough to allow individuals to use such an approach.

(See Robert X. Cringely's JUNE 28, 2001 PBS article, "Reach Out and Touch Someone: How Bob and His Binoculars Found More Bandwidth and Learned to Stop Worrying and Love the Bond" for an account of creating a line-of-sight link, at http://www.pbs.org/cringely/pulpit/pulpit20010628.html.)

A MAN may use the same networks as a WAN, or it may use leased lines from a local telecommunication provider; it may even use LAN technologies for some or all of its connectivity.

A recent addition to this acronym family, *SAN*, or *storage area network*, refers to a network of dedicated storage devices. When using a computer to mediate requests for data stored on a simple hard disk, the computer itself can become a bottleneck for applications in which a lot of data is accessed and/or modified frequently by many different users. The reduction in performance can be remedied by upgrading the computer's processor or other hardware, but a more scalable approach is to use smarter storage devices that respond to requests for data through a fast network connection rather than through a computer system bus. Work continues on applying IP networking tools to SANs.

2.6   Network Systems

As we continue to build our vocabulary, consider this syllogism:

- A system is an entity with observable and reproduceable behaviors
- A network links systems through a shared medium

- A network is a system
- A system is an entity with observable and reproduceable behaviors

Circular though this sequence may be, it also demonstrates that a network can behave like a black box with inputs and outputs. To understand networking, it helps to understand how networks can be networked, and how individual networks can be treated like systems—and how systems can behave like networks.

2.6.1 Autonomous Systems and Backbones

A system is an entity with observable behaviors. A PC is a system: certain inputs will elicit certain responses. A program can be a system, accepting inputs from entities with access to the software and producing outputs. A network can also be a system.

As a *black box*, a system has one or more ways to accept input, one or more ways to produce outputs, and inside the box something happens to the things that go in before they are sent back out.

An *autonomous system* (*AS*) is a network that can be seen to behave as if it is completely self-contained. Traffic going into an AS can be considered as entering a black box. What goes on inside the AS is not only irrelevant to anything or anyone outside of it, but the AS will very likely be opaque to anyone outside it. Figure 2–1 shows several ways to map a network into ASes. From any system in the right two thirds of the figure, Network A is an AS. And from Network A, the rest of the network behaves as an AS. And from within Network B, Networks A and C are clearly ASes.

While all three networks are ASes, from Network C, there appear to be only two ASes: Network C and Network B (which includes network A). Only from Network B is it clear that there really are three distinct ASes; thus, Network B acts as a *backbone* network because it can unambiguously link distinct ASes.

While *system* may refer to a device, a network, a software program, or some combination of those, the term *AS* is almost always reserved for a network or internet that may or may not be connected to the global internet.

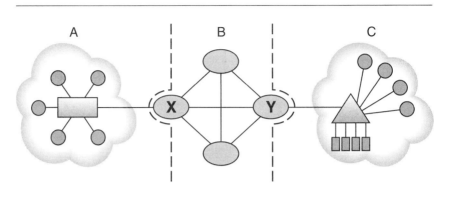

Figure 2–1: Autonomous system (AS) mapping.

2.6.2 ROUTERS AND GATEWAYS

Router and *gateway* are terms that describe systems that act as interfaces to other systems. Frequently confused or even used interchangeably, a gateway is not always a router, and vice versa.

A router is a system that applies intelligence to the movement of network data. Intelligence denotes both knowledge of the "current state of the internet" and the application of rules while processing network data. The router "knows" what connections are available, and it is also able to process data contained in packets to determine which connections should be used.

The function fulfilled by a router is similar to the function fulfilled by a shipyard freight terminal: as freight containers are unloaded from a ship, some entity (the "router") examines each container's manifest and assigns it to a freight train based on its destination.

Gateway is a more general term. A router usually operates only on network data, particularly the data's destination, without looking any further. A gateway looks beyond destination information and translates network data into a form that will be usable at its destination. One common type of gateway is the application gateway: a system that translates data from one application into a form that will make it accessible to another application.

Before commercial *internet service providers* (ISPs) offering internet mail service became common, commercial mail used proprietary formats. Mail from CompuServe, MCI Mail, and other commercial providers sometimes used different formats for message addressing and content. A gateway was necessary to translate addresses and content between different mail systems.

Back then a router might also function as a gateway in the sense that it had to translate data carried on a local network into a form that would be accessible to external networks. However, the two terms are not interchangeable, and gateway is generally preferred only when referring to a device that translates data.

2.7   Network Protocols

When systems communicate, they require rules. Network protocols define how systems communicate across networks.

The rules for handling internet communication must take into account the need for *interoperability* across various different network media (as well as different network link protocols, such as Ethernet, ATM, Fibre Channel, and others). Interoperability—the ability for systems to communicate and work together with no information about each other beyond compliance with certain standards—is a key component of any internetwork protocol because there are so many different network protocols used by different computing platforms and networking products.

One of the key goals of TCP/IP networking has always been to enable seamless interoperability across media as well as across computing hardware platforms. Ideally, the internet should make it possible for users to share data or resources without concern about what operating system, hardware, network medium, or software is being used at the other end.

A *protocol* is the complete set of rules governing the interaction between two systems. A medical protocol prescribes how a healthcare provider treats a patient. A diplomatic protocol prescribes how a person interacts and behaves with different people and groups. Likewise, a network protocol prescribes rules for how networked entities interact and behave with each other.

Protocols must specify:

- How entities initiate a protocol interaction
- What kinds of interactions are permitted

- Valid requests and responses from the entities interacting within the bounds of the protocol
- What to do when any invalid protocol message is received (in no possible case should the protocol be silent about what are correct behaviors)
- Proper formats for packaging data and protocol messages (requests/replies)
- Rules about what behaviors and data are acceptable (MAY), unacceptable (MUST NOT), or preferred (SHOULD)

In some cases, a network protocol may seem to avoid specifying some of these rules. This may mean the protocol is not completely specified, or it may mean that the protocol leaves some of the specification to processes controlled by some other protocol.

In any case, all communications require a set of rules to ensure that data can be transmitted and received, and that's what a network protocol is. Unlike medical or diplomatic protocols, network protocols are applied to computer communications that require explicit and comprehensive rules governing requests and responses.

2.7.1   A Protocol Example

Formal protocol specifications can make dry reading, but any act of communication will be governed by at least one protocol. To illustrate, consider this (incompletely specified) protocol for a telephone conversation (these rules will be more or less applicable to conversations taking place with most North Americans, and probably with English-speaking people from other parts of the world):

1. When the telephone is ringing, one SHOULD pick up the receiver, place the ear-piece to one's ear, the mouthpiece next to one's mouth, and clearly enunciate a call-receiver greeting.
2. Valid call-receiver greetings MUST include the following: "Hello", "<the answerer's name> speaking", and "<the answerer's organization>"
3. Valid call-receiver greetings SHOULD include the following: "Yo," "What's up?," and "Good [morning | afternoon | evening]."

4. Valid call-receiver greetings MAY include other words or phrases that indicate the answerer's readiness to begin speaking.
5. Upon completion of the greeting, the answerer stops speaking and waits for a reply from the caller.
6. The caller waits for the phone to stop ringing and listens to the greeting. Once the greeting is complete, the caller may begin speaking. The caller MUST respond to the greeting.
7. Valid greeting responses SHOULD include the following: a return greeting (e.g., "Hello"), an identification (e.g., "My name is Bob."), or a request (e.g., "May I speak with Alice?")
8. Caller and answerer continue the conversation, speaking in turn and waiting for the others' speech to end before speaking.
9. Repetition of greetings during the course of the conversation MUST be supported to allow interruptions, replacement of either the caller or answerer by other individuals, and call transfers.
10. The conversation SHOULD BE terminated by one party issuing a closing statement (e.g., "Well, I've got to go now") followed by a summary statement (e.g., "It was good talking with you") followed by a termination sequence (e.g., "Goodbye").

Network protocols often use formal specification languages to explicitly and precisely define data formats, requests, and responses. For example, telephone conversations between humans are typically carried out in human speech, preferably in the same language. Protocols typically define a set of functions and behaviors that all participants can be assumed to support as part of the protocol. For example, a complete telephone conversation protocol might state that the caller and the callee SHOULD speak the same language; it might specify that the caller and callee should each take turns finding a common language but that in the event the two have no language in common, the caller MAY terminate the call at any time. It might even further specify that the callee SHOULD not only try her own languages but also enlist help from any other person in the area before terminating the call.

Protocols also define the order in which communications take place. Some protocols impose a very strict order on when an entity may send data, while others allow data to be sent back and forth at will. A human caller must wait until a human answerer initiates speech; if she attempts to say something before the answerer has completed the greeting, the answerer may be confused and terminate the call prematurely (try it—it works!).

2.7.2   PROTOCOL DATA UNIT

Protocols define rules for packaging and transmitting data. The resulting packages of data are assigned a name, just like in the real world. For example, dishwashing liquid may be packaged in different forms depending on where it is in the chain of supply and demand: the factory may store the processed liquid in large tanks; the liquid may be transferred at some point to a railroad or truck tank car. Eventually, the liquid will be packaged in individual bottles, which will, in turn, be packed into corrugated cardboard cases, which may be loaded into multimode containers for shipment by sea, rail, or truck. Once purchased, the end-user may choose to transfer the liquid into a different container for dispensing.

Network data can be packed and unpacked in the same way as it travels from its source to its destination. The containers for protocol data will often enclose containers created by other protocols, just as a plastic bottle of dishwashing liquid may be packed into a case that is in turn packed into a shipping container. Giving names to the different data containers helps clarity when discussing protocols, and the specific term used by a protocol is referred to as the *protocol data unit* (*PDU*).

Specific PDUs will be defined as their protocols are introduced through the book. PDU names discussed in this book include *packet*, *frame*, *segment*, and *datagram*. *Datagram* is the more generic term, meaning a unit of data that contains just enough information to deliver it to its proper destination, along with whatever network data (if any) is being sent. *Packet* often is used for data passing through internets; *segment* for data passed between processes; *frame* for data passed on within a LAN.

Packet or datagram are often used to refer to a package of data for an unpsecified protocol, or for data packages in general. A PDU name may be used by only one protocol, or it may be used by more than one; whether or not the same PDU is intended depends entirely on the protocols being discussed.

2.8   Internetwork Terms

The thing we usually see called *the Internet* is increasingly being referred to, simply, as *internet*. There are several words that have been introduced over the years to describe networks that use TCP/IP as well as the global inter-network ordinarily called the internet. This section defines and clarifies these terms and their use.

2.8.1 CATENET, INTERNETWORK, AND THE INTERNET

At first, researchers who developed the protocols that allowed nodes on one LAN to interoperate with nodes connected to another LAN called such networks of networks *catenets*.[1] At the time, the term catenet was used to describe something that functioned as a "confederation of co-operating networks."[2] The term is likely derived from the term *cat* (originally from *concatenate*, a computer science term for what happens when you combine two or more things together into a single unit). Using those terms to describe an internetwork emphasized the fact that internetworking protocols allowed disparate networks to be concatenated into a single entity.

The word *catenet* was coined to describe a type of *internetwork*, although the specialized term did not catch on outside the research community. Ultimately, networks of networks continued to be called internetworks, a term that was shortened in its turn to *internet*. As a national and ultimately international network of networks developed, users began differentiating between *an internet* (perhaps a university network of networks) and *the Internet*, the national or global IP network. These terms were widely accepted and used within the TCP/IP community through the early to mid-1990s.

2.8.2 INTRANET AND EXTRANET

By the mid-1990s, two additional terms, *intranet* and *extranet*, entered the language. Arguably, these terms mean little: they are, perhaps, most often used in marketing materials rather than in technical discussions. However, they serve the purpose of differentiating private, shared, or smaller-scale internets from the global, capital-I, Internet.

---

[1]See Cerf, V., "The Catenet Model for Internetworking," Information Processing Techniques Office, Defense Advanced Research Projects Agency, IEN 48, July 1978, which refers to Pouzin, L., "A Proposal for Interconnecting Packet Switching Networks," Proceedings of EUROCOMP, Bronel University, May 1974, pp. 1023–36.

[2]See IEN 48.

As TCP/IP networking moved from the government-funded world of academic research into the corporate-funded world of end-users and commercial services, the terms *Internet* and *intranet* tended to confuse newcomers to TCP/IP.

The term *intranet* was coined to describe an organization's private TCP/IP internetwork, *intra* indicating that the *net* was "inside" the organization. The term often implied the use of an internally accessible web server to serve only the corporate community. Using intranet instead of internet, it was hoped, would eliminate the need to specify whether or not the spoken word internet had an upper- or lowercase "I." (Some people pronounce "intranet" and "internet" indistinguishably close, so rather than saying "lowercase internet, not THE Internet" they now say "INTRA-net, not INTERnet.")

The term *extranet* is a much harder term to nail down; despite having written a book about extranets, I am still hard pressed to define them.[3] Suffice it to say that an extranet is a sort of intranet turned inside out and strung across the Internet. Extranets generally allow employees, customers, and/or investors access to internal corporate network resources from anywhere within the organizational network or from outside the network. Extranets may be used to provide customer self-services (such as express delivery service package tracking web pages). Extranets also usually include facilities for identifying authorized users of the services provided, as well as other facilities for keeping data private.

All of these—intranet, internet, Internet, internetwork, extranet—are forms of IP-based network.

2.8.3   WEB AND INTERNET

To further add to the complexity and subtlety of internet terminology, non-technical users often equate the Internet with the World Wide Web. Although both are global networks, and the web may appear to comprise the entire Internet, they are distinct systems that overlap considerably but not completely.

The Internet is the global TCP/IP internetwork, linking network resources and users. The web, on the other hand, is an *application* distributed across

---

[3]*Extranet Design and Implementation*, SYBEX 1998.

the Internet. Web users access the application through web servers (see Chapter 12) that are linked through the Internet.

The Internet carries many different applications, including mail, news, the web, and others as we'll see in Chapter 7. The web, too, can carry many different applications, including mail, news, and others as we'll see in Chapter 12—but only between web-enabled nodes.

2.9   Chapter Summary

This chapter introduced important network vocabulary terms and concepts, independent (for the most part) of the specific instances. You may not know exactly what a router does or where one might use the Internet Protocol, but you will be able to knowledgeably discuss networks in general terms.

Key concepts covered here include:

Networks/Media: What are the different parts of a network, and what do the different (often familiar) terms really mean.

Interfaces: How network entities connect with each other.

Nodes/Hosts: What kind of systems are connected to a network.

Clients/Servers: What function do networked systems fill.

Networks: What kind of networks are in common use.

Network Systems: How a network can be a single system, and how different systems can become a network.

Protocols: The rules by which networked entities interact.

Internetworks: The different kinds of "networks of networks" that are the subject of this book.

3

Network Addresses, Network Names

Every network requires some mechanism by which individual nodes can be differentiated. In practice, this means every node is assigned a unique identifier or *address*, and in every network there is some mechanism by which this address can be associated with the correct node.

Network addresses provide the precision necessary for computers and other digital devices to interoperate across a network; *network names* offer people an easier way to interact with devices across a network. People do better with names than with numbers, particularly when the numbers are long and apparently random.

This chapter describes approaches to network addressing and network naming for commonly used network protocols.

3.1   Scalability and Network Naming/Numbering

Small and simple networks have small and simple naming and numbering problems: assign each node an address and a name, write all names and addresses into a file (known in internet terms as a *hosts* file), and put a copy of that file on all nodes. When a node's user needs to access another node by name, the node looks up the name in the hosts file and directs data to the address associated with the name.

The network administrator adds entries to the hosts file when nodes are added to the network, removes entries when nodes are removed, and changes entries when the node's name or address changes. For a small network of a few nodes, this network configuration file may take a few minutes to set up and distribute to networked nodes initially and may never need to be updated. Figure 3–1 shows the kind of simple network where this approach works best.

Centralized network naming and numbering becomes more difficult as the network increases in size. In fact, the task grows considerably as the size of the network increases. Adding one node to a five-node network means editing a hosts file on each of the five existing nodes and putting a copy of the file on the new node: six actions. Adding one node to a 100-node network means editing the hosts files on each of 100 existing nodes as well as putting a copy on the new node. The same event (adding a node) generates 20 times as much work in the larger network.

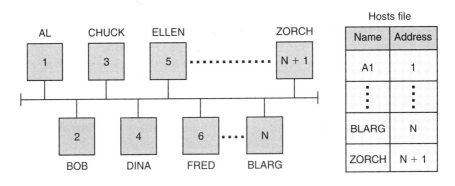

Figure 3–1: A simple naming and numbering scheme.

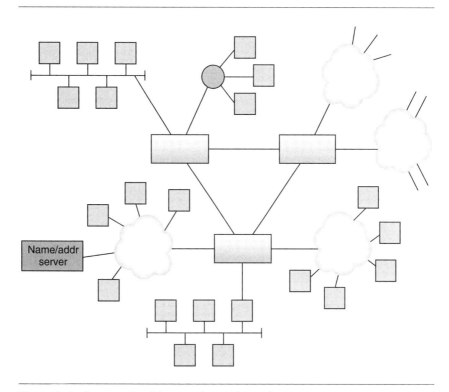

Figure 3–2: A network with a naming and numbering server.

Network naming and numbering in a network with hundreds, or even thousands, of nodes can be automated, with a centralized server managing the updates—or even providing the service of translating network names into network addresses. However, doing so requires having up-to-the-minute information about network nodes, and having a mechanism for propagating changes to all nodes without drowning the network in traffic.

Figure 3–2 shows the kind of network where a hosts file approach wouldn't work: while not messy, the network is big and complicated. Every time a new node is added to any of the networks, it must request name and address assignment from the name and address server. The difficulty of building such a server increases as the number of nodes increases because the server must be able to handle simultaneous requests. Complexity also increases as more networks are hooked together because the name and address server must find a way to uniquely identify where on the internet each node is located. If we're using the same sequential address assignment approach illustrated in Figure 3–1, the volume of information needed to locate each node explodes as the number of nodes increases.

As the internet continues to grow, any centralized approach to names and addresses fails. Networks with tens of thousands, hundreds of thousands, or millions of nodes, all located on thousands or hundreds of thousands of different interconnected networks, would overwhelm any centralized system.

Managing network naming and addressing centrally in such large internets would be a nightmare: any and all changes to any and all networks—new nodes, moved nodes, removed nodes—must be reported to the central authority, which must enter them into its system immediately and make sure that all changes are propagated out to all other networks and nodes as needed, and all without taking up too much of the internet's bandwidth.

Centralized systems capable of dynamically serving any significant percentage of the global internet are rare (if they exist at all). Depending on how they are implemented, they tend to work well with small populations but performance and effectiveness degrade as the size of the population being served grows; the point at which they fail will vary, but not the ultimate result.

The alternative is to distribute the system function across the network. Naming and addressing tasks are distributed throughout today's global internet, with different organizations dividing responsibility for allocation on a global scale. At the top level, a handful of groups manage information about the most broad categories of names and addresses; these groups delegate responsibility for naming and addressing within those categories to whichever organizations are best placed to do so. The top level organizations don't care about individual node names or addresses; the organization maintaining a network is assigned the task of keeping track of that kind of information.

This type of system, where parts of the system are managed by many different systems distributed throughout the internet, is called a *distributed system*. Most commonly seen as a distributed database, where data about the internet is stored on the internet (rather than collected and stored centrally), this approach has become a mainstay for several important internet applications and functions. (We'll see distributed systems used for addressing of LAN interfaces, internet addresses, internet domain names, internet network management data, and elsewhere.)

Here are some of the reasons centralized systems fail to scale well, and why distributed systems tend to do better:

- Centralized systems are susceptible to dramatic failures. When a single node provides an indispensable service to a network, pulling the plug on that node effectively pulls the plug on the entire network. When the indispensable service is provided by thousands of widely distributed nodes, the network is unlikely to be brought down by bringing down all of those nodes simultaneously. Also, whatever network connection feeds the centralized system also becomes a target for a dramatic failure.
- Centralized systems tend to generate a lot of network traffic. Every time a network or node changes in any way, information about that change must be communicated to the centralized name and address servers. The volume of traffic needed to keep everyone up to date increases much faster in a large internet than in a smaller one.
- Not only would that flow of data flood into the centralized system, it would also use a significant portion of available bandwidth throughout the network to carry updates as well as to carry requests for up-to-date information from nodes throughout the internet—even when a node seeks information about a local node, the request would have to travel all the way to the centralized system and back.
- Centralized systems tend to perform less well than distributed systems because any single system (whether or not that means a single computer or a parallel supercomputer) may have to handle millions of concurrent requests. That means ever-faster processors, more RAM, and bigger and faster data storage systems to support a growing network.
- Centralized systems tend to perform less well than distributed systems because all the extra network traffic they generate tends to slow down all network performance.
- Centralized systems perform less well than distributed systems because requests and responses to and from remote nodes must travel greater distances to get to the centralized server and back across the internet.
- Centralized systems must contend with the serious logistical problem of tracking addresses and names for every attached

node–all updates must somehow be sent in to the centralized system, processed and stored, and retrieved on demand. That means as the number of nodes increases the proportion of time that the centralized system is out of sync with the actual internet also increases.

It is ironic that demand for internetworking grew largely from the need to provide remote access to centralized systems, but rather than facilitating those centralized systems, the internet fosters decentralization of those systems.

These themes will repeat throughout this chapter as well as throughout this book. As will become clear with discussion of the Domain Name System (DNS), the Simple Network Management Protocol (SNMP), and IP addressing, this approach uses the networks connected to the internet to serve as the internet's name/address translation infrastructure and creates the ultimate in distributed relational database systems by storing network management information within the internet's own infrastructure.

3.2   Network Identification Terms, Defined

We've already discussed the differences and similarities among network designations such as intranet, internet, extranet, and so on. Individual networks and internets often have their own names, just as geo-political entities—whether cities, provinces, or nations—have names, but each is also an instance of a certain type of entity.

Hostname: Any node, whether or not is an actual host, may be assigned one or more hostnames.[1] While computers work best with numerical addresses, humans prefer names; a hostname is, therefore, a convenience to make networks more usable for people. Although a hostname and a network address may be strictly linked on a one-to-one basis, that is not a requirement. A single hostname may be shared by more than one node in order to improve responsiveness: all requests

---

[1]However, a node is not required to have a hostname under IP version 4 (the current version); IPv6-enabled applications rely on hostnames to determine whether a node supports IPv6. See Chapter 27 for more details.

to a particular hostname can be shared among several systems. A single node may respond to more than one name to improve efficiency: a single node may host many services, with many different names.

Domain name: Identifies the system within which hostnames are administered. In today's internet, hostnames consist of two or more parts separated by a "dot" or period (.). Top-level domains include .com, .org, .biz, and .net; the specifics of the system are discussed in Chapter 8. Below the top level domains, sub-domains can be assigned to organizations or individuals. The domain name is used to manage access to the domain name holder's internet systems, and is expressed in the form of *example.net* or *example.com*.[2]

Fully qualified domain name (FQDN): Completely identifies the hostname across the entire naming domain by concatenating a hostname with a domain name. Every network in an internet might have defined the hostname "dilbert", but each instance of "dilbert" can be differentiated by expressing its FQDN, like this: *dilbert.example.net* or *dilbert.example.com*.

Mail address: Often incorporates host and domain names, but each mail address must point to some entity. The entity may be a person (e.g., *pete@loshin.com* points to the author), a group (e.g., mail addressed to *support@example.com* may be delivered to any member of an organization's support group), or a function (e.g., mail addressed to *subscribe-mailing-list@example.com* may trigger an automated response from a mailing group system).

Domain name system (DNS): Is a system used in the internet for linking names with addresses. Submit a request to *resolve* (or determine an address that is associated with the name) a fully-qualified domain name to the DNS and it will respond with a numerical address to which to send any data intended for that name (or an error code if the FQDN is not valid).

---

[2]The domains *example.com*, *example.net*, and *example.org* have been reserved for use as examples in documentation. See RFC 2606, "Reserved Top Level DNS Names." By setting aside the example.* domains, the IETF insures that real domains are not flooded with well-intentioned attempts to "try things out." Domains such as acme.com, xyz.net, and abc.org are among those that are burdened in this way.

3.3   Binary and Hexadecimal Numbering

Understanding binary and hexadecimal numerical representation is a vital part of understanding computer networking. Computer networks, like computers themselves, use binary rather than decimal numbers. A binary digit, or bit, represents a single crumb of information: it is either on (1) or off (0). See the table below for more about binary and hexadecimal numerical representation.

The characters "1010," interpreted as a decimal number, represents the value one thousand and ten. The zero in the least significant (rightmost) digit means there are no ones (10^0), the one in the second least significant digit means there is one ten (10^1), the third least significant digit means no hundreds (10^2), and the most significant digit means one thousand (10^3).

However, these same numerals can be interpreted as a binary number. Each binary digit (bit) of a binary number represents a power of 2 in the same way that digits of a decimal number represent a power of 10. Just as a 4-digit decimal number can be given a value of anywhere from 0 (or 0000) through 9,999, the 4-bit binary number can be given a value of anywhere from 0000 through 1111. While the 4-digit decimal number can have any of 10,000 unique values, the 4-bit binary number can have any of only 16 values:

Decimal	Binary	Hexadecimal
0	0000	0
1	0001	1
2	0010	2
3	0011	3
4	0100	4
5	0101	5
6	0110	6
7	0111	7
8	1000	8
9	1001	9
10	1010	A

Decimal	Binary	Hexadecimal
11	1011	B
12	1100	C
13	1101	D
14	1110	E
15	1111	F

Computers have long used 8-bit binary numbers, which can represent the equivalent of decimal numbers 0 through 255, as a standard byte. A single byte consolidates the data contained in eight separate bits and provides humans with a more convenient and less confusing form of expressing data. Instead of using 256 different permutations of eight bits, we use 16 different symbols to represent each of 16 different permutations of four bits, and then we're able to represent our 8-bit bytes as the 256 different permutations of two of those 16 symbols.

So, an 8-bit value (e.g., the equivalent of 200) can be represented as an 8-bit binary number:

```
1100 1000
```

We've got 1 in the most significant bit (128) plus 1 in the second most significant bit (64) plus 1 in the most significant bit of the second 4 bits (8).

Another way to represent the same value uses a set of 16 characters to represent *hexadecimal* or base-16 numbers in the same way the characters 0-9 represent the decimal or base-10 numbers. Hexadecimal, or *hex* for short, numbers use 0-9 for the first ten values, and A-F for the values that correspond to decimal 10-15. Thus, expressing the decimal number 200 as hexadecimal gives us:

```
0xCA
```

Things to note here:

- Hex numbers are signified by the prefix "0x" to differentiate them from decimal values. When a hex number uses values A through F, it is easily differentiated from decimal numbers, but the hex value for the number "89" is not the same as the decimal value.

- Hex values may be represented with the upper or lower case values A-F, a-f; however, upper and lower case symbols are not normally mixed in the same number.

All hex values in this text will conform to this convention, using the "0x" prefix and upper-case A through F.

3.4   Network Addressing Spaces

Network nodes must be distinguished in some way for them to be reachable. In other words, a network node's address must be unique within its network.

The public switched telephone network (PSTN) provides the most obvious example of unique addressing within a network.

Within an entity such as a corporation, you can reach individuals using their internal extension numbers. These are often as short as two digits or as long as five or more. Each extension uniquely identifies a particular network interface (the telephone jack). There may be hundreds or thousands of individual businesses or branches that have assigned some or all of the same extensions to different people.

Knowing the extension alone is only enough if you are calling from within the domain in which that extension is unique.

Likewise, you may be able to use seven digits to reach a number that shares your three-digit area code within North America. That same number may be duplicated elsewhere in North America, with different area codes. In that case you would have to dial the entire 10-digit number, but only if you are calling from a number that does not share the same area code with the number being called. (This type of differential address length in the PSTN in North America is increasingly being eliminated as subscribers are being required to dial the country code (1) plus the entire 10-digit number.)

Three things can happen when you attempt to make a connection to a node whose address is not unique:

- The connection is completed correctly. In this case, there is no way to tell that there is a duplicate address.

- The connection is completed, but to the wrong destination. In this case, one or both endpoints may—or may not—become aware something is wrong.
- An error condition is produced. This may be an explicit error message of some sort, or the connection may be refused silently, or some other error that is apparently unrelated to the duplicate address may be reported.

Depending on the network, the nodes, and the protocols being used it may be difficult to predict which of these things will happen—or whether the same result will occur each time an attempt is made.

Thus, all nodes in a network are assigned unique addresses. As networks become larger, longer network addresses must be used to ensure all nodes can be identified uniquely. An "address space" refers to the general shape of a network's addressing domain.

For example, the North American PSTN address space consists of ten decimal digits. The absolute maximum number of nodes that can be uniquely addressed within this space is 10^{10}, or 10,000,000,000 (anything in the range of 000 000 0000 through 999 999 9999 would be considered part of the address space, for a total of 10 billion unique addresses).

Network address space lengths are usually discussed in bits, not digits. An 8-bit address space can have 2^8 unique addresses; everything from:

```
0000 0000 (in decimal, 0)
through
1111 1111 (in decimal, 255)
```

for a total of 256 unique addresses.

This book concerns itself with only a few network address spaces. These include:

- Ethernet and other IEEE standards–based networks use a 48-bit media access control (MAC) address scheme.
- IPv4, the version of the Internet Protocol (IP) in general use since the early 1980s, uses a 32-bit address space. (IP is the protocol that defines how all internet traffic is packaged and

delivered. IP version 4, or IPv4, is the current standard for virtually all internet traffic. Earlier versions [1,2,3] were used to designate earlier versions developed during research of what eventually became IP. Version 5 was assigned to an experimental protocol. IPv6 updates IPv4 to support much larger internets, and is discussed in Chapter 27.)

- IPv6, the version of IP developed to succeed IPv4, uses a 128-bit address space.

It is simple to determine the theoretical maximum number of nodes possible in a given address space: take the number of bits in the address space (call it N), and calculate 2^N. An 8-bit address space can support no more than 2^8, or 256, unique addresses; a 24-bit address space would support a theoretical maximum of 2^{24}, or 16,777,216, unique addresses.

In practice, network address spaces invariably support far fewer than their theoretical maximums. For more about address space utilization rates, see RFC 3194, "The H-Density Ratio for Address Assignment Efficiency: An Update on the H ratio." Each of these address spaces will be discussed in more detail (IPv4 in Chapter 19, IPv6 in Chapter 26, and Ethernet in Chapter 21), but looking at each briefly here will introduce some issues we will return to throughout this book.

There is also a network of sorts within all IP nodes, consisting of software entities that handle incoming and outgoing data on behalf of different applications within the system. This gives nodes a way to differentiate between data being sent to a mail application from data being sent to a web server application.

This internal "network" assigns unique "ports" to network traffic handled by each node program. Port numbering is not usually discussed in the context of network addressing, but it is an important component of the TCP/IP protocol stack and it helps to consider it as a form of address. Ports are discussed in more detail in Chapter 15.

At the same time, ports aren't really network addresses because early on in the TCP/IP protocol suite development process it became clear that assigning static addresses to processes—which by their nature are dynamic and mutable—would be a bad idea.

3.4.1 NETWORK AND INTERNET ADDRESSES

Nodes connected to any internet will be associated with at least two addresses, at two different levels: the local network interface and the internet interface. Note the wording: a node has network interfaces; the network interfaces are given addresses.

The address used to reach a node's interface on a LAN (or whatever medium the node's interface is connected to) usually has no nothing to do with the address used to reach its interface on an internet. Communication between nodes on a shared medium is brokered through the use of the interfaces' (local or network medium) network addresses; these may be dictated through hardware (see next section) or they may be assigned through some local network facility.

The network address may be a physical address, literally encoded physically into the interface; the internet interface is given a logical address that can be linked to the physical address. Why two addresses? Because the physical address may be subject to all the ills that can befall anything physical: the network interface device can break, be replaced by a better interface device, be turned off, and so on. If the logical address is linked irrevocably to the physical address, then a new logical address would have to be issued any time the interface device is replaced; by linking the two addresses more loosely, the logical address can be maintained when the network interface is changed or replaced, when the system with the network interface is moved to a different type of network, even when the entire system is replaced by a different system, on a different physical network, all moved to a different location.

The thing to keep in mind is that local or shared medium communications are not interoperable except (perhaps) when used between interfaces that use the same type of shared medium and protocols for communicating on that medium. Figure 3–3 illustrates how these two addresses work. Nodes A and B are on the same local network and can reach each other directly (from network interface to network interface) using their network addresses, 0001 and 0010.

They can also communicate using internet-level protocols by *encapsulating* (the process of wrapping data into a payload or package-packet defined by the protocol) their messages in the internet protocol and communicating over the local network medium. The data are addressed at the internet

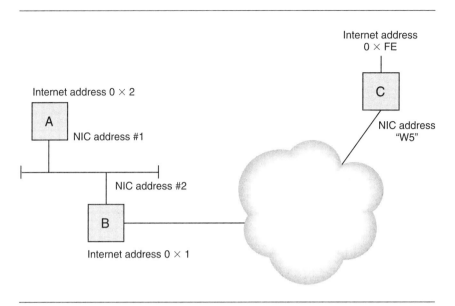

Figure 3–3: Network and internet addresses.

level, but no data can be transmitted until (somehow—we'll cover the details of how it works in increasing detail throughout the book) the sender figures out what network address corresponds to the internet level address.

Node A can communicate with Node C, only that node's network level address ("W5") is meaningless to Node A. Node A's address space doesn't support characters, only the numerals 0 through 9, so it has no way to use that information—but it doesn't have to. When a node must send data outside the local network, it will address it to the destination node's internet level address, pack it up with the appropriate local network protocol and send it to whatever local system has been designated to deal with moving data outside the local network.

How to assign internet level addresses? Here are some options:

- Sequentially. Not a good idea because it requires a central-ized system to keep track of which systems are using which addresses.
- Distribute sections of the address space and delegate address-ing authority to network administrators. A much better idea,

because nodes all get globally unique addresses, but remote networks need only know about who is responsible for the sections of address space without worrying about how to locate individual nodes.

Delegation works best. Local network addressing is a matter for the local network. Internet addressing is done separately, so each network interface will be associated with a local address having local significance, and with an internet address, having internet-wide significance. The two addresses are linked only within the local network.

Although one might think otherwise, there is no strict one-to-one correspondence between local network addresses and internet addresses. A single node may have a single internet address but several local network interfaces (a high-availability system that requires redundant network connections, for example). Another node may have a single local network interface, but may have several different internet level addresses (a system providing hosting or other connectivity services on behalf of several different organizations, for example). Finally, a node using a single internet address may, at different times, have different local network addresses (a system undergoing service or upgrade may use different network interface cards, with different network addresses, over a short time).

The internet address gives enough information to get data across the internet; the network address contains enough information to get the data across the local network once it arrives from its source.

3.4.2   IEEE MAC Addresses

The Institute of Electrical and Electronics Engineers (IEEE), a non-profit technical professional organization, provides various services to the community of engineers as well as engineering-related industries through its technical publishing, conferences, and consensus-based standards activities. IEEE network protocol standards form a vital core for many types of network, particularly for local networks and how data are transmitted across network media.

The IEEE maintains a local network interface address space for the world's network hardware manufacturers. To assign local network interface addresses to hardware interfaces, manufacturers must obtain an IEEE Organizationally Unique Identifier (OUI) company ID, defined on the IEEE web site this way:

> An OUI... is a 24 bit globally unique assigned number referenced by various standards. OUI is used in the family of 802 LAN standards, e.g., Ethernet, Token Ring, etc.

Manufacturers use their OUI (the privilege costs $1,650.00) as the left-most (most significant) 24 bits of their own portion of the interface address space.[3] This prefix identifies the manufacturer in the same way that the first 3 digits of a North American telephone number indicate an area code.

For example, Sega Enterprises, Ltd., is assigned the hexadecimal prefix 00-D0-F1 (in binary, that's 0000 0000-1010 0000-1111 0001). The hardware or MAC address of any network adapter built by Sega would use this prefix; Sega is permitted to assign the least significant 24 bits in any way it chooses.

IEEE-compliant network interface addresses are therefore 48 bits long; as many as 2 to the 24th (almost 17 million) OUIs can be supported, each supporting the same number of individual network interfaces. This addressing scheme can support an absolute maximum of no more than 281,474,976,710,656 (over 280 trillion) unique addresses.

These addresses demonstrate how a single address space, particularly a large one, can most easily be managed in a decentralized manner. Hardware manufacturers should be able to manage assigning unique identifiers to all their products, just as they can assign serial numbers to their products. They can also subdivide the part of the space they own by splitting off bits to associate with different factories. For example, a manufacturer can split their 24-bit address space into four 22-bit address spaces, or 16 20-bit address spaces.

The IEEE can likewise segment the other half of the 48-bit address space to simplify administration—or they can just build a database that they know will never exceed roughly 17 million OUIs.

---

[3]See the IEEE web page. Available at: http://standards.ieee.org/regauth/oui/oui.txt, for a complete listing of all assigned OUIs.

Delegating responsibility downward through an addre͜
lent way to turn a potentially unmanageable task (assign͜
unique addresses) into one that is very manageable. We wil͜
decentralization through delegation when we discuss the DNS in Cha͜
as well as in the discussions of routing in Chapters 22 and 23.

3.4.3   IPv4 Addresses

The most important aspect of the IPv4 address space is its size. At 32 bits, the absolute maximum number of unique addresses possible is over four billion. In practice, some experts claim that we have already exceeded the capacity of IPv4 to uniquely address nodes, with hundreds of millions of users already on the public Internet as well as perhaps billions more to be added with the implementation of IP on mobile telecommunicaions devices.

When the specifications for IPv4 were being written, computers were almost all large, expensive, multi-user systems; IPv4's creators anticipated neither the success of their protocol or of the PC itself. Had they imagined that their protocol would still be in wide use 20 to 25 years later, they would likely have built in more scalability. The largest early IP networks sported fewer than 100 nodes and grew relatively slowly for years before they reached tens of thousands of nodes, so the lapse is understandable.

Protocols that have been developed in an organic way, as those in the TCP/IP are, change in response to their environment. IPv4, however, is locked in to a 32-bit address space (as we shall see in Chapter 19). For reasons of performance, backward compatibility, and interoperability, IPv4 can not readily be patched to support more unique addresses. With prophets of gloom and doom proclaiming the imminence of the depletion of the IPv4 address space since the early 1990s, many network professionals believe that IPv6 is a solution in search of a problem.

However, researchers pursuing at least three general approaches have managed to prevent IPv4 from melting down. Some of those approaches have been so successful that opponents of IPv6 believe there is no reason to move to another version of IP for the foreseeable future. The details are discussed in Chapter 27; the use of these approaches, as well as others that are inappropriate, help illustrate how network protocols can evolve to address changing circumstances.

3.4.4 IPv6 Addresses

At 128 bits, IPv6 addresses are quite long and support an unimagineably huge number of network nodes. IPv6 addresses are intended to be split in half, with the most significant 64-bits used to identify the network and the least significant 64-bits to identify nodes.

IPv6 service providers will fall into several categories, from the huge to the small. The very largest providers will be given more bits in the most significant half of the address, while smaller providers get fewer bits to control.

The striking difference between IPv4 and IPv6 is that all IP service users, no matter how small—including individuals—get a network address. Individuals would be unlikely to have control over any network address space (the most significant 64-bits), but they do have control over the 64-bits of user address space. Thus, each individual subscriber would, potentially, be able to uniquely address as many as 2^{64} (roughly 18 billion billion—18,000,000,000,000,000,000) nodes.

The significance here is that the people developing IPv6 are building in plenty of room for future growth. As an experimental and experiential network, the internet requires scalability to be successful. What works for hundreds or even hundreds of thousands of users may not necessarily work for millions or hundreds of millions of users.

Though it's impossible to determine how many IPv4 nodes currently exist on the internet with any degree of certainty, it would be hard to argue that in early 2002 there are no fewer than several hundred million (10^8) and likely no more than a billion (10^9) or so. Considering that IPv4 was designed for an experimental network in which there may have been some tens (10^2) to tens of thousands (10^5) of nodes, the protocol scaled remarkably well and enabled internet growth over two decades of as many as 7 orders of magnitude with minimal change. (*Orders of magnitude* are used to roughly indicate scale, rather than for precise measurement. A group of 50 and a group of 200 are both considered to be on the same order of magnitude: 10^2. Growing by a factor of seven orders of magnitude is roughly equivalent to increasing by a factor of 10 million times the original size.)

IPv6 also teaches the lesson of building up relatively complex protocols based on relatively simple protocols. Lessons learned from IPv4 and IEEE

MAC/OUI addressing are applied to IPv6: delegation of responsibility for more or less local node addresses is extended to IPv6. Likewise, one key method for assigning IPv6 network addresses relies on network interfaces using IEEE MAC addresses. And experiences with IPv4 convinced the people working on IPv6 that splitting the address space in half, one half for uniquely specifying a network and the other half for uniquely specifying a node within a network, would help improve network performance over IPv4's more flexible approach to network and node addressing.

3.5   Network Names

Network names are most useful for humans, who have trouble dealing with apparently random strings of characters but are much better at remembering names to which they can attach some meaning. Networked computers can function happily without names but naming can be useful even in a small internet, especially when an important system must be moved from one network to another and its addresses must change: the name remains constant.

The dominant naming mechanism within IP networks, the DNS, will be discussed in Chapter 8.

For now, suffice it to say that any properly named network node will normally be associated with at least one network address. Properly addressed nodes may be associated with one or more (or no) network names. Though some networks may be composed of nodes that are all uniquely addressed as well as uniquely named, this is not a requirement. Nor is it necessary that the same node always have the same address.

Nodes in a network may share a pool of addresses, to be used for a set period and then returned to the pool. Thus, a node's address may change over time, while it retains the same name. Conversely, nodes may have their own unique network addresses but may all be associated with a particular network name; connecting to the network name does not necessarily guarantee that the connection will be with the same node every time a new session begins.

While it is possible to impose a simple one-to-one relationship between network names and addresses, doing so tends to limit the network.

Allowing more flexibility, as we will see in Chapter 8 and Chapter 27, makes possible a more scalable and extensible network.

3.5.1 Delegation of Naming Authority

Just as network addressing tasks are best delegated, so too are network naming tasks. Local names are handled locally; global names are handled globally. Thus, within a local naming domain (say, the author's family), a single name ("Pete") is enough. Outside the local name domain, the first name is irrelevant as long as it is possible to deliver a package to the right name domain. Thus, it is sufficient for someone in Europe to get enough information to address a package to "Loshin in Massachusetts in the USA"; they don't need to target their data any more accurately because I'll be able, locally, to sort through packages intended for me and those intended for other family members.

To oversimplify how DNS works, the top level domains can be queried to find out about names at the next layer. Consider a FQDN for a hostname within the example.com, naming domain:

elmo.boston.example.com

The DNS system that serves the .com domain will respond to a request for more information about reaching the domain example.com, and the DNS system serving example.com will respond to a request for information about reaching the boston.example.com domain. A DNS system serving the boston.example.com domain will respond to requests about the host elmo. At the .com level, DNS can answer only the question of where example.com can be reached. More details are available only by tracing through the hierarchy and getting increasingly localized information.

We'll return to naming authorities and distribution in Chapter 8, where DNS is discussed in greater detail.

3.6   Chapter Summary

In addition to expanding on the development of a networking language, begun in Chapter 2, in this chapter we look at the challenges of identifying networked systems uniquely, particularly when the network may consist of many millions of systems.

You should now be able to differentiate a hostname from a domain name, as well as understand how to express numerical addresses in decimal, binary, and hexadecimal numbering systems.

Although several different addressing schemes are introduced in this chapter, the primary objective was to illustrate the different challenges facing any protocol designer wishing to uniquely identify nodes on a network. Likewise, the primary goal of the section on network naming was to introduce the TCP/IP approach to network names.

In the next chapter, we will put some of these new vocabulary words to use as we discover how networks actually work.

Applying Networking
Concepts

In the last chapter we encountered network naming and addressing concepts; this chapter introduces fundamental networking concepts: how nodes manage to initiate, maintain, and manage connections. Rather than attempt to explain real technologies while demonstrating these concepts, we'll use imaginary network media and protocols that provide simple models for grasping the relevant components of each concept.

Although these imagined networks and protocols may mirror actual network protocols in a simple-minded way, they were created to demonstrate aspects of networking in a theoretical and general way rather than to accurately describe any actual protocols.

4.1   Virtual Circuits

The simplest type of network connects two nodes through a single medium. For example, two tin cans connected by a length of string. Data emanating from one node (words spoken into one tin can) has only one route available: through the medium (the string) to the other node (other tin can). This is a non-virtual circuit. The connection is direct.

Now, imagine a more complex network, consisting of several tin cans, each connected by a string to corresponding cans located centrally, with a human operating the central cans at all times (Fig. 4–1). All callers can connect directly only to a single location, yet all callers can connect indirectly through that central location.

A conversation proceeds like this:

1. The originating caller connects to the central office, saying "Hello, are you there operator?" into the can.

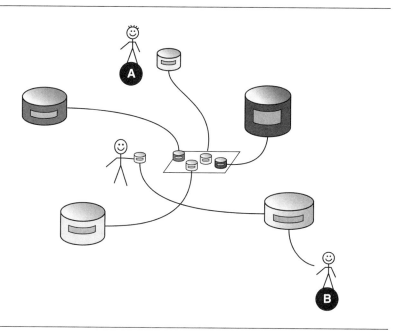

Figure 4–1: Tin can network.

2. The central office operator responds, saying, "Hello. I hear you. Can you hear me?"
3. The caller responds, saying, "Yes I hear you. Can you connect me with <subscriber name>?"

At that point, the operator has two options. First, the operator must ask the caller to hold on while he attempts to make a connection with the party being called. If that party is available, the operator initiates a connection; if not, the operator tells the original caller that the connection is not possible.

The protocol the operator uses to initate the connection with the intended callee will look very much like that used by the originating caller, except that the operator takes on the role of the originating caller. The operator opens the conversation by saying "Hello, are you there <subscriber name>?" And the subscriber responds by saying that she hears the operator, followed by the operator getting back to the original caller.

The caller and callee (A and B in Fig. 4–1) communicate through the operator. A says something to the operator, the operator repeats it to B; B responds to the operator, and the operator repeats it to A.

All data sent between A and B is delivered by the operator, but each end node on the network gets their data just as if the call had been direct. This is a *virtual circuit*. To ensure that all data is delivered accurately and completely, you can add rules to the protocol:

- If a speaker is talking too fast (sending too much data, too quickly), the listener can request her to repeat the last *n* words.
- If a speaker is talking too slow, the listener can let her know that she can speak faster, up to *n* words per minute.
- Data can be verified in different ways to increase confidence in the accuracy of the connection.
- Confirmation of receipt of data can be required to provide guaranteed delivery.

By including rules about confirming that the conversation is being received correctly, this protocol results in a connection that behaves in the same way as a real circuit.

4.2   Bandwidth and Throughput

As we talk about a network like this, one might suggest that a simple conversation could take considerably longer than conversations conducted either in person or over the PSTN. Two aspects of network performance regulate whether or not such a network can perform an adequate job of carrying human conversation. *Bandwidth* is the measure of a channel's data carrying capacity, expressed as an amount of data that can be delivered in a time period, while *throughput* is the measure of how much actual data is observed to be delivered in a time period.

Although bandwidth and throughput are often used as if they mean the same thing, bandwidth is usually used to mean the maximum theoretical capacity of a link, while throughput usually is used to mean how much data is actually being passed on that link.

4.2.1   MEASURING BANDWIDTH AND THROUGHPUT

Bandwidth and throughput are usually espressed as some number of *bits per second* (*bps*); most modern networks provide capacity for thousands (*kbps*), millions (*mbps*), or even billions (*gbps*) of bits per second.[1]

Strictly speaking, bandwidth is the maximum possible amount of data that can be transmitted over a medium, according to the laws of physics. Our tin can string is capable of carrying much faster speech, and there may be other protocols for encoding data into a string signal that can carry even more data.

We'll use a simple and accessible example to illustrate. For this example, we'll make some assumptions[2]:

- The average human speaks at an average rate of two words/second, or 120 words/minute.
- The average word consists of five characters, plus one character of punctuation (space, comma, period, and so on), for a total of

---

[1]Pronounced "kilobits per second," "megabits per second," and "gigabits per second," respectively.

[2]Perhaps most important is the assumption that we can reasonably pretend human language defines a protocol for encoding data (words) into signals (speech)—and that we can meaningfully measure words, letters, and sounds in terms of the bits and bytes they encode.

six 8-bit bytes of information in each word. Each word requires, therefore, 48 bits to encode.

• The average human can therefore transmit data, on average, at a rate of 12 bytes per second, or 96 bps.

• The absolute fastest comprehensible speech possible on string-connected cans is eight words/second, or 384 bps. This is the bandwidth of the string.

• Our tin can network allows only one speaker per line, so each line has a maximum throughput capacity of 96 bps for average human speech.

In practice, throughput rarely reaches the theoretical maximum.[3] A noisy machine, a crying baby, imperfections in cabling, errors in network infrastructure, and many more causes can reduce throughput.

For example, let's say that a tin can network link becomes so noisy that the speaker must say each word, spell it, and then repeat it. The average word, which can normally be encoded in 6 bytes, now requires far more information. Assuming an average of 4 letters per spoken character plus one for the space in between each additional word, the average word (5 letters plus one punctuation character) now requires 25 characters to spell (5 letters to be spelled out, at 5 characters/letter), plus 6 more bytes for the repetition of the word. That's 37 bytes, or 296 bits.

Throughput has plummeted: from 96 bps (2 words/second) to about 0.33 words/second.

4.2.2 OVERHEAD

The noisy environment described in 4.2.1 calls for saying, spelling, and saying every word transmitted. This is an example of a simple encoding protocol. It helps avoid errors, but it also raises *overhead*. This is extra data carried along with actual application data to enable network delivery. Protocol overhead reduces the amount of bandwidth available for application data, but some is always necessary. Simpler protocols may introduce less overhead; more complex protocols may increase overhead significantly.

---

[3] "The difference between theory and practice, in practice, always exceeds the difference between theory and practice, in theory."

To send a single word (48 bits) you burn up 296 bits. A tin can string can carry an absolute maximum of 384 bps, so the average speaker will be able to use at best only about one quarter of that bandwidth—while at the same time preventing anyone else from using it.

This say/spell/say protocol, especially when used with rules that allow the listener to tell the speaker to repeat a word or letter, is a form of error correcting protocol. It makes sense if you really need to know exactly what someone is saying. It is also costly: it slows throughput by a factor of six. However, another type of protocol could be used to compress the transmission and allow it to use more of the physical network's bandwidth. For example, the speaker could pre-record her transmission and then play it back through the transmitter at almost four times the normal speaking rate.

Now, instead of six seconds per word, the sender gets a more reliable encoding mechanism (say/spell/say) plus a throughput rate of about 1.33 words/second. At about 80 words/minute, this is noticeably slower than normal speech, but still usable as long as the sender can pre-record transmissions, and the listener can interpret them at high speed.

This example demonstrates some of the tradeoffs that are made in almost every network protocol. Sometimes, the most important factor to consider is speed; other times, accuracy, ease of use, or ability to detect, avoid, or correct errors are more important.

This example is also limited to the lower network layers: encoding data into speech and sending it out onto the tin can string medium. Let's go back to the higher level problems of pushing speech through a network with intermediaries such as operators involved.

4.2.3 THROUGHPUT STRATEGIES

Our tin can network suffers from limited overall bandwidth capacity because all inter-node traffic requires the mediation of the operator. With a single operator, no more than one transmission on the network can take place at any given time. Adding more operators increases overall network throughput and enables multiple simultaneous transmissions—until the number of operators equals the number of tin cans at the central office. The network illustrated in Figure 4–1 could increase overall capacity from by adding as many as four additional operators (for a total of five).

Another way to increase capacity would be to double the "cabling": install a second line between the central office and each node. All network users then have an inbound connection (to listen to) and an outbound connection (to speak into). In this way, a caller can listen to someone else speaking at the same time the caller is speaking. This doubling of capacity is called *duplexing*: it is a mechanism that allows a network node to be sending and receiving data at the same time.

Remember, tin can string has a bandwidth of 384 bps, while people typically transmit at a little more than one fourth that rate. Another form of duplexing lets more than one node share the same medium. In this example, that might mean having two or more speakers using the same line and synchronizing their speech so that whenever one paused, another one said something. Perhaps not too practical in this case, but in real world networks protocols often allow multiple nodes to share a single medium by breaking all their data into small chunks and then taking turns sending them out.

The full capacity for the network in Figure 4–1, when enhanced by duplexing the links and using a single operator for every in-bound or out-bound link, totals 3,840 bps or almost 4 kbps, because there are ten tin can string links, each with 384 bps of bandwidth. Without any additional duplexing, however, this network can support no more than 960 bps overall.

4.2.4 PROTOCOLS AND THROUGHPUT

However, let's stick with the original single-operator, non-duplexed network shown in Figure 4–1. In addition to being hobbled by our slow-speaking human operator, any attempt to build usable protocols for this network will cut down significantly the information-carrying capacity of the network. If we were to add any features from the list of possible protocol additions from Section 4.1, we immediately reduce our throughput.

Reduced throughput may not be so bad, if it can eliminate errors and increase the reliability of transmissions. Here are some options and how they affect throughput (in general, the more confidence you have in a link or the data you send and receive over that link, the more of that link's bandwidth goes into protocol overhead):

- The operator could repeat the caller's words as the caller is speaking, reducing overhead almost completely. The operator may not hear every word accurately, but throughput could approach (though never exceed) 120 words per minute. There is no protocol overhead related to *error checking* (a mechanism that reports whether data was changed in transit) or *error correction* (a mechanism that provides enough information to reconstruct data that was changed in transit).

- For better accuracy at a moderate cost of bandwidth, the caller can request a protocol that requires the operator to listen before sending to the other party. The protocol may permit the operator to transcribe or record transmissions; the protocol might include a mechanism to let a listener ask a speaker to speed up, slow down, or repeat or clarify some word or phrase. This approach reduces throughput by half (or more).

  Assuming that all transmissions are received with no detected errors (both by the operator and the speakers), the maximum potential throughput approaches 64 words per minute. Each word is transmitted at least twice, once each by speaker and operator. Any flow control mechanisms, as well as error messages, add to the overhead and further reduce maximum throughput.

- For more accuracy, more bandwidth must be sacrificed. A guaranteed accuracy protocol could use verification of all transmissions. For example, the operator could be required to repeat each message back to the calling party before passing it along to the called party. This halves throughput once again: sending 120 words requires 1 minute (at least) from caller to operator, another minute from operator to caller (to confirm content); another minute from operator to callee, and another minute for the callee to confirm content as well.

  Maximum throughput for this protocol is reduced to no more than 30 words per minute. In this case, the caller sends her words to the operator ("See ya later, Myrtle"); the operator confirms with the caller ("You want me to tell the other party, 'See ya later, Myrtle'?"); the caller confirms ("Yes"); the operator connects with Myrtle and passes on the message ("The other party says, "See ya later, Myrtle"); Myrtle confirms with the operator ("she said 'See ya later, Myrtle'?); the operator confirms and Myrtle can send a response. The same four words ("See ya later, Myrtle") are sent, at 120 words per minute, four times. Overhead in this case is even higher as well, including all the control and confirmation messages to be passed.

- Finally, the ultimate in accuracy can be attained by an even more rigid protocol, under which the operator confirms content at both ends of the conversation. In addition to the exchanges cited in the last example, once the operator confirms the content with the called party, the operator would also confirm with the calling party ("your party says she received the message 'See ya later, Myrtle'; is this correct?").

    With this protocol the same words are repeated five times, limiting maximum throughput to 25 words per minute. This protocol apparently provides error checking, but it isn't clear whether there is a mechanism for error correction. What happens when a transmission is garbled ("See ya later, Myrtle" becomes "Seagull ate her turtle", for example)? Error detection protocols include data that can be used to check that no errors occured during transmission; error correcting protocols resend data that has been garbled.

Throughput is, therefore, a measure of how much actual application information is being transmitted, not the speed of the link. Even more important, different applications will require more throughput while others can manage with lower throughput. Given the same bandwidth, application goals can be achieved with different approaches to the protocols used.

Real-time applications are those that rely on getting data from one point to another more or less as the data is created. Applications that depend on the transmission of existing files are affected by low throughput, but are not rendered unusable by lower throughput: it may be inconvenient and annoying to have to wait while a large file is downloaded, but eventually it will be downloaded. Voice or video transmission are real-time applications: the sound or images will not be comprehensible if they are not delivered more or less in order and more or less at the same speed they are transmitted.

Developers must be willing to settle for fewer guarantees about accuracy and delivery of their multimedia applications than they would be for applications, such as file transfer, that would fail if data is not transferred accurately. By the same token, a variety of protocols and mechanisms are available to the developer for choosing just the right combination of throughput and accuracy.

4.3   Latency

With current technologies, time will always elapse between the moment a packet is sent out the source's network interface and the moment it is received at the destination's network interface.[4] The average elapsed time is called the *latency* of a network link. Latency and bandwidth together describe the potential performance of any given link.

A link with high bandwidth and low latency offers the best of both worlds: lots of network data can be transmitted in a given time, and it will arrive at the other end quickly. A link with low bandwidth and high latency offers the worst: not much data can be sent in a given time, and it may take a while to arrive at the other end.

For many years, long distance telephone calls, particularly international calls, were routed through satellites maintaining a geosynchronous earth orbit (GEO). At roughly 22,000 miles above the earth, these satellites are able to "see" a large portion of the globe all at once. Any calls routed through these satellites suffered from relatively high latency. Transmitted at the speed of light (186,000 miles/second or 300,000 km/second), the signal must travel over 44,000 miles—adding roughly one fourth of a second to the link latency. The result was a noticeable and annoying delay of as much as a half second from the time you stop talking and the time you start to hear the other party's response.

Link latency may be related to the actual physical traversal of a link, as with satellite transmissions, or it may be related to the route data takes across different networks as it traverses the internet. The more routers a packet traverses, the more likely the link is yielding high latency. Intermediate routers and switches will always take some measurable amount of time to process and forward a packet.

Users prefer low latency for interactive applications, including telephony. Even if the bandwidth is relatively low, a comprehensible conversation can be carried over a link with low latency. Other types of application, particularly those that involve transmission of large amounts of data such as file transfer, will prefer a link with high bandwidth even if the latency

---

[4]Networks based on quantum physics may someday reduce the elapsed time significantly. There is some speculation that instantaneous interaction across vast distances might be possible, but much work remains before such networks become practical.

is moderately high. Consider an example:

```
A company uses a file transfer application to
distribute copies of the corporate database to a
backup facility every night. The database totals
10 Mb. The company can choose between three
transfer mechanisms, one with low bandwidth
(10 Kb/second) and low latency (10 ms)⁵; one with
high bandwidth (1 Mb/second) and high latency
(10 seconds); and a third with very high
bandwidth (100 petabytes/second)⁶ but also very
high latency (12 hours).⁷
```

Clearly, the best choice is the second one: total transmission time will be 20 seconds. It only takes 10 seconds to "fill up the pipe" with 10 Mb of data, but every bit of data spends 10 seconds in that pipe.

The low-latency, low bandwidth option will be more appropriate to an interactive application such as terminal emulation. In that case, one node is sending characters typed in by a person (roughly 5 bytes/second, or 40 bits/second); the other node is sending back terminal screens full of characters (roughly 80×25, or 2,000 bytes, or 16 kilobits per screen). The bandwidth will be more than sufficient, while the low latency ensures that the network won't be the bottleneck in the event of performance problems.

Finally, that last option—very very high bandwidth, very very high latency—makes sense for certain applications. For example, backing up or moving corporate archives might best be achieved by throwing all the tapes into a truck rather than dumping them down a data pipe.

4.4   Packet Switching and Routing

The term *packet switching* describes networks in which individual packets en route from their source to their destination traverse intermediate nodes

---

[5] milliseconds.

[6] Petabyte $= 2^{50}$ bytes, or 1,024 terabytes. Terabyte $= 2^{40}$ bytes. A terabyte is roughly 10 trillion bytes, or about 10,000 gigabytes. A petabyte is, therefore, equivalent to roughly 10,000,000 Gb.

[7] This last option does not, strictly speaking, describe a network solution but rather applies networking performance measures (latency and bandwidth) to a large truck screaming down the highway with a trailer full of high-capacity tapes.

independent of each other. *Routing* describes the process when intermediate nodes perform some level of analysis on packets, while *switching* occurs when the intermediate nodes use some much simpler algorithm for deciding how to pass the packet from node to node. Therefore, one packet traveling from a node in Berkeley to a node in Cambridge may pass through Evanston, while another packet traveling between the two nodes might pass through Austin.

To illustrate switching and routing issues, we'll use a new example: a high school math class, in which half of the students belong to a clique. The group (known as "the group") devises a system for passing messages from any member to any other member.

Students in this class are seated in a strict 6×6 array, so (assuming perfect attendance) students have between three and eight potential message forwarders. The student sitting in the front left corner can pass the message to her back, to her right, and on a diagonal to her right-back; any student seated on an "edge" (front-, rear-, left-, or right-most files) can pass the message to five potential message forwarders. Students seated in the interior have as many as eight potential message forwarders to pass messages (Fig. 4–2).

As with any form of communication, there are rules for transmitting messages. As with any form of communication among teenagers, those rules may not always be obvious to adults. Rules include:

1. All messages are passed from hand to hand to an immediate neighbor.
2. If more than one of the immediate neighbors are members of the group, the forwarder must pick the member who is closest to the destination.
3. If two or more of the immediate neighbors who are members of the group are equidistant to the destination, the forwarder can choose which to pass it to based on some "fair" metric. For example, the forwarder can determine who will forward based on whose turn it is, based on who is less likely to be caught by the teacher, based on who the forwarder likes better, or randomly.
4. If there is only one immediate neighbor who is also a group member, the forwarder must pass all messages to that member.
5. If there are no immediate neighbors who belong to the group, the forwarder must choose a non-member to forward the message. The forwarder may be chosen based on whose turn it is,

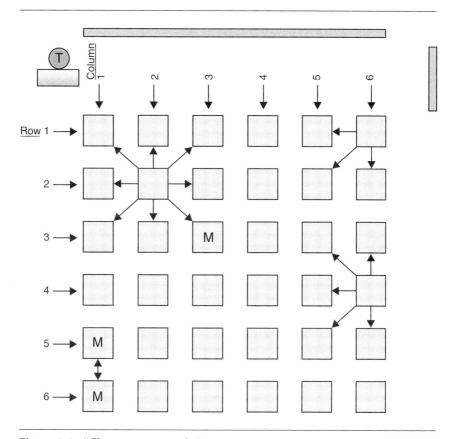

Figure 4–2: "Classroom network."

based on who is reliable and who is not, or based on who is least likely to get caught.

One difference between routing and switching occurs in the way forwarding decisions are formulated and implemented. In routed networks, the nodes handling the task of routing (in this case, the student members of the group) take an active part in determining optimal routes for messages. For example, consider what happens when the students seated at the far left in the last two rows are both members, but they are both otherwise surrounded by non-members. If the forwarding rules cited above were in use, any message passed between the two would (by rule #4) spend the rest of the class passing the same message back and forth between each other.

In a case like that, having more information about the network would help considerably. For instance, if the student in seat 1,5[8] is sending to a student in seat 3,3, then it would make far more sense to pass it along to seat 2,4, only one seat away from the destination. Network information can be distributed in different ways, as we'll see in later chapters.

In a switched network, members of the group would more likely set their forwarding policies at the start of each class based on who was sitting where. One simple policy might dictate that a member student (in seat X,Y) passes messages based on the coordinates of the destination (m,n). If the objective is to get the message closest to the destination, then the student would calculate (X-m) and (Y-n) for himself as well as for his neighbors and pass along the message to whichever neighbor is closer to the destination than he is. This set of calculcations can be made ahead of time, and can incorporate adjustments to keep messages in the hands of network members. The calculations then become a simple table listing destinations and linking them with neighbors.

4.5   Best Effort Delivery

In discussing throughput, and the way in which it can be affected by applications that require more or less assurance about whether or not their data has been received as sent, we talked about guaranteed delivery. The opposite of guaranteed delivery is *best effort delivery*. Best effort means that no guarantees are offered beyond the assurance that participating systems will make every reasonable effort to deliver packets, but if they don't, you shouldn't be surprised.

Packets sent by best-effort protocols either make it to their destinations, or they don't. The only mechanism provided by a best-effort protocol to allow a sender to confirm if a packet was received is to have the recipient reply. Packets may be dropped by intermediate systems for different reasons, many of which have nothing to do with either the sender or the recipient. For example, a system overwhelmed by demand for some service will often silently drop packets.

---

[8]Seats are identified by X,Y, where X is the column and Y is the row.

This is not to say that there is no way for a sender to ever determine if a packet has been dropped. Mechanisms for providing some sort of continuity are often provided at different protocol layers (see Chapter 5 for more about protocol layering). In other words, the protocol handling delivery of a packet may be best-effort, but protocols handling the data carried within the packet may provide mechanisms for checking in on remote systems to determine if they are still up and responding to network requests.

4.6   Unicast, Broadcast, Multicast, and Anycast

So far in this book we've been assuming that network communication occurs between a single source and single destination node. Although intermediate systems may participate in forwarding (see next section) packets along their paths, only the source and destination are concerned with the contents of a packet. Yet networks often provide mechanisms for transmitting the same packet to (or even from) more than one node.

Unicast describes the network traffic we've already met: unicast traffic goes from a single source node to single destination node. The source is identified by its network address, and the destination is identified by its network address. This is the "normal" mechanism for network transmission: one sender, one recipient.

There are situations in which it would be helpful to be able to send data once and have it be received by more than one node. We will cover three different instances of send once/receive many network transmissions in this book:

- *Broadcast* refers to a mechanism that allows a node to send a single message and have it be received by all nodes on the same network. Broadcasts may be used with a network interface layer protocol, or at the internet layer. Broadcasts can be used when there is reason to transmit the same message to all nodes on a network. There are advantages, in particular the need to transmit the broadcast data only once rather than having to unicast the message to every node, thus reducing overall traffic. Also, all nodes can be reached whether the sender is aware of their existence or not. Broadcast was thought to be a good idea when it was first implemented, but experience with it in large networks and the internet has shown that if not properly and carefully used, broadcasts can quickly overwhelm a network.

- *Multicast* refers to a mechanism by which members of a group of network or internet nodes receive messages directed to a group's address. Nodes may *subscribe* to multicast group. A member node sends multicast data only once to the multicast group address and members of that group receive copies. As with broadcast, multicast reduces traffic when one node must communicate with a group. The sending node send group data out only once. By limiting delivery to group member nodes only, multicast can be much more efficient than broadcast. As with broadcast, the sender need not be aware of all group members, although unlike broadcast, group membership can be limited.

- *Anycast* refers to a mechanism by which data is transmitted to one of a group of nodes, usually the one "nearest" the sender.

Brief examples of these transmission mechanisms will help clarify the differences as well as the reasons for each:

- Broadcasts are useful when a node is booting to the network and wants to announce its presence. As we'll see in Chapter 21, a node entering a network must identify itself to the other nodes on the network, to confirm that it is using a unique network address and to notify other nodes of how to reach it; broadcast is the best way to do so. A node may broadcast a request for a particular service if it is not configured with information about reaching that service directly. Broadcasts are most manageable when confined to local links. Allowing them out into the internet or an intranet may result in excessive traffic. Broadcast will be discussed at greater length in Chapters 19 and 21.

- Multicasts allow groups of nodes to communicate throughout the internet. For example, users on different local networks can subscribe to the same multicast group to listen to an internet broadcast or participate in a real-time discussion. Multicast packets are transmitted only on those networks where nodes belong to the multicast group; if no nodes on a network are subscribed, the packets are not passed to the network. And if there are one or more group members on a network, the packets are passed only once to the network itself (within the network, the packets may be reproduced for delivery to members). Multicast will be discussed at greater length in Chapter 24.

- Anycasts are intended to replace broadcasts for reaching specific services on a network. Rather than sending every node on a network a copy of a request, a request can be sent to an anycast address. All nodes that provide a particular service are configured to receive and respond to packets sent to an anycast address. Anycast is a relatively new internet mechanism, and will be discussed at greater length in Chapter 27.

4.7   Switching, Routing, and Bridging

Packets sent between nodes on the same local link are delivered through the network's local facilities. A LAN may use a hub to pass packets from one node to another; a wireless network may use its own network of transmitters and receivers to distribute data. When one network is connected to another network, however, something is needed to determine how to deliver packets sent from a node on one network to a node on the other network.

The devices that link networks and decide what to do with packets are called *switches* and *routers*. There are also things called *bridges* which don't get talked about as much as they used to. These things all look at network datagrams en route from their sources to their destinations, and they decide what to do with them.

We'll get into a more detailed discussion of the differences between bridges, routers, and switches in the next chapter; for now, it is sufficient to say that these devices share the function of forwarding packets on a network. How the forwarding is done, and to which networks, determines whether a device is a bridge or whether it is a router or switch. Differentiating routers and switches from each other has taken on greater subtlety over the past few years, and the differences will be detailed in Chapter 5.

4.8   Edge, Non-Edge, and Backbone Devices

Prior to its commercialization (in the early 1990s), the internet's structure was often portrayed as being an almost ad hoc collection of interconnected networks linking all nodes to each other, often with redundant links.

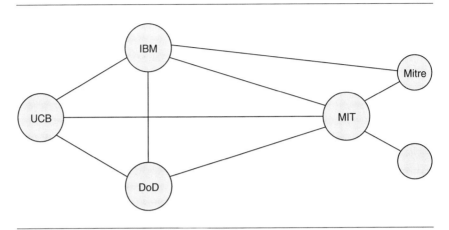

Figure 4–3: Primitive internet architecture.

Routers within an organization often provided internal routing services to nodes inside the organization as well as routing packets to nodes outside the organization's autonomous system (AS). Figure 4–3 shows how this worked in the days when many organizations had only one or a handful of mult-user mainframes; distinguishing between internal and external nodes makes little sense when there is only one internal node at a site.

This type of network may provide many different ways to reach any given node, depending on how many hops packets are permitted to take. It is well-suited to networks of individual nodes that may need to interact directly but unpredictably with nodes on any other part of the network. Distance between nodes did not always predict how often they need to interact: nodes within a single work group may interact frequently (or not) depending on what the users are working on. When a distant node begins offering some interesting service, those local nodes may need to interact more frequently with the distant node than the local ones. As a research network linking researchers, organizational boundaries might be blurred or at least less well protected as members of the network used it to interact.

In the early days, the ratio between the number of users and the number of nodes on the internet was fairly high because most nodes were multiuser systems and there were few if any TCP/IP implementations for PCs. The internet linked powerful computers that might or might not be local to each other, and the map of the internet had fewer nodes per network as well as a more ad hoc internet linkage process than we are now accustomed to.

As the internet became increasingly commercialized with widespread use of PCs and dialup internet access through internet service providers (ISPs), that ratio began approaching parity. It also changed fundamental assumptions about the way the internet worked. ISPs offering consumer internet access no longer needed to provide much in the way of internal routing and the focus became routing outside the ISP (though not exclusively, of course).

Figure 4–4 shows how today's internet resembles a circulatory system, with most of the connectivity provided by ISPs being offered in the form of access to a larger system that feeds into a central core. For the most part, people who connect to the same ISP have no interest in interacting with other nodes on the same ISP's network (e.g., their neighbors), but rather with nodes somewhere else.

By the late 1990s, a new distinction was clearly drawn between devices that exist and manage traffic on the edges of an AS and those devices internal

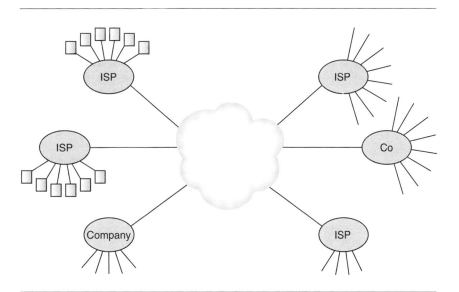

Figure 4–4: Circulating packets across the internet.

to the AS that also manage traffic. Edge devices include routers, but also switches and security devices (*firewalls*) that together act on behalf of the AS to the rest of the internet and that concentrate traffic entering and exiting the AS.

The distinction between edge and non-edge devices is important when considering what they do. An edge device acts as a gateway into and out of the AS, and it can be a single point of failure for connectivity for the AS. If the edge device (or devices) fail, the AS will seem to disappear from the global internet. Internally, nodes on the AS would lose access to external nodes on the global internet but all internal networking could continue without any problem.

On the other hand, if all nodes internal to the AS were to fail (e.g., a power failure) but the edge device continued working, the rest of the internet would view that AS as being reachable—but would not be able to reach any service running internal to the AS. An edge device moves packets between the inside and the outside of an AS; a non-edge device moves packets around inside an AS. A device could behave as an edge device for a small AS contained within a larger AS at the same time it behaves also as a non-edge device for that same AS. Edge devices and ASes are discussed at greater length in Chapters 22 and 23.

4.9   Chapter Summary

If the network components defined in Chapters 2 and 3 are the building blocks, in this chapter we begin to see how those building blocks can be assembled into functional structures, for example by building virtual circuits. And those structures can be defined and measured, for example by describing performance attributes (latency and throughput).

We also explored some of the ways those components can interact, through both switched and routed networks, by exchanging data packaged for delivery across network clouds. And we introduced some of the challenges facing protocol designers seeking to move packets across those networks, particularly as the networks grow larger and larger.

5

Network Models and Internetworking Concepts

The chapter about the OSI and IP internetworking models, complete with seven- and four-layer stack diagrams, has long been a mainstay for any book about TCP/IP networking. Unfortunately, the focus on network layer numbering often overshadows the fundamental concept of how those layers make it possible for IP (or OSI) to enable seamless and platform-independent interoperability between nodes.

In this chapter, we'll take an updated look at the OSI and IP internet models, but we'll concentrate on how encapsulation makes internetworking possible, and the different kinds of systems that move data across network boundaries.

5.1   OSI vs IP

When the International Organization for Standardization (ISO) created the Open System Interconnection (OSI) protocol architecture, they hoped to build, from scratch, a set of protocols from which a complete internet-working infrastructure could be built. The OSI design was based on the *OSI reference model* in which communication across the internetwork takes place in seven different layers, between seven different entities on each communicating system.

OSI and TCP/IP were developed virtually concurrently, with OSI formally starting in the late 1970s and matured by the early 1990s. The many significant differences between the two approaches might best be summed up in this way: The OSI effort aimed to completely specify protocols and then implement them, while the IP approach was to implement (and re-implement based on experimental results) and then specify the protocols.

As a result, the vast majority of networked systems now support TCP/IP, while OSI-compliant networks are an endangered species, surviving in far-flung corners of the world, usually in government agencies.

It is important to realize that OSI was not a failure, nor a misbegotten effort doomed to join 5.25" floppy diskettes, beta video tape, and DIVX in obscurity. The OSI effort produced many techniques that were incorporated into the internet protocol suite. Even so, there is little reason for most networking professionals to have more than a passing acquaintance with OSI protocols.

5.2   The OSI Reference Model

OSI is most famous for its layered network model. Seven groups of entities interoperate across an OSI internet. At the top, the application layer is where interactions happen between application entities: a user's browser and a company's web server interact with each other, exchanging requests and responses, oblivious to anything going on in between. At the bottom, the physical layer is where network interfaces communicate by exchanging signals through some physical medium. In between, there are five

Layer	Number	Description
Application	7	The entities with which people and other users interact to exchange network data operate here.
Presentation	6	Entities (applications) do something here to negotiate the form in which data is to be exchanged.
Session	5	Entities (applications) do something here to (possibly) manage how different protocols might be applied to a single application.
Transport	4	Processes on internet nodes interact by passing *messages* to each other.
Network	3	Nodes on an internet interact by transmitting and receiving data *packets* that may be forwarded across physical network boundaries.
Data Link	2	Nodes sharing a network medium interact by transmitting and receiving data *frames* over that shared medium.
Physical	1	Communication between the interfaces to the physical link, including raw signals over a wire, radio transmission over wireless.

Table 5–1: OSI model layers.

more layers of interactions between network nodes, internet nodes, and system processes.

Table 5–1 lists the OSI model's layers and describes, briefly, what each is supposed to do.

The OSI model was designed to cover all possible interactions between all possible entities. By creating seven different layers at which entities could interact, the OSI model complicated even the most simple interactions. On the other hand, such layering is quite useful in the world of telecommunications, where it is often necessary to exert a great deal of control over how data flows, and how it is ordered, and even how meta-data (information about information) related to managing connections can be transmitted and managed.

5.3   The DoD (IP) Reference Model

Originally named for the US Department of Defense, which funded the research, the *DoD reference model* (also known as the *IP reference model*) developed in tandem with experimental implementations of the protocols. By ignoring issues best handled individually by end nodes, such as application data formatting and flow, the IP model largely eliminated the presentation and session layers. Further simplifying matters, the physical expression of bits on a local network is a matter best left between the node and its network. In the course of traversing different networks, packets might be expressed in photons, electrons, or radio waves—but as long as the protocols used at the physical and network interface layers can communicate with the network layer protocols, the network layer protocols will be able to handle the data.

The OSI session and presentation layers often seem vague in the context of TCP/IP networking. Issues such as how data is to be formatted, or what a system does with network data before it presents it to the application, have (for most internet applications, at least) best been dealt with locally. As long as the mail or web page or other data gets where it's been sent, the local systems handle formatting and presenting it. Internet applications generally delegate responsibility for session layer issues like flow control to the transport layer, and either handle presentation layer issues within the protocol or allow the local system to deal with them.

The "IP model," to the extent that there is a formal model, is far less strict than the OSI model. Although many TCP/IP books use roughly the same pair of diagrams (Fig. 5–1) showing the seven layers of OSI on one hand and the four layers of IP on the other, in practice the IP model assumes far more flexibility and imposes far less structure on its related protocols.

Under the IP model, the functions of the session and presentation layers are largely subsumed into the application layer, and the physical layer

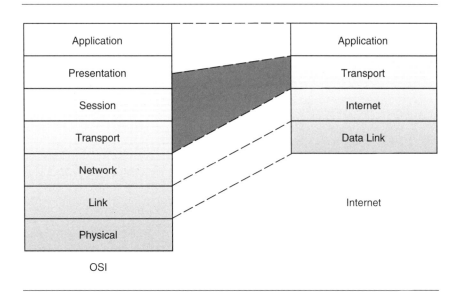

Figure 5–1: Traditional "OSI versus IP" illustration.

is ignored because it is accessed only indirectly, through the network interface layer.[1] Only the application, transport, network, and network interface layers are considered part of the IP model. As a result, IP networking focuses on application, transport, internet, and network interface layer protocols.

Figure 5–2 shows an approximation of the actual relationship among layers in the IP model. However, that figure doesn't express the flexibility available. Under IP, you could implement an application directly on top of IP with no transport layer protocol; you could layer one application on top of another, and one transport protocol on top of another, if you so desire (this sometimes makes sense, as we'll discover when we discuss encapsulation, as well as throughout the book).

Internet protocol specifications generally don't mandate which protocols are to be used above or below (although there are often strong practical, logical, and technical arguments for using certain protocols together). In general, application layer protocols are used over transport layer

[1]The primary importance of the link layer lies in its function of providing an interface between the internet and the physical layer.

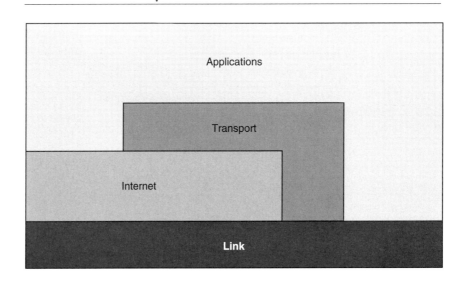

Figure 5–2: The IP "model".

protocols such as TCP (Transmission Control Protocol) and UDP (User Datagram Protocol), which in turn are used on top of an internet layer protocol (IP), but exceptions are possible and sometimes even useful. There is no technical reason one could not run a traditional internet application over a non-TCP/IP protocol suite (such as running HTTP between nodes on a Novell Netware network). Likewise protocol *tunneling*, running a network session that is enclosed within another network session, is not only possible but often required.

An extreme example is presented in RFC 3093, "Firewall Enhancement Protocol (FEP)," published on April Fool's Day, 2001 and describing a protocol that would allow any network protocol to be encapsulated within Hypertext Transfer Protocol (HTTP) packets. Because the only internet application protocol typically allowed through firewalls is HTTP, the result would allow any application protocol to pass through those firewalls. Nodes using FEP in effect treat HTTP as their transport layer protocol.

We will return to protocol tunneling when discussing IP security as well as multi-protocol networking.

5.4 Encapsulation

Whether a network uses 5 of 7, 4 of 4, or some other combination of available layers, effective use of those layers is enabled through *encapsulation*. The term may be unfamiliar, but the concept is not. If you've ever mailed a letter or package, you've used a form of encapsulation.

Consider the protocol for mailing a birthday present. First, acquire a present. Then, wrap it up in a box or appropriate container. In some cases, this means using tissue paper, packing peanuts, or other padding to make the present fit safely into the container. If purchased new at a store, chances are good that this packaging was already done by the manufacturer. Take the container, and enclose it in wrapping paper; the name of the recipient should be unambiguously and legibly written somewhere on the package. Then, the wrapped gift is placed in a shipping box, again with appropriate padding to make it fit. The recipient's name and address, as well as the sender's, are written on the package. At this point, the package can be taken to a post office and mailed.

The present itself can be thought of as the data; when the manufacturer creates the present, they package it appropriately by putting it in a box and padding it. The box carries information on it: the product's name and model number, instructions, and so forth. That box may be placed into a case, to be shipped to dealers. At that point the dealers unpack the cases and put the boxed products up for sale; you buy one as a gift, and then package it yourself to be shipped as a present.

Here's what happens: Each time the gift moves, the gift must be packaged; each time it arrives, the gift is unwrapped. To apply the concept to an internet, exchange "packet" for "gift" and "encapsulated (or de-encapsulated) with the appropriate protocol" for "packaged (or unwrapped)."

The process of mailing it from the purchaser to the recipient is particularly telling:

1. Buy the gift (don't forget to strip off all price tags or markings).
2. Wrap it, and mark it with the sender's and recipient's name ("From Alice, to Bob").
3. Put it into another box for shipping, padding it inside and marking sender/recipient names/addresses on outside.

4. The package is delivered through the postal system (using the recipient's address on the outside).
5. The package is opened by someone, who sees the recipient's name on the gift wrap; the package is then given to that person.
6. The gift wrap is taken off, and the present has been received (from sender to recipient).
7. The manufacturer's packaging is removed, and the item inside has been received (from manufacturer to end user).

In network terms, encapsulation is what happens when you start wrapping up data for delivery across a network.[2] The process of encapsulation begins at the very top layer of the network stack, where the application accepts data from the entity using the application. This data is broken down into some type of unit for transmission, and each unit is given a header containing all necessary application protocol information.

At each step, there are two parts to the protocol data unit: the *payload*, which is the data to be carried, and the protocol wrappings, usually *headers* containing data placed before the payload and sometimes *trailers*, additional data appended after the payload to indicate the end of the payload.[3] Protocols at each layer consider the data passed from a higher layer to be payload; the contents of the payload don't matter, just the appropriate headers.

So, the application begins with the actual application data, perhaps part of a file to be transferred or perhaps a login request, and adds its own protocol headers to that data before passing it along to the process that handles communication for the application. That process then wraps those bits up with its own set of headers to make sure the payload gets to where the application wants it to go—the appropriate process serving the appropriate application on the other end of the transmission. If the destination process resides on the same system, the package can be passed to it right there, and no further network processing has to take place. If the process is not local, however, further work needs to be done.

Once the process has encapsulated the payload it receives from the application, it adds its own headers and passes the whole thing to the entity handling internet layer activity. That entity may be a separate program or

---

[2]The term *de-encapsulation* has been used at times to mean the process of unwrapping data as it is being delivered, but this usage is neither wide or nor widely accepted.

[3]Sometimes also referred to, incorrectly, as *footers*.

part of the local computer's operating system, but in either case it packages the process's data into yet another payload and adds its own headers. Finally, at the network interface the system wraps the payload up one more time for transmission onto the network.

The reverse process of unpacking the data occurs at the destination,[4] where the network interface is responsible for accepting frames sent to it, stripping off the frame headers and passing the payload up to the entity that handles the network layer. As they progress up the stack, the headers of the nested protocol data units are stripped away until the only payload left is the actual data being communicated.

Note items 6 and 7 in the list of steps detailing the delivery of a birthday present: if you purchased a manufactured gift in its original packaging, the delivery of that unit (item plus packaging) completes the transaction between you and the recipient. At the same time, the item itself has actually been delivered from its original source (the manufacturing facility) to the end user only when the recipient opens the packaging. Even though you paid for and shipped the present, the underlying communication was one between the manufacturer and the end-user; you were merely the conduit through which that transaction took place.

This separation of different layers of interaction is fundamental to understanding how many different entities, often completely unknown to the endpoints of a communication, must interact to complete a data transmission.

The alternative to encapsulation of network data is to require every application to handle every aspect of the transmission and reception of data across the network. The prospect is daunting: each application would require access to information about the destination node(s) including data such as the destination's local network address as well as its internet address, what operating system or hardware is being used at the destination, what systems the data must pass through to arrive at the destination, and much more.

Encapsulation allows this single complex task—moving data from one application to another through a network—into several (perhaps even many) much simpler tasks. The application needs only to know enough to

---

[4]The process may also occur, at least in part, at one or more stops on the way to the destination, as we'll see later on.

format its data and commands in a standard format and pass it along to the appropriate interface at the next layer, and so on.

The huge success of the layered protocol model of the internet is undoubtedly due to this creation of simplicity out of complexity. However, the downside of encapsulation is that it, when strictly implemented, can introduce inefficiencies. The more protocols that need to be layered, the more opportunity for those inefficiencies to enter the process. The IP model with its four layers provides enough complexity for most applications to be broken down and delivered, while at the same time the model's flexibility about layer separation makes it easier for protocols to acquire and use information about network connections that can be used to optimize performance.

5.5   Internetwork Interface Devices

The OSI model was crucial in introducing and elaborating on the concepts of layers as well as encapsulation. Things that happen on a LAN or in some other homogenous network environment are often said to occur at the *network interface layer*, the *data link layer*, or *layer 2*. Internet layer activity occurs at *layer 3*, and transport layer activity at *layer 4*. Applications happen at *layer 7*. This segmentation is shown in Figure 5–3.

At layer 7, the application layer, two applications—a web browser and a web server—interact by sending requests and replies back and forth (the protocol for this application, HTTP, is discussed at greater length in Chapter 12). The browser and the server don't know, and don't care, about what protocols are being used to get the requests and replies back and forth; they are just concerned with application-type interaction, mostly requests to send over a data file or a reply containing requested files.

When discussing bridges, switches, and routers, it is more useful to concentrate on the lower layers. At the internet layer, or layer 3, network nodes use a globally unique identifier (IP address) to allow them to interoperate across many different networks, and many different types of networks. Network nodes on the same physical network interact at the data link layer, or layer 2. At the data link layer, communication is possible only over the local physical network; at the internet layer, communication is possible between any two network interfaces on any two physical networks connected to the same internet.

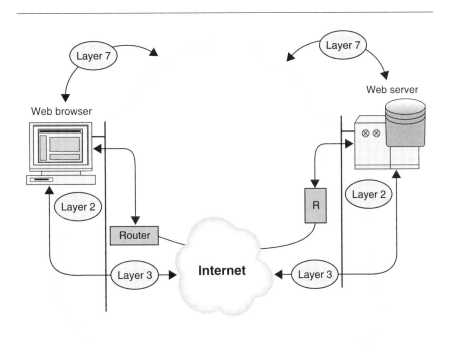

Figure 5–3: Using OSI layers to differentiate distinguish network interfaces.

Another difference is format: at the data link layer, data is formatted into protocol data units that are interpreted by the data link layer network interfaces. That means, for example, Ethernet frames comprise bits in a form that Ethernet network interfaces are able to decode. A Token Ring network interface would not be able to process an Ethernet frame. At the internet layer, data is formatted into protocol data units that can be interpreted by any internet network interface supporting the same internet-level protocol.

When an internet node emits an internet packet addressed to some non-local node, the internet layer interface produces a packet with an internet address. The internet connection is a logical construct, rather than a direct connection: the node is physically connected to a physical network on which it can actually send data through its data link layer interface. Thus the internet packet must be encapsulated within a data link layer protocol data unit to be sent anywhere. Understanding how bridges, switches, and routers work will help illustrate the distinction.

5.5.1 BRIDGES

A bridge is a device used to physically connect two (or more) networks of the same type. Bridges are layer 2 devices, because they operate at the data link layer to connect those networks. The bridge examines each network *frame* (the generic PDU for layer 2) to see which network the frame originated from and which network the destination is on (Fig. 5–4). If the frame originates on one network but is destined for the other network, the bridge repeats the frame on its interface to the second network.

Bridges vary in sophistication. A simple bridge called a *repeater* listens to all traffic on one physical network and repeats that traffic on the other network. *Learning bridges* examine all frames on both networks, recording the network on which frames from each source address appear. It repeats all frames at first, but as it gets more information about the nodes on the networks it connects, it become more discriminating. For example, assume the bridge in Figure 5–4 is a learning bridge and has just been turned on.

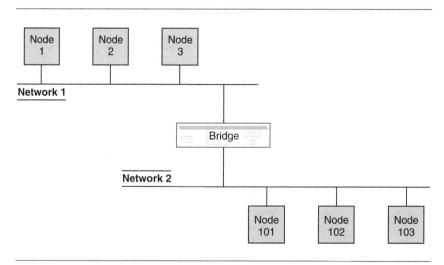

Figure 5–4: Connecting physical networks.

When Node 2 transmits a frame to Node 102, the bridge records that Node 2 is located on Network 1, and then repeats the frame on Network 2. When Node 102 replies to Node 2's frame, the bridge checks the destination address (Node 2) and, noting that it is on Network 1, repeats the frame. When Node 101 sends a frame to Node 102, the bridge records Node 101's address as being on Network 2, but does not repeat the frame, because the bridge checks the destination (Node 102) and notes that address as being on the same network as the source.

There are other types of bridges, for example those which answer on behalf of nodes on different networks by changing the layer 2 frame headers, but these depend on the type of network is being used. The concept of a network bridge is most useful when discussing internetworking only to illustrate why layer 2 internets tend not to scale well (for more information about network bridging, the reader can check the literature for the layer 2 network protocols to be bridged, or more general networking texts).

Although bridges work well with networks of dozens or even hundreds of nodes, they generate too much traffic (by repeating frames where the destination is not already known), and as the number of nodes in the networks increases, the memory and processing requirements increase beyond the capability of the devices. Furthermore, layer 2 internets require all connected nodes and netwroks to use the same protocol for transmitting frames locally. This presents a hardship for any nodes or networks that wish to be linked but that already use a different protocol.

5.5.2 SWITCHES

A switch also operates at layer 2, but rather than linking just two networks, a switch can link two or more networks. One definition of a switch is "a multiport bridge." The switch maintains a table associating layer 2 network addresses with the physical networks the switch connects. Switches tend to be more complex than bridges, especially when they are used for internetworks that do not depend on IP, for example, within automated teller machine (ATM) networks (see Chapter 21).

The complexity of switching protocols for ATM networks can approach the complexity of routing within IP internets. ATM switches don't just link individual networks, but often provide a fabric for moving frames (actually, ATM protocol data units are called *cells*) along many different paths in an internet depending on what kind of data they contain. The different paths may provide different levels of service, including higher reliability, lower cost, guaranteed delivery, higher bandwidth, or faster throughput. ATM switches are often highly configurable, and often support protocols that permit them to integrate ATM switching functions with IP routing protocols.

Though we will not revisit bridges in this book, we will discuss how ATM and IP protocols interoperate at greater length. As the internet continues to grow, ATM and other switching protocols become more important for providing high-speed internet backbone service.

5.5.3 ROUTERS

A router operates one logical layer above the network interface layer and is necessary whenever two different types of networks are to be connected. Consider what happens when we replace Network 2 in Figure 5–4 with a different type of network, that uses a different address space to number nodes. Let's say the original network interface layer addressing scheme assigns a unique number from 1 to 16 to identify the network, and a unique number from 1 to 1,024 to identify the node within the entire network. Now, if Network 2 is replaced by Network B, whose address space uses letters rather than numbers, a bridge will be incapable of dealing with the new network. Even if the two networks use otherwise identical protocols, any addresses on the new network will be seen as invalid and the bridge will most likely treat them as corrupted frames and discard them.

Two things are necessary: a global addressing scheme and a device capable of mapping local network interface layer addresses to the globally unique addresses.

Under a global addressing scheme, administrators working with each network assign unique addresses to each node in addition to the network interface layer addresses. When those nodes communicate using layer 3 protocols, they wrap their data up with headers that identify the internet—layer 3—addresses of the source and destination. When a packet (the name we'll most often use for layer 3 protocol data units) is destined for a local node—a node the sender can determine is on the same physical network—the sender will likely be able to handle layer 2 network processing on its own, through its own network interface.

However, when the sender determines that the packet's internet destination is not local, the packet is sent to the closest router for disposition and forwarding.

Routers may differ from switches in several ways, although the most important is that routers are able to map addresses between layers 2 and 3 (Fig. 5–5). Traditionally, switches were solid state, single purpose devices that used a fixed and static set of rules to very quickly determine where a frame should go and then send it there. Routing devices are available that use solid state electronics rather than traditional disk-bound computers to improve speed and efficiency, and manufacturers often call these devices *layer 3 switches*, to convey the differences.

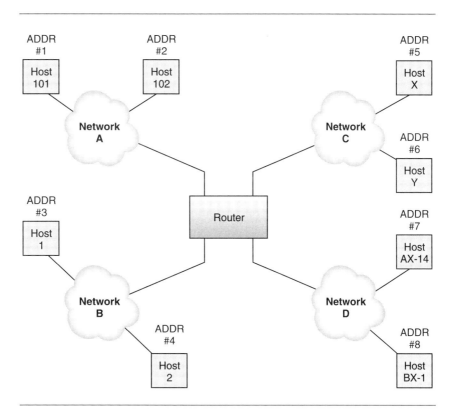

Figure 5–5: A routed network.

A router is any device that can behave as a gateway between two or more different layer 2 protocols, or between two or more physical networks using the same layer 2 protocol. When the packet is destined for a non-local address, a node sends it to a router on the same physical network. The router is connected to at least two physical networks, and is capable of sending and receiving layer 2 frames to and from all of them. When the router receives a packet to be forwarded out on an internet, it processes the layer 2 frame as well as the layer 3 packet headers to determine what to do with the packet. A router may use different protocols (to be discussed in Chapter 22) on which to base its decisions, but once it determines where the packet should go the router modifies the layer 3 header and creates new layer 2 frames to deliver the packet to its next destination. That destination may or may not be the packet's ultimate destination: it may be another router closer to that destination, at which point the packet is processed again. The process of handing a packet from router to router concludes only when the packet arrives at a router connected to the same physical network as the packet's destination. At that point, the router just delivers the packet to the destination node.

Figure 5–5 shows a routed network, in which there are four different networks connected through the router. Each of the networks uses a different physical host address scheme, but the router is able to communicate using all those schemes. Each node on every network has a logical address (the ADDR #X scheme), and the router keeps track of how best to move messages based on both their logical and physical addresses.

Of course, this brief discussion overlooks many of the subtle and not-so-subtle aspects of routing and packet delivery. Internet routing is a fundamental part of IP internetworking, and will be discussed at greater length throughout this book.

5.6   Defining the Internet

Attempting to put boundaries on the internet is as daunting a task as putting boundaries on the oceans of the world. One might say, all bodies of salt water, but then what to do with the Dead Sea in Israel or Utah's Great Salt Lake? One might say, all bodies of water that can be navigated with an ocean-going vessel, but then what do you do about the St. Lawrence Seaway and the Great Lakes of North America? Are tidal pools part of the ocean? What about estuaries like the rivers surrounding

New York City, alternately filled with salt and fresh water depending on the tides?

Unless you are an oceanographer, the answer is pretty much unimportant. As with other important transportation and communication networks such as the telephone system, national highway and local road systems, power grids, and more, the internet is increasingly something that most users simply plug into and get connected.

However, if you are reading this book you will surely want to understand what factors could be used to circumscribe the global internet, and why they may or may not be good indicators. A good place to start is with how a system makes its connections. The connections available to a system usually define what that system is connected to. This circular logic doesn't get you far: if you are connected to the internet, then you are connected to the internet, it seems to be saying. However, almost no one is ever connected directly to "the internet" (whatever that might mean). Systems (including networks) are connected to other systems (again, may be networks).

The problem lies in defining what it means to be connected. Here are some of the possibilities for ambiguity about connections:

- Is the connection permanent or intermittent?
- What systems can be considered connected?
- Must the connected system use internet protocols?
- Must the connected system support all internet or application protocols?

None of these possibilities is far-fetched; in fact, they call into doubt the "connectivity" of many systems that would normally be considered connected.

- Home users of dialup PCs routinely connect and disconnect their systems. Can those PCs still be considered to be connected to the internet when the phone line is not in use? The user may still feel "connected," reading and answering internet mail, perusing newsgroups, and browsing web content that has been downloaded during a previous session. And what about personal digital assistants, periodically downloading similar data from the PC? In the early days of the internet, many organizations provided only limited connectivity, perhaps internet mail and newsgroups only, to their users through a gateway system that connected directly to the internet only long enough to download and upload messages. Were the systems on those networks connected to the internet, or not?

- As broadband continues to expand, more individuals use these "always on" services. A cable or DSL modem is always accessible over the network, but can the home user's PC (or network) be considered connected if the system is not on? What about networks that are isolated from the rest of the global internet through a security system called a *firewall* that mediates all data transmissions between the inside and the outside?

- Although less common now that virtually all network operating systems are based on internet protocols, until the end of the 1990s it was still common for LANs based on proprietary protocols to provide transport and internet layer services for internet applications. A user might have a Netscape browser running over Novell NetWare protocols on the LAN, with those packets translated by a gateway system connected to the internet. The end user can connect to internet resources, but doesn't run TCP/IP; is that user's system connected to the internet?

- Subscribers to the America Online (AOL) ISP service use a proprietary protocol to connect to AOL's systems, which mediate access to internet resources. Are those users' systems connected to the internet, even though they might not support either TCP/IP or any internet application protocols?

Clearly, internet connectivity is not an either/or proposition but rather a question of degree. Rather than asking whether or not a system or network is connected to the internet, the more useful question to ask (and answer) is to what degree can that system or network be considered connected. Understand how the system is connected—by what network medium, through which network protocols, and using applications that interoperate with the internet in what ways—and you can begin to understand what that system can do and what might go wrong.

5.7 Chapter Summary

Building on the functional structures from Chapter 4, in this chapter we introduced the fundamental OSI and DoD/Internet internetworking models. Perhaps the single most important concept for internetworking is that of encapsulation: the process by which a message can be wrapped up for delivery by entities other than those doing the communicating.

We also revisited some of our fundamental network components, looking at them again as they behave within structure provided by the internetworking models: bridges, switches, and routers.

In the next chapter, we will take a high-level look at the protocols commonly considered part of the TCP/IP suite.

Internet Protocol Overview

This chapter briefly introduces the various protocols that are associated with TCP/IP networks. This includes required protocols such as IP or TCP, as well as recommended and other commonly used protocols. Most internet protocols either resemble or are based directly on some other protocol. For example, the Dynamic Host Configuration Protocol (DHCP), used to automatically configure nodes on demand across a network, builds on the earlier and less comprehensive Boot Protocol (BOOTP). Likewise, protocols for applications that depend on the transfer of files—such as the File Transfer Protocol (FTP) and the Hypertext Transfer Protocol (HTTP)—generally share one or more fundamental mechanisms for transferring those files. And applications that carry data streams—such as Telnet (terminal emulation) and the Secure Shell protocol (SSH)—are likely to share fundamental mechanisms for controlling those streams.

Although this chapter is intended to be a comprehensive list of internet protocols that are (or have been) in general use, only some of these protocols will be analyzed in greater detail later in the book. We'll delve into only a few application protocols, although once the reader has mastered

those few she should be able to understand others based on their specifications; this book will be more (but not completely) comprehensive at
the lower layers, and the same principles will apply. Technical protocol
details for selected applications (based on relevance and size) are provided
in Appendix B, including protocol headers and key protocol codes.

Internet protocols are presented in seven categories, beginning with the
network interface and moving up through the IP internetworking model to
the application layers; special attention is given three other categories: protocols related to Integrated Services (intserv) and Differentiated Services
(diffserv), different mechanisms for delivering network services; internet
security protocols; and internet management protocols. Each section introduces one of these categories, describes what protocols within the category
do, and includes lists of all relevant protocols with brief descriptions.

6.1   Network Interface Layer

When two IP network nodes interact directly, they do so at the network
interface layer. They may share the same physical network medium as well
as local network protocols, or they may be connected to a complex internet
and merely share the same set of protocols for passing data from a node to
a network.

Local area networks use protocols such as the IEEE 802.3 and Ethernet
specifications for packaging data and sending it on a physical medium.
In IP networks, there is a group of protocols that are used by local nodes
to interact by allowing them to exchange information about themselves,
and to pass that information up to higher layer protocols when necessary.
"Local" includes all nodes local to the same link layer, whether they connect
to the same Ethernet hub or link through the same wireless hub.

The most important of these protocols is the Address Resolution
Protocol (ARP) and related protocols which define mechanisms for map-
ping internet layer addresses onto network interface layer addresses.
The most common illustration provided for ARP is in its use with
Ethernet:

Scenario: A system connected to an Ethernet local area network (LAN)
has an IP packet to be delivered to another system connected to
the same LAN. The system sending the packet must discover the

destination system's Ethernet address by using the destination's IP address.

Solution: The source system sends out a broadcast Ethernet frame containing an ARP request. All systems on the LAN listen for broadcasts, but the ARP message contains a request for one of the connected systems to identify itself. The request includes the source system's Ethernet and IP addresses, as well as the destination system's IP address. Although all the systems are listening for broadcasts, the only system that should answer will be the one using the requested IP address.

Bonus: ARP requests are broadcast, so all systems on the LAN make note of the IP and Ethernet addresses of hosts requesting ARP services. They store these address mappings (along with any other address mappings they've received through replies to their own ARP requests) in an *ARP cache*. The cache is maintained according to a few set rules including a length of time that the cache value can be used before assuming it must be retrieved and verified; otherwise, a system sending data on the LAN will check the ARP cache first before broadcasting a new request. The result is that ARP broadcasts don't immediately overwhelm networks as they grow larger.

Ethernet was designed as a multi-access broadcast medium, meaning that LAN nodes connect to a single shared medium over which all nodes can listen to all network traffic and only one node can transmit on the network at any given time. Network collisions may occur in such networks when two systems, checking the medium and not sensing any transmissions, both attempt to transmit at the same time; various mechanisms have been defined to recover from such collisions in Ethernet networks. However, while ARP and its related protocols are quite simple, there are still some subtle twists even under Ethernet.

ARP is a much more complicated matter when the network does not support broadcasts natively. By its nature, Ethernet allows broadcasts because all nodes are always connected to a shared physical medium. High performance network protocols such as ATM and Frame Relay use virtual circuits over switched networks to link systems on the same network. Broadcasts cannot be supported natively because there is no way for all network nodes to be connected simultaneously and whether or not the sender knows of their existence. ATM, Frame Relay, and other *non-broadcast multi-access* (*NBMA*) networks must use a more complex system to simulate broadcasts for tasks such as ARP; instead of sending a message to a generic network broadcast address the sender transmits the broadcast frame to a server that keeps track of all nodes connected to the network and relays all broadcasts to them individually.

The Point to Point Protocol (PPP) is another important network interface layer protocol, designed to allow two systems at either end of a connection to set up a network link. Unlike network protocols such as Ethernet or Token Ring, PPP links support only two nodes on each "network". Because there are only two nodes on a PPP network, network addresses are not always strictly required: whether the node is sending or receiving, the data is always either going to or coming from the "other" node.

The Layer Two Tunneling Protocol (L2TP) is another network interface layer protocol, designed to encapsulate network interface layer data. When data is moved from one switched network to another, across a packet network such as the internet, the data must be de-encapsulated as it passes out of the source switched network, re-encapsulated for the internet, and the transformed again for its final leg inside the destination switched network. All that processing slows the data and mitigates considerably the advantages of using switched networks. L2TP allows the end-nodes to set up virtual circuits across the routed packet network by tunneling the switched protocol through IP (or other network layer protocols).

Table 6–1 lists key network interface layer protocols; these will be discussed at length in Chapter 21.

Acronym	Protocol
ARP	Address Resolution Protocol
RARP	Reverse ARP
inARP	Inverse ARP
NBMA ARP	ARP over Non Broadcast Multiple Access networks
PPP	Point-to-Point Protocol
L2TP	Layer 2 Tunneling Protocol

Table 6–1: Important network interface layer protocols.

6.2   Internet Layer

The internet layer provides an abstraction: a network that enables seamless interoperation between nodes on any local network, using any operating system, any hardware platform, and with no prior knowledge about communicating nodes beyond their internet addresses.[1] At the network interface layer there is often a degree of concreteness about networking: actual computers and other devices are plugged into outlets or other devices, with the flow of data readily verified by the flashing of green, yellow, and red lights; network transmissions must be directed to their specific destination nodes.

At the internet layer, we rise beyond physical realities and move into the realm of the mind. Packets destined for the same internet address may always arrive at the same physical system—or they may reach any one of dozens or even hundreds of different systems. Internet layer packets may always pass through the same intermediate systems as they are routed through the internet to the same destination—or each could (in theory, at least) take a different route. The internet layer makes it possible to create huge networks, but also dynamic networks in which the availability, cost, and speed of intermediate networks and systems may vary at any given moment.

The Internet Protocol (IP) itself describes how internet nodes communicate across this abstract network called the internet. It defines the internet address space as well as how to address outbound packets and interpret inbound packets. And it defines how IP nodes should handle IP packets that they receive and send. Related specifications of the form "IP over [X]," describe how IP packets are to be encapsulated within network interface layer protocols (see Chapter 21 for more details).

IP by itself is important, but it is not enough for rapidly growing and dynamic internets. Network managers require routers capable not only of processing packets quickly, but also of actively collecting and updating information about the networks to which the routers are connected. For the task of collecting routing information to be manageable without

---

[1]This statement is not entirely correct, inasmuch as nodes can actually communicate with other nodes over the internet even if they don't have access to the destination nodes' addresses—if all communicating nodes are members of the same multicast group. Although it has yet to be deployed widely for end user applications over the internet, IP multicast is an important part of IP networking and is covered at greater length in Chapter 24.

overwhelming intermediary networks, it is necessary to design protocols for propagating routing data across networks in the most efficient way. Internet routing protocols make this possible.

Most routing protocols are used either for *interior* routing (routing among nodes in an intranet or other localizable IP network) or for *exterior* routing (routing between and among autonomous systems such as is done on internet backbones). Key interior routing protocols include the Open Shortest Path First (OSPF) protocol and the Routing Information Protocol (RIP); the most important exterior routing protocol currently is the Border Gateway Protocol (BGP).

No IP network could function without the Internet Control Message Protocol (ICMP). Encapsulated within IP packets, ICMP messages afford IP nodes a mechanism for communicating to each other about the status of an IP destination, route, or router. When a node attempts to deliver a packet to a system that is not accepting packets (it may be powered down, flooded with other requests, or simply not accepting packets from that particular source), an ICMP message may be generated and sent back to the source. That interaction may happen entirely outside the view of either system because it is a communication within the IP infrastructure. In one sense, ICMP is an application carried directly on top of IP; in another sense, ICMP is a parallel channel by which nodes can notify each other about problems making deliveries.

The Internet Group Management Protocol (IGMP) is almost an administrative protocol for IP multicast, providing a mechanism for nodes to join in multicast groups, as we'll see in Chapter 25.

Although not widely used in North America as of early 2002, IPv6 is increasingly gaining acceptance in parts of the world where IPv4 addresses are hard to come by, such as Asia—as well as for applications where the IPv4 address is inadequate, such as for mobile telephony. As a revision to IPv4, IPv6 uses many of the same mechanisms in IPv4 as well as correcting many of its flaws. Chapter 21 provides an overview to IPv6.[2]

Table 6–2 lists protocols considered to be operating at the internet layer.

---

[2]For more in-depth and practical information about IPv6, see *IPv6 Clearly Explained*, 2nd ed.

Acronym	Protocol
IP	Internet Protocol
IPsec	Internet Security Protocol
IPv4	Internet Protocol, version 4
IPv6	Internet Protocol, version 6
ICMP	Internet Control Message Protocol
OSPF	Open Shortest Path First (a routing protocol)
RIP	Routing Internet Protocol (another routing protocol)
BGP	Border Gateway Protocol (an exterior routing protocol)

Table 6–2: Internet layer protocols.

6.3   Transport Layer

If the internet layer provides an abstraction that allows internet nodes to communicate independently of their respective network interfaces, then the transport layer allows processes running on those nodes to communicate independently of their internet layers. Without a transport layer between the application and the internet layers, all packets from one host to another would arrive in a big pile of data. There would be no good way for the destination host to differentiate data in the event that there were more than one process on the source host communicating with one or more processes on the destination host.

The transport layer gives processes an interface over which to communicate about how data is delivered to or accepted from the applications above. Until 2000, virtually all transport layer activity used one of two protocols:

UDP The User Datagram Protocol is an exceptionally simple protocol that provides nothing more than a mechanism for one process to pack and send a request or a reply to another process. A message is sent out, and that's that. If the message gets there, good. If not, then the process may send it again. There are no mechanisms for correcting a message that was corrupted in transit, no verifying that the message was received. With virtually no features, UDP is also incredibly lightweight, and perfect for applications that don't need guarantees of delivery, or acknowledgments, or virtual circuits.

TCP   The Transmission Control Protocol is very nearly the opposite of UDP. It offers delivery guarantees and acknowledgments, virtual circuit connections, and considerable flexibility in managing dynamic network conditions. Because TCP in its present form was documented in RFC 793 back in 1981, it has been tweaked in various ways to improve its ability to optimize performance for the applications that use it.

In 2000, a new transport layer protocol, the Stream Control Transmission Protocol (SCTP) was published in RFC 2960. Originally designed as a way to carry the signalling information required by publicly switched telephone network (PSTN) connections over IP, SCTP expands on many of the functions possible with TCP while at the same time adding new features to improve performance (see Chapter 18).

There are a handful of other protocols that can be considered to operate at the transport layer, including:

TLS   The Transport Layer Security protocol, the descendant of Netscape Communication's original Secure Sockets Layer (SSL) protocol for encrypting web data, operates between the transport protocol and the application protocol. Typically, TLS accepts data from an application (usually but not exclusively HTTP) and encrypts it before passing it along to the transport layer for processing.

SSH   The Secure Shell protocol was originally designed as a secure alternative to telnet for terminal emulation over the internet. As a remote terminal program, SSH encrypts and decrypts data sent and received at the application layer before passing it along to the transport layer. However, SSH can also be used as a secure transport for other applications. A web session, for example, could be tunneled through SSH. The result would be a completely encrypted session occuring between two nodes using SSH—no eavesdropper would be able to intercept the web session, let alone even discover what kind of data was being passed.

These protocols are all discussed in Chapter 15.

6.4   Application Layer

Any application that enables entities to exchange information across a network is a network application. There are different ways to characterize those applications:

- The kind of entities that use the application. Some applications enable direct communication between human people, some enable communication between people and systems, and some enable communication between systems and systems.
- The function or functions the application fulfills; network management or file sharing or real-time videoconferencing.
- Infrastructural or extrastructural applications. The infrastructural applications operate invisibly, within the network, to allow various *edge* and *intermediate* nodes to operate as part of the network infrastructure. The extrastructural applications are those that are carried over the infrastructure, and don't really care what protocols or applications are used within the network to carry data.

This last characterization is another way to differentiate between functions that are part of the internet, such as routing or managing service delivery, and functions that everyone can agree upon as being internet applications, such as internet mail or web browsing.

Although routing and other infrastructural protocols enable the exchange of data between nodes on a network, those protocols are designed to enable the transmission of end-to-end data between and among users of applications. A routing protocol operating inside of the internet cloud operates invisibly to the nodes using that cloud to communicate. As such, we'll cover these infrastructural protocols separately from end user applications.

Application layer protocols address the formatting of application as well the commands and responses that systems supporting those applications must support. Although some applications specify their own special

Acronym	Protocol/Description
FTP	File Transfer Protocol
Telnet	Terminal emulation
HTTP	Hypertext Transfer Protocol
Gopher	An early hypertext-like application protocol
SMTP	Simple Mail Transfer Protocol
SNMP	Simple Network Management Protocol
DNS	Domain Name System
SSH	Secure Shell Protocol (secure terminal emulation and more)
POP	Post Office Protocol
IMAP	Internet Mail Access Protocol

Table 6–3: Application layer protocols.

formats for packaging data, many popular applications use standards for data formatting that may have been defined for other purposes. For example, the Network News Transfer Protocol (NNTP) formats data and application headers similarly to the way specified for internet mail. Likewise, internet mail messages often contain data formatted to the HTML specification defined originally for the web. These formatting standards are important, although they are not a focus in this book beyond the way they are used with internet mail (web formatting standards are managed by the World Wide Web Consortium [W3C] and hardly need be repeated here). Table 6–3 lists common internet applications.

6.5   Internet Security and IPsec

Security may be applied at any layer of the protocol stack, and many protocols for doing so have been developed to secure internet communication. The field of security is vast, and simply describing all the issues raised by

Acronym	Protocol/Description
ESP	IP Encapsulating Security Payload
AH	IP Authentication Header
ISAKMP	Internet Security Association Key Management Protocol
IKE	Internet Key Exchange

Table 6–4: IPsec protocols.

Acronym	Protocol/Description
SSL	Secure Socket Layer
PEM	Privacy-Enhanced Mail
S/MIME	Secure Multimedia Internet Mail Enclosure
OpenPGP	Open version of Pretty Good Privacy encryption
RADIUS	Remote Authentication Dial In User Service
Kerberos	secure authentication and authorization protocol
	(after mythical three-headed Greek underworld guard dog)

Table 6–5: Security protocols.

internet security could take an entire book. This book simply introduces the components of the Internet Security Architecture (IPsec) and describes how they work together. Table 6–4 lists IPsec protocols, while Table 6–5 lists some of the many security protocols that have been defined within the internet standards process.

IPsec defines a framework under which IP nodes can encrypt and/or digitally sign packets. By doing so, users of those nodes can be assured that the data they transmit will arrive at its destination unchanged (if digital signature is used) and unseen (if encryption is used). IPsec can be summarized quite simply, in that it defines the process by which nodes initiate a secure connection, exchange encryption keying information, and send and receive encrypted (or signed) data. At the same time this simplicity belies the difficulty of designing protocols that make it possible to provably protect data in ways that are not vulnerable.

Security for internet applications can be provided at the transport layer, using TLS (see section 6.3); security may also be implemented directly in the application protocol itself. Privacy-Enhanced Mail (PEM), Secure MIME (S/MIME; MIME stands for Multipurpose Internet Message Extensions; see Chapter 9 for more about MIME), and OpenPGP are all protocols defining ways to protect application data that operate at the level of the application.

Although encryption and digital signature technologies are important aspects of network security, they are far from the only aspects. The so-called AAA area (access, authentication, and accounting) encompasses a number of network security protocols including those related to logging in to systems and networks. Likewise, internet firewalls have long been important elements in most organizations' security strategies; intrusion detection systems, network scanners, virtual private networks, and other types of system have also gained prominence in recent years.

Although these topics are mentioned here, they are largely out of scope for this book. Firewalls (along with Network Address Translators or NATs) are special forms of routers, and are, like the rest, best left to more specialized texts or to the source RFCs themselves.

6.6   Integrated Services, Differentiated Services

Some applications require specific levels of service from the network to work correctly. Telephony applications, for example, call for guaranteed bandwidth pegged at some minimum along with latency pegged at some maximum. One approach to providing guaranteed Quality of Service (QoS) within the internet, the Integrated Services (intserv) architecture provides mechanisms, including the Resource Reservation Protocol (RSVP), for applications to request QoS on an end-to-end basis.

The problem with intserv is that it adds a significant burden to the infrastructure of the internet. To guarantee QoS between endpoints, mechanisms must be put in place inside the internet to keep track of individual streams, to make sure no one gets too many resources or too few, and to make sure that resources aren't over (or under) allcoated. This is a lot of trouble, and the burden of enforcing intserv increases rapidly as networks grow.

The Differentiated Services (diffserv) architecture provides a simpler alternative. Rather than fine-tuning each and every application's service requirements, diffserv provides a framework in which there are only a few service options, and individual connections need not be tracked individually inside the internet. Packets requiring different handling are simply marked appropriately, and within the internet those packets are fast-tracked or otherwise treated specially as appropriate for their level of service.

The big problem for diffserv is figuring out what differentiated service levels are "appropriate" and how to use them. In the original specification for IP, a *Type of Service (ToS)* field was defined for the protocol header. Though there were different choices available, ranging from "best" to "worst" treatment for the packet, the tendency was for developers to seek the best treatment for packets generated by their own protocols and applications; no one really wanted to label their packets as being unworthy of rapid transmission. That much of the internet lacked any mechanism for differentiating between how packets are treated (other than perhaps artificially holding back non-priority packets) may also have contributed to the futility of the ToS field.

Since then the ToS field has morphed into the Differentiated Services field, though there is still much debate over how best to differentiate services. QoS issues are covered in Chapter 25.

6.7   Network Management

The internet manager's toolkit includes a wide range of technologies, from devices for testing cables to complex applications for gathering data from systems on networks around the world. The Simple Network Management Protocol (see Chapter 31), defines a method for managing, configuring, and administering any devices over any IP network.

Over the years, network vendors have used a multitude of hardware and software tools to configure and monitor their products. These devices have stored configurations and may have cached recent performance data on local hard drives, RAM or ROM, or even on other network devices; vendors provided many different tools, from software programs to knobs and dials, for changing configurations. The result was a sort of chaos: as the number of different vendors represented in a typical intranet rose, the number of different systems for managing those devices also increased.

SNMP offers network managers the option of using a single and standard interface for accessing current performance data as well as updating device configurations. The structure of management information (SMI), along with various management information bases (MIBs) form the framework for the world's most distributed distributed database. Rather than having all devices transmit their status and configurations to a central server, the devices store all their information in a standard database *schema*.[3] For example, all routers store their recent performance data in the same "place"; any SNMP management console will be able to gather that information from all routers in a given network without having to know beforehand anything about the routers.

The SNMP approach to configuration is equally simple. Device configuration data is also stored according to the standard schema, and SNMP consoles can be used to read as well as change or update that data. For example, a console operator can check the status of a network interface on a router by querying the router and asking it to respond with the value in the part of the database reserved for that information. The interface is either up or down; if it is up, the operator can turn it off by sending an SNMP request that changes the value to down.

6.8   Chapter Summary

The most important set of concepts to take away from this chapter have to do with the way in which TCP/IP and related protocols are interconnected at different network layers. At the network interface or network link layer, network protocols define how nodes actually exchange data across

---

[3]As traditionally defined for databases, a schema is a meta-format, a specification that defines how data is to be specified.

network media, but the protocols also provide for mechanisms by which data can cross network boundaries.

The internet layer provides a mechanism through which disparate networks can be linked through a logical, rather than a physical, internet structure. By imposing this virtual network architecture over the many different and interconnected literal network architectures, processes anywhere within the virtual network can communicate with each other. By enabling processes to communicate, applications can exchange information, thus enabling users to get value from using the global internet.

We also touched on some of the important issues facing the internet, including network security, network performance, and network management. In the chapters of Part II, we introduce the specific applications that are used over the internet.

Part Two

Internet Applications

Part Goals

- Provide a complete view of packets traversing the internet, from a high-level overview to the specifics of each relevant protocol.
- Understand how application, transport, internet and network interface layer protocols enable seamless and platform-independent interoperability.
- Enable reader to analyze network protocol data at all layers.

7

Meet Joe's Packets

A 30,000-foot overview of how packets move around the internet, starting with "Joe Surfer," the typical internet user. This chapter traces Joe's data as he initiates a connection to a web server from his browser. By examining it in depth, this simple process illustrates how the hypertext transfer protocol (HTTP) and domain name system (DNS) applications work, how transport layer user datagram protocol (UDP) and transmission control protocol (TCP) work, how IP works at the network layer, and how data moves around at the network link layer. We'll also take a look at what may be happening within the internet as packets leave Joe's system to be delivered to their destinations, as well as take a peek at how Joe's packets are routed from their source to their destination.

7.1 Meet Joe

For years, "Joe" was the single personality readers of *Readers Digest* magazine knew in the greatest depth: inside and out. Joe's various organs and parts were the subject of ongoing articles titled "I am Joe's [organ]," chatty and informative articles written from the organ's perspective. Invariably, Joe is either entirely unaware that he has this organ, or else he is woefully uninformed about the wonders it performs as well as the proper care that should be taken of it.

Our own "Joe" is a regular person who uses the internet for work and amusement, but who has no idea whatsoever how it works. Nor does he really need to know much about it, as long as it's working for him.

Joe starts each work day with a quick look at the news on his favorite news web site, TODAY.Example.net. He works in an average office, where internet access is screened by a firewall as well as a network address translator (NAT), both of which process all his packets as they go in and out. He uses a company personal computer (PC), connected to the local area network (LAN) with an Ethernet network interface card (NIC). All his software is generic, straight-out-of-the-box, internet standards–compliant software (no matter what operating system he uses).

Joe is just an entity sitting behind the keyboard on one end of the internet and using his systems to access resources elsewhere on the internet. Now that we've met him, we can bid him goodbye. We just want to see what happens to his packets; as far as we're concerned Joe is simply "J. Random User," just someone who makes systems generate packets. In this chapter, we'll begin by looking at what the end user (Joe) does, but only in terms of how it starts processes in motion. These processes may occur anywhere, but the interactions happen at several different levels, as described in Part I. Starting with Joe's keystrokes (his interaction with the network-connected system), we'll look at how systems interact at the application, transport, internet, and network link layers. We'll expose a fairly wide range of protocols in this chapter, including:

- Hypertext Transfer Protocol (HTTP)
- Domain Name System (DNS)
- Transmission Control Protocol (TCP)
- User Datagram Protocol (UDP)
- Internet Protocol (IP)
- Internet Control Message Protocol (ICMP)
- Network Address Translation (NAT)
- various routing protocols
- Ethernet
- Address Resolution Protocol

This chapter won't define any of these protocols in depth, but rather give the reader an idea of how data moves around on the internet and how systems interoperate across the internet. We will return to all these protocols later in the book to understand how they work in greater detail.

A protocol "sniffer" is an excellent tool for learning about how packets move around a network. Most network sniffing tools monitor LAN interfaces for transmissions, grab them, and can save or display them, often providing translation services for evaluating the contents of the packets. Sniffer software is available for almost any computing platform and both as open source and proprietary programs. You can use your own sniffing tool to confirm how the protocols described in this book actually work.

NOTE: The sample protocol messages used in this chapter were captured from actual sessions using a network sniffer program. Ethereal is a graphical front-end program (for the tcpdump network packet capture program running on Linux) which takes the raw packet data and makes it more accessible for analysis. Real packets consist of data (the stuff the protocol is designed to transport) and control information (protocol information); Ethereal interprets the protocol data and formats it to make the data more readable. This includes providing translation of status bits, translation of IP addresses (where available) into domain names, and evaluation of various protocol codes.

7.2   The Application Layer: DNS and HTTP

The first thing Joe does when he gets into his office is power on his PC and start up his web browser, which is configured to load the main TODAY.Example.net web page as his home page. Assuming that Joe's PC is properly connected to the LAN and properly configured, the internet connection is up and running, and the TODAY.Example.net server is functioning (along with all the systems in between), Joe will see the latest news being reported on that page.

What is really happening, though? The web browser, as it starts, is configured to make a request to download the contents of the web page at TODAY.Example.net. That's what's happening at the application layer: the browser gets set to initiate a request—or send an HTTP GET command—to the web server out on the internet. Or so one might think.

7.2.1 DOMAIN NAME SYSTEM

Actually, the first task is to map an IP address onto the server named TODAY.Example.net, so packets can be properly targeted. Why not start by putting the HTTP packet together? Because that packet must be encapsulated with transport and network layer information—including the server's IP address. Not only that, but if the server can't be properly identified, then it may not even be possible to make the connection.

The first step is to generate a DNS query. Joe's PC puts together a simple packet, consisting of a DNS query, specifying the name of the host and what kind of information is requested (the IP address). Somehow (we'll get to that later, as we discuss the transport and internet layers), that message is sent to Joe's PC's local DNS nameserver. That system maintains a cache of information about domain names, so if the information is available locally, the nameserver will just pass it back along in a reply to the DNS query. If not, the local nameserver will generate its own DNS requests and direct them to some other nameserver.

If the server name can be successfully linked with an IP address, the local nameserver will send off a response that includes all the information requested (which may be more than an IP address, depending on how the request was made).

The DNS request actually looks something like this, expressed in hexadecimal values corresponding to pairs of 8-bit values:

```
00 a0 c5 e1 47 8e 00 a0 cc 3b 38 a1 08 00 45 00
00 47 a5 28 40 00 40 11 11 bd c0 a8 01 6f c0 a8
01 01 80 02 00 35 00 33 cb 01 cc 42 01 00 00 01
00 00 00 00 00 00 03 77 77 77 11 69 6e 74 65 72
6e 65 74 2d 73 74 61 6e 64 61 72 64 03 63 6f 6d
00 00 01 00 01
```

In fact, if you were to read these values, they would look something like this:

```
.ÅáG.. Ì;8¡  ..E.
.GY(@.@.  .½Ã˙ .oÃ˙
```

```
.....5.3 Ë.ÌB....
.......w ww.inter
net-stan dard.com
.....
```

However, when we look at any kind of protocol headers, we'll use the framework provided by our sniffer to put it all into context, so the initial DNS request appears like this:

```
Domain Name System (query)
  Transaction ID: 0xcc42
  Flags: 0x0100 (Standard query)
    0... .... .... .... = Query
    .000 0... .... .... = Standard query
    .... ..0. .... .... = Message is not
    truncated
    .... ...1 .... .... = Do query recursively
    .... .... ...0 .... = Non-authenticated
                          data is unacceptable
  Questions: 1
  Answer RRs: 0
  Authority RRs: 0
  Additional RRs: 0
  Queries
    TODAY.example.net: type A, class inet
      Name: TODAY.example.net
      Type: Host address
      Class: inet
```

We'll get to the details of DNS later on, in Chapter 8, but for now it's enough to see that Joe's PC is sending out a request (directed to its local DNS server) for information about the server using the host name of TODAY.example.net, specifically that server's host address. The response comes back from the DNS server looking something like this:

```
Domain Name System (response)
  Transaction ID: 0xcc42
  Flags: 0x8180 (Standard query response,
No error)
  Questions: 1
  Answer RRs: 2
  Authority RRs: 2
  Additional RRs: 0

  Queries
    TODAY.example.net: type A, class inet
    Name: TODAY.example.net
    Type: Host address
    Class: inet

  Answers
    TODAY.example.net: type CNAME, class inet,
    cname internet-standard.com
      internet-standard.com: type A, class inet,
      addr 216.92.98.204

  Authoritative nameservers
    internet-standard.com: type NS, class inet,
    ns ns00.ns0.com
    internet-standard.com: type NS, class inet,
    ns ns130.pair.com
```

This is quite a complicated response, but it is what Joe's PC asked for in the original request: authoritative responses from all the web server's nameservers (the actual DNS response continues, reporting not just the responses from the nameservers but also identifying the IP addresses of those nameservers). This is enough for the PC to comfortably start sending data, and now the web application protocol can start to kick in.

7.2.2 HYPERTEXT TRANSFER PROTOCOL

All HTTP messages are either requests or responses. Clients make requests, servers make responses. HTTP defines headers to be used with messages; these headers tell first of all what the message is (a request or a response) and what version of HTTP is being used (as of 2002, HTTP version 1.1 is current). From there, more detail about the request or response can be coded in additional headers, as discussed in Chapter 12.

Joe's PC's first HTTP message will be a request to retrieve the contents of a particular Uniform Resource Identifier (URI). That message is sent off (again, we'll see how later) to the server, which responds in one of several possible ways:

- The server can decline to respond at all and ignore the request.
- The server can respond to the request by denying it.
- The server can fulfill the request and begin sending the requested resource.

In the first instance, the server might not be offering HTTP services and so would ignore any HTTP requests. Or, the server might be set up to ignore requests from clients outside the local network for security reasons.

In the second case, the server could deny a request for quite a few different reasons. The resource requested may not exist, or the request may not be an authorized one for that particular resource (but authorized for other resources), or the server may have encountered an internal error. The specification for version 1.1 of HTTP (in RFC 2616) defines almost two dozen different *response codes* that can be used to indicate different reasons a request is denied.

Server responses begin with the version of HTTP being used and a response code. Most application protocols define a set of response codes, usually three-digit values that correspond to different types of response; the first digit of the response code specifies a general status of the response, while the other digits refine the meaning of the code. The five levels of response for HTTP responses are:

1XX   Informational; the request is not being denied, but it has not yet been fulfilled. Different codes indicate what happens next or what must happen to fulfill the request.

2XX   Successful; the request was received, understood, and accepted by the server. Different codes indicate what actions have resulted.

3XX   Redirection; the request was received but further action is required by the client to fulfill the request. Different codes indicate what the client must do to complete the request, or what occured that prevented the request from being completed.

4XX   Client error; the request was received by the server but the server was unable to complete it due to perceived error in the request. Different codes indicate various reasons the request appeared to be incorrect, including the famous "404-File not found" error.

5XX   Internal server error; the request could not be fulfilled because the server encountered an internal error or unexpected condition that prevented it from fulfilling the request. Different codes indicate those reasons.

This response code system is either similar or identical to response codes defined for other file-transfer oriented protocols, such as File Transfer Protocol (FTP), Simple Mail Transfer Protocol (SMTP), and others.

A typical exchange between client and server is reproduced here. The initial request, from the client host, appears something like this:

```
GET / HTTP/1.1
Host: today.example.net
User-Agent: Mozilla/5.0 Galeon/1.0.3
(X11; Linux i686; U;) Gecko/20020205
Accept: text/xml,application/xml,application/
xhtml+xml,text/html;q=0.9,text/plain;q=0.8,
video/x-mng,image/png,image/jpeg,image/gif;
```

```
q=0.2,text/css,*/*;q=0.1
Accept-Language: en
Accept-Encoding: gzip, deflate, compress;
q=0.9
Accept-Charset: ISO-8859-1, utf-8;q=0.66, *;
q=0.66
Keep-Alive: 300
Connection: keep-alive
Referer: http://www.osdn.com/index.pl
```

Each line contains a separate header (the "Accept:" header displays as several lines but is only one header), with header names appearing first followed by a colon. The first line of the HTTP message indicates the version and the type of message; the rest of the headers pertain either to the request (in this case, the name of the host from which the client wants to get data, "today.example.net"), or to the client (in this case, the client software as well as preferences for the way in which the client would like data to be sent).

The response to this HTTP message appears next. The server exists and is able to fulfill the request, so it sends:

```
HTTP/1.1 200 OK
Date: Wed, 27 Feb 2002 17:56:17 GMT
Server: Apache/1.3.22 (Unix) mod_gzip/
1.3.19.1a PHP/4.0.6
X-Powered-By: PHP/4.0.6
Connection: close
Content-Type: text/html
Content-Encoding: gzip
Content-Length: 21204
```

The response from the server is "200," indicating that the request was successful, and (in this case) the requested data is included with the response; the last header indicates that the response contains 21,204 bytes.

And that's how the HTTP client (browser) and the HTTP server communicate with each other.

7.3   The Transport Layer

We've seen how two application protocols, HTTP and DNS, send requests and responses between clients and servers. It just so happens that each of these application protocols is usually associated with one of the two dominant transport layer protocols, TCP and UDP.

The application layer provides a mechanism for an entity on one side of the communication (in this case, a person trying to surf the web) to interact with an entity on the other side (in this case, a web server). The application protocol doesn't concern itself with identifying the client to the server, although the resource on the server may require some authentication or other identification; if identification is required, that data can be exchanged through the application's protocol (i.e., using messages).

However, the application protocol messages need more help to get from the client to the server. The application client and server communicate through the application layer protocol, sending messages to each other, but before the message can be sent, it must be wrapped up for shipping across the network. The first step actually is to wrap them up in a transport layer protocol so that the client process and the server process can communicate directly with each other.

Networks require unique identifiers to differentiate the network nodes. Within a host, processes can be considered something like nodes, capable of interacting with each other or with processes on other hosts. Each process gets its own unique identifier, called a *port*. This is the way that data can be directed not just to a particular host, but to a particular entity within the destination host.

Ports are defined as 16-bit integers, so valid values range from 0 through 65535. There are three types of port defined for use with internet transport layer protocols:

1. *Well known ports* (0 through 1023) comprise a set of ports that all TCP/IP hosts should be able to recognize as "belonging" to

a particular service, and are registered and managed by the Internet Assigned Numbers Authority (IANA). Well-known ports make it possible for Joe's PC to initiate a connection with any web server by addressing transport layer segments to port 80 (the well-known port associated with HTTP).

2. *Registered ports* (1024 through 49151) are ports that various organizations or individuals have registered with IANA and which should be used for the services registered. IANA registers these ports, and hosts should respect them.

3. *Dynamic and/or private ports* (49152 through 65535) are sometimes also called *transient ports* or *ephemeral ports*, and hosts use them once transport layer sessions have been set up using registered or well-known ports. As we'll see in more detail in Chapters 12 and 15, a web server operates by having a *daemon* process listening for requests on port 80; the client almost always uses its own, non–well-known, port from the start of any session. (A daemon is a process—an active, running instance of a program on a system—that does nothing more than wait to be summoned by a request for a service. The daemon responds to such requests by creating a new process to handle the request.)

TCP and UDP use the same values for well-known ports, where appropriate. HTTP messages can be carried in TCP or UDP, but in either case the initial session request is sent to port 80. The well-known port addresses that have already been assigned for TCP and UDP have been reserved for use with the Stream Control Transmission Protocol (SCTP), as appropriate. Additional registrations will occur as necessary.[1]

7.3.1 DNS AND UDP

Most hosts are configured with the addresses of at least two DNS nameservers; without a nameserver, people will only be able to access internet resources if they already know the 32-bit IP address for those resources. Having one is good enough for most purposes, but having two provides the benefit of redundancy in case one fails—and having two or more, each on a different network managed by a different provider, reduces the risk of losing service to a major outage.

---

[1]See RFC 814 for background on the use of ports, and RFC 2960 for details about SCTP.

By its nature, DNS does not require the kind of virtual circuit connection that TCP can offer; all it needs is a mechanism for sending out a request and for receiving a reply. There are lots of nameservers around, and if one is busy or unable for some other reason to respond, a host can try some other nameserver until it gets a response.

UDP is perfect for this kind of application: it provides a simple mechanism for sending messages, requests, or responses, and there is almost no overhead associated with building the packets (TCP, on the other hand, has considerable overhead for setting up, maintaining, and even terminating sessions).

When the DNS request (see above) is created, the data is passed down the protocol stack to be prepared for transmission. A source port number is selected for the process that requested the DNS information, and port 53 is selected as the destination port (that is, the well-known port number for domain name service). The rest of the UDP datagram consists of the DNS query—the stuff we saw in section 7.2.1. The UDP header for that query looks something like this:

```
User Datagram Protocol
  Source port: 32778 (32778)
  Destination port: domain (53)
  Length: 39
  Checksum: 0x98f0 (correct)
```

The length of the UDP datagram, 39, indicates that the entire datagram (including the headers) is 39 bytes long; the headers take 8 bytes, the data or *payload* of the datagram (actually, the DNS request) is 31 bytes long.[2]

Now, we have a better idea of how the original DNS request gets to a nameserver, or at least to the correct process once it arrives at the nameserver. The destination port, 53, identify the datagram as being intended for the domain name service, and the source port, 32778, indicates where the nameserver should direct its response, which looks something

---

[2]The checksum field provides a weak mechanism for detecting corrupt datagrams; more will be said about checksums and how they are created in Chapter 13.

like this:

```
User Datagram Protocol
  Source port: domain (53)
  Destination port: 32778 (32778)
  Length: 165
  Checksum: 0x5f33 (correct)
```

In this case, the nameserver sends a UDP datagram from port 53 to port 32778; the datagram is 165 bytes long. Eight bytes account for the UDP headers and the rest, another 157 bytes account for the payload–the response to the query. It's important to remember that the payload of the UDP datagram is actually an entire application layer protocol (DNS) message.

If for some reason the nameserver took too long to respond, the client would likely send out another request until it either got a response or until a *timer* (a process that keeps track of how much time has elapsed since some event) expired and the decision is made to consider the nameserver (or nameservers) unavailable. UDP does not use any timers, so applications that use UDP for their transport protocol must implement their own timers (or other mechanisms for keeping track of the application).

7.3.2 Hypertext Transfer Protocol and Transmission Control Protocol

Where DNS is message-oriented (a client sends a request and a server sends a response, and that's the end of the interaction), HTTP mediates the exchange of files rather than simple messages. Files are often much larger than the largest allowable packet size, so they've got to be broken up into smaller chunks for transport. Shifting even a single bit in the course of a file transfer can ruin the transferred file and cause the file to be resent, so a best-effort protocol like UDP may not be enough. The many pieces into which large files must be broken for transmission call for many different datagrams to carry them; dropping any one of those datagrams—a common enough occurence—means there must be a mechanism for keeping track of them all and making sure all have been received. Finally, one host may be able to send big datagrams very quickly while the other may need more time to receive and process the datagrams, and as a result drop some data on the floor. A mechanism for controlling how fast the data is sent would also help, as would a mechanism for detecting when network conditions are slowing transmission rates down.

TCP offers all these features, and has long been the transport protocol of choice for applications that require any degree of accuracy, acknowledgment, control over transmission for performance, or guaranteed delivery. Where UDP is an utterly simple protocol (RFC 768, "User Datagram Protocol", describes it in about 600 words), TCP is considerably more complex. It allows hosts to set up a virtual circuit, starting with the *three-way hand-shake* protocol for setting up the initial connection. It allows hosts to keep track of what bits of data have been sent and what bits have been received (actually, which have been explicitly acknowledged by the recipient, and which have probably been received), and additions to the basic protocol allow hosts to deal with transient network problems as well as resend the minimum amount of data when some goes missing.

However, we'll get to the details of transport protocols in part IV; here, we'll just take a quick look at how HTTP messages are encapsulated into TCP. In section 7.2.2, we saw an HTTP request from the client and a response from the server. Although this exchange required only two messages, one in each direction, at the transport layer many more messages are exchanged (in this particular case, about three dozen altogether). The first transport layer message for our HTTP exchange is a request from the client to open a TCP virtual circuit with the process listening to port 80 on the server, and looks something like this:

```
Transmission Control Protocol,
Src Port: 33463 (33463), Dst Port: http (80),
Seq: 579940142, Ack: 0
  Source port: 33463 (33463)
  Destination port: http (80)
  Sequence number: 579940142
  Header length: 40 bytes
  Flags: 0x0002 (SYN)
    0... .... = Congestion Window
    Reduced (CWR): Not set
    .0.. .... = ECN-Echo: Not set
```

```
    ..0. .... = Urgent: Not set

    ...0 .... = Acknowledgment: Not set

    .... 0... = Push: Not set

    .... .0.. = Reset: Not set

    .... ..1. = Syn: Set

    .... ...0 = Fin: Not set

  Window size: 5840

  Checksum: 0x3a2a (correct)

  Options: (20 bytes)

    Maximum segment size: 1460 bytes

    SACK permitted

    Time stamp: tsval 1826004, tsecr 0

    NOP

    Window scale: 0 bytes
```

Without delving too deeply into the actual meaning of all the different headers, note that the client selected its own source port, 33463, and set the SYN flag on. This indicates that the TCP segment is an initial request to *synchronize* or start up a virtual circuit between the client process requesting a web page and the server process listening for web requests. There is no payload for this segment other than the data carried in the headers and protocol options. The server process responds with a TCP segment looking something like this:

```
Transmission Control Protocol,
Src Port: http (80), Dst Port: 33463 (33463),
Seq: 372068242, Ack: 579940143
  Source port: http (80)
  Destination port: 33463 (33463)
  Sequence number: 372068242
  Acknowledgement number: 579940143
  Header length: 40 bytes
```

```
Flags: 0x0012 (SYN, ACK)
  0... .... = Congestion Window
  Reduced (CWR): Not set
  .0.. .... = ECN-Echo: Not set
  ..0. .... = Urgent: Not set
  ...1 .... = Acknowledgment: Set
  .... 0... = Push: Not set
  .... .0.. = Reset: Not set
  .... ..1. = Syn: Set
  .... ...0 = Fin: Not set
Window size: 32120
Checksum: 0xb029 (correct)
Options: (20 bytes)
  Maximum segment size: 1460 bytes
  SACK permitted
  Time stamp: tsval 1397385789, tsecr 1826004
  NOP
  Window scale: 0 bytes
```

This response from the server process is an acknowledgment (*ACK*) of the request to synchronize; the Acknowledgment and Synchronize flags are both set. This is the second part of the three-way handshake defined for setting up TCP connections. This is the fastest protocol for setting up a connection between two entities providing assurance that each party has agreed to the circuit. The first party sends a request to open; the second party sends an ACK to indicate that it, too, will open a circuit; the first party must respond, acknowledging the first ACK. Once the third message is received, the hosts can begin using the circuit to exchange application protocol data. The ACK from the client looks like this:

```
Transmission Control Protocol,
Src Port: 33463 (33463), Dst Port: http (80),
Seq: 579940143, Ack: 372068243
```

```
Source port: 33463 (33463)

Destination port: http (80)

Sequence number: 579940143

Acknowledgement number: 372068243

Header length: 32 bytes

Flags: 0x0010 (ACK)

  0... .... = Congestion Window
  Reduced (CWR): Not set

  .0.. .... = ECN-Echo: Not set

  ..0. .... = Urgent: Not set

  ...1 .... = Acknowledgment: Set

  .... 0... = Push: Not set

  .... .0.. = Reset: Not set

  .... ..0. = Syn: Not set

  .... ...0 = Fin: Not set

Window size: 5840

Checksum: 0x4595 (correct)

Options: (12 bytes)

  NOP

  NOP

  Time stamp: tsval 1826006, tsecr 1397385789
```

As with the first two messages of the handshaking protocol, the final message contains no payload beyond the TCP headers; only with the circuit created can the hosts start sending application data. In this case, the first TCP segment with an application layer protocol payload is sent by the client–the actual HTTP message requesting the server to send some data. The TCP headers for that datagram look like this:

```
Transmission Control Protocol,

Src Port: 33463 (33463), Dst Port: http (80),

Seq: 579940143, Ack: 372068243
```

```
Source port: 33463 (33463)

Destination port: http (80)

Sequence number: 579940143

Next sequence number: 579940615

Acknowledgement number: 372068243

Header length: 32 bytes

Flags: 0x0018 (PSH, ACK)

  0... .... = Congestion Window
  Reduced (CWR): Not set

  .0.. .... = ECN-Echo: Not set

  ..0. .... = Urgent: Not set

  ...1 .... = Acknowledgment: Set

  .... 1... = Push: Set

  .... .0.. = Reset: Not set

  .... ..0. = Syn: Not set

  .... ...0 = Fin: Not set

Window size: 5840

Checksum: 0x3a81 (correct)

Options: (12 bytes)

NOP

NOP

Time stamp: tsval 1826006, tsecr 1397385789
```

All TCP data must be acknowledged, so this TCP segment includes an ACK of the server's previous TCP segment; in the payload of this particular segment is the HTTP GET message we first saw in section 7.2.2. TCP needed three messages to pass between client and server before the client could actually make an HTTP request. Once the server starts sending, there may be any number of additional datagrams sent to the client, but each IP packet (see next section) may contain only part of the encapsulated TCP segment. For example, if the TCP segment size were to be defined as 2,920 bytes, but the most that IP could carry in any given payload is only 1,460 bytes, then it would take at least two IP packets to transmit that segment.

Compare these TCP headers with the UDP headers shown in section 7.3.1. UDP headers consist of just four pieces of information, while the TCP headers carry quite a bit, including a sequence number, an acknowledgment number, a set of eight single-bit flags, a window size, a checksum, and even more data is possible in the TCP options headers. We'll look at how this data is used to maintain the virtual circuit and control the rate at which data is transmitted to maximize efficiency.

Keep in mind that at the transport layer, we've got two processes communicating: the web server process denoted by port 80, and the client process using the transient port 33463. Only after the TCP circuit is set up do the TCP segments start carrying payloads of encapsulated data (in this case, HTTP messages). The TCP segments are encapsulated in their turn inside IP packets so that they can be exchanged between IP hosts.

7.4 Internet Layer

So far, we've dealt with end-entities interacting at the application level and processes interacting at the transport level. If all computing were done on a single gigantic computer capable of supporting all computer users around the world, this would be enough (more or less—you'd probably need a much, much bigger address space for system processes). However, internet communications presupposes the existence of an internet. If these TCP segments and UDP datagrams are to carry their encapsulated payloads (application messages) to their destinations, they (the segments and datagrams) must be properly encapsulated into an internet layer protocol packet and labeled with the appropriate source and destination IP addresses.

The IP is necessary for all inter-host communication between IP hosts. Nodes on a local area network can communicate at the network link layer, addressing link layer frames to each other using whatever addressing scheme the link layer protocols use. As we've seen, the entities using the applications use local processes to interact; the processes serving those entities interact through the transport layer. The internet layer serves as a mechanism for linking processes that may be on the same physical computer system, or on computers separated by thousands of miles, and allow them to interoperate across network link layer boundaries as well.

Processes use port numbers to identify themselves to other processes; the messages they send go out into the internet cloud through network interfaces. A network interface is usually associated with a specific hardware network interface into a local network. At the internet layer, IP lets us create an abstracted global network independent of any node's local hardware network interface. The task of linking IP addresses with network link layer addresses is a local one, not something that endpoints necessarily need be involved in.

Consider the IP headers used to send the server's response to the client's initial TCP SYN command in section 7.3.2:

```
Internet Protocol
  Version: 4
  Header length: 20 bytes
  Differentiated Services Field: 0x00
  (DSCP 0x00: Default; ECN: 0x00)
    0000 00.. = Differentiated Services
    Codepoint: Default (0x00)
    .... ..0. = ECN-Capable
    Transport (ECT):
    0 .... ...0 = ECN-CE: 0
  Total Length: 60
  Identification: 0x023f
  Flags: 0x04
    .1.. = Don't fragment: Set
    ..0. = More fragments: Not set
  Fragment offset: 0
  Time to live: 46
  Protocol: TCP (0x06)
  Header checksum: 0x0527 (correct)
  Source: today.example.net (10.28.67.35)
  Destination: 192.168.1.111 (192.168.1.111)
```

There is a lot going on in here, but for now the most important fields are the last two. The source and destination IP addresses, displayed here in the *dotted-quad* format, are abstractions imposed on the source (today.example.net) and the client (192.168.1.111). The host names map onto the IP addresses, which in turn map onto link layer network addresses—but neither the source nor the destination need ever be concerned with the other's link layer address. The link layer addresses don't matter until the IP packet arrives at the destination's link layer network.

Leave aside for the moment the problem of how an IP packet is carried from one link layer network to another; we'll get to that in section 7.7, on routing. Although we haven't mentioned any of the other data contained in the IP headers (in this case, 20 bytes' worth of data), all of that information is used to deliver the packet, either en route to or at its destination.

IP packets carry payloads, usually of upper layer protocol datagrams; there is even an IP header field that identifies the protocol carried in the payload. In this case, the packet payload contains a TCP segment (the response from the web server to the client's request to open a TCP session). This particular IP packet was encapsulated, in its turn, in an Ethernet frame at the network link layer for delivery on the local network.

7.5   Network Link Layer

It never hurts to be familiar with the leading network link layer protocols, including Ethernet and Asynchronous Transfer Mode (ATM), and to understand how they carry IP traffic. Ethernet is the more common protocol for most networked nodes, particulary end-user hosts. Ethernet's interaction with IP is also the simpler to understand; Ethernet is primarily a local link protocol and IP is an internet protocol. As we'll see in later chapters, ATM is more complicated, enabling internetworking at what appears to be the link layer.

7.5.1   ETHERNET AND ARP

Let's take a look first at a typical Ethernet frame and how IP addresses are linked to local network addresses.

Ethernet is a framing protocol,[3] meaning it provides a mechanism for formatting data so it can be sent on a local network. This means including a source and destination address as well as some way for nodes on the network to determine where the frame begins and where the frame ends. Ethernet frames are preceded by the *preamble*, a sequence of 8 *octets* or bytes, each containing the pattern "10101010" to indicate data is to follow, and are followed by a 32-bit *cyclic redundancy check* (CRC). The Ethernet protocol field indicates what upper layer protocol is being encapsulated in the frame.

Our typical frame appears here:

```
Ethernet II
  Destination: ff:ff:ff:ff:ff:ff
  Source: 00:ad:cb:3a:32:c5 (Acme_3a:32:c5)
  Type: ARP (0x0806)
Address Resolution Protocol (request)
  Hardware type: Ethernet (0x0001)
  Protocol type: IP (0x0800)
  Hardware size: 6
  Protocol size: 4
  Opcode: request (0x0001)
  Sender hardware address: 00:ad:cb:3a:32:c5
  Sender protocol address: 192.168.1.111
  Target hardware address: 00:00:00:00:00:00
  Target protocol address: 192.168.1.1
```

Here, we see two protocols in action: address resolution protocol (ARP) and Ethernet. The ARP is a simple and general protocol for *resolving* (mapping) an upper layer address onto a lower layer address. All ARP fields can be seen in this example, in which the sender is requesting the local

---

[3]There are actually two different relevant protocols that are often confused and used interchangeably. Ethernet, also known as *Ethernet II* or *DIX* (for Digital, Intel, and Xerox) Ethernet, is very slightly different from the IEEE 802.3 specification. We'll touch on some of those in Chapter 15, but for more details, see the author's *Internet Standards for Ethernet* from Wiley (or whatever it's called).

holder of IP address 192.168.1.1 respond with its hardware (Ethernet, in this case) address. The request includes the IP address of the requesting node as well as its Ethernet address: this makes it possible for the host at 192.168.1.1 to repond directly to the host at 192.168.1.111.

The Ethernet destination address is the *broadcast* address—all ones (ff is hexadecimal for 255, or 1111 1111 in binary: all ones). All nodes on the local network should see this message; all nodes on the network will take note of the requesting node's IP and Ethernet addresses while only the node using that IP address is supposed to reply to the request. The target hardware address is set to all zeroes because it is unknown; the responder will provide the information to fill in the blanks.

We'll look at ARP again in Chapter 21 (even though it is encapsulated within the link layer frame, ARP is usually associated with the link layer rather than the internet layer).

The Ethernet headers are even simpler: destination, source, and protocol type are all that are needed. The destination address is the Ethernet all-zeroes broadcast address, the source address is the Ethernet MAC address of the node requesting the mapping.

7.5.2 ASYNCHRONOUS TRANSFER MODE AND NON-BROADCAST MULTI-ACCESS NETWORKS

Ethernet encapsulates the ARP request, just as it would any other protocol such as IP or ICMP (see Chapter 20). ARP is easy with most Ethernet networks because the IEEE 802.3 protocol is specific for *CSMA/CD baseband networks*. CSMA/CD stands for *Carrier Sense Multiple Access/Collision Detection*. In other words, Ethernet nodes are all connected to the same medium at the same time and all frames are visible to all nodes, and there is a mechanism that allows nodes to sense when collisions—two or more nodes transmitting on the shared medium at the same time—occur.

(Although at one time Ethernet nodes could all sense all frames on the wire, this is not strictly true, particularly where Ethernet bridges or switches limit which frames are reproduced on which wires. Also, most Ethernet network interface cards must be explicitly put into *promiscuous mode* to process frames not addressed to them.)

ATM is known as a *Non-Broadcast Multiple Access* (*NBMA*) network protocol. In NBMA networks, there is no provision for broadcasting packets to all connected nodes: just individual point-to-point circuits (or virtual circuits) are possible. To attempt to broadcast in the same way as is possible with Ethernet, nodes would require complete lists of all other nodes on the network as well as sufficient information about those nodes to permit creation of virtual circuits with each node. Obviously, if nodes already have that information, they probably don't need to broadcast requests for address resolution—but even if they did, the overhead involved with setting up all those connections would be dwarfed by any mechanism for distributed current address information about all connected nodes.

In NBMA networks, *proxy ARP* is a mechanism in which a single node (a proxy ARP server) maintains contact information for all nodes on the network. Any time a broadcast would be necessary on a non-NBMA network, the NBMA node sends the message to the ARP server, which either responds on behalf of the system being queried or else contacts that system on behalf of the requesting node. You'll see this approach used for a variety of purposes in different internet protocols, from providing services in traditional NBMA networks to providing configuration services for mobile hosts.

7.6   The Big Picture

Figure 7–1 shows how these datagrams all fit inside each other, more or less like the Russian dolls. On the very inside, the HTTP command (and associated data inside that!), the HTTP message fits inside a TCP segment, which fits inside an IP packet, which is wrapped in a network link layer frame before being transmitted out onto the LAN.

We'll see more complicated nestings of protocols when we look at IP security tunneling (Chapter 26), but the ARP/Ethernet encapsulation is quite simple, as shown in Figure 7–2.

So far, we've been looking at how the protocols of the TCP/IP suite interact with each other, as well as allow interoperation between nodes, while we've mostly avoided the question of how packets move from source to destination across unknown and often unknowable intermediate networks. IP routing, covered in depth in Chapters 22 and 23, provides the answer. Routers sit at the edge of every network, (hopefully) always prepared to process outbound and inbound packets, checking destination IP

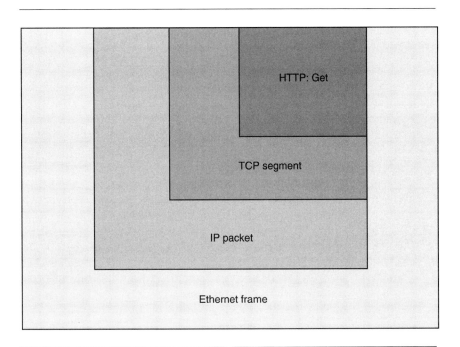

Figure 7–1: TCP/IP encapsulation of HTTP request.

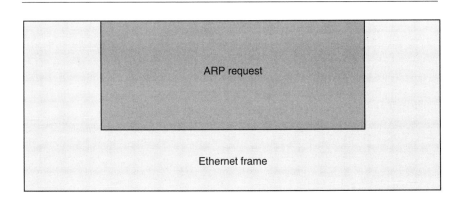

Figure 7–2: TCP/IP encapsulation of ARP request.

addresses and passing them along to the appropriate node or "dropping them on the floor"[4] and ignoring them.

7.7   Routing Joe's Packets

Without going into too many details, let's look at internet routing. Joe's PC sends its IP packets out on the local network, but where does it send them? If the destination IP address is local, the PC will send out an ARP request to discover the local link address, and send the packet directly to its destination at the link layer. But if the destination is not a local one, Joe's PC sends the packet to a router for forwarding.

Internet hosts are almost always configured with a *default gateway*; the router to which all packets go that the host can't deliver on its own. IP packets that can be delivered locally are like inter-office mail: just put it in an inter-office mail envelope and drop it in the proper receptacle, and it will be delivered directly to the recipient. Non-local packets are like mail destined for outside the organization, mail that must be sent to the mail room (no matter where the ultimate destination is) and then processed for further delivery.

Figure 7–3 shows a simplified approximation of what the internet looks like. The source host sends out a packet for the destination host; not being local, the source sends that packet to its local router. The local router accepts a link layer frame containing the packet, strips the link layer protocol headers off and examines the IP headers. Upon determining that the packet is destined for somewhere outside the local organization the router re-encapsulates the packet in the appropriate format for the ISP's router link layer and forwards the packet to the ISP's router. For clarity, only the source's router is shown in the figure; all links shown between network clouds imply the existence of routers on either end.

---

[4]This phrase may have been inspired by the infamous "I Love Lucy" episode in which Lucy and Ethel get jobs in a candy factory. Their task: wrapping and packing candies delivered by an ever-accelerating conveyor belt. As more candies are backed up, waiting to be packed, the two attempt to cope by eating or pocketing them. Eventually, they are overwhelmed by the onslaught and soon the floor is covered with candy. The metaphor is apt for routers, when overwhelmed with packets, may very well just ignore the packets they are unable to process.

It should also be noted that routers may silently drop packets for other reasons, as we'll see later on when we discuss firewalls and the IP *time-to-live* field.

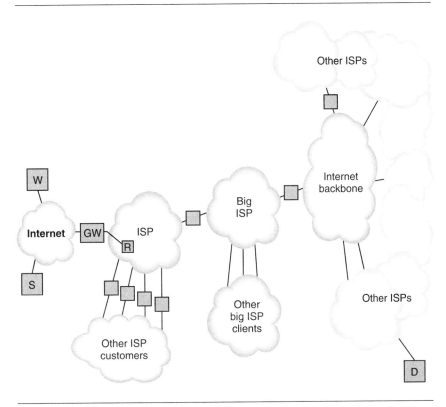

Figure 7–3: Overly simplistic approximation of the internet's architecture.

The ISP's router accepts the link layer frame from the source host's default router, strips the link layer headers off and examines the encapsulated packet's IP headers. If the destination is local to the ISP's router, then the packet will be re-encapsulated again and forwarded to its final destination. If not, the router forwards it to an appropriate router (within the ISP, or to one of the ISP's customers, or to the ISP's own ISP, or to an internet backbone router).

The process continues, moving from one router to another (or in some cases, switch to switch within switched networks that interoperate with IP networks) until the packet is finally delivered, or the packet is lost, or the packet is considered undeliverable for some reason.

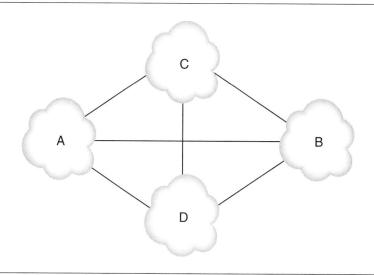

Figure 7–4: An extremely simple internet with extremely robust routing.

Routers implement a variety of different routing protocols to assist them
in doing the right thing with the packets they process. There are routing protocols for smaller organizations, for larger organizations, and
for backbone routing. Routing in small static internets like that shown
in Figure 7–4 can be quite simple: this is a *full-mesh* internet, with links
between every pair of networks in the internet. With only six links, no
single link failure can isolate any network; loss of any two links can
also be sustained with no loss of connectivity. If the internet loses three
of six links, at worst a single network will be isolated while the other
three will still be reachable to each other—in fact, to reduce connectivity
by 50%, you would have to eliminate 83% of the links and leave only
one active.

Of course, using a full-mesh architecture for an internet consisting of only
four networks requires only six connections; a full-mesh connecting 20
networks requires 190 links. There's no way a full-mesh routing structure could be deployed in today's global internet, with its hundreds of
thousands of networks. Building a reliable, efficient, and scalable internet
routing architecture continues to be one of the greatest challenges facing
the IETF.

7.8   Chapter Summary

The protocols described here are far from the only ones Joe's packets use, or cause to be used by other nodes—nor are they the only important ones. The objective of this chapter has not been to exhaustively demonstrate all internet protocols, but to give a sense of how those protocols work.

In this chapter, we've taken a lightning tour of the TCP/IP protocol suite, looking briefly at the ways in which data moves from one application to another. Many of the issues relating to the protocols have been omitted to avoid complicating matters; some of the subtleties of the protocols have been glossed over to avoid getting mired in specifics. However, for most people, this chapter should be more than sufficient to explain how the internet works and how internet mail, web browsing, and other applications work.

8

The Domain Name System

Because it is largely invisible to users (except when it is disrupted), domain name system (DNS) is not always spoken of as an application—but it is. The function it performs, providing a mechanism for translating the human-accessible hostnames to computer and network-friendly numerical addresses, makes the internet as we know it possible. DNS is a great place to begin looking at TCP/IP networking for a number of reasons:

- The protocol itself is relatively straightforward.
- DNS is implemented on all TCP/IP nodes.
- DNS illustrates basic protocol concepts.
- DNS also illustrates distribution of applications in IP networks.
- DNS also illustrates hierarchical organization in IP networks.
- DNS also illustrates networking issues such as security, scalability, and availability.

If you can grasp the DNS, the rest of TCP/IP networking should be simple.

145

8.1   Problem Statement

Although humans prefer to name the things with which they work, computers do better with numerical data—especially when the numerical data carries information that can be useful. At the same time people also need some patterns for naming in large namespaces. IP mandates globally unique 32-bit addresses for every node, within a format that simplifies packet routing and delivery.

IP itself provides no mechanism for simplifying those numerical addresses for use by people. Originally, internet hosts were named in a *flat* namespace, and hosts all relied the regular distribution of a *hosts* file, containing all those names along with their associated addresses, to link names and addresses. In a flat namespace, every host has a single name.

The hosts file approach failed to scale well as the internet grew in the 1980s for several reasons:

- "Host name to address mappings were maintained by the network information center in a single file (HOSTS.TXT) which was FTPed by all hosts (RFC-952, RFC-953). The total network bandwidth consumed in distributing a new version by this scheme is proportional to the square of the number of hosts in the network, and even when multiple levels of FTP are used, the outgoing FTP load on the NIC host is considerable. Explosive growth in the number of hosts didn't bode well for the future.
- The network population was also changing in character. The timeshared hosts that made up the original ARPANET were being replaced with local networks of workstations. Local organizations were administering their own names and addresses, but had to wait for the NIC to change HOSTS.TXT to make changes visible to the Internet at large. Organizations also wanted some local structure on the name space.
- The applications on the Internet were getting more sophisticated and creating a need for general purpose name service."[1]

The challenge was threefold:

1. Design a namespace that scales well and incorporates all the information necessary to locate named nodes.

---

[1]Mockapetris P. RFC 1034, pp 1,2.

2. Build a robust, scalable, and distributed system for distributing information that links resources with addresses.
3. Provide a mechanism for accessing that system.

The domain name system still operates substantially as described in two RFCs published in 1987: RFC 1034, "Domain names—concepts and facilities," and RFC 1035, "Domain names—implementation and specification."[2] As Paul Mockapetris describes in RFC 1034, the design goals for DNS included:

- "... a consistent name space which will be used for referring to resources. In order to avoid the problems caused by ad hoc encodings, names should not be required to contain network identifiers, addresses, routes, or similar information as part of the name.
- The sheer size of the database and frequency of updates suggest that it must be maintained in a distributed manner, with local caching to improve performance. Approaches that attempt to collect a consistent copy of the entire database will become more and more expensive and difficult, and hence should be avoided. The same principle holds for the structure of the name space, and in particular mechanisms for creating and deleting names; these should also be distributed.
- Where there [are] tradeoffs between the cost of acquiring data, the speed of updates, and the accuracy of caches, the source of the data should control the tradeoff.
- The costs of implementing such a facility dictate that it be generally useful, and not restricted to a single application. We should be able to use names to retrieve host addresses, mailbox data, and other as yet undetermined information. All data associated with a name is tagged with a type, and queries can be limited to a single type.
- Because we want the name space to be useful in dissimilar networks and applications, we provide the ability to use the same name space with different protocol families or management. For example, host address formats differ between protocols, though all protocols have the notion of address. The DNS tags

---

[2]Note that the Domain Name System has been significantly updated since 1987 by over a dozen more recent specifications; there are also dozens of other specifications that extend, describe best practices, or otherwise define how DNS and related protocols work in today's internet.

all data with a class as well as the type, so that we can allow parallel use of different formats for data of type address.

- We want name server transactions to be independent of the communications system that carries them. Some systems may wish to use datagrams for queries and responses, and only establish virtual circuits for transactions that need the reliability (e.g., database updates, long transactions); other systems will use virtual circuits exclusively.
- The system should be useful across a wide spectrum of host capabilities. Both personal computers and large timeshared hosts should be able to use the system, though perhaps in different ways."[3]

Basically, the DNS design team hoped to build a generalized directory service for the internet, rather than just a name resolution service for IP. That extensibility has permitted internet mail systems to use DNS as well as made it easier to extend DNS to add IPv6 and security support.

The team also brought several assumptions about the way DNS would be used:

- "The size of the total database will initially be proportional to the number of hosts using the system, but will eventually grow to be proportional to the number of users on those hosts as mailboxes and other information are added to the domain system.
- Most of the data in the system will change very slowly (e.g., mailbox bindings, host addresses), but . . . the system should be able to deal with subsets that change more rapidly (on the order of seconds or minutes).
- The administrative boundaries used to distribute responsibility for the database will usually correspond to organizations that have one or more hosts. Each organization that has responsibility for a particular set of domains will provide redundant name servers, either on the organization's own hosts or other hosts that the organization arranges to use.

---

[3]RFC 1034, pp 2,3.

- Clients of the domain system should be able to identify trusted name servers they prefer to use before accepting referrals to name servers outside of this "trusted" set.
- Access to information is more critical than instantaneous updates or guarantees of consistency. Hence the update process allows updates to percolate out through the users of the domain system rather than guaranteeing that all copies are simultaneously updated. When updates are unavailable due to network or host failure, the usual course is to believe old information while continuing efforts to update it. The general model is that copies are distributed with timeouts for refreshing. The distributor sets the timeout value and the recipient of the distribution is responsible for performing the refresh. In special situations, very short intervals can be specified, or the owner can prohibit copies.
- In any system that has a distributed database, a particular name server may be presented with a query that can only be answered by some other server. The two general approaches to dealing with this problem are "recursive," in which the first server pursues the query for the client at another server, and "iterative," in which the server refers the client to another server and lets the client pursue the query. Both approaches have advantages and disadvantages, but the iterative approach is preferred for the datagram style of access. The domain system requires implementation of the iterative approach, but allows the recursive approach as an option."[4]

The key to DNS lies in its use of a distributed network service in which there are many nameservers spread throughout the internet, with each nameserver responsible for, and providing information about, only a small part of the entire namespace. Without DNS or something like it, the internet may not have continued its rapid growth.

DNS continues to be a critical mechanism for the internet's growth and security. IPv6 with its 128-bit addresses will provide more than enough address space for future growth, but it relies even more heavily on DNS than IPv4. Secure DNS (DNSSEC) is expected to improve security against attackers who attempt to subvert the system for their own reasons.

---

[4]RFC 1034, p 3.

8.2   The Domain Name System Solution

Three components comprise the DNS, each corresponding to one of the three challenges cited above:

- "The DOMAIN NAME SPACE and RESOURCE RECORDS, which are specifications for a tree structured name space and data associated with the names. Conceptually, each node and leaf of the domain name space tree names a set of information, and query operations are attempts to extract specific types of information from a particular set. A query names the domain name of interest and describes the type of resource information that is desired. For example, the Internet uses some of its domain names to identify hosts; queries for address resources return Internet host addresses.
- NAME SERVERS are server programs which hold information about the domain tree's structure and set information. A name server may cache structure or set information about any part of the domain tree, but in general a particular name server has complete information about a subset of the domain space, and pointers to other name servers that can be used to lead to information from any part of the domain tree. Name servers know the parts of the domain tree for which they have complete information; a name server is said to be an AUTHORITY for these parts of the name space. Authoritative information is organized into units called ZONEs, and these zones can be automatically distributed to the name servers which provide redundant service for the data in a zone.
- RESOLVERS are programs that extract information from name servers in response to client requests. Resolvers must be able to access at least one name server and use that name server's information to answer a query directly, or pursue the query using referrals to other name servers. A resolver will typically be a system routine that is directly accessible to user programs; hence no protocol is necessary between the resolver and the user program."[5]

Mockapetris linked these three components with the perspectives of the three different classes of users:

- "From the user's point of view, the domain system is accessed through a simple procedure or OS call to a local resolver.

---

[5]RFC 1034, p 5.

The domain space consists of a single tree and the user can request information from any section of the tree.

- From the resolver's point of view, the domain system is composed of an unknown number of name servers. Each name server has one or more pieces of the whole domain tree's data, but the resolver views each of these databases as essentially static.
- From a name server's point of view, the domain system consists of separate sets of local information called zones. The name server has local copies of some of the zones. The name server must periodically refresh its zones from master copies in local files or foreign name servers. The name server must concurrently process queries that arrive from resolvers."[6]

For our purposes, we can discuss DNS in terms of these three components:

- Database: the domain name space and its component resource records (RRs).
- Service: the rules by which *nameservers* (programs implementing DNS services) store and make available their particular portions of the domain name space.
- Users: the rules by which *resolvers* (programs capable of retrieving information from DNS servers) access DNS information.

We'll look at each of these components in the next three sections, followed by illustration of the DNS protocol in action in section 8.5 and discussion of changes and additions made to DNS since RFC 1035 with emphasis on DNS security extensions.

8.3 The Database

The DNS is a huge, and hugely distributed, database, and the domain name space is the hierarchical database that DNS stores. Its hierarchical structure can be represented as a tree with the unnamed root represented at the top (more like a family tree than an apple tree). All nodes are descendants of the unnamed root. *Nodes* are points from which *leaves* sprout (or could sprout) off the domain name tree, and both are usually referred to as nodes because they are treated identically and can both be linked with a set of resources (information about the node/leaf). Nodes are identified by

---

[6]RFC 1034, p 6.

domain names, which consist of the sequence of node *labels* tracing a node's ancestry.

The *root* domain node is denoted by the null (0-byte) label, represented as ".", and usually left out of written domain names. Every domain name is represented as a sequence of node labels (labels may be up to 63 bytes long) separated by ".". Thus, the typical domain name "www.example.com", with the symbol "." pronounced "dot" and setting off the domain name's constituent labels.

Domain names start out with the most specific node label at the leftmost, with subsequent labels referring to increasingly general nodes. The *top-level domain* (*TLD*) refers to the highest-level node below the root in a domain name; the TLD appears directly to the left of the root (in most cases, the root being assumed, the TLD is the rightmost element of the node). In the "www.example.com" domain, ".com" is the TLD (see sidebar for more about TLDs). The label ".com" is most general, the label ".example." at the second level represents an entity that maintains its own subdomain, and the "www" label indicates the leaf node to be linked with a particular system ("www" within the "example" organization, which is registered under the ".com" TLD).

Sibling nodes have unique names at their own levels within their parent domains. In other words, under the root domain ".", there can be only one ".com" domain. Under the ".com" domain, there can be only one ".example." sub-domain[7]–but the ".example." sub-domain can be repeated once each under all other TLDs. Thus, "example.com" can co-exist with "example.net", "example.org", "example.gov" and so on. Node labels can be used only once under each parent node, but can be re-used at other layers. Thus, "example.com" can co-exist with "example.example1.com" as well as "example.example.com" (which is a child of the "example.com" domain).

Figure 8–1 shows a simplified example taken from RFC 1034. Although most readers will be familiar with two- or three-level domains (such as "example.org" or "www.example.com"), additional layers are also possible (such as the domain "XX.LCS.MIT.EDU" represented in Fig. 8–1). The parent of all domains is at the top: this node is unnamed, and (when it is referred to at all) is denoted by a single period ("."). Every *top-level domain*,

---

[7]Except for the root (or parent of all domains) ".", all domains are also sub-domains. The term sub-domain is relative (as are any further recursions such as "sub-sub-domain").

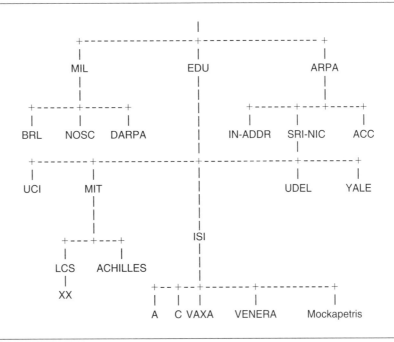

Figure 8–1: A sampling of the domain name space, from RFC 1034 (p 10).

or *TLD*, is a child of this unnamed parent. Figure 8–1 shows only three TLDs: .mil, .edu, and .arpa. As of 2002, there are several more TLDs (see next section) as well as .arpa, which is designated as an *infrastructure* domain (see section 8.6.1 for more about the *in-addr.arpa* and other miscellaneous domains).

8.3.1 TOP-LEVEL DOMAINS

Starting in the mid-1980s, the IETF defined a limited number of TLDs. In RFC 1591, "Domain Name System Structure and Delegation" defined the seven three-letter TLDs, adding that " It is extremely unlikely that any other TLDs will be created." The original TLDs included:

.com Intended for "commercial entities" i.e., companies; as early as 1994, the huge growth in registrations of .com domains was seen as a reason for caution (see RFC 1591, 'Domain Name System Structure and Delegation').

.edu Initially for all educational institutions, this domain was later reserved for 4-year colleges and universities.

.net Intended for naming systems associated with network service providers.

.org Was originally intended as a sort of catch-all category for organizations such as non-governmental organizations that didn't fit other categories.

.int Added in 1988, .int was reserved for international databases or for organizations formed as a result of international treaties, but by 2000 ICANN was recommending that use of this domain be reconsidered, and no new .int registrations have been permitted since then.

.gov Is used only for US government agencies or offices; initially, registration was open to state and municipal government organizations, but now only federal organizations may use the .gov TLD.

.mil Is used only by organizations within the US military community.

In addition to these TLDs are the two-letter country code TLDs, mostly taken from the ISO standard 3166. Networks can use these TLDs within their own countries; some countries with interesting two-letter codes offer registration services under those domains to anyone as an alternative to the crowded .com TLD. These include Tuvalu (TV), a small Pacific Ocean island nation; Cocos (Keeling) Islands (CC), a territory of Australia located in the Indian Ocean with fewer than 700 residents; and Ascension Island (AC), another tiny island in the South Atlantic Ocean 750 miles northwest of St. Helena.

Individual nations and territories are free to administer their TLDs as they see fit. In the US, a variety of sub-domains have been apportioned through the years, including two-letter state and territory sub-domains, K12 (for schools serving kindergarten through the 12th grade and associated educational organizations), and others. The registry has begun offering registration of individual and corporate names directly under the .us TLD in addition to registration under state and municipality subdomains (e.g., instead of registering the domain example.springfield.ma.us, you would be allowed to register example.us).

Starting in 2000, as the Internet Assigned Numbers Authority (IANA) was transferred to the Internet Corporation for Assigned Names and Numbers (ICANN), the process of adding seven new TLDs began; by early 2002 most were operational and accepting requests for registrations. They include:

.biz Is intended as an online business-oriented alternative to the .com TLD.

.info Is intended to be an unrestricted TLD (meaning anyone can register any domain name, within reason), and another alternative to the crowded three-letter TLDs.

.name Is intended as a non-commercial service for individuals. Registrants can opt for a domain in the format *lastname.name* or *firstname.lastname.name*.

.museum Is intended for use only by museums, museum organizations, and individuals working for museums.

.coop Is intended for use only by cooperatives and affiliated organizations.

.aero Is intended for use only by the aviation community (according to the .aero registry website, this includes "companies, organizations, associations, government agencies and individuals who participate in the efficient, safe and secure transport of people and cargo by air").

.pro Is intended for use by certified professionals including doctors, lawyers, and accountants. As of early 2002, .pro registrations had not yet begun.

Other TLDs may yet be proposed and approved, depending on the success of the existing alternate domains.

8.3.2 DOMAIN NAME SYSTEM DATABASE SERVICES

Segmenting the internet domain name space into this hierarchy significantly reduces the scope of the problem of doing domain name lookups.

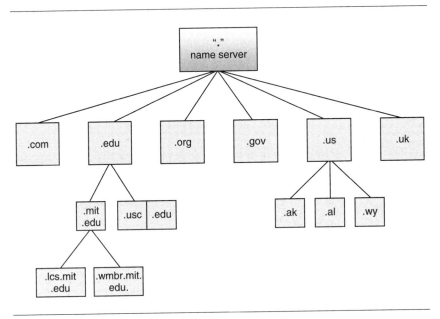

Figure 8–2: The DNS distributed database.

Although a central repository of global domain names and addresses could still be implemented (in theory, at least), DNS is much easier if responsibility for name lookups is delegated to each parent node. In other words, a node needs to maintain information only about its own children.

This means that the root nameserver needs to have domain name and address information only about the TLDs (the dozen or so *global TLDs* such as .com and .info, plus over 200 two-character country code TLDs); each TLD nameserver need only have information about its own child second-level domain nodes, and each of those second-level domains needs only maintain information about the third-level domain nodes.

Figure 8–2 shows how it works. At the tippy-top is the name service for the unnamed root DNS domain.[8] That service keeps track of all its child

---

[8]For many years, this function was performed by the TLD nameservers in addition to their own duties. In other words, the same systems that maintained DNS information about .com, .edu, .org, .net, and so on also maintained information about each other. Currently, the .com, .org, and .net domains were moved to new servers (*.GTLD-SERVERS.NET), separate from the root servers (*.ROOT-SERVERS.NET).

domain nodes—the TLDs. Any time a TLD needs to locate information about a sibling TLD, for example, when the .com nameserver needed more information about reaching the .uk domain, it would query this root name service. This root domain service maintains information on just the TLDs.

Each TLD has a domain name service for its own children. Thus, the service associated with the .info domain keeps track of only its own child domain nodes. If you needed to locate information about such a domain (e.g., example.info), you would query the name service associated with the .info TLD. By delegating domain name database duty to subordinate domains, no single domain is burdened with more than a portion of the entire domain name space. The .com domain, with roughly 10 million sub-domains registered as of early 2002, undoubtedly contains the most sub-domains to track; within each of those sub-domains, however, individual organizations will almost always administer considerably smaller domains.

The domain name system mandates that each node's children be administered through a single organizational entity, a *registry*. *Registrars* are entities that have been authorized to accept TLD registrations from customers; they are permitted to register domains with one or more domain registrars. Once a domain has been registered, such as example.com, child nodes are the responsibility of the owner of example.com. The TLD name service only knows about its own children; the example.com name service maintains information about child nodes of the example.com domain, such as www.example.com, hr.example.com, dallas.example.com, ftp.example.com, and any others. Assuming that the domain hr.example.com is a node with its own children, a name service for hr.example.com must also be set up to record information about any of that sub-sub-domain's children (such as www.hr.example.com, ftp.hr.example.com, payroll.hr.example.com, vacation.hr.example.com, and so on).

What's the difference between a host domain name and a domain name? A host name is assumed to refer to a single system (a leaf on the domain name tree hierarchy), while a domain name may contain child nodes of its own, which could be leaves or other sub-domains with their own leaves. As far as DNS is concerned, the difference may not matter. For example, the following domain names can be used with the web to connect to resources: mit.edu, www.mit.edu, lcs.mit.edu, www.lcs.mit.edu.

How many layers down can DNS go? Here is a functioning URL that uses a domain name with 25 nodes:

```
http://twas.brillig.and.the.slithy.toves.
did.gyre.and.gimble.in.the.wabe.
all.mimsy.were.the.borogoves.
and.the.mome.raths.outgrabe.
jabberwocky.com/
```

As of early 2002, this URL was functioning, although mostly as a stunt and to test the ability of users' software to cope with the deep domain name. RFC 1034 mandates an upper limit of 255 bytes for the representation of domain names to simplify processing and keep domain naming from getting out of hand.

8.3.3 RESOURCE RECORDS

No database can exist without records, and DNS was defined to store name and address information as well as provide the capacity to store other information as well. DNS data is stored in *resource records* (*RRs*). As defined in the internet standard for DNS,[9] "A domain name identifies a node. Each node has a set of resource information, which may be empty. The set of resource information associated with a particular name is composed of separate resource records."

Figure 8–3 is a graphical representation of the fields comprising an RR; those fields include:

NAME: The domain name where the RR is found; the owner may be implied by the contents of the RR.

TYPE: An encoded 16-bit value specifying what kind of abstract resource is referred to in the RR. RFC 1034 mentions several types, including *A* to indicate a host address, *CNAME* for the *canonical name* of an alias used to simplify access to the resource, *HINFO* for the CPU and OS used by the host, *MX* to identify the resource as a mail exchange

---

[9]STD 13, which includes RFCs 1034 and 1035.

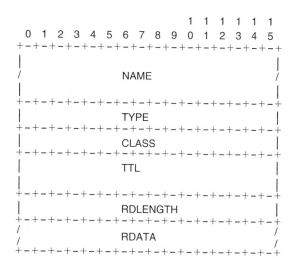

Figure 8–3: Layout of fields within an RR (from RFC 1034).

for the domain,[10] *NS* to indicate the authoritative nameserver for a domain, *PTR* to indicate a pointer to another part of the domain name space, and *SOA* to indicate the start of a *zone of authority*. These types will be discussed at greater length later in this chapter. (See Appendix B for the complete list of valid RR types.)

CLASS: Another encoded 16-bit value, the class specifies "a protocol family or instance of a protocol"; for example, the IN class, specifying the internet system. This value is rarely used.

TTL: The *time to live* of the RR. A 32-bit integer, TTL specifies the number of seconds before the RR should expire. This is used mostly after a resolver has retrieved an RR to indicate how long the cached value should be saved and used before discarding it as out of date.

RDLENGTH: Is a 16-bit value indicating the length of the resource data, in bytes, limiting the amount of data stored in any RR to no more than 65,535 bytes.

---

[10]See Chapter 10 for more about how internet mail uses DNS.

RDATA: The data associated with the RR. The composition and length of this field may vary, depending on the RR type.

8.3.4   RESOURCE RECORD TYPES

Different types of RR have been defined for different purposes, although we'll consider only the types defined in RFC 1034. Domain nameservers store all their information in these RRs, making the definition of each RR roughly equivalent to a database's design or schema.

Although DNS is most often associated with the process of matching hostnames with IP addresses, DNS makes other data available, for other purposes. One of the most important of these other purposes is making mail exchange (MX) information available. MX records allow internet mail addressed to one address be redirected for delivery to some other address, for a variety of reasons: to keep private details of an organization's intranet and internal mail systems, or to avoid going through a security firewall, or to provide a standard corporate address format (e.g., "firstname.lastname@example.com") while allowing users to receive mail on other addresses.

A number of RRs have been defined for use with DNS security extensions; these include the SIG (security signature), KEY (security key), and NXT (next domain) RRs defined in RFC 2535. Other special purpose RRs include the NAPTR (naming authority pointer) type defined in RFCs 2168 and 2915 and the AAAA and A6 types defined for IPv6 address resolution, and there is even an RR defined simply for storing text strings (TXT). A more complete list is available in Appendix B; the most up-to-date information about valid RRs is maintained by IANA at http://www.iana.org/assignments/dns-parameters.

The actual format and information stored in a particular RR are largely self-explanatory, or will be as we investigate how the DNS protocol works.

8.4   The Protocol

Under the DNS protocol, hosts making or responding to requests for DNS data do so by sending out messages with a minimum of fuss. DNS messages are usually encapsulated within UDP because of the low overhead; the assumption being that if a requesting host doesn't get a response fast enough, sending out another request, whether to the primary nameserver or to a secondary nameserver, poses no great hardship.

DNS protocols define formats for requests and responses, as well as a general architecture for interaction between the hosts making requests of DNS and the hosts fulfilling those requests. We'll look first at the general architecture and then at the specifics of the messages.

8.4.1 AUTHORITATIVE DOMAIN DATA

Some protocols are quite simple, involving only two entities exchanging information. Even though each component of the DNS protocol is straightforward, there are more components than many other protocols encountered on the internet.

At the risk of oversimplifying the DNS, the basic idea is that when a resolver requests domain information it generates a query, which is a DNS message sent to a nameserver (e.g., "What is the IP address of the host at www.example.com?"). The nameserver responds to the request by sending the requesting resolver a DNS message with the answer; that answer may be the data requested by the resolver (e.g., "www.example.com can be reached at 192.168.1.200"), where to reach another nameserver more likely to have the correct answer (e.g., "Try querying nameserver.example.com, which can be reached at 10.0.0.1"), or an error message.

This would be enough if there were only one nameserver in the network, maintaining all DNS information. Every resolver would query that nameserver, and that nameserver would respond to every request. However, as we have already seen, that solution does not scale well, so DNS differentiates between two different grades of domain data. There is *authoritative data*, which originates from the nameservers responsible for maintaining that data, and *cached data*, which is data received by a host in response to some prior request or interaction and stored for later use. In general, authoritative data is assumed to be "better" in the sense that it is more likely to be current and correct; however, most internet systems are sufficiently stable[11] that even cached data is very likely to be usable.

---

[11]The size of the internet guarantees that there will be many changes in DNS data every day, but the chances of any particular host's data changing from one moment to another are relatively low.

8.4.2 DOMAIN NAME SYSTEM ZONES

Authoritative data is maintained by nameservers that are serving their own *zones*; a zone is the portion of the name space for which a nameserver is responsible. A zone is defined by a set of authoritative data, contained in RRs, which includes:

- All the RRs for all the nodes within the zone (records concerning every named resource within the zone).
- The top node included within the zone (e.g., if a zone is defined as containing everything under the .example.com zone, then "example.com" is the top node of that zone). This indicates a boundary at the upper limit of the zone.
- *Delegated subzones* refer to zones that might be assumed to belong to the zone, but for which authority has been delegated. These represent boundaries at the lower limit of the zone. Within the .example.com zone, authority for a subzone under .hr.example.com might be delegated to the human resources department of Example, Inc. As part of the definition of the .example.com zone, a description of the .hr.example.com subzone would be included.
- *Glue data* regarding the delegated subzones, providing access to nameservers within those subzones.

A nameserver can be authoritative about some part of the namespace, even if that part is no more than its own node; nameservers also maintain cached data that has been received from other systems. Zones are important because they define how contact data is stored for all domains.

One important implication of this structure is that any organization seeking to manage its own zone must negotiate the process with whoever is responsible for the parent zone. Thus, Example, Inc., must get Network Solutions, Inc., to agree to delegate responsibility for the example.com domain. Once the agreement is reached, Network Solutions would "cut out" the delegated subzone (.example.com) and configure its nameservers to indicate that Example, Inc.'s nameservers are maintaining authoritative DNS data for that subzone.

Figure 8–4 should make things a bit clearer.

When a resolver needs to know how to reach the domain name `payroll.hr.example.com`, it would initially get contact information

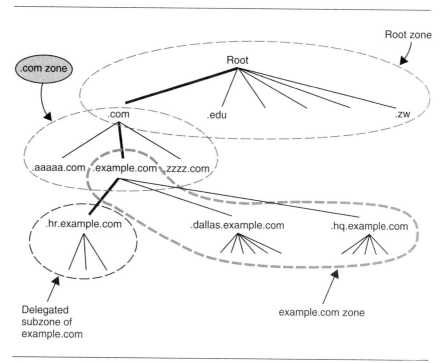

Figure 8–4: DNS zones and subzones.

for the `example.com` domain; the nameserver's response would indicate that some other nameserver was responsible for the `hr.example.com` domain. As long as the resolver can find an IP address for that name-server, all is well. However, if the subzone nameserver is situated within the subzone domain, the resolver has a problem: `dns.example.com` (the nameserver for `example.com`) tells it to ask `dns.hr.example.com` (the nameserver for the subzone) for the address—but now the resolver needs to find out the address of `dns.hr.example.com`.

The solution is to include *glue data* with subzone delegations. The name-server for the parent zone maintains full domain name and address data for the nameservers of its delegated subzones. That way, when a resolver goes to the parent zone for DNS data, the parent name-server can give complete contact information for the appropriate subzone nameserver.

8.4.3 DOMAIN NAME SYSTEM REQUESTS, RECURSIVE AND NON-RECURSIVE

The domain name space can be viewed as a huge quilt composed of these different zones; every part of the namespace belongs in one zone (Fig. 8–4 shows overlap between zones at their boundaries, that is, where a delegated subzone links with its parent zone, but this overlap merely shows where the interfaces are between the zones; the top nodes are authoritative for themselves and belong within their own zones).

Thus, while no single nameserver can respond to every DNS query with a complete and correct answer, it will always be able to respond reliably and accurately to requests. Either the nameserver stores authoritative information about the domain being requested (e.g., when a host on the local domain is requesting information about another host on the same domain), or else the nameserver will be able to direct the requesting host to a nameserver "closer" to the requested information.

In effect, a host sends a message to its local nameserver, making a request that is functionally equivalent to "How do I reach Bob at Example, Inc.?" The local nameserver, if it happens to serve the example.com domain, will respond with "Bob is at *<address>*". More likely, the nameserver has no information about example.com, and will respond instead, "I don't know, but you can try contacting *<nameserver>*, which is closer to example.com than I am."

With this type of response, a nameserver can respond reliably and accurately even when it does not have any information about the requested domain. The "closer" nameserver will likely be at the upper boundary of the queried nameserver's zone; when that nameserver is queried, it will either have authoritative information about the requested domain, in which case it will send that data to the resolver, or it won't have any information, in which case it will also send a response indicating a closer nameserver to query. The process continues until the resolver either succeeds or fails at reaching a nameserver with authoritative information.

This can be a tedious process, and not even necessary in most cases. There are two sets of options regarding the way requests are made and fulfilled:

1. DNS requests can specify whether or not authoritative data is necessary. In this way, cached data stored at a local nameserver

can be used, and that will be perfectly adequate to reach the desired domain.

2. Resolvers may specify that their requests be processed *recursively*, meaning the initial nameserver contacted must follow through on the request itself and respond to the original query with authoritative data. Nameservers can respond to *non-recursive* requests far more simply, either with authoritative data (if they have it) or a pointer to some other server.

    However, even if a resolver requests recursion, the server may respond with cached, non-authoritative data. The Recursion Desired flag is only relevant if the answer is not already cached.

When responding to a recursive request the nameserver takes on the role of resolver, making the same type of request as the original resolver made of the first nameserver. Figure 8–5 should make the process clearer.

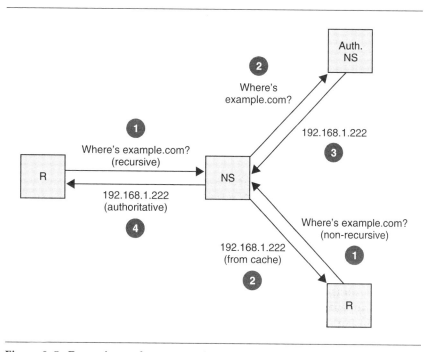

Figure 8–5: Recursive and non-recursive requests.

8.4.4 DOMAIN NAME SYSTEM MESSAGES

DNS is one of many internet protocols in which the same node can act as both a client and server at any particular time. Hosts that originate requests all have implementations of a resolver program that performs the domain name resolution function; nameservers also use resolvers when they seek information from other nameservers. A DNS request is not immediately triggered when some other process within a host initiates a request for domain information, but rather the resolver checks locally for that information (either in a cache or as part of a nameserver's authoritative domain data store). This improves performance and reduces the amount of traffic generated by DNS. A host may make a single DNS request and use the data received to address many packets before the locally cached data expires.

When a DNS request is required, it is encapsulated within a DNS *message*; Figure 8–6 shows the template for these messages, taken from RFC 1035.

Only the header section is always present in a DNS message; part of the information in the header indicates what other parts of the message are present (the header structure, along with descriptions of the header fields, is shown in Appendix B) shows the structure of the data within that section of the message. The rest of the DNS message consists of either a question or an answer and RRs associated with the query.

Let's look at the general form DNS messages take rather than attempt to reproduce and explain all the details of every DNS message type, field, and option. First, the initial query starts out with DNS header information

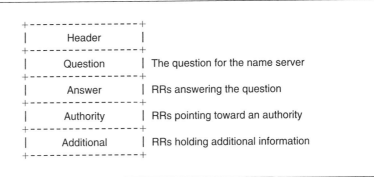

Figure 8–6: DNS message format.

```
                                        1  1  1  1  1  1
             0  1  2  3  4  5  6  7  8  9  0  1  2  3  4  5
            +-+-+-+-+-+-+-+-+-+-+-+-+-+-+-+-+
            |                      ID                       |
            +-+-+-+-+-+-+-+-+-+-+-+-+-+-+-+-+
            |QR|  Opcode  |AA|TC|RD|RA|   Z   |  RCODE  |
            +-+-+-+-+-+-+-+-+-+-+-+-+-+-+-+-+
            |                   QDCOUNT                     |
            +-+-+-+-+-+-+-+-+-+-+-+-+-+-+-+-+
            |                   ANCOUNT                     |
            +-+-+-+-+-+-+-+-+-+-+-+-+-+-+-+-+
            |                   NSCOUNT                     |
            +-+-+-+-+-+-+-+-+-+-+-+-+-+-+-+-+
            |                   ARCOUNT                     |
            +-+-+-+-+-+-+-+-+-+-+-+-+-+-+-+-+
```

Figure 8–7: DNS message header format (from RFC 1035).

(Fig. 8–7), including an ID number generated by the requesting process, whether or not the message contains a query, what kind of query it is, whether or not an authoritative answer is requested, how many queries are included in the message, and other relevant data.

This application header encapsulates the actual query, which includes the domain name (listed as a sequence of labels, each label including the length of the label plus the label string) in the QNAME field and the query type (QTYPE), which can match any RR type or may be some other query type.

In other words, the resolver opens the message with information about the request in the header, followed by the question: "Here's a domain name, and I want *<type>* information about that domain," where *<type>* could be type A (for a host IP address), or type NS (for an authoritative nameserver), or type CNAME (for a canonical, or "real", name associated with an *alias*, which is an alternate name commonly used by a host). Any of the RR types listed in Appendix B can be queried.

Replies from nameservers use the same header, including much of the data provided by the resolver in the original request (e.g., ID number and query type), but the successful response will include one or more RRs that either answer the resolver's question in some way (in the answer section of the message), relate to the answer (such as the RR for relevant authoritative servers), or additional relevant information (such as address RRs when the response to a request consists of a domain name, as happens with mail exchange queries).

In section 8.5, we'll look at two examples of DNS message exchanges, the first showing how a host is able to resolve a domain name into an IP address, the second showing how mail systems are able to determine where to send internet mail messages based on the destination mail address. There are other types of interaction, but in general, if a resource record has been defined for a particular type of data, then the basic DNS request/response messages can be used to access that data.

8.4.5   DOMAIN NAME SYSTEM AND THE TRANSPORT LAYER

Resolvers and nameservers exchange DNS messages over the UDP transport layer protocol (see Chapter 16 for more details). As previously mentioned, UDP provides a very simple mechanism for processes (in this case, processes running resolver and nameserver programs) to interact. The domain name system has been assigned the well-known port 53; this port is used whether the DNS message is sent over UDP or over TCP.

There are two issues relating to the transport layer that are worth raising when discussing DNS. The first is the limitations imposed by the use of UDP in terms of message size, and the second is the use of TCP for large transfers.

User Datagram Protocol Limitations

RFC 1035 specifies that DNS messages contained within UDP payloads must not be longer than 512 bytes. As we'll see later, in Part IV, this size is related to the maximum packet size that reasonably ensures there will be no *fragmentation*[12] of the packet. UDP offers no support for data streams spanning multiple messages—just single messages that must either stand alone or not. If an answer requires 1,000 bytes, it will be cut short (*truncated*) to stay within the 512 byte limit.

---

[12]Fragmentation occurs when a packet is too large for the local link protocol to handle. For example, Ethernet frames may be no more than 1518 bytes long; if a 2,000 byte packet must pass through an Ethernet network, the router handling it will break the packet up into frames smaller than 1518 bytes and those packets will be reassembled at the destination to re-create the original, larger, packet. Usually, it is preferable to avoid fragmentation; the topic is discussed in more detail in Chapter 14.

Truncation poses a problem, because if the answer to the resolver's question doesn't appear in those first 512 bytes, the resolver must retry the request using TCP, which provides a more reliable transport protocol than UDP. At the same time TCP uses greater bandwidth and resources so it should be used only when absolutely necessary.

Domain Name System Zone Transfers

Ordinary DNS messages between resolvers and nameservers are customarily encapsulated with UDP, which is a datagram service providing nothing more than a best-effort at delivery. Because these messages are usually brief (domain names are limited to 255 bytes, for example), and because they are typically limited to a single request matched with a single response, the use of a more complex protocol adds overhead, but no improvement in the service.

However, there is one DNS function that does need more than UDP can offer: the *zone transfer* process. DNS requires that every zone be served by at least two nameservers; the main nameserver is called the *primary nameserver* and the backup is called a *secondary nameserver*.[13] Backup nameservers periodically check their primary nameservers to get updates or even to reload an entire zone. The DNS protocol provides a mechanism for making this type of query, but the specification recommends using TCP for these exchanges. The virtual circuit and other controls on the connection that TCP provide make for a more reliable exchange of what may be a large volume of data.

8.5   Domain Name System in Action

The most common uses to which DNS is put are fulfilling requests for:

- IP addresses associated with a domain (requests for A RRs)
- Mail exchange binding (requests for MX RRs)

An example of the first of these was included in the previous chapter in section 7.2.1; another example will be provided here, including the complete request/response as well as more detail about the contents.

---

[13]Terminology for additional nameservers varies; some call the second backup the *tertiary nameserver*, while others refer to any non-primary nameserver as a secondary.

8.5.1 ADDRESS REQUEST

An initial request for an address to associate with the host name www.internet-standard.com appears below:

```
Domain Name System (query)
   Transaction ID: 0xcc42
   Flags: 0x0100 (Standard query)
     0... .... .... .... = Query
     .000 0... .... .... = Standard query
     .... ..0. .... .... = Authoritative Answer
(not set in requests)
     .... ...1 .... .... = Message is not
truncated
     .... .... 1... .... = Recursion desired
     .... .... .0.. .... = Recursion available
(not set in requests)
   Questions: 1
   Answer RRs: 0
   Authority RRs: 0
   Additional RRs: 0
   Queries
     www.internet-standard.com: type A, class inet
     Name: www.internet-standard.com
     Type: Host address
     Class: inet
```

Taking the headers one at a time, with the values represented in hexadecimal (for brevity):

0xcc42: The first 2 bytes of data are the *transaction ID*. This is purely administrative data for tracking the request and any responses to the request.

`0x0100`: The next 2 bytes comprise *protocol flags*, 3 reserved bits, and a 4-bit *response code* field. The listing indicates this is a query (if that flag was set on, it would indicate a response). The next four bits indicate the type of query (whether the message is a response or a query; this indicates the type of query in either case). The next flags indicate whether the message contains an *authoritative answer* (data received from authoritative nameserver—not a relevant flag for a request); whether or not the message was truncated (not in this case); whether *recursion* is requested (yes); and whether recursion is available (not relevant for requests). The three reserved bits are not assigned and must be set to 0; the response code is all zeroes because there is no associated response (this is the initial query).

`0x0001`: The next 2 bytes indicate the number of *questions* in the request. That is, the number of separate entries in the questions section of the request, which indicate the number of different records being requested. As a 16-bit value, up to 65,535 or so questions could be included in a single request, though the actual number is usually considerably lower.

`0x0000`: A 16-bit value indicating how many *answer RRs* are being sent; though up to 65,535 are possible, much lower values are more usual. For a request, this should be set to 0.

`0x0000`: A 16-bit value indicating how many *authority nameserver RRs* are included in the response; set to 0 for requests.

`0x0000`: A 16-bit value indicating how many *additional nameserver RRs* are included in the response; set to 0 for requests.

`[remainder]`: The rest of this DNS message consists of the *query*, itself consisting of three components, as follows.

`QNAME`: The name being queried. In this case, that is `www.internet-standard.com`. Domain names in DNS messages terminate with the hex value `0x00`, to indicate that the next data are not part of the name.

`QTYPE`: The query type is a 2-byte value indicating what kind of resource record is being requested. Any value that refers to a valid resource record type (see section 8.3.4 and Appendix B for details) is valid here as well.

QCLASS: The class type of the query specified by a two-byte value; inet is used for internet and IP queries.

The request is for the nameserver being queried to do a recursive query on behalf of the requesting host for an address resource record (A RR) from an authoritative nameserver for the domain name www.internet-standard.com.

After a short time (to allow the nameserver to make the recursive request) the response comes back from the DNS server. The transaction ID is the same as the original request value, so the requesting host can identify the message as a response to that particular query. The op code value and flags indicate a response, with no errors, to a standard query; the server not being an authority for the domain, the message (which is reproduced in full) contains a recursive response (recursion was requested originally, and the nameserver is able to do it).

The rest of the message header indicates that there is a single question, two answers, two RRs pointing to authoritative nameservers for the queried domain, and no additional related RRs.

The next part of the message contains the query or queries (in this case, just one), repeating the original request from the query message: an A RR for www.internet-standard.com. The answers section lists the answers received, followed by the authority section containing RRs for the nameservers that provided those answers.

```
Domain Name System (response)
  Transaction ID: 0xcc42
  Flags: 0x8180 (Standard query response,
No error)
    1... .... .... .... = Response
    .000 0... .... .... = Standard query
    .... .0.. .... .... = Server is not an
                          authority for domain
```

```
        .... ..0. .... .... = Message is not
                               truncated
        .... ...1 .... .... = Do query
                               recursively
        .... .... 1... .... = Server can do
                               recursive queries
        .... .... .... 0000 = No error
   Questions: 1
   Answer RRs: 2
   Authority RRs: 2
   Additional RRs: 0
   Queries
     www.internet-standard.com: type A, class inet
     Name: www.internet-standard.com
     Type: Host address
     Class: inet
   Answers
     www.internet-standard.com: type CNAME,
 class inet, cname internet-standard.com
        Name: www.internet-standard.com
        Type: Canonical name for an alias
        Class: inet
        Time to live: 1 hour
        Data length: 2
        Primary name: internet-standard.com
     internet-standard.com: type A,
 class inet, addr 216.92.98.204
        Name: internet-standard.com
        Type: Host address
```

```
     Class: inet
     Time to live: 1 hour
     Data length: 4
     Addr: 216.92.98.204
  Authoritative nameservers
    internet-standard.com: type NS,
class inet, ns ns00.ns0.com
     Name: internet-standard.com
     Type: Authoritative name server
     Class: inet
     Time to live: 1 hour
     Data length: 11
     Name server: ns00.ns0.com
    internet-standard.com: type NS,
class inet, ns ns130.pair.com
     Name: internet-standard.com
     Type: Authoritative name server
     Class: inet
     Time to live: 1 hour
     Data length: 13
     Name server: ns130.pair.com
```

Moving to the answers section, there are two RRs, but only one A RR; the first is a CNAME RR. We discover the name www.internet-standard.com is actually an *alias* for a different, *canonical* name (meaning the "real" name rather than nickname or alias). So part of the recursive response includes the RR for that. Also included are nameserver resource records (NS RRs) for each of two nameservers that are authoritative for the requested domain.

All these RRs share some fields in common:

Name: The name associated with the resource.

Type: The type of resource record.

Class: Refers to the naming/address domain in which the record occurs (again, this will be inet; other domains aren't often used).

Time-to-live: A 32-bit integer specifying (in seconds) how long the the information in the record is permitted to be cached before it must be updated.

Data-length: The number of bytes used by the record data. For example, an address record uses 4 bytes (32 bits), the same length as a standard IP address. The data length field indicates how many bytes are used, not necessarily how long the actual data is: a sort of compression is permitted in RRs that uses pointers (offsets) to indicate that part of one name is actually already used elsewhere in the message. For example, the actual data associated with the NS RRs above use pointers to the ".com" section at the beginning of the message; in this case, 1 or 2 bytes is saved; where longer domains repeat through a message, many more bytes can be saved.

[DATA]: The data fields vary depending on the RR type. NS RRs contain the domain name of an authoritative nameserver; the CNAME RR contains the primary name of the resource; and the A RR contains the 4-byte IP address.

This process demonstrates only the originating host (the one making the request) and the nameserver local to that host. As a recursive request, the nameserver had to submit its own query to its own nameserver, which either had the answer or had to refer the first nameserver to another nameserver even closer to the requested domain.

A response to a DNS query might arrive almost instantaneously, in fractions of a second, or there might be no response for several seconds. A DNS resolver will resubmit the same query after a certain time, during which it can be assumed that the first transmission either never made it to the nameserver or the nameserver was unable to handle the request immediately in which case the query would have been discarded silently.

8.5.2 MAIL EXCHANGE REQUEST

We'll cover mail in detail in the next chapter, but DNS serves as the repository of an important set of data about mail addresses. Rather than attempt to create a separate system for associating mail domains with mail servers that accept mail for those domains, DNS was designed to map the mail domain name space on top of the internet domain name space. With mail addresses taking the form user@domain.name, the section of the address following the @ symbol is based on the DNS domain of the organization hosting the user's mailbox. However, it is not enough for a mail resolver to get the IP address associated with a message's address domain: it must be directed to a mail server that accepts mail for that domain.

Thus, the *mail exchange resource record*, or *MX RR*, which contains two pieces of information:

Preference is a 16-bit integer that indicates a rank given to the RR by its owner. If a mail domain is served by more than one server, the owner of the domain may have one server as the primary, in which case that server's RR would have a lower value (higher preference) in this field. Secondary and other backup servers would have higher values, so that someone sending mail would try the primary first; if that server was unavailable, they would try the secondary server (with the second lowest value, or second most preferred RR) next.

Exchange is the domain name of a host that will accept mail on behalf of the holder of the mail address.

When a nameserver replies to a request for an MX RR, it automatically adds the A resource record for the mail exchange domain. An example of a recursive request for an MX RR is shown below. Quite like the query for an A RR, the primary difference is the query type—mail exchange—instead of host address.

```
Domain Name System (query)
 Transaction ID: 0x100e
 Flags: 0x0100 (Standard query)
   0... .... .... .... = Query
   .000 0... .... .... = Standard query
   .... ..0. .... .... = Message is not
                          truncated
   .... ...1 .... .... = Do query
                          recursively
```

```
    .... ... ...0 .... = Non-authenticated
                         data is unacceptable
  Questions: 1
  Answer RRs: 0
  Authority RRs: 0
  Additional RRs: 0
  Queries
    internet-standard.com: type MX,
class inet
      Name: internet-standard.com
      Type: Mail exchange
      Class: inet
```

As with the previous examples, we dispense with the intermediate steps involved in having the first nameserver query other nameservers on behalf of the original host that sent the query; the response (once that first nameserver gets all the data from upstream) appears below:

```
Domain Name System (response)
  Transaction ID: 0x100e
  Flags: 0x8180 (Standard query response, No error)
    1... .... .... .... = Response
    .000 0... .... .... = Standard query
    .... .0.. .... .... = Server is not an
                          authority for domain
    .... ..0. .... .... = Message is not
                          truncated
    .... ...1 .... .... = Do query
                          recursively
```

```
       .... .... 1... .... = Server can do
                            recursive queries
       .... .... ..0. .... = Answer/authority
                            portion was not
                            authenticated
                            by the server
       .... .... .... 0000 = No error
    Questions: 1
    Answer RRs: 1
    Authority RRs: 2
    Additional RRs: 3

    Queries
      internet-standard.com: type MX,
class inet
        Name: internet-standard.com
        Type: Mail exchange
        Class: inet

    Answers
      internet-standard.com: type MX,
class inet, preference 50, mx enek.pair.com
        Name: internet-standard.com
        Type: Mail exchange
        Class: inet
        Time to live: 56 minutes, 10 seconds
        Data length: 14
        Preference: 50
        Mail exchange: enek.pair.com

    Authoritative nameservers
      internet-standard.com: type NS,
class inet, ns ns130.pair.com
```

```
Name: internet-standard.com
Type: Authoritative name server
Class: inet
Time to live: 40 minutes, 46 seconds
Data length: 8
Name server: ns130.pair.com
```

```
internet-standard.com: type NS,
class inet, ns ns00.ns0.com
Name: internet-standard.com
Type: Authoritative name server
Class: inet
Time to live: 40 minutes, 46 seconds
Data length: 11
Name server: ns00.ns0.com
```

```
Additional records
enek.pair.com: type A, class inet, addr
209.68.1.148
Name: enek.pair.com
Type: Host address
Class: inet
Time to live: 1 hour, 59 minutes, 23 seconds
Data length: 4
Addr: 209.68.1.148
ns130.pair.com: type A, class inet, addr
209.68.1.148
Name: ns130.pair.com
Type: Host address
Class: inet
```

```
    Time to live: 1 hour, 59 minutes, 23 seconds

    Data length: 4

    Addr: 209.68.1.148

ns00.ns0.com: type A, class inet, addr
                216.92.60.60

  Name: ns00.ns0.com

  Type: Host address

  Class: inet

  Time to live: 1 hour, 20 minutes, 8 seconds

  Data length: 4

  Addr: 216.92.60.60
```

As can be seen here, there is a lot more information to gather, not to mention some records in every section of the message including queries, answers, authoritative nameservers, and additional records.

The query section includes a single query, the original one for a mail exchange for the `internet-standard.com` domain.[14]

The answers section includes the information stored in the authoritative servers MX resource record for the `internet-standard.com` domain; it happens to be a host known as `enek.pair.com`. Also stored in the MX RR is a value called the *preference*, which is used when more than one mail exchange server is available: the server with the lowest preference value gets priority over other servers (e.g., if one server has a preference value of 50 and a second server has a preference value of 100, a host would attempt to deliver mail to the first server first).

The rest of the MX RR contains many of the same fields as other RRs, including time to live, data length, class, and type.

Next comes the authoritative nameserver section, containing the NS RRs from which the answers were received. As with the MX record, the

---

[14]A mail exchange is a server willing to accept mail for the domain in question. See Chapter 10 for more details about how this data is used.

NS records are associated with the domain in question (`internet-standard.com`) and contain data concerning the nameservers that are authoritative for that domain. Everything is indexed to the domain name: nameservers, mail exchanges, addresses, and so on.

Finally, the additional records provide extra information—the IP address for the mail exchange server (`enek.pair.com`) as well as the IP addresses for the authoritative nameservers. Even though the query specified only an MX RR for the domain, the A RR associated with the mail exchange server clearly comes in handy if the host making the request wants to connect to that server.

8.6   Additional Domain Name System Issues

Over the years, DNS has held up remarkably well. Its hierarchical structure is well-suited to supporting very large networks such as the internet. Using distributed caches rather than overloading higher-level or very busy domains with a constant barrage of requests helps improve scalability, and resource records have been defined for a variety of different types of data (see Appendix B for a list of valid RRs, along with pointers to the RFCs in which they are defined). Such a robust system must have some modifications, extensions, and tweaks over the years to make it so, and this section highlights some of them.

8.6.1   INVERSE AND REVERSE ADDRESS LOOKUPS

One function that DNS, as described so far, does not provide but that the original *hosts* file approach did offer is the ability to as easily link an IP address to a domain name. The hierarchy of the DNS database is based on the domain name not on the IP address. The *hosts* file is a simple list; each host is listed on a single line and each line includes the IP address, host name, and any aliases associated with that address. Lookups on domain names, aliases, or IP addresses are all roughly equal in complexity.

The ability to lookup the domain name associated with an IP address—a *reverse lookup*—is useful in some cases:

- To determine whether a domain is being *spoofed* (an attacker is pretending to be originating packets from a different address).

- Some applications have used the domain name as a form of authentication (e.g., some *nix network applications).
- For trouble-shooting purposes.

Under DNS, however, one would have to query the domain name server for each domain to seek out information about the IP address in question. W. Richard Stevens writing in *TCP/IP Illustrated Volume 1* suggested such a query might take weeks to accomplish given the current size of the internet—in 1994! Clearly, such searches are impractical at best.

The solution, as defined in RFC 1035, was to create a special domain, in-addr.arpa, under which the entire IP network address space could be cross referenced. The arpa domain was originally intended for use by the US Department of Defense Advanced Research Projects Agency (ARPA); more recently, ICANN redefined this domain designation to stand for "Address and Routing Parameter Area." Doing so permitted the administrative task of further separating the internet's infrastructure from its DoD-funded roots while at the same time imposing no need for any systems to be changed.

Under this domain, a PTR (pointer) resource record could be defined so as to duplicate the IP network address space's hierarchy (see Chapter 19 for more details about IP addressing). The PTR RR consists of a domain name, and is associated with the in-addr.arpa domain name based on an IP address.

In this way, looking up a dotted-decimal IP address and finding the domain name with which it is associated can be as easy as using the domain name to find the address. Figure 8–8 shows how a portion of this part of hierarchy works. Just as DNS allows users to work their way up the hierarchy from the most specific to the most general part of the domain name, so too does the in-addr.arpa domain allow users to work their way up from the most specific portion of the IP address to the most general.

Assume the need to link an IP address 178.16.101.8 to a domain name. The most specific part of the IP address occurs at the rightmost part of the address, while the most specific part of a domain name occurs at the leftmost part of the name.[15] As a result, the IP addresses map in a reverse

---

[15]The most significant, or high-end, bits of an IP address comprise the network portion of the address, so 10.0.0.1 identifies a host (in this case, the 0.0.1 portion of the address) and a network (in this case, the 10. portion of the address. Domain names start with the most specific information, so that specific.example.net identifies a sub-entity of the example.net domain.

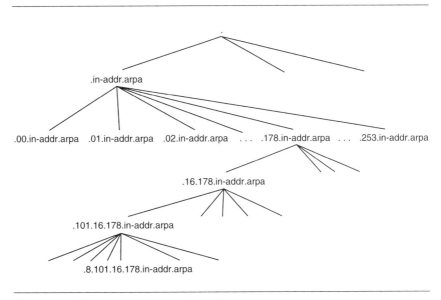

Figure 8–8: The `in-addr.arpa` domain.

format onto the DNS hierarchy and IP address `178.16.101.8` would map to this domain:

```
8.101.16.178.in-addr.arpa
```

Similar to the reverse DNS lookup is the *inverse query*. Nameservers may implement this as an option, allowing clients to request a PTR RR about a particular IP address. Unlike the reverse lookup, however, inverse queries do not go beyond the initial nameserver. If the nameserver does not have any information about the IP address stored locally, an error message is returned. Because the local nameserver is unlikely to have authoritative information about every IP address, and because it may not even have the function implemented, inverse queries are not particularly useful and are rarely used.

8.6.2 DOMAIN NAME SYSTEM CACHING

If the DNS server had to query all the way to one of the root domain name servers and then work its way down the domain names every time a system requested a connection to some other system off the local internetwork, things would get very slow very quickly. To avoid this, DNS servers cache responses they get from other servers whenever they do a name lookup with another server.

These caches depend on the time to live values reported by authoritative nameservers with each resource record. The time to live values may vary considerably because some DNS data is reasonably stable and other data isn't. For example, the IP address of a primary nameserver for a major domain is not likely to change very frequently—if it did, the owner of the domain would have to pay to support a very busy nameserver. By including a long time to live value in DNS answers, the domain could to some extent reduce traffic to its nameserver.

Likewise, addressing information concerning PCs that connect to the internet through the Dynamic Host Configuration Protocol (DHCP; see Appendix E for details) is quite likely to change from day to day if not from hour to hour.

Therefore, nameservers send out this time to live value as appropriate to the particular resource being queried; non-authoritative nameservers can offer their clients cached information as long as the data has not yet expired.

8.6.3   DOMAIN NAME SYSTEM SECURITY EXTENSIONS

The security of the internet requires that there be some assurance that resource names be linked with the correct IP addresses. If an attacker were able to hijack authoritative servers for a major online retailer or the US Internal Revenue Service, the resulting disruption could be quite costly indeed. Adding security extensions to DNS has long been a concern, and several standards that track RFCs have been published describing the DNS Security Extensions (DNSSEC).

As described in June 2001 in RFC 3130, "Notes from the State-Of-The-Technology: DNSSEC," securing DNS is, among other things, important but also difficult, and DNSSEC itself is still not a mature specification. This document also summarizes the components of DNSSEC. Not really a protocol, DNSSEC is more of a collection of mechanisms and solutions to securing DNS data. Edward Lewis of NAI Labs, the author of RFC 3130 identified several categories into which DNSSEC components could be sorted while at the same time noting that there was a good deal of arbitrariness about his categories, which included:

- RFC 2535, "Domain Name System Security Extensions," and RFC 3008, " Domain Name System Security (DNSSEC) Signing Authority," define mechanisms for adding digital signatures to DNS messages, which increase the degree to which clients can trust responses from name servers. These specifications describe protocols that are scalable to internet-wide deployment.
- RFC 2845, "Secret Key Transaction Authentication for DNS (TSIG)," defines a less-scalable but more efficient mechanism for authenticating DNS clients and servers to each other. According to Lewis, TSIG may not scale well but it has applicability for zone transfers.
- RFC 3007, "Secure Domain Name System (DNS) Dynamic Update," defines a mechanism for using TSIG to do dynamic updates of authoritative servers (as opposed to maintaining nameserver databases by hand, through static updating).
- RFC 2538, "Storing Certificates in the Domain Name System (DNS)," defines an RR for storing public key encryption certificates in the DNS. By doing so, hosts can retrieve these certificates (used to certify the identity of an entity using a particular public key) using an existing system (DNS) instead of requiring an additional protocol for the exchange of this information.

Whether or not these tools can eventually be made practical and useful remains to be seen. In any case, two aspects of unsecured DNS—the use of timers to expire cached data, and the degree to which the system is redundant and distributed—help reduce the potential for damage as a result of any single attack.

8.7   Chapter Summary

The DNS is more than a single protocol, but rather a system for maintaining and accessing a hugely distributed database. As a database system, DNS has a well-defined structure, with different types of data records and different types of systems capable of participating in the system.

Within the framework of this database system, DNS also defines a set of protocols that dictate how systems can request data stored in the DNS data repository, how DNS servers respond to those requests, and how to administer and update those DNS servers. Although the process of requesting a DNS record (and responding to that request) is straightforward, issues such as how to ensure that responses are correct, how to store new types of information in the DNS, and how to optimize DNS performance without affecting accuracy, tend to add interest as well as complexity to the protocol.

One of the most important functions of DNS, storing mail forwarding information, will be covered in the next chapter, along with other internet mail protocols and functions.

9

Internet Mail

The most popular and most widely used communication medium on the internet has always been mail. Internet mail, also referred to as electronic mail, e-mail, email, or just mail (as opposed to old-fashioned postal mail, postal service, or snail mail) permits individuals sharing nothing more than access to the internet to interact across virtually any boundary. Until the mid-1990s, internet messaging protocols mostly defined how to send, receive, store, and manage mail and news (an application through which individuals can post messages to a distributed message list accessible to anyone on the internet). Since then, additional message-oriented services have been added, including groupware, calendaring, and scheduling protocols; instant messaging protocols; and internet presence protocols.[1]

Nevertheless, internet mail is still processed by the Simple Mail Transfer Protocol (SMTP) in much same way as when the SMTP specification was published in RFC 821, back in 1982. An updated version of the SMTP

---

[1]Appendix B includes a section listing messaging protocols and relevant source documents. Readers who master the protocols that are discussed in this book should be able to master new protocols on their own, working from the original specifications.

specification was published in 2001 as RFC 2821; this specification made no substantive changes to the protocol itself but rather documented how it is being used and aggregated material from several separate RFCs to provide a complete picture of SMTP and how it works.

An integral part of any messaging protocol is the formatting of the messages. RFC 821 was published in tandem with a specification for message formats, RFC 822. An updated version, RFC 2822, was also published in 2001. "Internet Message Format" makes no substantive changes but rather provides a more complete and correct specification than the original.

All internet mail may be processed using SMTP, but SMTP by itself is not sufficient to handle all internet mail requirements. Some of these are discussed in section 9.3. Also discussed there is the use of extensions to the protocol (modern SMTP implementations that support extensions, as described in Section 9.3.1, are often said to support *Extended SMTP* or *ESMTP*).

9.1   Internet Messaging Architecture

The first electronic mail systems were developed for multi-user mainframe systems. Interactive users worked with terminals and were able to exchange mail with other users connected to the same computer. As vendors added networking functions to their systems, their proprietary messaging formats and mail exchange protocols meant users could easily communicate with other users of the same systems while at the same making communication with users of other systems more difficult.

Internet mail was developed to allow users to exchange mail messages with other users, no matter what either party uses for its computing platform, operating system, mail software, or network hardware. Several things are necessary to this type of interoperable mail:

- A standard format for mailbox addresses, with each mailbox unique across a single name space. Any system that uses a non-compliant format or proprietary name space can exchange mail with standards-compliant mail users only through the use of gateways to translate addresses between their own proprietary format and the standard format.

- A standard format for mail messages to make possible exchange of mail between the widest range of systems. With no way to tell what kind of systems will handle the transport of mail across the internet, messages should be formatted using the simplest possible set of characters to avoid having unusual character sets modified inadvertently by intermediate systems (or be incomprehensible to a recipient not prepared for non-ASCII text).
- A protocol for transporting mail messages from their source to their destination.
- A protocol for delivering messages to end users.

9.1.1 MESSAGING AGENTS

One of the original assumptions about internet mail was that it would work best if the functions of working with mail messages were kept separate from the functions of sending and receiving messages across the network. A *Mail Transfer Agent* (*MTA*) handled the transmission of messages across the internet, while a *User Agent* (*UA*) provided an application front-end for users reading, writing, and managing their mail.

The boundaries between the MTA and UA (now referred to as a *Mail User Agent* or *MUA*) have always been a bit blurred, even if most implementations of mail on *nix operating systems kept the two functions separate. However, while the two functions may rely on different sets of protocols, there is no inherent technical reason that they may not be implemented in a single application program. In fact, additional discrete functions have entered the mix in recent years. Three categories are addressed by IETF RFCs:

- The MUA provides a mechanism for users to interface with the messaging system, meaning a tool for writing, reading, sending, editing, and storing messages. In theory, at least, the MUA is intended to be separate from the process of actually sending or receiving message over any network. Once a message is ready to be sent, the MUA passes it along to the appropriate mechanism; inbound messages are likewise passed along to the MUA only after they have arrived at the local system.
- The MTA provides a mechanism for message delivery across the mail network from the point at which messages are *injected* into the network (pass from an MUA to an MTA). MTAs interact

with other MTAs, but they don't really interact with MUAs beyond accepting messages for delivery from the originating MUA or delivering messages to the destination MUA. Even these interactions are largely limited to reading or writing data from a message store rather than having explicit interactions.

- The process of injecting messages into the MTA network was not well defined under the original SMTP specifications, and over the years SMTP itself became the dominant mechanism for submitting messages to SMTP servers. The *Message Submission Agent* or *MSA* is defined in RFC 2476, "Message Submission," defines a more appropriate protocol for submitting messages from MUA hosts to MTA hosts.

Whether or not these functions are performed by the same application or by three different programs is not as important as being sure that the functions are performed. A fourth function is sometimes defined for performance by the *Mail Delivery Agent (MDA)* or *Local Delivery Agent (LDA)*; this is the delivery of mail to the MUA after it has arrived at the destination MTA.

Unlike mail delivery, however, message submission through SMTP has proven to be a problem over the years for a number of reasons; section 9.1.3 discusses these problems and how RFC 2476 helps solve them.

9.1.2 MAIL TRANSFER ARCHITECTURE

Protocols usually make some assumption about an overall architecture defining how hosts implementing the protocol interact; protocols are also defined by the data formats they require and the type of messages protocol-enabled hosts use to communicate. As we saw in Chapter 8, domain name system uses its own data formats, its own messages, and its own architecture.

SMTP has these elements as well. We'll cover the architecture first, followed by a discussion of the data formats used by SMTP and other messaging protocols (a general message format as well as format for mail addresses and message headers), an overview of SMTP's protocol messages, followed by some examples of SMTP in action.

Figure 9–1, taken from RFC 2821, shows SMTP's basic architecture: an SMTP client communicates with an SMTP server, exchanging commands and replies as well as mail messages. As the RFC states, "The responsibility

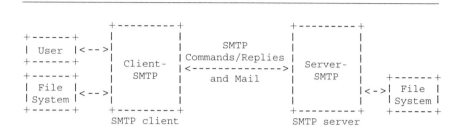

Figure 9–1: Basic SMTP architecture.

of an SMTP client is to transfer mail messages to one or more SMTP servers, or report its failure to do so." Part of the client's responsibility includes locating an appropriate server (see section 8.5.2 for more about using DNS to locate a mail exchange), opening a session with the server, and transferring the message(s) or else notifying the sender that the messages could not be sent.

SMTP is a protocol for interfacing with file systems, because messages are stored there. Sometimes called the *message store*, the local file system interfaces with the MTA—although there is no technical reason that a person could not use SMTP interactively to send mail. Doing so would require some mechanism for delivering commands and message contents to the SMTP server: that mechanism might be a user interface for an SMTP client application, or it might be nothing more than an application capable of sending commands from one host to another (such as telnet). However, there are few legitimate reasons for a person to interact directly with an SMTP server. Most applications would relate either to administration or trouble-shooting, or else to system attacks.

What is not shown in Figure 9–1 is that SMTP mail may require more than one *hop* to arrive at its destination. The originating client may not be able to send a message directly to the destination mailbox SMTP server. Figure 9–2 shows what path the message might take through the internet, as it passes from a personal computer (Pc) within Organization X to the recipient's Pc at Organization Y.

Why multiple hops? Consider the alternative: having the sender's host attempt to deliver the mail directly to the recipient's host. Any mail recipient would be required to keep their host up and running and accepting messages all the time—not always practical. It would also mean

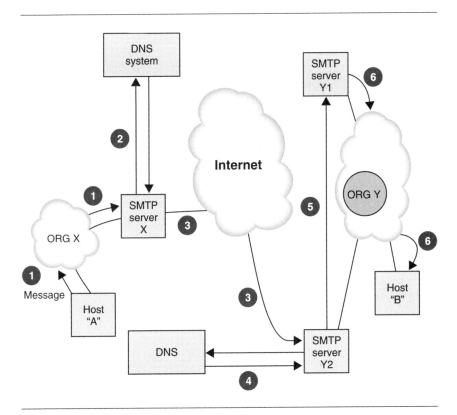

Figure 9–2: Following an SMTP-delivered message.

implementing SMTP on every host used by a potential mail recipient—
not often practical because of security issues. It would also complicate (or
even make impossible) receiving mail through a host that is not connected
to the internet.

Mail is useful because it is based on message stores. A message is written
and then passed from one system to another; if one system can't deliver it
right away, the message doesn't get lost but rather is stored and the system
tries to resend it again later.

Security is easier when an organization has all mail go in and out through
a single system. A single mail server is much easier to configure, maintain,
and monitor than if every host in an organization had to be able to respond
to requests for mail services. Likewise most individuals would prefer to

have their internet service providers take responsibility for managing their mail services by managing the mail servers they use.

Figure 9–2 labels the SMTP systems "servers," but any SMTP server that forwards mail to another SMTP server must by definition also act as a client. The entities involved here include:

- "A" and "B," two people who communicate via mail
- $Host_A$ and $Host_B$, the computers used by A and B
- "X" and "Y," organizations whose networks A and B use
- $SMTP_X$, $SMTP_{Y1}$, and $SMTP_{Y2}$, the SMTP systems serving X and Y

The steps in sending mail from A to B include:

1. A composes a message for B, places the message in $SMTP_X$'s message store and notifies the server that the message is ready to be sent. A may be using mail client software on $Host_A$ that sends messages to the server for delivery, or A may be using $Host_A$ as a terminal to use a mail application running on $SMTP_X$.

2. $SMTP_X$ must determine where to send the message, based on the message's destination(s). At this step, the server queries DNS for a Mail eXchanger (MX) resource record (RR) associated with the destination(s) mailbox address(es). This process was described in section 8.5.2. In this case, the MX RR indicates that there are two Mail eXchanger systems, $SMTP_{Y1}$ and $SMTP_{Y2}$, willing to accept messages for B's mailbox. The preference value for $SMTP_{Y2}$ would have been lower than that for $SMTP_{Y1}$.[2]

3. Having determined that $SMTP_{Y2}$ is the appropriate server to which mail for B should be forwarded, $SMTP_X$ opens an SMTP session (using TCP) to $SMTP_{Y2}$ and sends the message. At this point, $SMTP_X$ is acting as an SMTP client and $SMTP_{Y2}$ is acting as a server. As the message is received, $SMTP_{Y2}$ writes it to the local message store.

4. $SMTP_{Y2}$, having determined that it does not serve the message addressee (B) directly, must now determine where it should send the message. It does not provide mail service directly to B, even though it is willing to receive mail on behalf of B

---

[2] Alternately, the two servers might have been listed with the same preference, or $SMTP_{Y2}$ might have had a higher value (meaning it would not be the preferred server), but $SMTP_{Y2}$ would be preferred if $SMTP_{Y1}$ was not responding at all.

(and anyone else within Organization Y); if $SMTP_{Y2}$ served mail to B, it would write the message to the appropriate place in its message store for delivery to B.

Another DNS query is made, and the same MX RR will be returned listing $SMTP_{Y1}$ and $SMTP_{Y2}$ as Mail eXchangers for B's mailbox. Even if $SMTP_{Y2}$ has a lower preference value (higher priority), the server will not attempt to send mail to itself; instead, it will send the message to $SMTP_{Y1}$.

5. $SMTP_{Y2}$, acting as a client now, initiates an SMTP session with $SMTP_{Y1}$ (which is acting as a server) and sends the message, which $SMTP_{Y1}$ writes to its message store.

6. B uses whatever software is appropriate to retrieve and read the message from $SMTP_{Y1}$.

In this example, the originating SMTP host ($SMTP_X$) passed the message to an intermediate SMTP host ($SMTP_{Y2}$), which in turn passed the message along to the destination SMTP host ($SMTP_{Y1}$).

This example refers to SMTP hosts rather than clients and servers (except when indicating the role a particular host is playing) because most SMTP servers also act as clients when they transfer mail.

9.1.3 MESSAGE HOPS AND MESSAGE SUBMISSION

Two issues arise from this structure. First, messages often don't go directly to their destination's SMTP server but are routed through other SMTP systems before final delivery. Adding these extra hops in the mail delivery process may be done for several reasons, including security (to isolate inbound mail before it enters the organizational intranet), scalability (to distribute the task of processing inbound mail across a pool of servers), and availability (to provide backup systems in the even that the primary system is not reachable).

The other issue involves the ways messages are injected into the SMTP delivery network. This process requires passing the message to an SMTP server from a host being used by the sender. Although this does not sound like an alarming development, in fact it has significant security and administrative impact:

- *Open relays* are SMTP servers willing to accept mail from any host for delivery, which lets users send mail when they are away from their office or workstation—but it also allows anyone else to send mail from anywhere. This is a serious problem because *spammers* (senders of unsolicited commercial mail) use open relays to send mail without incurring fees or losing their own internet services (most ISP service agreements forbid sending unsolicited commercial mail because it is a huge drain on resources).

- Some organizations require inbound and outbound mail to be scanned for malicious software as well as for content. Having intermediate systems that can screen for security violations in either direction helps simplify the process.
- SMTP implementations can be difficult to configure properly, and when installed on end-user systems are easily misconfigured.
- Message submission often includes functions such as checking messages for all required header fields, something not provided for in SMTP.
- SMTP is an inherently insecure protocol, and servers must be configured with a balance of convenience and security, resulting in less or more restriction on who can use the server to transfer or submit mail. Strong authentication of users isn't widely implemented, although it would be quite helpful in reducing spammer exploitation of open relays while still permitting authorized users access to servers.

RFC 2476 addresses these issues by defining a protocol based on SMTP but using port 587 (instead of port 25) and tailored for use as a submission protocol rather than a full-blown mail transport protocol.

9.2   Simple Mail Transfer Protocol Details

Internet mail uses several specifications to operate, from the set of rules for creating a well-formed and usable mailbox address to the proper message format, including various message header fields, to the set of commands and responses defined for interaction between SMTP hosts. This section introduces the different specifications, starting from the basic commands and responses defined for SMTP interactions, and the message format and its header fields, to the formulation of internet mailbox addresses and response codes. The next section shows SMTP in action, with example protocol interactions.

9.2.1 Simple Mail Transfer Protocol Commands and Replies

SMTP packages internet messages into *mail objects*: the mail object consisting of an envelope (in effect, the SMTP protocol commands) and content (the internet message, itself comprised of headers and message body). SMTP commands and replies both consist of a sequence of characters and end with the carriage return-line feed (CRLF) characters.

Successful SMTP exchanges begin with the client attempting to open a TCP connection on port 25 with the server. A standard-compliant SMTP server will respond to this request by sending the protocol reply code 220, which includes the server's domain and indicates that the SMTP server is ready to accept commands from the client. This is step 1 in the SMTP session; the rest of a mail transaction takes this standard form:

1. The client (the system sending a message) initiates the TCP connection with the server (system receiving the message), and the server responds with a reply code (220) indicating that it is prepared to provide SMTP services.
2. The client starts the session by sending the EHLO ("Extended HELLO") command in which it identifies itself to the server and requests mail service. The server responds with a reply code—250—that indicates the requested action (in this case, requesting a mail service session for that particular host) has been successfully completed.
3. The client begins a message transfer by sending the MAIL command to indicate a mailbox to which error reports for the message should be sent; if the server is willing to accept the message, it responds with the 250 reply. The MAIL command is a part of the SMTP message envelope.
4. The client sends additional envelope information with the RCPT (recipient) command. There is a separate RCPT command for each destination mailbox being sent to the SMTP server. If the server will accept the message for the recipient in the RCPT command, the server responds positively; if the server will not accept messages for a particular mailbox, the response is negative–but the client can continue sending RCPT commands for other destination mailboxes.
5. The client sends the DATA command to signal it is ready to send the message; the server's response indicates it will interpret subsequent SMTP messages as the message itself.

This command is sent only after all recipients in RCPT commands have been submitted.

6. The client sends the message. The end of the message is indicated when the client sends a line containing only the period (".") character (in other words, the sequence <CRLF>.<CRLF> terminates the message).

7. When the client sends the "end message" sequence, the server responds with reply code 250.

8. The client may send more information or terminate the SMTP session at this point.

SMTP puts the client in charge of the entire process of transferring mail: the client indicates it wants to start a session, it has a message for a particular recipient (or recipients), that it is about to send data, and that the message is complete or the session is complete.

When the server acts as a relay, it must turn around and take on the client role with the appropriate SMTP server.

One other step the server must take whether it is acting as a relay or is delivering the message to its intended destination is to insert the trace record at the top of the message data (before the message header fields). These lines are also sometimes referred to as time stamps or "Received" lines, and contain the hostname of the system that sent the message, the IP address and hostname of the server that accepted the message, and the date and time the message was received.

SMTP is a simple protocol with relatively few commands: RFC 2821 defines only 11 commands, and a minimum implementation can still be standard compliant with 9 of those commands. The 11 commands described in RFC 2821 are:

EHLO: The *extended HELLO* command is the preferred command to start an SMTP session. It is a way for the client to introduce itself to the server; it does so by including its domain name. The command takes the form: `EHLO example.org`

There are three possible types of response from the server: indication that the command has succeeded (meaning the client can begin the session), indication that the command has failed (meaning the client is not permitted to begin a session), or an error response indicating that the server does not understand the command.

The last response means that the server does not support SMTP extensions (see section 9.3.1 below); this would indicate a very old or merely non-compliant SMTP server implementation. Although it should accept the EHLO command, when a server does not the client must use the older HELO command to initiate the session.

If the server responds positively, it also sends a return greeting, as well as a list of which SMTP extensions it supports.

HELO: The *original HELLO* command format is the same as for EHLO, but HELO should be used only when a server does not support SMTP extensions.

MAIL: The *MAIL* command indicates the *reverse path* for the message, meaning the mailbox from which the message originated. The command takes the form `MAIL FROM: <spiderman@example.net>`

RCPT: The *RECIPIENT* command is used to indicate the mailbox to which the message is being sent. The command takes the form `RCPT TO: <elvis@example.com>`

DATA: The *DATA* command (`DATA <CRLF>`) signals the server that the client is about to begin sending a message.

RSET: The *RESET* command is used by the client to abort the current mail transaction, reset all buffers and state tables, and discard any recipient or message data that may have been received as part of the current transaction. RSET does not terminate the session, and it does not have any effect if it is issued after a message has been transmitted and receipt by the server acknowledged. RSET may be used to indicate that another message is on its way instead of resending the EHLO command. The command is issued in the form `RSET <CRLF>`

VRFY: The *VERIFY* command, specified for use as a debugging tool, allows the client to request that the existence of a particular mailbox name or address be verified. The command takes the form `VRFY spiderman@example.org` (to verify that an address is correct) or `VRFY spiderman` (to see if there is a mailbox corresponding to the name).

The server may respond with the complete mailbox associated with the name or address specified by the VERIFY command, although allowing outsiders to use this command can compromise security or at the least allow spammers to collect valid mail addresses from the organization.

If the VERIFY command specifies an ambiguous name or mailbox, the server may respond with a simple message ("ambiguous result" for example), or with a list of names and mailboxes that might be correct.

Support for the VERIFY command, like EXPAND, is not required for a standard-compliant implementation of SMTP.

EXPN: Like the VERIFY command, *EXPAND* is defined as a debugging tool. Used to retrieve a list of all mailboxes that are included in a mailing list alias, servers may respond to EXPAND requests either with a list or with a message indicating that access to that data is prohibited. The command takes the form EXPN Example-List.

Support for the EXPAND command, like VERIFY, is not required for a standard-compliant implementation of SMTP.

HELP: *HELP* is provided for people using SMTP interactively rather than for normal host-to-host SMTP interactions. HELP is not strictly required in SMTP hosts, but when implemented it may return information about using the system or information about using some particular command.

NOOP: The *NOOP* command does nothing other than elicit a response from the server.

QUIT: When the client is finished with a session, it may send the *QUIT* command to terminate the session.

SMTP responses are based on a standard framework for application protocols (see section 8.2.2 above) with three-digit codes starting with the numbers 1 through 5 to indicate different levels of response. The second and third digits indicate the specific response at each level. The meanings of each digit for SMTP are provided in Appendix B, as are the complete set of replies defined in RFC 2821.

9.2.2 INTERNET MESSAGE FORMAT

RFC 822, "STANDARD FOR THE FORMAT OF ARPA INTERNET TEXT MESSAGES" defined a format for internet messages that remained stable (if modified in practice) for almost two decades. In 2001, RFC 2822, "Internet Message Format," replaced RFC 822. The new Proposed Standard specification was intended to revise the original spec, reflect incremental changes made in that specification by other RFCs, and bring it in line with actual practice rather than to introduce new features or make significant changes in message formats. The RFC number of the new specification, 2822, was reserved for the updated version of RFC 822 to reflect the continuity of the original protocol.

The RFC 2822-compliant message reflects a number of attributes:

- The message is composed of ASCII characters[3] (US-ASCII characters with values of 0 through 127)
- The message is composed of lines separated by the carriage return (CR, also known as ASCII 13) and line feed (LF, also known as ASCII 10)
- Message lines MUST BE no more than 998 characters long
- Message lines SHOULD BE no more than 78 characters long (excluding the CR-LF characters)
- Messages contain *header fields*, consisting of a header field name followed by a colon (":") and the contents of the header body
- Messages may include a *message body* following the header
- If the message body is present, it MUST be separated from the headers by a single blank line
- The CR and LF characters may not appear anywhere in the message except in the CR-LF pairing

Much of the work done by the group revising this specification centered around how to define header fields, particularly header fields that might have gone on longer than the default line length of a particular messaging implementation. The details of how to properly include "white space" and multi-line headers are interesting, and can be found in RFC 2822, in Section 2.2.

Also beyond the scope of this chapter are the details of the message format syntax (RFC 2822, Section 3). This section is reproduced in Appendix D, however, because it provides an excellent introduction to the use of the Augmented Backus-Naur Form (BNF), also called Augmented BNF (ABNF) or just ABNF. This is a format for building formal specification of protocol structures, and is documented in RFC 2234, "Augmented BNF

---

[3]Messages can contain non-ASCII content by encoding it with the multipurpose internet message extensions specifications; see section 9.3.5 for more about MIME.

for Syntax Specifications: ABNF." Many internet protocols use this format, so it helps to understand how to read it, and since mail messages are so familiar to most readers (and can be viewed in full through most mail readers), the mail message format is a good place to start with ABNF (section 9.2.3 uses the ABNF notation to show how internet mail addresses are formed).

To summarize what we know so far about internet messages, they consist of US-ASCII characters, grouped into lines of no more than 998 characters (with 78 as the recommended maximum), and separated by the CR-LF characters. Messages always have headers fields; a message body is optional. If included, the body is separated from the header fields by a blank line.

9.2.3 MESSAGE HEADER FIELDS

The message headers carry information about the message, most importantly to whom the message is addressed. However, much more information may be included in typical internet messages. RFC 2822 defines the basic message header fields (section 3.6) as well as a format for new header fields, permitting anyone to create new (optional) header fields (section 3.6.8). According to the specification, "The only required header fields are the origination date field and the originator address field(s)."

Other than the origination date header field, header fields fall into several categories:

Originator: The originator fields indicate who sent the message and/or how to reply to the message. They consist of appropriate type of data to indicate the source (either a mailbox list, a mailbox, or an address list; see section 9.2.5 for more details).

Destination: Destination address fields give the sender options as to how the addressee(s) receives the message.

Identification: Identification fields provide a mechanism to pass information about the message, including a message ID number, whether or not the message is a reply to a previous message and, if so, the message ID number of the original message, and so on.

Informational: Informational fields provide information about the message, including the subject as well as keywords or comments.

Resent: The specification provides an option for "reintroducing" (resending) a message into the internet mail system. Though not clear from the RFC, the *resent-* fields are used to allow the user to re-send a message that has already been sent to someone else. In other words, if you send a message to Bob in the morning, and then decide to send the same message to Carol later in the day, you can (if your mail client permits it) use the resent- fields to make the message appear to Carol with the same original headers as were sent to Bob as well as an extra set to get the message to Carol. You may also resend a message that you've received from Bob to Carol, and the resent-fields will show Carol that the message came from Bob originally but was resent to her by you (and it allows her to reply to Bob directly).[4]

Trace: Trace fields are used by intermediate systems as they move messages to their destination, and include name and IP address of the host from which the message was received, a timestamp indicating the time the message was received, and the name of the host that received the message. This information must not be modified by intermediate hosts, but should not be used in any way to determine how the message is processed.

The field names, as appearing at the start of a header field, are almost always the same as the name of the header field; the notable exception is the `orig-date` header field, which uses the string `Date` (followed by a colon) as its field name. The list of field names (including colons) shows the header field names as they appear in a message header; included in each definition is the name of the header field if it is different from the field name as it appears in messages.

Date: The `orig-date` header field indicates the date and time that the message "entered the mail system"—in other words, when the sender "pushed the button" to send the message.

From: The mailbox(es) of the person(s) responsible for writing the message.

---

[4]Re-sending a message is different from forwarding, in either sense of the word: (1) Forwarding a message you've received from one person to another—MIME defines a format for doing that; or (2) having a mail client automatically forward a message that it receives for a particular mailbox to a different mailbox.

`Sender:` The mailbox of the agent (person or system) that sent the message on behalf of the writer (the entity identified in the `From:` header). If there is a single mailbox that can be used to unambiguously identify the entity that wrote and sent the message, the `Sender:` header is not necessary. This field may be used when an assistant sends a message that his or her supervisor wrote; it may also be used when there are more than one entities involved in writing the message (multiple mailboxes in the `From:` header)—only one of those can actually be the sender.

`Reply-to:` The address(es) to which replies to the message should be sent. This is an optional field, and is used in cases when the message originator wants to send the message from one address but have replies returned to a different address or additional addresses.

`To:` The address(es) of the primary recipient(s) of the message.

`Cc:` The address(es) of recipient(s) who may be receiving the message as a courtesy or as interested parties. The usage comes from the common office practice of using "cc:" (for "carbon copy") and a recipient's name to indicate they were to receive a carbon copy of the original message.

`Bcc:` The address(es) of recipient(s) who may be receiving the message as a courtesy or for some other reason, without their identity being known to the primary sender. The usage comes from the practice of using "bcc:" (for "blind carbon copy") to indicate a recipient who was to receive a copy of the original message without the knowledge of the primary recipient. There are three options for implementing this header: (1) Recipients (including the Bcc: addressees) receive a copy of the message without the Bcc: header; no one, including blind-copy recipients, know blind copies were sent. (2) Recipients listed in the To: and Cc: headers receive a copy of the message without Bcc: headers, the Bcc: addressees get a copy of the message that includes the Bcc: header with their address(es). (3) Everyone gets the message with a Bcc: header, only Bcc: recipients get a copy with their address(es) listed—everyone else gets an empty Bcc: header.

`Message-ID:` Data that uniquely identifies the message among all messages sent by the originating host. This data is intended for use by computers and may not be human-readable.

In-Reply-To: Used in replies only, this header indicates the message ID of the original message.

References: Similar to the In-Reply-To header, this header includes the message IDs of other messages related to the current one. This header helps identify *threads*, or series of messages on the same topic.

Subject: A short description of the contents of the message body.

Comments: Additional comments about the message.

Keywords: Words that may be useful to the recipient or sender for referencing the message.

The *trace* or *timestamp* header fields may also be included, but they are purely optional and the protocols don't allow them to be used to make any decisions about handling mail, just for adding information to a message as it is processed through the internet messaging system to its destination.

There are no particular rules about the order in which headers must appear in a message, as long as all the headers appear before the message body. Though intermediate systems could move the headers around, the specifications urge strongly against doing so.

RFC 2822 includes a section describing obsolete syntax, most of which are included as allowable options in the current specification. This is a demonstration of a crucial tenet of IP networking: "Be liberal in what you accept, and conservative in what you send." Most internet specifications use this philosophy, which basically calls upon implementers to assume that other implementations may be outdated, or perhaps not even properly coded, while at the same time admonishing them to be scrupulous in adhering to the specifications themselves.

In practice, being liberal means programming in exceptions for software that is known to generate improper but still comprehensible data. That allows the organizations or individuals using the software a wider window for upgrades; the alternative would impose catastrophic failures on those users. As for being conservative in what you send, that practice helps reduce the volume of non-compliant network traffic, again helping reduce catastrophic failures.

9.2.4 ENVELOPES AND HEADERS

One frequent point of confusion is the differentiation of the terms *envelope* and *headers* when applied to SMTP messages. A traditional postal envelope contains the sender and recipient of the postal mail; this information is also available in an internet message. Internet messages use header fields to store data about the message: where it is being sent, who is sending it, and when it was sent. Is this not the envelope?

No.

The message is composed of two parts: the headers and the message itself. They represent actual application data, and could be considered a part of the highest layer of the internet mail application.

SMTP is an application protocol in the sense that it provides a mechanism for moving data from one end user to another, but it could be more accurately characterized as an application *transport* protocol. This means it provides a mechanism for some data (entire messages) to move around the transport network (the parts of the internet that move mail). The message header fields provide a mechanism to communicate at the user layer (above the application layer, where people interact); the SMTP commands serve as the envelope.

Internet messages are encapsulated within an SMTP envelope as they pass from one SMTP host to another, allowing the systems to interact at the application layer as they exchange messages.

9.2.5 MAILBOX ADDRESSES

Here's the ABNF definition of an internet mail address compiled from RFC 2822:

```
address     = mailbox / group
mailbox     = name-addr / addr-spec
name-addr   = [display-name] angle-addr
angle-addr  = [CFWS] "<" addr-spec ">" [CFWS] /
                 obs-angle-addr
group       = display-name ":" [mailbox-list /
                 CFWS] ";" [CFWS]
```

```
addr-spec        = local-part "@" domain
local-part       = dot-atom / quoted-string /
                   obs-local-part
domain           = dot-atom / domain-literal /
                   obs-domain
display-name     = phrase
mailbox-list     = (mailbox *("," mailbox)) /
                   obs-mbox-list
address-list     = (address *("," address)) /
                   obs-addr-list
local-part       = dot-atom / quoted-string /
                   obs-local-part
domain           = dot-atom / domain-literal /
                   obs-domain
domain-literal   = [CFWS] "[" *([FWS]
                   dcontent) [FWS] "]" [CFWS]
dcontent         = dtext / quoted-pair
dtext            = NO-WS-CTL /
                   ; Non white space controls
                     %d33-90 /
                   ; The rest of the US-ASCII
                     %d94-126
                   ; characters not including
                   ; "[", ; "]", or "\"
```

This definition is relatively easy to puzzle out once you realize that the term CFWS means "a comment, or folding white space (FWS)," and that FWS refers to "folding white space." In these specifications, FWS refers to the use of non-printing characters (spaces, tabs, carriage return/line feeds) with extra long headers that need to "fold" or wrap from one line to another.

ABNF starts from the very basic elements of a protocol component, specifying from which characters any particular element can be composed. Earlier in the RFC, NO-WS-CTL is defined as the set of all characters in the US-ASCII set, not including the white-space characters. Another basic component defined by the specification is the atom, a string of one or more characters set off by a comment or white space (CFWS). A dot-atom is the same as the atom, except that it begins with the one or more characters followed by zero or more instances of a "." dot symbol followed by one or more characters. Valid `dot-atoms` include:

```
elmo
elmo.example.net
elmo.e.x.a.m.p.l.e.net
```

Neither the string `.elmo.anything` nor `elmo.` is a valid `dot-atom` because the first starts with a bare dot and the second ends with one.

To read the ABNF specification, start at the top and read each line, like this, based on the spec listed above:

1. An `address` is composed of either a `mailbox` or a `group`.
2. A `mailbox` as either a `name-addr` or an `addr-spec`.
3. A `name-addr` must be composed of an `angle-addr`, option-ally preceded by a `display-name` (anything inside square brackets is an option).
4. An `angle-addr` may optionally open with a comment or fold-ing white space, be followed by an `addr-spec` set off by angle brackets ("<" on the left and ">" on the right), option-ally ending with a comment or folding white space. Or, the `obs-angle-addr`, which is the obsolete version of the angled address object. (We'll skip the obsolete forms from here on, since they are included only for backward compatibility.)

   We're making progress now: one kind of an `address` looks like this "DISPLAY_NAME <addr-spec>". We still don't know what an `addr-spec` or a `display-name` looks like, or other key components, but we're making progress.
5. A `group` is a `display-name` followed by a colon, followed by an optional `mailbox-list`, CFWS, and if desired, additional CFWS set off by a semicolon.
6. An `addr-spec` is a `local-part` followed by the "@" symbol followed by a `domain`. This is the "@" that appears in internet mail addresses, so we're getting close.
7. A `local-part` is either a `dot-atom` (at least one word, fol-lowed by one or more ".words") or a `quoted-string` which is a string that includes characters not normally permitted in an `atom`, in particular non-printing white-space characters.
8. A `domain` is either a `dot-atom` or a `domain-literal`. The `dot-atom` looks like a domain name ("something.example.net" for example); the `domain-literal` turns out to be the literal IP address of the host (instead of the domain name).

9. A display-name is a phrase (or a quoted string, basically the same thing only with quotes around it); elsewhere in the RFC, a phrase is defined as one or more instances of the word object; a word is composed of least one atom, so a phrase is more or less the same as a regular phrase, made up of words and letters. We know a dot-atom looks like a domain name (using the form "word.example.net"), so at this point we realize that an address can look like this:

```
Peter Parker <spidey@example.net>
```

or any of the following:

```
Pete Parker <web.slinger@example.com>
"Peter Q. Parker" <pqp@example.org>
Mary <mj@example.net>
maryjane1001@example.com
```

This is all a very roundabout but extremely precise way of describing what an internet message address looks like. The ABNF notation can serve as a specification for a programmer to write a program for recognizing valid and invalid internet addresses as well as for creating addresses based on data provided by a user (or some process) and extracting information from addresses for processing them.

9.2.6 PROTOCOL STATE

One of the reasons SMTP is really a simple protocol is that it has relatively few *states* or conditions in which the server and client can be in at any given time. In other words, if the client has sent a MAIL command, the server can either be ready to accept that mail or not. If the server has indicated its willingness to accept mail, then it expects the next message from the client to be a RCPT command (or, a NOOP or RSET command). Possible sequences for the protocol are listed below (from RFC 2821):

```
CONNECTION ESTABLISHMENT
  S: 220
  E: 554

EHLO or HELO
  S: 250
  E: 504, 550
```

```
MAIL
  S: 250
  E: 552, 451, 452, 550, 553, 503

RCPT
  S: 250, 251
  E: 550, 551, 552, 553, 450, 451, 452, 503, 550

DATA
  I: 354 ->data-> S: 250
  E: 552, 554, 451, 452
  E: 451, 554, 503

RSET
  S: 250

VRFY
  S: 250, 251, 252
  E: 550, 551, 553, 502, 504

EXPN
  S: 250, 252
  E: 550, 500, 502, 504

HELP
  S: 211, 214
  E: 502, 504

NOOP
  S: 250

QUIT
  S: 221
```

This chart shows each command with the possible replies that the server can make to the command. For example, the first command is session initiation, which the server can either respond to by allowing the session (reply code 220) or indicating that the service is not available (reply code 554).

The only complicated command is DATA: it generates either an intermediate reply code (354) or one of several error codes (451, 554, 503); if the intermediate code is received, the client sends message data. If the server receives the message successfully, it indicates that by sending reply code 250; if not, the server may send any of the reply codes listed (552, 554, 451, 452).

There are only a limited number of states the SMTP server can be in: waiting for a session to begin, waiting for a command, waiting for recipients or data, accepting recipients or data, writing data to the local file store, etc. This means that very simple SMTP hosts can be built based on these states rather than using more complex software to examine and process all the data.

9.3 More Simple Mail Transfer Protocol Issues

Some successful protocols are perfect the way they were originally written and require little if any elaboration over the years despite their ubiquity and importance. For example, UDP (see Chapter 16) is utterly simple and almost entirely unchanged and uncommented despite its age.

Although SMTP has also been shown to be extremely useful over the same time period as UDP, it has generated considerably more de jure as well as de facto modification (formally, by the IETF and as required or desired by software developers). This section looks at topics related to SMTP and internet mail that have required further attention over the years:

Extensions Adding functions to an existing protocol can be difficult: At what point must you stop adding functions? How do you decide whether a function should be required, recommended, or just permitted? Modern protocol specifications often include provisions for adding extensions or additional functions, but older protocols must be revised to enable extensions. SMTP extensions provide a good example of such extensions.

Delivery SMTP is not ideal for getting messages to an end-user's desktop PC. The Post Office Protocol (POP) and the Internet

Message Access Protocol (IMAP) were developed to fill this void. SMTP "pushes" messages out onto the network and (it is hoped) to their destinations, but this approach works well only when it can be assumed that the destination hosts will be up and running. To receive mail on a personal computer, "pull" message delivery protocols (such as POP and IMAP) work better, as they are used from the PC only when the PC is in the proper state to receive mail.

Security　　Internet mail was not originally designed with security in mind, and there are several security issues related to using SMTP and internet mail.

Attachments　　Internet mail messages can carry only US-ASCII data, which means sending binaries (software programs, graphic images, video, audio, or anything else but textual ASCII data) can be difficult. Proprietary formats have been used over the years, but they invariably posed problems for users as mail moved across gateways.

9.3.1　SIMPLE MAIL TRANSFER PROTOCOL EXTENSIONS

Although some protocols remain fairly constant over time, most evolve as implementers discover problems with the way the protocol was originally specified or discover that some new feature could help improve or extend the usefulness of the protocol. Early application protocols frequently incorporated no mechanism for adding functions or commands, which means adding a new command almost requires revising the entire protocol—with the result that implementers must also revise all the systems that support that protocol.

Part of the problem has been that the original designers often tried to design their protocols as simply as possible so as to make it easy for anyone to deploy a standard-compliant implementation. As new uses for the protocol cropped up later, or as existing commands proved incomplete, protocols would have to be revised to incorporate the new features. It wasn't until the 1990s that protocol designers began consistently building in mechanisms for adding new features through *extensions* to their protocols.

Protocol extension is usually done by having the client and server exchange with each other information about some or all functions each supports or desires the other to support. For example, SMTP with extensions requires that, in a successful response to the EHLO command from a client, the server must list the functions that it supports.

The SMTP protocol extension mechanism is specified in RFC 2821, and a list of registered SMTP extensions is available at:

```
http://www.iana.org/assignments/mail-parameters
```

9.3.2   Post Office Protocol Version 3

When RFC 821 was published (1982), most mail was composed and sent from the same systems. The mail client software used by a human was running on the same host as the SMTP client sofware, or else people were using proprietary mail over their local area networks that were gatewayed into the SMTP transport system. Just as basic SMTP is not always ideal for injecting mail into the delivery transport network from user systems, it is also not always appropriate for delivering mail to the end user desktop. Mail delivery protocols have come into use to allow users easier access to their mail.

Two trends created a need for supplemental mail protocols. First, more and more people used PCs rather than multi-user systems for mail, which meant that their PCs either had to implement SMTP or else use some other mechanism to inject their mail into the SMTP delivery system. The other trend was that PC mail client software was increasingly written to interface directly with the internet mail infrastructure, reducing the need for the gateways that had formerly performed the task of sending messages onto the internet.

Defined as a full internet standard in RFC 1939, "Post Office Protocol - Version 3," POPv3, or simply POP, provides a mechanism for getting messages from the *maildrop* (where messages are stored on the destination SMTP server) to the node on which the user wants to manage those messages. The form of a POP session has some similarities to SMTP interactions, but is also different in significant ways:

- Like SMTP, POP servers wait for clients to open a TCP connection (POP uses port 110, SMTP port 25). On successfully opening the connection, the POP server sends a greeting response to the client. Client and server exchange commands and replies (respectively) until the session is terminated.

- Unlike SMTP, POP provides only two reply codes, +OK and -ERR, indicating respectively the successful or unsuccessful completion of the command.
- Like SMTP, POP servers exist in different states during any particular session; different sets of replies to client commands are allowed in these different states.
- Unlike SMTP, POP sessions open with an authorization of the client. The client sends a user ID and passphrase to the server before the server sends any messages.
- Unlike SMTP, POP provides mechanisms for managing mail in the server's maildrop. A POP client may delete mail that has already been downloaded or leave it on the server. Likewise, a POP client may download all mail in the maildrop or just those messages that have not been marked as having already been seen.

The protocol summary, taken from Section 9 of RFC 1939, is included in Appendix B. RFC 2449, "POP3 Extension Mechanism," defines the mechanism for extending POPv3 as well as several extensions.

POPv3 is a quite simple protocol, with only seven mandatory and five optional commands defined in RFC 1939; RFC 2449 only adds another eight functions and two new reply codes.

9.3.3 INTERNET MESSAGE ACCESS PROTOCOL

Basic internet mail provides basic functions, but users brought up with proprietary mail products often desire more. For example, products designed to be implemented on a LAN and served from a single organizational server offer the ability to store messages on a central server, making backup more convenient as well as permitting access from any host, not just the user's own PC.

Internet Message Access Protocol (IMAP), defined in RFC 2060, "Internet Message Access Protocol - Version 4rev1," was designed to provide a more complete set of mail function to users than previously implemented in SMTP and POP. Rather than allowing commercial vendors such as Microsoft and Lotus to attempt to lock users into proprietary mail products that might have reduced the ability of other mail implementations to interoperate, the IMAP specification provides a framework within which an open standard can be applied to the more complex needs of commercial mail vendors and consumers.

Users of systems that support IMAP can access and manipulate messages stored on a remote server. IMAP allows users to read messages, move them into folders, and otherwise manipulate messages and folders on their IMAP server as if they were stored on their local host.

Unlike SMTP and POP, IMAP can be quite complex: more than two dozen commands are defined for IMAP, and over a dozen different replies. Also unlike SMTP, IMAP replies are not based on the usual three-digit codes.

In some ways, IMAP is more of a design specification for a generalized mail management system than a typical internet application protocol. This complexity is largely due to the broad problem that IMAP was designed to solve: managing mail. Unlike POP and SMTP, which must only move mail between a source and a destination, IMAP provides a framework within which a local host (the client) manipulates data that is stored on the remote host (the server). Issues such as allowing access, copying, moving, deleting, and adding to the server's message store are far more complex than merely requesting that data be transmitted from one node to another.

9.3.4 SMTP Security

Security is increasingly an important aspect of every internet protocol, and mail has several areas in which it may be vulnerable to attack. Some mail vulnerabilities are related to technical issues such as open relays, but often mail poses security problems that have more to do with management and policies than to changes in technology.

The SMTP architecture as originally designed was largely insecure. Messages are exchanged in plain text, there is no control over what servers the messages traverse before they arrive at their destinations, no authentication mechanisms for clients and servers. Exposures include:

- Local link sniffing of packets. Attackers with access to a protocol sniffing tool on the local network will be able to view any messages sent on the local link. All data is sent as US-ASCII, so the attacker would have no problem interpreting it.

- Attackers could use open relays (see above) to forward unsolicited bulk mail or to hide their identities.
- Modification of DNS MX records could cause all mail from a site to pass through an attacker's server; the attacker could collect information from those messages or modify those messages undetected.

Approaches to mitigating these vulnerabilities include:

- Using public key cryptography to encrypt and/or digitally sign all messages. This protects the messages from unauthorized viewing and/or modification en route to their destinations.
- Closing of open relays and using alternative mechanisms to allow users to send mail when they are away from their offices.
- Implementation of the DNSSEC protocols (see section 8.6.3).

Other approaches are available at the lower layers, including the transport layer security protocol discussed in section 15.4.1 and the IP security protocol discussed in Chapter 26.

9.3.5 MULTIPURPOSE INTERNET MESSAGE EXTENSIONS

Standard internet mail assumes that all data in the mail message, from the header to the body, consists of ASCII text characters. Binary data as found in graphic image files, video, audio, and executable software, therefore, poses the problem of how to attach files with binary data to ASCII-based messages.

The Multipurpose Internet Message Extensions (MIME) structure and encode other types of data into a form that can be attached to mail messages, using two sets of headers to do most of its work:

> `content-type` headers identify what kind of material is being enclosed
> `content-transfer-encoding` headers identify how the content is encoded

MIME content types consist of a type, which provides a general description of what kind of data is enclosed; and a subtype, which provides a more specific description of what kind of data is enclosed. Parameters may be present to provide additional customization for the content description. Valid types include application, text, image, audio, video, message, and multipart. Each different type has its own set of valid subtypes. For example, a Microsoft Word document MIME enclosure would be identified with the content-type header value of application/MSWord. The type is application, the subtype is MSWord. A text file would be identified with the value of text/plain, where the type is text and the subtype is plain.

There are many different MIME content types, and the IANA maintains a registry at http://www.iana.org/assignments/media-types/index.html.

MIME multipart enclosures are worth mentioning as they enclose more than one item in a single enclosure. Multipart enclosures are used to include security data related to the message; for example, a multipart enclosure might include an encrypted file and a digital signature for that file.

MIME offers a set of three encoding mechanisms for the representation of the data included in the enclosure. Although all systems process mail messages as if they are ASCII text, other types of data can become mangled if treated as seven-bit ASCII characters. Binary data or non-ASCII text (for example, character sets for non-English languages) tends to be difficult to transmit in e-mail bodies, unless MIME is used to enclose the data.

One of MIME's three primary encoding mechanisms is *7 bit,* which is used to indicate that the content can be treated as standard ASCII text. Another encoding mechanism is called *quoted-printable,* which is used to indicate that the content is mostly ASCII, but may have some non-ASCII characters included. Quoted-printable enclosures retain the non-ASCII characters so that the recipient can use the data as originally sent.

The *base64* encoding mechanism is used for binary data. The danger with sending binary data through e-mail is that e-mail processing systems treat all messages as if they were ASCII text; the characters are treated as if they are seven-bit characters even though the binary data uses all eight bits of each available byte. The binary data would often have the last bit truncated and would appear at the receiving end as nonsense streams of ASCII characters. The base64 encoding mechanism avoids this problem by mapping 24 bits (three bytes) of binary data onto four ASCII characters. When a MIME enclosure is received, the recipient determines whether it was encoded with base64, in which case the ASCII characters are converted back into binary data.

MIME, MIME types, and related topics are the subject of many RFCs. The specification is defined in a series of five RFCs (2045-2049), starting with RFC 2045, "Multipurpose Internet Mail Extensions (MIME) Part One: Format of Internet Message Bodies."

9.4   Internet Mail Lessons

Internet mail provides an excellent introduction to a range of internet application protocol concepts. Understanding the mail specifications provides an excellent foundation for understanding how other internet protocols operate. Although SMTP is the *Simple* mail transfer protocol, it is simple in a fairly sophisticated way. Some of the lessons that can be derived from understanding how SMTP and internet mail work include:

Commands: The basic SMTP commands provide only the most basic functions, but those are enough to move the mail. All the commands are issued by the client, and all responses are made by the server. In most applications the client issues commands and the server replies to those commands; when a command cannot be successfully completed for some reason, the server still responds but with an indication that the command failed and (possibly) with a message indicating why the command failed.

Replies: SMTP uses the three-digit server response code format that is common to so many other internet protocols. The codes may be accompanied by text strings for people to read, but the codes themselves may also be interpreted by local software for end users. Protocols that define the transfer of data files are particularly likely to use reply codes; these include the file transfer protocol as well as hypertext transfer protocol and others.

States: Because the hosts supporting SMTP may be in only a handful of different states, the protocol can be implemented with minimal resources by setting up state tables indicating what actions should be taken in each different state.

Translations: Interoperability requires either that systems be capable of translating any format into any other format—or that systems be capable of translating local formats into a "lowest-common denominator" format and back. Internet mail mandates the use of US-ASCII characters as the lowest common denominator fomat for messages; MIME-encapsulated binary files are still represented in 7-bit format to fulfill this requirement. The use of a lowest common denominator format to create a universal translator function for gateway systems is apparent in other application protocols. For example, Telnet uses the concept of a *network virtual terminal*, a basic set of terminal functions that all client hosts can be assumed to provide to users (e.g., keyboard mappings, video display attributes) and that all server hosts are expected accept input from and produce output to.

Interactions: SMTP clients and hosts interact with each other, but they also interact with the domain name system to determine where to send mail, and they interact with the hosts associated with a message's source or destination. SMTP systems also interact with other mail protocols such as IMAP and POP, as used by the people sending and receiving mail.

Extensions: SMTP basic commands are enough for most purposes, but not for every purpose. One problem that arises with many programs is that the designers don't always know what commands will be necessary when the protocols are first specified. Attempting to add commands to a protocol after it has been deployed is troublesome: that type of change is essentially a revision to the protocol, and it requires widespread system updates.

Formats: Internet mail offers several different format specifications, from formatting proper addresses to formatting messages, message header fields, SMTP protocol commands and trace fields added by intermediate SMTP hosts, and MIME attachments. Much of the mail exchanged over the early internet was based on proprietary rather than open standards, and thus often had to traverse one or more mail gateways where proprietary formats, headers, and addresses may have undergone translations. As a result, the IETF has produced a large body of RFCs documenting protocols and techniques for making all these different systems interoperate. These approaches may be faintly echoed in other application layer protocols, but they are more strongly evoked in protocols at the network link layer (where there is no single open standard) and at the internet layer.

ABNF: Formal specifications require formal methods. Early protocol specifications sometimes used ABNF notation, but since the mid-1990s it has become the preferred tool for specifying internet protocol formats. Although in this chapter we have referred to ABNF specifications mostly for mail message and address formats, it is used throughout mail specifications to specify everything from what characters are allowed in any protocol data to how protocol commands are properly formatted.

Distribution of architectures: The mail address namespace is largely but not completely mapped onto the internet DNS. DNS uses a highly distributed architecture to provide access to information about mail delivery. SMTP relies on DNS not only for these pointers but also to hold SMTP transport information in the form of MX preferences.

9.5 Chapter Summary

Although the architecture devised for internet mail, with its user, message transfer, and message injection agents, may seem unwieldy to us today, it still serves us remarkably reliably and at low cost. The SMTP protocols and formats have survived substantially unchanged since 1981, and could conceivably continue to function far into the future with the use of SMTP extensions.

The POP makes SMTP more accessible to users of laptop or desktop PCs, while the IMAP increasingly enables users to access their mail from any location, any PC. Message privacy is still a problem that most users are either unaware of or unconcerned about, but S/MIME provides one approach to the problem.

Like other application protocols, SMTP uses a simple protocol for exchanging textual command and response information: Telnet. As discussed in the next chapter, Telnet provides a basic tool with which systems can interact.

10

Telnet

The two first application protocols were terminal emulation (Telnet) and the file transfer protocol (FTP). Telnet allows people to work interactively with a remote host, FTP allows people to move files from one host to another. Neither of these applications is nearly as important today as it was in 1982, but both are probably more widely used now than they were then.

This chapter provides an introduction to the telnet protocol, the next highlights FTP, and the ones after that cover hypertext transfer protocol (HTTP) and other important internet applications. However, these chapters won't go into as much detail about the protocols as earlier chapters, in part because some of that detail is redundant (many applications share similar if not identical mechanisms) and in part because concentrating on the details can make it more difficult to grasp the fundamental concepts.

10.1   Problem Statement

Unlike the other application protocols discussed so far, Telnet's purpose is to enable the transfer of data between a user and a computer. Simple mail transfer protocol (SMTP) and domain name system (DNS) (for that matter, HTTP and FTP as well) include mechanisms that mediate interaction between hosts: the client requests some data, and the server sends it.

Telnet differs in that it is a mechanism for a person to send commands to programs running on the server, as if she were sitting in front of a directly connected terminal (or the server itself). Speed of data transfer is not as important as latency: in many cases, the user will need to transfer only a byte or two or data (for example, when pressing the Enter key in response to an application prompt). The server will usually send no more than about 2,000 bytes at most because that is all that is needed to fill the typical terminal display of 25×80 characters.

Telnet is the oldest of the internet terminal emulation protocols, but it is not the only one—nor necessarily the best one. But it provides a good example of an application protocol that does something other than send files back and forth. Measuring the performance of an interactive protocol such as telnet means looking at very different attributes than those important to bulk transfer protocols such as SMTP and FTP. Unlike relatively straightforward applications based on simple queries and responses, terminal sessions also require more attention to the client-host connection.

10.2   Terminal Functions

Many internet users have never used either a hardware terminal or a terminal emulation program, so it is worth reviewing the terminal emulation function. Early computers used a variety of mechanisms for accepting input from users and for producing output for those users, including toggle switches, paper tape, punch cards, and teletype consoles for input and including flashing lights, paper tape, punch cards, printers and teletype consoles for output. The introduction of the personal terminal, a combination of keyboard and cathode tube display monitor, provided a more practical means of interactive computer control for end users (printer/terminals provided the same functionality as the cathode ray tube monitor, but were noisy, slow, and consumed endless volumes of paper).

Initially, computer manufacturers sold terminals that matched their computers, but not anyone else's, as a means of increasing revenues by locking customers (large corporations, usually) into buying all their computing hardware from one vendor. Although vendors might optimize their terminal offerings for their mainframes, eventually most vendors adhered to some basic standards for interoperability. The notable exception was IBM, whose terminals and mainframes long relied on an entirely different character encoding system.

For many years, terminal emulation was done locally, but remote network terminal emulation function was one of the earliest TCP/IP applications because the researchers working under ARPA/DARPA funding needed a way to control systems remotely, over the network.

Terminals allow users to connect to a remote host, log in with their user ID and passphrase, and use applications that are running on the server. Many corporations use mainframes for key applications such as accounting, payroll, inventory, and others; those employees using those systems for their daily work would have a terminal on their desks wired directly to the mainframe. Companies with mainframes from more than one vendor might have employees with two or even three different terminals on their desks to allow them to access the systems they needed to do their work.

The telnet application was designed to allow a user running the telnet client software on any computer to communicate with the telnet server on any other computer, no matter the vendor, hardware, or operating system of either system.

This means a user with a DEC terminal would use a telnet client running on her local DEC mainframe to connect to a server program running on a remote mainframe. That server accepts telnet transmissions, converts them into the appropriate local format, and passes them to the user's session on the mainframe. Once that session returns some result (usually in the form of data to be displayed on a terminal), the server program accepts it from the local mainframe session and sends it off to the client software, which sends the properly formatted results to the user's terminal.

Figure 10–1 shows how this works. Although this may not be terribly complicated, it may be a bit subtle for users accustomed to PCs and workstations.

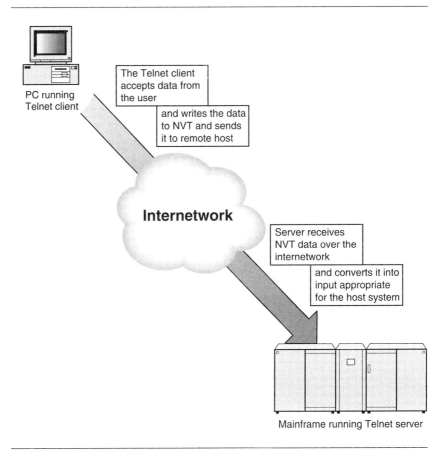

Figure 10–1: Terminal emulation between incompatible mainframe and terminal.

The steps in the telnet interaction depicted here pass demonstrate how telnet works:

1. The user sends a signal of some sort (e.g., types a command to be processed in her remote mainframe terminal session running on B) by pressing one or more keys on the local terminal keyboard. The terminal sends the signal through the local network to the telnet client running locally on mainframe A.

    The local telnet client translates the signal into *network virtual terminal* (NVT) format. The NVT is a lowest common denominator for terminal signals, providing a basic set of signals to which telnet clients translate inputs from the terminal keyboard and from which telnet clients translate outputs from the remote session for local display. Telnet servers also use the NVT to translate client inputs into a format that the server host can understand and to translate the output into a format that the client will be able to display.

For example, some terminals may lack a *Return* key; in those cases, some other key is used locally to represent the characters generated by the Return key. The telnet client translates whatever character(s) is (are) generated by that key into the appropriate sequence for the NVT emulation and send them to the server.

2. The telnet client on mainframe A sends the NVT inputs to the telnet server on mainframe B.

3. The telnet server on mainframe B translates the NVT inputs into the appropriate format for local processing by the server host. For example, if the server host is an IBM mainframe that uses the EBCDIC character set rather than the ASCII character set, the telnet server will convert the inbound ASCII data into EBCDIC data.

   Once converted into the appropriate local format, the telnet server passes the data along to the end-user's mainframe session on host B.

4. The mainframe session accepts the data and does whatever it would do with any other terminal session. The results, generally some screen output, are sent back to the telnet server.

5. The telnet server converts the data from local format to the NVT format and sends it back to the telnet client program running on host A.

6. The client converts the data (in NVT format) into an appropriate format for display on the user's terminal, and sends it to that terminal for display.

10.3   Telnet Protocol Basics

Telnet is specified as an internet standard in RFC 854, "Telnet Protocol Specification," and RFC 855, "Telnet Option Specifications." There are over 100 different RFCs about telnet published; the first, RFC 97, "First Cut at a Proposed Telnet Protocol," came out in 1971; 14 new RFCs were published about telnet during the year 2000.

This multitude of specifications indicates two things: telnet is important, and it's needed a lot of fixing over the years. Special versions of telnet have been created specifically to handle IBM mainframe terminal sessions (emulating the IBM families of terminals designated 3270 and 5250). Telnet is marginally more secure than the remote shell commands (rsh and others) but is still susceptible to many different attacks, including interception of terminal session data, hijacking of terminal sessions, and even sniffing of system passphrases.

Nevertheless, telnet is still useful, even if it is increasingly being replaced by the secure shell protocol (SSH) to be discussed later in this chapter.

Telnet sessions begin with a client opening a transmission control protocol (TCP) connection to the appropriate well-known port. As defined in RFC 854, the Telnet protocol may be used for communication between a client and a server; remote terminal emulation servers listen for Telnet service requests on port 23. The Telnet protocol is used to exchange data in other application protocols, in particular with FTP (see Chapter 11) or SMTP (see Chapter 9). This means that a telnet client can be used to communicate directly with an FTP server (it is standard operating procedure for implementers to reuse telnet code in their ftp implementations), or with an SMTP server (it is standard operating procedure for attackers to use telnet to interactively communicate directly with target mail servers).

TCP is the preferred transport protocol for telnet because it provides a reliable virtual circuit between the interacting hosts. TCP guarantees that if the connection fails for some reason, both client and server will be able to recover gracefully. With TCP's transmission control functions, both client and server can determine whether a lull is the result of a failed connection or whether it just means nothing has been happening.

Servers must be able to both receive commands from the clients reliably and send system responses to the client reliably.

10.3.1 TELNET PROTOCOL EXCHANGES

Telnet sessions have two sets of interactions: the user interacts with his client software running locally and his terminal session running on the remote host, and the client and server interact by sending data back and forth over the internet. First, the user-session interaction looks like this:

1. The user commands the local host to open a telnet session with a remote host (specified by hostname or by IP address).
2. If the client software is successful in opening the session, the user sees whatever other message the remote host would normally display when a terminal session is opened. In most cases, this will be a short "welcome" message,[1] followed by a login prompt.
3. The user enters her user ID and passphrase (or goes through whatever login process is normally required), and the terminal session is conducted.
4. When the user is finished, she logs off.
5. The user may log on to another terminal session (with the same or a different host) or else close the client software.

The user sees a terminal session just like any other terminal session. The session may happen inside a window sitting on top of a GUI desktop, but it is still nothing more than a terminal session.

The client and server programs, however, go through a bit more work to support the session:

1. Once the user command for opening a session is received, the client software starts (if it is not already running) and requests that the server hostname be resolved to an IP address (as described in Chapter 8).
2. The client attempts to open a TCP circuit (see Chapter 17) with the server IP address and the telnet port (23).
3. If it is to be successful, the host responding for the specified IP address must be responding to requests for TCP circuits on port 23 and running a telnet daemon. It must also be available to serve clients, in particular the client making the request. If those conditions are all met, the server responds with an acknowledgment of the request and then starts sending data (the welcome/login screen, for example).

---

[1] "Welcome" is in quotes because the message may include warnings against unauthorized intruders as well as summaries of penalties that may be applied to those who break applicable laws.

4. At this point, the session may proceed, with the client software
    sending the user's login information or any other keyboard
    (or mouse) input to the server and the server responding with
    the results of entering that input into the session with the server.
    Client implementations are expected to buffer keystrokes until
    an end-of-line naturally occurs or some other event (such
    as pressing the Enter key) triggers the equivalent of the
    end-of-line.

    Mostly, telnet sessions consist of these exchanges of data
    plus session negotiation messages (see no. 5, below) and telnet
    protocol commands (see no. 6 and Table 10–1, below).

5. As the session opens, the client and server software may also
    negotiate which telnet *options* (added features that may be sup-
    ported by either client or server but are not required) are to be
    used for the session. Option negotiation begins with one party
    (either client or server) sending a DO, DONT, WILL, or WONT
    message.

    The sequence is shown in Table 10–2; the effect is of a conver-
    sation between asker and askee. The asker starts out: "Please,
    do (or don't) use <some special option>, if you can" with the
    response like this: "Sure, I'll do (or not do) <special option> in
    this session."

    The hosts need not wait for answers as they exchange requests
    and responses; for example, a server might send a list of requests
    to the server to be responded to sequentially.

    The official list of telnet options is available at http://
    www.iana.org/assignments/telnet-options from the IANA
    web site, and in Appendix B.

The user opens a telnet session by opening the telnet client with a hostname
(to be resolved to an IP address as described in Chapter 8). The client
software opens the session with the remote host by opening a TCP circuit
on the server's port number 23, for telnet, at the requested server. The
client assigns itself a local, arbitrary, port to differentiate each terminal
session.

Both client and server can maintain more than one telnet connection
at any given time, as long as there are enough resources to maintain
additional TCP connections. A client may open more than one telnet session with the same remote host: although it uses the same IP address
and TCP port (port 23) as destinations for the telnet traffic, the client

Cmd	Stands for	Explanation
AO	Abort Output	Finishes process but doesnt output results
AYT	Are You There	Requests response from other side, to indicate link is still functioning
BRK	Break	Used as an attention key on NVT
DM	Data Mark	Places mark in data stream to allow urgent data to be transmitted
DO	Do <option>	Announces host willingness for other host to enable <option>
DONT	Dont do <option>	Announces host unwillingness to permit another host to enable <option>
EC	Erase char	Erases the last character sent EL 0xf8 Erase Line Erases the last line sent
EOR	End of Record	Indicates end of data sent; part of a negotiated option
IP	Interrupt Process	Interrupts the current process being executed on the server
NOP	No Operation	Acts as a place holder
SB	Suboption	Used when options have Negotiation suboptions
WILL	Will Do <option>	Announces host willingness to enable <option>
WONT	Wont do <option>	Announces host unwillingness to enable <option>

Table 10–1: Telnet protocol basic commands (from RFC 854).

Host	Wants to	Host	Response	Result:
client	WILL XXX	server	DO	client begins XXX
client	WILL XXX	server	DONT	nothing
client	DO XXX	server	WILL	server begins XXX
client	DO XXX	server	WONT	nothing
server	WILL XXX	client	DO	server begins XXX
server	WILL XXX	client	DONT	nothing
server	DO XXX	client	WILL	client begins XXX
server	DO XXX	client	WONT	nothing

Table 10–2: Option negotiation.

assigns non–well-known port numbers for its side of the TCP connection. As a result, two or more different telnet links to the same server could be active on a host: the only difference between segments intended for the different sessions would be the TCP port numbers on the client host (the rest of the addressing information, IP addresses of both hosts, and the TCP port number for the server, would remain the same for all segments).

If the server offers telnet, it opens negotiations with the client to determine what options are supported (see below). A telnet server may be configured to accept requests for a session on ports other than 23, and telnet clients may open sessions with any application protocol server that sends and accepts ASCII data. For example, you may connect to an SMTP server with a telnet client and send SMTP commands interactively.

The use of the NVT convention that the client and server send each other will be mutually comprehensible; thus there is little need for further application layer protocol formatting. It also allows the telnet client to interoperate with other servers. The most obvious application level protocol needed for telnet is a mechanism to allow transmission of character sequences in the terminal session that might be interpreted as part of the protocol such as commands and to permit transmission of protocol commands that might otherwise be interpreted as part of the terminal session. The usual approach to this problem is to use "escape" characters or codes, sequences of characters that indicate how the next character(s) is to be interpreted.

Minimal protocol formatting simplifies the exchange information between client and server. The client program sends whatever it has, whenever the user indicates she is ready to send that data; the server sends whatever it has, whenever the host system (interacting through the terminal session) indicates the transmission is complete. The sending continues until all the data has been delivered. If the host system would send a cascading stream of output to a terminal (as when displaying hundreds of filenames in a directory listing), the same stream is sent to the telnet client. When the volume of data to be sent exceeds the amount that can be incorporated into a TCP segment or an IP packet, the lower layer protocols break the data up—telnet implementations aren't required to provide any mechanisms for managing such transmissions.

10.3.2 TELNET PROTOCOL COMMANDS AND OPTIONS

The telnet protocol itself has relatively few commands. These include options negotiation commands (see the next section), as well as a few commands regarding the flow of data. Commands are set off from the rest of the flow of data by a special one-byte character, 255 (or 0xff, in hexadecimal) that is called the Interpret As Command (IAC) character. The commands are also single bytes and follow the IAC character.

One of the important features of telnet is the ability to negotiate options between the server and the client. By allowing options, telnet implementations permit either client or server programs to extend functionality between two hosts if they both agree. Option negotiation between the telnet client and server is symmetric, meaning that either side can initiate a request to honor any option. Either side also has the authority to veto any option requested by the other side.

Negotiation begins when one participant sends a request that it wants to turn on (or off) a certain option for itself, or a request that it wants the other participant to turn on (or off) an option.

As mentioned in section 10.2.3, telnet hosts negotiate options by exchanging DO/WILL requests. The DO <option> command is a request for the other host to turn on an option; the WILL <option> command is a request for the other host to allow the requesting host to turn on the option. A host may respond WILL or WONT to a DO request, signifying that the host either will or will not turn on the option (the requesting host must accept that response). A host may respond DO or DONT to a WILL request, signifying that the host is willing or not to allow the other host to turn on the requested option. Table 10-2 shows all eight possibilities for option negotiation for option XXX.

Either host can initiate a request to enable (or leave disabled) any particular option, and all hosts must support the four option commands. However, telnet hosts don't necessarily have to support any options—although they must be able to recognize that a remote host is requesting an option, and be able to respond to that request negatively.

Options are an important aspect of telnet implementations, because they allow the most primitive telnet server (or client) to support sessions with the most modern and fully featured telnet client (or server).

Because an option request (DO and WILL) can look like a request acknowledgment, a telnet host need not acknowledge requests for services already on: the request is ignored to avoid looping requests between hosts.

Telnet options vary from implementation to implementation, but some of them relate to terminal characteristics, like negotiating the size of the window represented on the terminal: how many characters wide and how many high can be represented on screen. This type of option must first be negotiated, and then the two hosts can exchange information about terminal type. Line mode or character mode is another option, which determines whether characters are sent individually or grouped together to be sent one line at a time. Other options include choices about whether or not to allow a host to echo data it receives or whether or not to use a special end of record code to indicate the end of a data transmission.

10.3.3   INSECURE TELNET ALTERNATIVES

Telnet may be the most grizzled and time-tested of internet terminal emulation protocol, but it is not the only one. Two other terminal emulation families should be mentioned here: the r-utilities and the SSH. The r-utilities are considerably less secure than telnet, while the SSH is considerably more secure.

Telnet is widely implemented and deployed in large part because it has always been widely implemented and deployed. Despite its weaknesses, telnet has been used for years for robust, reliable, and remote logins across the internet. At the same time, system administrators in smaller TCP/IP networks, where *nix operating systems dominated, were taking a different approach to remote sessions. Generally simpler (supporting fewer options) than telnet, the r-utilities were designed to operate mostly between *nix systems.

Foremost among these utilities is the *rsh* ("remote shell") program, which allows a user on a local system to connect to a remote system and open a shell on that system. There are a number of other "remote" programs, including *rcp* ("remote copy") and *rlogin* ("remote login"). As with the Network File System (NFS), a protocol produced by Sun Microsystems and submitted to the IETF for publication in a non-standards track RFC, the r-utilities rely on hostnames and local user IDs for authentication.

The r-utilities restrict remote access based on the hostname of the source host from which the request for access is made. *nix systems use the .rhosts file, listing authorized hosts and use IDs. If the user ID and hostname are in the file, the request is allowed.

This approach to security is easily defeated simply by sending a false user ID and hostname with a request to open a session. Although this risk would likely have been acceptable in a research organization or small workgroup network, that is no longer the case. In addition to being insecure, r-utilities are less useful in environments with a broader range of operating systems in use (although r-utilities have been ported to many if not most non-*nix* OSes).

Like telnet, r-login uses the TCP transport protocol to initiate a connection between the client and the server. However, once the connection is initiated, the client sends user information to the server. This includes the user's ID on the client system and the user's ID on the server system; the server may also prompt for a password. The password prompt and response are not handled any differently from other data passed between the two hosts. If the server gets a valid password, it continues the session; otherwise it will terminate the connection.

10.4   Secure Shell Protocol

SSH was first created as an open source project by Tatu Ylonen in the 1990s (who later founded SSH Security Communications, Inc., with a set of

SSH implementations as its flagship product). Since then, SSH (for "secure shell" and in contrast to rsh, or "remote shell") has been adopted by the Secure Shell (SECSH) IETF working group. Although no RFCs have been published, SSH is widely used as a secure alternative to telnet as well as a tool for securing other applications.

SSH consists of three pieces, as described in an internet draft published in 2002:

- The transport layer protocol provides server authentication, confidentiality, and integrity. It may optionally also provide compression. The transport layer will typically be run over a TCP/IP connection, but might also be used on top of any other reliable data stream.
- The user authentication protocol authenticates the client-side user to the server. It runs over the transport layer protocol.
- The connection protocol multiplexes the encrypted tunnel into several logical channels. It runs over the user authentication protocol.

As far as terminal emulation, SSH is similar to telnet—but before establishing the terminal session, SSH allows the client and server to negotiate the exchange of security data, creation of a secure connection, and user authentication.

However, SSH is far more than a terminal emulation protocol. It defines a framework within which two hosts can negotiate a secure circuit. Although the most basic use of that circuit is the exchange of terminal session data, SSH-secured circuits can be used to encapsulate almost any other type of application session. The connection protocol allows multiplexing—the aggregation of different data streams—over a single SSH session, making it an ideal mechanism for securing other applications. This use of SSH is discussed in Chapter 16.

10.5   Chapter Summary

Telnet provides a simple protocol for the exchange of textual data, whether those exchanges be of protocol commands and responses for other protocols (including FTP and SMTP) or the exchange of terminal commands and system responses that make up a remote terminal session between a user and a remote system.

One of the most notable aspects of Telnet is the use of the network virtual terminal: the imaginary device to which and from which all inputs and outputs can be mapped. By building this idealized entity, Telnet can accept input from any kind of input device, as long as the inputs can be mapped onto the NVT. Likewise, as long as an output device can interpret NVT outputs, those can be displayed on the local output device. Rather than requiring a separate translation between each and every input and output device (which would result in a huge number of different translations), each device must be translated only once—to and from the NVT—to ensure interoperability with all other devices.

11

Internet File Transfer

The two fundamental and most basic problems that a network solves are these:

1. How do users connect to, and control sessions with, remote hosts?
2. How do users move data files from one host to another?

Telnet and other terminal emulation protocols help solve the first problem; the File Transfer Protocol (FTP) solves the second problem.

Although we've already introduced the concept of transport layer ports (in Chapters 5 and 7), transmission control protocol (TCP) ports are more important to FTP than the other protocols discussed so far. Readers may wish to review the relevant sections of those chapters, or to read this chapter in parallel with Chapters 15 and 17, in which transport layer issues are discussed at greater length.

11.1 Problem Statement

Telnet offers a basic mechanism for passing data from the client to the server, and back. The client sends data the user inputs through her keyboard, while the server responds by sending terminal output from the terminal session to the remote client, for display on the client's output device. Terminal sessions tend to be *bursty*, meaning data is sent in short bursts or flurries of activity with lots of waiting around time in between. While the client initiates a connection, the user sits and waits for a response from the server; the user enters user ID and passphrase, and waits while the remote host determines whether the login should be accepted. Data sent from the terminal session to the telnet client is displayed, and the server sits around and waits while the user reads that data.

If a telnet message is dropped somewhere along the line, resending the message is likely to impact performance virtually imperceptibly. If the connection is flaky, and one in a hundred or even one in ten packets are corrupted or lost, the session can still be usable.

File transfer is different:

- Files may be very short, but more often are large. File sizes of hundreds of megabytes are routinely downloaded over the internet. File transfer applications must permit hosts to maximize transmission speeds.
- A single error in a transferred file can render the entire file useless. File transfer applications must permit hosts to check for errors as data is received, without waiting for the entire file to be downloaded.
- File transfer may or may not be an interactive activity. Terminal sessions almost always involve a person sitting in front of a computer and entering commands via keyboard at one end of the connection and a host at the other accepting those commands. File transfer may be an interactive task, but it may just as likely be an automated task set up to run at night when bandwidth is cheaper.

File transfer must also be differentiated from *network file sharing*, where networked hosts share access to a network file system. Local area network (LAN) operating systems such as Novell's NetWare and Microsoft's network services allow individual hosts to access files, disk storage space, and other network resources such as printers as if those resources were directly connected to the host. Figure 11–1 shows how two client hosts appear (at least to their users) to be directly connected to the server's disk and printer. A user of either of those systems might not realize that her files are not being stored locally but on a portion of the network disk.

However, a host with an FTP client across the internet or across the LAN could access the same files—but only by treating the server as a distinct file system from which files would first have to be copied across the network. The FTP user must copy a file before it can be used locally, but the local copy is distinct (and can be changed) from the original file stored on the FTP server.

In Figure 11–1, the FTP clients are shown with arrows between the server's shared disk and their own local disk because files are copied across the network in their entirety before they can be manipulated locally.

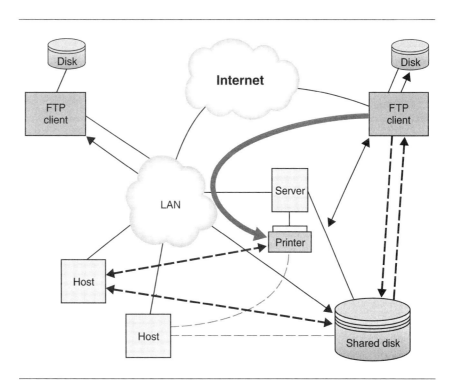

Figure 11–1: Network file sharing.

Users can treat network file systems as if they were directly connected to the users' hosts, but files on FTP servers must be transferred prior to being manipulated (or even viewed) in any way.

11.2   File Transfer Protocol Basics

Like telnet, FTP is an ancient protocol, tracing its roots back to 1971 and RFC 114, "A File Transfer Protocol." Published in 1985, RFC 959, "File Transfer Protocol," is still curent. As defined in RFC 959 and updated in subsequent RFCs, FTP displays greater complexity than telnet—and even uses the telnet protocol for exchanging transfer commands and control information.

The complexity of the FTP protocol arises from segregation of the file transfer process from the exchange of command and control information. Hosts exchange information about the transfers (e.g., requests for files) through one channel, while the actual file transfers are conducted through a separate, dedicated, channel. Even more unusual is that data transfer connections are initiated by the server, rather than the client, after a request for a file is made.

Figure 11–2, adapted from RFC 959, shows how the FTP architecture works; the entities involved are:

Server-Filesystem: This is where the server physically stores files that can be accessed through FTP. Files transferred to a client are read from this filesystem; files transferred from a client are written to this filesystem.

Protocol Interface (PI): FTP defines two separate PIs, one each for client and server. The PI is the process that manages the exchange of protocol data; the PIs set up the control connection (see below), send and receive protocol commands and responses, and control the data connection.

Server-PI: The server's protocol interface listens for requests to open a TCP connection on the standard inbound FTP control port (port 21), and interprets FTP commands sent by the client.

Data Transfer Process (DTP): The DTP manages the actual transfer of file data over a separate data connection (see below).

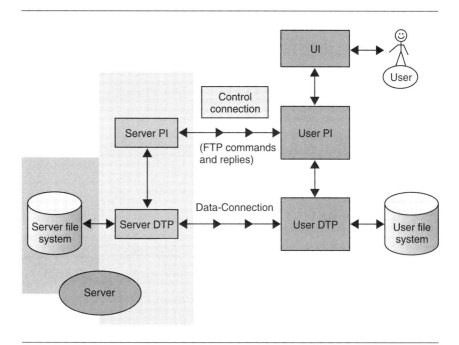

Figure 11–2: FTP architecture (from RFC 959).

Server-DTP: The server-DTP is the part of the server's FTP process that initiates a data connection when in its *active state*. The server DTP listens for a client initiation on port 20 when in its *passive state*.

Server-FTP: The server-FTP is the process that does FTP; this may be one or more processes that incorporate the data transfer and protocol interface functions for the server.

Control-connection: The circuit over which the user and server protocol interpreters exchange commands and responses.

Data-connection: The circuit over which the user and server protocol interpreters exchange data and acknowledgments.

User Interface (UI): The UI allows the user to enter commands and see the results of those commands. Most FTP user interfaces in use through the early 1990s (and beyond, in some cases) relied on a command

line UI. By the mid-1990s, most software publishers had begun shipping fully graphical UIs for FTP. The user interface issue will be
revisited in Chapter 28.

User-FTP: The user-FTP does FTP; this may be one or more processes that
incorporate the data transfer and protocol interface functions for the
client, as well as the client user interface.

User-PI: The user-PI orchestrates files transfers by linking the user
(through the UI), the local data transfer process and the server's
protocol interface.

User-DTP: The user-DTP sends and/or receives file data, and reads/
writes it from/to the local filesystem. The user DTP also listens for
requests to open data circuits on port 20 from an FTP server.

User-Filesystem: Where the user's FTP process stores data transferred
from the server or to be transferred to the server.

Unlike any of the protocols we've discussed so far, FTP uses two circuits,
one for commands and the other for data. Also unique is the use of the
active and passive modes for transfer: by default, the protocol requires
that client commands be sent over the command circuit, but when data
is to be transferred, the server must be allowed to initiate the data circuit. This is most unusual, because it assumes that inbound and outbound
connectivity are roughly equivalent. In practice, however, servers are far
more frequently configured to allow just anyone to connect than clients.
There are security implications of allowing external hosts to open a data
transfer circuit with a user's system inside a corporation or other organization, foremost among them the need to differentiate between legitimate
file transfers and those made by attackers.

Using the passive mode, however, the client may request that a server
allow the data transfer circuit to be set up in the same direction as the
command circuit. Rather than having the client initiate the command
circuit but require the client to allow an outside host to initiate the
data transfer circuit, the passive mode permits the client to initiate both
circuits.

Figure 11–3 shows the steps in an FTP session. Figure 11–2 shows several different entities, with the client and server host each having its

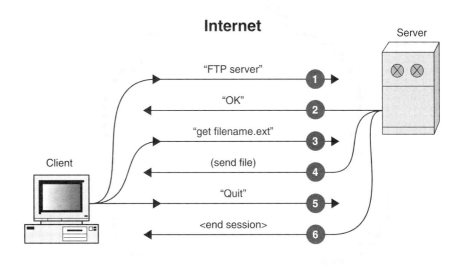

Figure 11–3: An FTP file transfer session.

own separate PI, DTP, and FTP; but in practice all of these functions are combined into an implementation of FTP.

A file transfer, such as a user downloading a file from a remote server using FTP, might proceed as follows:

1. The user starts the client FTP process, identifying the server from which a file is to be downloaded.
2. The FTP client process initiates a control connection with the FTP server. The control connection uses the telnet protocol for the exchange of command/response data. Commands include requests for file transfers as well as requests to set various options, list directories, change directories on the server, or manage the connection itself.
3. The FTP client requests that a file be transferred from the FTP server by sending a command over the control connection.

4. The FTP client then waits for the server to open a connection, assuming that the active mode is in use. If the passive mode has been specified, the server waits for the client to open the connection.

5. The client and server exchange file data. FTP provides no reliability or guaranteed delivery services, relying on TCP to provide those. FTP data may be transferred in *block mode*, or in *stream mode*. Block mode means the format of each chunk of data transmitted by an FTP host includes a protocol header which may specify the size of the chunk or provide information about where the block begins and ends. Stream mode is when the sending host reads data directly from the file into the transmission queue. Because the receiving host can clearly identify to the sender how much of the file was actually received, block mode makes possible the resumption of transfers interrupted by system or network. In stream mode, the recipient of the file has no way to determine the end of a chunk of data until the sender completes the transmission; if there is a failure in the circuit, the sender won't know for sure how much of the file got through, and the recipient has no way to notify the sender where to begin resending (other than from the start).

6. The control connection remains active during transfer to allow either host to transmit information about the data transfer (this is not to be confused with acknowledgment data passed between the hosts at the transport layer via TCP). For example, if a user decides to terminate a file transfer before it is complete, the appropriate command to abort the transfer is passed over the control connection.

7. When the file transfer is complete, the server closes the data connection. The server terminates the control connection when a file sent in stream mode is complete (because there is no other way to indicate the end of the file).

To further muddy the waters, the FTP specification defines a set of commands and responses to be exchanged between the client and the server. At the same time, early command-line FTP implementers used the protocol to build a basic set of user commands. Table 11–1 includes a typical list of FTP client software commands. However, FTP user commands are not the same as the FTP protocol commands. Part of the FTP implementation is a mechanism for accepting input from the user and turning that input into the appropriate protocol commands.

Command	Purpose
!	Open operating system shell
?	Get help
ascii	Set file type to ASCII transfer
binary	Set file type to binary transfer
cd	Change default directory on remote host
close	Terminate connection with remote host
delete	Remove file on remote host
dir	Get directory listing on current directory on remote host
get	Retrieve file from remote host
hash	Display # (hash character) for each block of data transferred
lcd	Change directory on local host
ls	Get directory listing on current directory on remote host
mdelete	Multiple delete of files using wildcard
mdir	Make directory
mget	Retrieve multiple files from remote host
mkdir	Make directory on remote host
mput	Send multiple files to remote host (from local host)
open	Open connection with remote host
put	Send file to remote host (from local host)
pwd	Return current working directory on remote host
quit	End FTP session
quote	Execute command on server
recv	Same as get
rmdir	Remove directory
send	Same as put
type	Return current file transfer type (ASCII or binary)
verbose	Toggle verbose mode—start or stop plain-language prompts

Table 11–1: Some commonly encountered FTP commands.

Looking at Figures 11–3 and 11–4, you can appreciate how the session differs depending on whether you are looking at a transcript of an FTP client program session or at a protocol trace of the same session.

Some of the protocol commands defined in RFC 959 include:

USER: Sends the user's account ID, to identify the end user to the server.

PASS: Carries the user's account passphrase, to allow authentication to the server.

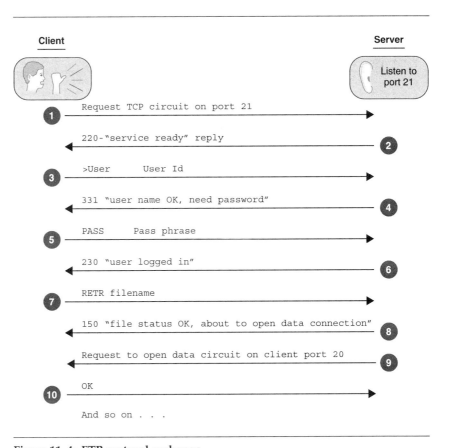

Figure 11–4: FTP protocol exchange.

CWD: Changes the current working directory on the server.

CDUP: Changes the current working directory to the parent of the current directory.

SMNT: For "structure mount;" allows the user to retain the current session and session settings but to mount a different file system.

REIN: For "reinitialize"; resets the session (while allowing transfers in progress to finish). After this command, a user would have to log back in again (the next command is assumed to be USER).

QUIT: Allow transfers in progress to finish, but otherwise terminate the session by closing the control circuit.

PASV: Requests the server to go into passive mode so the client can initiate the file transfer circuit.

TYPE: Sets the format used for data represenation; options originally defined included ASCII and EBCDIC (the format used by IBM mainframes), as well as IMAGE, for binary data. The protocol allows selection of a local byte size if necessary.

STRU: Specifies the type of structure to be used in a transfer; options include F (for "file," meaning no structure), R (for "record"), and P (for "page").

MODE: Specifies the transfer mode; options include S (for "stream"), B (for "block") and C (for "compressed").

RETR: Requests that a file be copied from the server to the requesting host ("retrieved").

STOR: Requests that a file be copied from the requesting host and be "stored" at the server.

STOU: Requests that a file be copied from the requesting host and be stored under a unique filename at the server.

APPE: Appends the file being copied to the named file on the server (unless the file does not yet exist, in which case the file is created with that name).

ALLO: For servers that require it, this command allocates space for a file to be sent by an append or store command. Servers that don't require it should treat it as a NOOP command by ignoring it.

REST: Indicates a file marker from which the server should restart sending the file. This command is followed by a command that initiates the actual file transfer.

RNFR: Paired with the RNTO command, the RNFR command specifies the old filename and path to be renamed (rename from). RNFR is always sent first. Together, the two commands cause a file to be renamed.

RNTO: Paired with the RNFR command, the RNTO command specifies the new filename and path to which the file should be renamed. RNTO is always sent second.

ABOR: Aborts a current file transfer.

DELE: Delete a named file.

RMD: Remove a directory.

MKD: Create a new directory.

PWD: Print (display) the current working directory.

LIST: Lists directory or file information about a specified file or directory.

NLST: Sends a directory listing (names of files/directories) of the specified directory.

SITE: Lists site parameters that affect file transfers but are not sufficiently universal to require being addressed in FTP.

SYST: Requests information about the server's operating system.

Appendix B includes a list of FTP response codes (from RFC 959).

11.3   What's Special About File Transfer Protocol

Several things are worth noting about FTP:

1. FTP incorporates a different application protocol, telnet, to be used for the transmission of commands.
2. FTP requires two separate channels be open for file transfer, one for commands and replies to commands, the other for actual data transfer.
3. FTP originally required that a client be able to permit the server to open up a circuit for data transfer.
4. FTP originally required that all file transfers be conducted over the same TCP circuit.

Now, it is worth noting that the active mode for file transfers is a more or less unnecessary complication. Item no. 4, the requirement for all transfers to be made over the same circuit, is the reason Item no. 3 was mandated in the first place.

The TCP connection from server to client is done from the server's port 20 (the well-known port for FTP-data) to the same port the client used as the originating point of the control connection. In this way, all file transfers during the same session would be conducted over the same circuit. The TCP circuit originating from port 20 on the server and arriving at port X on the client (where X is the port chosen by the client for the control circuit).

But, it turned out that no one really implemented FTP this way: doing so tended to cause problems with a TCP timer. Instead, in most implementations the client notifies the server of a new inbound port for every new file. This approach solves the problem of dealing with a TCP timer on a circuit whose activity varies considerably: quite active during the actual file transfers, but dormant in between file transfers. And it also solves the problem of requiring the client to allow remote hosts to open on non–well-known ports, by rendering the normal active mode unnecessary. RFC 1579, "Firewall-Friendly FTP," describes why PASV should be used to eliminate or at least reduce the impact of these problems.

Not yet mentioned, but also quite special, is the FTP feature allowing transfers between two hosts, initiated by a third host. The protocol defines a mechanism by which a user connects to two FTP servers, setting up two separate control connections (one to each server). The client host then directs one of the servers to send a file (or files) to the other server. The control connections between the client and each server must remain active during the entire session, but the data transfer connection is set up between the two servers. The client sends commands to and accepts responses from both servers, mediating the transfer process. This *proxy FTP* function is particularly useful when the client uses a slow network connection (for example, with a modem over a telephone line) but needs to have files moved between hosts with faster links.

Although sometimes useful, proxy FTP opens a vulnerability through the *bounce attack*, in which the attacker (using an FTP client host) has one FTP server send a file to the target server being attacked. The attacker does not open a true proxy session, but only pretends to be doing proxy FTP—there is only one control connection, to the "dupe" FTP server. The file uploaded to the dupe contains a sequence of protocol commands for the target server. For example, an attacker could use SMTP commands to forge mail from the target system, while having the attack appear to originate from the dupe FTP server.

The attacker sends a command to the dupe server, directing it to open a connection on the target server's service port (e.g., on port 25 for an SMTP attack). Because FTP clients send data file contents over the data transmission connection without any protocol information to encapsulate the data, the target server treats the file as if it were a sequence of protocol commands—and may be tricked into executing them. Figure 11–5 shows how the attack progresses.

11.4   Trivial File Transfer Protocol

The Trivial File Transfer Protocol (TFTP) was published as an internet standard in 1992, in RFC 1350, "THE TFTP PROTOCOL (REVISION 2)." The use of TFTP for remote booting was described in 1984 in RFC 906, "Bootstrap Loading using TFTP." In light of today's wealth of RAM, disk space, and processor speed, FTP was often too big a protocol to implement for systems used in the 1980s and early 1990s, particularly network terminals with minimal resources that loaded their boot image from their networks.

FTP required a full TCP/IP protocol stack as well as the ability to set up at least two concurrent TCP circuits; additional functions such as the ability

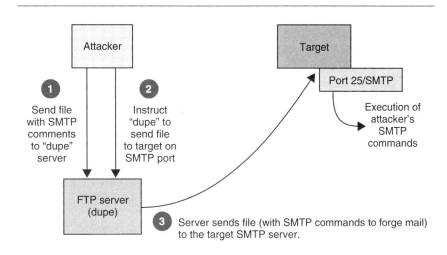

Figure 11–5: FTP "bounce attack."

to change directories or list directories were certainly not necessary for remote booting.

TFTP was created to provide a minimal protocol to be used by a system with minimal resources. RFC 1350 specified only two applications for TFTP–remote booting and transfer of mail—though remote booting has always been its dominant use.

TFTP was originally defined with only two commands: read a file or write a file (extensions have since been added to provide greater security, among others), and to use UDP, a much simpler transport protocol, instead of TCP. Data is transferred in 512 byte chunks; each chunk must be acknowledged before another may be sent. The end of the file is indicated by sending a chunk of data that is less than 512 bytes long (if the file contains an exact multiple of 512 bytes, a data message containing zero bytes is sent).

Relatively recent updates to the TFTP specification include:

> **RFC2349** TFTP Timeout Interval and Transfer Size Options (May 1998)
> **RFC2348** TFTP Blocksize Option (May 1998)

RFC2347 TFTP Option Extension (May 1998)
RFC2090 TFTP Multicast Option (February 1997)

More recently, however, IETF participants have been urging that use of TFTP be discontinued because its simplicity can be used by attackers.

11.5   File Sharing

File sharing is the application that provides users access to networked files, filesystems, and other computing devices such as printers, as if they were directly connected to the user's host. Typically offered locally, on LANs, file sharing applications include Novell's NetWare, Microsoft's peer-to-peer and client/server networking solutions, and the Network File System (NFS).

Originally developed by Sun Microsystems, NFS was submitted to the IETF for publication as an Informational RFC in 1989; since then NFS has been put on the IETF standards track and the latest specification published as RFC 3010, "NFS version 4 Protocol." NFS is used in much the same way as other file sharing protocols, and most of its complexity arises from the need to reproduce file system functions, such as the ability to sense when a file is being used by another user or process, to handle file input and output as well as caching of data as it is being written or read.

NFS clients and servers exchange data using the eXternal Data Representation (XDR) format, defined in RFC 1832, "XDR: External Data Representation Standard," as their "least common denominator" so that systems with different operating systems may exchange data transparently. The other key standard for NFS is the Remote Procedure Call (RPC) defined in RFC 1831, "Remote Procedure Call Protocol Version 2." RPCs provide a mechanism for NFS hosts to exchange requests for various actions such as reading and writing data from and to files.

11.6   Anonymous File Transfer Protocol

FTP provides a popular mechanism by which file sharing has traditionally been accomplished over the internet. File sharing with FTP is straightforward when the people who need access are a well-defined group: the FTP server administrator adds user IDs and passphrases for authorized users, who use their login information to access files.

Often, FTP servers contain files that are intended for unlimited public consumption. Distribution of those files would be hindered if every person who wanted to download them had to contact a system administrator to be assigned login credentials; likewise, system administrators would be swamped with such requests. Anonymous FTP is a method by which administrators can open up portions of the server filesystem for unrestricted access. Usually, anonymous FTP service requires users to login as "anonymous" and use their mail address when prompted for a passphrase. Anonymous FTP service may also include an upload area, where anyone can contribute their own files for public use.

Anonymous FTP may be used for many purposes, including distributing commercial and non-commercial program files, patches, and support material; distributing data files; and maintaining file stores for collaborative work. However, allowing virtually unrestricted access to a server filesystem opens up some security vulnerabilities so anonymous FTP deployments should be closely monitored. Many organizations, preferring greater control over access to such data, are moving to HTTP and custom applications for file transfer.

11.7 FTP Updates

Although almost as venerable as telnet, FTP has survived with fewer modifications since its publication as a standard in 1985. RFC 959 is updated by only two later proposed standards:

RFC2228: "FTP Security Extensions" adds several protocol commands and a new set of protocol responses intended to provide strong authentication, encryption, and integrity protection to FTP data and commands (e.g., they protect not only the files being transferred but also the commands used to control the file transfer session).

RFC2640: "Internationalization of the File Transfer Protocol" suggests and describes approaches to make FTP more accessible to users throughout the world, without undue dependence on the ASCII 7-bit character set.

FTP is far from perfect, yet it has retained relevance and usefulness over many years. However, FTP is increasingly under pressure from web applications, which have the benefit of the years of experience with FTP.

11.8   Chapter Summary

As with many other protocols that originated in the early days of the internet, the FTP serves not only as a protocol but also as an example of what doesn't work well and an experiment pointing to future solutions that will work more smoothly.

The original specification for FTP called for the client to initiate a connection with the server, but then to have the server initiate a second connection to the client in order to transfer a file. This approach has become increasingly unpopular, as attackers have used it to cause system breaches and as firewalls usually do not allow such connections to be initiated from external hosts.

As with many other application protocols, FTP implementations include their own set of commands that are built upon FTP protocol commands—but not always identical to them. FTP also has a lightweight version (Trivial FTP) and a flavor for public access file uploads and downloads (Anonymous FTP). Although web surfing may seem to have little in common with file transfers, the truth is that file transfer is fundamental to the web, as we'll see in the next chapter.

12

The Web

The most popular application on the internet is undoubtedly the web, which relies on the hypertext transfer protocol (HTTP) to move data between client and server (or, the web browser client implementation and web server). HTTP shares some attributes with both file transfer protocol (FTP) and simple mail transfer protocol (SMTP), but it goes much further to make the end-user experience pleasant and easy. Originally designed to allow users to browse *hypertext* documents (non-linear documents that allow readers to jump around to interesting or relevant areas of the document through *links*), HTTP has been extended and supplemented over the years by a number of additional protocols.

The web is based on the HTTP, which very likely generates more internet traffic than any other application protocol. For many, the internet and the web are virtually synonymous. HTTP does not stand alone, however. It relies on several important protocols, and is in turn relied upon by other protocols.

If FTP, Telnet, and internet mail (SMTP/post office protocol) represent the first generation of internet applications, the web is surely an important part of a second wave of internet applications. The original internet applications helped end-users because they turned the complexity of internetwork communication into a black-box. Users no longer had to do anything special to access remote file systems (through FTP) or remote operating systems (through Telnet)—these early applications made using the internet as simple as (or, rather, no more complicated than) using any connected host as a directly connected user.

The second generation of applications, like the web and internet message access protocol (IMAP), make further abstraction possible. They make the local operating system effectively irrelevant to the end user; no longer must the end user understand how the operating system works, or how to use the system from the command line. With the web (as well as with IMAP mail, and other applications), the user needs only to interface with a basic program that acts on behalf of the user in getting and using network as well as local resources.

This chapter introduces HTTP, explaining the fundamental structures of the protocol while not getting bogged down in the detailed description of every command, response code, or header. For reference, some of these are included in Appendix B, and the interested reader who needs a full and detailed description of the HTTP protocol workings can read the relevant RFCs. More interesting is the way HTTP has developed into a multifarious and ubiquitous application protocol, as well as a "substrate" protocol used by other applications.

Specifications and protocols commonly associated with HTTP and the web include:

URI: The uniform resource identifier (URI) specification defines how web resources are located and named, and is discussed below.

HTML: Hypertext markup language, the mechanism by which web content is prepared for display. Though an HTML specification was published in RFC "1866 Hypertext Markup Language - 2.0," HTML is no longer considered relevant to the activities of the IETF. Good HTML references abound, and the interested reader will find numerous books and web sites offering guidance on learning and using HTML; it is outside the scope of this text.

WebDAV: For web distributed authoring and versioning, this is the protocol specified for remote updates of web content. WebDAV is defined in RFC 2518, "HTTP Extensions for Distributed Authoring—WEBDAV," and updated in RFC 3253, "Versioning Extensions to WebDAV (Web Distributed Authoring and Versioning)." Discussion of the WebDAV protocol is beyond the scope of this text, but the interested reader will find these RFCs a good starting point (books about web publishing will also provide some helpful coverage).

MIME: Multipurpose internet message extensions. HTTP uses a slightly different protocol for its "MIME-like" data objects, as will be explained below.

SOAP: Simple object access protocol is a protocol that uses HTTP as a transport and enables many interesting new applications. SOAP will be discussed in Chapter 13.

We will mention only in passing protocols and specifications used to create web content—hundreds of other books, devoted solely to teaching about creating web content and managing websites, will provide better and more complete discussions of those.

12.1   Specifying Web Resources

The web is more than an application: it is a network of content that rides on top of the internet. As a network, the web requires mechanisms by which *resources* (the things people use on the web, such as documents, images, multimedia content, applications, and more) can be identified.

The URI specification is a Draft Standard, documented in RFC 2396, "Uniform Resource Identifiers (URI): Generic Syntax." Two types of URI are the Uniform Resource Locator (URL) and the Uniform Resource Name (URN). Tim Berners-Lee and his co-authors explain in RFC 2396 that:

```
URI are characterized by the following definitions:

Uniform Uniformity provides several benefits: it
    allows different types of resource identifiers to
    be used in the same context, even when the
    mechanisms used to access those resources may
    differ; it allows uniform semantic interpretation
    of common syntactic conventions across different
```

types of resource identifiers; it allows
introduction of new types of resource identifiers
without interfering with the way that existing
identifiers are used; and it allows the
identifiers to be reused in many different
contexts, thus permitting new applications or
protocols to leverage a pre-existing, large, and
widely used set of resource identifiers.

Resource A resource can be anything that has identity.
Familiar examples include an electronic document,
an image, a service (e.g., ``today's weather
report for Los Angeles''), and a collection of
other resources. Not all resources are network
``retrievable''; e.g., human beings, corporations,
and bound books in a library can also be
considered resources.
     The resource is the conceptual mapping to an
entity or set of entities, not necessarily the
entity which corresponds to that mapping at any
particular instance in time. Thus, a resource
can remain constant even when its content—
the entities to which it currently
corresponds—changes over time, provided that
the conceptual mapping is not changed in the
process.

Identifier An identifier is an object that can act as
a reference to something that has identity. In the
case of URI, the object is a sequence of
characters with a restricted syntax.

A URI might identify the resource by providing enough information
to locate that resource, in which case the URI is a URL; a URI might
also name the resource, being a persistent label that can be applied to
the resource over time.

A URI can be both a URL and a URN, but most URIs in common use are
URLs. To understand the difference between URN and URL, imagine a
global web in which every individual is identifiable by their unique name
and by their location (in this future, we've all received global positioning
implants).

You could use the name itself as the destination address of a message; for example, "Craig_Shergold.name" might be assigned to a person named "Craig Shergold" as his official resource name. Any message sent to that address would be forwarded to the person, wherever the person happens to be (there must be some mechanism to translate the name into a location, a non-trivial requirement).

Or, the URI could specify a location. Instead of the person himself, perhaps the phone number that "Craig Shergold" usually answers, or the street address where he lives, or his office address.

Although it is much easier to use the location type of URI, a URL works only as long as the resource stays put. "Craig Shergold" may not be the one answering a telephone he shares with family members; he may not be at his office if he goes out of town on business. With a URN, you should be able to send something to "Craig_Shergold.name" and have it delivered to him whether he is sick at home, at work, taking a long lunch in the pub down the street, or preparing for a business meeting in room 204 of the Manchester Hotel.

A URI may be either or both a URN and a URL.

We'll focus on URL syntax here. The objective of the URL is to use a single format to locate any internet resource be it web document, FTP file, telnet server, internet mail address, or any other type of service available through TCP/IP. URLs were originally defined to use only ASCII characters, although provision for other character sets is available. Web clients use URLs to locate network resources; URLs may incorporate non–well-known port numbers (or may, optionally, include the well-known port numbers) to direct a TCP connection to a specific port.

URLs are formed of the following components:

Scheme: This is the service identifier, and schemes include `http`, `ftp`, `mailto`, and other application services. Although the scheme may specify a particular protocol associated with an application service, it does not have to (e.g., `mailto` specifies a mail address rather than a protocol).

Scheme-specific-part: This is the rest of the URL, containing the information necessary to locate the resource.

RFC 2396 provides an informal (as well as a formal) specification for the URI format:

```
<first>:<second>;<third>?<fourth>
```

The first "part" is the scheme, separated by a colon (":") from the second part; the only required part of the URI is the scheme (first part), which indicates what type of resource is being accessed. Most common URIs include two parts, the scheme (http) and a resource (www.example.com). Details on the third and fourth parts of the URI can be found in RFC 2396.

The form of the scheme-specific part of the scheme depends on the scheme itself; valid schemes recognized by the IETF and listed on the IANA web site as of April 2002, are listed in Appendix B.

URLs can become quite complex, carrying different variables and parameters to be used to locate a particular resource, such as search parameters to retrieve resources from a database.

12.2   The Hypertext Transfer Protocol (HTTP)

Originally envisioned as a fairly simple application protocol, by 1996 HTTP 1.0 was documented in 60 pages in RFC 1945, " Hypertext Transfer Protocol – HTTP/1.0." From RFC 1945's abstract:

> *The Hypertext Transfer Protocol (HTTP) is an application-level protocol with the lightness and speed necessary for distributed, collaborative, hypermedia information systems.*

Things changed with HTTP 1.1, as this excerpt from the abstract for RFC 2068, "Hypertext Transfer Protocol – HTTP/1.1," published less than a year later, shows:

> *The Hypertext Transfer Protocol (HTTP) is an application-level protocol for distributed, collaborative, hypermedia information systems. It is a generic, stateless, object-oriented protocol which can be used for many tasks, such as name servers and distributed object management systems, through extension of its request methods. A feature of HTTP*

*is the typing and negotiation of data representation, allowing systems
to be built independently of the data being transferred.*

RFC 1945 was only 60 pages, but RFC 2068 expanded to 162 pages; the
revised specification for HTTP/1.1, RFC 2616, bulged to 176 pages. Clearly,
the degree to which HTTP had been embraced by internet users was
unprecedented and the uses to which it was applied were unanticipated.
RFC 2324, "Hyper Text Coffee Pot Control Protocol (HTCPCP/1.0)," was
published as a joke on 1 April 1998, but it demonstrates how well-adapted
HTTP has become to implementation on virtually any platform, including
a broad range of server configuration tools, user interfaces for printers,
and many more.

Yet HTTP 1.1 is still considered a simple request/reply protocol. As
summarized in RFC 2616, HTTP works like this:

1. An HTTP client sends a request to the server. The request
   includes a *request method* (essentially equivalent to and used
   instead of referring to an HTTP "protocol command"), a URI
   (usually a URL, as described previously), and the HTTP version
   in use (usually 1.1). For the purposes of the HTTP server (and
   as defined in RFC 2616), URIs are "formatted strings which
   identify—via name, location, or any other characteristic—
   a resource." The request also includes a MIME-like message that contains assorted information related to the client
   and the request (e.g., client information such as the browser
   name and version or parameters to be included with the
   request).
2. The HTTP server responds to the request with a status line that
   includes the HTTP version being used and the protocol response
   code to the request (e.g., 404: File Not Found). The server also
   sends a MIME-like message with its own information as well as
   (if appropriate) the *entity information* or the actual content being
   requested.

That's pretty much it for HTTP, although not entirely. Although HTTP
can be used to transfer any type of data, a markup language, the hypertext
markup language (HTML), has long been the specification of choice for
web content. Although at one time HTML was placed on the internet standard track, responsibility for web content specifications has been passed
to the World Wide Web Consortium (W3C).

A *markup language* provides a mechanism for identifying certain parts of a document as having particular functions. Originally intended to be used for computer document creation, markup languages assign *tags* to specify the start and end of each functional entity within a document. With traditional word processing programs, users define different functional entities by changing fonts, font size, line spacing, and other physical attributes of the displayed document. Doing so, however, means that the document cannot easily be ported to another format, where font size or line spacing are irrelevant. For example, the same content might be destined for publication both as a printed book and as online, text-only, help files. In this case, the author or editor would have to go through the content to verify that every heading, subheading, and other functional entity was properly formatted for printing as a book—and then repeat the process, verifying that the document was properly formatted for online help display.

With a markup language, the document writer need only "tag" functional entities within the document; the tags are interpreted appropriately for the output form chosen to display the document. Perhaps the most important types of HTML tag are those that *link* to other files or documents. Users use the links to move to other parts of the same document, to other documents on the same server, or to other resources elsewhere on the internet.

HTTP permits the client to specify a *scheme* in a URL that identifies the resource being requested; the scheme refers to the type of resource or service and comprises the first part of the URL. So, to access a web resource (from an HTTP server), the URL reads `http://webserver.example.org/`; HTTP client users could also just as easily access an FTP server by specifying the URL `ftp://ftp.example.org` or a telnet server via `telnet://terminal.example.org`.

The HTTP specification does not mandate any particular transport protocol, other than stating it should be reliable. Internet HTTP clients and servers usually communicate over TCP, through the HTTP well-known port 80. In the early days of the web, many if not most people used Novell or Microsoft networking protocols to connect to a LAN. Vendors published browsers that could operate over proprietary LAN protocols through application gateways.

HTTP *methods* (what might be called HTTP application protocol commands) allow servers to send data to clients, as well as allow clients to submit data to the server. Clients usually request data from servers using the GET method, while clients may submit data using the POST method. Clients frequently submit data, in particular when the end user is submitting data in a web page fill-in form.

RFC 2616 defines methods and server responses, as well as specifying the proper use of MIME-like headers for data transmissions, formats for dates and times, how to determine whether data may be cached, and if so, how and when that data expires.

Originally, HTTP interactions were one-time events: each time the client requested a resource, a new TCP connection had to be set up, only to be closed when that resource was received. This is not a problem when web pages are small and simple, but became a problem as web pages became increasingly complex. A single page might incorporate dozens of images as well as textual data files; TCP connections are resource-intensive and add latency to a session. The addition of persistent connections to HTTP improved performance significantly because it allows the client to set up a single TCP connection that remains in effect for the download of all resources from a website.

An HTTP protocol summary is included in Appendix B; RFC 2616 is reasonably readable and accessible for those who need all the details for implementations or troubleshooting. Rather than focus on protocol details here (for details of the interaction between TCP and HTTP, see Chapter 12), we'll examine some of the following issues:

- HTTP clients and servers don't always communicate directly, but rather the client accepts data that has been cached on a host "closer" to the client. Cached data should be data that is not likely to change during a specified lifetime but that is likely to be requested more than once during that lifetime. Large organizations use caching to serve clients to reduce the amount of bandwidth necessary to download data from a popular server (if hundreds of users all download the same pages, the caching server downloads the data once and distributes it locally to all those users). Popular web sites use caching services to distribute their content around the world, reduce their reliance on their own network links, and improve download performance for users around the world.

The specification acknowledges that such indirect connections are made, and provides mechanisms to accommodate the use of caching.

• Data is transferred using a "MIME-like" format to allow virtually any type of data to be transmitted. There are several other protocols upon which HTTP depends for continued operation as well as development and support of new functions, including URI/URN, WebDAV, SOAP, HTML, and XML.

• HTTP's popularity combined with growing concerns about security have led to a situation in which very few well-known ports are available for users connecting to internet servers from within an intranet—in many cases the only well-known port permitted is port 80. As a result, many protocols have been made to piggyback over HTTP (use HTTP as their substrate protocol). There are various security issues as well as usability issues related to this practice, some of which are addressed by the development of the Blocks architecture for developing new protocols, to be covered in the next chapter.

12.3 Hypertext Transfer Protocol and Multipurpose Internet Message Extensions

HTTP messages carry data in the form of "MIME-like" structures. Briefly introduced in Chapter 9, HTTP messages contain MIME-like objects; this means all messages from a browser look very much like MIME objects, and all data coming from a server will be packaged as a MIME object (or objects).

What is the difference between HTTP's "MIME-like" objects and RFC 2045-compliant MIME objects? They are quite similar, one of the most obvious differences being that HTTP MIME-like objects include a header field, Content-Length, that indicates the number of bytes needed to transfer the object. The other major difference is in the way HTTP MIME-like objects use the Content-Encoding and Transfer-Encoding header fields instead of the MIME-standard Content-Transfer-Encoding header field.

In regular MIME, the `Content-Transfer-Encoding` header field carries two pieces of information about the content of the MIME object. First, is the *transformation* used on the content. Because some protocols can't carry binary data, or data with a line length of greater than 1,000 lines (specifically, SMTP, which has both those restrictions), MIME objects containing binary data need to be transformed so that the data will be transportable by protocols that can't normally handle binary data correctly.

There are three transformations for data defined in the original MIME specification:

identity: This is equivalent to saying that no transformation has been applied to the data.

quoted-printable: Encoding means the data is converted into 7-bit values. This encoding is used when converting data from a 7-bit character set that includes unprintable ASCII characters; these are represented either with replacement characters or with their hexadecimal value.

base64: Encoding means binary data is being converted into a form that uses only printable ASCII characters, and in which lines are no longer than 76 characters long.

The transformations indicate what has been done to the data in the object; the other piece of information provided in the `Content-Transfer-Encoding` header field is the *domain*, or the appropriate context in which to interpret data in the object. Three domains were defined in RFC 2045:

binary: Data is to be treated as a stream of raw bits rather than text-based.

8 bit: Data uses an 8-bit character encoding, such as a Cyrillic, Latin, or other language-specific encoding.

7 bit: Data uses the basic set of 127 ASCII characters and symbols.

HTTP supports 8-bit transfers without any limitation; thus, there's no point to converting binary or 8-bit data to an ASCII-only, printable format.

Instead, the `Content-Encoding` header field is used to specify how the content of the MIME-like object is encoded. RFC 2616 defines the following values for this field:

chunked: Indicates that the message body has been split into two or more "chunks" to allow easier download of large objects.

identity: Indicates that no transformation encoding has been applied to the data.

gzip: Indicates the use of an encoding format produced by the file compression program "gzip" (GNU zip). This format is described in RFC 1952, "GZIP File Format Specification, version 4.3."

compress: Indicates the use of an encoding format produced by the *nix file compression program "compress."

deflate: Indicates the use of an encoding format produced by the "zlib" format used in combination with the "deflate" compression mechanism. These are described in RFC 1950, "ZLIB Compressed Data Format Specification Version 3.3" and RFC 1951, "DEFLATE Compressed Data Format Specification, Version 1.3."

The `Transfer-Encoding` header field is also defined in RFC 2616, with the same initial values as are defined for the `Content-Encoding` header field; the difference between the two HTTP MIME-like header fields is explained in RFC 2616:

> *Transfer-coding values are used to indicate an encoding transformation that has been, can be, or may need to be applied to an entity-body in order to ensure "safe transport" through the network. This differs from a content coding in that the transfer-coding is a property of the message, not of the original entity.*

In other words, the transfer encoding refers to the HTTP message; the content-encoding refers to the original data entity.

Figures 12–1 and 12–2 show an example of an HTTP exchange, with MIME-like objects; the different parts of these messages will be discussed in the next section.

```
GET / HTTP/1.1
Host: www.loshin.com
User-Agent: Mozilla/5.0 Galeon/1.2.0 (X11; Linux
    i686; U;) Gecko/20020326
Accept: text/xml,application/xml,
application/xhtml+xml,text/html;
    q=0.9,text/plain;q=0.8,video/x-mng,
image/png,image/jpeg,image/gif;
    q=0.2,text/css,*/*;q=0.1
Accept-Language: en
Accept-Encoding: gzip, deflate, compress;q=0.9
Accept-Charset: ISO-8859-1, utf-8;q=0.66, *;q=0.66
Keep-Alive: 300
Connection: keep-alive
```

Figure 12–1: An HTTP GET message, with MIME-like object.

12.4   Hypertext Transfer Protocol in Action

To get an idea of how HTTP operates, refer back to Figure 12–1. This figure shows a message passed from a client to a server, requesting the contents of the URL www.loshin.com (Fig. 12–2 shows the server's response). The IP and TCP headers have been omitted here for clarity's sake.

Look at the first line of the first message:

```
GET / HTTP/1.1
```

GET indicates that the client wants to retrieve some resource (in this case, the "/" or root resource) from the host indicated in the message body (the string HTTP/1.1 indicates that the client supports version 1.1 of HTTP).

```
HTTP/1.1 200 OK
Date: Wed, 10 Apr 2002 20:11:55 GMT
Server: Apache/1.3.23
Last-Modified: Sun, 07 May 2000 19:21:36 GMT
ETag: ''5d091-8f7-3915c240''
Accept-Ranges: bytes
Content-Length: 2295
Keep-Alive: timeout=5, max=100
Connection: Keep-Alive
Content-Type: text/html

<html>
<head>
<title>Pete Loshin's home</title>
<meta name=''description'' content=''World-famous
author ...
```

Figure 12–2: An HTTP response message, with MIME-like object.

The rest of the message consists of the message body that uses the MIME-like HTTP object format.

The first header field (on the second line of the message) indicates the host being queried (www.loshin.com); however, even though the client and server have already opened communication through a transmission control protocol and internet protocol session, the hostname is still required so as to distinguish among virtual servers (representing different websites at different domain names, but hosted on a single host).

The third line (second header field) is the User-Agent: header, and it carries information about the web browser software running on the client. In this case, it indicates that Mozilla, Galeon, and Gecko (all part of the local browser) are running in X Windows on a Linux host. The next three lines, the Accept: header, provides information to the server about the types of data the client is willing to accept (this header appeared on a single line with no breaks).

The `Accept-Language:` header indicates that English ("en") is the language of choice for the browser; `Accept-Charset:` and `Accept-Encoding:` headers indicate the browser's preferred character set(s) and character encodings. In this case, the ISO set of US characters and extended ASCII (UTF-8) characters, and the gzip, deflate, and compress encodings. These two headers include some additional characters. The figures that follow a semicolon (";") indicate the degree of preference given to that character set or encoding. In these two header fields, gzip, deflate (in the `Accept-Charset:` header), and ISO-8859-1 (in the `Accept-Encoding:` header) get the default preference of 1 (the highest value). The `utf-8;q=0.66` indicates the utf-8 character set has a lower preference (0.66; the lowest value is 0); the `*;q=0.66` indicates that all other, unspecified, character sets receive the same 0.66 preference value. Likewise, the preferred encodings are gzip and deflate, while compress is slightly less preferred with its 0.9 preference value.

The `Keep-Alive:` and `Connection:` headers are two of several "hop-by-hop" header fields, meaning they do not persist from the originating client through to the destination server, but are used only as needed between a client and a directly connected server (such as a cache server or other intermediary system, as discussed in the next section). The hop-by-hop headers indicate how to manage those direct connections.

The first HTTP message, then, is little more than a request for the web server to deliver the content it holds in its root directory. The response, shown in Figure 12–2, opens with the line `HTTP/1.1 200 OK`, the standard HTTP response format consisting of the protocol and version numbers, along with the three-digit response code number (200, meaning a positive response) and the string associated with that response ("OK"). The rest of the HTTP message is a MIME-like object. The header fields are largely self-explanatory: the `Date:` header contains the date of the response, the `Server:` header indicates the name and version of the web server program, the `Last-Modified:` header indicates the date on which the content being delivered was last modified.

The next four headers are less obvious. The `ETag:` header indicates an *entity tag*, a value associated uniquely with each content object; the entity tag is used to help identify whether an object is a cached copy or the original content.

The `Accept-Ranges:` header indicates if the server allows *acceptable byte ranges*—an option that allows a client to specify that only certain ranges of bytes of the content object be sent, rather than the entire object. If the server does allow them, the value of this field indicates the units by which those ranges are specified; in most cases, the ranges are specified in byte values, offset from the start of the object. This option is useful for situations in which the connection between client and server may be unstable, and the client either needs a certain chunk of data or the client wishes the data to be sent in chunks to reduce overhead associated with corrupted data transfers.

The `Content-Length:` header indicates the length, in bytes, of the content being transferred in the message content body. This header differs from the MIME header of the same name which is an optional header for the message/external-body content type (a MIME type that includes a pointer to an external resource instead of the resource itself). The HTTP version is not required, but RFC 2616 states that the `Content-Length:` header SHOULD be included in any message for which the body length can be determined before sending.

As with the GET message, the `Keep-Alive:` and `Connection:` headers are hop-by-hops options.

The last header is the MIME `Content-Type:` header, indicating in this case that the content is text/html. This means the object body contains text only, and the text is formatted with HTML. Other valid MIME types are available; see http://www.iana.org/assignments/media-types/index.html for details.

The rest of the server's response message contains the HTML-tagged text of the server's root directory (the server typically delivers the content of a file named `index.html` in response to requests for the root document).

12.5   Web Caching and Intermediaries

Early on it was clear that web servers and clients would not always be in direct communication. Even in RFC 1945, the protocol designers acknowledged that some but not all web interactions would be "accomplished via a single connection" between the client and server; three categories of intermediary system have been identified: proxies, gateways, and tunnels. Figure 12–3 shows how a single web intermediary operates.

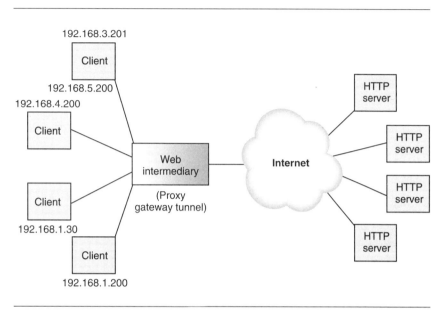

Figure 12–3: Web intermediary system.

As defined in RFC 2616, the proxy acts as a forwarding agent for the client, accepting requests from the client and passing them on (possibly after rewriting some or all of the request) to the destination server. A proxy server operates on behalf of all the clients it serves, so the servers responding to many requests from many different clients would be able to identify only one destination for the responses to those requests: the proxy server. In Figure 11–8, all four client hosts communicate with internet servers through a proxy server (note that IP addresses in this figure are not valid for the public internet; see Chapter 19 for more details on IP addressing).

Every time one of the clients submits a request, the proxy server rewrites the request to make it appear as if it originated from the proxy server. Responses from the internet servers are sent to the proxy server (not the client hosts making the original requests), and the proxy server rewrites the responses to make them appear as if they were sent directly from the servers to the clients.

A gateway acts as a "receiving agent" for the clients, "acting as a layer above some other server(s) and, if necessary, translating the requests to the underlying server's protocol." In other words, the gateway accepts

HTTP requests and responses and translates them to and from TCP/IP and whatever other protocol(s) are being used locally or remotely. The gateway might even translate locally used non-HTTP protocol messages into HTTP protocol messages and back, if the gateway was linking a local or proprietary application with HTTP. In this case, the web intermediary system shown in Figure 12–3 is a protocol gateway, but the architecture is similar to that used with proxy servers. The difference is that in this case, the gateway must do some protocol translation on behalf of the clients.

A tunnel acts as a "relay point" between client and server, making no changes at all to the messages, but rather encapsulating the HTTP exchanges in some other protocol to go through some network obstacle such as a non-IP network or a firewall (see below for more about this approach). For example, an intranet might be linked to the internet through a non-IP network, in which case all IP traffic would be encapsulated within the non-IP network protocol and then forwarded as appropriate as it exits the non-IP network. With a tunnel web intermediary between HTTP client and server, the basic architecture is similar to that shown in Figure 12–3, but packets remain unchanged, being encapsulated as they enter the tunnel and unwrapped as they exit.

All three (or any combination of these) intermediaries may exist between an HTTP client and server, and more may exist to provide cached versions of web content on behalf of the server. Gateways and proxies may maintain cached HTTP data (tunnels cannot do so), and the distinctions among the three are drawn so as to differentiate them for the purpose of certain types of HTTP communications (that are beyond the scope of this discussion).

No internet protocol can achieve any degree of success unless it can scale up to allow hundreds, thousands, or even more users to access it simultaneously. As the web has become more popular, the most popular web sites have attracted so many users that concentrating content on any single network would overwhelm it. As a result, companies such as Akamai, Digital Island, Speedera, Cisco, and Inktomi provide either content delivery network (CDN) services for popular web sites or the tools with which to build private CDNs.

The basic HTTP specification offers some facilities for dealing with content caching—but not quite enough to support global CDNs capable of serving data to the millions of users who visit the busiest web sites. The problem is that a cache may contain data that is accurate but not the latest version, for example, when a news web site updates an article. The remedy in this case is to shorten the data's lifetime within a cache. While that works, it also defeats the purpose of having a CDN, in that all of the web intermediaries serving the data must update more data, more frequently—even if no one wants it. The result is increased bandwidth use.

Content delivery and web content caching have presented a substantial barrier to web scalability over the years. In 1997, RFC 2186, "Internet Cache Protocol (ICP), version 2," was published as an informational document. ICP is a lightweight protocol intended to provide a mechanism for web intermediaries that maintain caches of content to query each other for pointers to the most appropriate source for a particular URL.

ICP relies on UDP as its transport because UDP can be very fast when network conditions are good—and if network conditions are *not* good for communicating with a particular web cache system, then there is nothing to gain from connecting to it (however, TCP is not ruled out as a transport). The protocol was originally developed for use in the Internet Research Task Force resource discovery project, Harvest, and is also used by the popular open source Squid web proxy cache program.

ICP is simple: a host sends out a request for a particular URL; if a host receiving the request has the latest version, it sends back a HIT message (indicating the presence of the URL); if not, it sends a MISS message. There's a bit more, and an introduction to the way ICP is used by web cache hosts is available in RFC 2187, "Application of Internet Cache Protocol (ICP), version 2."

However, ICP was not enough, because it was designed for HTTP 0.9, which did not provide for anything other than the exchange of a URI for a piece of content. HTTP 0.9 makes no provision for the possibility that a single URI might be available from multiple hosts—such as the origination server and any number of possible caches. To fill the void, next came RFC 2756 "Hyper Text Caching Protocol (HTCP/0.0)," defining a more complete but still experimental protocol for "discovering HTTP caches and cached data, managing sets of HTTP caches, and monitoring cache activity."[1]

Another effort to provide a framework for the task was embodied in the Web Replication and Caching Working Group of the IETF. By the end of 2000, the group had made a good start at identifying some of the technical

---

[1]RFC 2756, p 1.

issues related to web caching and built a vocabulary to use while discussing the problems—and the group had also been replaced by the Web Intermediaries (WEBI) Working Group. WEBI takes a more systematic approach to the problem, starting from the very beginning. Its first task is to develop a resource update protocol so that web intermediaries (whether they be caches or other components of a CDN) can easily and quickly determine whether or not their content is synchronized with its source, and whether it should be updated. The next task for WEBI is developing a mechanism by which intermediaries can "discover" other web intermediaries and describe themselves to each other.

Our ability to meet the challenge of managing web replication and web caches in a growing global web will determine how much impact the web will have on our cultural as well as economic lives going forward. Development in this area will continue as well.

12.6   State and Statelessness

As originally specified, HTTP is a stateless protocol. Unlike the mail protocols discussed in Chapter 9, HTTP servers are always in essentially the same state: requests come in, and the server responds to the requests. The server does not maintain "sessions" with clients (beyond keeping the TCP circuit open to avoid the overhead associated with reinitializing that circuit for every object downloaded). Clients are not required to go through any session initiation (again, beyond the TCP circuit setup), or progress through any particular series of commands and responses. If a user clicks on a button on a web page, the server responds by delivering the associated content object. If the user wants to retrieve that same object again, and clicks the same button, the server will deliver the object, again. It is not required to keep track of what the user is doing; in fact, HTTP originally offered no way to do so.

The use of state within a session makes possible many useful functions. For example, if you are going through a registration process, submitting various data to a server (perhaps making a purchase), the server needs to be able to keep track of what you've done, what data are missing, and what data you've submitted. If you are shopping online, it helps to have a *shopping cart* function that allows you to select items and have the server keep track of what you've chosen—even if you leave the site and return another day.

Netscape Communications was the first to add a mechanism to maintain state: the *cookie* was a part of early browsers and allowed servers to store small amounts of data on the client system, and then have the client return that data on subsequent queries. RFC 2965, "HTTP State Management Mechanism," defines a slightly different mechanism from the original one used by Netscape, but the broad outlines are similar:

1. A client requests a resource from a server. Unlike ordinary resources, however, some resources will trigger the server to request the start of a session with the client. Designers of a retail web site, for example, might want to set up sessions with all clients, to keep track of what users are looking at and how they go about making buying decisions. Web sites that provide user interfaces to other systems that require a login procedure also generally require a session be initiated.

2. The server will request that the session be started by asking permission to set a cookie on the client host. The cookie is often an identifier used by the server to link activity to the session user.

3. The client may respond by allowing the cookie to be set, or not. If the cookie is refused, the server will not be able to store state about the session; that doesn't mean the server can't respond to client requests, just that the server won't be able to track those requests and link them together.

    If the cookie is set, then cookie information will be incorporated into the HTTP messages exchanged during the session. The server can then keep track of the activity by storing the data it needs and associating that data with the cookie data stored on the client.

Although many important web functions, especially online transactions, would be difficult or even impossible without some mechanism for maintaining state, cookies offer web publishers a powerful tool for tracking users' activities online. Web ads are placed by a handful of large agencies serving large web publishers; they are able to keep track of what web sites a user visits because each time the user's browser downloads an ad, a cookie is set. This allows the ad agency to make a list of all the web sites a user visits, and what the user does on each site.

Modern web browsers often provide users the option of turning off cookies altogether, or of choosing which cookies to set and which to reject.

12.7   Hypertext Transfer Protocol as Substrate

As recently as 1990, the lowest common denominator of network connectivity was a character-only terminal capable of displaying no more than 80 characters on 25 lines; text-only applications such as internet mail, command-line file transfers, and terminal emulation were dominant on the internet. Most of the earliest internet service providers[2] offered shell accounts on *nix servers connected to the internet. That meant that even if the home personal computer (PC) were running a full TCP/IP network stack with graphical applications (such as NCSA Mosaic, the original graphical web browser) the user would only be able to use that PC as a terminal to connect to the ISP's *nix server—and only use whatever applications were installed on that *nix server.

As processor and memory costs continue to decrease, developers can now reasonably assume that most users will have access to a system capable of running a graphical user interface and an HTTP client. While HTTP was originally intended to serve as a simple interface for end users wishing to browse through sometimes complex hypertext documents, it has become the protocol of choice for many different applications. Although FTP continues to be a popular protocol for file transfers, most of those transfers are initiated through HTTP sessions. Telnet, formerly used as a way for users to access legacy mainframe applications, has been supplanted by middleware that maps those legacy systems to a web interface. Internet mail is frequently available through popular web sites such as Hotmail.com and Yahoo! as well as offered to employees through corporate intranets, rather than directly through a mail client. Maintaining mail services through a web interface allows users to access all their mail from anywhere an HTTP client is available; with standard mail clients, mail and mail-reading preferences are usually stored on a single system.[3]

---

[2] Software Tool and Die's World service, was the first ISP to offer publicly accessible dialup internet access, starting in 1989. World subscribers received a shell account on a UNIX server, through which they could send and receive mail, use network newsgroups, run telnet and ftp sessions with other servers, and other basic command line applications—including web access through ASCII-only web browsers such as lynx. Even after most ISPs had begun offering full connectivity services between home users' PCs and the internet, World subscribers still got nothing more (and nothing less) than a shell account.

[3] Although the Internet Mail Access Protocol (IMAP) allows clients to access the user's mailbox from any system, most providers still prefer to offer Post Office Protocol (POP) services instead. IMAP calls for the provider to maintain storage for all messages to all users using the system; POP users generally download their mail so server storage requirements are lower. IMAP also requires the server provide greater functionality than POP, so servers must not only have more disk storage but must also have more processing power.

Web mail also allows the service provider to maintain reliable backups of all mail.

By the late 1990s, the trend of using HTTP as a *substrate* protocol for many different applications was already apparent. RFC 3205, "On the Use of HTTP as a Substrate," also published as Best Current Practices (BCP) 56, spelled out some of the issues involved in encapsulating application data inside HTTP message exchanges (this is what is meant by using HTTP as a substrate for other applications). Several reasons for this choice are cited in the RFC:

Familiarity: Everyone can be assumed to know how to use an HTTP client (e.g., a web browser), so training costs of rolling out a new application can be minimized.

Compatibility: HTTP-compliant web browsers are available on virtually any platform, from web-enabled telephones to supercomputers.

Reuse: Encapsulating an application within HTTP allows existing servers to be reused for the new application more easily than requiring a new application server to be written.

Ease: Prototyping new application servers is simple, using CGI scripts and other extension mechanisms.

Security: HTTP already has a significant security infrastructure, including widespread client and server support for transport layer security and secure sockets layer protocols for encryption and authentication, as well as the HTTP digest authentication specification spelled out in RFC 2617 "HTTP Authentication: Basic and Digest Access Authentication."

Transparency: Firewalls are usually configured to filter out traffic from applications other than HTTP, which is almost universally allowed in and out of corporate intranets (inasmuch as access to the web provides important benefits to the corporation). A completely new application would normally be assigned its own well-known port, and that port would be blocked by most firewalls. That application would only be accessible to corporate users when (and if) the firewall is reconfigured to permit it. Application developers seeking a broad audience find it much easier to encapsulate their application within

HTTP sessions than to require potential users to petition for changes in corporate security policies.

Convenience: In many cases, the new application server would also be required to support HTTP as well as the new application anyway, for example when a single server provides web and all other application services.

HTTP's transparency to most internet firewalls makes it an ideal vehicle not only for carrying traffic associated with legitimate applications but also for more harmful traffic. This problem was highlighted in the 2001 "April Fool's" RFC 3093, " Firewall Enhancement Protocol (FEP)," which specifies a protocol mechanism for encapsulating any IP packets within HTTP messages, thus bypassing firewall security. Although FEP is presented as a joke, it is a serious joke that makes an important statement about how using HTTP as a transport can easily create security headaches.

Although HTTP is useful for some applications, the protocol has certain characteristics that make it better-suited for some applications than others. For example, applications that communicate with very short messages will likely be hampered by the generally high overhead associated with the use of TCP as a transport layer protocol. Likewise, security requirements may constrain the degree to which HTTP is applicable to an application. Although security issues associated with HTTP and other web protocols have been the focus of considerable effort since the commercialization of the internet in the early 1990s, some applications will be best served with new protocols, while others can be secured satisfactorily using the standard tools associated with the web.

Issues related to choosing HTTP as a substrate include:

- What kind of data interchange does the new application call for? If the exchanges are brief, HTTP may be too "expensive"; however, if there is a sequence of exchanges that can be accomplished using a persistent connection between client and server, then HTTP (with TCP) may be appropriate.
- Does the new application require modification to existing servers and/or clients? If so, the incentive for using HTTP is reduced: if new software is required, it may be easier to design a new protocol than to adapt HTTP.
- What kind of security is required? HTTP security is oriented toward authenticating the server rather than the client.

Most commercial servers (or any server using TLS or other encryption/digital signature oriented protocol) have up-to-date digital certificates that allow client systems to authenticate data from the server. Clients with digital certification are far rarer. If the application calls for client authentication, HTTP may be inappropriate.

- Does HTTP make sense for the application? Audio- or video-conferencing might not fit well into the HTTP model of requests and delivery of data. Mail and other file transfer protocols, on the other hand, make more sense to adapt to HTTP.

Of great concern is the continued use of port 80 for applications that run over HTTP. As noted in RFC 3205, the telnet protocol for transmitting commands and responses was adopted for use as a substrate protocol with both SMTP and FTP, but each of those protocols was given its own well-known ports to differentiate them from telnet. Most applications designed to piggyback over HTTP do so to avoid getting a new well-known port assignment. The author of RFC 3205 recommends the use of new well-known ports for any applications that differ significantly from the familiar web application—not a popular position.

Whether by remapping a text-only terminal application to a GUI browser–based web application, or by creating entirely new protocols that are encapsulated within HTTP messages, the reuse of HTTP for new applications will continue.

12.8   Chapter Summary

Creating web content is only a small part of the web: it is necessary first to be able to identify and differentiate web resources, through URLs. The HTTP provides the mechanism by which content is requested by clients and provided by servers. The content itself must not only conform to the HTML but must be encapsulated within MIME objects for transmission by HTTP.

Although the exchange of web data between client and server seems straightforward, the process may be quite complicated. For example, web caching can improve performance while potentially running the risk of delivering outdated data. While the inherent statelessness of HTTP is often an advantage, it is also an impediment to using the web in the ways that people wish to use it: incorporating cookies, to add statefulness to the protocol, can be an effective (though controversial) solution.

And the ubiquity of the web, with browsers available to almost anyone, makes it a tempting platform on which to piggyback other applications. As we'll see in the next chapter, a new generation of applications that need more than the web can offer are coming down the road; either they will succeed (and perhaps supersede) the web, or they will fail to gather a critical mass of implementations and deployments.

13

Third-Generation
Application Protocols

This chapter introduces third-generation internet applications. Telnet and file transfer protocol (FTP) allowed users to access *resources* on remote systems as easily as they could on local systems; the web and internet message access protocol (IMAP) allowed users to access *data* on remote systems as easily as they could on local systems. The latest wave of new applications allows users to access *applications* as easily on remote systems as on local systems using a combination of protocols.

The eXtensible Markup Language (XML) provides a format for delivering self-describing data, carrying its own context with it. In other words, XML allows content creators as well as developers to produce data objects that can be easily used by any application. If an application receives an XML-formatted message containing data the application can use, that data will be used; if the data is irrelevant, the application can ignore it safely.

The Simple Object Access Protocol (SOAP) is a lightweight protocol designed to allow the exchange of XML-formatted messages between network nodes. Early work on SOAP was conducted within the IETF, but the working group eventually landed at the World Wide Web Consortium (W3C), where it is being developed as a mechanism for delivery of network content and data services. The original SOAP specification did not mandate any particular protocol in which SOAP messages should be carried, but hypertext transfer protocol (HTTP) and RPC seem to be the protocols of choice at this point.

More relevant to TCP/IP is the Blocks Extensible Exchange Protocol (BEEP), which provides a meta-protocol for application protocols. Before BEEP, network designers building a new application had to choose between creating a new application protocol, from scratch, to accommodate the new application, or else somehow try to shoehorn the new application into an existing application protocol.

As discussed in Chapter 12, many new applications have been adapted for use within HTTP. As discussed in Chapter 9, mail submission and delivery are two applications separate from (but similar to) mail transport. All three of those functions have long been handled by a single protocol (simple mail transfer protocol [SMTP])—an appropriate situation when virtually all mail users had accounts on multiuser systems, but less appropriate in modern networks dominated by single user systems.

A third alternative, one that allowed reuse of protocol components to streamline application protocol development, would enable much more flexibility for the developers as well as for users. Looking to the future of internet applications, Marshall Rose, creator of simple network management protocol (SNMP) and other protocols, began work in the late 1990s on a new architecture for specifying new application protocols. Rather than starting from scratch each time a new application protocol is to be created, Rose thought that protocol elements could be designed as building blocks—as long as the application domain is appropriately limited.[1]

---

[1] "An interesting tidbit is the fact that Marshall Rose was an early proponent of open system interconnection (OSI). The OSI application layer architecture describes the application layer as consisting of a set application service elements. . . that are used as building blocks to construct an application. Thus only the specific application elements need to be specified. The rest of the application interactions can be constructed using the standardized ASEs. After his initial enthusiasm for OSI, he proceeded to denounce it as a failure. BEEP appears to be a resurrection of the OSI application layer architecture concept (with a different implementation) within TCP/IP." (from Reviewer #1, Instructor.)

The Blocks Architecture, along with the BEEP was quickly brought into the IETF development process; the first RFCs describing the protocol were published in 2001, as were specifications for applications using BEEP. This chapter examines the new architecture, first to see why it is necessary and then to see how it works (and how it differs from traditional application protocol development) in the context of BEEP-based application protocols.

Another approach to managing multimedia applications is provided by the Session Initiation Protocol (SIP), an application layer control protocol that

> *"...can establish, modify and terminate multimedia sessions or calls. These multimedia sessions include multimedia conferences, distance learning, Internet telephony and similar applications. SIP can invite both persons and "robots", such as a media storage service. SIP can invite parties to both unicast and multicast sessions; the initiator does not necessarily have to be a member of the session to which it is inviting. Media and participants can be added to an existing session."*[2]

These new application layer protocols define interactions between hosts as they carry application data, while at the same time they extract all of the system or software-specific features of the applications. The implications of this approach to applications are serious.

Prior to FTP, file transfers between hosts required direct connections of some sort between systems as well as a knowledge not only of the differences between filesystems of the source and destination hosts but also knowledge of the attributes of the circuit over which the file transfer takes place. With TCP/IP networking, the details of the circuit between hosts become irrelevant; with FTP, the details of the remote host become irrelevant as well.

Before HTTP, users could only access a file stored on a remote system by downloading it to the local system and then opening it with an appropriate application.[3] HTTP freed users from having to deal with local and remote filesystems or even with local applications: click on a web link, and the resource opens.

---

[2]RFC 2543, "SIP: Session Initiation Protocol," p 7.

[3]Or, use a resource-sharing protocol, but that option was far more common on local area networks (LANs) than on the internet, and not usually considered practical over internetworks.

The third-generation application protocols will further simplify matters for end users as well as applications developers. "Universal client" software can be deployed on any type of connected system, and permit any kind of internet interaction.

13.1   Markup Languages

HTML and XML were mentioned briefly in Chapter 12; although both standards are being developed within the W3C, XML is becoming a vital part of many fields of computing and networking. A brief introduction to XML is therefore in order.

First, the concept of markup language should be reviewed. Most documents are *marked up*, meaning that parts of the document are bracketed by *tags* (codes associated with certain attributes) that indicate something about those parts. For example, most word processing documents contain some sort of marking to indicate that the characters that follow the tag should be printed in boldface, and another tag that indicates when to stop using the boldface font.

Most word processing software uses tags to prescribe specific attributes: boldface, underline, font size, spacing between lines, paragraph indentations, and so on. These tell us nothing about the text being tagged: a writer might decide to set the title of one chapter of a book in a 24 point Helvetica boldface font, while the next chapter might be a 28 point italic font. In neither case do the tags tell us anything about the text, beyond how to display or print it.

The Standard Generalized Markup Language (SGML) defined a specification for creating descriptive tags that describe the function of a part of a document rather than how that part should be displayed. This approach frees the writer from having to keep track of what characteristics a chapter title should be given—all the writer needs to know is that a chapter title should be set off by start-chapter-heading and end-chapter-heading tags. Descriptive markup tags can also be used for document "grammar" verification. Certain types of document (such as books) consist of different elements (table of contents, preface, chapters, index, etc.). If the writer, by mistake, puts the preface at the end of the document and the index at the front, structure verification will report errors.

Most important, however, is the separation of content and presentation format by markup languages. A book must be laid out in a certain way when it is printed out on paper, but that format won't be appropriate when the book content is presented in an online format. The same content might be developed for use in several formats: a technical manual might be printed out in its entirety, abstracted for a quick reference guide, made available online through a help system, made available through a fax-back service, or even made available over a telephone interface.

The different output formats are designed to accept standard, marked-up documents and output them as appropriate.

13.1.1   eXtensible Markup Language

SGML is a meta-markup language in that it defines rules for creating markup tags and applying them to documents. HTML is a markup language created using the SGML specifications; XML is another meta-markup language (like SGML).[4]

XML is important because it allows application developers (among others) to create their own sets of markup tags, register them publicly, and deliver self-describing messages. The application developers may also use common XML tags defined by others. XML data can be delivered through web servers, but it can also be delivered through any other protocol capable of exchanging messages. SOAP uses XML to format application data, as do many other protocols.

A good example is provided by applications that allow browser users to store personal data on their local host. One way to store this data is to put it into a simple ASCII file using standard field delimiters such as tabs or commas. Applications that are aware of the format need only read the file and parse it according to the standard rules (the user's name, last name first, followed by first name and initial, followed by street address, and so on). However, many different applications are more likely to create their own "standard" format for this file rather than using a single, shared, file.

With XML, a true standard for personal information can be created, with each data field tagged (e.g., <first_name>Pete</first_name>) so that any

---

[4]So XML and SGML are both meta-markup languages, but at the same time, XML is based on SGML—it is defined as an SGML application. XML is a subset of SGML, at the same time being easier to use and deploy.

application can access a single file and determine the user's name, address, and phone number (if the user agrees to permit it).

13.1.2 SIMPLE OBJECT ACCESS PROTOCOL AND EXTENSIBLE MARKUP LANGUAGE

SOAP was literally created for XML. With XML, *self-describing* messages are possible. Different applications can use the same tags to indicate the same type of data. For example, a stock symbol is a stock symbol, no matter what application needs to use it. A stock quote might normally include, at the least, a stock symbol and a currency value for the stock; other elements might include optional elements that contain the stock trading volume, the date and time of the quote, the size of the most recent trade, and so on.

Full information about XML data element definitions is stored in repositories, where they can be accessed by applications. For example, a SOAP-based stock quote program might accept requests for stock quotes, as long as they include a valid stock trading symbol (required) and any optional parameters (such as a date to get historical data, or a flag to indicate the level of detail desired on current quotes).

A client application might request a series of stock quotes from an internet quote service by specifying the type of request and other parameters to be included with the request. The underlying application might be anything from a desktop stock ticker display for current stock prices, to part of a web page, to a newspaper publishing program for typesetting stock quotes. The application server doesn't need to know what the application is, as long as both server and client can recognize and process the data.

A request for the current price of the XYZ Corporation might look something like this:

```
<SOAP-ENV:Envelope
   xmlns:SOAP-ENV=
``http://schemas.xmlsoap.org/soap/envelope/''
   SOAP-ENV:encodingStyle=
``http://schemas.xmlsoap.org/soap/encoding/''>
   <SOAP-ENV:Body>
     <m:GetLastTradePrice xmlns:m=``Some-URI''>
```

```
        <symbol>XYZ</symbol>
      </m:GetLastTradePrice>
    </SOAP-ENV:Body>
  </SOAP-ENV:Envelope>
```

The meat of this message is in the three most deeply-indented lines: get the last trading price for the stock symbol XYZ. The rest of the message provides information about how to get enough information to comprehend the request and where to direct the request.

SOAP is a simple message protocol, so the response to this request would undoubtedly be an XML message indicating a value (the last trading price for XYZ) and some other other information about the requested data (perhaps the stock symbol, or perhaps more detailed information about the last trade) as well as about the XML message itself.

Although SOAP is usually carried over HTTP, there is no reason it could not be encapsulated in any message-oriented protocol. A specification detailing the use of SOAP over BEEP was approved for publication (but not released) as a proposed standard RFC in February 2002. Microsoft's .NET initiative, as well as other Microsoft projects, is based on XML, as are an increasing portion of the web.

13.1.3 EXTENSIBLE MARKUP LANGUAGE AND OTHER PROTOCOLS

Publishing XML-tagged data takes web content one step beyond the custom displays possible with HTML. While properly marked HTML content can be displayed on any HTML-compliant web browser (whether graphical or text-only), properly marked XML content can be used by applications other than web browsers for display or for further processing. Online news providers can use XML tags to identify their headlines and to create links to those stories—to make those headlines accessible to new applications. For example, a news aggregation program can automatically check an XML-based news site for headlines and search them for user-specified keywords, downloading only those headlines and links likely to be of interest to the user.

At the same time that increasing volumes of web content are published as XML content (or derived from XML content), so too are applications developers using XML as a universal encoding standard. Commands, protocol responses, and virtually any kind of data can be expressed within XML bodies—and decoded by XML-compliant systems. Although not required, XML is strongly recommended for use with applications that use the Blocks architecture.

13.2   Blocks Architecture and BEEP

As Rose explains in RFC 3117, "On the Design of Application Protocols," there is a lot of wasted effort in the creation of new application protocols. There are only a limited number of problems that an application protocol must solve, and each of those problems has only a limited number of valid solutions. To further simplify the issues, Rose (in RFC 3117) limits the domain of applications to those meeting three criteria:

1. The application must be connection-oriented, meaning that there is a concept of a session, in which hosts may exchange a series of requests and replies, and/or exchange sequences of data (as with file transfers). At first, this criterion included only those applications using TCP, but support for the Stream Control Transmission Protocol (SCTP) described in Chapter 18 was in development as of mid-2002.

2. The application must use requests and responses to exchange messages. Rose defines message-oriented applications as those exchanging structured data between loosely coupled systems, and contrasts those applications with tightly coupled applications such as network file system (NFS), in which the exchange of data between client and server is not highly structured but resembles more closely the activity occuring within a system that accesses a local filesystem.

3. The application must permit asynchronous message exchange. The first and second generation of internet applications allow clients to send requests and servers to send responses, but they often don't allow the server to send requests (as would be necessary in a peer-to-peer application). This type of request would be asynchronous by virtue of having requests and responses going in both directions, at the same time. Another type of asynchrony is found in applications that allow a client to submit multiple requests and have the server respond to those requests independently of each other. While clients can submit

multiple requests (through *pipelining*, or sending a sequence of requests without waiting for responses), the servers almost always respond to those requests serially. The ability to respond to multiple requests in parallel is rare in modern applications, and certainly is desirable in some cases.

These criteria exclude many important applications. Domain name system (DNS), for example, is not connection oriented, depending on transmission of a single request and a single response between hosts in most cases. NFS, as noted, is excluded because it requires a tight-coupling between client and server. However, Rose notes that many of the most popular internet applications (the web, FTP, internet mail, telnet) do meet the criteria—and that if this family of protocols has been important in the past, it's a safe bet that these kinds of protocols will continue to be important in the future.

13.2.1 Defining Protocol Components

Whether or not one agrees with that assessment, the Blocks architecture is intriguing because it isolates the pieces of an application protocol that are unique to each application from the pieces of protocol that are more or less constant across applications. As Rose writes in RFC 3117, as much as 90% of an application protocol can be attributed to solving the following problems, with only about 10% attributable to the specific application.

- **framing**, which tells how the beginning and ending of each message is delimited;
- **encoding**, which tells how a message is represented when exchanged;
- **reporting**, which tells how errors are described;
- **asynchrony**, which tells how independent exchanges are handled;
- **authentication**, which tells how the peers at each end of the connection are identified and verified; and
- **privacy**, which tells how the exchanges are protected against third-party interception or modification.

To put it in context, consider how HTTP solves each of these problems. Framing is done by adding a field containing a byte count of the

HTTP message. Encoding is done by putting HTTP messages into MIME-like structures. Error reporting is done with the familiar 3-digit response codes. Asynchrony is achieved in HTTP from the client to server by pipelining requests, and from the server to the client by *chunking* (see Chapter 12). Users are authenticated with a user ID/passphrase login, and privacy is provided through the Transport Layer Security (TLS) protocol (see Chapter 15)

In contrast, SMTP's approach to framing, based on transmission of messages on a line-by-line basis (see section 9.2), is known as *octet-stuffing*. SMTP encodes data using the RFC 2822/822 specification, reports errors with the 3-digit response codes, allows pipelining for client to server asynchrony, and implements authentication with the Simple Authentication and Security Layer (SASL) mechanism described in RFC 2222. Privacy is available through either SASL or TLS.

Rose cites the following relatively limited options available for the problems listed above:

> **Framing:** Three options are discussed, including *octet-stuffing*, which allows data to be sent line by line (as in SMTP) before the size of the data is ascertained; *octet-counting*, which calls for the application to specify message lengths before sending (as in HTTP); and *connection-blasting*, in which the application simply passes raw data through to the network and continues sending until the connection is terminated (as in FTP).
>
> **Encoding:** The method by which data is to be represented within the application protocol. Although there are many options, Rose cites multipurpose internet message extensions (MIME) and RFC 2822/822 as the dominant mechanisms. There are no other alternatives for encoding that are as universally acceptable, and MIME tends to be the preferred encoding protocol because it allows inclusion of virtually any type of data as well as virtually any combination of data files.
>
> **Reporting:** The mechanism for the application to report success or failure, errors, or other system responses. Most internet protocols rely on some form of three-digit response code, usually in combination with a short "human-readable" component.[5]

---

[5]Interestingly, this is another instance of an artificially constrained address space. Although up to 1,000 unique values are available (000 through 999), typical internet application response codes use only four or five, or more rarely, six values for the first

Asynchrony: The method by which an application host can send more than one command at a time, or that both communicating hosts can send commands to each other over a single connection. Three options include *pipelining*, in which a host can send a series of commands without waiting for responses to the first command (as with SMTP); *persistent connections*, in which a single connection is used for multiple transactions (as with HTTP), and *chunking*, in which messages are broken up into two or more pieces and sent separately (as with HTTP).

Authentication: The method by which an application user logs in; generally, SASL is becoming a preferred method, while many applications still rely on the basic transaction of login prompt and userID/passphrase.

Privacy: The method by which application data is kept private from anyone not participating in the application exchange (e.g., eavesdroppers). The TLS protocol provides one mechanism, though it applies only to data while it is "in flight" between hosts, and SASL, which is a simple framework for adding security to applications (see RFC 2222, "Simple Authentication and Security Layer [SASL]").

13.2.2 THE BLOCKS EXTENSIBLE EXCHANGE PROTOCOL CORE

BEEP itself, defined in RFC 3080, "The BEEP Core," specifies a framework within which BEEP-based protocols can operate. A BEEP session begins at the transport layer (we'll return to BEEP in Part Three when we discuss TCP and SCTP), but once the session has been opened, the hosts open a single *channel* (defined as a "binding to a well-defined aspect of the application, such as transport security, user authentication, or data exchange") using BEEP. Through this first channel, other channels will be opened, depending on what the application protocol requires. During the start of every session, the hosts exchange information across this first channel to *tune* the session, or to open additional channels, for example to set up transport security. Once the session is underway, the tuning

---

digit of the code: 1 (or 2) through 5 (or 6) in the first digit of the code. The middle digit often provides an encoding for some aspect of the response, while the last digit is reserved for a specific response value associated with a (possibly) unique human-readable reply message. As a result, some applications are limited to only 10 distinct error codes for certain families of errors. Response categories (middle-digit values) are not cleverly defined, and applications may run out of valid codes. This occured with SMTP, with a remedy defined in RFC 1893, "Enhanced Mail System Status Codes."

channels become dormant, and channels will be used for the real business of the application, including one or more to transfer commands or
data.

BEEP enables asynchrony through channels: either host can open a channel to transmit a request, for example, so that a host may send a request
to a client at the same time that it is responding to a request made by the
client. Likewise, a client may make multiple requests of the server to be
fulfilled in parallel rather than in sequence; the server would respond to
all those requests more or less simultaneously.

Taking the rest of the criteria cited in RFC 3117, we can see how BEEP
solves each one:

> **Framing:** Like HTTP, BEEP adds a byte-count to its header, but
> also indicates message completion by adding a trailer at the end
> of each message. This gives implementations an added method
> of checking messages to determine whether they've arrived
> whole or have been corrupted en route.
>
> **Encoding:** Again, like HTTP, BEEP uses a MIME encoding. Any
> type of data that can be represented in MIME is permitted,
> although text/xml (XML tagged data) is preferred.
>
> **Reporting:** In addition to the standard three-digit response code
> scheme, BEEP specifies whether a response is positive or neg-
> ative so that very simple decisions about "what next" can be
> made without interpreting the response.
>
> **Asynchrony:** BEEP uses channels, which enable asynchronous
> interaction. BEEP encapsulates all channels within a single TCP
> circuit, which allows the application protocol to define what
> kind of data is to flow over each channel, and how it should be
> parsed, using *profiles*. A profile may specify that a channel is to
> be used for authentication, or negotiating an encrypted connec-
> tion, or the channel may be used to transfer commands from
> client to server or data from server to client.
>
> The use of channels can complicate matters at the same time.
> Because only a single TCP circuit is shared by all channels,
> many of the same issues related to flow control and conges-
> tion (to be discussed in detail in Part III) become apparent
> at the application layer. BEEP needs some mechanisms for
> preventing any single channel from adversely affecting per-
> formance of other channels. These issues will be revisited in
> Chapter 18.

Authentication: BEEP uses SASL, with only one user identity allowed per session. In other words, once the user is authenticated, channels may be opened and closed without further authentication. This property makes BEEP appropriate only for applications that require no more than one user identity to be authenticated per session.

Privacy: BEEP uses both SASL and TLS to ensure privacy. Profiles are defined to use either of those specifications within a channel when setting up the session; TLS for transport layer encryption and SASL for adding encryption at the application layer.

Not only does the channel mechanism allow asynchronous protocols, but it provides a mechanism for extensability: adding new features is as simple as adding a new channel and defining an appropriate profile.

13.2.3   WHAT'S LEFT?

Applications developers using the BEEP framework have relatively little left to do:

- Specify a format for application messages. The default encoding type is XML, so the process should be one of defining the data to be used by the application and writing the appropriate XML definitions to support that data.
- Define a naming domain. While authentication and encryption (privacy) are provided by BEEP, authorization (the process of determining what degree of access a user entity has to system resources) requires that the application be associated with some population of entities with names. There is no single such namespace, so BEEP leaves the task of choosing (or creating) that namespace to the application developer.
- Define an authorization mechanism. This task is linked to the namespace, and is also left to the developer.
- Register XML-related structures with the appropriate repository.
- Register a well-known port with the internet assigned numbers authority (IANA), to be used with the application.

That last step may be easier said than done; there is a limited number of well-known ports available. However, in the event that this address space is exhausted, there is additional space available below the transient ports. The next section introduces some of the first applications of the BEEP framework.

13.2.4 HOW DOES BLOCKS EXTENSIBLE EXCHANGE PROTOCOL WORK?

Technically, BEEP is a complete application protocol, in the sense that BEEP hosts exchange data using the BEEP protocol. The process begins once some underlying transport protocol session has already been initiated (e.g., TCP or SCTP) between the two hosts. At that point, the two hosts send each other "greeting" messages; these may be sent simultaneously—the greetings do not follow a request/response form.

There are two forms to referring to BEEP hosts during interactions. First, as *listener* and *initiator*; second, as *client* and *server*. The listener is the host that listens to requests from the initiator; the client is the host that starts a BEEP exchange and the server is the host that responds. Usually, the listener will be the same as the server and the client the same as the initiator, but that is not a requirement of the protocol. Because BEEP is designed to be an asynchronous, peer-to-peer protocol a host may act as a client at one moment and a listener at the next.

Thus, the greeting messages are sent by both hosts (presumably their paths cross en route) at the same time; assuming that both hosts' greetings indicate their readiness to proceed, the first BEEP channel (*channel zero*) is opened. The server's (listener's) greeting includes a list of its supported BEEP profiles.

The BEEP session is now in operation, but with only one channel (zero), which must be used to manage any application channels. The next step is to open one or more application channels. Either peer can send a *start* to open a channel with the other. The start message consists of a channel number and a profile uniform resource identifier (URI). The initiating host always uses odd channel numbers and the listener always uses even numbers to avoid channel number collisions: it wouldn't do to have both hosts attempting to open a channel with the same number but different profiles.

Some profiles may allow hosts to include channel initialization information with the start request, such as data needed to initialize an encrypted session (as with TLS). In any case, these BEEP messages are encoded with XML and sent as MIME elements using the application/beep+xml content-type. Channels, once initialized, are then used (when needed) to exchange application data associated with the channel's profile. When TLS is being used, for example, the requesting host initiates a TLS channel, over which the two peers exchange all the same data that would normally be exchanged by two hosts setting up a TLS session—except that all the TLS data is encoded in XML-tagged MIME elements.

To illustrate, consider an application that required an encrypted session be setup between hosts for the exchange of medical information between physicians and insurance companies. The protocol might be defined to include the following steps:

1. Initiate a BEEP session over TCP.
2. Client requests a channel (channel 1) for setting up encryption using TLS.
3. Client and server initialize an encrypted session with TLS over channel 1.
4. Channel 1 is closed and channel zero re-initialized (standard whenever transport security is reset).
5. Server requests a channel for an application-specific authorization profile (channel 2).
6. Client and server exchange authorization information over channel 2 (allowing the physician to login and the insurer to determine what access the physician is entitled to), and close the channel.
7. Client initiates channel 1 to carry file transfer commands.
8. Server initiates channel 2 to carry the file transfers.
9. And so on...

The application protocol is specified separately from the specification for the protocol over BEEP. This allows application developers to specify sophisticated techniques for things such as authentication, encryption, encoding, and other basic protocol functions by choosing existing profiles instead of having to reinvent those functions.

BEEP also makes it possible to develop simple, inexpensive BEEP boxes–network appliances with support for BEEP. Any network device that supports BEEP will be usable (in theory) for any BEEP application, making the local OS far less important than the BEEP-based applications to be used on those devices.

13.3   BEEP-Based Protocols

Before the BEEP specifications were approved for publication as RFCs on the standards track within the IETF, implementers were using BEEP as the basis for new protocol applications. These applications are defined as BEEP profiles. Like HTTP, BEEP is a protocol that is used to carry other application protocols—but BEEP was designed for the task. Not only are new protocols being developed using BEEP, but existing protocols are also being defined as new BEEP profiles.

Several BEEP profiles have already been developed, and some have even been registered with the IANA, having been approved for publication on the IETF standards track. The rest of this section covers BEEP profile development underway in the IETF, starting with the most mature (based on publication dates). As author of the BEEP framework, Rose has been active in seeking and describing applications that make sense for use in BEEP, and is also an author or co-author of several BEEP-based protocols. Although several of these protocols have already been approved for publication as IETF standards track specifications, others are defined in Internet-Drafts that have already passed their expiration dates.

The rest of this section discusses each of the BEEP profiles listed in Table 13–1. Some of these, including TLS, SASL, and TUNNEL, are defined to be used as part of the BEEP tuning process. In BEEP, application *tuning* occurs before the exchange of any actual application data. *Tuning* is the process of setting up the application channel(s), and a key aspect of BEEP is the way it allows application developers to include existing protocol components to provide authentication, privacy, or other application requirements, as part of the tuning process.

Other profiles, including IDXP and reliable delivery for syslog, define applications that use other profiles (such as TLS and SASL) during their tuning processes. At the same time, profiles are defined for the applications to specify the messages to be exchanged between hosts over their BEEP channels.

The Application Exchange (APEX) specification adds an additional layer of abstraction to internet applications that use it, making possible an entirely new type of application, as we'll see in section 13.4.

Profile	Specification	STD?
TLS	RFC 3080, ``The Blocks Extensible Exchange Protocol Core''	Y
SASL	RFC 3080	Y
syslog	RFC 3195, ``Reliable Delivery for syslog''	N
APEX	RFC XXXX, ``The Application Exchange Core''	Y*
SOAP	RFC XXXX, ``Using SOAP in BEEP''	Y*
IDXP	``The Intrusion Detection Exchange Protocol''	N[†]
xmlrpc-beep	``Using XML-RPC in BEEP''	N[†]
WCIP	``The WCIP Profile''	N[‡]
PDM	``Profile for PDM protocol''	N[‡]
TUNNEL	``The TUNNEL Profile''	N[‡]

* Draft has been accepted for publication but not yet published.
[†] Draft-only; work in progress.
[‡] Draft-only; work in progress (I-D expired).

Table 13–1: BEEP profiles.

13.3.1 TRANSPORT LAYER SECURITY (TLS) PROTOCOL IN BEEP

RFC 3080, defining BEEP, also defines the use of the Transport Layer Protocol (TLS) within a BEEP channel. The specification requires that negotiations be done during the tuning of the BEEP session, and once complete the session is reinitiated with a new exchange of greeting messages between peers.

13.3.2 SIMPLE AUTHENTICATION AND SECURITY LAYER (SASL) IN BEEP

Also defined in RFC 3080 as a basic element of BEEP, the SASL channel permits use of the Simple Authentication and Security Layer protocol within a BEEP channel for authentication or setting up encrypted sessions.

SASL is defined in RFC 2222, "Simple Authentication and Security Layer (SASL)," as a protocol for defining mechanisms that provide authentication support to connection-based application protocols. It provides a generalized interface through which a client can submit login information (or a server can solicit login information from the client), as well as, subsequently, set up digital signature or encryption for the data passing over the connection.

Whereas the TLS in BEEP profile defines a mechanism for using encryption and digital signatures on data at the transport layer, SASL in BEEP defines a mechanism for providing security services at the application layer. Security services at the transport layer can be subverted by an attacker successfully breaking into the system, because inbound messages are decrypted as they pass through the transport layer of the stack. By adding security to the application layer, successful attacks require breaking into the application as well as breaking into the system.

13.3.3   THE TUNNEL PROFILE

Protocol tunneling is the practice of taking data being passed between two entities and encapsulating it within some other protocol for transmission across intermediate systems. One example of tunneling was described in Chapter 12, in which new applications are packaged into HTTP messages. In HTTP tunnels, the application tunneling over HTTP typically uses the same hosts that are acting as web server and client, but other types of tunnels allow hosts to transmit untunneled data to tunnel entry points, and receive data from tunnel exit points.

Security tunnels are often used to provide secure links across the internet, accepting traffic from within an intranet, encrypting it (to keep it private) and sending it through to the tunnel endpoint, at the entry to another intranet, where the data is decrypted (to permit its use locally). This profile is an important part of BEEP because it makes available to applications an important service.

A BEEP TUNNEL allows source and destination hosts to connect through proxy systems. According to a work-in-progress document of the BEEP TUNNEL profile, one use of such a profile would be to provides BEEP applications a path across security firewalls. In that case, the tunnel proxy would sit on the firewall system and accept requests from hosts inside the intranet for tunnels out as well as accept requests from

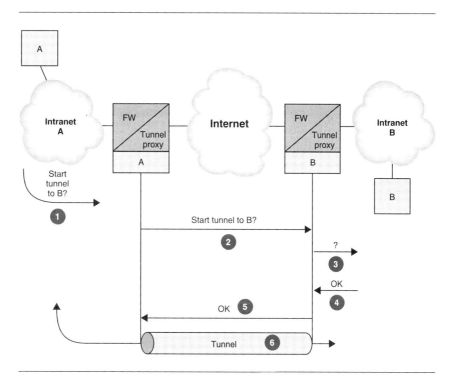

Figure 13–1: BEEP TUNNEL architecture.

hosts outside the intranet for tunnels in. Figure 13–1 shows a typical setup.

Shown here are two hosts, A and B, both supporting the same BEEP application, and both sitting behind firewalls on their respective intranets. In this case, A is requesting that a BEEP TUNNEL be set up between A and B. Because both hosts are behind firewalls they can't simply connect—the firewalls would not allow it—so a tunnel is necessary.

The gist of the conversations among systems in this instance is this:

1. Host A connects to the BEEP TUNNEL proxy running on the local firewall, and then requests that the proxy set up a tunnel between A and B.
2. Proxy A does not answer A, but immediately connects to Proxy B and submits the request to open the tunnel.

3. Proxy B does not answer Proxy A, but immediately connects to B and submits the request for the tunnel.
4. Host B responds to Proxy B, indicating that the tunnel should be set up (if appropriate and authorized).
5. Proxy B now responds not to Host B, but to Proxy A, also indicating that the tunnel should be set up.
6. Proxy A now responds to Host A, indicating the tunnel can be set up.

Now, Hosts A and B can communicate directly; the tunnel proxies serve only to relay data between the two hosts.

The BEEP TUNNEL profile is intended for use during the tuning process, to set up a tunneled connection on behalf of some other application.

13.3.4   THE PASSWORD DERIVED MODULI PROFILE

Another work-in-progress, the Password Derived Moduli (PDM) profile defines the mechanism by which application hosts may authenticate themselves or for securely exchanging encryption keying material. PDM itself is a new mechanism, described by Radia Perlman and Charlie Kaufman in a paper presented at the 10th USENIX Security Symposium, held in Washington DC during August 2001; the PDM profile provides a format by which PDM can be applied to BEEP applications during the tuning process in much the same way that SASL or TLS profiles allow the exchange of messages on behalf of those protocols.

13.3.5   RELIABLE DELIVERY FOR BSD SYSLOG

The BSD syslog protocol has long been used within networks for the reporting and recording of system events that occur on different network-attached devices. Syslog messages use a standard format to describe system events (disk failures, failed logins, etc.). *Devices* are anything on the network to which something might happen of interest to a sysadmin. *Collectors* are the systems to which the devices send their events, and *relays* are systems that may act on behalf of the collectors to accept events from devices and on behalf of the devices to deliver those messages.

As a fairly simple, message-oriented application, syslog has long been implemented with UDP as a transport layer protocol. The sheer volume of events and the overhead associated with TCP sessions that would have to be set up and torn down for each message exchange ruled out using TCP to achieve reliability or even secure syslog exchanges.

Whether or not reliable or secure syslog is desirable, RFC 3195, "Reliable Delivery for syslog," specifies two profiles for using it over BEEP to deliver both security and reliability. RFC 3195 authors Darren New and Marshall Rose clearly acknowledge the possibility that no one really wants secure or reliable syslog; as they write in the abstract, "It is beyond the scope of this memo to argue for, or against, the use of reliable delivery for the syslog protocol."

Two profiles are defined, RAW and COOKED. The RAW profile is easier to implement, mostly being a specification for encapsulating in BEEP messages the same syslog data that would otherwise be sent in UDP datagrams. Using a separate BEEP channel to set up SASL authentication and TLS encryption makes even the RAW profile secure, but the COOKED profile makes possible extensions to the syslog protocol itself. In any case, since it is being encapsulated in BEEP messages–which are transmitted over TCP (or SCTP)—syslog over BEEP provides reliability (see Chapter 17 for more about TCP and reliability).

13.3.6 THE eXTENSIBLE MARKUP LANGUAGE-RPC IN BLOCKS EXTENSIBLE EXCHANGE PROTOCOL PROFILE

Interoperability has always been a key goal for IP networking. One way to attain interoperability is to develop versions of the same applications for all platforms, resulting in versions of telnet for Windows, *nix, Mac OSX, and so on. Another approach is to design an application programming interface (API) that permits programs running on one host to submit a remote procedure call (RPC) to some other host.

The XML-RPC specification defines an XML encoding for remote procedure calls (RPCs), making such interoperability possible. First implemented in 1998, the original intent for XML-RPC was to use XML to encode the RPCs, and to transport the resulting elements over HTTP. The XML-RPC BEEP profile extends the use of XML-RPC to BEEP.

13.3.7 SIMPLE OBJECT ACCESS PROTOCOL IN BLOCKS EXTENSIBLE EXCHANGE PROTOCOL

Most often carried over HTTP, SOAP-based applications require nothing more than some network transport mechanism to move messages between the host requesting a service to the host offering the service. BEEP is likely a better transport mechanism than HTTP, if only because it allows different SOAP applications to specify different BEEP session requirements. A lightweight SOAP service requiring rapid responses rather than reliability or privacy could specify a minimalist BEEP session (no encryption, no authentication), while transaction-oriented SOAP services (credit card approvals, for example) could specify encryption, authentication, and other, application-specific, profiles for BEEP sessions.

SOAP in BEEP makes it possible for existing SOAP in HTTP application to be ported fairly easily to BEEP, at the same time providing a more appropriate protocol for carrying SOAP applications.

13.3.8 THE INTRUSION DETECTION EXCHANGE PROTOCOL PROFILE

As large organizations began connecting to the internet in the 1990s, the *firewall* (a system that filters unwanted internet traffic based on certain characteristics) became an integral part of any corporate security strategy. Entering the 2000s, the *intrusion detection system* (IDS) joined the firewall as a fundamental corporate internet security tool.

An IDS *analyzer* monitors network and system activity, looking for suspicious patterns of behavior that can be correlated to attacks; when such behavior is detected, a message is sent from the analyzer to an IDS *manager*, which provides an interface to the system for human users.

Intrusion detection messages, therefore, represent an important part of an organization's security strategy. An attacker who can successfully forge IDS messages indicating "all is well" will be able to attack with impunity; an attacker who can successfully forge messages that falsely report an attack will be able to probe an organization's security infrastructure to see how the organization responds to different attacks. The attacker may even use forgeries to stage a *denial of service* (DoS) attack, in which the attacker's goal is to prevent authorized use of a system by bringing it down (rather than penetrating it).

Clearly, there is a need for a secured protocol for exchanging intrusion detection-related messages. The Intrusion Detection eXchange Protocol (IDXP) is a work-in-progress defining such a protocol that uses BEEP to tune secure connections between managers and analyzers. IDXP enables the exchange of Intrusion Detection Message Exchange Format (IDMEF) messages, another work-in-progress specification.

In addition to the IDXP profile, the protocol also specifies the use of TLS, SASL, and TUNNEL profiles during the initial tuning process, to provide security as well as permeability to firewalls.

As noted earlier in this chapter, the TUNNEL profile enables hosts to communicate across firewalls. As used with IDXP, TUNNEL makes it possible for managers and analyzers to exchange information through intermediary application proxies. Figure 13–2 illustrates how this works.

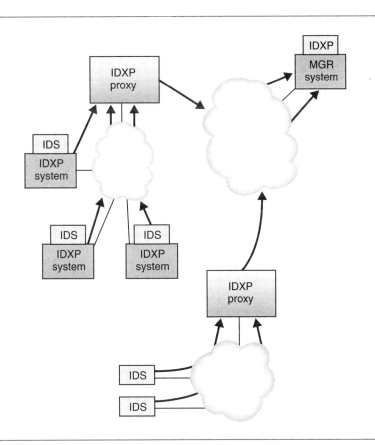

Figure 13–2: BEEP TUNNEL as used with IDXP.

Real-world networks can be big and messy. Distributing any type of network monitor (which is what the analyzers are) across a large network can have a great impact on network performance, particularly if there are any bottlenecks in the internal network. In Figure 13–2, a portion of a typical network is portrayed; tunneling the IDXP application through proxies reduces the need for each IDS to maintain a separate session directly with the MGR system. Individual monitors set up tunnels through the proxies, which are able to concentrate all the separate, tunneled, sessions into a single BEEP session. Overhead related to setting up circuits between every analyzer and the manager system across a large network can be costly, but bundling many sessions into a single BEEP session drastically reduces that cost.

13.4   Application Exchange (APEX)

The APEX protocol is on the IETF standards track, but had not yet been published with an RFC number as of mid-2002. APEX is an "extensible, asynchronous message relaying service for application layer programs" that provides a best-effort datagram service at the application layer. As a result, the application sits all the way at the top of the APEX stack sending out application messages; the messages are wrapped up in BEEP messages, which are in turn wrapped up in TCP frames and sent out over the network.

Why would all that extra encapsulation be useful? APEX makes it possible to create "one-to-many" applications. These are applications in which one entity communicates simultaneously with one or more other entities.

Most internet applications are one-to-one, meaning that there is one client and one server (or to be more accurate, one requesting host and one replying host). File transfers are always between two hosts, one sending the file and the other receiving it; telnet sessions always have one host sending commands and the other sending responses. Although we usually perceive these applications as inherently one-to-one, in large part that format has been forced on users by the choice of transport protocols available: TCP offers reliability and guaranteed delivery, while UDP offers a best-effort datagram delivery service.

While the applications may not be inherently one-to-one, TCP requires no more and no less than two hosts.

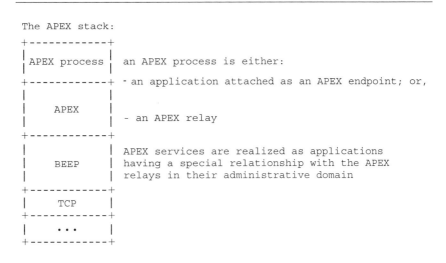

```
The APEX stack:

+------------+
|            |
| APEX process |   an APEX process is either:
|            |
+------------+   - an application attached as an APEX endpoint; or,
|            |
|            |
|    APEX    |
|            |   - an APEX relay
|            |
+------------+
|            |   APEX services are realized as applications
|    BEEP    |   having a special relationship with the APEX
|            |   relays in their administrative domain
|            |
+------------+
|    TCP     |
+------------+
|   ...      |
+------------+
```

Figure 13–3: The APEX protocol stack.

Why not permit a server to transmit a file once, to many different clients? Why not allow a single telnet session on a remote host be shared by an entire class of individual telnet clients? Mostly because TCP could not support the multiple clients, and UDP could not support the connections required to transport data reliably.

Until APEX, such applications could run only over UDP because TCP allows communication between no more and no fewer than two processes. With TCP, the two communicating processes negotiate a connection; UDP has no connection process, providing only a datagram message service: the messages go out, and it is hoped that the recipient(s) receive them. Because multicast requires that transmissions be one-to-many (or even many-to-many), UDP must be used (see Chapter 24 for more details on multicast) and reliability and guaranteed delivery, if needed, must be built into the application itself rather than handled at the transport layer.

APEX provides basically the same type of service that UDP provides (see Chapter 16). Figure 13–3 shows the APEX "stack" as it appears in the APEX core specification.[6] The APEX core itself provides an asynchronous, message-oriented, best-effort delivery service—on top of TCP.

---

[6]Published as draft-ietf-apex-core-06, and approved as of February 2002 to be published as an RFC, pending edits.

In effect, APEX makes possible best-effort application layer networks that operate on top of networked hosts linked through reliable TCP connections. APEX may not be best utilized to create a protocol for multi-client telnet, but it could certainly be used to enable efficient delivery of the same data to many different recipients. Anyone sending data over such an application network could be confident that anyone who receives the data will receive all of it—yet that sender does not necessarily need to specify who those recipients might be ahead of time.

APEX allows the creation of *publish/subscribe* applications, for example, when used with the security and TUNNEL profiles. Publish/subscribe is a form of middleware application in which systems can subscribe to information that other systems publish, without having to be explicitly connected. Before APEX, publish/subscribe middleware was available only in the form of costly cross-platform development tools and programming interfaces. Those products were well worth the costs for the financial institutions who bought them, because publish/subscribe tools enable financial transactions; APEX enables secure and reliable multicast publish/subscribe, enabling publication of financial (or any other) information among three or more hosts.

13.5   Chapter Summary

Early network applications, such as file transfer and remote terminal emulation, provided the means to eliminate the network as an impediment to using remote systems, but users still had to know their way around a *nix (or other multi-user OS) command line. The second generation of applications, represented by the web and IMAP, required less of their users: no longer was direct OS experience required, but the users still had to learn new software applications (browsers or mail readers) that could access the remote data.

The coming generation of applications take the progression a step further, by further and seamlessly integrating the network application into existing non-networked system functions. Part of this trend is the move toward the use of standards for data and meta-data representation, provided by XML.

Another part of the trend is the use of protocols that transport requests for information between whatever entities want or have information. Although a web server may publish some information, when data representation is controlled through XML any type of client can retrieve the data and format it (or use it) in the most appropriate manner.

SOAP offers one approach to seamless interoperability between data consumer and data provider, by packaging requests for data or services within a basic message unit: the HTTP message. BEEP and APEX offer a different approach, in which each network application is developed wholly from a set of basic application protocol components.

The trend in network application protocols over the past decades has been to put more and more of the network into a "black box," a system that accepts requests and magically responds to those requests. With FTP and Telnet, users still must be aware of their own local host and their remote host: how they work, what they do, what files to access. With IMAP and the web, users can access the same content from different hardware platforms and independent of operating system issues. The next chapter examines these trends, along with what the future holds for network applications.

14

Thinking about Internet Application Protocols

So far we've looked at several different protocols in this book. Starting with a simple one, domain name system (DNS), used mostly under cover by systems connected to the internet, we moved on to simple end-user applications such as Telnet, file transfer protocol (FTP), and simple mail transfer protocol (SMTP); then, the web and hypertext transfer protocol (HTTP); and finally the third generation of applications such as those enabled by simple object access protocol (SOAP) and blocks extensible exchange protocol (BEEP). This chapter examines the evolution of internet application protocols over the years, and into the future.

The first applications—telnet, FTP, and the first incarnation of internet mail using SMTP and post office protocol (POP)—vary in complexity and function, but are alike in that they extend what would otherwise be basic system functions across systems and networks. In 1977, most computing was done through terminal sessions; the obvious network application would be to enable users to conduct terminal sessions with all the hosts connected to the network. Likewise, once logged in to a host, the user would normally be able to move, copy, or remove files from some portion of the system's filesystem (depending on the user's authorization). The need for a file transfer network application then becomes obvious: if you can log onto a remote host, you should also be able to manipulate files on that host. Mail, as well, was a common mainframe application, allowing users of the same system to communicate with each other (and, where gateways existed, to communicate with others linked through similar gateways). Internet mail makes it possible for users to communicate with each other from any networked host.

The common thread here is that these first-generation internet applications made accessing data and applications on any host on the internet as easy (or at least, no more difficult) as using the same data and applications when logged into each of those hosts locally. If you could manage a *nix, VAX, or MVS terminal session on a dumb terminal with a direct connection to the mainframe, Telnet made it possible to reproduce that terminal experience across a network. If you could use the local mail on a mainframe or *nix workstation, you could use internet mail on that same system. And if you could copy a file from one local filesystem to another, you could certainly copy a file from a remote filesystem to a local one.

The next generation, with HTTP and hypertext markup language (HTML), made it possible for those lacking command-line interface skills (the ability to issue commands at a bare operating system (OS) prompt, and do what needs to be done) to become productive on the internet. And the latest wave of new applications, based on BEEP, SOAP, and XML, allow developers to take yet another step away from the inner workings of the network protocols and concentrate on building applications that work better.

14.1   File Transfer Protocol, Telnet, and Mail

In the early days of the internet, telnet was a sort of universal connector allowing end users to interact with any computer, anywhere on the internet. However, the nature of telnet ensured that only skillful users could benefit from it: telnet acts as little more than a pipeline for sending commands and receiving the results of those commands to and from remote hosts. If you don't know how to use a computer from its command line interface, telnet offers relatively little benefit.

FTP, like telnet, helps knowledgeable users—the ones comfortable working with filesystems and files—most. Whether used at a command line interface, or with a graphical interface, FTP extends the host operating system to be able to treat remote internet resources (servers, directories, and files) as if they are local resources.

Although telnet and FTP both can be used non-interactively, such as when a process is set up to do unattended batch file transfers, or to automatically log on to a remote server to perform some function, they are usually considered interactive end-user applications. The user sits in front of a keyboard and monitor and enters commands, the client and server exchange data, and the session has a beginning (when the user logs on and/or authenticates herself to the server), a middle (during which the user issues commands or interacts with the server), and an end (when the user logs off or otherwise terminates the session). And both telnet and FTP serve to extend the user's client system OS: the user can run processes on the remote system with telnet, as if issuing commands to a local system, just as FTP allows the user to copy, move, and delete files and other system resources on the server.

Internet mail is different from telnet and FTP in several ways. Mail allows interaction between individuals, rather than systems (although some systems can notify people of specific events by mail); mail allows asynchronous interaction, meaning neither the sender or the recipient of a mail message needs to be online at the same time to communicate. Mail is a store-and-forward application, meaning that intermediate hosts can store messages, to be passed along to their destinations at some later time or date; if a telnet or FTP server is down, there can be no telnet or FTP session.

What these three applications share is this direct link to the client host platform. Internet mail protocols define how mail is packaged, sent, and delivered from one host to another. The tasks of creating messages and receiving them are left to the end-user application developer; ultimately, the internet mail protocols prescribe mechanisms for moving raw data from one system to another—just like telnet and FTP. All three of these applications are fairly simple, or at least straightforward in concept, and all three leave most of the complexity of dealing with the data being transferred to the people using them.

14.2   Gopher, the Web, Internet Access Message Protocol, and Instant Messaging

By the late 1980s, internet use was growing beyond the borders of the research/academic communities as students and faculty outside the engineering and computer science departments began using it. Network staffs were overwhelmed by the task of teaching all those new users about operating system functions and *nix shell accounts; a new protocol that could be used easily and intuitively, without significant computer skills, was needed. The Gopher protocol (see RFC 1436, "The Internet Gopher Protocol (a distributed document search and retrieval protocol)") defined an application that was more user-friendly than telnet or FTP, but that still fell short of HTTP's adaptability and extensibility.

Briefly, Gopher servers provided access either to one or more menus or to documents. The menus provided a hierarchical and reasonably accessible tool that end users used to search for and retrieve those documents (which might actually be programs, or multimedia files, or even telnet sessions with mainframe systems). To a great extent, Gopher interfaced to public FTP file archives and offered a front-end for retrieving files from those archives. Although helpful, Gopher merely stitched together existing protocols.

Although Gopher was better than nothing, users found it lacking. The menu-driven structure ensured that novices could navigate Gopher-space, but it also hobbled more expert users who knew exactly what they wanted but were still bound to the menus. Offering no basic format for display of data beyond plain text, users still had to download (often quite large) data files before they could tell whether or not the file contained what they wanted.

However, Gopher was doomed to fail for the same reasons users prefer graphical client/server applications running on PCs to menu-driven applications running over a terminal session to a mainframe: slow and clunky, it lacked a truly intuitive interface. Graphical interfaces are preferred because they allow users to quickly make decisions based on a glance, while text-based interfaces mean the user must read through—and comprehend—*all* the options before a choice can be made.

The web made Gopher obsolete almost immediately. Unlike Gopher, HTTP uses a standard format, based on multipurpose internet message extensions (MIME), for transmission of any type of data. HTTP's use of HTML meant that publishers could easily create graphical content that was truly platform-independent.[1] Before the web, developers wishing to offer internet access to resources with a graphical interface had to program a separate client/server application for every OS platform: DOS, Windows, Macintosh, *nix, and any other OS deemed worthy. After the web, a few simple HTML tags made it possible for anyone with an HTTP client to click a button and access the same resource.

Web protocols allow developers to make not only the internet but also the operating system transparent to the end user; Gopher merely put a menu-driven interface on top of the existing applications that offered an interface to the OS. Even though the original applications (FTP, telnet, mail) made the internet transparent to the end user, they still required considerable skill in using the local host operating system. The web makes the local OS irrelevant, at least to the end-user.

The other key element in the web's success is its immediacy. The web allows transfer of any type of data, and if the client host can output the data, it can output it automatically. With Gopher, you could download audio files from an archive, but you still needed to start up an audio file player, outside the Gopher session, to listen. With the web, audio plays automatically and instantaneously (more or less, anyway)—bypassing the complexity of executing a command to start an audio player, load a file (from some filesystem), and start playing it.

Although we lumped the internet mail application in with other first-generation internet applications such as FTP and telnet, but in truth, IMAP should be differentiated from SMTP- and POP-based internet mail. SMTP and POP make the internet itself transparent, but still require the user to interact with his local OS to make sense of the mail. IMAP makes the local OS irrelevant by allowing access to mail and mail directories that are stored on a central repository, within a server. An IMAP mail user might access her mail from a laptop running Eudora over Windows, from a Palm Pilot, from a web kiosk in an airport, or from a Linux system using pine.

Interactive text-based communication between people has also become a key second-generation application, augmenting the function fulfilled by

---

[1] At least in theory. In practice, content producers quickly learned ways of making their content unintelligable to text-only users and to users of particular browsers or particular OSs. The eXtensible Markup Language (XML) promises to enable true platform-independence, eventually.

internet mail. Multi-user systems often provided a *talk* function, permitting terminal-based users to send short messages to another user's terminal. Perhaps not too useful if all users work in the same room, but these programs allowed individuals to communicate across hallways, down stairs, or even across buildings.[2]

Internet mail is still one of the most important internet applications, but by the late 1990s proprietary *instant messaging* applications offered by America Online and Microsoft were quickly gaining ground. In many ways identical to the early talk programs, these applications allow users to interact with other users in real-time over the internet, rather than asynchronously as with mail. With one user's (let's call her Alice) unique identifier (within a particular application domain), another user (in the same domain; we'll call him Bob) can check to see if Alice is online and accepting messages. If so, the two can exchange messages directly; if not, Bob might send Alice a mail message asking her to contact him.

Published early in 2000, RFC 2778, "A Model for Presence and Instant Messaging," and RFC 2779, "Instant Messaging/Presence Protocol Requirements," laid the groundwork for the IETF to begin work on developing open standards for instant messaging. Although owners of dominant proprietary systems have been resisting the opening up of internet presence protocols, work continues with more or less wholehearted cooperation from all players.

14.3   Beyond Interactivity

If the second wave of applications offered users more opportunity to interact with each other as well as with internet resources, users were still fairly passive participants in the process. Users are able to access a database only if some programmer implements a web interface to it. Even dynamic web data, which changes as the underlying systems incorporate new data, limits the user to whatever the content designers and programmers choose to offer—and to using some kind of device or system that will access the web.

---

[2]Internet relay chat (IRC) provides a similar case of "nothing new under the sun." IRC makes possible *chat rooms* online, with access wide open. Discussions among many individuals, often anonymous individuals, are similar to those offered within the bulletin board systems (BBSs) of the 1970s and 1980s.

The development of internet applications tracks the development of computer applications. At first, programmers controlled systems directly, through machine language, often entering programs directly to the hardware by flicking switches. Among the first computer applications were programs that allowed programmers to enter encoded instructions with names rather than binary representations and other user-friendly features such as named variables. As computers proliferated and more and more people had to program them, more features were added: programming languages performed more and more of the interaction between user and system.

These developments parallel the introduction of early proprietary network end-user applications, such as local area network (LAN) resource sharing. Users could safely ignore what was going on at the hardware level, and work productively. Once the hardware and software development environments could be separated, programmers could concentrate on software.

Eventually, with easier-to-use languages available on different hardware platforms, programmers could use their programming skills on many different platforms rather than just one: a development akin to the introduction of open standards for networking. Improved interoperability meant that companies could often continue to use the same programs even when the hardware was upgraded, programmers could be more productive over time, and programs could be adapted for use on many different platforms more easily.

Internet applications such as telnet and FTP provided a similar improvement in interoperability, allowing those with certain skills to apply those skills on a wide range of systems and across many systems and networks all at once. For both computing and networking, the next step would be to simplify applications to the extent that end users without programming or system administration skills could easily work productively. In both cases, that step required use of the graphical user interface (GUI).

Text-based systems allow only two modes of operation: menu-driven and command-driven. End-user applications on mainframes almost always rely on menus, listing all the options and allowing the user to pick one by pressing a particular key. Users face an endless round of either re-reading menus every time they use the program to choose the correct options, or else learning sequences of menu options and waiting as every menu and submenu is redisplayed. Command-driven systems usually depend on a command-line interface (CLI) with a *prompt* to indicate that the system is ready for commands. Expert users prefer these to menu-driven systems because they are much faster—if you know what you are doing.

GUIs provide a third, graphical, alternative. Users can see what happens to their documents as soon as they make a change, rather than waiting for a printed version to be output; users can choose options based on icons that look (more or less) like the functions they perform, rather than searching menus for an appropriate option. Most importantly, users need not be concerned about mundane tasks like command grammar and syntax when the system can more easily handle them. Operating systems such as the Macintosh OS, Windows, and the X Window system, allowed creation of applications through which end users could more easily interact with their data—just as the internet allowed creation of network applications through which end users can more easily interact with networked systems.

There is still a tendency to rely on menus and commands, both online and off: early GUI desktop applications often did nothing more than translate ASCII menus into more visually pleasing menus; just as many (if not most) web sites still rely on menu-like structures to some degree. However, in both cases the user is screened more completely than ever before from the dirty work of the hardware and network.

The next step, as evidenced by development of protocols such as XML, SOAP, and BEEP, is to continue making the internet (and any other network) invisible to the end user of whatever product uses that transport. Electricity and telephone connectivity provide two models for the future internet application. Anyone can use an electric appliance or telephone without knowing anything about the underlying networks, how the voice signals are transmitted, how the electrons are delivered to the electric outlet, or anything else beyond how to work the buttons on the telephone or washing machine or video cassette recorder. The less is required of the end user, the closer we'll move to applications that use an *internet dialtone*. There will be an assumption that any connectible device will be connected; the user won't have to use a particular OS, browser, or type of connection. Using this dialtone, BEEP can be used to develop applications for remote control of heating systems by pager, for example, or SOAP for online trading through a pay telephone or even a television remote control unit.

14.4   Chapter Summary

Internet and related protocols are always evolving; the successful ones are developing useful features and growing in popularity, the unsuccessful ones will eventually wither and die. The earlier applications operated much closer to the bare metal of systems (metaphorically speaking, at least) by providing a means only of making the network connection transparent to the skilled user. As the protocols continue to develop, we will increasingly see a disconnect between the applications themselves and the protocols that operate at the lower layers.

This disconnect is already apparent in the way in which important internet applications, from web site design to digital commerce applications, can be created and maintained with little knowledge of the deeper protocols concerning transport and network functions. The telecommunications industry deploys vast networks, but the protocols that define those networks are of little or no concern to most of the people who work with telephone equipment.

Part III brings us, finally, to these lower layers as it introduces the transport layer.

Part Three

Transport Protocols

15

The Transport Layer

The transport layer lies between the applications layer, where real data is entered or viewed by a user, and the network layer, where IP routes the traffic from its source to its destination. It is at the transport layer that information from the application layer is packaged and routed from one process to another. The application layer enables interaction between a flesh-and-blood user and a mainframe computer. The transport layer enables interaction between the user's terminal emulation client program and the mainframe's terminal emulation server program, as well as interaction between a Web browser and Web server.

This chapter elaborates on the need for a transport layer, as well as the mechanisms common to transport layer protocols and how they are used. Topics covered include:

- Processes and ports
- Port addressing
- Reliable delivery
- Ordered delivery
- Acknowledged delivery

- Message size
- Synchronization (virtual circuit or message service)
- Flow control and congestion
- Multiple processes
- Transport layer protocols (UDP, TCP, SCTP)
- Other transport layer protocols (SSH, TLS)

The transport layer provides an interface not only between processes, but also an interface between the application layer and the internet layer. It is at the transport layer that recognizable data from the application layer is packaged for transmission over the internet. Until quite recently, all internet traffic used either user datagram protocol (UDP) or transmission control protocol (TCP). UDP was easy but unreliable, TCP more complicated but more reliable and more appropriate for most data transfer applications. With publication of RFC 2960 documenting stream control transmission protocol (SCTP), a third option was made available in 2000. This chapter introduces the transport layer functions that these three transport layer protocols provide (or don't provide) and concludes with a special section on transport layer security protocols.

15.1   Problem Statement

Without a transport layer protocol, application protocols would interface directly with the internet layer protocol being used. The implications of such a setup are considerable. For instance, the task of determining what should be done with the data in any given packet, once it arrives at its destination, would have to be added either to the application layer or the internet layer protocol being used. As has been mentioned, the Internet Protocol (IP) delivers packets to a network interface; essentially, it drops the packet off at the destination host's network connection.

Once the host receives a packet, it must do something with it. IP has no facilities for doing anything but pass the packet's payload up the stack[1]; internet application protocols have no facilities for accepting data from

---

[1] As will be discussed in Chapter 20, IP packets include a header for "next layer protocol." This value currently indicates what transport layer protocol is being used, but could (at least in theory) be used to indicate what application protocol is being used.

the internet layer. Lacking a transport layer protocol, the application pro-tocols would have to include mechanisms for the application to accept data from the internet layer. Likewise, the application protocols would have to include mechanisms for packaging data to be sent to the internet layer protocol. Even that might not be enough to allow more than one application to accept inbound network data simultaneously.

At the internet layer, packets are delivered to destination hosts. If the destination host is a single-user and single-processing system, in which only one process can run at a time, then a transport layer protocol might not be necessary: whatever process is running at any given time is the only one running, so there is no question of what to do with inbound data. However, most modern systems support both multiple users and multiple processes concurrently, so there must be some mechanism by which inbound data can be linked with a process on a host.

Services that a transport layer protocol can provide touch on a number of issues:

> **Data Delivery:** IP is a best-effort delivery protocol, meaning there are no guarantees that packets will be delivered if they encoun-ter problems along the way to their destinations. Packets might be delivered out of order, or there might be a delay between delivery of packets. An application that is very sensitive to deliv-ery issues may fail if packets arrive out of order, and may time out if data doesn't arrive quickly enough.
>
> It is inappropriate to address delivery issues (such as order of delivery) at the internet layer because doing so places too much burden on routers, which must quickly process packets and route them correctly; addressing the issue at the applica-tion layer is possible, though it requires significant tinkering with applications to add transport layer function. The trans-port layer has long been considered appropriate for these tasks.
>
> **Acknowledgment of Receipt:** Does the sender need to be noti-fied that data has been delivered? What happens if the same data is delivered more than once? What happens when the data takes longer to receive than was anticipated? Applications often need to be notified that data has been received, but the pro-cess by which data receipt is acknowledged is irrelevant; again, the transport layer provides an appropriate home for this task,

particularly in conjunction with the issues of delivery order and
delivery delays.

Connection Orientation: Does the application call for connections between hosts (such as are used to link telephone callers)?
Can the application perform adequately without any connections? Most application protocols do not mandate particular
transport layer protocols. There are cases of connection-oriented
applications using a datagram (best-effort and messge-oriented)
transport protocol (e.g., TFTP and NFS), as well as cases
of message-oriented applications using a connection-oriented
transport protocol (e.g., any instance of an application that
requires the use of encryption at the IP layer with IPsec, as
described in Chapter 26). However, just because something
is possible does not always make it worthwhile: in general,
message-oriented application protocols work better with connectionless transport layer protocols and connection-oriented
applications work best with connection-oriented transport layer
protocols.

Reliability: Do communicating hosts need mechanisms by which
they can confirm that their transmissions are being received?
Do they need mechanisms by which they can determine that
their transmissions are *not* being received? The aggregation
of data delivery reliability, acknowledgment, and message
or connection-orientation determine the degree to which a
transport layer protocol can offer reliability to application
protocols.

Message Framing: Can the application send messages/data of
any size? Some applications require transmission of arbitrary
flows of data (e.g., very large file transfers, audio/video transmissions, terminal sessions). How does a host know when a
transmission is complete? The application protocol does not
usually concern itself with issues of formatting or framing
data for network transmission, but that task must be done.
The transport layer should offer mechanisms allowing the
host receiving data to properly identify the boundaries of that
data.

Control: How fast should a host send data? Some systems can
be overwhelmed by incoming data, while others may be idle
while awaiting transmissions. Is there a way for hosts to
request senders to either speed up or throttle back on data
transmission?

Congestion: Packets en route from source to destination may encounter *congestion*, meaning that some intermediate system is delaying delivery. How can an application cope when it encounters congestion?

Multiprocessing: When more than one process on a host is accepting data from the same network interface, there must be some mechanism by which the inbound packets can be passed along to the appropriate processes.

Two transport layer protocols, one minimalist and the other full-featured, have been sufficient to serve all IP networking needs through the end of the 20th century: The UDP provides a bare minimum, best-effort, message-oriented transport mechanism, while the TCP offers a connection-oriented, reliable, guaranteed delivery service capable of adapting to network congestion and end-point delays.

However, in October 2000 the SCTP joined UDP and TCP as a standards-track transport protocol. Capable of offering a different combination of features than either of the two older protocols, SCTP provides both greater flexibility than either.

The Transport Layer Security (TLS) and Secure Shell (SSH) protocols are not necessarily transport protocols in the same league as UDP, TCP, or SCTP, but because they operate conceptually just below the application layer they will be discussed briefly in this chapter.

15.2   Transport Layer Components

The transport layer links application layer entities with internet layer entities: the applications don't need much information about the structure of the network over which they operate, and application data is just part of the payload to be transported in packets over the internet. The transport layer offers a mechanism to interface between the application and internet layers, and as such it interacts more directly with applications and the internet layer of the protocol stack than might be inferred from the reference models discussed in Chapter 5.

Transport layer protocols use a system for addressing the instances of programs running within a system (already introduced in Chapters 3 and 7);

some transport layer protocols use the concepts of circuit, connection, and data channel, and servers use special programs to "listen" at the transport layer for requests from clients for services.

15.2.1 PROCESSES AND PORTS

Already discussed at some length in Chapters 5 and 7, the network of *processes* running in a computer uses an address space consisting of *ports*. These constructs allow a host to send and receive data on behalf of many processes, all through a single network interface.

A process is the instance of a program running on a system. The same program may have two or more instances running on a system at the same time. For example, a multiuser system might have three users all running a Telnet client, to connect to several different remote hosts. A single user might have two or more Telnet client instances running, to connect to different hosts (or to have different sessions on one remote host). Each of these instances of telnet is assigned a process number. In this way, five telnet sessions initiated by users of a single host can be carried on concurrently: all of the packets from server to client host will be sent to the same IP address, but the telnet server will send session A packets to the port assigned to session A, session B packets to the port assigned to session B, and so on.

The combination of a port and an IP address is enough to specify the exact source or destination of a piece of network information: a single host may accept data from many different sources and for many different applications, all at the same time, through this mechanism. When you put together a source port/IP address with a destination port/IP address, you've fully specified the connection between communicating processes: a circuit.

Transport layer protocols identify source and destination processes in much the same way that a suite or apartment number identifies where to deliver a piece of mail within a building, even though all tenants of the same building share the same street address. The systems on which those processes are running are specified by the lower layer protocols, and once you arrive at the transport layer it is no longer possible to identify in any way the source or destination systems simply by looking at the protocol headers.

Hosts that offer services to other hosts "listen" to certain ports for service requests. When an unexpected message is received on certain ports, the message will be relayed to a special process associated with that port. These processes are known as *daemons* because when they receive a request they spawn off a new process to handle the request and then go back to listening for more requests.

TCP, UDP, and SCTP use port numbers in a 16-bit address space. Any value, from 0 through 65535, is valid (however, port 0 is reserved, and is used to indicate that a transient port is requested). Port numbers are divided into three ranges: *Well Known Ports*, *Registered Ports*, and *Dynamic Ports* (also known as *Private Ports*). As a reminder, internet assigned numbers authority (IANA) specifies the following ranges for port types:

```
Well Known Ports:              0 through 1023

Registered Ports:              1024 through 49151

Dynamic and/or
Private Ports:                 49152 through 65535
```

Two other types of port are often referred to interchangeably: *ephemeral ports* and *transient ports*. Even among experts there is some confusion over the precise status and boundaries of these different types of port.

Well-known: Well-known ports, defined by the IANA, refer to ports that are assigned by the IANA and that, "on most systems can only be used by system (or root) processes or by programs executed by privileged users."[2] These ports are intended to be used as *contact ports* for well-known services, and are a de facto mechanism by which inbound messages are passed to applications.

Registered: The IANA lists registered ports but does not assign them; the listing is provided as a convenience for the community. Registered ports may (again, "on most systems" per the IANA) be used by ordinary users or processes, and registered ports are registered for use by particular services as contact ports for those services.

Dynamic/Private: There are no restrictions on the use of these ports. They may be used for any purpose, including contact ports for services that are not registered with or assigned by the IANA as well as for other purposes.

---

[2]See IANA web site, at http://www.iana.org/assignments/port-numbers, as of mid 2002.

Ephemeral/Transient: As their names imply, these ports are used as needed but are not retained from session to session. When hosts connect to well-known services, they assign themselves a transient port on which to listen for responses from the server. Likewise, once a well-known service session is requested, a server may transfer the session to a non–well-known port.

The RFCs say relatively little (or nothing) about ephemeral, transient, or even dynamic ports: many implementations relied on a passage in Richard Stevens' seminal *TCP/IP Illustrated, volume 1,* in which the range for ephemeral ports was given as being between 1024 and 5000; the 5000 turned out to be a typo. The actual value intended was 50000. As a result, many implementations still use the range 1024 to 5000 for ephemeral ports.

The IETF, through the IANA, created the range for dynamic ports (49152 through 65535) some time prior to 1999; as of 1994, all ports were either well-known (0 - 1023) or registerable (1024 - 65535).

Further confusing matters, some implementers have used any port value (from 0 through 65535) for ephemeral port assignment. Their reasoning is that a host requesting services from some host will likely not be offering the same service back to that host. For example, a host could (in theory) wind up accepting incoming data on port 23 during an FTP session (if that was the number the system chose to assign as a transient port for the transfer)—the same port that a telnet server listens for inbound requests. Depending on the configuration of any intermediate firewalls, which may restrict delivery of packets sent to well-known ports inside an intranet, the application would likely fail when inbound packets are blocked. However, most modern implementations no longer allow transient ports less than 1024 to avoid security vulnerabilities related to such practices.

In short, if you are building a TCP/IP stack, you should check current best practices for port selection. However, application implementers need only specify port 0 when they require a transient port.

15.2.2 CIRCUITS AND CONNECTIONS

A connectionless protocol such as UDP needs only a port number and an IP destination address to operate, because UDP does little more than bind an address for a process (the port) on a host to the host's IP address. The combination of port and IP address is also known as a *socket*; a *socket pair* consists of two sockets: one for a source host and one for a destination host. A socket pair completely identifies a *connection* between two processes. If the processes coexist on the same host then the source and destination host addresses would be identical, but the port numbers would be different (pointing to two different processes). If the two processes are on different hosts with different IP addresses, they could conceivably use the same port number. In either case, there would still be no way for transport layer protocol PDUs (protocol data units) intended for that connection to be confused.

When data flows in only one direction, there would be only one connection: from host address A, port a; to host address B, port b. When data flows both ways, however, there must be two connections: one from A to B, and another from B to A. The socket pair implies both flows, making it a *duplexed* connection, meaning data flows in both directions (at the same time—as we'll see in Chapter 17).

As a connectionless protocol, UDP can be used when it is necessary to send data out even if the destination is not known. For example, protocols specifying discovery mechanisms provide techniques for hosts to, in effect, yell out "Are there any local hosts offering service *foo*[3] here?" with any foo servers responding by indicating their presence. Lacking a known destination, UDP allows the request to be sent out to a broadcast or multicast address. Circuit-oriented protocols require a destination address as well as a destination port—which explains, in part, the need for well-known ports (they permit hosts to make an initial contact with a server).

15.2.3 Daemons

A server *daemon* listens for traffic coming in on the well-known ports assigned to that service. When a client initiates an interaction, the daemon assigns an ephemeral port to that client. In this way, the daemon can continue listening to the well-known port for new sessions, even new sessions from the same host. Interaction between the client and server is conducted using the ephemeral port rather than the well-known port. It is the computer equivalent to meeting someone in front of the big statue in the park and then going off to a coffee shop to continue a meeting.

---

[3]A *metasyntactic variable*, *foo* is used a word to stand in for some other, unspecified word. Foo, along with *bar*, *baz*, *foobar*, and others serves a function similar to the terms *Joe Sixpack*, *Joe User*, *Company XYZ*, and *Plan B*.

For example, web servers are most frequently implemented in the form of HTTP daemons, usually named *httpd*, the final "d" indicating that the program is a daemon. The daemon itself "listens" to the well-known port with which the service is associated, and when a request is made to open a transport layer session using port 80 (the HTTP well-known port) the daemon responds.

In the absence of a daemon process, the alternative is to design the web server program to respond to each request on port 80 directly. In other words, there is a single instance of the HTTP server running on the server system and that instance of the program handles all HTTP sessions. This approach does not scale well because it requires the server software to cope with multiple simultaneous sessions—the more requests for service there are, the more likely that the performance of the server in every session will suffer.

The daemon approach avoids this problem by separating the function of responding to initial requests from the function of exchanging data in response to requests from an established session. The daemon immediately refers the client to a different port, while continuing to monitor new requests on port 80. The web session is managed on a the server side by a new process that was created (instantiated) specifically to deal with that particular session.

Daemons are mostly used for connection-oriented applications that run over TCP; UDP-based applications, which usually depend on the exchange of messages with no need for an ongoing connection, can also do without a daemon. In a fraction of the time it takes to spawn a new process and set up a connection with a client, a UDP-based application server can respond to a request with its reply.

15.3   Reliability, Congestion, and Flow Control

Best-effort datagram protocols such as IP and UDP make no promises to upper-layer protocols. They send messages; if the message gets through, fine, and if the message doesn't get through, that's also fine. Application protocols could and sometimes do incorporate mechanisms for verifying that data sent was received, that data was received in the proper order and that data was received without any corruption introduced en route. Likewise, mechanisms can be applied at the application layer to allow hosts to modulate the rate at which data is sent, or even how the data is packaged for transmission. However, applying these mechanisms at the application layer can result in chaos when two or more applications compete for system and network resources. Not only does it increase the difficulty with which applications can coexist on one system, it increases the complexity of each application protocol.

Conventional wisdom has long held that it is much simpler to apply these functions at the transport layer, where the network stack can balance the needs of all applications running on the host, and where each function need be implemented only once. However, this is not always the case: there are congestion-aware applications that require some form of congestion management but which must use a low-overhead transport layer protocol to avoid performance issues. Detecting congestion at the internet layer (or even lower) might also be useful. Work on the Congestion Manager (CM) and DCP will continue as the need to reduce congestion also continues.

To a great extent, any discussion of transport layer protocols in general turns into a comparison of UDP and TCP. UDP offers nothing more than a pass-through binding of ports to IP addresses, while TCP offers the full range of transport layer services. The situation is a bit more complex than that, but for our purposes here, the UDP vs TCP scenario will suffice.

15.3.1 DATA PACKING

UDP datagrams include a 16-bit message size field to carry the message (plus header) length in bytes; the maximum UDP datagram size is, therefore, 65,535 bytes. The header itself takes up 8 bytes, so the maximum payload size is 65,527 bytes. In practice, most UDP datagrams are considerably smaller (see Chapter 19 for more about IP packet fragmentation), so clearly, UDP is not a good choice for transporting very large messages. However, if you can fit all of your message into a relatively small package, UDP makes sense because the receiving host only needs to read the message length field and then calculate when that many bytes have been received to determine where the UDP datagram ends.

TCP, on the other hand, sends bytes. Streams of bytes. This makes TCP a good choice for sending streams of data, especially when the precise data length could not be calculated ahead of time (e.g., interactive sessions, or downloading files as streams of data). As a byte-stream protocol, TCP imposes no limits on how the data is to be packaged for sending or receiving. In other words, the sending host's TCP might package data up in chunks of 5,000 bytes, but the receiving hosts's TCP might read data in from TCP segments 100 bytes at a time.

One advantage of byte-streaming is that there are no restrictions on the amount of data that can be sent in one stream. Another is that the data can be handled in the most efficient ways for both sender and recipient.

15.3.2 DELIVERY GUARANTEES

Best-effort protocols offer no guarantees, other than that they will attempt to deliver datagrams. Neither IP nor UDP offers a guarantee that a datagram will be delivered. They offer no mechanism for a recipient to indicate that a datagram has been received, either.

TCP, on the other hand, specifies that every byte sent over a connection be acknowledged (ACK'ed) by the recipient. If some part of a data stream is lost, the sender will resend it.

TCP provides other mechanisms for guaranteeing the connection between two hosts, including a very conservative approach to setting up the connection, a two-step process for terminating a connection, and mechanisms for resending data and for receiving it in the correct order.

15.3.3 CONGESTION AND FLOW CONTROL

Data flows along networks, sometimes faster and sometimes slower. Datagram protocols don't usually specify any mechanisms for controlling the rate at which hosts exchange data, mostly because datagram protocols tend to be used for best-effort, message-oriented connectionless deliveries. Unfortunately, the internet layer is where a significant portion of internet *congestion* (situations in which the amount of network traffic is sufficient to cause slowdowns or failures in the delivery of packets) occurs. IP offers little help in dealing with congestion for various reasons (see Chapters 17 and 25), and applications would not normally be expected to deal with network congestion without additional information passed to them from lower layers.

Flow control, as performed by TCP, uses a *sliding window* mechanism, allowing sender and recipient to exchange information about how many bytes per segment they can process comfortably. Other mechanisms are available to signal senders that they should change the rate at which they transmit data. TCP specifies the use of four different timers to keep track of when data is sent, received, and acknowledged, so that transmission can be optimized for the most amount of data to be sent and received most quickly and in the largest chunks (yet not so large that losing one would affect performance).

Doing flow control at the transport layer, where one entity can control it, makes more sense than allowing applications to do it because each application will attempt to maximize the network and system resources that it consumes. Some applications running on top of UDP have implemented congestion response mechanisms, but in general they do not work as well as those provided at the transport layer. A proposed standard, RFC 3124 "The Congestion Manager," specifies an approach to congestion management that allows any software module, whether at the transport or application layer, to use a congestion management entity within a system to coordinate. This approach allows UDP applications to respond appropriately to congestion without the added overhead of running a heavier-weight transport layer protocol such as TCP.

Congestion response should be distinguished from flow control, even though they seem similar. Flow control comprises a set of mechanisms that sender and recipient use to stabilize (and optimize, it is to be hoped) the rates at which they exchange data. There is an implicit assumption that flow control is concerned with conditions at the endpoints of the connection: a host with a slow connection, for example, might have to indicate limits on the volume of data it can accept in a given period; a host with high latency might have to indicate that a sender should expect a longer delay between transmitting data and getting an ACK for that transmission.

Congestion, however, tends to occur unexpectedly, within the network. Endpoint hosts have little or no control over congestion, although there are strategies for dealing with it.

15.4   Security at the Transport Layer

Good arguments can be made for implementing security at the application, transport, internet, or data link layers; there is no technical reason not to apply security at all those layers even though there may be performance and budgetary reasons to avoid that approach. Security for network data means maintaining data integrity, authentication, and privacy. The typical approach to achieving all three of these goals typically relies on strong public-key cryptography to encrypt data for privacy, digital signatures, or secure hashes to ensure data integrity and authentication (see Chapter 26 for more about IP security).

The highest degree of network data privacy can be achieved if all data input and output to and from networked systems is encrypted. In other words, the only data ever entered has already been encrypted off-line; in this way, the data is never in an accessible form while on any system. This approach is also highly impractical for the vast majority of users.

Encrypting at the application layer is more practical, because data is encrypted earlier in the process of transmission (by the application, before it even arrives at the protocol stack) and decrypted later in the process (only after it has been received by the application). Until someone actually runs the application that uses the data, it can be stored in encrypted form on the system. While more practical, application layer privacy presents complications: application protocol designers and implementers build or borrow the appropriate security mechanisms and design the interface linking the application with those mechanisms, and make sure it is all secure. Sensible protocol designers want to avoid building security into an application for at least two good reasons: first, secure protocols are not easy to design. And second, why reinvent the wheel? Transport layer security has proved to be good enough for most current applications.

Although security is available at the internet layer through the IP Security Protocol (IPsec), applications can't ordinarily initiate or control IPsec sessions, so while IPsec is an excellent tool for securing data in flight between two points across a public network[4], it is less helpful for securing application layer data on demand.

The transport layer offers a good compromise for implementing security because it eliminates the need to re-invent the wheel every time an application protocol needs security mechanisms and also because application protocol can most easily interact with security protocols that operate at the transport layer. An important point to keep in mind, however, is that when security is implemented at some given layer, the assurance provided

---

[4]As it is used to implement virtual private networks (VPNs); see Chapter 34 for more about VPNs.

by that security relates to entities at that layer. Thus, adding security at the internet layer means encrypting packets as they their source IP node and decrypting them as they enter their destination IP node—even with perfect internet layer security, the data is still vulnerable before it is encrypted and after it is decrypted.

This section examines the two most commonly used transport layer security protocols: the TLS protocol and the SSH protocol.

15.4.1 TRANSPORT LAYER SECURITY (TLS)

Until the commercialization of the internet—and the web—during the early 1990s, there was little demand for secure applications. When Netscape published the Navigator web browser, they included support for their proprietary Secure Socket Layer (SSL) protocol. SSL offered security at the transport layer, by facilitating the negotiation of a secure channel for communication over a TCP circuit. Netscape was able to capture most of the early internet's market for web browser as well as web server software[5] by making the SSL specification public and encouraging other software publishers to incorporate it into other web server and browser programs. Within a short time SSL had become the de facto standard for securing web transactions, succeeding so well that at least two other web security protocols were effectively throttled in their cribs.

Secure HTTP (S-HTTP) is currently designated an experimental specification defined in 1999 in RFC 2660, "The Secure HyperText Transfer Protocol," despite its long history of IETF-sanctioned development. Although some vendors incorporated S-HTTP support in web clients and servers, the protocol offered no significant competitive advantage over SSL (and later, TLS). Interoperability required all web software to support SSL, while S-HTTP was less important to software buyers.

The Secure Electronic Transaction (SET) standard, another fairly spectacular failure, was backed by a substantial number of big companies including major credit and charge card vendors, hardware and software vendors, banks, and other financial institutions. Intended to provide a comprehensive protocol for enabling every step of a web commerce transaction, SET also failed for a number of reasons, not least of which was the inability of all its backers to cooperate on the project. Other problems were

---

[5]A lead that was to prove illusory once Microsoft turned its attention to the internet.

the length of time it took for the designers to release usable specifications, the ambitious scope of the project, and the lack of industry enthusiasm for yet another digital commerce protocol that seemed to offer little or no benefit over and above that offered by SSL and/or TLS.

TLS is specified in RFC 2246, "The TLS Protocol Version 1.0," published in 1999. By design, TLS provides a mechanism by which application clients and servers can communicate securely. In this case, security refers to both privacy and data integrity. Encrypting data keeps it private, and using a cryptographic function such as a digital signature or a secure hash allows recipients to determine whether or not an attacker (or some naturally occuring event) has modified or corrupted the data in some way.

Two different types of TLS protocol are defined:

TLS Record Protocol provides an encapsulation layer for TLS data, and provides functions similar to those performed by UDP and TCP. The Record Protocol accepts messages from higher layer protocols (such as the TLS Handshake Protocol, see below) and packages those messages for secure transmission. The Record Protocol breaks up messages into manageable chunks, and then may apply one or more types of compression, data integrity, or encryption to the data before passing it along to the transport layer protocol.

TLS Handshake Protocol offers what is in effect a security application, applied between client and server before any actual application data passes between them but after the client initiates a request for service. The Handshake Protocol helps by (1) authenticating one or both peers, (2) negotiating the secure exchange of a *shared secret* (to be used for encrypting or digitally signing data), and (3) detecting when data has been tampered with.

The Record Protocol frames data for security purposes: it contains a payload of secured data as well as minimal plaintext header information. The headers are kept terse to reduce the possibility of an eavesdropper from doing *traffic analysis*: examining all intercepted data, secure or not, and attempting to extract as much information out of the data as possible. For example, suppose there were a "document title" header transmitted in plaintext. Even if it is encrypted, knowing that there exists a document titled "List of Terminated Employees" gives the eavesdropper some information; more information can be extracted from looking at the length of the encrypted document.

The Handshake Protocol is just one of the protocols that can be encapsulated within the Record Protocol, but it is necessary for starting a TLS session. The "handshake" is the process by which the two TLS peers negotiate the algorithms and protocols to be used for encrypting, authenticating, and exchanging keying material with each other. Other encapsulated protocols include:

TLS Alert Protocol is used to pass information about the session from peer to peer. Alerts may be used to indicate that a session is over, that a session has been compromised, or that a protocol error has occured.

TLS Change Cipher Spec Protocol consists of a single message type (change cipher spec), consisting of a 1-byte value (1), sent to indicate that the sender is about to change the way it is encrypting or digitally signing data, starting with its next transmission. The protocol is used during the Handshake Protocol.

Application Protocol is the application protocol being encapsulated within the TLS session.

The existence of TLS, and even the use of TLS with an application protocol, does not by itself ensure a secure session. As noted in RFC 2246, although TLS can be used to secure applications, it "does not specify how protocols add security with TLS; the decisions on how to initiate TLS handshaking and how to interpret the authentication certificates exchanged are left up to the judgment of the designers and implementors of protocols which run on top of TLS."

15.4.2 SECURE SHELL PROTOCOL

The SSH can function as an application protocol (see section 10.4) but also as a secure transport protocol.

As described in the work-in-progress internet draft, "SSH Protocol Architecture," the SSH architecture consists of three protocol components:

SSH Transport Layer Protocol performs many of the same functions as the TLS Record Protocol. Once the SSH connection is established, encryption, data authentication, and integrity checking are done at the Transport Layer Protocol; compression is optional. Also like the

Record Protocol, the Transport Layer Protocol typically runs on top of TCP.

SSH Transport Layer sessions are opened with requests on the well-known port 22, with session negotiation taking place after host authentication is done. This protocol supports only host authentication; user authentication takes place only after the transport layer session is set up.

SSH User Authentication Protocol provides a mechanism for user authentication, running over an SSH Transport Layer Protocol session.

SSH Connection Protocol enables the creation of different channels to carry different application sessions over a single SSH connection. It also enables the use of port forwarding, by which an application session can be redirected to flow through a secured channel. By specifying a port and IP address, the client can tunnel the application data through an encrypted tunnel capable of bypassing firewall scrutiny.

Although SSH and TLS address a similar set of needs, TLS is most often implemented in web client and server software and configured to operate transparently to the user. Although most commonly encountered by end users as a client application for securely connecting to other hosts, SSH is more often viewed as a system administrator's tool requiring a higher degree of expertise to use safely. Part of that reputation stems from the different uses to which SSH can be put. Not only does SSH allow the replacement of the notoriously insecure r-utilities, but it permits secure tunneling of X window system sessions, creation of encrypted channels for virtual private networking, and other secure applications.

15.5   New Approaches to the Transport Layer

UDP and TCP are no longer the only transport layer protocols available. Although not yet widely deployed, the SCTP offers an alternative that is more than UDP and different from TCP. Although still in the earliest stage of development, support is gathering for another transport layer protocol, the Datagram Control Protocol (DCP). Both these protocols will be discussed in more depth in Chapter 18.

However, even these protocols do not exhaust the possibilities for transport layer protocols. A UDP-like transport protocol could be imagined that added guaranteed delivery, or a TCP-like transport that used a transmission rate rather than a transmission window (e.g., suggested rates at which the recipient could accept data instead of indicating the sliding window mechanism described in Chapter 17).

Just as application protocols use certain fundamental mechanisms that could easily be reused (as with BEEP, described in Chapter 13), a modular transport protocol could also be designed at some point in the future. In the meantime, SCTP was designed to provide applications developers with a wider range of capabilities than UDP or even TCP, and a greater degree to which those capabilities could be turned on and off.

As we'll see in Chapter 18, SCTP uses many of the features offered in TCP, particularly in terms of providing reliability and guaranteed delivery; datagram control protocol (DCP) takes UDP, with its barebones approach and lack of guaranteed delivery, but drops UDP's connectionlessness in favor of support for data streams and connections. By doing so, DCP explicitly incorporates the ability to specify a range of options for handling congestion control. Although still very much an early-stage work in progress, DCP will be discussed in Chapter 18 as well.

15.6   Chapter Summary

Many networked systems offer only a single interface to the internet, yet they can run many different tasks for many different users. The transport layer provides a mechanism by which multi-tasking computers can maintain multiple network sessions: every application that needs access to network resources (or that provides network resources) can use its own transport layer process to get in and out of the lower layer interface.

The transport layer is also a convenient "place" to resolve networking issues such as packaging data for transmission, creating circuits (for reliable services), monitoring traffic performance for responding to network congestion, and as the proper layer to provide session security.

Until 2000, all network transmissions were carried over two transport layer protocols: TCP for virtual circuit guaranteed delivery and UDP for best-effort datagram delivery. These two protocols shaped generations of network professionals, who often viewed them as almost polar opposites—as well as the only possible solutions for the transport layer. With the additon of SCTP to the internet standards track, the dualistic view of the internet transport layer must fade as the new family of transport protocols offers a new set of transport layer attributes.

The next chapter introduces the simplest of the transport layer protocols, UDP.

16

User Datagram Protocol

Jon Postel wrote and published RFC 768,"User Datagram Protocol" in August 1980; unlike most internet protocols from that era it has not been made obsolete or updated or modified. It is probably the simplest of internet protocols. The entire specification is reproduced in the first part of this chapter with commentary following. For those who have never read an RFC, this should be an interesting introduction.

16.1 RFC 768: User Datagram Protocol

16.1.1 INTRODUCTION

This User Datagram Protocol (UDP) is defined to make available a datagram mode of packet-switched computer communication in the environment of an interconnected set of computer networks. This protocol assumes that the Internet Protocol (IP) [1] is used as the underlying protocol.

This protocol provides a procedure for application
programs to send messages to other programs with a
minimum of protocol mechanism. The protocol is
transaction oriented, and delivery and duplicate
protection are not guaranteed. Applications requiring
ordered reliable delivery of streams of data should
use the Transmission Control Protocol (TCP) [2].

16.1.2   FORMAT

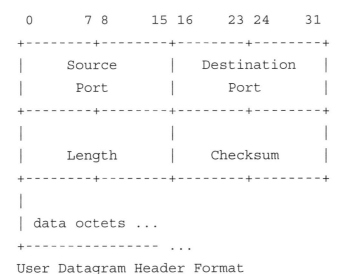

```
     0        7 8        15 16       23 24       31
    +--------+--------+--------+--------+
    |        Source   |     Destination |
    |        Port     |        Port     |
    +--------+--------+--------+--------+
    |                 |                 |
    |        Length   |     Checksum    |
    +--------+--------+--------+--------+
    |
    | data octets ...
    +--------------- ...
```

User Datagram Header Format

16.1.3   FIELDS

Source Port is an optional field, when meaningful, it
indicates the port of the sending process, and may be
assumed to be the port to which a reply should be
addressed in the absence of any other information. If
not used, a value of zero is inserted.

Destination Port has a meaning within the context of a
particular internet destination address.

Length is the length in octets of this user datagram including this header and the data. (This means the minimum value of the length is eight.)

Checksum is the 16-bit one's complement of the one's complement sum of a pseudo header of information from the IP header, the UDP header, and the data, padded with zero octets at the end (if necessary) to make a multiple of two octets.

The *pseudo header* conceptually prefixed to the UDP header contains the source address, the destination address, the protocol, and the UDP length. This information gives protection against misrouted datagrams. This checksum procedure is the same as is used in TCP.

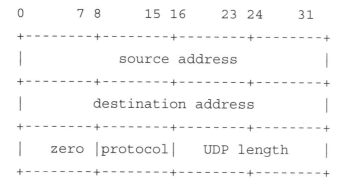

If the computed checksum is zero, it is transmitted as all ones (the equivalent in one's complement arithmetic). An all zero transmitted checksum value means that the transmitter generated no checksum (for debugging or for higher level protocols that don't care).

16.1.4 USER INTERFACE

A user interface should allow

* the creation of new receive ports,

- receive operations on the receive ports that return the data octets and an indication of source port and source address,
- and an operation that allows a datagram to be sent, specifying the data, source and destination ports and addresses to be sent.

16.1.5 IP Interface

The UDP module must be able to determine the source and destination internet addresses and the protocol field from the internet header. One possible UDP/IP interface would return the whole internet datagram including all of the internet header in response to a receive operation. Such an interface would also allow the UDP to pass a full internet datagram complete with header to the IP to send. The IP would verify certain fields for consistency and compute the internet header checksum.

16.1.6 Protocol Application

The major uses of this protocol is the Internet Name Server [3], and the Trivial File Transfer [4].

16.1.7 Protocol Number

This is protocol 17 (21 octal) when used in the Internet Protocol. Other protocol numbers are listed in [5].

16.1.8 References

[1] Postel, J., ``Internet Protocol,'' RFC 760, USC/Information Sciences Institute, January 1980.

[2] Postel, J., ``Transmission Control Protocol,'' RFC 761, USC/Information Sciences Institute, January 1980.

[3] Postel, J., ``Internet Name Server,'' USC/
     Information Sciences Institute, IEN 116, August
     1979.

[4] Sollins, K., ``The TFTP Protocol,'' Massachusetts
     Institute of Technology, IEN 133, January 1980.

[5] Postel, J., ``Assigned Numbers,'' USC/Information
     Sciences Institute, RFC 762, January 1980.

16.2   A Bit More About User Datagram Protocol

As the original RFC makes clear, UDP is a lightweight protocol: there are no protocol commands, there are only four fields in the protocol header. The UDP header indicates the source and destination ports (addresses of the communicating processes), a field indicating the length of the datagram and a checksum on the entire datagram plus *pseudo header*, a logical construct built on parts of the encapsulating IP header meant to provide a very slight degree of protection against misrouted packets or malformed headers.

UDP offers nothing more than a simple mechanism for associating application data with a particular pair of processes at either end. There's little more to say about it.

UDP provides no error correction, no connection-oriented links, no handshaking, and no verification of delivery order. UDP offers basic datagram delivery and nothing more. The UDP header checksum provides only the most basic check on datagram integrity: if the checksum doesn't match on arrival, the datagram is assumed to be corrupted and is discarded silently by the receiving host.

Applications based on UDP are often simple ones that don't need to maintain connections. UDP application may consist entirely of requests and replies to requests, as with DNS; UDP may also be used to provide the simplest transport layer protocol possible while the application layer protocol provides flow control, authentication, acknowledgment, verification, error detection, and so on.

A simple datagram delivery service like UDP, without any added features, is easy to implement and requires minimal overhead. UDP is often built into the limited memory of diskless workstations, where it is used for remote booting. UDP is also used for low-intensity tasks performed in the background, such as resolving hostnames with DNS, or routine network monitoring through Simple Network Management Protocol (SNMP, Chapter 31). Some UDP applications operate mostly over local networks that are usually reliable, and so don't need transport layer reliability. Other applications can trade the uncertainty of delivery for lower overhead, because retransmitting requests is easier and usually has minimal impact on network traffic.

The Trivial File Transfer Protocol (TFTP) was designed to be used by the Boot Protocol (BOOTP) to bootstrap terminal systems from the network. TFTP was intended for implementation in systems with minimal resources: no disk drives and just enough RAM to support UDP and IP; most TFTP transfers were done over local area networks (LANs). UDP was a perfect solution for TFTP.

16.3   User Datagram Protocol Datagram Format

Source and destination ports are 16 bits each; the source port is assigned by the originating host, and the destination port is usually the well-known port associated with the application using UDP. The UDP message length field is also 16 bits, and it indicates the length of the entire UDP datagram including header in bytes, giving an upper limit to UDP datagram size of 65,535 bytes.

The UDP checksum is an option (when not used, this field must contain all-zeroes) that is not strictly necessary on LANs (such as Ethernet) already using a *cyclic redundancy check* (*CRC*) on network frames. When the datagram will be passing over unreliable links, use of the checksum is advised.

The pseudo-header uses IP addressing information taken from the IP header. The source and destination IP addresses, 8 bits of padding ("0"s), and the UDP protocol code (17) compose the pseudo-header, which is then appended to the UDP header and payload; the checksum is then calculated on the entire datagram.

The UDP payload is raw data. Maximum datagram length can be configured, but is usually set to 8,192 bytes. Although the 2-byte datagram length field sets the upper limit on the datagram size at 65,535 bytes, the maximum datagram length (8,192 bytes) generally implemented is determined more by other issues like programming interface and the way that TCP/IP is implemented. For example, application programs like NFS that use UDP by default use chunks of data that are 8,192 bytes long, so creating UDP datagrams any longer would add to the processing overhead without adding any benefits.

16.4   Where User Datagram Protocol Data Fits In

UDP and IP are tightly integrated: IP identifies a packet's destination and source nodes on the internet, while UDP identifies the destination and source processes within those systems.

At first glance, UDP seems almost pointless: it adds no features on top of IP and pushes reliability functions up a layer to make the application responsible. IP is a connectionless and unreliable protocol; so is UDP. However, UDP adds value by performing transport layer functions for several different categories of application, including:

- Applications requiring minimal implementation. For example, diskless workstations used TFTP over UDP rather than full-blown FTP over TCP for remote booting because they lacked resources (disk, memory, and processor power) to implement the more complex FTP and TCP. The SNMP uses UDP in part because some managed devices also lack the resources to support TCP.
- Applications that don't need any transport layer services. For example, DNS (see Chapter 8) uses UDP because most protocol interactions between individual hosts consist of a single request followed by a single reply. There is no benefit from setting up a circuit, and the cost is high. Instead of two packets, total, for DNS over UDP (one message sent in each direction), DNS over TCP requires at least seven packets (three to set up the connection, two to terminate it, and two for the UDP messages).
- Applications that can withstand data loss better than increased latency. For example, a live audio transmission needs reasonably stable bandwidth more than it needs bursts of high bandwidth: a telephone-quality connection might be possible

at lower bandwidths, while higher fidelity becomes possible at higher bandwidths. However, there's no point in making sure every bit of audio data is delivered if the data arrives seconds after it's needed—that bandwidth is put to better use moving current data. Real-time applications may implement whatever flow control services they need at the application layer or else use some other mechanisms (such as RSVP or RTP) to create predictable channels.

- One-to-many applications (see Chapters 14, 18, and 24). Until recently, any application that required TCP-like services had to use TCP; because TCP uses virtual circuits, only two hosts can communicate with TCP (one host at either end of the virtual circuit). Collaborative applications such as video conferencing and any others linking more than three hosts were required to use multicast, and by implication, UDP, because (unlike TCP) UDP permits the transmission of a packet from a single host to any number of different hosts. (Unlike TCP, UDP does not require a checksum or any other control linking the packet body and the transport layer headers. If you attempted to send a TCP segment to a multicast address, the packets would be discarded at their destinations because the checksums calculated there would not match the original checksums calculated by the sender.)

16.5   User Datagram Protocol Examples

There's not much to say about UDP headers, except that they're quite simple. The examples shown below in Figure 16–1 are from an exchange of DNS messages; the first was a request for domain name resolution, the second the reply from the DNS server.

The checksums can be verfied using the IP packet headers; in this case, the pseudo-header for the first UDP message is based on the source and destination IP addresses, eight bits of 0, the protocol code (in this case, 0×11, or 17, representing UDP) and the UDP length value (39). After creating the pseudo-header (as described in section 16.1), the checksum is calculated on the headers, pseudo-headers, and datagram contents.

```
UDP Header from DNS Request:


Source port: 32778

Destination port: 53

Length: 39

Checksum: 0x98f0


UDP Header from DNS Reply:


  Source port: 53

Destination port: 32778

Length: 165

Checksum: 0x5f33
```

Figure 16–1: UDP headers from a DNS exchange.

16.6 Chapter Summary

By opening with the short, official, UDP specification (RFC 768), we see how truly simple UDP can be. There is little more to say about it, and there are few additional RFCs that extend, explain, or modify UDP in any way.

Yet UDP fills an important role in providing a lightweight transport protocol offering little more than a simple binding function, connecting process to the internet interface.

17

Transmission Control Protocol

If you can understand the Transmission Control Protocol (TCP), you can understand just about any internet protocol as well as TCP/IP networking in general. Unlike most of the other protocols discussed so far, TCP engages many of the real problems related to running actual applications across real-world networks. User datagram protocol (UDP) provides no help when data fails to arrive at its destination; the application protocols covered so far leave the task of managing transmissions (and making sure that data arrives in the correct manner) to some other protocol. Over the years, that other protocol has almost exclusively been TCP.

Covered in this chapter are:

> **Problem Description:** What problems does TCP solve?
> **Protocol Description:** What does the TCP protocol do, and how does it work?
> **Protocol Examples:** What do TCP protocol exchanges look like?

Protocol Issues: Whereas UDP has remained unmodified since 1982, TCP has been updated and added to over the same period. Modifications focus on mechanisms for improving performance.

Although both protocols are useful, neither TCP nor UDP provides the perfect balance of transport layer functions for every application layer protocol; however, for most modern internet applications TCP is the transport layer protocol of choice for its adaptability to changing network conditions as well as for its reliable, guaranteed data delivery.

17.1   Problem Statement

Internet datagram service (as defined by the Internet Protocol, discussed in Chapter 19), whether today or during the 1970s, when TCP was developed, is a service without any guarantees. IP is a best-effort protocol, and when intermediate systems are overwhelmed by traffic or fail for other reasons, there is no promise of notification. Systems running over upper layer protocols are left to determine for themselves whether or not their requests and responses have been delivered or not. As discussed in Chapter 15, the transport layer has long been deemed the appropriate venue for handling such tasks. Although UDP provides a pass-through protocol at the transport layer, the TCP was designed to provide a more feature-rich set of transport services.

Application layer protocols that depend on the reliable and accurate transfer of data require that there be mechanisms to provide:

Connection-oriented transmissions. A connection implies that there is a sender on one end of the link and a receiver on the other, and that there is a way to determine what has been sent and in what order it should be interpreted.

End-to-end transmissions. Users must trust that their application data has been sent from their application client to server without any intermediate changes having been made. Often, changes are mandatory, such as when a segment sent over a local area network (LAN) must be redirected to a destination outside the LAN. In that case the segment will have to be changed to reflect a different link layer address, and the entire segment translated into a format appropriate for a new link layer. However, applications typically require that their data be delivered exactly as submitted by the sender.

Reliable transmissions. Users must also trust that their client application receives all the data being sent to it, and that all data being sent by the client is being received by the application server. Guaranteeing delivery is one way to build reliability into the protocol, and to provide the guarantee it is necessary for all data transmitted between processes be acknowledged upon receipt; if data is not acknowledged, it must be retransmitted.

Interprocess communication. Just as UDP provides interprocess communication with a minimum of fuss, TCP allows processes to address each other within the context of specific ntework hosts. For UDP, this is the only service provided; for TCP, this is one service of many.

These four functions are taken from the current internet standard for TCP, RFC 793, "Transmission Control Protocol: DARPA Internet Program Protocol Specification." In order to fulfill these requirements, the authors of RFC 793 concluded that certain facilities must be provided with TCP; those facilities are described next.

17.2   Transmission Control Protocol Attributes and Features

As described in RFC 793, to provide connection-oriented, end-to-end, reliable interprocess communication, TCP offers these protocol facilities:

Basic Data Transfer A TCP implementation can send and receive data as a continuous stream of bytes. Each implementation determines how to package the bytes into *segments* (the TCP protocol data unit), how many bytes to include in each segment, and when to send segments. The exception is when the application requires that all data up to a certain point must be submitted, for example, when a user enters data to a terminal session and wants to submit the data to the remote host. Designed for those cases, the *push* function causes the sending TCP implementation to send all data that is being queued for transmission or that is in the process of being framed for transmission.

Unlike other protocols that impose a structure on their data, TCP offers *byte stream service* meaning that segment data is delivered in order but without any other constraints—the process may send data to the local TCP implementation 100 bytes at a time, or in smaller or larger chunks (e.g., a terminal session will consist of variably sized streams of data). Once the data is transmitted, the receiving TCP implementation can send the receiving process the data in 50-byte chunks, or whatever is most appropriate. The goal is to permit the recipient to duplicate exactly the byte stream being sent; for the same reason, TCP sends data exactly with no reference to whether the data is ASCII or binary or any other representation.

Reliability TCP was designed to be resilient even when data is received out of order, is damaged during transmission, is not received at all, or is received more than once. Sequence numbers are used to ensure proper data delivery order as well as to prevent duplication. A checksum on the segment contents allows rejection of damaged segments. TCP implementations are required to positively acknowledge (ACK) receipt of all data. The sender times receipt of ACKs on segments that have been sent, so that when an ACK is not received in a timely fashion, the sender assumes the segment was not received and it is re-sent. The timeout value has to be sufficiently long so that transient network problems don't affect performance, but also sufficiently short so that more permanent network congestion conditions do not cause retransmission of all segments.

Flow Control Datagram protocols offer no mechanisms by which communicating hosts can tune the rate at which they are sending because (by definition) they don't offer any connection over which to exchange such information. Flow control is possible with TCP by allowing implementations to signal each other the amount of data they are prepared to accept as they acknowledge segments already received. The acknowledging host sends this *transmission window* value to the sending host; the sending host then calculates how much data is "in flight" and subtracts that amount from the window to calculate how much more data it can send before another ACK is received.

Multiplexing The use of ports as described in Chapter 15 allows a host to accept multiple connections over a single socket—in this way, the host is able to multiplex on a single socket. In addition, multiplexing occurs over any given TCP connection because hosts can send

TCP data and ACKs in the same segments—the sender acts also as a recipient by ACKing previous data.

Connections Two hosts construct a TCP connection through a process known as the *three-way handshake*. This is an important part of the protocol, because it makes possible a reliable connection despite the inherent lack of reliability of lower layer protocols. TCP connections have specific attributes, including the socket pair addresses and ports, sequence numbers used by the hosts, and their window sizes. As long as the hosts can interoperate using these attributes, the connection active.

TCP connections are characterized as virtual circuits, meaning that each circuit behaves as if there is a direct, two-way connection between the communicating hosts. TCP provides end-to-end reliability, requiring that communicating hosts coordinate and agree to make connections and acknowledge receipt of network traffic. Each TCP segment bears a relationship with the segment that came before and the segment that comes after. And that means the first and last segments in a sequence require special treatment. TCP also supports out-of-order delivery of segments, reassembling data streams from IP datagrams that may have been delivered out of order.

A TCP virtual circuit resembles any other (non-virtual) circuit in that there can only be two nodes on either end: one to send, the other to receive. Being connection oriented means that TCP can only be used for host-to-host communication. As a result, TCP can be used only for unicast transmissions (see Chapter 19 for more about unicast) from one host to another.

TCP connections behave as if there were a hard-wired connection between processes on the two connected hosts. When a process initiates a TCP connection with another process, the two processes negotiate to open the connection. Each process must agree to participate. The TCP virtual circuit is similar to a telephone link: one person (process) initiates the telephone call (TCP circuit), but the person (process) at the other end has to answer the telephone (agree to open the TCP circuit). A conversation (TCP circuit) ensues if both individuals (processes) agree to start and continue the conversation (TCP circuit).

Under certain circumstances, when a telephone call is made a telephone conversation won't follow: a wrong number is dialed, the person being called is unavailable, there is a bad connection, or the person being called can't talk. Similarly, there is no guarantee that a TCP circuit can be initiated and maintained: the requesting system wants a service that the other end does not provide, there is no connectivity between the two hosts, the server is unable to handle the request for service.

Each connection is identified uniquely with a combination of each host's IP address and port number for the connection. As with UDP, servers using TCP for their transport protocol use well-known port numbers for offering different network application services. The process specifies a port number to establish the connection, and the IP layer of the networking software indicates the host address. A client process attempting to connect to a Telnet server process specifies the Telnet port number (port 23). The port number and IP address of the host on which the process is running create a TCP socket. The client assigns some other TCP port number (not a well-known port) as its own TCP port, resulting in its own TCP socket: the client's IP address and TCP port number.

The combination of these two pairs of IP address and TCP port numbers, or two TCP sockets, uniquely identifies each TCP connection. A single host can maintain more than one TCP connection through a single TCP port because incoming TCP segments are differentiated by different source sockets. For example, a telnet server at address 10.0.0.1, listening to port 23, maintains any number of unique connections through the socket {10.0.0.1 | 23} because the other sockets (identifying the host IP addresses and port numbers of the client processes) are all unique.

In fact, a server can even maintain multiple connections made through a single client host. Consider what happens when several users of a mainframe system (10.0.0.1) all attempt to telnet to a remote mainframe (192.168.1.1). The server side socket will be { 10.0.0.1 | 23} in all cases; the client side sockets will be of the form { 192.168.1.1 | /nnnn/} where /nnnn/ is some randomly selected port number. The server distinguishes incoming TCP segments not only by the IP addresses of the clients, but also by the port numbers so that the server can send the appropriate session data to the appropriate Telnet session.

17.3   Transmission Control Protocol Basics

One of the hallmarks of TCP is its use of a three-step protocol for establishing a connection. The steps in the three-way handshake can be inferred, at least in broad outline, from the stated goals and features of TCP. Because TCP is connection-oriented, it must have two participants; because TCP provides a reliable transport, all data transmissions must be acknowledged when received. Thus, the following steps are necessary:

1. A process sends a request to open a TCP circuit with a target process. Unlike TCP messages sent in most other situations, this segment contains no acknowledgement—because the process is asking to initiate a circuit (a request that may be declined), there is nothing to ACK. The substance of this initial message will be along the lines of "Requesting to open a TCP session from my socket {host(A) | port(A)} to your socket {host(B) | port(B)}."

2. If there is a process willing to open that socket, it responds to the request with an ACK. At this point, the circuit is half complete: host(A) has sent a TCP segment and received an ACK from host(B).

3. The only thing remaining to establish the connection is for host(A) to send an ACK to host(B). At this point, both ends of the connection have sent data and sent acknowledgments of having received data from the other.

The TCP headers are designed to support TCP protocol interactions such as this three-way handshake as well as a formal disconnect procedure; other aspects of the protocol such as flow control and segment check-sums are also best introduced with the TCP headers. Other basic aspects of TCP, such as how acknowledgements are sent, how data is re-sent, compression, and congestion response strategies, are also covered in this section.

17.3.1 TRANSMISSION CONTROL PROTOCOL HEADERS

Figure 17–1 shows the basic TCP header structure; header fields are described below.

The standard TCP header is 20 bytes—five 32-bit words—long, but may be longer if options are present. Figure 17–1 represents the TCP header fields in digital *words* of 32 bits (or four octets) in length. Thus, the first two fields, source and destination port numbers, are 2 bytes (16 bits) each.

The smallest possible TCP segment header is 20 bytes; options are optional, as is segment payload data. TCP segments may be as small as 20 bytes.

```
    0                   1                   2                   3
    0 1 2 3 4 5 6 7 8 9 0 1 2 3 4 5 6 7 8 9 0 1 2 3 4 5 6 7 8 9 0 1
   +-+-+-+-+-+-+-+-+-+-+-+-+-+-+-+-+-+-+-+-+-+-+-+-+-+-+-+-+-+-+-+-+
   |          Source Port          |       Destination Port        |
   +-+-+-+-+-+-+-+-+-+-+-+-+-+-+-+-+-+-+-+-+-+-+-+-+-+-+-+-+-+-+-+-+
   |                        Sequence Number                        |
   +-+-+-+-+-+-+-+-+-+-+-+-+-+-+-+-+-+-+-+-+-+-+-+-+-+-+-+-+-+-+-+-+
   |                    Acknowledgment Number                      |
   +-+-+-+-+-+-+-+-+-+-+-+-+-+-+-+-+-+-+-+-+-+-+-+-+-+-+-+-+-+-+-+-+
   |  Data | Rsrv'd|C|E|U|A|P|R|S|F|                               |
   | Offset|       |W|C|R|C|S|S|Y|I|            Window             |
   |       |       |R|E|G|K|H|T|N|N|                               |
   +-+-+-+-+-+-+-+-+-+-+-+-+-+-+-+-+-+-+-+-+-+-+-+-+-+-+-+-+-+-+-+-+
   |           Checksum            |         Urgent Pointer        |
   +-+-+-+-+-+-+-+-+-+-+-+-+-+-+-+-+-+-+-+-+-+-+-+-+-+-+-+-+-+-+-+-+
   |                    Options                    |    Padding    |
   +-+-+-+-+-+-+-+-+-+-+-+-+-+-+-+-+-+-+-+-+-+-+-+-+-+-+-+-+-+-+-+-+
   |                             Data . . .                        |
   +-+-+-+-+-+-+-+-+-+-+-+-+-+-+-+-+-+-+-+-+-+-+-+-+-+-+-+-+-+-+-+-+
```

Figure 17–1: TCP headers (from RFC 793 and RFC 3168).

Although TCP implementations know the length of the TCP segments they receive, that information is not included in the TCP headers but rather calculated from data carried in the IP headers. The TCP Data Offset field (see below) indicates the size of the header; the IP header length field indicates the size of the IP header, while the datagram length field indicates the total size of the datagram (see Chapter 19). By subtracting the length of the IP and TCP headers from the length of the entire datagram, a network protocol stack implementation is able to infer the length of the TCP segment contained in the IP datagram. Thus, TCP segments are complete within an IP datagram.

For more about determining a maximum segment size, see section 17.3.2 below.

Source Port/Destination Port: These are the addresses of the communicating processes. The initiating host assigns itself an ephemeral port number, usually a randomly assigned value greater than 1,023. The destination port number will initially be the well-known port associated with the service desired from the remote host.

Sequence Number: Each octet in a TCP data stream is numbered; the sending process chooses an arbitrary number when it begins sending. Each host has its own data stream and each selects its own arbitrary starting point for numbering bytes in that data stream. The initial sequence number (ISN) typically is set to some arbitrary 32-bit value, and wraps around to 0 when the highest allowed value is exceeded. The sequence number field contains the 32-bit value assigned by the sending host to the first byte in the current segment—except when the segment is the first in the sequence. For initial segments in a sequence, this field contains the ISN (see section 17.3.3, on protocol establishment).

Sequence numbers are chosen arbitrarily (instead of starting at 0) to avoid confusion when a connection unexpectedly fails. In that case, one or both processes may be waiting for an ACK from the other; meanwhile if a new connection is attempted (with sequence number starting from 0) the receiving process may interpret that as a duplicate of a segment it already received. To avoid problems, implementations would either be required to examine segments to differentiate duplicates from new transmissions or else time out connections relatively quickly. Performance suffers in either case, so arbitrary sequence numbers are preferred.

Acknowledgment Number: The sending process identifies its data with a sequence number; the receiving process acknowledges receipt of data in this field. This field contains the value of the next expected sequence number from the sender, and serves as an ACK of all data up to that sequence number, minus 1. If the sequence number value of the last complete segment received was "4e09 881a 0000 1000" then the acknowledgment number field will have a value of "4e09 881a 0000 1001".

When the segment contains no data (as during connection initialization and termination) the acknowledgment number is still incremented by 1.

Data Offset: The number of 32-bit words in the TCP header, the data offset value, indicates where the TCP header ends and the segment data begins. TCP allows options, so although the segment header will never be less than 5 words (20 bytes) long, with options it may be longer. *Padding* (inclusion of extra bits in a field, all with value of "0") is used with options to ensure that all TCP headers end on a 32-bit word boundary. At 4 bits, the maximum value for the data offset field is 15, meaning that the maximum TCP header length is 60 octets (15 4-octet words) or 480 bits (15 32-bit words).

Reserved: RFC 793 left a 6-bit portion header undefined to allow modifications to the protocol later; RFC 3168, "The Addition of Explicit Congestion Notification (ECN) to IP," defines the use of these bits (designed bits 8 and 9 of the fourth word of the TCP headers).

Flags: RFC 793 defined six *flags*, single-bit fields that are either "on" (set to "1") or "off" (set to "0"); two more were defined in RFC 3168. The six original TCP header flags are used during the three-way handshake protocol, as well during other protocol interactions; the two flags added in RFC 3168 are used to add support for explicit congestion notification (ECN). The use and meaning of these flags is discussed below.

Window: As defined in RFC 793, the window field value is the "number of data octets beginning with the one indicated in the acknowledgment field which the sender of this segment is willing to accept."

The workings of the TCP *sliding window* are discussed in greater detail below.

The window size reported by a receiving process will vary depending on how much data the process is willing to accept. A large window means the efficiency of the connection is increasing—the process is willing to accept more data, more quickly. A smaller window will cause the sender to reduce the rate at which data is being sent.

Checksum: This is a "standard" transport layer checksum, used by UDP.[1] Unless one is implemented RFC 793, the most important aspect of the TCP checksum is that it reliably (in most cases) can indicate whether or not the segment has been modified or damaged. The TCP checksum procedure is defined in RFC 793 as follows:

```
The checksum field is the 16 bit one's complement
of the one's complement sum of all 16 bit words
in the header and text. If a segment contains an
odd number of header and text octets to be
checksummed, the last octet is padded on the
right with zeros to form a 16 bit word for
checksum purposes. The pad is not transmitted
as part of the segment. While computing the
checksum, the checksum field itself is replaced
with zeros.

The checksum also covers a 96 bit pseudo header
conceptually prefixed to the TCP header. This
pseudo header contains the Source Address, the
Destination Address, the Protocol, and TCP
length. This gives the TCP protection against
misrouted segments. This information is carried
in the Internet Protocol and is transferred
across the TCP/Network interface in the arguments
or results of calls by the TCP on the IP.
```

---

[1] This checksum is also specified for the work-in-progress Datagram Control Protocol (DCP). The Stream Control Transmission Protocol (SCTP) uses a 32-bit checksum; see RFC 2960 and Chapter 19 for more about both.

```
+--------+--------+--------+--------+
|             Source Address         |
+--------+--------+--------+--------+
|          Destination Address       |
+--------+--------+--------+--------+
| zero   | PTCL   |   TCP Length     |
+--------+--------+--------+--------+
```

The TCP Length is the TCP header length plus
the data length in octets (this is not an
explicitly transmitted quantity, but is
computed), and it does not count the 12 octets
of the pseudo header.

Urgent Pointer: When the URG (urgent) flag is set (URG = "1"), this field's
value indicates the sequence number of the last byte considered to
be part of the urgent data. A common example of urgent data is the
interrupt key in a Telnet session: it is used to interrupt other processes
on the remote server, and it should be accepted even though the
server may be waiting for a process to end or waiting for some other
data.

Options: Protocols are typically extended or modified over time, without
loss of interoperability with earlier implementations, both by using
portions of the protocol header that were previously undefined or
reserved and by adding new options. TCP options may be added to
the header immediately following all the required fields and immediately preceding the segment data. TCP options are discussed in more
detail later in the chapter.

Padding: When options are used, padding (up to 2 bytes with value
of "0") is added to the header to ensure that the header ends on a
4-octet word boundary. A TCP option must be at least 1 octet, but no
more than 40 octets long.

Data: The segment payload, if present, follows the header. As mentioned
above, the end of the data portion of the TCP segment is inferred
from the TCP and IP header fields related to datagram and header
length.

TCP flag bits are used in the course of protocol interactions, particularly related to initiating sessions, acknowledging receipt of data, and terminating the session. Before discussing those processes it helps to know a bit about the defined flags. The six flags originally defined for TCP include:

URG: The URGENT flag indicates that the segment being sent should be considered urgent. The urgent pointer field described earlier is valid only when this flag is set.

ACK: The ACKNOWLEDGMENT flag indicates that the acknowledgment number in the segment header is valid. This flag is set for all segments after the very first segment of an active connection; the first segment can't include an ACK because there is no prior segment to refer to. Put differently, only the first segment of an connection will have the ACK flag off; all others should have it set. Also, when the ACK flag is off, the value in the acknowledgment field is ignored. This bit should always be on once a TCP connection has been established.

PSH: The PUSH flag indicates that the data in the TCP segment should be pushed out to the application as soon as possible. This might be used during a terminal session, for example when the data to be sent would not normally be enough to fill up the TCP send buffer. The sending TCP implementation might normally wait for 1,000 bytes of data before sending to achieve better performance; however, if the data consists of a carriage return sent by a user during a terminal session, the application would cause the PSH flag to be set to avoid waiting for more data.

RST: The RESET flag is used to signal the receiving process to reset the connection. The RST flag may be set in response to segments sent to an inappropriate (non-existent or non–well-known) port or to abruptly terminate (abort) a connection. Such a termination is not orderly: data in flight (but not received) and data received (but not ACK'ed) won't be properly acknowledged. If the session is re-established, that data will have to be retransmitted.

SYN: The SYNCHRONIZE flag is used to indicate that the TCP connection is being established. The "syncrhonization" is that of setting and exchanging sequence and acknowledgment numbers.

FIN: The FINISH flag is set when the sender has no more data to send; this is the preferred method of terminating a connection, a process by which all outstanding data is accounted for and acknowledged.

Finally, it is worth noting that TCP segments need not be carrying data. In particular, when initiating or terminating a connection, the segments have no data other than that contained in the header to pass between hosts.

RFC 3168, as mentioned above, adds two new flags for using ECN with TCP. Congestion is of great concern for TCP, as until recently the only protocol mechanisms that TCP offered to detect congestion relied on the timing of dropped segments. ECN uses fields in the IP header to indicate that congestion is occuring at the internet layer. TCP implementations can detect Congestion Events (CEs) and respond to them appropriately and more quickly than previously. The two new TCP flags are:

ECE: The ECN Echo (ECE) flag is used to negotiate the use of ECN during the session initialization, as well as to indicate that a CE notification was received.

CWR: The Congestion Window Reduced (CWR) flag is used to indicate that the congestion window has been reduced in response to an ECN flagged segment.

17.3.2   SEGMENT SIZE

A TCP segment should be complete within a single IP datagram. It makes little sense for a sending process to allow a segment to be broken into more than one IP packet—to do so would mean that if one of those packets is lost, all of the packets carrying the segment would have to be retransmitted. Chapter 19 provides more insight into how IP packets might be broken into pieces by intermediate systems, but communicating TCP implementations need to determine a packet size, somehow.

One approach is to use the implementation default segment size. The default *maximum segment size* (MSS) should be 536 bytes, according to RFC 879, "The TCP Maximum Segment Size and Related Topics." This figure is derived from the requirement for all hosts to be able to handle IP packets that are 576 bytes long. In other words, all IP hosts can be assumed capable of accepting IP packets up to 576 bytes—it is acceptable for a host to refuse a 1,000-byte packet because it is too long, but not acceptable for a host to refuse a 500-byte packet for that reason.

Working backward, a 576-byte IP datagram will consist of at least a 20-octet IP header and a 20-octet TCP header; thus, 536 bytes for the minimum MSS. Other implementations have been known to set the default MSS at 512 bytes, perhaps to allow an additional margin for TCP and IP header options or perhaps to use the "even" number of bytes (512 is "0000 0010 0000 0000" in binary or 0×0200 in hexadecimal) or bits (4096 bits, or "0001 0000 0000 0000" in binary and 0×1000 hex) for improved processing efficiency—the more likely reason, as physical disk sectors are also 512 bytes.

However, this is a minimum value for the maximum segment size. Larger segment sizes (within limits) are preferred because they reduce the proportionate cost of protocol overhead required to send each segment. All TCP/IP packet/segments "cost" at least 40 bytes for their respective headers. For 512-byte segments, the protocols take up roughly 8% of the bandwidth used. Double the size of the segment to 1,024 bytes, and the protocol headers take only about 4% of the bandwidth. With segments of 40 K bytes, the protocol headers would take only 0.1% of the bandwidth used.

As segment size increases, the likelihood of its IP datagram being corrupted, dropped, or fragmented (see Chapter 19) as it travels from source to destination also increase. As a result, any gain in protocol efficiency is likely to be outweighed by the loss in efficiency caused by the need to retransmit. Ideally, the communicating TCP implementations should negotiate an acceptable compromise: large enough to be more efficient than the minimum default, yet small enough to avoid unnecessarily frequent retransmissions.

This negotiation is done within TCP using the MSS option (see section 17.5.1) during the connection initialization (discussed next).

17.3.3 THREE-WAY HANDSHAKE

All TCP connections are initiated through the process known as the *three-way handshake*, also referred to as the *syncrhonization protocol* or *syncrhonization process*, already mentioned earlier in this chapter. The process is illustrated in Figure 17–2, and is described here:

1. Process A (on Host A) sends a segment to process B (on Host B), requesting process B to open a TCP circuit with process A and telling process B its opening sequence number. The SYN flag is set to indicate that the circuit is in the process of being synchronized.

2. B responds to A's initial segment by sending an acknowledgment of the initial segment. It sets the ACK flag and takes A's initial sequence number, adds 1 to it (the next expected byte in the sequence), and puts that into the acknowledgment field. The SYN flag for this segment is also set, to indicate that synchronization is still not yet complete. At this point, when A receives this segment, it knows that B acknowledges the request, the connection from A to B is valid, but the link back from B to A won't be validated until B receives A's acknowledgment.

3. A acknowledges B's acknowledgment by putting the correct value in the acknowledgment field: B's sequence number plus 1. The ACK flag is also set, since A now knows the correct sequence number for the next segment from B. The SYN flag is no longer set, however, because once A sends this segment the synchronization process is complete.

Once the handshake is complete, the two processes continue to acknowledge each other's transmissions, but now they can start sending data in the segments as well, so the applications using TCP can communicate with each other. To improve performance, implementations may start sending data with the third segment—the connection can be considered active once the initiator sends the second ACK, so there is nothing preventing the initiator from including data in that segment as well.

17.3.4   THE TRANSMISSION CONTROL PROTOCOL–SYNCHRONIZE FLOOD ATTACK

An interesting attribute of the TCP synchronization protocol is that, as originally defined, there is a simple exploit of the protocol that can result in a *denial of service* (*DoS*) attack. Such attacks are intended to prevent anyone from using a host by tying up its resources in some way: perhaps by overloading the system, or perhaps by causing it to crash, or both.

When a single, legitimate request to open a TCP circuit is accepted by the host and processed, a synchronization response is sent out (the SYN and ACK flags are set) and the requesting host sends back the final segment

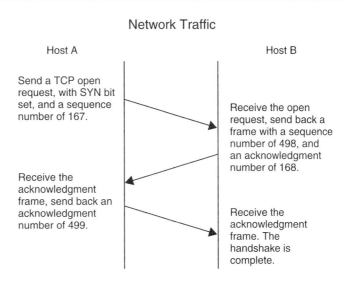

Figure 17–2: The sequence number and acknowledgment number represent byte counts in the streams of data being sent between two hosts connected using TCP.

in the handshake. Depending on the type and configuration of the host hardware, it may be able to handle many legitimate requests in a short period.

In the *SYN flooding* attack that first appeared in 1996, attackers send a flood of phony synchronization requests (segments with the SYN flag set) to open TCP connections with the targeted host. Even relatively small numbers of such requests, sent over relatively low-bandwidth dialup lines, were capable of disabling systems across the internet since 1996.

Interestingly, this vulnerability is implicit in the TCP protocol; there is no way to eliminate it entirely. However, there are strategies that can be used to minimize the impact of such attacks and to deter many of them. These include:

- Improved firewall filtering can deflect some attacks. Because many of these attacks use *spoofed* (forged) IP addresses, filtering should be done to block IP packets that appear to be originating from the wrong places. For example, a router should never accept an inbound packet (a packet it receives on its interface with the external internet) that claims to be originating from a host inside the router's network.

- Configure hosts to wait longer before responding to synchronization requests; the requests can then be safely ignored if a SYN flood attack is detected.
- Reduce the timeout value for synchronization ACKs. An attacker can unleash many SYN requests in a short time; reducing the wait for the attacker to complete the handshake makes it easier to cut such attacks short.
- Use appropriate tools (intrusion detection systems, for example) to detect attacks in progress.

Hardware and software vendors have generally been quick to respond to these attacks, so there are numerous fixes, patches, and upgrades available to reduce the exposure to such attacks.

17.3.5 TRANSMISSION CONTROL PROTOCOL CONNECTION TERMINATION

Although there is only one way to initiate a TCP connection, termination is a different story. Because the connection is duplexed with two flows of data, one in each direction, an orderly close calls for a termination announcement in each direction. And because all TCP data is acknowledged, each termination announcement requires an ACK. Thus, orderly termination requires the exchange of four segments.

An orderly termination begins when one process sends a segment with the FIN flag set. This indicates that the process has no more data to transmit. When the receiving process gets this segment, it sends an ACK and then (usually) sends its own FIN segment, to which the first process also sends an ACK.

It is possible for a TCP connection to be half closed and half open. This would occur when one side (A) sends a FIN segment and the other side (B) sends an ACK but does not send its own FIN segment. In this case, B can continue to send data to A, and A will continue to ACK that data—but A can't send any new data to B. For example, an application might send a single command to a remote host and then terminate transmission; the remote host could return the results of that command without needing any additional data from the application.

During an orderly circuit termination, the communicating processes must continue to acknowledge data even if it arrives after a FIN segment. When that happens, the receiving process will be aware that there is something missing when it checks the sequence number; if some intervening segment has been lost, the receiving process will ignore the FIN segment and wait for the missing segment. The sender, waiting for ACKs of both the missing segment and the FIN segment, will likely have to resend both.

As mentioned earlier, it is also possible for a process to abort a connection unilaterally by sending a segment with the RST flag set. When this occurs, no more data or ACKs are transmitted.

17.3.6 ACKNOWLEDGMENT, RETRANSMISSION, AND FLOW CONTROL

Once the connection has been established, each side may transmit but usually one participant will do the bulk of the transmission. For example, any application stream involving file transfers (whether SMTP deliveries or FTP transfers) will invariably consist mostly of file data being sent from the server to the client. However, the client must still ACK data that has been received, and as a result will periodically transmit a TCP segment to do so. Because TCP provides a byte stream service, a single ACK can be used to acknowledge receipt of more than one segment. The process sending the bulk of the data also sends acknowledgments along with that data—to acknowledge receipt of the other host's acknowledgments!

Assuming that conditions are optimal, both systems will transmit TCP segments back and forth, receiving each other's acknowledgments and continuing to transmit new segments. However, when conditions are sub-optimal, such as often happens in large internets, network traffic can be delayed, fragmented, or corrupted (or all three). Unlike underlivered/underliverable UDP datagrams, a response is required when TCP segments are lost or damaged. Because TCP is a reliable protocol and because all TCP data must be acknowledged, when data is lost or when an ACK for data is lost the data must be resent.

Instead of waiting for acknowledgment of receipt of every individual TCP segment before sending another one, TCP implementations determine some number of bytes they are willing to send before expecting to receive acknowledgments.

Calculating that number depends on the receiving TCP implementation's transmission window—what the host at the other end indicates is the maximum number of bytes it is willing to accept—as well as the time it takes to move a packet from host to host and back, or the *round-trip time* (*RTT*). More than one mechanism may be used to estimate the RTT in a circuit, but that value and the receiver's transmission window are used to help calculate how long the sender should wait for an ACK. The most obvious approach is to check the system clock when a segment is sent out and then check it again when an ACK for data in that segment is received, but there are others.

Getting the RTT value right is important: wait too short a time, and the sender will start retransmitting data that hasn't yet reached its destination; wait too long a time, and the receiver will wait too long a time to restart when the connection is lost. When it sends a segment, the host starts a countdown; if an acknowledgment for the segment is not received when that time is up, the segment is retransmitted.

For example, if the receiving TCP implementation signals at the start of the connection that it can handle up to 10 K bytes of data (its transmission window), and the sender determines that the RTT is 10 seconds. In that case, the sender can send 10 TCP segments of 1-K bytes each, pausing for 1 second between each, and the first ACK should arrive at the sender just as the last segment is sent out.

TCP lets communicating processes determine how much data they are willing to process at any given time. Every time a segment is sent it includes a value indicating a current window size, so the host at the other end can modify the amount of data it is sending to accommodate the receiving host. This helps avoid flooding a smaller, slower computer's buffers when communicating with a larger or faster computer. The window size indicates the number of segments that can be considered to be "in transit" and the size of the window affects how fast segments are sent.

The optimal size of a transmission window depends on how fast data can be transmitted between hosts and how much latency there is in the connection. The problem is to make sure that the pipeline between hosts is always full of data, while never being too full of data. Imagine the TCP connection as a conveyor belt carrying bits of data to be processed (for the sake of the analogy, imagine that there is a second conveyor belt running in the opposite direction to carry responses and acknowledgments back to the sender—see Figure 17–3).

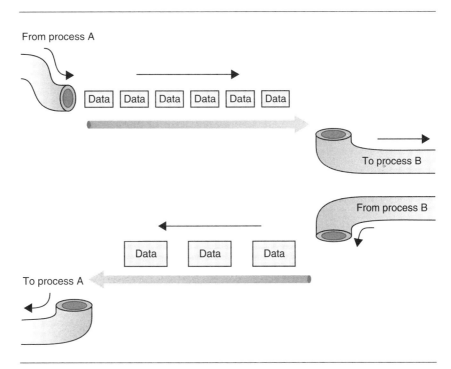

From process A

Data Data Data Data Data Data

To process B

From process B

Data   Data   Data

To process A

Figure 17–3: Data moving between processes using TCP.

The distance between the sender and recipient can be short, meaning that there is low latency, or it can be long, meaning there is high latency. Assume that the conveyor belts move at 4 units per second, and that the two hosts are separated by 10 units. Thus, it takes a little more than 5 seconds for a round-trip: you send a chunk of data from one process to another, it takes 2.5 seconds to arrive and some small amount of time is taken to create an acknowledgment and put it on the belt going back to the sender, 2.5 seconds later.

Five seconds is a long time to wait for an ACK without sending anything. If the receiving process can handle four chunks/second, the sender could actually just start sending its packages at that rate. In this case, the transmission window is about 5 units wide. If it doesn't start getting ACKs after 5 seconds, though, the sender might have to resend some or all of the packages—as well as consider making the window smaller. If the ACKs start coming sooner, the receiving process might indicate it can handle more segments in a given time—in other words, it wants a bigger transmission window. Transmission windows allow the sender and receiver to adapt to variations in network conditions: when a link is congested, segments are lost and the sending process can slow down the rate at which data is transmitted.

17.4   Transmission Control Protocol Performance

Responding to congestion with a sliding transmission window is one important mechanism specified for TCP; four other performance enhancements have been added to the standards track specification for TCP. These techniques, all developed by Van Jacobson, are documented in RFC 2581, "TCP Congestion Control." Co-author of RFC 2581, the late W. Richard Stevens, also wrote an earlier version of the specification in RFC 2001 as well as the seminal reference, *TCP/IP Illustrated*. Without these enhancements TCP would be a considerably less powerful transport protocol and TCP/IP would be a less useful protocol suite. The rest of this section provides brief descriptions of each algorithm as it is used for TCP.

17.4.1   Slow Start

Early TCP implementations did nothing special for the first few segments sent after the connection was established. As soon as the connection was made, as many segments as filled the window would be transmitted down the line. Although this works when the hosts are on the same local network, it presents a problem when the hosts are connected across a routed internetwork. Intervening routers may have to queue the traffic carrying the segments, so some part of that initial set of segments can be lost and cause significant performance problems.

The *slow start algorithm* addresses this problem of regulating the speed of transmission of segments by observing how fast the other side acknowledges the segments that have already been sent. If the ACKs come in quickly, the transmission window can be made larger; if the ACKs dribble in slowly, the transmission window may need to be made smaller.

With slow start, the sending process maintains a *congestion window*, whose value is initially set at one segment, and is increased every time an ACK is received. To determine the number of segments a sender can have in transit at any given time, the sender compares the values of the congestion window and the transmission window and is limited to the smaller of the two values.

With slow start, TCP implementations are able to gradually work their way up to a mutually acceptable value for the rate at which segments are transmitted, while minimizing the impact of sending too fast. In theory, the sender starts by transmitting a single segment (at which point the congestion window is set to one). When it receives an ACK of this first segment, the congestion window is increased to two—at which point it sends out two segments. When the recipient sends out ACKs for those two segments, the congestion window increases to four. Now, the sender can transmit four segments; when those are ACK'ed, the congestion window doubles again to eight. Eventually, if the congestion window exceeds the transmission window, the smaller value will be used to limit the window size. The other possibility is that the capacity of some intermediate system will be exceeded, in wihch case the sender will have to reduce the size of the congestion window.

Let's consider the vehicular analogy:

A vehicle traveling at 1,000 kilometers per hour along a reasonably clear road encounters a huge boulder. Slamming on the brake, the driver waits until it is clear to go around the boulder and then starts accelerating again, starting at 1 kph, then 2 kph, doubling every second until achieving a maximum sustainable rate.

17.4.2 Congestion Avoidance

Almost always implemented in conjunction with slow start, the *congestion avoidance algorithm* helps reduce packet loss by acting as a brake, to slow down transmissions when the sender receives indications that packets are being lost somewhere along the line. Congestion occurs in networks for the same reasons it occurs in motor vehicle traffic: a high-volume roadway is being routed into a lower-volume roadway, two or more roadways are merging into a single roadway with lower overall capacity than the others put together, or a roadway is operating at a lower than normal capacity (a lane is blocked by a stalled vehicle, for example).

With slow start, all segments (or vehicles) would come to a halt at any obstacle and then gradually speed up again until they hit another obstacle.

This is as bad a strategy for network traffic as it is for vehicular traffic. The congestion avoidance algorithm increments (increases by one segment for each acknowledgment received) the congestion window when congestion is detected.

Congestion is assumed to be occuring when a segment acknowledgment timer expires (meaning that no ACK has been received for that segment) or when duplicate ACKs are received (meaning that the original ACK segment timer expired). In either case, a timeout occured usually due to a complete stop to traffic somewhere along the route. In this case the sender begins the slow start algorithm from scratch, setting the congestion window back to 1. From there, slow start continues until the congestion window is half as large as it was when the timeout occured.

This is where congestion avoidance begins: rather than doubling the window back to the same value it was when the congestion occured, the window increases only by one segment at a time. Let's consider the vehicular analogy:

A vehicle traveling at 1,000 kilometers per hour along a reasonably clear road encounters a huge boulder. Slamming on the brake, the driver waits until it is clear to go around the boulder and then starts accelerating again, starting at 1 kph, then 2 kph, doubling every second until reaching 512 kph—at which point, the acceleration is slowed down to 1 kph/second. This approach is only prudent, given that there may be more boulders around; if the vehicle accelerates up to 600 kph before it hits another boulder, it will stop, accelerate rapidly to about 300 kph, and then more cautiously.

Network traffic may not hit boulders, but if it is going "too fast," then segments may be lost. Gradually reducing the rate at which a sending process attains its top speed helps prevent overloading the congested link.

17.4.3 FAST RETRANSMIT

Duplicate ACKs may be caused either by lost segments or by segments that have been delivered out of order. If the segment was actually lost, early TCP implementations had to wait for a timer to expire before retransmitting the missing segment. If the segment was delivered out of order, then it will eventually be ACKed and the sender won't have to retransmit it.

Fast retransmit is a simple algorithm: if three or more duplicate ACKs are received in a row, the TCP implementation can assume that there is a missing segment and therefore resend it. If the segment was merely delivered out of order, waiting for one or two duplicate ACKs should be enough to clear up the matter. If it takes longer, just resending the missing segment will be the right choice in almost all cases.

17.4.4 FAST RECOVERY

When a duplicate ACK is received, it means that there may be some congestion to avoid. When the fast retransmit algorithm is put into play, the *fast recovery algorithm* dictates that the TCP implementation invoke the congestion avoidance algorithm.

17.5 Improving Transmission Control Protocol

By the time RFC 793 was published, TCP had been under development for much of the preceding decade. By 1982, it was largely considered complete. A TCP implementation published in 1982 could (in theory, anyway) be interoperable with a TCP implementation published in 2002—despite all the changes that have occured in the intervening 20 years: more available bandwidth, more powerful computers, larger networks and internets, and more.

Rather than attempt to upgrade TCP to meet new challenges, changes have been made manageable in TCP by incorporating them as TCP options. New implementations add support for more options but they continue to interoperate with other implementations that don't support those options. Upgrades, after which older versions of a protocol can no longer interoperate with newer versions, threaten to fragment the interoperable internet by preventing hosts that don't support the new version from communicating with hosts that do (and vice versa). As we'll see in Chapter 27, attempting to upgrade a fundamental internet protocol can be a frustrating process.

This section introduces the most common and important TCP options, followed by discussion of an important performance-related modification: Selective Acknowledgment (SACK). The last section lists many of the RFCs that describe TCP and ways in which it can be improved.

17.5.1 Transmission Control Protocol Options

The TCP header allots up to 40 bytes for options following the required header fields and before the segment data. As already mentioned, when the options do not terminate on a word boundary, up to 2 bytes of data are added as padding.

TCP options always start with a single octet, containing a "kind" value (as in, "what kind of option is this?"). Two types of option are defined, the first consisting of a single byte; the other are longer than 1 byte. Multiple byte options are at least 2 bytes long, consisting of the 8-bit kind value and an 8-bit option length value. The length includes the first 2 bytes, and up to 38 bytes of data are possible.

RFC 793 defines three basic options:

End of option list: This option indicates that there are no more options to follow and consists of a single octet with a value of 0; it is different from padding only in that it immediately follows the last option data. It is not used when the option ends on the 4-octet word boundary; when the option ends at the first octet of a word, the end of option list option will be used, followed by 2 bytes of padding.

No-operation: This option consists of a single octet with a value of 1 and causes the recipient to do nothing other than continue processing the segment options. It may be used to separate options, particularly if the first option does not fall on a word boundary. While the end of option list option indicates that no more options are to be processed and signals the recipient to begin processing the segment, the no-operation option acts as a placeholder between options. If the no-operation option is present, there will be at least one more option yet to process.

Maximum Segment Size (MSS): This option consists of 4 octets, the first, with a value of 4, identifying it as the MSS option; the second octet indicates the option length is equal to 4 octets. The last 2 octets indicate the maximum segment size to be sent. As a 16-bit value, the maximum segment size possible under RFC 793 TCP is 65,535 octets long.

This option must be used during the initialization sequence, otherwise it will be ignored. If an MSS value is not specified during the initialization sequence, senders can use any segment size they wish. As already mentioned, all TCP/IP-compliant hosts can be assumed capable of handling a segment of 536 octets, so in the absence of a specific MSS the sender is most likely to opt for the highest value known to be acceptable to any host—even though the specification permits the sender to use any size if no MSS is specified. Sending a large segment will only be more efficient if the recipient can accept it; as the segment size increases, so do the odds that it will be rejected as being too large.

Since 1982, almost two dozen other options have been identified, although only about half have been specified in published RFCs. Valid TCP options are listed at the internet assigned numbers authority (IANA) web site (http://www.iana.org/assignments/tcp-parameters). Of these, the most important is undoubtedly the SACK option, to be discussed in the next section.

Two other important options include:

WSOPT (Window Scale) option: RFC 793 limits the TCP window size to a maximum of 65,535 octets. This may be enough for processes running on hosts connected to 10-Mbps Ethernets, but it seems much smaller on gigabit (1,000 Mbps) Ethernets. This option permits the negotiation between the two hosts of window scaling. The option uses 3 bytes, 1 for option kind and 1 for length, with the third indicating a scaling factor (a factor of 2) to use on the sender's receiving window. Window scaling may be performed on both transmission and receiving windows, so a host might send this option (during the initialization sequence only) with a scaling factor of 1, meaning it is willing to do scaling on its own transmission window but not on its receiving window.

Timestamps option: Given that TCP sequencing numbers are limited to 32-bit values, two communicating processes transmitting over (and saturating) a 10-Mbps Ethernet would need about an hour to move the roughly 4 billion or so octets necessary to cycle through all available sequence number values. Increase the bandwidth by a factor of 100 by moving to gigabit Ethernet, and the sequence number space can be cycled in less than a minute. The timestamps option allows both hosts to check each others' clocks, to make sure that neither has cycled through the sequence numbers and to avoid ACKing old segments.

TCP options like windows scaling and time stamping make it possible to support the new faster networks by allowing larger window sizes. Time stamping segments helps to eliminate ambiguity caused by the wrapped sequence numbers, as well as improving flow control by making roundtrip time estimation more accurate.

17.5.2   SELECTIVE ACKNOWLEDGMENT

TCP's acknowledgment mechanism is quite elegant: the ACKer sends a single value to indicate that all numbered octets in the sequence, up to the ACK value, have been received. The receiver does not have to ACK every segment, particularly if they are being delivered in a nice steady stream. Depending on many factors, a single ACK might notify the sender that 536 octets have been received, or 5,000 or even 50,000.

This elegance can be expensive, especially when in a flow of many segments, one is lost. Under RFC 793, if a host receives every segment in a stream except for the first segment, it must discard all those segments and wait for the first segment to be retransmitted (after the sender times out while waiting for an ACK for that initial segment).

This can be a waste of bandwidth, particularly as more bandwidth becomes available and more data is shoved down the data pipeline before any ACKs are received. The solution for TCP, called *selective acknowledgment* (*SACK*), was first published in the experimental RFC 1072, "TCP Extensions for Long-Delay Paths," in 1988. Selective acknowledgment had already been tried in other experimental protocols in the 1980s, and the experience to that point had been positive. By 1996, RFC 2018, "TCP Selective Acknowledgment Options," was published as a standards track specification.

Hosts negotiate the use of SACK during the circuit initialization process; the SACK-permitted option is 2 octets long and simply indicates that the sender will support SACK. Once negotiated, SACK itself is straightforward: instead of using a single acknowledgment value to indicate the last byte received, the recipient uses the SACK option to indicate that it will be ACKing one or more ranges of bytes received.

The SACK fields consist of pairs of acknowledgment numbers: the first indicating the ACK number for the first byte received in a block of received data, and the second indicating the ACK number for the last byte in the block. Each ACK number is 32 bits, and the SACK option itself uses 2 octets, so no more than four discrete blocks of data can be selectively ACKed in a single TCP segment (TCP options may use no more than 40 octets; each block requires 8 octets, and the option itself requires 2 octets, for a total of 34 octets plus padding).

17.5.3 TRANSMISSION CONTROL PROTOCOL EXTENSIONS AND REVISIONS

In addition to the modifications, options, and additions to TCP already noted, the IETF has published dozens of RFCs that bear on TCP in some way. These RFCs provide a good resource for the interested reader:

RFC 3168: The Addition of Explicit Congestion
Notification (ECN) to IP

RFC 3155: End-to-end Performance Implications of
Links with Errors

RFC 3042: Enhancing TCP's Loss Recovery Using
Limited Transmit

RFC 2988: Computing TCP's Retransmission Timer

RFC 2923: TCP Problems with Path MTU Discovery

RFC 2884: Performance Evaluation of Explicit
Congestion Notification (ECN) in
IP Networks

RFC 2883: An Extension to the Selective
Acknowledgement (SACK) Option for TCP

RFC 2861: TCP Congestion Window Validation

RFC 2760: Ongoing TCP Research Related to
Satellites

RFC 2757: Long Thin Networks

RFC 2582: The NewReno Modification to TCP's
Fast Recovery Algorithm

RFC 2581: TCP Congestion Control

RFC 2525: Known TCP Implementation Problems

RFC 2488: (BCP0028) Enhancing TCP Over Satellite
          Channels Using Standard Mechanisms

RFC 2416: When TCP Starts Up with Four Packets
          into Only Three Buffers

RFC 2415: Simulation Studies of Increased Initial
          TCP Window Size

RFC 2414: Increasing TCP's Initial Window

RFC 2398: FYI0033 Some Testing Tools for TCP
          Implementors

RFC 2267: Network Ingress Filtering: Defeating
          Denial of Service Attacks Which Employ
          IP Source Address Spoofing

RFC 2018: TCP Selective Acknowledgement Options

RFC 1693: An Extension to TCP: Partial Order
          Service

RFC 1323: TCP Extensions for High Performance

RFC 1263: TCP Extensions Considered Harmful

RFC 1146: TCP Alternate Checksum Options

RFC 1144: Compressing TCP/IP Headers for
          Low-Speed Serial Links

Searching the RFC Editor's archive for TCP-related documents (at www.rfc-editor.org) returns over 100 RFCs; those listed here are among the more interesting and important. Simply browsing the titles will give some idea of the extent of the issues related to TCP. Perhaps most important is a quest for improving performance in the form of recovering quickly from network congestion, reducing the impact of network congestion before errors occur, and calculating the optimal values for TCP variables such as transmission and reception windows, timeouts, and segment size.

Other issues relate to using TCP over networks with different attributes. For example, the *long thin networks* (*LTNs*) and *long fat networks* (*LFNs*) pose different problems for TCP. A "long" network is one in which the latency is high and it takes a long time for a segment round trip: from source to destination, and back (for the acknowledgment). A network is "thin" or "fat" depending on how much bandwidth is available. High-bandwidth networks can carry a lot of data, and can be compared to "big fat" pipes carrying vast quantities of fluids; thin networks are those with skinny little pipes (such as those based on low-speed modems or early wireless networks). The higher the latency of the network, the longer hosts should wait before resending unACKed segments, compared to networks with lower latencies.

Sending TCP over satellite channels, as described in RFC 2488, "Enhancing TCP over Satellite Channels Using Standard Mechanisms," has its own unique problems: long round-trip delays to high-orbit satellites can result in very high latency as well as high error rates due to radio transmission noise, low earth orbit satellite networks can result in highly variable latency over time due to variations in distance a transmission travels to reach the nearest satellite, and often low bandwidth. RFC 2488 outlines how standard TCP flow control responses behave in these circumstances and discuss how other mechanisms such as *forward error control* (*FEC*) and *path MTU* (the *maximum transmission unit* [*MTU*] is the largest packet size that can be sent between two IP hosts, and the path MTU is the largest packet size possible in a particular route between two hosts) can be applied at the lower protocol layers. Path MTU will be discussed in Chapter 19.

17.6 Chapter Summary

UDP is the minimalist transport layer protocol, but TCP is the full-featured version: TCP is documented in many RFCs, with many revisions, additions, and adjustments, not to mention reports of research and development to improve it.

TCP is complicated, from the demanding protocols for initiating a TCP connection to the mechanisms for keeping track of which segments have been

sent, which acknowledged, how many should be sent before an acknowledgment is received, and sliding windows for sending and receiving data.
Where as UDP offers nothing more than the bare minimum, TCP offers
almost as many features as can be imagined at the transport layer.

Many years of practical experience on untold numbers of hosts and networks as well as on the global internet, coupled with the vast research and
development efforts over the years as documented in RFCs and elsewhere,
ensure that although TCP may not always be the only transport protocol
for most applications it will remain an important one. TCP will continue
to dominate the internet as an important transport layer protocol for years
to come.

However, in recent years we have seen the introduction of SCTP as a
standards-track protocol as well as an increasing willingness of network
engineers to consider alternatives to TCP (and UDP). As we see in the next
chapter, not only is TCP not the only possibility for full-featured transport layer protocol, but neither is UDP the only possibility for barebones
transport layer protocol.

18

Transport Layer Protocols of the Future

For many years, transmission control protocol (TCP) and user datagram protocol (UDP) were sufficient to handle all transport layer needs—just as some ice cream sellers offer only chocolate and vanilla to their customers. TCP offers reliable transport with flow control and many other features, while UDP provides only the most basic transport function of providing an interface linking application layer protocols with the internet layer protocols. Limiting the number of transport layers reduces the complexity of implementing application protocols because there are three choices for the designers at the transport layer: implement an interface with TCP, with UDP, or with both. Likewise, internet layer implementers need only design interfaces for two transport layers protocols, so the internet layer protocol implementation does not require any special accommodation for particular applications.

It has been unusual for a set of modern computing standards to remain largely unchanged and unchallenged for decades, but new alternatives for application implementers are slowly gaining acceptance. This chapter presents a new internet standards-track protocol, the Stream Control Transmission Protocol (SCTP), and one work-in-progress protocol, the Datagram Control Protocol (DCP). Each takes a different approach to the transport layer, and each will succeed or fail on its ability to solve a networking problem better than existing solutions. "Better" might mean at a lower cost, with improved efficiency, with higher performance, increased services, higher degree of interoperability, or some combination.

18.1   Stream Control Transmission Protocol

As long as an application can use all of its features, TCP is an acceptable solution. However, TCP imposes limitations as well in its lack of flexibility: although with selective acknowledgment (SACK) TCP provides a limited mechanism for out-of-order delivery, some applications don't really care whether data is delivered in order or not. Likewise, some applications work well with TCP's byte stream delivery, while others tend to be oriented to well-defined formats for data that must be delivered when the data units are complete rather than whenever a buffer fills with enough data for a complete segment payload (TCP uses PSH or URG flags to designate data that needs to be sent immediately).

During the 1990s, researchers working on the problem of transmitting publicly switched telephone network (PSTN) signals[1] across the internet found that UDP offered too little while TCP offered too much for their new application. TCP works well for traditional data transfer tasks such as moving files around the internet, but it performs less well for carrying telephony signaling data. Although telephony in general includes the task of carrying a voice (or data) signal from one telephone set to another, there is a great deal more that must be accomplished to provide telephony services such as:

- Carrying the dual-tone multi-frequency (DTMF) signals, otherwise known as the sounds generated by pressing a telephone set's keypad.

[1]Signaling System 7 (SS7) is the dominant protocol for telecommunications signaling, and the SIGTRAN (Signalling Transport) working group of the IETF proposed the move to a new transport protocol capable of handling SS7.

- Transmitting signals indicating call status, such as a busy signal, fast-busy (no available lines), call-waiting, and telephone call ringing.
- Transmitting call information, including caller ID.
- Allowing the negotiation of special services such as conference calling and delivering of calls to internal extensions.

Telephony signaling, it turns out, benefits from a transport protocol that provides a more or less ordered delivery service (rather than TCP's strict ordered delivery service) as well as a record-oriented data transfer (rather than TCP's stream orientation). In addition, PSTN signaling can be much more complicated than typical data transfer-based applications. Whereas TCP provides applications a single socket (IP address and TCP port number) for each half of a connection, telephony signaling is more likely to involve *multi-homed hosts*, which are hosts with more than one IP address, usually on more than one network; routers, for example, are multi-homed hosts. TCP offers no obvious mechanism to allow a single connection to be carried through more than one network path. Finally, once it's been decided to design a new transport layer protocol, why not directly address the problem of SYN flooding attacks?

The rest of this section outlines the architecture, protocol elements, and function of SCTP.

18.1.1 STREAM CONTROL TRANSMISSION PROTOCOL ARCHITECTURE

SCTP grew out of the needs of applications that must do PSTN signaling over the internet. The decision to create a new protocol was not taken lightly, as efforts to implement IP telephony and similar applications over either TCP and UDP have been ongoing since the late 1980s. As described in RFC 2960, "Stream Control Transmission Protocol," SCTP is similar to TCP in that it provides "a reliable transport operating on top of a connectionless packet network" (in other words, IP) and offers these services:

- Acknowledged error-free non-duplicated transfer of user data.
- Data fragmentation to conform to discovered path maximum transmission unit (MTU) size.
- Sequenced delivery of user messages within multiple streams, with an option for order-of-arrival delivery of individual user messages.

- Optional bundling of multiple user messages into a single SCTP packet.
- Network-level fault tolerance through supporting of multi-homing at either or both ends of an association.
- Appropriate congestion avoidance behavior and resistance to flooding and masquerade attacks.

SCTP is similar in some ways to TCP, but it provides a more flexible transport capable of handling multiple flows of data through a single logical connection between two nodes. Although both transport protocols support flows, which imply two endpoints, SCTP allows application layer processes to maintain flows even when data might pass in and out of the node over different internet layer interfaces. In other words, two hosts can communicate with SCTP.

Of the services SCTP provides, the newest one is the "sequenced delivery of user messages within multiple streams." SCTP nodes are able to take advantage of multi-homing, meaning data from a sending node might arrive on any active network interface, but the user applications may also define multiple streams of data. Unlike with TCP, an SCTP-based application can define one stream of data as an unstructured byte stream for data transmission and another for managing the connection (and others for other purposes, if needed). The same functionality can be approached with TCP only by defining completely separate TCP connections for each function, an approach that can be costly in terms of application performance.

18.1.2 STREAM CONTROL TRANSMISSION PROTOCOL ELEMENTS

SCTP can be said to consist of some new protocol constructs, as well as its basic set of protocol functions. These are introduced in this section.

Connections made between processes are permitted to communicate with SCTP over broadly defined *association*, the complete set of ports and IP addresses that each node advertises as being available as *transport addresses* (port and IP address pairs). Therefore, SCTP can be used completely only when implemented on multi-homed hosts.

TCP nodes exchange data over a circuit defined by a single port and IP address for each node. If a node's IP address becomes unreachable (perhaps the hardware fails or there is a network failure), the TCP circuit will, eventually, time out. SCTP nodes are able to specify more than one port/address through which they can send and/or receive data, and the SCTP association is defined as the complete set of possible combinations of the advertised transport addresses.

For example, the table below lists transport addresses for two nodes, A and B.

```
Node A                    Node B
192.168.1.1:343           10.1.1.1:3454
192.168.100.10:343        10.1.1.244:3494
192.168.232.50:343        10.200.50.100:4444
```

The SCTP association, therefore, consists of the set of combinations of all of those transport addresses (corresponding to all the different circuits that are possible between nodes A and B):

```
192.168.1.1:343::10.1.1.1:3454
192.168.1.1:343::10.1.1.244:3494
192.168.1.1:343::10.200.50.100:4444
192.168.100.10:343::10.1.1.1:3454
192.168.100.10:343::10.1.1.244:3494
192.168.100.10:343::10.200.50.100:4444
192.168.232.50:343::10.1.1.1:3454
192.168.232.50:343::10.1.1.244:3494
192.168.232.50:343::10.200.50.100:4444
```

The same SCTP connection may be carried over any (or all) of these connection specifications, while a TCP circuit would have to be set up and maintained for each. Figure 18–1 shows how this association would look graphically.

The two communicating processes can send data over nine different internet routes in this case, using a single SCTP association. Of course, the number would vary depending on how many internet interfaces each host allows to be used in the assocation.

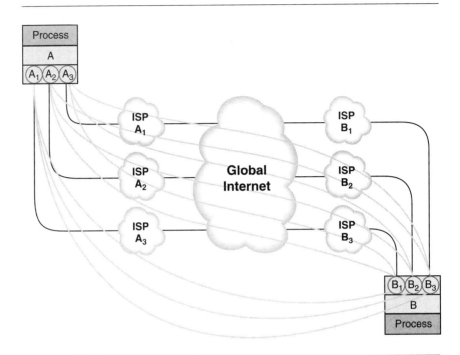

Figure 18–1: Connecting two multi-homed hosts with a single SCTP association.

The authors of RFC 2960 define the SCTP *stream* as "a sequence of user [application] messages that are to be delivered to the upper-layer protocol with respect to other messages within the same stream." A stream might consist of the sequence of words a person is speaking, while another stream might consist of commands that same person issues with respect to the voice connection (e.g., to put the caller on hold, add another caller to a conference, and so on). As the RFC authors explain, this definition contrasts with the way it's used in TCP, where it refers to a sequence of bytes.

One more concept should be introduced here: the SCTP *chunk*. Per RFC 2960, a chunk is a "unit of information within an SCTP packet, consisting of a chunk header and chunk-specific content." In other words, it might be considered a PDU (protocol data unit) in the same way that a segment is TCP's PDU, except that SCTP packets can contain more than one chunk, as will be made clear in the next section.

18.1.3   STREAM CONTROL TRANSMISSION PROTOCOL FUNCTIONS

The SCTP protocol itself consists of several protocol functions, which will be described here briefly:

Association Startup and Takedown: The SCTP association is similar in function to the TCP connection, and initializing the association requires an exchange of protocol messages. To prevent attacks similar to TCP SYN flooding, a four-step handshake protocol, using a *cookie*, a small piece of data used to store a system's status at a given time, and used in this case to maintain information about the association. Each node exchanges initialization and acknowledgment messages, including information about transport addresses.

Also like TCP, a formal and orderly termination process is specified; unlike TCP, when one node terminates the session, the other node must also terminate the session. Likewise, a session can also be aborted (terminated unilaterally and without formal exchange of messages).

Sequenced Delivery Within Streams: Again, SCTP functions similarly to TCP, assigning sequence numbers to data being transmitted. However, unlike TCP, SCTP nodes negotiate during the association initialization process how many separate streams will be supported. Thus, there are separate sets of sequence numbers assigned to data sent within each separate stream.

User Data Fragmentation: SCTP implementations are permitted to break up user application messages to avoid having a lower layer protocol (such as IP, as discussed in Chapter 19) fragment the messages. In contrast, TCP gets the maximum transmission unit size from IP, and then builds segments that will not need to be fragmented. The difference is that under SCTP the transport layer protocol has more control over the process of fragmenting and reconstructing the messages.

Acknowledgment and Congestion Avoidance: SCTP uses a *transmission sequence number (TSN)* to keep the acknowledgment process separate from the stream sequence numbers. Doing so allows nodes to ACK every message it receives in the sequence, without any reference to whether they are received in order, or whether there are missing messages.

Congestion avoidance and packet retransmission use mechanisms similar to those used in TCP.

Chunk Bundling: An individual chunk is a data unit that occurs within the context of an individual SCTP stream. For example, the data in a stream dedicated to SCTP control messages would consist of chunks containing the protocol messages, while the data in a stream dedicated to carrying voice data would consist of chunks containing voice data. SCTP provides a mechanism by which chunks from different streams can be bundled into a single SCTP packet. This allows SCTP nodes to efficiently package data, although receiving nodes may request that senders disable chunk bundling when they experience congestion.

Packet Validation: In addition to the robust 32-bit Adler checksum (see RFC 1950, "ZLIB Compressed Data Format Specification, version 3.3," for the details), SCTP mandates use of a *verification tag* to validate transmissions. The verification tag value is set during association initialization, and must be included with each message.

Path Management: SCTP nodes are responsible for monitoring all the transport addresses in an association for "reachability" (determined by how easy or difficult it is to communicate over that address), as well as determining appropriate paths based on the application configuration. When some transport addresses are not being actively used, the SCTP nodes use "heartbeat" transmissions—short messages whose only function is to verify the address is reachable—to monitor reachability.

18.1.4 USING STREAM CONTROL TRANSMISSION PROTOCOL

SCTP was borne out of the efforts to map SS7 over IP, mostly because it requires guaranteed and reliable delivery of high volumes of unrelated streams of data, a framing service at the transport layer level (as opposed to the byte stream service TCP offers), and improved security (resistance to DoS attacks as well as data integrity attacks), among other needs. By allowing multi-homed hosts to specify multiple interfaces over which data can be transmitted, SCTP makes it possible to improve drastically performance in an unreliable network environment. With each additional interface, the implementers add redundancy to the network; if one interface fails, there is at least one other interface that is likely to still be active.

Although at first blush, SCTP seems a very specialized protocol, many of the same attributes that make it useful for PSTN signaling also make it attractive for transporting web applications. Modern web sites often incorporate data from many sources, offering that data in different forms and with different methods of access. More to the point, SCTP offers companies and other organizations that host their own web sites the potential to better serve their clients.

SCTP could improve web performance in several ways:

Redundant internet access and path management means that customers would be less likely to experience long delays during peak periods, and that catastrophic connectivity losses at one ISP could be overcome almost instantly.

Streams and chunk bundling allow web servers to transmit data as it becomes available, rather than having to transmit all data sequentially. Anything that improves web performance can be considered a competitive advantage for businesses offering their services over the web.

Packet validation provides a more robust mechanism for protecting data integrity, reducing the exposure to malicious attacks.

The added security features in SCTP merely make it even more attractive for deployment over the web. As of mid-2002, there are still only a few SCTP implementations, and a broad deployment to end-user personal computer is still way off on the horizon. SCTP may still need years of research, testing, and additional development before it can become a viable alternative to TCP for mainstream applications.

18.2   Datagram Control Protocol

While SCTP has already been annointed by the IETF as a standards track protocol, as of 2002, the DCP is still very much a work in progress. Specifications have been submitted to the IETF as internet drafts, and DCP supporters have been lobbying the IESG for approval of a new working group, but there is a long way to go before DCP can be considered on a par with SCTP (let alone TCP or UDP).

This section describes DCP briefly, not so much as an exemplar of protocol design as to offer another alternative transport layer protocol. Interested readers should monitor the IETF mailing lists to see how DCP fares in the future.

One might suppose that between UDP, TCP, and SCTP, every application could be matched with an appropriate transport layer protocol. However, the deck is stacked in favor of applications that can use the reliable and connection-oriented services offered by TCP and SCTP. Applications that need no transport layer services can use UDP, but another set of applications can be imagined needing more than UDP can offer while not quite everything that TCP and SCTP promise.

DCP advocates suggest that streaming media applications, such as those in which voice or video transmissions are carried, can benefit from a more relaxed approach than is possible with either TCP or SCTP. Although those transports provide delivery guarantees for applications in which a single error can corrupt an entire data file or change the meaning of a control signal, streaming media applications are less sensitive to lost or corrupt data.

When transmitting a video feed, for example, a significant portion of the data can be lost or scrambled while the entire stream is still comprehensible. The difference between 99.9% accuracy and 70% accuracy might be similar to the difference between watching a television broadcast over a cable system and watching the same broadcast on a set with rabbit ear antennae, but in both cases the broadcast will convey information.

As described in the most recent available draft,[2] DCP is intended for applications that can use a transport with the following features:

- Acknowledged, but unreliable, datagram flow transmission. The receiving node ACKs all datagrams it gets, but missing datagrams do not have to be retransmitted.
- A formal connection orientation, with communicating hosts initializing DCP connections and using an orderly connection teardown procedure.
- A reliable mechanism for negotiating connection options. The specification explicitly mentions that this mechanism

---

[2]Internet drafts are published with explicit warnings against referencing them in more permanent documents; for the most current documents regarding DCP, the interested reader should check the RFC Editor web site at www.rfc-editor.org and search in both the RFC and internet draft archives ("DCP" should be sufficient to retrieve all current documents).

be available for negotiation of appropriate congestion control strategies.

- Mechanisms allowing a server to avoid holding any state for unacknowledged connection attempts or already finished connections.
- An option to provide some mechanism to inform the sender about which packets reached the receiver.
- Congestion control incorporating explicit congestion notification.
- Path MTU discovery, as per [RFC 1191] (see Chapter 19).

In large part, the objective for DCP is to provide a subset of the features offered by TCP and SCTP, while at the same time offering unique features such as negotiation of congestion control while at the same time improving efficiency and reducing overhead.

However, just because there is a void between UDP and TCP/SCTP, it does not follow that there must be something to fill that void. The goal of DCP is to provide a transport protocol appropriate for streaming media as well as other applications for which reliability is not necessary. Network gaming is the other commonly cited application for DCP: Quake or Starcraft participants are better served with timely data than with complete and reliable data. After all, it's better to have 80% information about a game event immediately after it occurs than to have certainty about that event when it is too late to respond to it.

18.3 The Future

Transport layer protocols will evolve as surely as application and internet layer protocols have. As will become apparent in Chapter 27 with discussion of IPv6, the upgrade to IP, the lower the layer the more difficult it is to replace a successful protocol. Application layer protocols are relatively easy to replace or at least to upgrade because the data involved can usually be fairly easily adapted to new uses. The same data can be used in parallel by an existing application protocol and a new application protocol; eventually, the newer protocol will replace (or at least displace) the old one.

Lower layer protocols are more difficult to upgrade because there is less interoperability and there are more interfaces to deal with. End users are far less likely to clamor for a new transport layer protocol than they are to demand a new application protocol. If a lower layer protocol can be demonstrated to offer significant benefits (such as gigabit Ethernet compared to 10-Mbps Ethernet), then chances are good that the new protocol will eventually triumph. However, the process can only occur as infrastructures are replaced. For the transport or internet layer, that means replacement of the operating system.

TCP and UDP will continue to dominate the internet for the immediate future—and perhaps longer. Ultimately, however, SCTP and perhaps other protocols will find their places as well.

18.4   Chapter Summary

Although TCP and UDP have long filled all transport layer needs for the internet, SCTP provides a more adaptable and potentially better performing protocol for the transport layer. Whereas TCP was developed to meet the needs of IP networking in the 1970s and 1980s, it is still widely used even in applications for which it is not well-suited. SCTP provides many of the same features and functions as TCP, but allows greater lattitude in choosing and using those features as well as providing features and functions not available anywhere else.

While it is too early to tell whether DCP will achieve any degree of success, it is important because it demonstrates the need for a wider variety of transport layer protocols—and because it further demonstrates that TCP and UDP may not be best suited to all possible situations.

In Part IV, we examine the lowest layers of the network protocol stack, beginning with the Internet Protocol itself.

Part Four

Internet Layer and Below

19

The Internet Protocol

The Internet Protocol (IP) defines the rules for packaging network traffic into IP datagrams—also known as *packets*—and it defines the rules for moving these datagrams across network boundaries. Internet traffic is carried inside IP packets; transport layer protocols interface with local IP implementation as segments (or datagrams, as appropriate) are put together at the transport layer. As data arrives at its destination, the local IP implementation accepts packets and presents the payloads to the appropriate local transport layer implementation.

Operating across possibly widely separated internets, IP provides a best-effort datagram service. *Datagram* means that these IP protocol data units are individual and unrelated messages that can stand on their own; *best-effort* means that intermediate systems transporting them treat all datagrams equally. Those systems make as much (and as little) effort as necessary to successfully route or transport *all* packets.

It is at the internet layer that the relatively tidy logical internet model, with its globally unique IP addresses and extensive routing infrastructure, is mapped onto the rather messy real-world of local networks. It is possible

397

to create a working model of an internet all within a single computer system, with no local physical network interface (the size depends only on the memory, processing, and other aspects of the system). All "network" traffic can be routed virtually through system software, with applications interacting through processes that interact through the transport layer implementation, which pass segments and datagrams down to the IP layer. In this imaginary internet model, the IP implementation would do little more than accept data from the upper layers, package it, pass it along to a different logical interface, accept it and unwrap the packet, and pass it up to the appropriate upper layer entity.

In real life, IP has considerably more to do: IP nodes must be able to determine where to send packets on the local link (the local network), as well as how to handle inbound packets. All IP nodes must have some mechanism that handles routing issues whether or not they act as routers, as well as ways to map IP addresses onto appropriate local link addresses.

IP uses a variety of tools to deliver datagrams across any internet. For example, there are mechanisms to prevent data loss due to sending packets that are too big to be carried across local networks with very small maximum protocol data unit (PDU) sizes. The *path maximum transmission unit (MTU)* mechanism lets nodes probe the path a packet will take and determine just what the *MTU* is; failing that, *fragmentation* allows packets to be broken up into small enough pieces to fit on intervening networks. Other mechanisms prevent undeliverable packets from bouncing around the internet forever, and even to mark packets to be handled differently as they are routed to their destination.

This chapters covers a great deal of material, from the basics of IP addressing to issues such as network renumbering and IP mobility. Because IP interfaces directly with the real link layer protocols as well as the transport layer protocols, it can be the part of the transmission control protocol (TCP)/IP suite that is most difficult to understand. However, IP concepts are straightforward if not always simple. Topics covered in this chapter include:

- IP address space and addressing, concepts, nomenclature, and practice
- IP datagram headers and structure
- Introduction to the Internet Control Message Protocol (ICMP)
- Introduction to internet routing

- Introduction to IP "helper" protocols and applications
- Network Address Translator (NAT)

AUTHOR'S NOTE: This chapter introduces the basic vocabulary for working with IP, but it is only a start: consider it an introduction to all the material in Parts IV and V. All of the chapters in this and the next parts of the book are integral parts of the IP. At times, it may be necessary to refer backward or forward to material in other chapters because of the high degree of inter-relatedness among internet concepts. Some readers may find it helpful to read Chapter 21 before this one, just as some readers may prefer to read Part I first and then read backward from Chapter 21. There is no wrong way to learn TCP/IP, just as there is no single right way to learn it.

I started learning TCP/IP networking in 1988 or so, from a coworker who insisted on explaining things in the same order as in Douglas Comer's excellent text, *Internetworking with TCP/IP (volume 1)*: from the bottom up. Every time he started talking about packets or segments or frames, my head would spin and I'd start asking impertinent questions about where the packets were going, and what was in the payload. Previous editions of this book used the same approach, as does virtually every other text I've ever seen.

This time around, I've started from the top. It always made much more sense to me to understand what was inside each protocol data unit, and where those payloads were going, before trying to understand what was happening underneath. At the same time, it helps to have a general awareness of what might be happening under the covers while discussing the upper layers, so this book begins with a general overview to the problems of networking in general and then becomes progressively more specific. All the while, the direction is from the top of the protocol stack down, to give you, the reader, something real and immediate to connect to all the discussion of headers and protocols.

19.1   Internet Protocol Addressing

Internet addresses refer to network interfaces. All internet-connected hosts must have a globally unique [1] IP address assigned to each network interface

---

[1] When discussing IP networks, "globally unique" means unique for the routing domain in which the host operates. All nodes on an isolated network, with no connections to any other

over which they will accept IP traffic. A host with one network interface device (an Ethernet LAN card, a serial modem, a wireless network adapter, etc.) requires one IP address to communicate over an IP internet.

There is often—but certainly not always—a one-to-one relation between IP addresses and domain names (see Chapter 8). An IP address can be associated with one or more domain names through the Domain Name System (DNS) just as a domain name can be associated with one or more IP addresses. For example, internet service providers (ISPs) offering web hosting services may host many different web sites on a single server. In that case, the server's IP address will appear in DNS records for all hosted domains. Likewise, popular web site domain names will resolve to DNS records that list more than one IP addresses through which clients may access the service.

Although personal computers will generally have a single IP address and a single network interface, multi-user systems, switches, routers, and other infrastructure-related systems may have more than one network interface on more than one network. Such redundancy provides greater reliability in the event of network outages.

Because so much of IP revolves around the IP address—determining where a packet comes from and where it should be sent—it makes sense to get a basic understanding of IP addressing before looking at the protocol specifications.

Already introduced in Chapter 3, the current standard for IP, version 4,[2] defines a fixed-length 32-bit address. As originally defined, every value can uniquely identify a single network interface. Network devices process these values as binary data, but humans do better with shorter strings, so hexadecimal and decimal notation are more common.

Not every IPv4 address can be used to identify a unique network interface. Different sections of the IPv4 address space have been allocated for individual hosts, reserved for future use, or set aside for special uses.

---

networks, must have unique addresses—but may use the same addresses as are used on some other isolated network. Even if these networks are linked through protocol gateways, they are still considered isolated routing domains—even when IP is the protocol being gatewayed.

[2]As IP version 6 continues to gain ground, slowly but surely, the term "IP address" becomes increasingly ambiguous: does it mean IPv4 addresses only, or all IP (IPv4 and/or IPv6) addresses, or IPv6 addresses only? Usually, the meaning can be inferred from the context, though I try to be specific wherever there is the possibility of ambiguity.

The use of IPv4 address classes further divided the address space as originally defined, although the notion of network address classes has since been deprecated. Even so, understanding network classes is important from an historical perspective and to ensure greater understanding of older books and articles.

19.1.1 ADDRESS NOTATION

IPv4 addresses can be expressed in three number systems: binary, hexadecimal, and decimal. In all cases, the first part of the address identifies the network and the last part identifies the unique node on that network (Fig. 19–1).

IP addresses for these examples are drawn from the private IP address ranges that were reserved for use on networks not connected to the global internet; they are not supposed to be forwarded onto a public network. See also the discussion of NAT later in this chapter. A binary address might look like this:

11000000101010000000000100000001

This is hard to grasp, so let's break it up into octets:

11000000 10101000 00000001 00000001

Still not so easy; eight groups of four are easier to manage than four of eight:

1100 0000 1010 1000 0000 0001 0000 0001

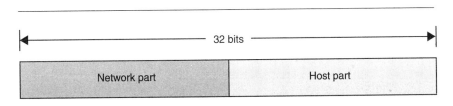

Figure 19–1: General form of IP address (valid for all versions of IP).

But that's still binary, and still not easy for people to work with. Hexadecimal is easier to handle (fewer characters), and network engineers eventually learn to do hex-decimal/decimal-hex (as well as hex-binary/binary-hex) conversions in their head. Here's the hex version:

```
C0 A8 01 01
```

The spaces added between each octet's worth of data help make the numbers easier to read, but hex is not always the easiest form to use. Decimal numbers are better for many uses, especially for people who can't convert hex to decimal in their heads. The address, in decimal, is:

```
192.168.1.1
```

Table 19–1 shows the decimal, binary, and hexadecimal representations of values from 0 to 16.

Note the use of the periods to separate the octets. This format is called *dotted decimal* or *dotted quad* notation, because it uses "dots" to separate the four octets of the address. This address is pronounced "one-ninety-two dot one-sixty-eight dot one dot one."

IP addresses are assigned through national registries that distribute network addresses (Appendix A introduces various Internet organizations). Network addresses are distributed to organizations, which in turn are responsible for making sure that all attached hosts are properly numbered.

The network address is an IP address in which the least significant (right-most) bits are set to zero. The most significant bits identify the network itself, while the least significant bits are used within the network to identify individual nodes.

19.1.2 Internet Address Types

IPv4 addresses are limited to the four billion or so values between 0.0.0.0 and 255.255.255.255, but there are other limitations. IP *network address classes* are discussed in detail in the next section, but large chunks are unavailable because of the way RFC 791 allocated network addresses

Decimal	Binary	Hexadecimal
0	0000	0
1	0001	1
2	0010	2
3	0011	3
4	0100	4
5	0101	5
6	0110	6
7	0111	7
8	1000	8
9	1001	9
10	1010	A
11	1011	B
12	1100	C
13	1101	D
14	1110	E
15	1111	F

Table 19–1: Table for decimal, binary, and hexadecimal counting.

back in 1982. Here are six other types of internet address commonly encountered, in order of specificity:

Loopback Networked nodes usually define a *loopback* interface over which the node can send live network data to itself. This is similar to the telephone number a telephone technician uses to send a ring signal to the line she is calling from. Data sent to the loopback interface (usually referred to as lo on *nix and similar systems) is processed down the protocol (and back up, on receipt) just like any other network data—it is just never transmitted over any local link. Loopback transmissions are often used for testing purposes, as well as for processes on the same system to communicate over TCP/IP.

The *loopback address* for any host is usually defined as any address starting with the first bit off (0) and the next seven bits on—or `127` in decimal. On most systems the only valid loopback address is `127.0.0.1`; but in the range from `127.0.0.0` to `127.255.255.255` no addresses are unavailable for assignment, a matter of roughly 16 million unique addresses.

Unicast All internet nodes have at least one interface through which they can send and receive internet packets; each of these interfaces has an IP address. Packets sent from this interface show this as their *source address*, while packets from other nodes intended for this interface show it as their *destination address*. This type of address is called *unicast:* one address, one interface. Knowing that this type of address has a name, one can infer that there are other addresses to which one can send packets that will be delivered to more than one interface.

Multicast Nodes can send the same packets to more than one destinations by individually addressing separate copies of each packet to each destination. This solution becomes increasingly impractical as the number of destination nodes increases; it is impossible in cases where the sender does not have addresses for all destination nodes wishing to receive packets.

A *multicast address* can be used in these cases as the destination address, with packets forwarded to all nodes that have *subscribed* to a particular multicast *group*. Chapter 24 discusses IP multicast at greater length; although multicast makes some difficult applications possible, multicast itself is not always easy to get right.

A portion of the IPv4 address is reserved for multicast addresses: the range from `224.0.0.0` to `239.255.255.255`, a total of over 250 million unique addresses unavailable for assignment to internet nodes.

TCP (and other connection-oriented transports) cannot be used with multicast addresses, because there is a one-to-many relationship between the sender and the recipients so TCP circuits are impossible (at least, not without having a separate circuit for each destination node). User datagram protocol (UDP) (or another connectionless datagram transport) is required when using IP multicast; this is the case for all IP traffic with more than one possible destination, as we'll see for the next two address types.

Anycast Multicast groups are usually open to all internet nodes, subject to certain limitations. All group members are supposed to receive packets, and perhaps even participate in the data stream and act as peers. Some multicast group addresses have been set aside for use of specific applications or types of systems, for example, "all local routers." Allowing nodes to multicast to all systems of a particular type on the local network with a reserved address makes automatic configuration when adding new systems to a network much easier. However in these cases the node doesn't need to contact all local configuration servers (for example), just one server, presumably the one "closest"[3] to it.

For these cases, RFC 1546, "Host Anycasting Service," introduced the concept of *anycast* back in 1993. Though there hasn't been huge demand for anycast support in IPv4 networks (despite its usefulness), anycast has been incorporated into the requirements for IPv6 (see Chapter 27). More than one destination may receive anycast packets, and more than one may respond to anycast requests, but the node sending the original anycast will continue to communicate only with the closest responder (e.g., the first one). Other nodes that respond to an anycast do nothing else after their initial response.

No part of the IPv4 address space has been allocated for anycast addresses, although some multicast addresses are associated with certain types of node (e.g., routers) on a network.

Broadcast When it is necessary to transmit data to all nodes on a network the *broadcast address* is used. Sometimes called the *all-ones* address because all bits of the address are set to 1, IP broadcasts are easy to transmit over local links such as Ethernet, where all nodes can easily receive a single transmission simultaneously), but less easy over *non-broadcast multi-access* (*NBMA*) networks in which all transmissions are point-to-point, as will be seen in Chapter 21.

An IP broadcast can be a *limited broadcast*, addressed to 255.255.255.255 (all ones) and never forwarded beyond the local IP network; or a *network-directed broadcast*, in which the first part of the address identifies an IP network and the rest of the address is

---

[3]The "closest" being the one able to respond to the request most quickly. A server with a very high capacity for responding quickly, over a fast link, to many requests may turn out to be "closer" than a much smaller server that is operating at its capacity—even if it is in the same room as the requesting node.

"all ones". For example, `10.255.255.255` is a network-directed broadcast intended to be received by all hosts in network `10.0.0.0`; `192.168.1.255` is a network-directed broadcast intended for all hosts in network `192.168.1.0`.

Every network address will be linked to one network-directed broadcast address, making the number of addresses made unavailable for assignment to IP nodes roughly equal to the number of globally routable networks; that number is something over two million.

Broadcast transmissions are not specified for IPv6, because broadcast turned out not to be as good an idea as it originally seemed for IPv4. Indiscriminate broadcasting can generate huge volumes of traffic, particularly when a broadcast is addressed to all nodes on a large network. Applications for which broadcast was envisioned tend to work more efficiently with multicast or even anycast.

Reserved and Special A significant portion of the IPv4 address space is reserved or otherwise restricted from use. Some of these restrictions are intended to save some space for future, undefined or unknown, purposes, such as the Class E addresses (see next section). This allocation may have originally been set aside for use as anycast addresses, but as of 2002 it has not be assigned for any use. Class E addresses are those in the range `240.0.0.0` to `247.255.255.255`, a total of over 130 million unique addresses unavailable for assignment to internet nodes.

There are other addresses that are "special" such as the broadcast addresses and the *all-zeros address* (e.g., `0.0.0.0`, `192.168.1.0`, or `10.0.0.0`); these add another two million or so addresses that are unavailable for assignment to nodes.

The all-zeros addresses are used as source addresses, to indicate "*this* network" or "*this* node" as the source of packets sent by a node attempting to get configured over the network (i.e., the node does not "know" it's own address yet).

Private Network Addresses: Three sets of network addresses, `10.0.0.0` through `10.255.255.255`, `172.16.0.0` through `172.31.0.0`, and `192.168.0.0` through `192.168.255.255` (altogether about 25 million addresses taken out of circulation), that can be used by anyone in private networks. As defined in RFC 1918, routers

connecting such private networks with public networks cannot forward packets from these private networks; their use is discussed in
more detail later in this chapter in the section on Network Address
Translators.

There are other quirks of IP addressing that will be addressed later in
this chapter, particularly IP network classes, subnetting, supernetting,
and issues of usable addresses within a network. The total number of
IPv4 addresses unavailable for addressing individual network interfaces
because they are assigned or reserved for other uses may be as high as half
a billion or so, reducing the theoretically available IPv4 space from over
four billion.

19.1.3   NETWORK ADDRESS ARCHITECTURE

During the 1970s, as the protocol that turned into what we know as IPv4
was being developed, two concepts steered the protocol in a direction that
has been found in retrospect to be less than optimal. One of these was that
network processing efficiency benefits from well-formatted data. This idea
resulted in the high degree to which protocol headers are strictly defined
into 32-bit words. Another result is the tendency to define header fields
in octet units, to simplify processing header data by allowing systems to
process chunks of 8 or 32 bits at a time.

The other important thought was about the nature of the IPv4 network.
Commercialization of the internet was still 15 to 20 years in the future
when the IPv4 address space was being formulated, computers were far
from ubiquitous even in academic environments, and what computers
existed in internets were far more likely to be multi-user systems than
PCs. It's not clear that IPv4 was intended to provide a fully featured production network environment, nor is it clear that it was designed for use
over three or more decades.

These two factors resulted in the creation of the IPv4 network address
classifications. RFC 791 defined three network address classes: A, B, and C.
Two more, D (for multicast addresses) and E (reserved for later use and
as yet still unused), were defined later. Like the OSI seven-layer reference
model, IPv4 network classes have had enormous impact on the way people
learn about IP as well as the way it has been used; however, also like the OSI
model, network classes are currently relevant only in providing historical
background.

Class A networks were intended for the hugest of global networks. The most-significant bit of all Class A network addresses is "0," and the network part of the address is the most-significant octet. Thus, Class A network addresses can have values of from `0.0.0.0` to `127.0.0.0`. Since `127.0.0.0` is reserved for the loopback address, there is a total of 126 possible Class A addresses (the `0.0.0.0` network is theoretically usable but has been reserved).

Node addresses in Class A networks consist of an 8-bit network part and a 24-bit host part; 24 bits of address space means that each Class A network can address no more than 2^{24} nodes—16,777,216, minus the all-ones broadcast and the all-zeros "this" addresses.

Class A networks were originally intended for the very largest of organizations such as the very biggest countries and companies. In practice, early recipients of Class A network addresses included US government and military agencies, research organizations such as those at Xerox, AT&T, MIT, Stanford, and IBM, and others.

Class B addresses, whose first two significant bits are `10`, have their most significant 16 bits as network address (`10` plus 14 bits), and leave 16 bits of network address space for addressing nodes. There can be no more than 2^{14} (16,384) unique Class B networks, but each network can uniquely address no more than 2^{16} (65,536) unique nodes. It was thought there would be enough Class B networks to accommodate the largest corporations and other large organizations; Class C networks used the first three octets as the network part of their addresses, started with the first three bits set to `110`; with 21 bits left over to provide a theoretical maximum of 2^{21}, or 2,097,152 networks with no more than 254 node addresses (2^8, minus the all-ones and all-zeros addresses).

Table 19–2 shows the permissible IP address ranges for each network class. The most significant bit of Class A network addresses is always 0, thus the first octet of Class A addresses ranges from 1 to 126. The two most significant bits of Class B addresses are always 10, thus the first octet of Class B addresses range from 128 to 191. And the three most significant bits of Class C addresses are always 110, thus the first octet of Class C addresses range from 192 to 223.

Classes were supposed to make processing packets easier: packets destined for destinations on one of the super-large Class A nets are processed faster because routers must only examine the first octet of the destination address

Network class	Address range	Maximum networks in class	Maximum hosts in network
Class A	0.0.0.0 to 127.255.255.255	126	Over 16 million
Class B	128.0.0.0 to 191.255.255.255	16,384	65,534
Class C	192.0.0.0 to 223.255.255.255	2,097,152	254
Class D	224.0.0.0 to 239.255.255.255	Reserved for multicasting	N/A
Class E	240.0.0.0 to 247.255.255.255	Reserved for future use	N/A

Table 19–2: IPv4 Address Classes.

to determine where the packet is headed; packets headed for Class C nets called for routers to examine three octets before a routing decision could be made.

In practice, however, network classes proved problematic: Class A networks with over two million possible node addresses are very difficult to use efficiently, while each Class C network, with an absolute limit of 254 node addresses, tends to be an acceptable size for a single local area network (LAN) but not nearly enough for most larger organizations. Class B networks are just about the right size for many organizations, but are also quite scarce, with no more than about 16,000 available.

As a result, the available IPv4 address space is further reduced by up to 16 million addresses for every Class A network assigned to an organization with far fewer unique network interfaces to address.

Another problem with network classes lays in the way *routing tables* are used. Somewhere in the internet there must be at least one router that can handle packets addressed to any network address in the internet. Local routing of packets to their destinations isn't considered part of this process, but there has to be some router that can route packets intended for any network—which means that the IPv4 routing table could (in theory) have over two million entries. Class A networks account for

126 entries at most, Class B for no more than 16,384, and Class C for over two million.

To some extent, address space shortages and the routing table explosion are problems implicit in IPv4 and ultimately will be resolved by adoption of IPv6 (see Chapter 27); however, recognizing that network classes are a bad idea, the IETF has made them obsolete.

19.1.4 INTERNET PROTOCOL SUBNETS

One benefit of network classes was that they made *subnets* easier to understand and work with. *Subnetting* an IP network means subdividing it into subnets by borrowing bits in the host part of the address to be used for a *subnetwork* address. Limitations on bandwidth and physical connections to local network media limit the number of nodes on most networks to fewer than a thousand or less. Although large IP networks can and usually do span more than one physical network, mapping IP subnets to those physical networks can help improve network performance and efficiency.

For example, consider what happens when a single organization has the equivalent of a Class A network address—this circumstance occurs often as more organizations opt to use private network addresses (see section 19.4) such as the 10.0.0.0 address. Assigning numbers sequentially to nodes will not work very well because there is no correlation between the host number and where the host connects to the internet. Subnetting the network address allows a hierarchical network architecture. A fairly simple example is illustrated in Figure 19–2, where the 10.0.0.0 network is shown with a link to the global internet, through Router I.

As a private network address, packets addressed to any destination in the 10.0.0.0 network are never supposed to be forwarded from the internet, but this is an example and so we use the private address rather than actual addresses.

Router I treats the address as a Class A network address, meaning that the router examines only as much of the address as is necessary to determine the proper route. Router A reads the first octet, identifies the destination as a Class A network, and then compares the relevant portion of the address (the first octet) to its *routing table*, or list of network addresses and local addresses to which packets addressed to those networks should be forwarded. Packets destined for network 10.0.0.0 are listed as being

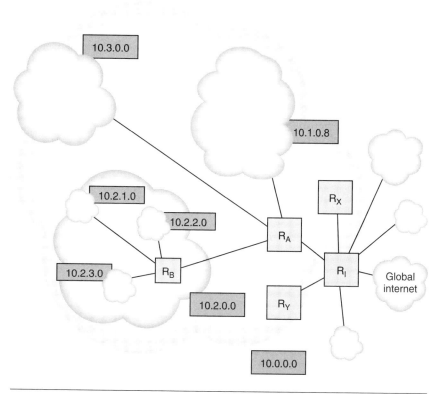

Figure 19–2: Subnetting the equivalent of a Class A network.

forwarded to Router A, with the last three octets of the address serving as the host part of the address.

The `10.0.0.0` network is subdivided into three subnets: `10.1.0.0`, `10.2.0.0`, and `10.3.0.0`. In this simple example, the first octet of all node addresses in this network represents the network part of the address, network `10.0.0.0`, and the second octet (rather than being a part of the node address) is used to indicate a subnet address. When it receives a packet addressed to any node within the `10.2.0.0` network, Router A forwards it to that subnet where Router B must figure out what to do with it.

Unlike Router I, Router A treats the first *two* octets as the network part of the address. In this case, the network is said to be subnetted on eight bits of the Class A host part of the address: the "real" network part (the first octet of the Class A) plus eight more bits of the host part. The *subnet mask* is a 32-bit value that is used to determine which part of the IPv4 address is to be treated as host part and which as network part.

In this case, the subnet mask would be `255.255.0.0`, which is the equivalent of `1111 1111 1111 1111 0000 0000 0000 0000`; the 1's indicate the portion of the address to be treated as network part while the 0's indicate the portion of the address to be treated as host part. Sometimes, a subnet mask can be expressed as the number of bits that is not part of the official network part of the address but that is used locally as a subnet. Thus, for Router A the subnet mask might also be indicated as eight bits.

One oddity of the original protocol specification is that subnet masks need not use contiguous bits for the subnet (atlhough most subnet masks do). For example, it would be possible to mask off every third bit of the host part of the address or some other odd arrangement. There are some circumstances under which such an arrangement might be useful, but in most cases non-contiguous subnet masks result in more confusion than they are worth.

Router A will forward packets destined for `10.2.2.0` to Router B, as well as packets destined to any address within the `10.2.0.0` *prefix* (network part + subnet part, as far as Router A is concerned). Router B has a longer subnet mask, spanning 16 bits beyond the Class A prefix and expressed `255.255.255.0`. Router B thus looks at the first 24 bits of the address to identify an appropriate route match, and then forwards the packet to the appropriate destination—which may be yet another router on a further-subnetted link, or it may be the destination node.

In this example, each different router processes the same destination address differently: Router I looks for a route match only on the first eight bits of the address, while Routers A and B match on the first 16 bits and 24 bits (respectively) of the address. Router I treats only the first eight bits as the network part of that address (ignoring the least significant 24 bits), while Router A processes the packet based on the 16 bits of network + subnet part of the address, and Router B processes the packet based on 24 bits of network + subnet part of the address.

Subnetting provides important benefits, not least of which is the ability to improve router performance. Consider what the alternative would be in the example illustrated in Figure 19–2. Router I would pass all packets destined for network `10.0.0.0` to Router A. Note that Router A would require a separate routing table entry for each network but not for every node attached to the entire network. The router must examine each destination address to determine its responsibility for delivering each packet bound for network 10.0.0.0. For packets destined for the local network, Router A would have to map the destination address to a link layer address (see Chapter 20).

Using eight bits of the address part as a subnet part of the address means that Router A can completely route all inbound packets with no more than 255 routes (corresponding to the eight bits' worth of subnet address space, less the all-ones broadcast address). Rather than a single router, as many as 255 (more, if some subnets have more than one router) might be required to serve all of those subnets—but system requirements for Router A would be far lower than if it had to deal with tens of thousands of routes.

Likewise, Router B and its peers within the 10.0.0.0 network can manage with no more than 255 unique routes for internal subnet datagram delivery, while sub-subnet routers within 10.X.X.0 networks can handle delivery to no more than 254 nodes each (256, less the all-ones and all-zeros addresses).

This approach to routing hierarchies made possible with subnetting also allows network designers to reduce the amount of traffic that has to be routed as well as improve reliability and disaster resistance. In a *flat* network (no subnets), all packets must be routed—but only once. That puts tremendous loads on the router, as well as turning that system into a single point of failure. If the main router goes down, no traffic can be forwarded to any node. More routers means more routing redundancy is possible, as we'll see in later chapters.

Reducing traffic volume can be done by grouping together nodes that interoperate most often as well as by placing more accessibly any servers used by nodes throughout the network. Departmental servers should be located on the same subnets as the hosts used by members of each department; corporate mail servers should be located centrally.

Subnet masking can be done on any network class address, or even on any length subnet, as long as there is enough address space left to address individual nodes. That means at least two bits of host address space, allowing a total of two unique addresses (along with the all-ones and all-zeros addresses), corresponding to X.X.X.1 and X.X.X.2. Because at least one of those addresses must be allocated to a router, this smallest subnet would have only one node on it other than the router (in practice, it is possible for a host to function as a router as well as a server or client host). In this case, the subnet mask would be `1111 1111 1111 1111 1111 1111 1111 1100`, or `255.255.255.252`.

Subnet masks established 1 or 2 bits on either side of an octet boundary act to increase or decrease by a factor of two or four the number of subnets possible in a network or the number of nodes possible on each subnet. An organization with relatively few logical network divisions but many nodes within each one might use a Class A address with a 6- or 7-bit subnet, limiting the number of subnets to fewer than 64 or 128, respectively, (instead of fewer than 256), while supporting up to 260,000 or 130,000 unique nodes on each subnet (instead of fewer than 65,536). An organization with hundreds of locations, each of which supporting only a relatively few nodes, could use a 9- or 10-bit subnet mask on a Class B network to allow them an upper limit of 512 or 1,024 on the number of subnets while allowing no more than 62 or 126 nodes on each subnet.

An 8-bit subnet mask on a Class B network address (such as `172.16.0.0`, from the private network reserved address assignment) looks just like a 16-bit subnet mask on a Class A network (such as `10.0.0.0`): in both cases, the mask can be represented as `255.255.255.0`. A 10-bit subnet mask for a Class A network would be `255.192.0.0`, while a 6-bit subnet mask on a Class B network would be `255.255.252.0`.

Although network classifications are helpful in understanding how subnetting works, as well as how subnet masks work, the classful internet no longer exists. Subnet masks are rarely specified as a number of bits any more, although subnet masks are still widely used for configuration purposes. With the advent of Classless Inter-Domain Routing (CIDR), discussed later in this chapter, a different notation for describing network prefixes has become the preferred, and unambiguous, way to refer to unique network routes.

19.2   Internet Protocol Datagrams

IP datagrams consist of headers and a payload. Figure 19–3 shows how the IP header fields describe routing information for the datagram. IPv4 headers are all at least 20 octets long. All IP headers are organized into four-octet words, for ease of processing (nodes and routers process four octets at a time); IPv4 headers may include options, which

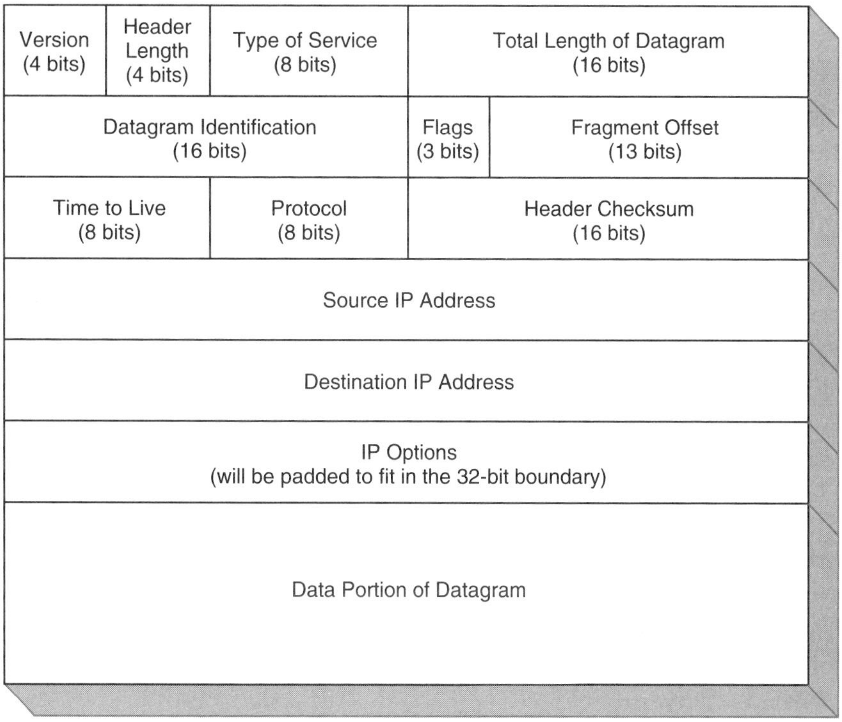

Version (4 bits)	Header Length (4 bits)	Type of Service (8 bits)	Total Length of Datagram (16 bits)	
Datagram Identification (16 bits)			Flags (3 bits)	Fragment Offset (13 bits)
Time to Live (8 bits)		Protocol (8 bits)	Header Checksum (16 bits)	
Source IP Address				
Destination IP Address				
IP Options (will be padded to fit in the 32-bit boundary)				
Data Portion of Datagram				

Figure 19–3: IP header fields.

may add as many as 40 octets to the header length (in four-octet word units).

The fields in the first word identify the datagram as far as version of IP, header length, how the datagram is to be handled (Type of Service) and datagram length. The next word includes information about fragmentation: a unique ID number for the datagram, flags for fragmentation control, and the fragment offset. The third word includes time to live, the originating transport protocol of the content being carried, and a checksum for the header itself. The fourth and fifth words are the source and destination IP addresses, and an optional options field can be added when IP options are needed.

Understanding what information about the packet the different IP header fields contain helps considerably when discussing how IP works.

19.2.1 HEADER FIELDS

Protocol header fields provide the mechanisms by which network entities can interact. IPv4 protocol header fields carry considerable information about the IP packet, the source and destination of the packet, and the contents of the packet—not to mention instructions about how to process the packet as it moves from source to destination.

The current (2002) standard for IP packet header fields are as follows:

Version: This 4-bit field indicates the version of IP being used. The current version of IP is v4, although the latest version, IPv6, has been specified and has been deployed experimentally for some time. IPv6 will become increasingly important as more products are rolled out and more organizations upgrade.

Possible values for this field are in the range from 0 through 15; 0 and 15 have been reserved, while 1–3 and 10–14 are unassigned. Version 5 is allocated in RFC 1190, "Experimental Internet Stream Protocol, Version 2 (ST-II)," while 7–9 were used by protocols submitted for consideration as the next generation of IP.

For most implementations of IP, the node examines this field and if it contains anything other than 4, the packet is discarded.

Header Length: This 4-bit field indicates the length of the header in four-octet words. The maximum length of an IPv4 header is 60 octets (15 four-octet words). The required IPv4 headers take up 20 octets, allowing up to 40 octets for IP options. The minimum valid value is 5; anything less would indicate missing fields or some other malformation.

Differentiated Services and ECN Fields: These fields replace the Type of Service (ToS) field defined in RFC 791 and provide mechanisms by which scalable service discrimination can be deployed in the internet and active congestion responses can be incorporated into TCP/IP nodes. Some documents refer to the entire octet as the diffserv field, while others identify only the first 6 bits with that field and the last 2 bits with the ECN field.

What is clear is that the first 6 bits contain the Differentiated Services CodePoint (DSCP), while the last 2 bits contain the Explicit

Congestion Notification codepoint field, also known as the ECN or ECN codepoint field.

IP traffic engineering and ECN will be discussed in Chapter 25; we will return to this octet there.

Datagram Length: This value represents the entire datagram length, including the header, in units of single octets. At 16 bits, this limits IP datagrams to a maximum length of 65,535 octets. With a standard header length of 20 octets, an IPv4 packet's maximum payload length is therefore 65,515 octets (65,475 octets when the header includes the full 40 octets allowed for options). Nodes use the header length and datagram length to determine where the header ends and the packet payload begins because IP has no end of datagram character or sequence.

Datagram Identification: This is a unique 16-bit identifier assigned to a datagram by the originating host. At the source, there is a one-to-one relation between datagrams and datagram identifiers; however, as the datagrams pass through an internetwork, they may become fragmented (fragmentation is discussed later in this chapter). When datagrams are split, the identification field contains the same identifier for all of the resulting datagrams, making it possible for the destination node to identify which fragments go with which original packet.

Fragmentation Flags: The first of the three flag bits is unused; the other two are used to control the way the datagram is fragmented. The *Don't Fragment* (DF) bit, when set to 1, means that the datagram must not be fragmented. If the datagram has to be fragmented to be routed (it must be forwarded to a network that cannot handle the datagram without breaking it up into smaller pieces), the router will throw it away and send an error message back to the originating host. When the *More Fragments* (MF) bit is set to 1, it means the datagram is one of two or more fragments, but not the last of the fragments. If the MF bit is set to 0, it means there are no more fragments (or that the datagram was not fragmented). Receiving hosts use the MF flag and the fragment offset to reassemble fragmented datagrams.

Fragment Offset: This number tells the receiving host how many units from the start of the original datagram the current datagram is. This value represents units of eight octets; with 13 bits, the maximum value is 2^{13} to 1, or 8,191. Thus, the furthest from the start of the original datagram that a fragment can begin is 65,528 octets.

To illustrate, a 64,000 octet-long datagram divided into eight fragments of 8,000 octets each will cause the fragment offset value for the first fragment datagram to be set to 0: the fragment begins at the start of the original datagram. The fragment offset for the second fragment will be 1,000 because the second fragment starts after the first 8,000 octets of the original datagram.

Time to Live (TTL): This 8-bit field indicates how long the datagram should be allowed to exist after entering the internetwork. The node sending the packet sets the value of this field appropriately (see below) and every time the packet is received by a node for processing this value is decremented by one. If the TTL field contains the value 0, the packet should be discarded—but a node may not automatically discard packets whose TTL value is less than 2. The reason is that by doing so, the intended destination node could discard packets that arrived just before they expired.

Protocol: This field identifies the protocol of the next higher layer data being carried in the datagram. This field might indicate that the payload data is a TCP segment or a UDP datagram, or some other protocol. The IANA maintains a list of protocol codes at www.iana.org/assignments/protocol-numbers; however, the most common ones will be those representing TCP (6), UDP (17), and ICMP (1).

Header Checksum: This field contains a checksum on the IP header only. The header is treated like a series of 16-bit binary numbers with the checksum field itself set to zero. These values are added together and then ones-complemented. This checksum is calculated only on the IPv4 header, and provides an adequate integrity check for the header only; no integrity check is done on the rest of the packet.

Inasmuch as some IPv4 fields change as the packet if forwarded from one node to another, the header checksum will change as well (if only to accommodate the changes in the TTL field). This means each intermediate node must recompute this checksum before forwarding a packet.

As RFC 791 defines this field, "The checksum field is the 16 bit one's complement of the one's complement sum of all 16 bit words in the header. For purposes of computing the checksum, the value of the checksum field is zero."

Source/Destination: These are the actual 32-bit (four octet) IP addresses of the originating host and the destination host.

Options: These are optional, and are discussed later in this chapter; suffice it to say that IPv4 options must be padded out to a four-octet border and the entire options field may not exceed 40 octets in length.

Payload: Typically, the payload will consist of a transport layer datagram (e.g., UDP), a transport layer segment (e.g., TCP), or a "helper application" message (e.g., ICMP). The protocol ID for the payload contents is specified in the IPv4 header so the destination IP implementation can determine what to do with the payload once the packet is processed and received.

More than most of the protocols discussed in this book, IPv4 relies on its headers to determine how packets are processed through the internet. Several issues are raised when introducing these header fields, including the incorporation of traffic engineering features in IPv4, maximum transmission units (MTUs) and datagram fragmentation, calculating the TTL value, and the use of IPv4 options.

19.2.2   IPv4 Type of Service and Diffserv

Although IPv4 is fundamentally unchanged since RFC 791 was published in 1981, there have been some changes that might cause incompatibility between early and modern TCP/IP stacks under certain circumstances. The most obvious change over the years can be seen in the way the original *ToS* field has evolved over the years. This octet has undergone various modifications and changes before arriving at its present configuration.

With the internet's growth have come unexpected challenges in terms of how packets are routed and handled in a very large network. Some applications are able to trade off one or more performance attributes (reliability, throughput, latency) to get the best of one of those attributes. For example, real-time multimedia applications require lower latency and/or higher throughput while reliability is a less important factor.

The ToS field was originally defined to allow applications to specify (through the programming interface to the IP implementation) how their packets should be treated while en route to their destinations. However, ToS proved to be the wrong solution, and the Differentiated Services and Integrated Services working groups were established to come up with solutions that would work for applications that required specific traffic guarantees (such as guaranteed throughput or an upper limit on latency). Traffic engineering, congestion response, and quality of service issues are all covered in greater depth in Chapter 25.

Inasmuch as the ToS field has undergone the greatest degree of change since IPv4 was specified in 1981, in this section we summarize how the field has been used over the years:

RFC 791: "Internet Protocol" specifies that the *ToS* field contain a set of parameters (in the form of a 3-bit precedence field [for use only by the Department of Defense] and three flags for delay, throughput, and reliability) governing how routers process packets.[4] Although well thought out, this scheme gained little support as it demanded that implementers flag some or all of their applications' packets as being less important than others. The last 2 bits of the ToS octet were reserved for future use.

RFC 1122: "Requirements for Internet Hosts–Communication Layers," modified the original use only slightly by including the "reserved" bits in the ToS field. At the same time, the authors noted that while (as of 1989) the ToS field had been "used little in the past," it was expected to become more important in the future.

RFC 1349: "Type of Service in the Internet Protocol Suite," added a fourth flag bit for minimizing the monetary cost of handling the packet when set. This specification also deprecated the use of these four bits as flags and mandated five permitted values for this ToS field, one each to indicate normal service or the minimization of delay and cost, or maximization of reliability and throughput. Published in 1992, this proposed standard was also doomed.

RFC 1455: "Physical Link Security Type of Service," specified an experimental use of the four flag bits to set a level of security for the packet. This, too, failed to catch on in any meaningful way.

---

[4]For details, see p 12 of RFC 791.

RFC 2474: "Definition of the Differentiated Services Field (DS Field) in the IPv4 and IPv6 Headers," replaced the ToS field in 1998 with the diffserv field consisting of a 6-bit Differentiated Services Codepoint (DSCP) while leaving the last two bits designated as "currently unused."

RFC 2481: "A Proposal to add Explicit Congestion Notification (ECN) to IP" defined the addition of the ECN field to IP as an experimental protocol.

RFC 3168: "The Addition of Explicit Congestion Notification (ECN) to IP" added the revised specification published in RFC 2481 as a proposed standard, which established the ECN field as a preferred use of that part of the IPv4 header.

Although the ToS/DS field has evolved, IPv4 implementations at any point are still likely to interoperate as long as they don't attempt to use the ToS/DS fields. In RFC 3168, the authors note that the many uses to which the same header octet has been put over the years means that when the different specifications have been implemented there will be a significant lack of compatibility with the newest specification. Had the original specification been widely deployed, such a disregard for backward compatibility would likely not occur—but when some portion of a protocol header is not used, it becomes fair game for anyone who has a better idea.

19.2.3 PATH MAXIMUM TRANSMISSION UNIT

Traffic through tunnels is limited to vehicles that can fit, and vehicles over set weight limits may be restricted from using certain bridges. Likewise, some networks limit the size of the data they can handle in a single chunk.

Minimum sizes are generally decreed by the need for certain specific information about the packet, frame, or datagram, but the *MTU* size of a network medium is generally determined by the bandwidth (amount of data that can be handled in a given time) of the medium and the reliability of the infrastructure. Network media that can move large volumes of data quickly can afford to pack the data up in big chunks, but media that move data more slowly may need to break it up into smaller chunks to keep it moving smoothly across the network.

MTUs (exclusive of headers) for different network media range from as high as 65,535 octets for Hyperchannel, a high-speed medium, down to 4,352 for FDDI (fiberoptic), 1,500 octets for Ethernet, 1,006 octets for SLIP, 576 octets for X.25 networks (a WAN technology), to as low as 296 octets for point-to-point links with low delay. These figures come from RFC 1191, "Path MTU Discovery," which discusses typical MTUs for different network media.

Although Asynchronous Transfer Mode or ATM (see Chapter 27) transmits data in chunks called cells, each of which is only 53 bytes, ATM cells are created only after the upper layer protocol data has been organized into considerably larger frames. These frames are then divided into cells, each of which is transported and switched within the ATM network.

The *path MTU* specifies the maximum transmission unit that can be carried without fragmentation between two actual nodes. Doing so eliminates the need for fragmenting packets sent from source to destination. In some cases, the path MTU will be the same as the local MTU. For example, two widely separated nodes each connected locally to their own Ethernet LAN, will both have local MTUs of 1,500 octets. Assuming that all intervening networks are capable of carrying larger frames, the path MTU for the two nodes will be the same as their local MTUs. However, if the two nodes are separated by an X.25 network, their path MTUs will be 576 octets.

The mechanism for determining the path MTU is defined in RFC 1191. The source host sends an IP packet, using its preferred MTU size, to the destination with the Don't Fragment flag set. If an intervening router sends back an error message (using ICMP, as discussed in Chapter 22) indicating that the packet could not be forwarded without fragmenting it, then the source host tries again with a smaller packet. The process repeats until the source host discovers the path MTU for the destination—or until the source host gives up and allows packets to be fragmented.

19.2.4 FRAGMENTATION

IPv4's datagram fragmentation option has long caused controversy.[5] Fragmentation squanders IPv4 header real estate, accounting for 20% of the basic IP header (the datagram ID, fragmentation flags, and fragment offset field). Fragmentation adds a computational burden on routers

_____

[5] IPv6 omits fragmentation entirely.

and destination nodes. Fragmentation makes IPv4 more complicated to implement, as well.

Ultimately, fragmentation was permitted because the alternatives seemed even less appealing. Placing an upper limit on IP datagram size lower than the smallest allowed PDU on any network medium using IP would unreasonably limit the PDU size for media that can handle very large chunks of data efficiently. Limiting the IP datagram length to under 1,500 octets (the maximum allowed size for Ethernet frames) or to 576 octets (the *MTU* for the X.25-wide area network protocol) would likewise limit more efficient network media.

Alternatively, placing a lower limit on the size of PDU of any network medium using IP and thus requiring all network media to support some minimum PDU size determined by the IETF would unnecessarily restrict the types of media capable of carrying IP. Because one of the most basic tenets of IP networking is that it is a universally interoperable protocol, this option is also unacceptable.

Datagrams can potentially be fragmented any time they cross different types of network media. For example, a 1,492 octet-long IP datagram is just long enough to fit inside an Ethernet frame—but it would have to be fragmented in order to cross an X.25 network, which can handle only datagrams as large as 576 octets.

A node sets the length of its datagrams based on its local MTU. IPv4 has an upper limit on datagram size of 65,535 octets because the IP header field for datagram length is 16 bits long. However, most common network media have much smaller maximum network frame sizes, as discussed in the previous chapter. When there are several different networks across which network traffic passes, there will be a path MTU. This is the largest size unit that can pass unfragmented across all the intervening networks in a datagrams route; in other words, the smallest MTU of any of those networks.

Figure 19–4 shows an internetwork consisting of an FDDI network (Network A), an Ethernet (Network B), and a 16-Mbps IBM token ring network (Network C). Traffic staying entirely on Network C could maintain an MTU of 17,756 octets because the high-speed token ring network allows frames to carry that much data. However, traffic going from Network C to Network B would be limited to the much smaller Ethernet MTU of 1,500 octets. Each of the token ring frames (assuming they used that MTU) would

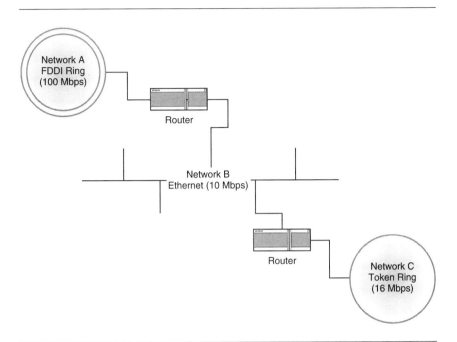

Figure 19–4: An internet with different MTUs for each local network will result in the lower MTU being used as the path MTU for all traffic between the two networks.

be broken into a dozen or so smaller Ethernet frames as they are processed by the router between the two networks.

Traffic moving from Network C to Network A would also have a Path MTU of 1,500 octets, even though the FDDI network can sustain an MTU of 4,352 octets since datagrams would have to traverse the Ethernet before arriving at the FDDI network, they would already be fragmented.

Intermediate routers do not bother reassembling fragmented datagrams. Because each datagram is routed independently over the internetwork, not all intermediate routers could be certain of processing all fragments of any particular datagram. And because datagram fragments may be delivered out of order with considerable delays between fragments, reassembling datagrams at every intermediate router would hurt overall performance.

A router fragments a datagram only if it is too large for the next-hop network. Most of the original datagrams header fields are simply copied, although the router modifies the fragmentation-related fields. The datagram length is recomputed for the datagram fragment, though the datagram identifier remains the same. The router sets the MF bit to 1 for all the fragments except the last one, and computes the fragment offset value for each fragment. The router decrements the TTL counter and recalculates the header checksum for each fragment header, but other fields remain the same and each fragment is forwarded onto the next leg of its route.

19.2.5 TIME TO LIVE

In versions of IP predating IPv4, researchers were puzzled by a gradual but steady and unexplained degradation in network performance that would be eliminated only by rebooting the entire network. It turned out that packets that encountered routing loops (see Chapter 22) or packets that were improperly addressed could bounce around the internet indefinitely. Adding the TTL field prevents these immortal packets from clogging networks.

Assigning a maximum lifetime for an IP packet serves also to ensure that "stale" packets aren't accepted as valid. This is especially when packets are carrying TCP segments, which might have timed out.

There are circumstances under which a packet can be caught in a loop (see Figure 19–5), where data can be passed along from one router to the next without ever arriving at its destination, which has lost its only link to the rest of the internetwork. The TTL field remedies this situation by setting a limit on the amount of time network traffic can remain in the internetwork before it is discarded.

RFC 791 defines TTL as the maximum number of seconds that a packet can exist within an internet. However because the field allows only integers (with values from 0 through 255), and because every node accepting a packet must take some non-negative, non-zero amount of time to process it, the TTL behaves almost exactly like a hop counter. Presumably no system will take more than 1 second to process a packet, although processing is simplified considerably by programming the IP stack to simply decrement the value rather than computing the actual number of seconds a packet takes to traverse the node.

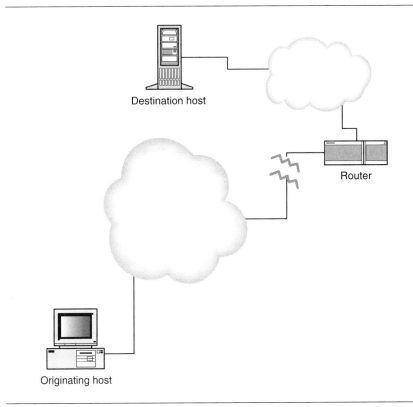

Figure 19–5: A failed router can isolate a network from the rest of the internet and cause route looping.

As an 8-bit field, the maximum possible TTL is 255. RFC 1122, "Requirements for Internet Hosts–Communication Layers," suggests that the default value for new packets should be set to "at least big enough for the Internet 'diameter,' i.e., the longest possible path. A reasonable value is about twice the diameter, to allow for continued Internet growth." The current (2002) figure for suggested TTL default is 64, unchanged since 1994. RFC 1122 requires that this value be configurable on all internet hosts so that the value may be changed as and when necessary.

Some software vendors set the default for their implementations at higher values, although the actual diameter of the internet may be receding a bit since 1994 when there was considerably less coordination among commercial internet service vendors. Different TCP/IP implementations may also use different TTL defaults for different transport layer protocols, depending on whether there is a need for reliable or guaranteed delivery.

19.2.6 OPTIONS

IPv4 options, as the name implies, are strictly optional. Implementers and applications developers have in the past tended to avoid IPv4 options. Routers tend to be optimized for the general case of IP datagrams, which means non-optioned packets. Packets with options must get special treatment, which means that routers often shunt such packets off until enough processing resources are free to handle the IP options properly, causing performance to suffer. IPv4 options are commonly used for application debugging and testing.

Options were intended to be the way the protocol handled special functions related to routing. IPv4 options include:

End of Options List: Indicates the end of the options list, this option was defined in RFC 791.

No Operation: Used to indicate the presence of an option that causes no operation to occur. Used for padding.

Source Routing: Defined in RFC 791, this type of option specifies a list of routers through which the packet must pass on its way to the packets destination. *Loose source routing* means that *all* the routers specified in the list must be traversed, but other routers may be traversed in addition. The *strict source routing* option lists all the routers, and the only routers, that the packet may pass through.

Attackers can hijack transmissions by using source routing by directing a packet that would otherwise be processed through a local or the global internet to a router controlled by the attacker.

Time Stamp: Requests every router to record what time it handled the optioned packet. Time is represented as a 32-bit value representing the number of milliseconds since 12:00 midnight, UTC. Three options are available: time stamp only, showing nothing more than a series of 32-bit values; time stamp plus address of each entity adding the time stamp; and a time-stamp for specified routers, where only routers specified by IPv4 address are required to add a time stamp. A field in the option header is also set aside to indicate the number of entities that wanted to set a time stamp but were unable to because the options part of the IP headers was full. Defined in RFC 791.

Record Route: Requests every router handling the optioned packet to append its IP address. Defined in RFC 791.

Traceroute: Defined in RFC 1393, "Traceroute Using an IP Option," an experimental protocol specified to improve on the *traceroute* function described later in this chapter.

IP in IP: Defined in RFC 2003, "IP Encapsulation with IP," IP tunneling is useful for *mobile IP nodes* or hosts that connect to the internet through different networks (e.g., laptops taken on business trips or used at home and office, where the same LAN interface is plugged into and configured for more than one IP network depending on where it is being used).

IP mobility is discussed in the last section of this chapter, but IP tunneling allows a mobile node to register with a server on its "home" network when it will be connecting to the internet remotely. When nodes attempt to connect to the mobile node, their packets are intercepted by the mobility server and then forwarded to the mobile node at its current IP address. Rather than rewriting the destination header address in the original packet (which would be a violation of the protocol), the mobility server creates a new packet addressed to the mobile node's current network and with the entire original packet as the new packet's payload.

IPv4 options are restricted to a total length of 40 octets; where data is carried in the option header, there will be limitations on the number of data points that can be handled. Where IPv4 addresses are recorded, there is an upper limit of nine addresses (36 octets for data and three or four octets for option header fields); where addresses and time stamps are recorded, the upper limit is four sets of data (32 octets for data and three or more octets for option header fields).

Options can cause problems because they are special cases. Most IP datagrams have no options, and vendors optimize their routers to handle standard IP datagrams. The IP header without options is always 20 octets long and is easy to process when the router design is optimized to process 20-octet headers. Network managers prefer faster routers and because most traffic does not use IP options the routers tend to handle those packets as exceptions, shunting them off to the side to be handled when it is convenient and when it wont affect the routers overall performance.

When used, IP options are strung together with no delimiting characters, and if they do not end on a word boundary padding characters are added. As already noted, the options field is limited to 40 octets of options and options data.

19.3   IPv4 Routing

When a host receives a network link layer frame it must *decapsulate* (or unwrap headers from) the frame, as we'll discuss in Chapter 21. In doing so, the host determines whether or not to pass the contents of the frame up its protocol stack. If the contents of the frame are intended for the host that just received it, then the frame is unwrapped and the payload passed up the protocol stack. If the contents of the frame are intended for some other node, then the receiving node repackages and forwards the payload to its intended destination if the receiving node is a router.

Routing allows individual hosts to address packets to any destination on the internet without knowing anything but the first step toward that destination.

All IP nodes, be they hosts or routers, can receive IP packets, but only routers are permitted to forward them to other systems. If a host receives a network frame addressed to it, but containing an IP datagram addressed to some other host, the host must ignore that datagram. Routers, however, must determine the correct route for that datagram, re-encapsulate it for its *next-hop destination network*, and retransmit it.

Hosts can ignore incorrectly addressed frames; if they were obliged to respond to all incorrectly formatted and addressed frames the resulting traffic would adversely affect network performance. Routers, on the other hand, use a special protocol specifically for exchanging information about routing issues like delivery failures, timeouts, and unexpected circumstances like gateway failures: the *ICMP* allows routers to generate error and control messages.

Data passing between nodes connected to the same link layer network (such as a LAN) does not require any IP layer processing: just package the data for local delivery and transmit. Chapter 21 covers some of the issues related to link layer networking, especially as they relate to IP. Every IP packet sent between network interfaces will be carried over at least one link layer network, and possibly more. The vast collection of physical networks that comprise the internet use many different link layer protocols and addressing schemes; as noted in Part I, the problem is to somehow map all these disparate local networks into a single IP network through which any two nodes can communicate.

IP specifies how internet data is to be packaged and addressed; IP routing protocols define ways in which routers exchange the network topology information that must be used to specify how those packets are to be delivered.

The process of exchanging this routing data may be quite simple or quite complex, and several routing protocols will be discussed in Chapters 22 and 23. In this section, we'll look at what happens when a node receives a link layer frame containing an IP packet and how the node processes that packet.

In this section, we'll discuss what happens to a packet as it is sent and received, the differences between direct and indirect routing, and the function of routers and routing tables.

19.3.1   MOVING PACKETS

One of the fundamental problems to be solved by IPv4 is how to move packets from their sources to their destinations without requiring the senders to have any knowledge of the internet infrastructure. Further complicating matters is the requirement that routers be capable of routing packets even when some of their links are unavailable, and again, without requiring detailed infrastructure knowledge.

A node will, barring error conditions, accept any frame transmitted over the local network addressed to the node's network interface.[6] There is no question that the frame contents are intended for that node.

---

[6] As well as link layer broadcasts and multicasts, if they exist in that medium.

However, when the frame contains an IP packet, the node must do further processing, primarily consulting the local routing table to determine whether there is a match for the packet's destination network. At that point the node may accept the packet for local delivery, forward the packet on to another IP node, or discard it.

19.3.2   HOSTS AND ROUTERS

An IP host may either be a source for an IP packet or a destination, but it is permitted to send or receive only those packets whose source or destination address fields contain the node's own address.

An IP router, on the other hand, can *forward or route* packets for which it is neither source or destination.[7] An IP host may send packets destined for a remote node to a local router, but that transmission does not occur at the network layer in IP. The host encapsulates IP packets for transmission at the link layer on the local network link.

Routers, because they have more than one IP address, are also known as *multi-homed hosts* because they have more than one "home" on the internet. A multi-homed host is not necessarily a router, however; a router must be configured to forward packets, and it normally has physical links on two or more different networks.

RFC 1122, "Requirements for Internet Hosts—Communication Layers," specifies not just which protocols an IP host must support but how those protocols are to be supported. It provides an excellent overview to anyone interested in how IP and TCP operate. It also specifies, on page 28, that an IP implementation must take certain steps when it receives an IP packet. The node:

1. verifies that the datagram is correctly formatted;
2. verifies that it is destined to the local host;
3. processes options;
4. reassembles the datagram if necessary; and
5. passes the encapsulated message to the appropriate transport-layer protocol module.

---

[7]Routers can also be the source or destination for packets, just like any other host.

Step 2 is of particular importance: if the packet is *not* destined to the local host, then something else must be done with it. A host, upon receiving a packet addressed to some other destination than itself, may *silently* (no error messages sent) discard the packet. A router's function is to accept such packets and forward them after determining the proper course of action.[8] Once the packet has been accepted and processed by a router for forwarding, it becomes an outbound packet and subject to the rules for outbound packet processing discussed next.

19.3.3 INTERNET PROTOCOL PACKET PROCESSING

When a node emits an IP packet, certain steps must be taken. RFC 1122 notes, on page 28, what must be done at the IP layer when a packet is about to be sent. The IP implementation:

1. sets any fields not set by the transport layer;
2. selects the correct first hop on the connected network (a process called "routing");
3. fragments the datagram if necessary and if intentional fragmentation is implemented (see section 3.3.3); and
4. passes the packet(s) to the appropriate link-layer driver.

Routing is nothing more complex than "selecting the first hop on the connected network." Making the selection for any given host should be relatively easy; RFC 1122 (on pages 47 through 51) provides some answers:

1. Remote/Local Decision: Determine whether the destination is *local*, meaning it is on the same network and subnet as the source host and therefore directly accessible; or *remote*, meaning it is accessible only through a router. The decision is made by comparing the network/subnet for source and destination addresses. Multicast and local broadcast packets need not go through this process.
2. Gateway Selection: Consult the *route cache* (all hosts are required to maintain a list of routes, see below) to choose. If a gateway is specified for the destination address, the host should send the

---

[8]Routers may also silently discard packets, for example, when they are unable to respond due to network or hardware problems, but that is not their primary function.

packet to that gateway. If there is no gateway specified for the destination, the host must:

a. Send the packet to the *default gateway* (or default router) configured for the host and open a new entry in its route cache for the destination.[9]

b. If the default gateway isn't the best choice, it will send an ICMP redirect message to point the host in the right direction (to a different gateway).

c. The host must update its route cache to reflect the proper gateway for the destination.

The route cache must contain entries with the following information:

- The local IP address from which packets originate [only if the host is multi-homed]
- An IP address (either a complete destination address or a network/prefix designation)
- Diffserv information (if present)
- Next-hop gateway IP address to be used for the entry IP address

When the destination is local, *direct routing* comes into play: the source node can send the packet directly to the destination, encapsulated in the appropriate PDU for the local network. The only problem remaining is that of correlating a local network address to the IP address. The *Address Resolution Protocol* (*ARP*), described in Chapter 21, offers the principle solution to linking network and IP addresses.

Indirect routing occurs when there is no shared local link available to the sender, and an intermediary chosen from the route cache (or default gateway) must be called upon to forward the packet. Packets are shunted from one router to another on the way to their destinations, typically first up a routing hierarchy, across a global internet backbone, and then back down another routing hierarchy. Figure 19–6 shows the typical route, where the packet moves from the router serving a small local network to a local ISP's router to a national ISP's backbone router. At that point, the packet is exchanged across the backbone to the backbone router that serves the cascade of networks serving the destination node.

---

[9]RFC 1122 also mandates that IP implementation be able to operate in minimal networks where they may not be any routers; in these cases, the IP implementation should generate an unreachable error message.

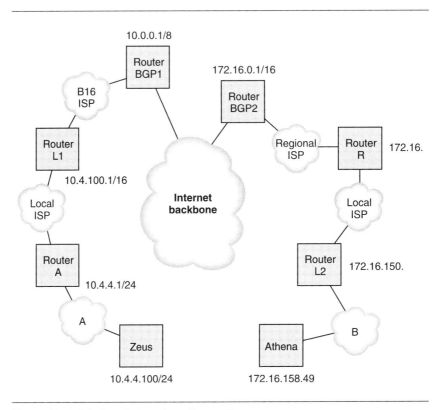

Figure 19–6: Modern internet routing path.

Two families of routing protocol govern the exchange of routing information. Within smaller private networks, routing structures are usually
straightforward: there will likely be a centralized authority for overall
routing information and router management, internally routed traffic
will be predictable. *Interior routing* protocols such as RIP and OSPF
(see Chapter 23) are designed to allow routers to share route and link
information among themselves within these internets.

In contrast, the size and complexity of the global internet quickly demonstrated that these interior protocols would not scale, and *exterior routing*
protocols such as Border Gateway Protocol (BGP, see Chapter 24) came
into use to allow routers to exchange routing information across internet
backbones. Backbone routers must be *non-default routers*—there is no

backup router to which these routers can pass packets whose destinations are not listed in the routing table.

19.3.4 SOURCE ROUTING

Discussed earlier in this chapter as an IPv4 option, source routing permits sources to designate the routers through which datagrams are forwarded to their destinations. Source routing permits the originating host to specify the route its packets should take. Unlike other routing methods, source routing requires that the sender have knowledge of the internetwork architecture; otherwise, it wouldn't be able to specify a correct route to the destination host. Source routing is useful for testing different routes between two hosts.

Source routing is invoked by the originating host adding an option to the IP header. The option includes a code to indicate whether strict or loose source routing is to be used, a length field indicating how long the options field is, and a pointer field that points to the currently relevant address in the options field. The options header also includes a list of IP addresses of routers specified for the route.

19.4 Network Address Translation

Despite the fact that NATs were introduced earlier in this chapter, they deserve more scrutiny for a number of reasons. NATs are hailed by some as the remedy for some if not all of what ails the internet and IPv4, while others consider them the network equivalent of kudzu: a hardy and fast-growing plant that was imported to parts of the US southeast to alleviate soil erosion earlier in the 20th century. Despite the lofty goals, kudzu turned out to be a superweed and with no natural checks on its growth; kudzu has displaced almost everything in its path. It grows so quickly that visitors may be cautioned not to nap on the porch unless they want to wake up tangled in the vines that are known to grow as much as a foot or more in a day.

19.4.1 REASONS FOR NETWORK ADDRESS TRANSLATION

There are times when it is preferable for packets not to be forwarded directly from inside an internetwork. NAT is an approach used for those instances. The two most commonly cited reasons for using NAT are for security and to map a large network onto a small IP address space.

Perhaps more common is the use of NATs to preserve IP address space. As the IP address space is depleted, more and more organizations have been denied Class B or even Class C networks. One solution is to use the private network space allocation to set up a private network with a Class A, B, or C network address. Routers within the private network can route packets within the network, and packets destined for the global Internet are passed through a network address translator that acts on behalf of the internal systems when interacting with Internet hosts.

NATs were originally introduced to help alleviate network address allocation shortages, so that organizations could build their intranets as large as they wanted without going through a lengthy and largely pointless process of trying to get an appropriate allocation from a service provider or regional registry. In the meantime, they have propagated across the internet and have been incorporated into networks as simple and small as single-system home networks and as complicated as any that requires a full Class A-equivalent network address.

Much of the controversy over the need for IPv6 (see Chapter 29) revolves around the question of whether or not NATs make things better or make them worse. In the meantime, people continue to deploy private networks and NAT boxes of various types while the IETF continues to publish RFCs that attempt to clarify matters or even to solve the entire problem with ever more end-to-end friendly versions of NAT.

19.4.2 NETWORK ADDRESS TRANSLATION BASICS

Whether you call it a network address translator or NAT box, a NAT acts as an old fashioned telephone operator, mediating all inbound and outbound traffic through a switchboard. Inside the NAT, private IP addresses are used for all internal communications; outside the NAT, standard global internet addresses are used. The NAT box has one interface on the internal network with a private IP address and another interface on the global internet with a globally unique IP address.

When a node in the private network wants to send a packet to a node on the outside, it creates a packet with its own, private, IP address as the source and the remote node's IP address as the destination. Following the rules of IP routing, the privately-addressed node will determine that the destination is on a different network and therefore the packet must be sent to a router.

NAT boxes often double as routers, both to reduce costs and to simplify their function. When the NAT box/router receives the outbound packet, it takes that packet and rewrites it so that the original source address (which will not be usable outside the private network) is replaced with the NAT box's own global internet IP address. The packet is then sent along to its destination. The destination node perceives the packet as originating with the NAT box.

Any response to the packet is addressed to the NAT box, which keeps track of the internal hosts for which it is serving as go-between. When a packet comes in, the NAT box accepts it, repackages the packet for delivery on the private network, and sends it along to the original source node.

19.4.3   ELABORATING ON NETWORK ADDRESS TRANSLATION

Basic NAT poses difficulties when it is necessary to host internet servers within the private network: there is only one well-known port for each service available on the NAT box, which makes it difficult if more than one web server are inside the network. Network Address Translation/Port Translation (NAT/PT) solves this problem by adding a port translator module onto the NAT box.

Various other developments and proposals have been considered and implemented over the years to make NAT friendlier with more or less success; some indication of these developments can be inferred from the quantity and titles of the NAT-related RFCs listed later in this section.

19.4.4   NAT ISSUES AND MISCONCEPTIONS

Rather than attempting to cover NATs exhaustively here, we will list relevant and current RFCs after a short list of NAT-related problems and concerns:

> **NATs break IPsec:** IPsec (see Chapter 28) is not made any easier by NATs, but it is still often usable. When packets from inside the private network are tunneled securely with IPsec (i.e., IPsec

secures packets which are then encapsulated in unsecured IP packets), NATs do not modify the tunneled packets and thus do not harm them. However, end-to-end, untunneled authenticated packets cannot be carried intact across a NAT.

Another area where NATs affect IPsec is in the reuse of the private IP addresses. Non-unique addresses can result in confusion, at the least, especially when security information is linked with IP addresses.

NATs complicate organization change: NATs provide a limited number of options for network addressing to the network designer. The odds of having address space collisions are great. Most people naturally assign their small private network the network address `192.168.0.0`, with hosts assigned IP addresses starting at `192.168.0.1` and increasing by one. When two such networks are merged, pandemonium ensues as networked systems stop working and network engineers rush madly to renumber at least one of the original networks.

NATs break applications: Most NAT-related problems with internet applications are manageable and have been or will be imminently resolved through one fix or another. More relevant to corporate network administrators, the most notable application broken by NAT so far has been the multi-player game, Quake.

NATs improve security: IP routers are not supposed to forward datagrams addressed in the private address ranges. If a backbone router receives a datagram bound for one of these addresses, it is supposed to drop it. However, these addresses can be used within an organizational internetwork.

Allowing outsiders access to information about a network's hostnames and IP addresses can expose that network to security risks. Some network administrators prefer to put their entire network behind a network address translator, which accepts datagrams from outside the internetwork and translates them to the NAT addresses used by the hosts inside the private network.

However, NATs can often open more holes than they close, especially when routers are not properly configured to drop packets addressed from or to private networks—or when routers can be reconfigured by an attacker. Likewise, network administrators typically use a fairly predictable set of addresses for NATted networks, so attackers may have an easier time locating sensitive systems.

NATs are easy: Solid-state NAT/router/hub/firewall/internet appliances capable of linking small numbers of systems in home office/small office environments are widely available at reasonable prices. These devices often include a Dynamic Host Configuration Protocol (DHCP) server, making the NAT a plug-and-play as well as a install-and-forget proposition.

NATs are complicated: Deploying NATs in complex internet environment can generate network administration nightmares, particularly if there are other NATs already in the network (such as in branch offices). Some engineers have reported that the actual cost of maintaining such a network far exceed the cost of paying for enough globally unique internet address space to serve the organization's needs—if that address space were available.

All NATs are pretty much the same: As previously noted, there are basic network address—only translators as well as network and port translators; a NAT box may be an inexpensive solid state appliance, a piece of software running on a PC, a dedicated router. There are many different types of NAT, and there are many of each type already in use throughout the world.

19.4.5 Realm-Specific Internet Protocol

The greatest problem with NAT is that lacking a globally unique address to link to privately addressed node, "end-to-endness"—that quality of having data transmitted directly, without modification, and with assurance of data integrity from source node to destination node—becomes difficult to impossible.

Having been proposed as a method to avoid depleting the IPv4 address space, NAT has been an easy and safe answer for some years now; the only alternatives for much of the late 1990s seemed to be either further rationing of IPv4 addresses or a rapid migration to IPv6 support. Neither of those options is particularly appealing, but there was no other mechanism by which the existing IPv4 internet infrastructure could be preserved while at the same time relieving the address squeeze by adding new globally unique addresses.

That is, until the Realm-Specific IP (RSIP) arrived, published in late 2001 in a series of four experimental RFCs (see RFC list in the next section for titles of RFCs 3102 through 3105). As explained in RFC 3102, "Realm Specific IP: Framework," NAT "has become a popular mechanism of enabling the separation of addressing spaces. A NAT router must examine and change the network layer, and possibly the transport layer, header of each packet crossing the addressing domains that the NAT router is connecting. This causes the mechanism of NAT to violate the end-to-end nature of the Internet connectivity, and disrupts protocols requiring or enforcing end-to-end integrity of packets."

Rather than depending on an artificial pool of non-unique IP addresses and the NAT to interoperate with the global internet from inside a private network, RSIP defines a mechanism by which a host in one addressing realm (i.e., a private network) can be allowed to use network resources from a second addressing realm (i.e., the global internet).

RSIP gateways, which replace the NAT boxes, must have the ability to permit the use of those resources—"addresses and other routing parameters," according to RFC 3102—and the (private) RSIP node can interoperate directly with an internet node, without any lower layer protocol tinkering as is done by a NAT.

This turns out to be a possible solution to some of the problems that NATs pose in terms of end-to-end interoperability. However, as the authors of the specification make quite clear, RSIP is intended neither to replace NAT or to solve the IPv4 address shortage. At best, they write, RSIP is a stopgap measure (as NAT was when it was first proposed).

However, RSIP does offer an interesting solution to the problem of interoperating between networks using different internet layer protocols, such as IPv4 and IPv6, or even IPv4 and some other as yet undetermined protocol. We'll return to RSIP in Chapter 29, when we discuss IPv4/v6 interoperability issues.

19.4.6 NETWORK ADDRESS TRANSLATORS AND RELATED RFCS

As of 2002, these RFCs had been published about NAT and the issues related to its use. A good place to start is RFC 3022, "Traditional IP Network Address Translator (Traditional NAT)," defining traditional NAT functions. RFC 2663, "IP Network Address Translator (NAT) Terminology and Considerations," is another good basis for discussion of NAT issues, as are RFC 3027, "Protocol Complications with the IP Network Address Translator," and RFC 2993 "Architectural Implications of NAT."

RFC 1631 *The IP Network Address Translator (NAT)* INFORMA-TIONAL (obsoleted by RFC 3022)

RFC 2391 *Load Sharing using IP Network Address Translation (LSNAT)* INFORMATIONAL

RFC 2663 *IP Network Address Translator (NAT) Terminology and Considerations* INFORMATIONAL

RFC 2709 *Security Model with Tunnel-mode IPsec for NAT Domains* INFORMATIONAL

RFC 2766 *Network Address Translation-Protocol Translation (NAT-PT)* PROPOSED STANDARD

RFC 2962 *An SNMP Application Level Gateway for Payload Address Translation* INFORMATIONAL

RFC 2993 *Architectural Implications of NAT* INFORMATIONAL

RFC 3022 *Traditional IP Network Address Translator (Traditional NAT)* INFORMATIONAL

RFC 3027 *Protocol Complications with the IP Network Address Translator* INFORMATIONAL

RFC 3102 *Realm Specific IP: Framework* EXPERIMENTAL

RFC 3103 *Realm Specific IP: Protocol Specification* EXPERIMENTAL

RFC 3104 *RSIP Support for End-to-End IPsec* EXPERIMENTAL

RFC 3105 *Finding an RSIP Server with SLP* EXPERIMENTAL

RFC 3235 *Network Address Translator (NAT)-Friendly Application Design Guidelines* INFORMATIONAL

RFC 3257 *Stream Control Transmission Protocol Applicability Statement* INFORMATIONAL

This list does not necessarily include every RFC that mentions NAT, only those that are particularly relevant. Only one of these, RFC 2766, is published as a proposed standard; that the rest are all either experimental or informational RFCs shows the degree to which NAT is still very much a topic of research and discussion.

19.5   Chapter Summary

We covered a great deal of material in this chapter, starting with IP addressing. We examined IP addressing notation, IP address types (including "special" addresses), the network addressing architecture used for IP, and the use of subnetting within IP networks.

Just as important as addressing to the IP protoocol, the IP datagram—its header fields and options—was also examined here. Beyond simply describing the datagram components, we also looked at some of the mechanisms that the IP datagram structure incorporates:

Type of Service/Diffserv: providing a mechanism for differentiating datagram handling en route to their destinations.

Fragmentation: allowing larger packets to be broken up for delivery across intermediate networks with smaller maximum transmission unit sizes.

Path MTU: defining the MTU size for a particular IP route.

Time to Live: for timing packets out, keeping them from endlessly cycling around routing loops.

IP options: providing a method for extending the protocol to include new functions.

IP routing topics were also introduced, focusing on the ways in which routers move packets around networks and the ways in which IP hosts and routers process packets they send and receive.

Finally, we looked at the NAT specifications, under which increasing numbers of hosts are attached to the global internet, examining how this short-term solution for the IP address shortage has become a long-term solution for millions of hosts.

In the next chapter, we will study the ICMP, which defines a set of mechanisms by which network control messages are exchanged between IP systems.

20

Internet Control Message Protocol

Although carried within IP datagrams, *Internet Control Message Protocol* (*ICMP*) messages comprise a protocol running side by side with IP at the network layer. Routers use ICMP to notify hosts and other routers that a route is unreachable, that there is a problem with a particular path, or that a router is being overloaded. Although ICMP can also be used to provide certain information to hosts (like the current time or the subnet mask for a particular network), these functions are less vital and are often available in other ways.

ICMP is part of the STD-5 specification that includes the Internet Protocol, and it is documented in RFC 792, "Internet Control Message Protocol (ICMP)." All IP hosts must implement ICMP so that they can receive and send:

- error messages about unreachable destinations
- error and status messages about routes and gateways
- echo requests and replies to indicate status of reachable hosts

- error messages about traffic that has timed out (the time to live [TTL] value reaches 0)

ICMP provides an important adjunct to internet protocol (IP) as the channel through which nodes can exchange error and other types of message about packet exchanges.

20.1 Internet Control Message Protocol Headers and Messages

As shown in Figure 20–1, ICMP messages have a simple structure: a one-octet type field, which indicates what function the message is fulfilling, and a one-octet code field, which may be used to further clarify the contents of the message. For example, the code field is not used with echo requests or replies (see the section on Ping), although there are many codes to go with destination unreachable error messages.

A two-octet checksum follows the type and code fields, and the contents of the ICMP message will vary, but will always include the header and the first eight octets of the datagram that caused the error message to be sent. ICMP provides no error correction: it simply reports routing errors by sending error messages back to the source.

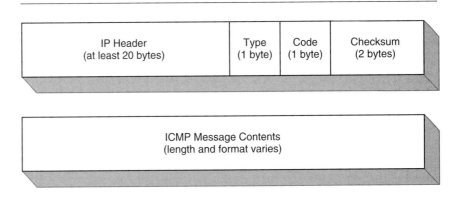

Figure 20–1: ICMP messages are encapsulated within IP datagrams, but they operate at the same layer as IP.

The message contents field contains the IP header and the first 64 bits of the original datagram that caused the ICMP message to be sent. This is enough to permit higher level protocols (such as transmission control protocol [TCP]) to examine their own headers and take corrective action based on the ICMP message. The message may also contain the IP addresses of intervening routers between systems or a list of available routers on a network with corresponding preference levels, depending on the ICMP message type.

Mostly to avoid having the cure be worse than the disease, ICMP has certain limitations built into the specification. For one thing, ICMP error messages cannot beget ICMP error messages. For another, broadcast or multicast messages also cannot beget ICMP error messages. Both these rules help avoid cascading errors which would result in broadcast storms that could easily flood a network.

20.2 Unreachability and Routing Messages

ICMP unreachability messages indicate there has been a failure somewhere in the process of addressing the datagram that triggers the message. For example, an incorrectly addressed datagram can cause an unreachable message to be sent to the host originaly sending the datagram. The message usually indicates that the host or the network is either unreachable or unknown. This happens when a host is turned off, when a network link is down, or even when the specified protocol is not available (for instance, attempting to connect to a network application port that is prohibited or restricted).

The most obvious uses for ICMP routing messages are requests for lists of available routers and the replies that include lists of other available routers (each router listed with a priority level). Hosts often use ICMP to request a list of available routers when they boot up, to initialize their routing tables. Routers advertise gateways when they boot up, and they will also periodically broadcast this information.

These routing messages include a field to indicate how long to retain the enclosed information because sometimes routers fail, are taken down, become overloaded, or lose connectivity to remote networks. By periodically broadcasting the current routing preferences, routers ensure that hosts on their networks don't attempt to use a default router that is inappropriate.

Another type of routing message is generated when a router becomes overloaded. Routers can be overwhelmed by a high-volume of traffic from a single host or from a generally high load generated by many hosts on the network. Although routers attempt to process all network traffic as it is received, when volume is high this is not always possible. The use of memory buffers to store incoming traffic before processing can help, but it no longer takes a Cray or Thinking Machines supercomputer to saturate a typical 10 Mbps Ethernet wire–nor does it take that many video-conferencing sessions to saturate a 100 Mbps Fast Ethernet local area network (LAN).

Routers may send out source quench messages when they are overloaded (although this is not required). Each time the router receives a datagram it can't handle, it discards the datagram and sends back a source quench message, basically asking the fast transmitter to slow down. The originating host then drops its speed until it stops getting the error messages, slowly building up speed again until it starts getting the error messages again.

Another instance where an ICMP message may carry routing information occurs when a host sends traffic to one router when a different router advertises a better route (a route with fewer hops). This is called a redirect. This is a common occurrence on networks with more than one router, where the hosts start out with only a single default router in their routing tables.

Figure 20–2 demonstrates this situation. Host A is attempting to send a datagram to Host C and is using Router AB as a default gateway. Since Host A knows that the datagram is destined for a nonlocal network, it sends it to the default gateway. However, Router AB has to route that datagram to Router AC to get it to Host C, taking an extra step (the first step is from Host A to Router AB, then Router AB to Router AC, then Router AC to Host C; the optimal route is from Host A to Router AC to Host C).

Redirects occur when a router forwards a datagram onto the same network on which the datagram was received by the router this means that the originating host could have sent the traffic directly to another router on the same network. Although the router still forwards the datagram, it also generates a message back to the originating host that there is a better route.

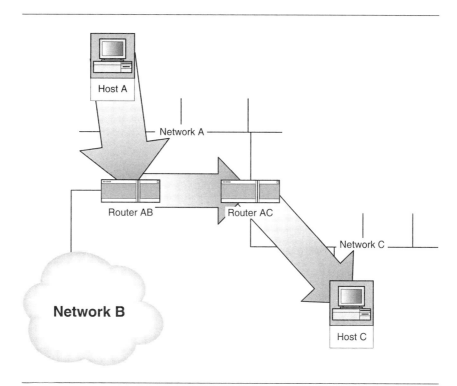

Figure 20–2: ICMP can be used to help a host learn about optimal routes.

The host can then incorporate the new, more efficient, route into its routing table.

20.3   Ping and Internet Control Message Protocol Echo Messages

Probably the most common explicit use of ICMP is the ping application. Written in 1983 by the late Mike Muuss at the University of California at Berkeley, ping behaves like the "ping" sent out by warships using sonar, prompting the name of the utility.[1] Ping sends an ICMP echo request

---

[1]Writing on his web site (http://ftp.arl.army.mil/~mike/ and still available as of 2002) Muuss denied that PING was an acronym for anything, and was chosen strictly on the sonar analogy. However, Dave Mills, currently a professor at University of Delaware, claimed on an IETF mailing list in 1988 to have coined the term "ping" as an acronym for "Packet InterNet Groper" in 1980.

out to a specific host, and the host responds to ICMP echo requests by sending out an ICMP echo reply. Pings purpose is to see if anything is out there.

Ping represents the simplest level of connectivity possible between two hosts on an internetwork, so it is useful for testing whether a remote host is reachable or whether the network connection for a local host is properly configured and installed. Most ping applications use the command format:

```
ping <IP host name | IP address>
```

By using the IP host name instead of the address, it is possible to verify not only that the two hosts have connectivity, but also that the local host is resolving names properly (see Chapter 11 for more on network name resolution).

Because organizations connected to the Internet are increasingly using firewall gateways (see Chapter 24 for more about network security issues) to protect against unauthorized use of their hosts, some hosts that may be visible to network applications won't respond to ICMP echo requests. However, ping continues to be useful as a diagnostic tool on unconnected internetworks as well as (usually) within organizational internetworks.

Ping implementations can vary a surprising amount, but all do the same task: send out at least one ICMP echo request and report back whether the host is reachable or not. Some implementations simply send a single ICMP request, and report whether the pinged host responds. Most implementations also report the amount of time it took between the request being sent and the response being received, which helps diagnose slow links between hosts.

Also fairly standard is the use of multiple pings for each invocation of the program, one request per second. In these cases, a sequence number is recorded for each request and is reported when the response is received. Again, this is useful for identifying links that are dropping traffic (there will be missing numbers in the responses received) or that are sending traffic out of order or with varying routes (replies will not be received in the same order the requests were sent out).

Ping implementations usually pad out the datagram with some amount of data to simulate actual traffic. Some implementations allow the user to modify the amount of padding, making the ping datagrams larger or smaller. This function can be subverted into a denial-of-service attack known as the ping of death. Sending a ping datagram that is larger than it should be has been known to crash some systems.

20.4 Traceroute

Ping offers a tool to test connectivity between two individual hosts. The IP record route option (see above) will report the route taken by any IP datagram, including an ICMP echo request. This option causes every system handling the request to add its own IP address to the IP options field. Although useful, record route is severely limited. It records every system, every time that system handles the message, which includes the destination host and every intervening router, every time the router is traversed. So a packet traveling from Host A to Router AB to Router CD to Router EF to Host N, and then back to Router EF, to Router CD, to Router AB, to Host A would have nine routing entires.

This would not be a problem except that the route must be stored in the IP header options field, which can be no longer than 40 octets. Nine routing entries would take up 36 octets (IP addresses are 4 octets long each). A simple route like the one just described, with only three routers between source and destination, is as long a route as can be recorded by this option. A single octet of the options field identifies the option type, another indicates the length of the options field, and a third indicates where in the field the IP address of the next stop in the route is recordedleaving room for a maximum of nine IP addresses.

Some implementations of the *traceroute* program (including the Microsoft version, TRACERT and some *nix versions) offer a different strategy to trace the route between hosts on an internetwork. Rather than attempting to collect all the intermediate routers in a single pass, traceroute takes advantage of rules about handling IP datagrams that are about to expire because their TTL (time-to-live) field is almost 0. Routers wont forward a datagram with a TTL of 0 or 1; the datagram is thrown awaybut the router also sends an ICMP message back to the originating host. The message indicates that the offending datagram expired on the network.

ICMP messages are addressed from the router that discovered the error to the originating host, so that when the host gets the ICMP error message, it then can know where the original ICMP echo request was in its route when the TTL counter expired. Traceroute determines the route between hosts by sending out pings with varying TTL values. The first ping has a TTL field value set to 1. The first router receives the ping, throws it out (because the TTL is too low to pass it on), and generates an ICMP error message back to the originating host.

Traceroute stores the address of the first router, then pings the remote host again with the TTL counter set to 2. This time the echo request gets past the first router, but causes the second router to return an ICMP error message. Traceroute keeps this up until the TTL counter is just large enough to reach the remote host, which sends back an ICMP echo reply. The program then outputs the IP addresses of all the routers that sent ICMP error messages in the proper order.

Traceroute is not foolproof. Because IP provides no connections but simply delivers datagrams, it is possible that traffic between two hosts may be sent over more than one route. Over time it is likely that the route between any two hosts on the Internet will vary due to changes in internet connections, modification of routers, and changes in service. However, over the short term these changes will usually not be present, making traceroute a useful tool. In any case, traceroute normally sends multiple probes per hop so that short-term changes in routing can be seen, and also to handle occasional packet losses.

20.5   Using Ping

Ping is most often used as a connectivity verifier, although it can verify only that there is connectivity; failure is not an infallible indicator of lack of connectivity. Network software installers often ping a remote host from a newly installed workstation to verify that the host is truly connected to the internetwork. Pinging a host by name rather than by IP address adds the ability to check that name resolution is being done correctly. When ping fails in these instances, the problem is almost as likely to be with the configuration of the host as with connectivity.

Ping is much more useful as a diagnostic tool when used from a host suffering from a problem connecting to some other host or hosts. For an example,

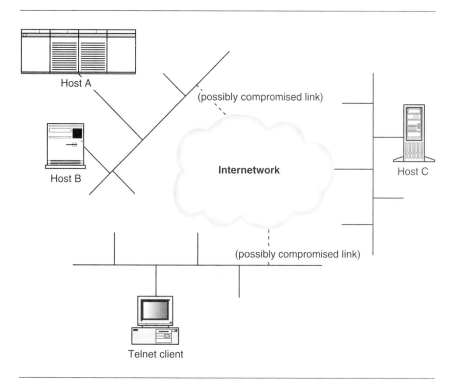

Figure 20–3: Connectivity problems can sometimes be diagnosed with ping.

look at Figure 20–3. A user attempts a telnet session with remote host A but fails to connect and gets an error message that indicates the host is down.

Depending on the result, different actions may be taken:

1. If the users system is not properly configured to resolve host names, connecting to Host A by its IP address should work.
2. If attempting to connect by IP address instead of host name still doesn't work, the telnet server may not be running, the host may be down, or the hosts network may be inaccessible (its link to the internetwork is down).
3. If after sending a ping to host A (by its IP address) the local host gets a response from host A, then the remote hosts telnet server may not be running, or it may have been temporarily down, or the local hosts telnet client may not be working properly.

The user can verify that the telnet client is working by initiating a telnet session with another host, perhaps a local one.

4. If host A doesn't respond to the ping, it may mean that host A is down or that the network is temporarily inaccessible. To find out, the user could attempt to connect to another host on the same network as host A (for instance, host B) or send another ping to host B. If the client cannot connect to any host on host As network, the user could check on connectivity to other networks, which can help determine if the local network is disconnected from the internetwork or if it is the remote network that has connectivity problems.

Ping is also useful for generating traffic on a network between two hosts. Many ping implementations permit the user to specify a size for the packet, a delay between packets sent, and the number of times to retry the remote host. This controlled transmission can help the administrator identify problems, like systems that can't handle lots of traffic, or hosts that have sporadic outages, that could not be diagnosed with a single ping.

It should be clear that ping can be a helpful diagnostic, as long as the user understands all the different variables that may be at work. By itself ping may sometimes be sufficient to indicate that a problem exists, but it is not always sufficient to pinpoint problems.

20.6   Using Traceroute

Traceroute offers an ingenious use of the ICMP TTL Exceeded message to determine the route taken between a client and a server. The output from traceroute includes the names of the different routers forwarding packets between the two hosts as well as the round-trip time for the messages from source to router.

Network managers may use traceroute to diagnose slow response time between a client and a server: by checking what path network traffic is taking from one host to another it is sometimes possible to identify bottlenecks (routers that are responding very slowly) or instances where traffic is being routed over an unnecessarily long path.

Like ping, however, traceroute cannot be regarded as a formal and infallible management solution but rather as a useful diagnostic tool and guide.

20.7   Chapter Summary

As we've seen in this chapter, ICMP provides an invaluable and ingenious tool for generating network reachability information. Ping and traceroute are two fundamental network troubleshooting tools as well as important learning tools for new network engineers seeking to explore the ways in which their networks interoperate. The next chapter takes us to the data link layer, where physical systems communicate over a shared medium.

21

The Data Link Layer

Mapping a logical (internet protocol [IP]) network onto the real-world physical networks requires that the logical network protocol entities be able to communicate with data link layer protocol entities, if only to figure out how to deliver data. IP and the link layer protocols interact in a variety of ways; as discussed in Chapter 20, ICMP operates in parallel with IP to deliver messages about IP system status.

The protocols governing communication between entities on the same link layer network, such as Ethernet, must provide some mechanism for IP (or any other network layer protocols) to map addresses from IP to the link layer network. IP originally used link layer broadcasts, with nodes effectively shouting, "who here is using the IP address X.X.X.X?" A single message, but all nodes would hear it.

Not all network media support this kind of broadcasting because they have no way for more than one node to receive the same message at the same time. This type of network is called a *Non-Broadcast Multiple Access* (*NBMA*) network, and it just means that all communication is done on

455

a one-to-one basis. (Think of the difference between a simple telephone system, where the only calls possible are from one instrument to another—no extra instruments on the same line, no conference calling, not even a public address system or intercom system.)

Increasingly, these NBMA media have become important for IP networking, and if there is no mechanism for broadcasting at the link layer, address resolution must be accomplished some other way.

This chapter examines three of the most common link layer protocols used with IP: Ethernet, the Point to Point Protocol (PPP), and Asynchronous Transfer Mode (ATM). Some might argue that of these three, only Ethernet is the only true link layer protocol because it specifies how data is to be framed, transmitted, and received over a local network medium. PPP is most often used for linking home personal computers to internet service providers. Strictly speaking, ATM is an internetworking protocol in its own right, defining activity at layers 2 and 3 for traversing circuit-oriented networks of networks.

Some might also argue that if we talk about ATM we must also talk about Frame Relay (FR), another key NBMA medium. However, most of the protocols we'll cover in this book are generalized for NBMA networks rather than specifying; ATM is presented largely as an example, one type of NBMA network; just as Ethernet is presented as an example of a broadcast network.

Of even more concern to some might be the inclusion of ATM (and FR) in a chapter about the data link layer: these protocols have traditionally been treated as sort-of link layer protocols by IP engineers, yet actually they are designed as internet protocols capable of supporting large, interconnected internets on their own.

However, Ethernet, ATM, and PPP are all examples of protocols used to convey IP packets across networks, they all interact to a greater or lesser degree with IP entities, and they're all examined in this chapter.

We start with a look at how IP interacts with the link layer protocols, followed by an overview of fundamental Ethernet specifications. Inasmuch as the basic IP mechanism for address resolution, the Address Resolution Protocol (ARP), is strongly linked with Ethernet, we cover ARP and variations such as Reverse ARP (RARP), and Proxy ARP next. After ARP, we look at ATM, which is representative of the NBMA family of protocols over which ARP will not work without significant modification—so we also discuss how ARP has been adapted.

PPP, over which IP/link layer addressing issues are simplified (a signal can have only one source and one destination on the link), is discussed next. The last section introduces the family of "IP over X" specifications defining how IP packets are to be handled over various different link layer protocols.

21.1   Internet Protocol and the Link Layer

Strictly speaking, TCP/IP should not be concerned with the data link layer. Networked hosts use the data link layer to move data between the network interfaces of two different computers on the same physical network. At this level, network traffic is just one level above the physical signal: whether the signal is a variation in current on a conducting medium, a variation in light signals on a fiberoptic medium, or a variation in sound on an analog telephone wire. The data link layer is concerned with properly sending and receiving these signals between communicating hosts through their network interfaces.

The most important function transacted between IP and the link layer is linking an IP address with a local network address. ARP solves this problem handily—as long as the local network uses a *broadcast/multiple access* medium, such as Ethernet, in which there are mechanisms for broadcast (one datagram reaches all nodes on the network) and for allowing all nodes to monitor the medium simultaneously. Early Ethernet networks based on coaxial cables used a *bus* topology, with all nodes interfacing to the network through a physical tap into the wire; likewise, wireless networks lend themselves to protocols similar to Ethernet because all nodes can monitor the local network simultaneously and all can be reached with a single broadcast packet.

Important IP functions, starting with local link address resolution, require a broadcast mechanism to work. If a network supports only unicast datagrams, then address resolution for IP based on standard ARP becomes difficult if not impossible. Although Ethernet, and increasingly wireless, dominate the market for organizational networks,[1] ATM, Fibre Channel,

---

[1] Token Ring and others are increasingly viewed as legacy systems to be replaced when possible.

and other high-performance, circuit-oriented data communications proto-cols are based on point-to-point connections. They are known collectively as *NBMA* networks. There is no support for broadcast in these networks; since there is no common bus or medium through which a single packet can be received by more than one node, there is no support for multiple access either.

As illustrated in Figure 21–1, broadcast is simple on an Ethernet network because it is transmitted once, but all nodes on the network (including the sender) can detect the transmission and determine that they should accept it for processing. In this case, host A sends a broadcast message out on the LAN, and all nodes identify it as a broadcast, accept it, and process it. If the message had been intended only for host D, all the nodes would still check the message just enough to determine that it was not a broadcast and that it was not intended for them, and ignore it (except for the recipient, D).

In an ATM network, all communication is done through circuits, shown here as a pipeline through the network cloud from E to H. IP over NBMA networks is further complicated by the fact that many NBMA networks are

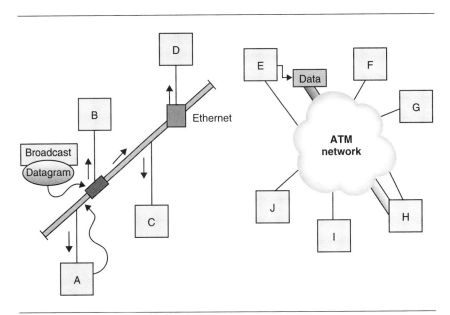

Figure 21–1: Broadcast/multiple access networks and non-broadcast/multiple access networks.

not simple local area network/link layer protocols but are rather full-blown internetworking protocols themselves. Many NBMA network protocols are aimed at accomplishing the same function in their protocols stacks that IP does in the TCP/IP suite: routing data across internets.

This section introduces the fundamentals of Ethernet networking, ATM networking, and the PPP.

21.2   Ethernet

Ethernet is actually a set of standards specifications that define network MAC addresses, frame formats, and transmission standards. Ethernet took its basic form in research labs during the mid-1970s and its modern form by 1982. The commercial version that came to dominate the market runs at 10 Mbps and is sometimes referred to as DIX Ethernet, where DIX stands for Digital Equipment Corporation (DEC), IBM, and Xerox—the companies that underwrote the specification (DIX Ethernet is sometimes also called Ethernet II; both of these terms are now rarely used).

The IEEE maintains the IEEE 802.3 of standards that define what is now more commonly known as Ethernet. There are minor differences between the IEEE 802.3 standards and the Ethernet standard, some purely semantic in the use of different nomenclature for the same frame fields.

The IEEE called their Ethernet standards group Project 802 because it was started in February 1980, and they came up with several sets of standards relating to the standard networks of that time (Table 21–1).

Ethernet is considered a *CSMA/CD* network; the acronym stands for *Carrier Sense Multiple Access/ Collision Detection*, and it represents Ethernet's most important characteristics:

Carrier Sense: All nodes on an Ethernet share the medium, so only one can transmit at a time. Before a node can transmit on the network, it must check to see if any other node is already transmitting—carrier sensing is the process of checking the wire to see if anyone else is using it.

Multiple Access: This means that all nodes on an Ethernet share the medium *and* any or all of them can, at any time, detect any signals traveling over it.

IEEE	Standard	Area Standardized
IEEE	802.2	Logical Link Control (LLC)
IEEE	802.3	Standardization for Ethernet (CSMA/CD baseband networks)
IEEE	802.4	Token Bus network standards
IEEE	802.5	Token Ring network standards
IEEE	802.11	Wireless networks

Table 21–1: The IEEE 802 standards apply to various types of networks, with the 802.2 standard applicable to all. 802.3 refers to Ethernet-type networks, while 802.11 is for wireless.

Collision Detection: This means that not only does each node have to check to make sure that no other node is transmitting before it sends anything, but also that nodes must have a mechanism by which they are able to detect if any other node (having also determined that the medium was available) has also attempted to transmit at the same time. Such events are known as *collisions* and call for specific action on the part of both nodes.

The IEEE standard numbers aren't version numbers as one might think, but rather differentiate the standards. The 802.2 standard provides transparency to the physical layers for all the 802 network standards (802.3, 802.4, and 802.5). So, if a CSMA/CD baseband network runs IEEE 802.2, it generates 802.3 frames and uses the 802.2 Logical Link Control (LLC) specifications within those frames. Likewise, if a network uses the IEEE 802.3 standard, one should expect that it uses the 802.2 extensions (but this is not always the case).

21.2.1 ETHERNET FRAMES

The protocol data unit for Ethernet is the *frame*, consisting of header fields and a field for a payload. The payload will almost always contain network traffic relating to a higher layer. In TCP/IP internetworks the payload is invariably an IP datagram, though in heterogenous networks IP datagrams can coexist with other types of network traffic. The nodes that process the frame are unconcerned with the payload: the frame functions as a

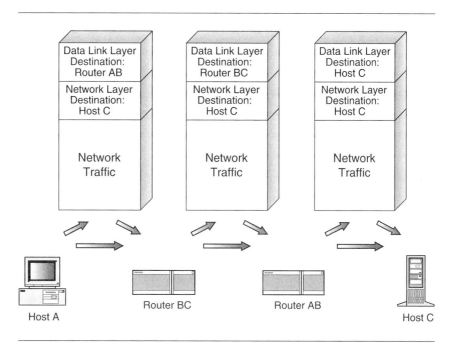

Figure 21–2: **The data link layer addresses of a frame change as the frame passes from one network to another, but the IP source and destination addresses remain unchanged.**

container in which to deliver the payload to the correct destination host on the local network.

The source and destination hosts may or may not be the source and destination hosts for the frames payload. Consider Figure 21–2, a simple internetwork. Host A is sending a piece of data to Host C across an internetwork. Host A begins (at the application layer) collecting the application data, adds TCP headers to address it to a specific remote process (at the transport layer), then adds IP network addressing to address it to a particular host (at the network layer). Before the resulting IP datagram can be sent out on the Ethernet, the originating host adds network link layer information to create an Ethernet frame.

There are three different PDUs involved here:

Transport layer PDU: In this case, a TCP segment addressed to a particular process running on the destination node.

Network layer PDU: In this case, an IP datagram addressed to a particular hosts IP address somewhere on the internet in the figure.

Link layer PDU: In this case, an Ethernet frame addressed to a specific network interface directly connected to the same network as the source.

Host A knows the ultimate destination for the IP datagram is off the local network; therefore, the originating source host addresses an Ethernet frame to the local router. Even though the IP datagram is addressed to Host C, the Ethernet frame sent by the originating host is addressed to Router AB.

Although Network A and Network C in our example are both Ethernets, intermediate internet B could just as easily be a high-speed ATM backbone, a token ring network, or something else. Once the frame is received by Router AB, it strips away the Ethernet frame headers, checks the IP destination address, and determines that the IP datagram is intended for a host on a different network.

Because Router AB is configured to send all packets destined for Network C to Router BC, it creates a new network frame (perhaps an Ethernet frame, perhaps not) containing the IP datagram (from Host A to Host C). The new network frame, traveling from Router AB to Router BC, will have Router AB as the source and Router BC as the destination—but the IP packet itself remains unchanged, and the packet's destination IP address remains unchanged. Figure 21–2 shows that the headers are stripped off and the router converts the frame into the proper format for Network B; Router BC in turn must accept the resulting frame, determine the local network address of the destination host, Host C, and create a new Ethernet frame for Network C. The final network frame in this example will show Router BC as the source and Host C as the destination—but the IP destination address is still unchanged, with the IP destination still Host C.

21.2.2   ETHERNET AND IEEE 802.3 FRAMES

The host requirements specification (RFC 1122) mandates IP nodes connected to an Ethernet network MUST be capable of handling Ethernet frames. The requirements specification indicates only that nodes SHOULD

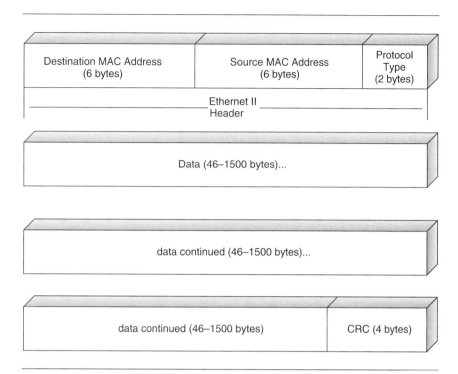

Figure 21–3: An Ethernet frame contains from 46 to 1500 octets.

accept frames formatted with the more strict IEEE 802.3 specification (most IP nodes on Ethernets do support both, however).

Network frames literally frame the data being sent, with header fields (and often with *trailer* fields, which indicate the end of the frame). Network data fits in the data field. Figure 21–3 shows the structure of an Ethernet frame, and Figure 21–4 shows the IEEE 802.2/802.3 frame.

First, note the similarities: Ethernet and IEEE headers both begin with the destination and source *media access control* (MAC) address, six-octet values typically hard-coded into the network interface, and both terminate with a four-octet *Cyclic Redundancy Check* (CRC) as their trailer. Both specify a two-octet header field following the source and destination fields. The differences between Ethernet and 802.3 frames lie in the definition of this field and in the use of the eight octets following it.

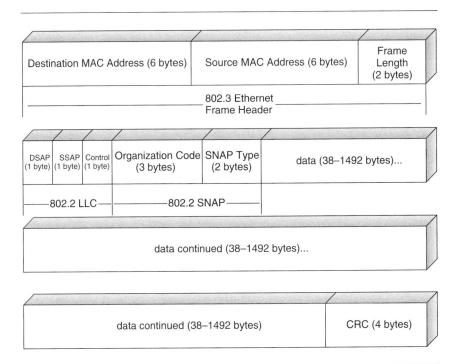

Figure 21–4: The IEEE 802.2/802.3 frame varies slightly from the original Ethernet specifications, but is compatible with those specifications.

Following the addresses, Ethernet defines a two-octet *ethertype* field identifying the frame's payload protocol type to indicate the upper layer protocol to receive the payload once the frame is processed. The value of this field is used to distinguish frame payload encodings. For example, IPv4 traffic is indicated by the hex value of 0x0800, IPv6 by 0x86DD, and ARP messages by 0x0806.

IEEE 802.3 specifies that these two octets be used as a *length* field, indicating a value in octets representing the frame payload length; this value may be no smaller than 46 octets (frames containing less than that much data are padded to that length to enable collision detection) and no longer than 1,500 octets.

IEEE standard permits further classification of the frame's contents by using additional fields for *Logical Link Control* (*LLC*) and *Subnetwork Access Protocol* (*SNAP*) fields, while Ethernet uses the *ethertype* (a value that indicates the protocol being carried in the payload) field to identify a frame's contents.

Because valid ethertype values are all higher than 1,500 (the maximum number of octets for the data portion of the network frame), IEEE 802 frames are distinguished from Ethernet frames simply by checking the two octets that follow the destination and source addresses: if the value is larger than the hexadecimal for 1,500, the frame is an Ethernet frame (and the value defines a protocol type); if it is 1,500 or less, it is an IEEE frame. Because the original Ethernet specification limited payload length to 1,500 octets, the IEEE 802.3 committee was able to specify the use of ethertypes whose values are greater than 1,500 while maintaining compatibility with Ethernet.

The important part of the frame, the actual payload, differs between Ethernet and IEEE in the first eight octets, assigned by IEEE to LLC and SNAP functions. As a result, an Ethernet data field can be no longer than 1,500 octets and no smaller than 46 octets; valid IEEE data fields range from 38 octets to 1,492 octets.

One further difference (semantic though it may be) between IEEE and Ethernet is in the name given to the 64-bit sequence with which each frame opens. Ethernet defines a *preamble* sequence:

```
10101010  10101010  10101010  10101010
10101010  10101010  10101010  10101011
```

IEEE 802.3 defines a seven-octet preamble:

```
10101010  10101010  10101010  10101010
10101010  10101010  10101010
```

followed by the *Start of Frame Delimiter* (*SFD*):

```
10101011
```

Ethernet/802.3 frames have strict size limitations, which in turn affect the size of the IP packets that may be carried in each frame. A complete frame may be no larger than 1,518 octets: a maximum of 1,500 octets for the payload, 14 octets for the headers, and 4 octets for the CRC.

The lower bound for the entire frame size is set at 64 octets (14 octets for the headers, 4 octets for the CRC, and 46 octets of data or padding) to put enough data on the wire at any given time during the transmission so that it will collide with data sent by any other node.

While the minimum Ethernet frame is limited to 64 octets by the nature of the medium, the upper value for frame length is more flexible. The 1,500-octet frame limit was chosen apparently because it balances overall network efficiency, by maximizing the time during which the network is actually carrying traffic, while minimizing network delay, which is increased when larger frame sizes are permitted. Larger frame sizes are possible, and *jumbo frames*, up to 9,000 octets long, are allowed in gigabit Ethernet. To ensure compatibility with "standard" 10-Mbps Ethernet, the 1,500-octet payload is enforced for Fast/100-Mbps Ethernet, but the jumbo frames at higher-bandwidth Ethernet to improve overall performance. The 32-bit CRC becomes less reliable as the frame length increases, with 12-K octet frames the largest for which a 32-bit CRC is adequate.

The use of 8 octets of the Ethernet payload for LLC/SNAP encapsulation in 802.3 frames results in maximum payload size of 1,492 octets, but most modern systems and networks support an IPv4 MTU of at least 1,500 octets, which in turn implies that non-optioned IP packet payloads will be 1,480 octets in length (1,500 octets for the packet less 20 octets for IP headers). The IP payload can therefore encapsulate TCP segments whose payloads are no greater than 1,460 octets (1,480 octets of IP payload less 20 octets for TCP headers).

Other link layer protocols, with other limitations on frame size, may support local MTUs that are greater or smaller than 1,500 octets, but the predominance of Ethernet and similar protocols means that a path MTU of 1,500 octets is often a safe bet. The minimum path MTU allowed for IPv4 is 576 octets, a figure that should accommodate even the most archaic systems.

21.3   Address Resolution

If you could make IP addresses and physical addresses (so called because they refer to the physical device receiving network data; also referred to as link layer or MAC addresses) match, linking an IP adress to a network address becomes trivial. Unfortunately, this is not feasible for the most common network media. MAC addresses are 6 octets long, and cannot be mapped directly onto four-octet IP addresses. You could try padding the IP addresses and inserting them into the MAC address, but MAC addresses are hard-coded into network interface cards.

You could also try copying all the physical addresses of hosts on the local Ethernet into a file and associating them with the hosts IP addresses. However, this approach is flawed. Although the IP addresses are associated with specific hosts, the network addresses are bound to the network interface cards. When a card fails or a new card is installed, that link layer/IP address list becomes useless. A more dynamic approach is required.

When a host determines that an IP datagram is destined for a node on the local network, it uses the Address Resolution Protocol (ARP) to get that address, as documented in RFC 826, "An Ethernet Address Resolution Protocol - or - Converting Network Protocol Addresses to 48-bit Ethernet Address for Transmission on Ethernet Hardware." Reverse Address Resolution Protocol (RARP) takes a similar approach to allow hosts to find out their own IP address on the basis of their network address.

ARP is simple. The host that wishes to send the IP datagram broadcasts an ARP request to the local physical network. The request is for the system assigned to the specified IP address to respond with its physical address. All the systems on the network process these requests, but only the host with the specified IP address responds. The system originating the ARP request then uses the physical address supplied to address the local network frames.

One might ask whether it would be more sensible for nodes on an Ethernet to dispense with ARP entirely, and process all network frames. Unwrapping all frames' Ethernet headers would reveal the true destination of the payload, allowing the intended recipient to further process the packet and all others to discard it. Of course, this is hugely wasteful: in effect, it would turn all network traffic into broadcast traffic with all nodes required to allocate resources to process all frames. Also, modern Ethernets typically rely on switches that transmit frames only to their intended destinations; broadcasting all frames to all nodes would impose much greater demands on switches.

A few elaborations make ARP less unwieldy than it appears at first glance. The first is the ARP cache: each system maintains a list of network address and IP address pairings, which is consulted before sending out any ARP requests. The next is that ARP requests include the network address/IP address of the requesting system; if host A needs a network address to direct traffic to host B, chances are good that host B will soon be sending some kind of traffic to host A. Finally, even though only the requesting and responding hosts generate any traffic on the local network, all the hosts on that network listen in and update their own ARP caches with the network address/IP address of the requesting node.

21.3.1 ADDRESS RESOLUTION PROTOCOL MESSAGE FORMAT

Most often, ARP is used to correlate 6-octet link layer addresses with 4-octet network layer addresses, but ARP can be used to link any size network addresses with any size link layer addresses. ARP operates at the data link layer, so ARP messages are carried in network frames rather than in IP datagrams. Figure 21–5 shows a typical Ethernet ARP frame. To conform with the standard Ethernet frame, the Ethernet destination will be "all ones": the Ethernet broadcast address. Every host on the network will receive the frame. The Ethernet source address is the originating host's Ethernet address, and the Ethernet frame protocol type value is 0×0806, indicating the frame carries an ARP message.

The first two fields within the Ethernet frame indicate the kind of network hardware address (Ethernet) that must be located to match the address of the network protocol type (IP). The next two fields, hardware length and protocol length, indicate in octets how long the hardware and protocol addresses are. These four fields may vary for different network and protocol types, but for IP over Ethernet they specify that the ARP packet will be 28 octets long: 8 octets for the header fields, 10 octets for the originating host's IP address (4 octets) and Ethernet address (6 octets), and 10 octets for the target host's IP address and Ethernet address (which the originating host leaves blank when it sends the ARP request).

Finally, the operation field indicates the function the ARP packet is fulfilling. An ARP request has the value of 1 here, and an ARP reply has the value 2. RARP requests are indicated by the value 3, and RARP replies by the value 4. The requests have all the fields filled in except for the address being sought: the network address of the host with the specified IP address,

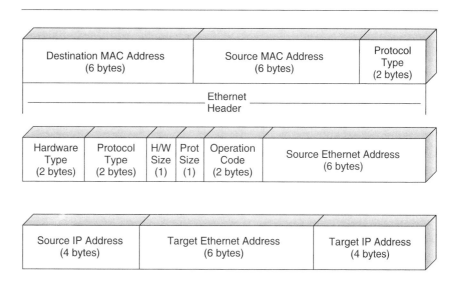

Figure 21–5: An ARP packet, as encapsulated in an Ethernet frame, will result in a 28-octet Ethernet payload.

for ARP requests, or the IP address of the host with the specified network address, for RARP requests.

ARP requests and ARP replies differ only in the values held in the operation field (indicating request or reply) and the requested address field (replies will contain the requested address).

21.3.2 ADDRESS RESOLUTION PROTOCOL CACHE

ARPs are broadcasts, and broadcasts are a nuisance to almost all hosts that receive them. We try to keep broadcasts to a minimum because they can really cut into network performance. So, to keep the number of broadcast ARP requests to a minimum, hosts store the addresses they receive from ARP replies in an ARP cache. When a host needs to send an IP datagram, it first looks in the ARP cache to see if it has a data link layer address for that datagram. If it does, the host can forego sending out an ARP request.

Hosts build up their ARP caches by adding the address mapping in every response they receive to their own ARP requests. Because all ARP requests are broadcast, all nodes will receive all those requests—if a node already has an entry for the requested address, that node can update its own cache (but if the node doesn't already have an entry for that address, the data in the request is ignored).

Gratuitous ARP also enhances ARP cache efficiency. Every host, as it boots, sends itself an ARP request. The purpose is not to try to determine its own address so much as to verify that its IP/network address is not already being used by some other host on the network, as well as to register the IP/MAC address pairing in other nodes' ARP caches.

21.3.3 PROXY ADDRESS RESOLUTION PROTOCOL

Proxy ARP is a method used when two parts of the same network are divided by a router. Hosts on one side need to be able to address Ethernet frames that encapsulate IP datagrams for hosts on the other side. Although the originating host thinks the remote host is on the same physical network, network traffic is actually being directed through the router. Addressing the network frame to the remote host would not work, since it isn't on the same physical network, so the router performs the proxy ARP service, filling in its own Ethernet address in response to ARP requests for hosts on opposite sides of the network.

This is also the approach to ARP used in nonbroadcast networks like ATM. An ARP server keeps track of all connected nodes and maintains a list of data link layer and network layer addresses. When a node needs a data link layer address, it sends out an ARP request to the ARP server, which responds on behalf of all connected nodes.

21.3.4 REVERSE ADDRESS RESOLUTION PROTOCOL

As the name implies, RARP is simply the reverse of ARP. Used by diskless workstations to get their assigned IP addresses, RARP requires that at least one host on the internetwork be designated a RARP server. The RARP source fills its own network address in both the source and target network address fields, and the RARP servers respond to the requester with the required IP address. RARP packets use a different set of values for the operations field and use the value 0×0835 for Ethernet frame type (instead of the value 0×0806 used by ARP).

Whereas ARP is handy when the transmitting host knows the IP address of the destination host, RARP is useful when a host knows a hardware address but does not know the IP address it desires. The most common situation in which this occurs is booting a diskless workstation. The workstation reads its own MAC address, but needs to send a request to a RARP server to map an IP address to itself.

Multiple RARP servers are desirable to allow nodes on a subnetted network to access the RARP service locally. Because RARP requests are broadcasts, and therefore not forwarded by routers, there must be a local RARP server on every subnet with nodes that require one. In the case of multiple RARP servers on the same subnet, requesting nodes use the first reply and ignore any additional responses.

RARP must be distinguished from the Boot Protocol (BOOTP) and Dynamic Host Configuration Protocol (DHCP). Those protocols permit hosts to boot (BOOTP) and configure (DHCP) themselves as IP nodes—and those protocols operate at the IP layer, with BOOTP using a minimal UDP/IP and Trivial FTP implementation to download a boot image and DHCP allowing a host to request an IP address as well as routing and DNS configuration information. RARP operates at the link layer and may be used before BOOTP.

21.3.5   INVERSE ADDRESS RESOLUTION PROTOCOL

Inverse ARP, or InARP, was first described in RFC 1293 in 1992 and updated in RFC 2390 in 1998. InARP lets a node find the IP address of another node to which it already has a data link layer connection. ARP and RARP are used to determine an IP address to link to a data link layer address through the use of broadcasts. In contrast, InARP is used in networks where broadcasts must be replicated across all virtual circuits. Instead of sending the request to all connected nodes, the requesting node can just send a single request down a single virtual circuit to ask the node at the other end what its IP address is.

InARP adds two values to the ARP operation type. The InARP request uses the value 8, and the InARP response uses the value 9. Other than this and their use of unicast rather than broadcast to make requests, InARP messages are identical to ARP messages.

21.4   Asynchronous Transfer Mode

Unlike Ethernet, ATM protocols were devised to be independent of the physical layer, and to be used for transmission of any kind of digital information, voice as well as network data. The objective was to build a technology capable of handling a lot of data at very high speed over large internets. ATM differs from IP in several important ways and can be made to coexist in more than one way. This section covers these differences as well as the approaches to coexistence.

21.4.1   VIRTUAL CIRCUITS AND ROUTES

IP packets are (at least in theory) each delivered independently. A host sending a stream of packets must somehow check for the proper destination for every packet before sending it; the routing decision process is repeated at every hop, whether or not a similarly addressed packet was just processed. The routers must check each packet against a routing table and make a next-hop decision, adding incrementally to delivery overhead and latency throughout the data exchange. However, packets can be generated and immediately sent on their way by nodes that have no detailed knowledge of the internetwork topology in which they exist.

ATM is virtual circuit (VC)–based, meaning that when two nodes set up a communication link, they use often complex protocols to identify a stable path through the network cloud (based on the switches through which the data must pass), and then they blast data back and forth through those switches. Rather than carrying complete source and destination node addresses within each switched *cell* (ATM's unit of transport: 53 octets each, 48 for data and 5 for cell header fields), they carry short labels indicating how each switch should process the cell.

With less data to process and fewer decisions to make, switched circuit networks can move data extremely quickly. However, the process of setting up the circuit at the start of an exchange (or during the exchange when network conditions change) can add significantly to the delay in the connection, unless virtual circuits are set up in advance, just in case they are needed.

21.4.2 INTERNET PROTOCOL AND ASYNCHRONOUS TRANSFER MODE ISSUES

IP leaves the framing of data to link layer protocols such as Ethernet; ATM, on the other hand, performs many of the functions associated with the network layer as well as the link layer. ATM cells contain small fragments of the data that ATM frames into larger chunks, in much the same way that Ethernet organizes data and header information into 1,518-octet frames. ATM frames data by gathering it into appropriately sized chunks and adding addressing information, and then slices those frames up into 53-octet cells for speedy delivery.

If ATM is treated as a link layer protocol, however, it means that any given ATM network cloud may consist of more than one distinct IP network. What happens then is that IP traffic is passed to the ATM cloud by way of a router that seeks a next-hop IP router. Packets can be routed around inside the ATM cloud from one IP network to another, each packet being decapsulated and encapsulated over and over as ATM/IP switch/routers put the cells together into frames and then unwrap the packets to determine what to do with them.

The performance benefits of ATM are in this way negated unless the routing/switching systems can find a way to map an optimal route across an ATM internet using the ATM network layer. This is particularly relevant when a packet from outside an ATM network is sent to a destination within the ATM nework. The distance between any two stations on an ATM network is (for all practical purposes) one hop, because all circuits are direct links between two stations. This means that since the ATM network may be composed of more than one logical IP network, a packet might take several trips across the IP networks within the ATM network when only one would be sufficient.

To clarify this last point, consider what happens when an ATM network contains IP internets. Figure 21–6 shows what can happen, with a packet entering the ATM network via Router A, destined for host 10.1.100.99. The entire destination network (10.x.x.x) is interconnected through a single ATM network, so it should be possible to switch a packet directly from its entry point to its destination.

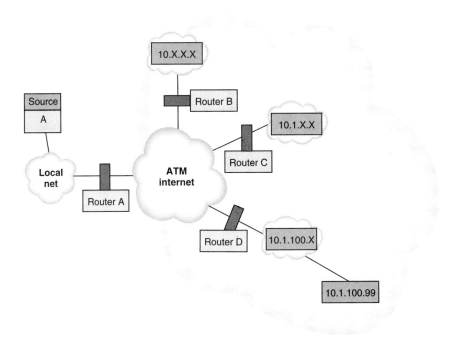

Figure 21–6: ATM and IP are both internetworking protocols, but the traditional approach to IP over ATM treats ATM as a link layer protocol, while ignoring ATM's internetworking function.

However, when the ATM network is treated purely as the link layer network, Router A will forward the packet to Router B (because that is the router responsible for all packets destined for network 10.x.x.x), which forwards the packet to Router C, before it is ultimately delivered to the destination host. The packet passes through four routers en route to its destination, and is processed from ATM to IP at each stop.

This is the traditional approach to layering IP over ATM, described in RFC 2225, "Classical IP and ARP over ATM," and the ATM Forum's contribution, LAN Emulation (LANE). As defined in the eponymous RFC 2332, *Next-Hop Resolution Protocol* (*NHRP*) allows IP routers at the edges of an NBMA network to determine the best next hop for a packet: if the destination is inside the NBMA network, the next hop will be the destination–even though the destination node may be on a different logical IP network.

As shown in Figure 21–6, Router A would be able to determine that the packet should be routed through directly to Router D. This protocol allows IP and ATM networks to get the best of both worlds when data passes across both.

Multiprotocol Label Switching (*MPLS*), specified in RFC 3031, "Multiprotocol Label Switching Architecture," allows routers to assign a *Forwarding Equivalency Class* (*FEC*) to packets just once, as they enter a network, to designate how the packets are to be treated by systems within the network.

Standard IP routers can be said to assign packets to FECs based on their destination addresses: if the destination addresses of two packets indicate to the router that both should be sent to the same next hop, then they are in the same FEC. MPLS provides a mechanism that allows routers to process packet headers, determine the best path for it to take through the network, and then attach a *label* specifying its FEC. As that packet transits the ATM network, the label changes at each switching point, to indicate how the upstream switch should treat the packet (or any other packet within the same FEC).

MPLS makes possible some interesting things. Connectionless IP datagrams are ordinarily divorced from their past and future: when they arrive at a router, the router looks at the headers and determines the next best hop. Where the packet came from and where it is going don't really matter— even if the packets were treated specially for some reason on an earlier hop. With MPLS, packets can be tagged for special treatment as they enter a network and be accorded the same treatment at all hops within that network.

Also now possible is the use of networks (such as ATM and other high-performance NBMA networks) where there are no routers capable of evaluating headers and selecting a best next hop. ATM switches are well adapted to this approach, and MPLS is becoming an increasingly important part of the global internet infrastructure as well as organizational internet infrastructures.

For detailed discussion of MPLS and related protocols, the interested reader is referred to *MPLS: Technology and Applications* by Bruce S. Davie, Yakov Rekhter (Morgan Kaufmann Publishing, 2000). Rekhter and Davie are the principal authors of many key MPLS specifications.

21.4.3   BROADCASTS

Another important implication of a circuit-based network is that there are no free rides for broadcasts. All transmissions require that a circuit be set up (as with TCP, see Chapter 18), with the result that ATM networks look more like a collection of ad hoc point-to-point links between pairs of nodes. As a result, broadcasts and multicasts must be repeated once for every intended recipient—once for each node on the ATM network. Ethernet and wireless make broadcasts easy, which in turn makes them well suited to IP networks where multi-recipient packets are used frequently. ATM does not have a native facility for broadcasting, so to support IP over ATM a mechanism that behaves like broadcast must be put in place. We'll discuss this mechanism in section 21.4.6, below.

Despite all these issues, ATM and IP are well on their way to learning to play well together.

ATM is representative of the family of NBMA network protocols that include Frame Relay and others. Many of the issues raised, and solved, for IP and ATM apply equally to other protocols; in fact, many of these solutions have been generalized in specifications that refer to NBMA networks rather than ATM–only or Frame Relay–only. We'll first look at the ATM cell and then move on to a general solution for address resolution in NBMA networks.

21.4.4   ATM CELLS

ATM cells are small; 5 octets for the header and 48 octets for payload. Such small units make very high performance, solid-state switches easier to design and build; ATM switches can provide higher throughput using the same resources necessary to build a router. The benefits even outweigh the relatively heavy (roughly 10%) overhead associated with the small cell sizes, not to mention overhead associated with framing activity.

Figure 21–7 shows the 5-octet header in detail. ATM header fields include the following:

Generic Flow Control (GFC): This 4-bit field carries data that governs how traffic flows across the interface, indicating whether an interface should slow down or speed up its transmission rate. ATM provides

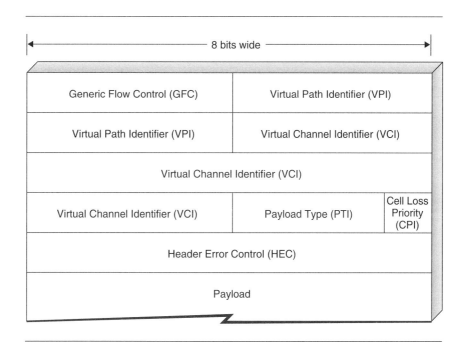

Figure 21–7: ATM header fields.

no cell-buffering mechanisms so it uses the GFC field to control traffic flow.

Virtual Path Identifier (VPI): Eight bits for user-network interface links or 12 bits for network to network interface links, the VPI identifies the cell's source and destination.

Virtual Channel Identifier (VCI): This 16-bit field, with the VPI, is used to route the cell within the ATM network.

Payload Type (PT): This 3-bit field identifies the cell's payload data type, useful for distinguishing data that may require special handling or that may be necessary for maintaining the network.

Cell Loss Priority (CLP): This flag bit indicates whether the cell is expendable or whether network resources must be allocated to guarantee its delivery (not all cells will have the same priority, even within the same circuit).

Header Error Control (HEC): An eight-bit data integrity field used by the physical layer to verify that the cell has not been damaged in transit.

ATM framing creates large chunks of data, while the cells are merely individual units taken from those chunks and formatted for rapid transmission. A cell by itself will usually have no protocol information relating it to either its upper layer (e.g., IP) destination or source.

Issues of framing, ATM station addressing, signaling, and circuit management are outside the scope of this book, but a short list of resources, including relevant RFCs, is included at the end of the chapter.

21.4.5 NON-BROADCAST MULTI-ACCESS ADDRESS RESOLUTION

Traditional address resolution over ATM networks is described in RFC 2225, "Classical IP and ARP over ATM," where ATMARP is specified as a service provided on each logical IP subnet within an ATM network. The ATMARP server maintains an ARP table whose entries are created whenever a new station registers its IP/ATM station link layer addresses with the server. ATM client stations are responsible for notifying the ATMARP server periodically to refresh and/or update their listings.

Traditional ARP, as defined in RFC 826, works "normally" on NBMA networks, except that instead of broadcasting an address resolution request over the local network the requesting station unicasts the address resolution request to the NBMA ARP (NARP) server. The requesting node gets its response from the NARP server, acting as a proxy, instead of directly from the station associated with the requested IP address.

21.4.6 NON-BROADCAST MULTI-ACCESS BROADCAST

ARP over an NBMA network does not require the emulation of broadcast, as a proxy ARP system operates on behalf of attached nodes and eliminates the need for broadcasts. However, broadcasts are still useful for other protocols (including some IP routing protocols to be discussed in Chapter 23).

NBMA networks emulate broadcast capability using a system that acts on behalf of all connected stations for the purposes of dealing with broadcasts. Figure 21–8 shows how it works: the system works as a proxy for

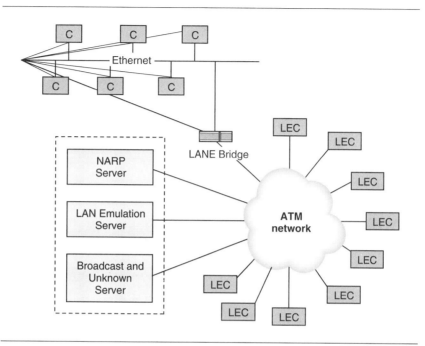

Figure 21–8: Using "proxy" systems in an ATM network allows NBMA networks to operate similarly to broadcast media.

"all systems on the network" (a similar arrangement can be made for "all systems subscribed to the multicast address" as well). When an NBMA station needs to broadcast, such as when doing address resolution, it sends over a preconfigured circuit between the station and the proxy system. That proxy system then resends the broadcast (or multicast) message to all the appropriate nodes.

Multicast (see Chapter 25) and broadcast are similar enough that the solution for multicast over ATM described in RFC 2022, "Support for Multicast over UNI 3.0/3.1 based ATM Networks," a *Multicast Addresss Resolution Server* (*MARS*) can be used for broadcasts as well. Broadcast is a sort of special case of multicast: an address to which all nodes on the network subscribe.

The MARS keeps track of all stations on the logical IP network it serves and repeats all broadcasts and multicasts as appropriate.

21.5   Point to Point Protocol

The simplest useful network consists of a pair of nodes connected only to each other. In this special case network, many of the complications that multi-node networks face are absent. For example, when one node emits a signal, there is only one other node that can detect it; naming and addressing issues are simplified as well.

In addition to consumer-oriented dialup internet access services, this type of *point to point* connection is commonly used in high-performance circuit-oriented networks such as ATM and FR. A protocol capable of encapsulating IP (or other network layer protocol) packets for transmission over a point-to-point link, the PPP provides a mechanism for two nodes to initiate and carry on data communications over such a link.

The Serial Line IP (SLIP) protocol is explicitly referred to as a "non-standard." It began as an ad hoc solution for engineers who wanted to access IP networks over their phone lines with a basic PC and a modem. SLIP provided a mechanism for running IP over a serial line (most commonly a telephone link) with a simple protocol for encapsulating IP data in modem signals.

Though once the primary protocol mechanism for dialup internet connection, SLIP has long been replaced by a formal, and standard, specification for the PPP.

PPP uses a frame format that includes a protocol field, so the remote host can connect to the network and use IP (or any other supported) network protocols. It includes a protocol to control the actual link, and it can negotiate connection parameters as well as compression. And it includes a CRC to protect against transmission errors.

PPP defines a network frame with a 5-octet header and a 3-octet trailer. As shown in Figure 21–9, the PPP frame starts and ends with an octet control value. The address and control octet values are constant, and many implementations drop these octets upon negotiation.

The 2-octet protocol field indicates the contents of the PPP frame. This field may indicate whether the data portion of the frame contains an IP or an IPX datagram, or it may indicate that the frame is carrying information relating to the link itself.

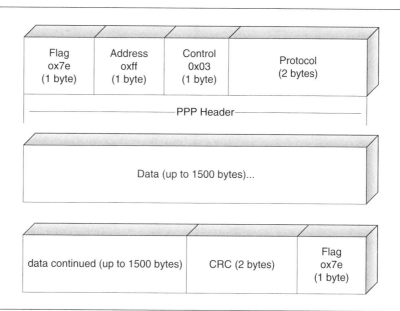

Figure 21–9: PPP network frame format.

PPP uses the link control protocol to control the data link layer connection: starting and ending the actual serial connection and negotiating line parameters are done through this protocol.

Likewise, various sets of protocols are defined for controlling the network layer. Called *network control protocols*, these are defined for different network protocols, including NetWare/IPX, DECnet, AppleTalk, and others. For example, header compression options (like Van Jacobson compression, discussed in Chapter 18) may be negotiated through these protocols.

21.6   Internet Protocol on Everything

IP is designed to operate over virtually any network medium capable of carrying packets. The motto "IP on everything," introduced as a t-shirt motto by IP pioneer Vinton Cerf in 1992, has inspired (and been inspired by) much serious work.

To interoperate independently of lower layer protocols, standards for how IP and the various link layer protocols over which it operates are required. Table 21–1 lists most of these specifications. Many are full standards, most are on the standards track. As with most IETF specifications, the earlier RFCs tend to be shorter and the later ones longer, in part becuase standards for writing RFCs were not formally spelled out until well into the 1990s, so earlier RFC authors might not cover all aspects of a protocol, all implications of the protocol, or portions of the protocol that might have been considered "common knowledge." In general they follow the same pattern: describe the link layer protocol or refer to its specifications, describe how IP packets can be encapsulating within the link layer protocol's frames, and discuss any issues involved along with appropriate solutions or workarounds.

STD 36 RFC 1390: Transmission of IP and ARP over FDDI Networks

STD 41 (RFC 894): A Standard for the Transmission of IP Datagrams over Ethernet Networks

STD 42 RFC 895: A Standard for the Transmission of IP Datagrams over Experimental Ethernet Networks

STD 43 (RFC 1042): A Standard for the Transmission of IP Datagrams over IEEE 802 Networks

STD 46 (RFC 1201): Transmitting IP traffic over ARCNET Networks

STD 47 (RFC 1055): A Nonstandard for Transmission of IP Datagrams over Serial Lines: SLIP

STD 51 (RFC 1661): The Point to Point Protocol (PPP)

STD 52 (RFC 1209): The Transmission of IP Datagrams over the SMDS Service

RFC 1188: Proposed Standard for the Transmission of IP Datagrams over FDDI Networks

RFC 1469: IP Multicast over Token-Ring Local Area Networks

RFC 2067: IP over HIPPI

RFC 2176: IPv4 over MAPOS Version 1

RFC 2225: Classical IP and ARP over ATM

RFC 2549: IP over Avian Carriers with Quality of Service

RFC 2625: IP and ARP over Fiber Channel

RFC 2728: The Transmission of IP over the Vertical Blanking Interval of a Television Signal

RFC 2734: IPv4 over IEEE 1394

RFC 2834: ARP and IP Broadcast over HIPPI-800

RFC 2835: IP and ARP over HIPPI-6400 (GSN)

21.7   Chapter Summary

After an overview of the interaction between IP and related link layer protocols, this chapter introduced the Ethernet and IEEE 802.3 protocols that are so commonly used in corporate and home networks. Although address resolution is required to allow IP hosts to communicate over any link layer protocol, ARP is most readily understood as implemented for Ethernet; we examined ARP as well as ARP messages, ARP caches, and Proxy ARP and related address resolution protocols including RARP and InARP.

Although the ATM protocols span both Layer 2 and Layer 3, in this chapter we look at how ATM and IP have traditionally interoperated, with IP treating ATM as a link layer protocol. We also examine the use of non-broadcast media with IP, particularly the mechanisms necessary to allow address resolution and multicast/broadcast under NBMA protocols.

While Ethernet and ATM are both recognizably network protocols, PPP is less obviously a link layer protocol: it does not even require nodes to be addressed, but that is only because addresses are superfluous when only two nodes are allowed on the medium—all outbound packets are destined to the "other" node, while all inbound packets are destined for "this" node.

These three link layer protocols account for a significant portion, if not the majority, of all internet transmission; however, there are many other link layer protocols over which IP can be carried. This chapter concluded with a listing of current (as of mid-2002) specifications for IP over various link layers.

The next chapter digs deeper into the intricacies of IP routing protocols, which specify how IP routing information is exchanged and interpreted by IP routers across sometimes quite large networks.

22

Internet Protocol Routing

As described in Chapter 20, internet protocol (IP) routing can be defined strictly in terms of a node choosing the best next hop for a packet to take based on the information available. A host sending a packet makes a routing decision based on whether the packet is destined for a node on the local IP network; if not, most hosts will send the packet to a *default gateway*—the local router that handles traffic destined outside the local IP network.

As soon as a packet is passed to a router, the process by which the routing table is created may be more complicated than what happens on a regular host, but the actual process, already described in Chapter 20, remains the same. Complications arise because routers link two or more distinct *logical IP subnetworks* (*LISes*) and the routers must choose the best route for those packets.

One way to route packets would be to have every system that forwards packets maintain a complete map of the entire internet: comparing the destination address to this master map, the router can determine how best to handle the packet. This approach might be acceptable in smaller internets that are stable and centrally administered; however, it won't work for the global internet or most other routed intranets, all of which change too frequently, too fast, and with little or no coordination.

Routers must be able to keep track of which networks they have direct connections to and which networks they are connected to through inter-mediaries; routers in the same AS will communicate with each other periodically to update network and link status as well as to verify their own connectivity. Routing protocols define the ways in which routers com-municate with other routers in order to exchange information about their network and link status, and use that information to build up their own maps to the internet: their routing tables.

In this chapter we introduce the fundamentals of routing in general, starting with the options available for any network routing protocol stra-tegy, followed by an overview of the different types of routing protocol we'll encounter in internets, both private and global. The next section introduces distance-vector and link state routing, two important algo-rithms for the distribution of routing information within a network, followed by an introduction to the routing protocols based on those algorithms, the Routing Information Protocol (RIP) and Open Shortest Path First (OSPF) protocols for interior routing. The chapter ends with a discussion of routing issues such as slow convergence and routing loops.

22.1 Routing Protocol Objectives

Routing protocols are designed to distribute routing information, with routers sharing information about which networks and links are available and which are not. In the venerable textbook for university-level net-working students, *Data and Computer Communications*, (Macmillan, 1985), William Stallings breaks down the elements of routing techniques into six different categories, each with its own selection of strategies (see p 254, Table 9-2 in Stallings, 1985). The categories he cites are:

> **Performance:** What criteria form the basis for routing performance decisions? Should routing performance be measured by how many hops a packet takes en route (fewer hops means higher performance), or should performance be measured by through-put? Can a cost basis be applied to routing performance over

different links? Should latency be considered a key part of the performance equation?

Decision time: At what point in a packet's transmission should a route be determined? Datagram services, in which each packet is treated individually, allow routers and intermediate systems to make routing decisions as each packet is accepted; just because one packet from source X to destination Y used a particular path through network doesn't mean the next packet from X to Y must take the same route.

The other alternative is to use a circuit-based approach to routing, in which case a session path is determined at the start of each session. The routing problem is solved once for all data in that session.

Decision place: Where are routing decisions made? In a distributed network, the decision to route (or not route) a packet is made everywhere: all nodes that receive data over the network may participate in the routing determination process.

A centralized routing structure provides a single routing terminus through which all packets are processed: every packet is sent to the central router, which determines how best to route the packets to their destinations. This offers a simple, though far from scalable, solution.

Or, the originating node can generate the route for its packets itself, by somehow having access to complete and current network routing information.

Information source: Where do the routing nodes get their information about network paths? Maybe they aren't able to handle any information at all; maybe they access routing information from a local routing table. Other sources might be neighboring nodes, nodes that are encountered by a packet traveling from a source to a destination, or even all nodes in the entire network.

Routing strategy: How do routing nodes approach the problem of determining the best next hop for a packet? A simple, fixed routing strategy uses a static routing table that matches sources and destinations. A packet from source X will always be routed the same way to arrive at destination Y. ATM and other switched protocols use an approach of this type.

A less efficient but more flexible and robust approach is to *flood* the network: source X sends a copy of the packet to every node with which it has a direct link. Those nodes then repeat the packet to every node with which they are linked (except for the link on which they just received the packet). The process generates huge volumes of network traffic, particularly as the network increases in size, but it also reduces the need for complex routing architectures and protocols—no information about the network is required, other than how to send packets to a neighbor.

A variation on the flooding approach is to use a random approach to routing. A node can pick an interface at random over which to forward an inbound packet (other than the interface over which the packet arrived). Eventually, the packet will arrive at its destination; network load will be higher than optimal (some packets taking many hops before they arrive) but considerably lower than in the flooding approach.

The adaptive routing approach is the one most frequently encountered, especially in modern networks. Routers collect information about the network, usually in the form of the status of various links and routers as reported by other nodes, and try to use that information to determine optimal routes. As conditions change, the routers adapt so as to maximize one or more of the performance criteria listed in the first item of this list.

Adaptive update strategies: When adaptive routing is chosen (as it invariably is), choices must be made as to whether to have routers update their data continuously, periodically, whenever there are significant changes to network traffic patterns or to the network itself.

The original IP routing strategy for the ARPANET (the US military research network), as described by Stallings, was to minimize network delay (performance), allow routing decisions to be made individually for each packet with a datagram service (decision time), distribute the routing task to all nodes (decision place), allow nodes to gather information from adjacent nodes (information source), and periodically update its adaptive routing strategy. Strategy for ARPANET later was changed to allow all nodes in the network to provide routing information, not just adjacent nodes. This description still applies to the global internet to a great extent.

Routing as we know it can be discussed in terms of *routing algorithms* that define the abstract process by which a router determines the appropriate path for a packet, and *routing protocols* that define the concrete processes by which routers exchange information about routes and routing.

22.2 Routing Fundamentals

As noted in section 20.3.3, RFC 1122 provides an excellent rundown of the process by which IP hosts route packets. Although we often speak of routing infrastructures and routing complexity, IP routing is a process that is done one hop at a time, from source host to destination. Although we often speak of routing as the aggregated result of the individual routing decisions made by all the intermediate devices through which a packet passes from source to destination, each node that receives a packet must process it and determine an appropriate route for it based on data in its own routing table and configuration.

The primary difference between an ordinary host and a router is that the router is configured to accept packets intended for another destination, and to forward those packets to what the router determines is the best next hop. The router usually also supports at least one routing protocol, through which it can acquire current information about network routes.

22.2.1 GATEWAY ROUTING

The simplest of routers are those serving a single network with two interfaces: one for the local network and the other for sending all other traffic. These routers function as *gateways* for the local network. Local hosts recognize two types of destinations: those hosts that are on the local LIS and that can be reached directly over the local link, and those hosts that are not local (everywhere else). Hosts on this network are configured to deliver local packets directly, on their own, over the link layer, and all other packets are sent to the IP gateway system (the local router) which forwards them along its "other" interface.

The typical small office/home office (SOHO) network uses a simple gateway like this, as do almost all networks connected to the internet via broadband services. The local router (or gateway) will typically be

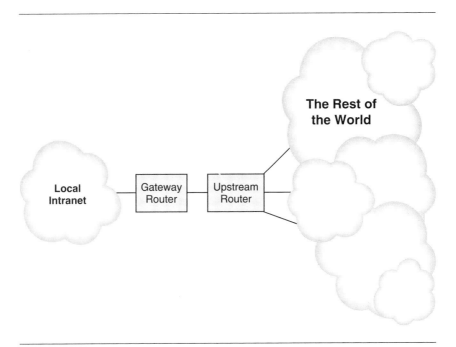

Figure 22–1: Simple local gateway router architecture.

configured to accept inbound packets destined for the local network and
to forward any packets it receives from within the network to its own
upstream router. If the gateway is on a point-to-point link, as is frequently
the case, the gateway does nothing more than pass along packets from the
local network to the system on the other end of that link. See Figure 22–1.

22.2.2 ROUTED NETWORKS

As intranets become more complex with more than one internal LIS spanning multiple local area networks, metropolitan area networks, or wide
area networks, internal routers become necessary. These routers provide
connectivity to hosts within the intranet as well as (perhaps) the rest of the
global internet. The number and type of routers, as well as the number of
networks each router links, all depend on the intranet's design and organization's goals and requirements for that network. Figure 22–2 shows a
simple multi-router intranet, in which internal routers must decide how
best to forward packets not intended for the local network.

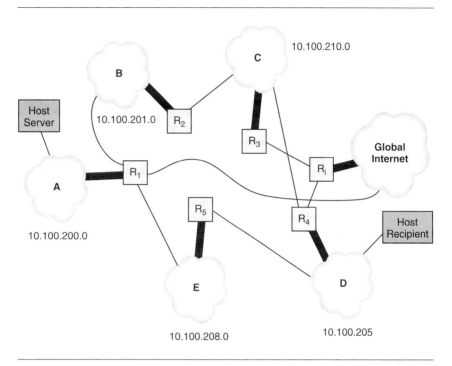

Figure 22–2: Increasingly complicated intranet routing domain.

Using the example in Figure 22–2, it becomes clear that packets sent from a host on network A and destined for a host on network D would have to be sent to Router$_1$, which would then forward it to Router$_5$ on network E; from there the packet is forward to Router$_4$ on network D. Router$_4$ then forwards the packet directly to the destination host.

When that same packet is to be delivered but Router$_5$ is unavailable for some reason, Router$_1$ will have to forward the packet to another router that is capable of, ultimately, delivering the packet to network D. The only other options open in that case are to forward the packet to the global internet (not acceptable) or to Router$_2$ on network B. Router$_2$ forwards the packet to Router$_3$, which forwards the packet to Router$_4$, which delivers the packet to its destination. Router$_i$ is the internet gateway, forwarding packets to and from the global internet; Router$_1$ is a backup internet gateway.

With five internal LISes, and the global internet, there are six different LISes to contend with; fully interconnecting them all so that all networks are reachable from each other in one hop requires 15 dedicated links. By permitting more than one hop between local LISes, full interconnectivity can be achieved with fewer links.

However, the routers need information—which of their own links are up and which down, what portions of the network the other routers can reach. The exchange and update of this information is the primary goal of internet routing protocols; in support of this goal is the corollary need to avoid propagating false information or acting on faulty information while at the same time optimizing performance (by minimizing the number of hops it takes from source to destination).

The routers in Figure 22–2 are *interior* routers, because they route packets inside an AS or other *routing domain*; inside that domain, the LISes are separate *administrative domains* (ADs). An AD is comparable to an AS, except on a smaller scale. As we'll see later in this chapter and in Chapter 23, *exterior routing*, which occurs between routers linking different ASes through a backbone, requires a different approach to the exchange of information and determination of optimal routes.

22.2.3 INTERIOR AND EXTERIOR ROUTING PROTOCOLS

The two basic routing tasks are, first, making sure that all networks within internets route traffic appropriately among themselves (interior routing), and second, making sure that all internetworks connected to a large internet (such as the global internet) are able to route reliably between each other (exterior routing). Simple routing strategies like default gateways and internet control message protocol route advertising will be sufficient to move network traffic inside most intranets.

However, routing protocols do not define the routing process—they define the process by which routers exchange information about the network. Routing table information must be kept current, and routers are constantly communicating with each other to announce their own connectivity.

Typically, hosts acquire routing information either as part of their static configuration or through the Dynamic Host Configuration Protocol (DHCP). The host uses address resolution protocol (ARP) to acquire a physical address for all local internet traffic, and everything else is passed to the default gateway router. In smaller networks, that router connects directly to the ISP's router, connected in turn to an internet *backbone*, a network linking more than one AS. Routers on backbone networks must maintain far more comprehensive routing tables because they must route between and among all networks—they don't usually have a default gateway specified, and backbone routers are sometimes referred to as *non-default* routers.

Exterior or backbone routing protocols must allow communicating routers to report frequent changes in conditions and connectivity, quickly and efficiently. An interior routing protocol enables routers within smaller internets to report their own conditions and connectivity, but generally support less complicated routing architectures. The interior routing protocol supported by a router is often referred to as its *Interior Gateway Protocol* (*IGP*), where "gateway" is used as a synonym for router; an exterior routing protocol is likewise termed an *Exterior Gateway Protocol* (*EGP*). In this chapter, we focus on IGPs, starting with RIP and then moving on to OSPF.

22.2.4 ROUTING ALGORITHMS

The simplest formulation of a routing strategy is to opt for the *shortest-path* route whenever there is a choice. How to determine which is the shortest path presents the greater challenge. There are two dominant strategies for determining the shortest path for interior routing, each of which is implemented in its own protocol. The *distance-vector routing* algorithm[1] is described in RFC 1058, "Routing Information Protocol," which also defines the RIP routing protocol for IP networks. Another approach to interior routing is called Dijkstra's Algorithm, and is also known as the *link state* or *open shortest path first* algorithm. OSPF is also the name of the interior routing protocol defined in RFC 2328, "OSPF Version 2," which, as of 2002, is also STD 54.

Together, RIP and OSPF represent the IGPs you are most likely to find on an internet or intranet.

22.3 Distance-Vector Routing

Routing protocols can use two basic methods to measure connectivity across internetworks, as exemplified by the RIP and OSPF protocols.

[1]This algorithm may also be identified as *Bellman-Ford*, or other combinations of the names of the researchers who did the original work on it.

We begin with RIP, which uses the *distance-vector* approach: routers share their routing tables and make additions and corrections based on reports from other routers.

The distance-vector algorithm takes its name from the way routers share their routing tables. A router expresses each route as a pair of values, the *vector* or destination network, and the *distance* from that router to that network (usually measured in hops, or the number of intermediate routers a packet would have to traverse to arrive at the destination network).

A router sends *advertisements* of its routes, containing all the routes (vectors) and distances to those routes, to neighboring routers. In this way, routes can be propagated across an internet, as can changes in available routes.

22.3.1 The Distance-Vector Algorithm

A distance-vector router begins with no knowledge of the internet other than the networks to which it is directly connected. When it first boots, this router will have a routing table that consists of only as many entries as the router has network interfaces; it might look like this:

```
Destination     Distance    Route
10.0.0.0            0        direct
192.168.100.0       0        direct
```

The router then begins building its routing table up by listening to other router announcements that are broadcast on whatever network interfaces each router is connected to. In other words, routers advertise their routes to any neighboring router, where "neighboring" means connected to the same link.

For example, consider what happens when this router (let's call it router X) receives an announcement from router Y. The announcement lists routes as pairs of destination and distance values, like this:

```
Destination     Distance
192.168.200.0       0
10.5.0.0            0
```

```
10.10.0.0              3
10.0.0.0               4
192.168.100.0          4
```

Router X can now update its own routing table by comparing it to the distance-vector data supplied by router Y. The first two distance-vector pairs are not already in router X's routing table, so they can be added; the distance to those networks is 0 hops from router Y, which means they are only one hop from router X (router Y is a neighbor to router X, so it is only one hop away). Router X adds those networks to its routing table, with a distance value of 1.

The third pair is also for a network heretofore unknown to router X, but at a distance of three hops from router Y; router X adds this network to its routing table, with a distance value of 4.

The last two routes are the only networks that router X started out with in its routing table; after comparing the distance value, router X ignores those pairs. Router X's routing table now looks like this:

```
Destination       Distance       Route
10.0.0.0                 0        direct
192.168.100.0            0        direct
192.168.200.0            1        router Y
10.5.0.0                 1        router Y
10.10.0.0                4        router Y
```

Distance-vector routers may be thought of as street hawkers who advertise their routes by shouting them out to their neighbors; in the example above, router Y in effect yelled out, "I can reach 192.168.200.0 in zero hops; I can reach 10.5.0.0 in zero hops; I can reach 10.10.0.0 in three hops; I can reach 10.0.0.0 in four hops; I can reach 192.168.100.0 in four hops."

Router X, listening to this advertisement, could be anthropomorphized to be thinking, "Y can reach 192.168.200.0 in zero hops, so now I can reach it in one hop; Y can reach 10.5.0.0 in zero hops, so now I can reach it in one hop; Y can reach 10.10.0.0 in three hops, so now I can reach it in four hops; Y can reach 10.0.0.0 in four hops, but I can reach it directly; Y can reach 192.168.100.0 in four hops, but I can reach it directly."

When Router X sends out its route advertisement, router Y will undoubt-edly amend its own routes for 10.0.0.0 and 192.168.100.0, changing the distance from those networks from 4 to 1.

22.3.2 BASIC ROUTING INFORMATION PROTOCOL

All systems on an internetwork can use RIP, but hosts generally are pas-sive participants, listening to the routing information and updating their routing tables, whereas routers can both listen to routing broadcasts and transmit routing information. Routes can be propagated on request by a router that has just booted up, although routers typically broadcast their routes every 30 seconds.

Routes are broadcast as distance-vector pairs: a network and a hop count. Other routing protocols use the convention that a hop indicates a trans-mission to another router, so the hop count from a gateway to a network to which the gateway is connected directly would be 0. RIP counts that as one hop, so the lowest number of hops possible with RIP is one; with other protocols zero hops are possible.

The rules for RIP are fairly simple:

1. Active routers broadcast their routes every 30 seconds by default (although this may vary if the network administrator wishes).
2. All listening systems compare these broadcasts to their own routing tables and update their routing tables IF
   a. there are routes to new networks previously unlisted,
   b. there are better (e.g., shorter) routes to existing networks,
   c. a route is reported unreachable (it should be removed).
3. A route is kept until a better route is reported.
4. If there are two equivalent routes (same hop count), the first received goes into the routing table.
5. Routes are timed out if they are not updated after 3 minutes; in other words, a route must be assumed down if it is not being reported.
6. Routers broadcast route changes as they occur, without waiting (triggered updates).
7. A hop count of 16 is considered unreachable (which means RIP is unusable in any intranet wider than 15 hops).

RIP tends not to propagate corrections to routing tables very quickly, although errors are passed along more quickly. RIPs relatively low maximum hop count and the use of triggered updates help minimize some of the inherent problems with the distance-vector method of sharing routing information, as described in the next section.

22.3.3 ROUTING WITH ROUTING INFORMATION PROTOCOLS

Implemented for IP before any actual standard specifications had been agreed upon, RIP is currently documented in RFC 2453, "RIP Version 2," (also published as STD 56). RIP's success has more to do with the way it was implemented—in the *routed* program that was a part of the original BSD/UNIX distributions—than with its technical merits.

RIP is a protocol implementation of distance-vector routing: RIP messages, encapsulated in UDP datagrams, are sent out with a header and at least one and no more than 25 *RIP entries*. The header has three fields (followed by 1 to 25 RIP entries):

Command: A one-octet field, whose value may currently contain either 1, indicating a request for all or part of a routing table; or 2, indicating a response, containing all or part of a router's routing table. An advertisement is a response, even though it may not have been sent in response to a particular request.

Version: RIP versions 1 and 2 are valid values for this one-octet field.

The RIP entry itself is 20 octets and consists of the *address family identifier* (*AFI*) field, a two-octet value indicating the type of address family (i.e., internet addresses, or some other type of address), and a second 2-octet field that, for RIPv1, is left set to 0. In RIPv2, this field is the *route tag* field, and it contains a tag that can differentiate internal routes (those pertaining to the local routing domain) from external routes (those imported from adjacent interior or exterior routing domains).

RIPv1 uses the next 4 octets for network destination IPv4 address, followed by 8 octets set to 0, followed by a 4-octet *metric* field containing a value from 0 through 15 indicating the "distance" of the route.

This is an important limitation, and it is imposed on RIP rather than imposed by RIP: the field is large enough, at 32 bits, to accommodate

huge distances but the protocol designers felt that RIP should not be used
for networks that have a diameter greater than 15 hops. Routing changes
take too long to propagate across a larger RIP network, and the volume of
router network traffic also becomes a burden as the internet grows larger.

The RIP headers are shown here (from RFC 2453):

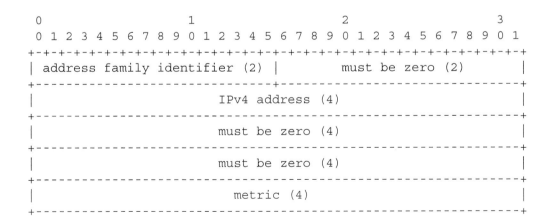

```
RIP headers:



 0                   1                   2                   3
 0 1 2 3 4 5 6 7 8 9 0 1 2 3 4 5 6 7 8 9 0 1 2 3 4 5 6 7 8 9 0 1
+-+-+-+-+-+-+-+-+-+-+-+-+-+-+-+-+-+-+-+-+-+-+-+-+-+-+-+-+-+-+-+-+
|  command (1)  |  version (1)  |        must be zero (2)       |
+---------------+---------------+-------------------------------+
|                                                               |
~                     RIP Entry (20)                            ~
|                                                               |
+---------------+---------------+---------------+---------------+



RIPv1 entry:



 0                   1                   2                   3
 0 1 2 3 4 5 6 7 8 9 0 1 2 3 4 5 6 7 8 9 0 1 2 3 4 5 6 7 8 9 0 1
+-+-+-+-+-+-+-+-+-+-+-+-+-+-+-+-+-+-+-+-+-+-+-+-+-+-+-+-+-+-+-+-+
| address family identifier (2) |       must be zero (2)        |
+-------------------------------+-------------------------------+
|                        IPv4 address (4)                       |
+---------------------------------------------------------------+
|                        must be zero (4)                       |
+---------------------------------------------------------------+
|                        must be zero (4)                       |
+---------------------------------------------------------------+
|                          metric (4)                           |
+---------------------------------------------------------------+
```

```
RIPv2 entry:


0                   1                   2                   3
0 1 2 3 4 5 6 7 8 9 0 1 2 3 4 5 6 7 8 9 0 1 2 3 4 5 6 7 8 9 0 1
+-+-+-+-+-+-+-+-+-+-+-+-+-+-+-+-+-+-+-+-+-+-+-+-+-+-+-+-+-+-+-+-+
| address family identifier (2) |         Route Tag (2)        |
+-------------------------------+------------------------------+
|                       IPv4 address (4)                       |
+--------------------------------------------------------------+
|                       Subnet Mask   (4)                      |
+--------------------------------------------------------------+
|                         Next Hop (4)                         |
+--------------------------------------------------------------+
|                          metric (4)                          |
+--------------------------------------------------------------+
```

22.3.4 ROUTING INFORMATION PROTOCOL: v1 vs. v2

As is clear from the differences in the RIP entry formats for RIPv1 and RIPv2, RIPv2 can transmit considerably more information about each route, including a subnet mask value and a next hop value (to be used in concert with the route tag). RIPv2 incorporates an extension facility and in addition to transmitting more routing information, it uses an algorithm for multicast routing and improved security.

RIP does not send subnet mask information in routing updates, so there is the potential for routing problems in internetworks that are highly subnetted, particularly if more than one subnetworking scheme is being used in the internetwork. RIP-2 addresses many of the shortcomings of RIP, and adds support for subnets something that the original RIP lacks simply because subnets had yet to be accepted as part of the IP networks at the time that RIP was first designed.

Despite RIPs flaws, development of RIP-2 continued for several reasons. RIP is widely implemented on many different platforms, partly because it is an easy protocol to implement. On small intranets, RIP can be a very efficient routing protocol making few demands on system overhead and bandwidth. Finally, RIP is relatively easy to configure and manage.

22.3.5   ROUTING INFORMATION PROTOCOL ADVANTAGES AND DISADVANTAGES

Distance-vector algorithms are relatively easy to implement: the routers need only be able to transmit and process two types of message (requests and responses), process a routing table and compare routing table entries with the distance-vector pairs contained in router advertisements. These algorithms also result in all routers maintaining reliable and complete routing tables for the interior routing domain, eventually.

RIP is still widely implemented throughout the world, so there is a huge installed base making for a high degree of interoperability with new RIP nodes. And RIP provides an easy routing solution for smaller networks that uses relatively little bandwidth for routing protocol exchanges.

On the down side, however, RIP is limited to small networks (15 hops across is the maximum permitted, but in practice RIP is probably best used in even smaller networks). RIP is also subject to routing loops (see next section) that may take either lots of time (when router updates are infrequent) or lots of bandwidth (when router updates are more frequent) to resolve when they involve many different networks.

Another important limitation of RIP is that it is inflexible in the way it measures network hops: one hop is always considered equivalent to one hop. A one-hop route that is experienced high delay may be more "costly" (take longer) than a three-hop route where delay is minimal. While the protocol provides no way to accommodate the evaluation of actual network conditions and take that information into account when deciding on a route, many RIP implementations do allow administrators to configure different hop increments as a remedy.

22.3.6   SLOW CONVERGENCE

One common dynamic routing problem occurs when a router or network goes out of service. Consider the example in Figure 22–3. Assuming that all routers advertise all known routes to all other routers, if the internet router goes down, it might take some time before all the other routers would become aware of the failure.

What happens is this: Router ACD would know that its one-hop link to the internet was no longer available, but Router AB would be advertising

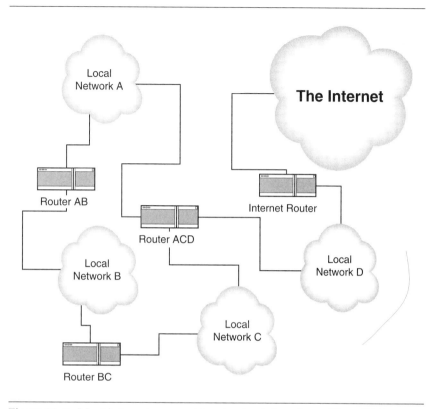

Figure 22–3: Most internets connect local subnets together with multiple interior routers, but only one connecting to the global internet.

a two-hop route to the internet (actually via Router ACD). Router ACD would then say to itself, the direct route via the internet router is down, but there is an indirect, two-hop route to the internet via Router AB. It would then reset its own routing table to show a three-hop link to the internet.

This problem is called slow convergence because it means that it takes quite a few routing table updates before all the participating routers become aware of the fact that they are all actually routing through the failed link. There are several solutions to this problem, which is already limited by the maximum number of hops that the routing protocol allows (e.g., RIP allows no more than 15 hops before it considers the route to be unreachable).

22.3.7 Routing Loops

Changes to internet topology require changes to routing tables; one of the drawbacks to RIP is that it may take a while for changes in the routing domain to propagate to all routers in the domain. *Active* (meaning they advertise routes) RIP routers advertise once every 30 seconds; *passive* (they listen only) RIP routers accept those advertisements and incorporate them into their routing tables. However, consider what happens when something changes.

In Figure 22–4, Network A is reachable only through Router AB. Router AB advertises to the other routers that it can reach Network A in a single hop. Router BC receives this information and incorporates it into its routing table, indicating that it can reach Network A in two hops (one from Router BC, and one more from Router AB). If the link to Network A fails just before

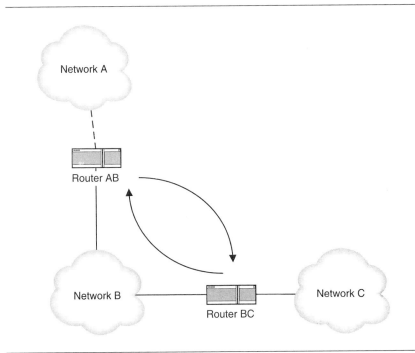

Figure 22–4: The interval between routing reports can cause a routing loop when the only link to a network fails.

Router BC advertises its own routes, Router AB, knowing that its link to Network A is down, may add Router BC to its own routing table as the way to get to Network Ain three hops (the two that Router BC advertised and itself, again).

With timers that expire advertised routes, Router BC may drop the link that (it thinks) gets it to Network A and may add it again when some other router advertises this three-hop link to Network A as a four-hop link. This could go on forever, but it is a well-known problem with distance-vector routing, and protocols based on distance-vector routing usually also include fixes that do things like put limits on the maximum number of hops allowed in a route.

22.3.8   RIP FIXES

There are several strategies that can be used to fix RIP's slow convergence and loop problems. One solution is to use a *split-horizon update*. This method calls for routers to keep a record of each interface for which they received a route. When a router sends out routing information, it avoids sending information to any interface over which it originally heard about a particular route. In other words, it assumes that the routers on a particular interface already have more current information about routes reported over that interface. Routers thus are made aware of changes on connected networks without incorrectly propagating status about those connections.

Another solution to this problem is called *hold-down*. Instead of updating routing tables right away, any changes are ignored for a long enough time that the changes are likely to have been propagated to all participating routers. Usually, the hold-down period is twice as long as the normal reporting period, so if routers advertise routes every 30 seconds, the hold-down period would be 60 seconds.

Another approach is called *poison reverse*. This approach mandates that routers continue to advertise any failed routes, even after the link has been dropped, but advertise them as accessible only as unreachable (i.e., hop count of 16 for RIP) for a number of reporting periods. This is especially effective when used in conjunction with triggered updates, which require routers to broadcast a failed route as soon as they become aware of it.

22.4 Link State Routing with Open Shortest Path First

Defined in RFC 2328 (STD 54) "OSPF Version 2," the current version of the Open Shortest Path First (OSPF) protocol uses the link-state method to let routers create their own internetwork maps. Developed partly in response to some of the shortcomings of RIP, OSPF propagates routing information more quickly and stably than RIP, handles subnets appropriately, can balance loads where equivalent routes are available, supports type of service routing, and uses multicasting—all advantages over RIPv1.

Link state routing protocols, of which OSPF is an example, mandate that each router in an AS maintain a *link state database*. This database represents a map of the entire AS's topology, a map that is shared by all routers in the AS. Each router *floods* (see section 22.1, above, in discussion of routing strategies) the AS with its own reachable neighbors and usable network interfaces—known as the router's *local state*. In short order, all routers in the AS can build their own map by aggregating the data in these advertisements and connecting the dots. If router A announces that it is directly connected to routers B, C, and D, on network 10.0.0.0, and router E on network 192.168.100.0, then any router in the AS can start assembling the map: routers A, B, C, and D all have interfaces on 10.0.0.0; routers A and E have interfaces on 192.168.100.0.

Once the map is assembled, each router calculates the *shortest paths* to any given route by walking the map from its own location in the network. Figure 22–5 shows how a simple network map can be created. The link state approach to routing keeps the volume of information passed along to other routers to a minimum. Each router periodically checks on the status of neighboring routers, reporting which links are alive to all other participating routers. With this information, each router can then create its own map of the internetwork.

Link state routing addresses most of the problems posed by distance-vector protocols like RIP. OSPF adds features not available in RIP, and calculating routes based on the link state database is easier than mapping routes based on periodic RIP advertisements. Link state routing protocols even have less impact on the network because they generate a lower volume of data and because that data is passed to neighboring routers, which pass it on to other routers. By virtue of being a link state protocol OSPF also makes changes propagate in a more orderly and reliable fashion. Since a link is either up or down, there is no reason for hosts to retain looped routes.

Network A connects to Networks B and C

Network B connects to Networks A and D

Network C connects to Networks A and D

Network D connects to Networks B and C

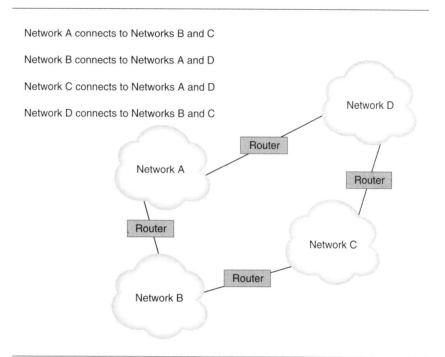

Figure 22–5: Routers using a link state routing protocol can deduce the structure of their AS.

OSPF allows routing decisions to be made explicitly in cases where there are equivalent alternate routes, as is required for applications such as load balancing. Under RIP, the first of any group of equivalent advertised routes is the route that will be recorded; OSPF allows network managers to distribute traffic across these equivalent routes.

Another OSPF feature that offers greater flexibility is the use of separate routes for different types of IP services. For example, it supports routing of FTP traffic over one route (perhaps a faster link, to give better overall file transfer performance) and Telnet over a different route (perhaps a link with lower latency or roundtrip time for better interactive response).

Support of subnet addressing is an important feature, as is the use of multicasting to routers. OSPF also includes an authentication mechanism that prevents routers from accepting routing information from unauthenticated sources.

Whereas RIP is relatively straightforward, OSPF presents a higher degree of complexity than RIP. As defined in RFC 2328, OSPF takes over 240 pages to specify; RIP, in RFC 2453, takes under 40 pages to specify. The interested reader is urged to read RFC 2328 for more details about how routers exchange routing information using OSPF.

With the acceptance of RIP-2 as an Internet standard alongside OSPF, these two routing protocols will continue to coexist. Neither is likely to dominate TCP/IP interior routing any time soon.

22.5   Chapter Summary

The task of routing in an IP network requires only that the router have a routing table and be capable of using it to make appropriate decisions about where to forward packets. However, as we have seen, IP routing protocols provide the mechanisms by which routers are able to exchange information about their links and update their routing tables to reflect changes reported by other routers.

The difference between interior and exterior routing is an important one, inasmuch as interior routers usually have the simpler task of routing packets within smaller internets. When the interior router encounters a packet with a destination address outside its routing domain, it passes the packet along to its upstream default gateway. Exterior or backbone routers do not have the luxury of default gateways, and must be able to route packets to any destination. That means the exterior router must maintain routing table entries for every valid destination network in the entire routing domain—in the case of the global internet, this domain may contain over 100,000 routes.

Routing protocols generally rely on either the distance-vector or link state approaches to distributing routing table data. RIP is a simple distance-vector routing protocol, while OSPF is a more complex routing protocol based on the link state algorithm. As we saw at the start of this chapter, routing is a task that has several different and sometimes contradictory measures of success—is it better to be fast at the risk of being inaccurate, or to be accurate at the risk of slowing network traffic? The attempt to somehow balance these strategies means that other problems can arise, including slow convergence and routing loops—most of which are remediable in some form.

In the next chapter we focus on exterior routing, in particular looking at how classless inter-domain routing changed the task of routing within the global internet, and how the border gateway protocol works to keep backbone routing tables up to date.

23

Exterior Routing

In the early days of the internet, routing that happened outside organizational networks—internet routing—was accomplished through centrally managed routers called *core gateways*. We've already discussed the term gateway as it relates to providing an interface system between different protocols; however, when speaking of IP routing, a *gateway* is defined as a router that passes packets from one autonomous system to another.

Non-core gateways were controlled by the organizations connected to the internet and needed some connection to core gateways for proper routing of internet traffic. The connection from organization to core doesn't necessarily have to be direct, meaning that one organization can function as a gateway to the core gateway for other organizations. But there does have to be some connectivity between the organization and the core.

This was effective, but the mechanism did not scale well as the internet grew. Tracking all possible routes rapidly increased in difficulty, especially as more organizations linked to the core indirectly. Finally, as the Internet grew more complex, with multiple, parallel backbones, the routing

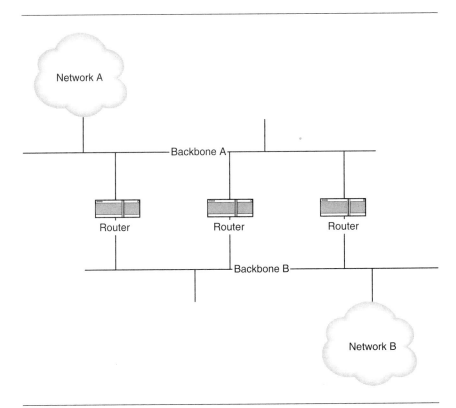

Figure 23–1: Routing between backbones can be direct, moving from one to another just once. If routing tables aren't properly maintained, however, a packet might zigzag back and forth between backbones.

problem became more intractable. Figure 23–1 shows that with more choices there are more opportunities for making the wrong choices, and the right choice is often far from obvious. Choosing the right route between two networks separated by backbones can be considerably more efficient than choosing what might appear to be a slightly worse route.

23.1   Interior vs. Exterior Routing

Interior routing requires that participating gateways be able to exchange information about which networks they can reach and which networks they can't reach. In simple intranets, particularly those with only a couple of networks and routers, static routing tables can be maintained by hand. However, it doesn't take much complexity before this task can overwhelm the network managers, and dynamic routing protocols are required.

To illustrate, look at Figure 23–2. Before adding the new router between Network B and Network D, all the networks were reachable in just one way. Traffic from Network B destined for Network D all was routed to Router BC to Router CE to Router DE to the destination on Network D. With the new router in place, there are now two routes from Network B to Network E, both apparently equivalent just as there are now two routes for traffic from Network A to Network E. Routing protocols allow routers

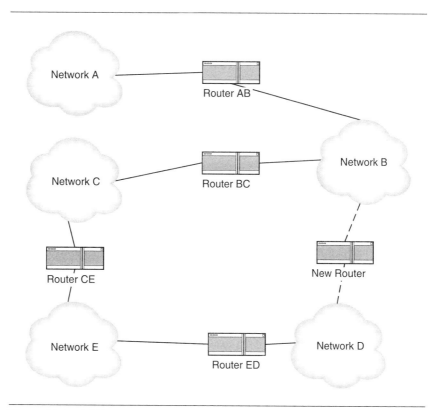

Figure 23–2: Adding a router in a simple internet shows why reachability advertisement is so important; when a router or link fails, routers need to know how to decide which route to choose.

to communicate network connectivity across network boundaries to other routers. Reachability data can be passed along, as well as changes in reachability: if the new router fails after being installed, routing protocols allow the other neighboring routers to report the failure to their neighbors.

Look at the same internetwork, as it relates to the rest of the internet, as shown in Figure 23-3. For one thing, there is only a single point of contact between the local internetwork and the connected internet, that is, the internet router itself. This router knows directly about Networks A, B, C, and D it is connected to Network B, just as Routers AB, BC, and the new router are, so it can exchange routing information with those routers. However, it may not know about Network E or other more remotely connected networks.

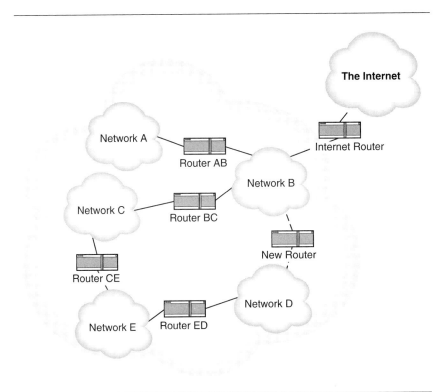

Figure 23–3: Interior routing, within an AS, presents a different problem from routing over the global internet.

Rather than requiring that the internet router in this example be able to notify other internet routers of all internal routes automatically as well as keeping track of internet routes, interior routing is assigned to the organization that runs the local internetwork and internet routing is reserved for routing systems that run on the backbones of the internet.

Exterior routing, on the other hand, is done externally to organizational internetworks. There are a number of issues, not the least of which is the number of different networks (and the rapid pace of change to the internet overall) to track. You could require each organizational unit to arrange somehow for internal routes to be reported to its internet router, but all core routers for the Internet would then have to communicate those routes to each other.

Figure 23–4 illustrates one of the main reasons why internet-connected gateways need to be able to route traffic dynamically to the internet. Each of the autonomous systems is actually an organizational internetwork, but for the purpose of the internet, each autonomous systems router passes traffic from the interior out into the internet and routes traffic in from the Internet. When there are few internetworks connected to the internet and a single backbone to carry all internet traffic, routing traffic by default gateways might almost make sense: give each internet router another gateway to send internet traffic to, as shown in Figure 23–4. If each unit routes to the right along the backbone (which is as reasonable a scheme as any), traffic intended for the neighbor on the left will have to transit the entire internet before it arrives at its destination a single hop away.

The problem is compounded as soon as more than one backbone appears; in today's internet there are many different backbones and carriers to consider and special routing protocols have been introduced to handle this kind of exterior routing.

23.2   Exterior Routing Problems

Global internet backbone routing is different from interior routing:

- Exterior routers need only interconnect ASes while interior routers need only interconnect hosts and networks inside a single AS.

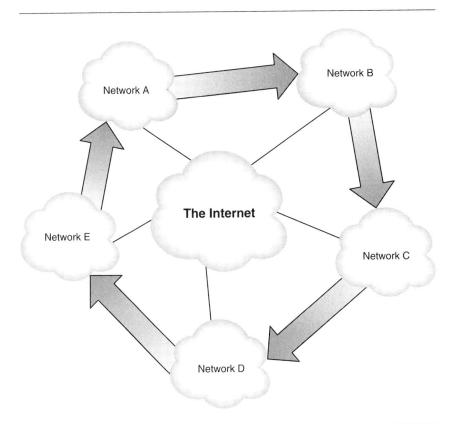

Figure 23–4: Multiple ASes all linked through an internet backbone cloud. All networks are technically "neighbors" but if routers use a simple algorithm for routing such as "pass packets clockwise around the backbone" then from A to B is only one hop while from B to A becomes a four-hop trip.

- *Border* routers, which link ASes to *core* networks (backbones) should be able to route packets from a source AS to a destination AS in a single hop, as long as both ASes are directly connected to the same backbone.

A major factor in complicating exterior routing has been the addition of the Classless Inter-Domain Routing (CIDR) protocol which removes class limitations from IP networks. As described in the next section, with CIDR, a single network may be considered as a single autonomous system in the context of the network owner's ISP routing domain, while at the same time being an interior network within the ISP's autonomous system—which may in turn be viewed by global internet backbone routers as just a part of some larger AS.

The concept of relative addressing, as discussed later, demonstrates how routers at different locations in a packet's route can treat the source and destination networks. Exterior routers don't care about destination or source hosts—they move packets from one AS to another, leaving the actual delivery of packets to interior routers.

23.2.1 CLASSLESS INTER-DOMAIN ROUTING

Classful addressing, as we've seen, turns out to be incredibly wasteful of IPv4 address space. For a complete discussion of address space efficiency, see RFC 1715 "The H Ratio for Address Assignment Efficiency," and RFC 3194 "The H-Density Ratio for Address Assignment Efficiency An Update on the H ratio," both of which discuss the degree to which it is possible to use the IPv4 address space efficiently. Although a 32-bit address space places an unalterable limit on the number of unique addresses possible (something over four billion), the practical limit is considerably less. The authors of RFC 3194 conclude that as host density increases, the "pain" of maintaining the address space increases as well. The authors also explain how to calculate the number of nodes on any particular network that correspond with more or less painful densities. They conclude that 240 million nodes in the IPv4 address space likely represents a practical maximum.

The *CIDR* protocol extends the idea of subnetting in the opposite direction: taking contiguous blocks of Class C networks and stealing bits from the first 3 octets of the address to aggregate routes. In other words, just as all datagrams addressed to a single Class B address are routed to a single router, all datagrams addressed to any of a block of Class C addresses could also be routed to a single router.

This is known as classless routing because it tells the router to ignore the network class (Class C) address and walk up higher in the network address than usual to determine where to send the datagram. And unlike subnetting, where the subnet mask is irrelevant outside the network, the supernet path is used externally for routers to slim down their routing tables. For example, an ISP might be granted a block of 256 Class C addresses. This can be considered the equivalent of a Class B address, only the first three bits will be set to 110, instead of 10x. With supernetting, routers can be set to include the first 16 bits of the address block and treat it as a single route with 8 bits of supernet, instead of having to deal with as many as 256 different routes for each of the included Class C network addresses. ISPs are given these blocks because they often provide the routing for their customers' networks, so all datagrams for those customers will be routed through the ISP's router anyway.

Due to the relative scarcity of Class B networks, the relative abundance of Class C networks, and the fact that Class C addresses can be bundled in blocks that work well for moderate-sized organization, this approach makes a lot of sense. CIDR also reduces the size of routing tables, thereby improving routing performance. However, while CIDR improves the efficiency of network address allocation, it does not do anything to increase the total number of host addresses possible under IPv4 and should be considered purely a short-term tool rather than a long-term solution to the problems of IPv4.

More recently, some organizations assigned Class A network addresses have returned them. Though they weren't able to use them efficiently, the regional registries are starting to allocate portions of them to ISPs (especially broadband internet providers) that need them and can fill them.

23.2.2 INTERNET PROTOCOL ADDRESS PREFIX NOTATION

With classful addressing, determining how much of an address should be processed as the network part is easy: the first octet of Class A addresses, the first two octets of Class B addresses, and the first three octets of Class C addresses. However, classless addressing removes this mechanism, and requires a new notation for nodes to indicate how much of an address should be treated as network address.

The *address/prefix* notation for CIDR addressing takes the form of a network address followed by a slash and the number of bits of the address to be considered the network part. For example, when discussing the reserved private IP network addresses, the following notations can be used:

```
Address Range                          Prefix Notation
-----------------------------------------------------
10.0.0.0    - 10.255.255.255     10/8
```

```
172.16.0.0   - 172.31.255.255      172.16/12
192.168.0.0  - 192.168.255.255     192.168/16
```

The first address range, 10/8, can also be referred to as a *24-bit block* because it provides the owner of the network with 24 bits of host addressing space. The second address range, 172.16/12, indicates that 12 bits of the address are treated as the network part and may also be referred to as a 20-bit block because it offers the owner 20 bits of host addressing. The last address range covers a 16-bit block, where the high-order 16 bits define the network and the low-order 16 bits are used for host addressing.

This notation is used in routing tables and elsewhere, and has replaced the use of a number of bits to specify a subnet mask which was made obsolete when network classes were made obsolete.

23.2.3 RELATIVE ADDRESSING

As mentioned earlier, the *network part* of the address uniquely identifies the administrative network on which the node is found. This is all that a remote system needs to know in order to properly deliver a packet to its destination network (or to determine that the address is a local one). The *host part* of the address is useful only within the local administrative domain, where it is used for delivery to individual destinations.

The network part of an address may vary, depending on who is interpreting the address. In general, the network part of any address will be the longest string of bits (starting from the left, or most significant, bit of the address) that a non-destination node must examine to determine how to handle the packet.

Postal analogies help clarify matters. If I have a letter for my next-door neighbor, I know that he is local to me and I need not use the postal system to deliver it. In this case, almost the entire address matches my own address, and I don't need anyone to route my mail for me.

When I mail my water bill payment to Town Hall, I put it in the "local delivery" slot at the post office. The network part of the address is my town, state, and country. I know what to do with letters going to my own town; the host part of the address is everything else. I can pick the correct slot, but after that, it's all just a postal cloud to me—the postal service has to figure out how to deliver the letters from there.

Consider the world's global postal network and a package sent from:

```
Joan Smith

123 High Street

London, Ontario N6B 1X1

Canada
```

to:

```
John Smith

321 High Street

London SW19 5

England
```

The information in these addresses becomes increasingly general as you progress through the data in them—this is different from IP addresses. But if you read them from the bottom line (indicating the country) to the top (individual's name) as is typically done at a post office processing mail, the data starts out general and becomes specific:

1. Joan drops the package off at the local London, Ontario, post office, where a postal worker checks the bottom line of the address. That worker notes that there is a country name there, so it's an international package which must go to the international sorting station. The worker puts it into a bin designated for international mail.

    This postal worker doesn't need to know that much about geography, just that an extra line at the bottom of the address means "international."

    Host JoanSmith emits a packet into the interpostalnet, sending it to the local post router. The router directs the packet to its international link.

2. At the international mail sorting center, another postal worker checks the bottom line of the address. This worker needs to

know more about geography and very likely has a sheet of paper holding a list of country names that will tell her what to do with each item. Mail bound for England goes in a bin labled "NWEurope."

The international link router forwards the package to a router called NWEurope for further processing.

3. The northwestern Europe-bound mail is put on a jet to London; when it arrives, the package is sorted into a bin bound for the postal facility serving all London SW postal codes.

After traveling over the intercontinental link to router NWEurope, the packet is forwarded over NWEurope's LondonSW link.

4. At the London SW postal facility, the package is passed along to the SW19 post office.

LondonSW forwards the packet to the SW19 router.

5. At the SW19 post office, a local postal worker sorts the package into a bin to be placed in the mail van driven by the letter carrier serving High Street in the SW19 5 zone. That letter carrier delivers the package to John Smith.

SW19 routes the packet to the areas router named 19-5, which passes it to the local router HIGH-STREET, which delivers it directly to host JohnSmith.

The list above includes, in italics, a "translation" of the postal analogy into network-speak. Figure 23–5 shows what's happening in steps 1 through 3, which should give an idea of what's going on in the remaining steps.

When Joan emits her packet into the global postal network, she has to specify a complete address. For the local postal worker who initially receives the packet, the network part of the address is "international"—the fact that the packet is even going to another country is sufficient for them to determine the postage needed and to put it in the right bin. At the next step, the country name actually becomes the network part—the smallest chunk of address the international mail sorter can use to correctly route the packet.

As far as Joan is concerned, there are three "postalnets" to choose from: the local one for London, Ontario, everywhere else in Canada, and the rest of the world. They are just clouds to her—she doesn't need to know what the rest of an address means, as long as it is accurate. When she realizes she's

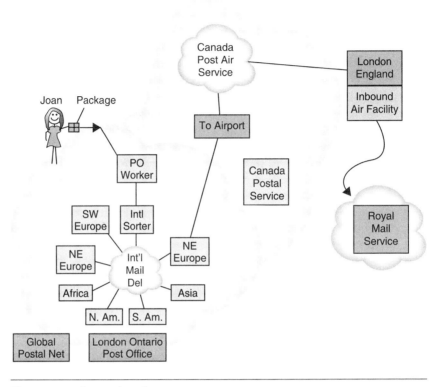

Figure 23–5: A postal analogy.

got to send the package out of the country (to England, though it could be Mauritius or San Marino or anywhere else), she has enough information to completely and correctly process her package.

For Joan, the network part of the address is the existence of a country (indicating international mail). She sees that part of the global postalnet as a huge network, and the bulk of John's address is the host part as far as Joan is concerned.

As the package moves through the global postalnet, more and more of the entire address becomes relevant to making decisions about how to handle the mail. At the airport in London, England, as the mail is processed into the postal service there, someone checks that the destination country is

England—but they've also got to check the city, because there's no point to sending the package to a distribution center for southern England in Bristol when the packet is going to be delivered locally. So, at that point, the network part of the address includes the country and the city (and perhaps even part of the postal code).

The length of the network part of an address won't necessarily be the same for all addresses being processed by the same system. Consider the inbound British mail processor. A destination address in London will have a rather long network part, while the network part of a destination address in France will be shorter since all mail for France goes through the Chunnel.

How does this all relate to IP addresses? Quite simply: think 4 octets instead of five address lines, and the analogy is quite close. IP nodes all have some understanding of the nature of their network. A simple node might understand nothing more than "me" (the node itself) and "everyone else." In that case, any data bound for an external node would be forwarded based on the contents of the node's *routing table*. For that node, the network address for a destination could be as short as 1 bit if the most-significant bit of the destination is different from the node's own address, or as long as 30 bits if the destination address is identical to the node's own except for the last 2 bits. If the network address part were 31 bits, the very most nodes possible on the remaining 1 bit of network would be 2—except the all-ones and all-zeros addresses in any network are usually reserved to indicate "this network" (all zeros) and the local broadcast address (all ones).

As the packet progresses toward its destination, intermediate nodes will interpret more of the IP address as network part, and less of it as the host part, until it arrives at its final destination network where the local router will pass the packet along directly over the local link.

23.3   Exterior Gateway Protocols

Historically, internet exterior routing protocols have evolved over the years to accommodate increasingly large and complex routing environments. An early such protocol, the Gateway to Gateway Protocol (GGP) was described in RFC 823, "The DARPA Internet Gateway," in 1982. GGP uses a distance-vector routing algorithm similar to that incorporated in RIP: gateways boot up assuming that all their links are down and no networks are reachable, but as they test out their own links and receive routing updates from other gateways, they are able to build up their routing tables to reflect the current state of the internet. RFC 823 has been assigned "Historic" status.

Also historic, the Exterior Gateway Protocol (EGP) formally specified in RFC 904 "Exterior Gateway Protocol Formal Specification," in 1984. GGP failed to address the issue of organizational internets that could not be connected directly to a *core* or backbone router. Extra hops were often added when non-core routers would send traffic to their own local default routers instead of forwarding them to a more appropriate internet router that might be closer to the destination. Figure 23–6 shows the problem.

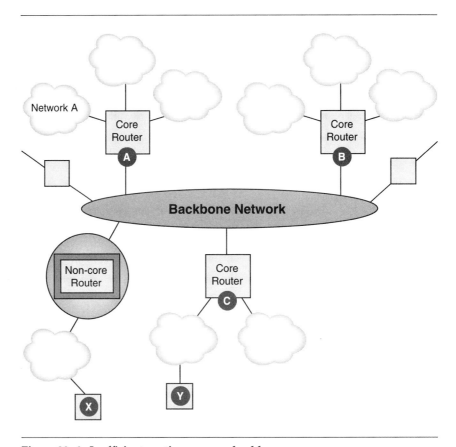

Figure 23–6: Inefficient routing across a backbone.

The figure shows a non-core router that is connected to a backbone on which various core routers are available. All of the core routers are, in theory at least, equally capable of routing any packets from any other routers connected to the backbone. Node X wants to communicate with node Y; ideally, the non-core router sends packets directly to Core Router C, but that can only happen if there is a way for the core routers to advertise their routes directly to non-core routers. EGP provides such a mechanism, by which EGP routers, as they come online, attempt to acquire some other router to act as a *peer*; peers exchange routing information about which networks they can reach. One of EGP's flaws was that it provided no way to compare two or more advertised routes to the same destination.

23.4   Border Gateway Protocol

If routing across a single backbone can be complicated, imagine routing over multiple backbones—some of which overlap, and many of which offer routes to the same destination networks. Figure 23–7 illustrates some of the entities involved, as well as the problems.

By 1989, a version of today's core internet routing protocol was published in RFC 1105, "A Border Gateway Protocol (BGP)," as an experimental specification; BGP version 4 is currently an internet draft standard (one step away from full standard status), and specified in RFC 1771, "A Border Gateway Protocol 4 (BGP-4)," and RFC 1772, "Application of the Border Gateway Protocol in the Internet."

Backbone Z is operated by a backbone service provider, and offers a *transit* service, meaning that they carry packets to and from client networks, such as the internet service providers I and J. Backbone Z is called a *transit AS*, because it is an autonomous system that moves packets from one AS to another—this implies that it has connections to at least two other ASes. Traffic from one AS to another is called *transit traffic*, to be distinguished from *local traffic*, or traffic that remains within a single AS.

In the modern internet topology, a routing entity may also be a *multi-homed AS*, which differs from a transit AS because it does *not* carry transit traffic but it does carry local traffic. For example, network X in Figure 23–7 might represent a large organization that maintains connections to several backbone networks but that carries traffic only intended for network X.

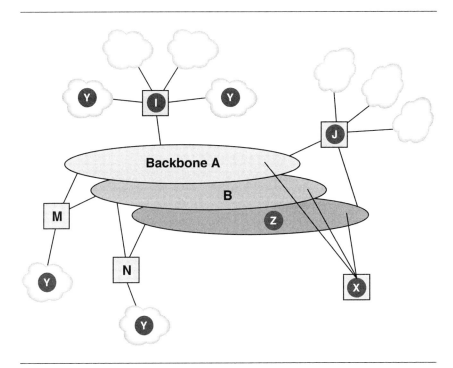

Figure 23–7: Modern internet topology with multiple backbones.

Finally, a *stub AS* is one, like network Y in the figure, that can carry only local traffic; a stub router connects a single AS to one other AS.

EGP worked reasonably well, but was unable to differentiate between advertised routes: a router notified other routers only whether or not it could reach an AS. With no basis for comparing directness of routes offered by two or more routers, a border router could only guess at which router was better for a particular packet. Neither the link state nor the distance-vector routing approaches will work well for this kind of network: the complexity is too great for any single router to handle all of the routes between all of the networks.

BGP addresses the problem by extracting the inter-AS routing issues from the intra-AS routing issues. In a BGP-routed network, each AS is connected to the rest of the network by at least one each of two different entities:

BGP speaker: Every AS in the network needs at least one BGP representative, to exchange reachability information with speakers for the other ASes.

BGP gateway: Every AS in the network needs to be connected to the network through at least one BGP gateway.

A gateway and a speaker may be deployed on the same system, but they may be deployed separately. And unlike RIP or OSPF routers, which exchange information about their own connectivity only, BGP routers exchange complete routes. With a RIP-like protocol, a router in network I (Figure 23–7) would have a routing table full of entries from every other router it can reach directly for all the other networks on backbone A: network X would be reachable in two hops through networks M and J, even though network I can reach X in a single hop on its own.

By including not just the number of hops but also the specific path for each route, BGP routers can eliminate routing loops. Using speakers, separate from routers, to communicate reachability information allows BGP network administrators to implement routing and forwarding policies that affect how packets are routed to and from particular networks that would otherwise be indistinguishable.

Table 23–1 lists some RFCs that document BGP and related issues.

RFC #	Title
1265	BGP Protocol Analysis
1266	Experience with the BGP Protocol
1771	A Border Gateway Protocol 4 (BGP-4)
1772	Application of the Border Gateway Protocol in the Internet
1773	Experience with the BGP-4 Protocol
1774	BGP-4 Protocol Analysis
1863	A BGP/IDRP Route Server Alternative to a Full Mesh Routing [EXP]

1930	Guidelines for creation, selection, and registration of an Autonomous System (AS) [BCP 6]
1997	BGP Communities Attribute
1998	An Application of the BGP Community Attribute in Multi-home Routing
2042	Registering New BGP Attribute Types
2270	Using a Dedicated AS for Sites Homed to a Single Provider
2385	Protection of BGP Sessions via the TCP MD5 Signature Option
2439	BGP Route Flap Damping
2519	A Framework for Inter-Domain Route Aggregation
2547	BGP/MPLS VPNs
2796	BGP Route Reflection - An Alternative to Full Mesh IBGP
2842	Capabilities Advertisement with BGP-4
2858	Multiprotocol Extensions for BGP-4
2918	Route Refresh Capability for BGP-4
3065	Autonomous System Confederations for BGP
3107	Carrying Label Information in BGP-4
3221	Commentary on Inter-Domain Routing in the Internet

Table 23–1: Current RFCs about BGP.

The BGP replaced EGP as the current solution to Internet routing. Routers pass along distance-vector reachability information, but instead of just including networks and distances, BGP includes the actual route needed to reach each destination. This allows the router to lay down the distance-vector routes into an actual map of the internet and eliminate the routing loops to which distance-vector protocols are prone.

23.5   Chapter Summary

Backbone routers operate in an environment where traditional interior routing protocols are insufficient: they don't scale sufficiently well to allow all routers in a very large network to exchange routing information without overwhelming parts of the network with routing protocol messages, and they don't offer the right tools for mapping routes to the backbone.

The introduction of CIDR and hierarchical network addressing was an important step forward in reducing routing complexity in a global internet consisting of many small (/24 and even smaller) networks.

Exterior routing protocols, such as BGP, make the distribution of routing information more scalable and more reliable across very large networks.

In the next chapter, we examine IP multicast.

24

Internet Protocol Multicast

Server capacity and network bandwidth are water and air to networks: without them, the network dies. Anything that preserves bandwidth or reduces server load is good, and anything that wastes bandwidth or server capacity is bad.

Internet protocol (IP) broadcasts might have once been considered a good thing, within limits—they have always been restricted to the local network. Yet broadcast can be wasteful or even dangerous to modern networks, wasting bandwidth as well as server capacity, especially in non-broadcast multiple access networks. Global internet broadcasts would be disabling to the global internet, rapidly filling all bandwidth with broadcasts from every conceivable source.

However, certain desirable applications, such as streaming multimedia and audio- video-conferencing, require transmission of the same data to many different recipients—often on the same local network. Sending individual copies to each recipient can also overwhelm networks in which more than a few hosts receive the same streams of data. *Push* applications rolled out in the middle and late 1990s on the internet, in which individual users subscribed to news or other broadcast services, alienated corporate IT departments as they flooded internet links.

IP multicast provides a middle path, eliminating the indiscriminate retransmission to everyone, no matter whether they're interested or not, of broadcasts while minimizing the transmission of duplicate packets over networks with multiple subscribers. However, for IP multicast to work well it must be implemented in a balanced manner.

An important tool for using bandwidth more efficiently, IP multicast has long been an important part of IP but it is still not used very often for internet transmissions. In this chapter, we examine how multicast works, why it is useful, and why organizations have been slow to deploy multicast across the internet.

24.1   Network Multicasting

With broadcast transmission of data across a network, all nodes on the network receive the data. This is one way to get information to more than one node at a time, while sending only one copy of the message. The alternative is to send a separate copy of the message to each recipient.

Each of these alternatives has serious drawbacks. Broadcasts can be inefficient, despite conserving network bandwidth in broadcast/multiple access networks like Ethernets: every connected system must process every broadcast message. NBMA network broadcasts, which require a server to repeat all broadcast messages over circuits to all connected nodes, are arguably just as inefficient as unicast to all network nodes. Although IP broadcast is hardly likely to disappear entirely, it is gradually being deprecated; IPv6 does not include support for broadcasts, for example.

Sending a separate copy of the message to each recipient takes far less of a toll on the systems receiving the messages. However, each copy of the message takes up network bandwidth—even applications that are not bandwidth intensive can overwhelm a network if data must be retransmitted enough.

A middle path exists in the form of network multicast. Messages sent to a multicast address are sent only once on each network link, but any number of connected nodes can listen to messages sent to that address. Broadcast can be viewed as a form of multicast in which all nodes on a network link are subscribed, by default, to the broadcast address.

Like broadcast, multicast is most transparent when implemented on a broadcast/multiple access network medium such as wireless or Ethernet, where all nodes can process all frames. Subscribing to a multicast address on this type of network is a simple matter of configuring the network interface to accept frames addressed to subscribed multicast addresses.

Multicast over NBMA networks is more efficient than broadcast over NBMA because the multicast proxy needs to repeat data only to the nodes that are subscribe to a multicast address—not to all nodes.

24.2 Applying Multicast

Applying multicast across internetworks poses a problem similar to that of using multicast (or broadcast) within an NBMA network. Routers (or some other systems) must act on behalf of subscribing nodes to accept and forward messages sent to a multicast address. To understand how IP multicast works, consider an actual application that could have benefited from it.

When Pointcast rolled out its news service to internet users in the late 1990s, it was heralded as a milestone application. Users signed up for the news categories and sources they preferred, and Pointcast *pushed* those items out to users automatically, regularly transmitting updates and new content automatically. Individuals could specify the types of content they wanted, as well as how often their clients would be updated with new material.

Users loved it, network administrators hated it: Pointcast chewed through bandwidth faster than a school of piranha through a cow. As users subscribed to essentially identical content streams, Pointcast transmissions flooded organizational internet links, and intranets. Instead of a single copy of an article, hundreds of copies of the exact same article were transmitted to an intranet with hundreds of subscribers.

Pointcast and other internet push services eventually implemented proxy servers to accept updates and new content on behalf of all users within a network, and then distribute them locally. A more elegant solution

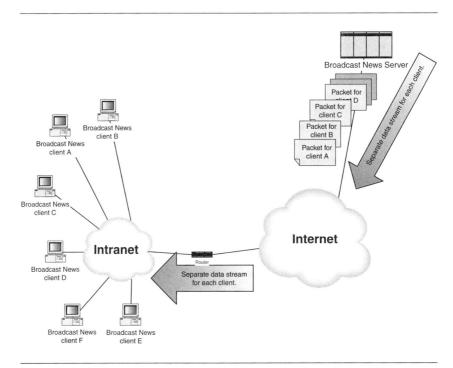

Figure 24–1: Unicast transmission can waste bandwidth when the same messages must be repeated to many nodes on the same network.

is available with multicast, but only if all routers operating between subscribers and the Pointcast server support multicast routing.

Figure 24–1 shows how a Pointcast-like service works. Subscribers may be connected to the same local networks or directly connected to an internet service provider, but in each case every subscriber gets a direct stream of data sent to its own unicast address. This approach is expensive in terms of bandwidth: every new subscriber requires a discrete amount of additional bandwidth capacity from the server. Within the intranet users clog up their organizational internet connection with duplicated inbound messages.

One way to cut down on the waste is to have organizations with many users of this service set up a system designated as a proxy or agent for internal subscribers. Rather than have a separate stream of messages for each subscriber within the intranet, the service sends a single stream of messages to the proxy agent, which distributes the messages to local subscribers. Within the intranet, the agent might make duplicates of every message and send it out individually to subscribers, or it might make use of network multicast functions to reduce the amount of internal bandwidth wasted. However, this approach reduces the wasted Internet bandwidth both for the organization receiving the messages and also for the organization sending the messages.

IP multicast offers an even better solution to this problem. If all our ISP's internet routers support multicast (still not always the case), a broadcast news service can send a single stream of messages to a single multicast address. The multicast-enabled IP routers within the internet act on behalf of subscribers. Nodes subscribe to an IP multicast address by notifying its local routers; that router now subscribes to the same multicast address on behalf of its client node.

Figure 24–2 shows an ideal result, in which the multicast originator sends material once to a multicast group address. Each node subscribes to the group by sending a multicast subscription request to Router A. Router A sends a request to Router B, subscribing to the same multicast group; Router B subscribes through Router C, which subscribes through Router D, which is connected to the multicast source.

When the multicast sender transmits a packet to that multicast address, Router D forwards a copy to Router C, which forwards it to Router B, which forwards it to Router A, which forwards it to all the subscribing nodes.

Now something similar happens with the other subscribers connected to an ISP. Those nodes tell Router E they are subscribing, which tells Router F to subscribe, which tells Router D. Thus, Router D sends out two copies of that datagram, one to Router F and the other to Router C. Router F forwards the packet to Router E, which forwards the packet to the two subscriber nodes.

In practice, the route that a datagram takes is likely to be more complicated than what is shown in Figure 24–3. And it assumes that all the routers in the paths between subscribers and the broadcaster are multicast-enabled— not a likely situation. Internet service providers still can't be assumed to routinely enable their routers and backbones for multicast, at least not so far.

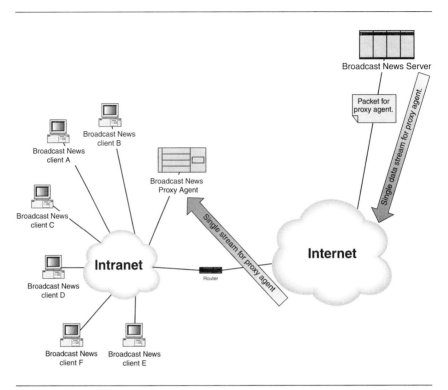

Figure 24–2: Proxy agents, or proxy servers, can act on behalf of a service to reduce duplication of messages within an intranet.

24.3   Internet Protocol Multicast

Multicast has long been an integral part of the IP standard: RFC 1112, "Host Extensions for IP Multicasting," published in 1989, defines IP multicast. Though RFC 1112 is integral to IP, by 1995 when RFC 1812, "Requirements for IP Version 4 Routers," was published, the authors stated that forwarding of IP multicasts is still somewhat experimental. That document suggests that IP multicast forwarding "should" be supported by routers. As a recommendation rather than a requirement, standard-compliant implementations are possible without multicast forwarding support.

RFC 1112 specifies three levels of conformance to IP multicast. At level 0, the host has no support for IP multicast. When such a host improperly

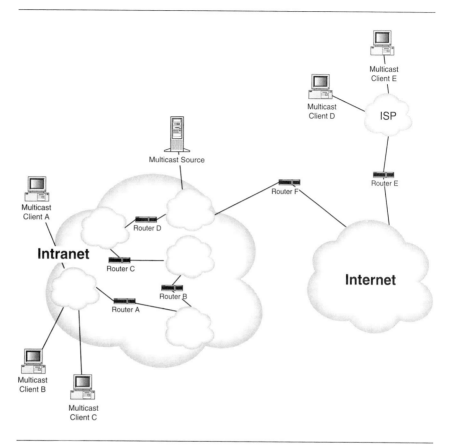

Figure 24–3: IP multicast has the potential to improve efficiency of propagating a message to many destinations across the internet.

receives a datagram addressed to a multicast address, its proper response is to quietly discard the datagram. Level 0 hosts should be able to identify Class D addresses as multicast addresses, but do not have to support multicast in any other way.

Level 1 hosts are able to send multicast datagrams, but not receive them. Converting a level 0 host to level 1 conformance is relatively simple, and allows such hosts to participate in applications that require hosts to report their status or submit other information to a multicast address, but which do not require such hosts to be able to accept multicast datagrams.

To achieve level 2 compliance, a host must not only be able to send multicast datagrams but also to join and leave host groups, which are the sets of hosts that are identified as being associated with a particular multicast address. By joining a host group, a host can receive multicast datagrams.

24.4   Internet Group Management Protocol

Earlier in this chapter, we spoke of hosts telling routers about which multicast addresses they wanted to subscribe. The *Internet Group Management Protocol* (*IGMP*), specified in RFC 1112, describes the mechanisms by which hosts can notify any multicast routers that are in the immediate neighborhood of the host's multicast group memberships.

IGMP specifies two types of messages relevant to multicast hosts. Multicast routers send out the IGMP membership query message to a standard multicast address that identifies the all-hosts group (224.0.0.1). This address differs from the broadcast address in that only level 2 multicast-enabled hosts respond to it other hosts ignore messages sent to this address.

When a multicast host receives an IGMP membershp query it begins to send IGMP membership replies, one for each multicast group to which it belongs. The replies are addressed to the multicast address of the group. This helps reduce traffic if there are other members of the same multicast group on the local link. Once the first member of the group responds to the IGMP query, the other members don't have to notify the router of their own memberships.

Multicast routers periodically send out IGMP membership queries to keep track of which multicast addresses they should be listening for on their other networks. Hosts usually send out IGMP membership replies in response to these queries or as soon as the host joins the group.

As defined in RFC 1112, routers need not keep track of which hosts are subscribing to which multicast addresses—if a host is a member of a group, it simply listens to multicasts forwarded at the link layer multicast address. However, things are different for NBMA networks, where broadcast and multicast are more complicated. Such networks require some mechanism to keep track of which nodes need multicast retransmissions.

24.5 Multicast Routing

Routing multicast datagrams is more complicated than routing either unicast or broadcast datagrams. A router that forwards packets on several networks might find itself forwarding the same multicast packet on all or some of those networksor on none, depending on whether or not hosts on those networks are members of the multicast group in question.

These protocols generally use a mechanism to discover the shortest path for multicast datagrams by looking at the source address of the datagram. If a router receives a multicast packet on an interface that is on the shortest path back to the sender, then the router can forward the packet on to other network interfaces to other group members. If the router receives the multicast packet on some other interface, then it just discards the packet because there is no need to forward it.

There are two approaches to multicast routing. *Dense-mode multicast routing* algorithms work on the assumption that there are likely to be multicast group members on all or most connected networks. *Sparse-mode multicast routing* algorithms work on the assumption that there are relatively few members of each multicast group and that most routers won't be involved in forwarding multicast packets. Each of these approaches has advantages and disadvantages, and each has specific types of situations in which it works best.

24.5.1 DENSE-MODE MULTICAST ROUTING

Dense-mode multicast routing protocols are best suited to networks with plentiful bandwidth where most routers are connected to networks that may have multicast group members. These protocols are built on the assumptions that there will be many other multicast routers in the routing environment and that there will be many hosts that are members of multicast groups. Routers implementing these protocols use IGMP messages to build routing tables, and share their results with other multicast routers.

One dense-mode protocol, the *Distance Vector Multicast Routing Protocol* (*DVMRP*), was published as an experimental protocol in 1998, in the eponymous RFC 1075. IETF members currently are engaged in work on a very different, modern version of this protocol. DVMRP routers are used to calculate multicast delivery trees that include the optimal routes to all members of the multicast group. As members join or leave the group, the routing trees are modified. As its name implies, DVMRP uses distance-vector routing and has some features in common with RIP (see Chapter 22).

Multicast Open Shortest Path First (MOSPF) is another dense-mode multicast protocol. Described in RFC 1584, Multicast Extensions to OSPF, MOSPF extends OSPF to enable OSPF routers to exchange multicast routing information.

The *Protocol Independent Multicast-Dense Mode (PIM-DM)* protocol is still (as of 2002) an IETF work-in-progress, described in Internet-drafts. In PIM-DM, it is just assumed that all downstream routes will want copies of a multicast datagram. Routes on which there are no group members will eventually be pruned off the PIM-DM routing tables.

24.5.2   SPARSE-MODE MULTICAST ROUTING

Sparse-mode multicast routing protocols are built on the assumption that there just aren't that many multicast group members or multicast routers around. Common to sparse-mode multicast routing protocols is an approach that uses the concept of a core router or rendezvous point (RP). In each case, the core or RP acts as a reference point for multicast groups. Rather than attempt to build routing maps, as is done by the dense-mode protocols, in sparse-mode protocols the routers route multicast packets to and from the core routers or RPs. This approach reduces the overhead of keeping track of a multicast routing map.

RFC 2362, "Protocol Independent Multicast-Sparse Mode (PIM-SM): Protocol Specification," specifies a multicast routing protocol that is largely identical to PIM-DM, except that it uses rendezvous points through which to route packets. The Core-Based Trees (CBT) routing protocol is described in RFC 2189, Core-Based Trees (CBT version 2) Multicast Routing, and in RFC 2201, Core-Based Trees (CBT) Multicast Routing Architecture. CBT is also specified as an experimental protocol, and uses the concept of a core router from which multicast routing trees sprout. Other multicast routers must determine routes to these trees for multicast group members.

24.5.3   SPARSE VS. DENSE MODE MULTICAST

The two approaches to multicast, sparse- and dense-modes, reflect two different styles of multicasting. The dense-mode approach works best when it can be assumed that most networks will include at least one host that is a member of the multicast group. The dense-mode approach is often said to be *data-driven* meaning that the sender effectively broadcasts the data to everyone, and then *prunes* the routing tree as routers on networks with no group members respond with a request to be removed from the distribution.

Sparse-mode multicast works best for *demand-driven* applications, where group members must request (demand) to be added to the routing tree for the group. Multicast routers accept requests to join a multicast group from individual hosts, and then report (to a *core* router, designated to coordinate sparse-mode multicasting) whenever a host joins or leaves the group.

Dense-mode multicasting does not scale well, certainly not to the global internet, but it can be useful for corporate intranets. For example, an investment firm might use data-driven multicast to push out stock quotes to all employees' workstations. Sparse-mode multicast is deemed more global internet-friendly, in that packets are sent only to group members that have explicitly opted to receive them.

24.6   Internet Protocol Multicast Applications

Multicast lends itself to applications that require the systematic transmission of identical information to many different recipients. Financial firms often use multicast to enable applications to transmit financial ticker and news information to every workstation on a trading floor.

Multicast is seen as a key enabling technology for the broadcast of audio and video over the internet, especially for audio and video conferencing applications. These applications can withstand delivery delays or interruption in transmission of datagrams, but still require some degree of feedback from recipients as well as some kind of framework for the data being delivered. The Real-Time Transfer Protocol (RTP), described in RFC 1889, helps provide quality of service feedback to multicast originators from multicast recipients.

The Real Time Streaming Protocol (RTSP) described in RFC 2326 defines the way data is carried and controlled within the transport layer, and provides mechanisms for setting up recipients to receive multicasts.

24.7   Chapter Summary

Although not often supported on the public global internet, IP multicast can be useful within private internets, where it can reduce network traffic for widely used applications as well as improve efficiency of subscription services. In this chapter, we looked at how multicast works generally: while it is almost trivial to implement in broadcast media like Ethernet, NBMA networks pose a challenge for multicast implementation. Layering IP multicast over these different families of network media requires the participation of multicast proxy agents in many cases.

IP multicast requires solutions to two important problems: allowing individual hosts to join multicast groups, and delivering multicast packets to all subscribed hosts without overwhelming the internet with unnecessary copies while also making sure that all subscribed hosts get at least one copy (but no more than one). Hosts and routers use IGMP to easily join or leave a multicast group, while the dense-mode and sparse-mode approaches to multicast routing enable routers to make the correct decisions about where and when to forward multicast packets.

In the next part, we introduce internet infrastructure protocols and issues, starting with Quality of Service.

Part Five

Internet Infrastructure

25

Quality of Service

We've already touched briefly on the *Quality of Service (QoS)* issue in Chapter 20, if only by mentioning the DiffServe/ECN header fields in Section 20.2.1. Rather than introduce more complexity than absolutely necessary, we've treated the internet as a reasonably reliable and fair packet delivery system. This is a convenient simplification (some might call it a fiction), particularly for most of the classic internet applications: a file transfer happens one packet at a time, whether those packets are delivered quickly or not. A delay in the network may cause a delay in the application session, but delays don't cause the application to fail (although if the delay is long enough, the session may time out, of course).

The phrase Quality of Service implies that there is a way to guarantee a host that it will have a certain level (or quality) of network services. For example, "quality" may refer to how much bandwidth the host can use or it may refer to a ceiling on the delay that can be expected. While classic internet applications can deal with delays and bandwidth variations reasonably robustly, newer applications such as real-time multimedia streaming require some minimum service guarantees to work.

The problem is that a real-time application may gobble up all the available bandwidth on a network link because that's what the destination node requires; other applications would be starved and fail. QoS is aimed at making it possible for network systems to negotiate their minimum requirements and to allocate some portion—but not all—of the available network resources for applications that need service guarantees.

When using switched, virtual circuit-based networks, such as those carrying telecommunications signals, QoS features are already available: voice telephony requires service above certain thresholds if users are to be able to carry on conversations, and telecommunications networks provide far better QoS than is possible under internet protocol (IP). For example, although multiple conversations can be multiplexed over a single link, each conversation is still guaranteed its own dedicated subchannel of 64 kbps.

IP, on the other hand, which started out as a datagram service, has been used mostly for the transmission of data—loss of data cannot be tolerated, but uneven performance is more acceptable. Losing a bit or an octet of a file being transferred means that the entire file is worthless and must be retransmitted; while losing even a relatively large proportion of a voice transmission is acceptable because the remaining signal will still convey the spoken voice.

Quality of Service and related issues represent one of the most challenging issues facing network engineers, and the technical details are beyond the scope of this book. For the sake of completeness, however, it is worth introducing some of these issues. in this chapter, we discuss network congestion and traffic engineering efforts, including the Explicit Congestion Notification (ECN) protocol. We also take a look at the Differentiated Services and Integrated Services approaches to traffic management, how diffserv has been added to IPv4, and more.

25.1   The Quality Problem

The IP model is a democratic one: all packets are (in theory) treated equally, getting a "best effort" delivery service from the systems in the internet. This has several implications for application performance and in some cases limits applications in a number of ways:

1. Packets may be delivered in order, or out of order.
2. Packets may be delivered smoothly, or in spurts.
3. Packets may be delivered, or not.

In the case of real-time applications, this can require that receiving hosts buffer data as it comes in, adding delay on top of whatever network delay exists. Instead of passing incoming network data directly to the application, the incoming data is stored temporarily as the host waits for all data, including out of order data and data that may be temporarily delayed, to arrive.

The unpredictability of the IP datagram service is due to the way routers handled traffic: packets come in from various sources, arriving at the router on different interfaces with different networks, and the router processes those packets in the order they are received.

Despite the first pass at the problem through assignment of Type of Service values, IP as originally defined lacks mechanisms for differentiating between packets that have quality of service requirements and those that don't:

- Transient congestion, such as caused by a surge of packets from one source, can cause unpredictable results. A packet surge may delay other traffic passing through a router. Or it might not.
- All datagrams are created equal, which means that there is no way to give one datagram priority over another.
- Individual routers can be configured to favor packets being sent to or from some particular network interface, but once the packet is routed it will be treated just like any other packet by other routers. IP lacks a mechanism for flagging packets at their source and indicating that they should be treated differently in some way from source to destination.
- Even if packets can be flagged for special treatment, IP lacks the mechanisms for tracking packets and monitoring performance and resource use.

QoS protocols are intended to differentiate between packets on an end-to-end basis, and adding the mechanisms necessary to allocate resources throughout a path for packets that require them.

25.2   Approaches to Quality

The two basic approaches to adding QoS to the internet are the Integrated Services (intserv) and Differentiated Services (diffserv) models. Introduced and defined in 1994 in RFC 1633, "Integrated Services in the Internet Architecture: an Overview," the intserv effort grew out of implementation experience with multicast of IETF meetings. According to RFC 1633 authors, real-time applications work poorly across the global internet "because of variable queueing delays and congestion losses."

In addition to QoS for real-time applications, the intserv model would allow network service providers control over how bandwidth is shared. Allowing all the available bandwidth to be allocated among different classes of traffic even when the network is under a heavy load means that applications can count on having a minimum amount of bandwidth to work with even when the network is congested—instead of being summarily cut off when packets are dropped silently and the hosts on the other end drop the connections.

The ability to control which traffic categories are allowed how much of the available bandwidth is called *controlled link sharing*. The intserv approach defines a service model in which best-effort and *real-time services* (services over which there is some control of end-to-end packet delay) coexist and are facilitated through controlled link sharing.

Whether or not overly influenced by their experiences with multicast, the intserv working group was agreed that any QoS solution would have to support multicast: real-time applications such as videoconferencing require the ability to handle multiple recipients of the same packets.

Ultimately, intserv has proven inadequate to the task of providing a single solution to the QoS problem: the intserv mechanisms are not seen as being scalable to the global internet, and they can be difficult to implement.

The next pass at the problem became known as *diffserv* to differentiate it from intserv. Cursory examination of the RFCs may not shed much light on the differences between the two, but there are considerable differences. Where intserv is focused on ways of sharing available bandwidth among unique *flows* (series of packets with the same source and destination IP and port addresses), diffserv approached the problem by suggesting that a less granular classification of packets could provide the desired result.

25.3   Reserving Resources

The process of provisioning circuits, as in asynchronous transfer mode (ATM) and other telecommunication-oriented network protocols, is necessary before any communication can occur between a source and a destination. The *Resource ReSerVation Protocol (RSVP)*, defined in RFC 2205, "Resource ReSerVation Protocol (RSVP)—Version 1 Functional Specification," defines a mechanism by which hosts can, in effect, provision a connection across the connectionless IP internet. RSVP, a required part of the intserv model, also requires intserv-capable routers in the network over which services are to be provided.

This reservation infrastructure can be dispensed with when services are provided to more general categories of packet, rather than the very specific intserv flows. Diffserv does not specifically require any mechanism on hosts, but vests the responsibility for managing bandwidth with the network itself. Diffserv packets are marked for special treatment by their applications, but the specific way in which those packets are treated is left to routers.

25.4   Intserv in a Nutshell

Central to intserv is the concept of the flow: if packets share source and destination IP addresses as well as source and destination ports, then one can assume that those packets are all part of an application's stream of data flowing between source and destination, with all that entails.

The intserv approach requires that routers keep track of all these flows, examining each packet to determine whether or not it belongs in a flow, and then computing whether or not there is enough available bandwidth to accept the packet. In other words, intserv requires the following functions:

Admission control: Can the router, or the network at large, provide service to the flow? Can it provide service to the individual packets that comprise the flow? What about other, non-QoS packets?

Packet classification: Every packet that is admitted must be classified. What flow does it belong to? What level of QoS does it get? The three options are to treat the packet "normally" giving it best-effort, *controlled load* for allocating some portion of an uncongested network, and *guaranteed service* for real-time delivery with delays minimized to within preset levels of service.

Packet scheduling: Once a packet is classified, how is it scheduled? Should some packets jump ahead of others? How are packets within a queue treated when the queue exceeds its limits?

Combined with RSVP, intserv tends to be cumbersome to implement and it certainly is not scalable to the global internet—but it is quite good at managing flows of data within smaller networks.

25.5   Diffserv in a Nutshell

There is no way that internet backbone routers could contend with the demands of tracking individual flows in an intserv-enabled global internet, but network customers and service providers both increasingly demand some form of QoS that can scale well in the global internet. Differentiated services, diffserv, answers the call by streamlining the process. Diffserv over IP is documented in RFC 2474, "Definition of the Differentiated Services Field (DS Field) in the IPv4 and IPv6 Headers."

Rather than building an elaborate infrastructure for emulating a circuit-based network on top of IP, diffserv allows communicating endpoints to classify their packets into different treatment categories. These categories are identified with a *per hop behavior*, or *PHB*. The PHB is the action that a diffserv routing node can be observed to take when it receives a packet. When a PHB is defined (and a Differentiated Services Code Point value assigned, as described in Chapter 20), diffserv routers are supposed to treat packets marked with that value in a certain way.

For example the Expedited Forwarding (EF) PHB (specified in RFC 2598, "An Expedited Forwarding PHB") is billed as "premium service" and indicates that the packets in that *behavior aggregate* (*BA*) should all be processed as they are received, rather than be queued or dropped. Unlike intserv with its traffic flows, the diffserv model calls for the use of BAs at each diffserv router: these are associated with a PHB which indicates how the router will treat the packet.

Aggregates or *aggragated flows* may also be referred to as *classes* of packets; routers are configured to respond to these different classes in different (appropriate) ways. Routers may also be configured to break up these classes into sub-aggregations to be treated slightly differently. For example, a router might be configured to forward premium-service packets from preferred customers over links that are more reliable than premium-service packets coming from customers subscribing to a "budget-premium" service.

Diffserv brings with it the ability to create network service policies specific to a single router, some part of a network, or an entire diffserv routing domain. As long as their policies don't affect the ability to provide guaranteed QoS, network providers can fine-tune their diffserv routers to differentiate how they treat packets.

The diffserv model distributes the task of allocating resources to the routers within a diffserv domain, providing greater flexibility as well as more efficient routing. A backbone router could process diffserv traffic far more easily than it can process intserv traffic: there is no need to negotiate RSVP reservations with all intermediary routers—and no overhead necessarily associated with failure to maintain an RSVP session with one particular router. With diffserv, the PHB mandates how the packet is treated, and different routers can provide the same service without having to maintain state for a particular connection, as with intserv.

25.6   Diffserv vs. Intserv?

At first glance, diffserv and intserv may seem to be competing with each other. However, the two models are complementary, with intserv working best within smaller domains while diffserv provides somewhat less precise handling of packets across much larger networks; the two can even be used together, as documented in RFC 2998, "A Framework for Integrated Services Operation over Diffserv Networks."

In this informational document, the authors see intserv, RSVP, and diffserv as "complementary technologies" each of which is intended to achieve end-to-end quality of service. "Together," they write, "these mechanisms can facilitate deployment of applications such as IP-telephony, video-on-demand, and various non-multimedia mission-critical applications. Intserv enables hosts to request per-flow, quantifiable resources, along

end-to-end data paths and to obtain feedback regarding admissibility of
these requests. Diffserv enables scalability across large networks."

25.7   Chapter Summary

What was originally considered an almost trivial problem—assigning priority to certain packets while marking others as less important and more
expendable with the Type of Service field in the IP header—turns out to be
one of the thorniest issues facing the internet community. Quality of service, whether achieved through the differentiated services approach or the
integrated services approach, is difficult to achieve in the connectionless,
best-effort network environment provided by IP network protocols.

In this chapter we introduced both Diffserv and Intserv, highlighting their
differences and their approaches to providing QoS. Readers seeking additional information about any of these topics are urged to read the RFCs
cited here, as well as the book *Internet QoS: Architectures and Mechanisms
for Quality of Service* by Zheng Wang (Morgan Kaufmann, 2001).

The next chapter introduces the IP security protocol, the set of protocols
that, together, can be used to protect network traffic by enforcing privacy
and providing authentication.

26

The Internet Security Protocol

The desirability and utility of authentication and security features at the internet protocol (IP) layer have been debated for years. This chapter discusses how authentication and security, including secure password transmission, encryption, and digital signatures on datagrams, are implemented under IP through the *Authentication Header* (*AH*) and *Encapsulating Security Payload* (*ESP*) options. Before examining the *IP Security Protocol* (*IPsec*), however, we will take a look at the IP security architecture described in RFC 2401, "Security Architecture for the Internet Protocol," and the different pieces of that architecture.

IPv4 as originally designed offered no real security features; it was intended simply as an internetworking protocol. While not necessarily a problem for a networking protocol used largely in research and academic settings, the increase in importance of IP networking to the general business and consumer networking environments makes the potential harm resulting from attacks more devastating than ever. This section examines:

- Issues of security for IP.
- Security goals defined for IP.
- Cryptographic elements of IPsec.
- Protocol elements of IPsec.
- Implementing IPsec.

The next section takes a look at the specifics of IPsec, as well as some of the tools being assembled to achieve these goals.

26.1   Internet Protocol Security Issues

IPsec as defined in RFC 2401 provides a security architecture for the IP—*not* a security architecture for the internet. The distinction is important: IPsec defines security services to be used at the IP layer, both for IPv4 and IPv6. It is often said that IPv6 is "more secure" than IPv4, but the difference is that IPsec is required for all IPv6 while it is optional for IPv4 nodes.

The IP Security Protocol (IPsec) provides an interoperable and open standard for building security into the network layer, rather than at the application or transport layer. Although applications can benefit from network layer security, the most important application IPsec enables is the creation of virtual private networks (VPNs) capable of securely carrying enterprise data across the open internet.

IPsec is often used in conjunction with tunnel management protocols including the Layer 2 Tunneling Protocol (L2TP), the Layer 2 Forwarding (L2F) protocol designed by Cisco Systems, and Microsoft's Point to Point Tunneling Protocol (PPTP). RFC 2661, "Layer Two Tunneling Protocol 'L2TP'," defines L2TP as a standards track specification (as of 2002, a proposed standard) for tunneling packets sent over a PPP link.

While the tunnel management protocols provide access security services, they don't provide authentication or privacy services, so they are often used in conjunction with IPsec—which does provide those services. However, saying that IPsec specifies protocols for encrypting and authenticating data sent within IP packets is an oversimplification, and even obscures IPsec's full potential. IPsec enables:

Encryption of data passing between two nodes, using strong public and private key cryptographic algorithms.

Authentication of data and its source, using strong authentication mechanisms.

Control over access to sensitive data and private networks.

Integrity verification of data carried by a connectionless protocol (IP).

Protection against *replay* **attacks,** in which an intruder intercepts packets sent between two IP nodes and resends them after decrypting or modifying them.

Limitation of *traffic analysis* **attacks,** in which an intruder intercepts protected data and analyzes source and destination information, size and type of packets, and other aspects of the data including header contents that might not otherwise be protected by encryption.

End-to-end security for IP packets, providing assurance to users of end-point nodes of the privacy and integrity of their transmissions.

Secure tunneling through insecure networks such as the global internet and other public networks.

Integration of algorithms, protocols, and security infrastructures into an overarching security architecture.

As defined in RFC 2401, "Security Architecture for the Internet Protocol," the goal of the IP security architecture is "to provide various security services for traffic at the IP layer, in both the IPv4 and IPv6 environments." This means security services that are:

Interoperable: As with all internet protocols, interoperability is a fundamental goal. This means that any IP node supporting IPsec can communicate with any other node supporting IPsec. There is a basic set of cryptographic algorithms for encryption and integrity checking that all IPsec nodes must support, although individual nodes and implementations may support many more, optional, algorithms. Although some nodes are configured to prefer newer or less open algorithms, all nodes are required to support the basic ones.

High-quality: The baseline for security through IPsec must be set high enough to guarantee a reasonable degree of actual security. Algorithms and key lengths that are to be vulnerable to attack are not acceptable. For example, data encrypted with 40-bit encryption keys can be *brute-forced* or successfully and quickly decrypted by trying every combination. The number of possible keys is $2^{40} - 1$, or roughly 1,000,000,000,000; on average, the correct key will be discovered after trying half (about 500 billion) of those combinations. Such attacks are almost trivially easy with commercial off the shelf hardware, and thus 40-bit keys are not considered to provide "high-quality" security.

Cryptographically based: Cryptographers work with algorithms for encryption, secure hashing, and authentication. Encryption algorithms allow regular data to be transformed into *cyphertext*, data scrambled so that only the entity holding an appropriate *key* can decrypt it. Secure hash algorithms operate on any size chunk of data to generate a fixed-length sequence of bits (the hash). An entity can confirm the integrity of the data by running the hashing algorithm on received data; if the transmitted hash and the calculated hash agreee, the data is verified as having been sent without change. Authentication of entities through the use of digital signatures depend on public key algorithms. Data encrypted with the public key of a public/private key pair can be decrypted only by an entity with access to the private key; likewise, if an entity encrypts something (such as the text of a message) with their *private* key, then anyone with access to the public key can decrypt the message and confirm that the sender has access to that key.

By basing IPsec on cryptography rather than on any other mechanisms for security, the protocol designers place limits on the security goals possible to attain through its use while at the same time insuring that those security goals will be achieved through the use of verifiable and reliable mechanisms.

The IP security architecture allows systems to choose the required security protocols, identify the cryptographic algorithms to use with those protocols, and exchange any keys or other material or information necessary to provide security services.

As may be evident from its highly qualified description, public key cryptography-based mechanisms require that all participants can be confident that public keys are issued only to the entities identified with those keys. When a public key is published purporting to represent Microsoft Corporation, the possibility that the key has been properly issued to

Microsoft and not to a computer criminal should approach 100% certainty. Unfortunately, as was demonstrated in early 2001 when it was reported that leading public key infrastructure vendor Verisign, Inc., issued two public key certificates to an imposter claiming to represent Microsoft, this is not always possible.

As a network layer protocol, IPsec provides security only at the network layer. This means that packets can be protected from the point at which they enter the IP network (the source node's IP interface) to the point at which they leave the IP network (the destination node's IP interface). IPsec cannot substitute for proper application or transport layer security mechanisms, and IPsec cannot protect against attackers taking control of the source or destination nodes or processes.

26.2   Security Goals

Computer security can be said to embody three general goals:

Authentication: The ability to reliably determine that data has been received as it was sent and to verify that the entity that sent the data is what it claims to be. Successful authentication means preventing attackers from impersonating an authorized entity.

Integrity: The ability to reliably determine that the data has not been modified during transit from its source to its destination. Successfully maintaining data integrity means preventing an attacker from modifying authentic data without detection as well as preventing the acceptance of data that has been corrupted somewhere in the network clouds (as happens occasionally).

Confidentiality: The ability to transmit data that can be used or read only by its intended recipient and not by any other entity. Successfully maintaining data confidentiality means preventing anyone other than the intended recipient(s) from being able to access private data.

Developments in modern cryptography, specifically in the use of *public key cryptography* (discussed in the next section), make possible the combination of these three goals in one set of functions. These goals, authentication, integrity, and confidentiality, are achieved through three related functions:

Digital Signatures: unequivocally link the holder of a particular secret with data represented as having been *signed* by that entity.

Secure Hashes: digitally "summarize" a sequence of data using a repeatable process that will produce identical results only if the data sequence being verified matches the data sequence produced by the sender.

Encryption: the process of performing a reversible transformation on readable data so as to render it unreadable by anyone other than the holder of the appropriate decryption key.

Some or all of these functions are possible in combination or individually in protocols at every layer of the TCP/IP stack, from IP (through IPsec) to TLS (Chapter 17) to application protocols such as BEEP (Chapter 14).

The goal of IPsec is to provide security mechanisms for all versions of IP.[1] IPsec provides security services at the IP layer, and systems may require other systems to interact with it securely with IPsec and a particular set of security algorithms and protocols. While IPsec mandates support for a basic set of algorithms, it also allows nodes to negotiate acceptably secure interaction with other systems with optional algorithms. IPsec provides the framework within which nodes can negotiate appropriate algorithms, protocols, key lengths, and other aspects of secure communication.

IPsec allows maintenance of:

Access control: IPsec allows security protocols to be invoked governing the secure exchange of keys, allowing authentication of users for access control purposes.

Connectionless integrity: IPsec allows nodes to validate each IP packet independent of any other packet. There is no need to verify sequences of packets or even to have access to other packets exchanged by the same nodes. Connectionless integrity is enabled through use of secure hashing techniques, similar to the use of check digits but with greater reliability and less likelihood of tampering from unauthorized entities.

---

[1] IPsec support is mandatory for IPv6 nodes, while optional for IPv4 nodes.

Data origin authentication: Identifying the source of the data contained in an IP packet is another security service provided by IPsec. This function is accomplished through the use of digital signatures.

Defense against packet replay attacks: As a connectionless protocol, IP is subject to the threat of replay attacks, where an attacker sends a packet that has already been received by the destination host. Replay attacks can harm system availability by tying up receiving system resources. IPsec provides a packet counter mechanism that protects against this ploy.

Encryption: Data confidentiality—keeping access to data from anyone but those with proper authorization—is provided through the use of encryption.

Limited traffic flow confidentiality: Encrypting data is not always sufficient to protect systems; merely knowing the endpoints of an encrypted exchange, the frequency of such interaction, or other information about the transmissions can provide a determined attacker with enough information to disrupt or subvert systems. IPsec provides some limited traffic flow confidentiality through the use of IP tunneling, especially when coupled with security gateways.

All of these functions are possible through proper use of the encapsulating security payload (ESP) header and the authentication header (AH). A handful of cryptographic functions are specified for IPsec and are described briefly in the next section.

Public key encryption provides a mechanisms for performing almost all of these functions with a single set of processes. AH provides mechanisms for applying authentication algorithms to an IP packet, while ESP provides mechanisms for applying any kind of cryptographic algorithm to an IP packet including encryption, digital signature, and/or secure hashes.

IPsec is aimed at eliminating certain types of attacks, including:

Denial of service (DoS) attacks: These occur when an entity uses network transmissions to prevent legitimate users from using network resources. For example, an attacker may flood a host with TCP SYN requests (see Chapter 18) and thereby crash a system, or the attack may consist of repeated transmission of long mail messages with the intention of filling up a user's or site's bandwidth with nuisance traffic.

Spoofing attacks: These occur when an entity transmits packets that misrepresent the packets' origins. For example, one type of spoofing attack occurs when the attacker sends a mail message with the From: header indicating the source of the message as, say, the president of the United States. More insidious and almost as easy to engineer are those attacks that occur when packets are sent out with an incorrect source address in the headers.

Man-in-the-middle attacks: These occur when an attacker (Alice) positions herself between two communicating entities (call them Bob and Carol) and intercepts all their transmissions. Alice poses as Bob when communicating with Carol, and as Carol when communicating with Bob. Alice, as a result, is able to send whatever data she wants to Bob instead of what Carol wants to send to Bob. These attacks are relatively easy when transmissions are not encrypted or authenticated, but if Alice can successfully attack even a protected data stream if she is able to either gain access to Carol's secret keys or be issued a set of her own public/secret key pairs that is sufficiently similar to Carol's that Bob will be fooled.

This last attack is important because it raises the issue of handling keys. As previously noted, encryption and digital signature functions require the use of *keys* to decrypt and/or verify data, and *digital certificates* are one mechanism by which public keys can be distributed. Although all *public key infrastructure (PKI)* providers, including Verisign, make their own efforts to validate all applications, the problem is not a matter of technology. As previously noted, Verisign issued two digital certificates to someone who improperly posed as a representative of Microsoft; a sufficiently motivated attacker will presumably use every possible tactic to get a desired certification. An attacker's ability to forge credentials (from letterhead on which to type a request for a corporate digital certificate to passport, birth certificate, or other documents submitted to support a fraudulent application) may exceed the ability of the PKI provider to detect them.

As a result of this potential vulnerability, IPsec requires a mechanism by which keys can be securely administered and distributed in a way that associates public keys with the entities they are supposed to owned by.

As previously noted, IPsec secures IP—not the internet, and certainly not the systems connected to the internet, or the processes running on those systems. IPsec must be considered only one part of the organizational security strategy. While IPsec-protected traffic may pass unscathed across the global internet, before it leaves its source and after it arrives at its destination, that traffic will be vulnerable to attacks on local links, local systems, processes, and the protocols used there.

26.3 Encryption and Authentication Algorithms

Rather than relying on secrecy to protect an encryption or authentication scheme, an approach known as "security through obscurity," TCP/IP security protocols always specify that cryptographic algorithms be well known and accessible. This is done for several reasons, not least of which is that as an open protocol suite, TCP/IP protocol specifications must be published freely. The most important reason, however, is that secrecy is a poor safeguard over security.

Attempting to keep an encryption algorithm secret is almost impossible, particularly if it is being used by anyone other than the person who knows the secret. Attackers have many cryptanalysis tools at their disposal for breaking codes, and they need only have access to ciphertexts to break them. Having access to the software used to encrypt and/or decrypt data with the secret algorithm makes the task much easier: the attacker must only determine what the software does to the data to figure out how to reverse the operation.

The greatest advantage that published algorithms provide is the benefit of scrutiny by researchers and others seeking to find ways to further improve or break the algorithms. The more trained experts examine an algorithm, the less likely they are to overlook an "obvious" attack.

Security algorithms and protocols are hard to design because there are so many different ways to attack them—and designers can't always imagine them all. Although national security organizations as well as corporations may have their own top-secret codes, secrets are hard to keep. Spies and other criminals are well known for their skill at motivating (through bribery, extortion, or other means) people who know secrets to share them.

The prevailing wisdom in security holds that a good encryption or authentication algorithm should be secure even if an attacker knows what algorithm is being used. This is particularly important for internet security, as an attacker with a sniffer will often be able to determine exactly what kind of algorithm is being used by listening as systems negotiate their connections.

In this section we'll cover five types of important cryptographic functions:

- Symmetric encryption
- Public key encryption
- Key exchange
- Secure hashes (message digests)
- Digital signature

26.3.1 SYMMETRIC ENCRYPTION

Most people are familiar with *symmetric encryption* if only at a visceral, intuitive level: plaintexts are encrypted with a secret key and some set of procedures, and decrypted with the same key and the same set of procedures. If you have the key, you can decrypt all data that has been encrypted with that key. Sometimes known as *secret key encryption*, symmetric encryption is computationally efficient and is the most frequent type of encryption for network transmission of volumes of data.

In October, 2000, the National Institute of Standards and Technology (NIST) announced that the *Rijndael*[2] data encryption algorithm had been selected for the *Advanced Encryption Standard* (*AES*), to replace the outdated *Data Encryption Standard* (*DES*) algorithm originally developed during the 1970s by IBM. DES uses 56-bit keys, although a variation called *triple DES* encrypts data three times with the DES algorithm, providing improved security.

Using a secure encryption requires using sufficiently long keys. Shorter keys are vulnerable to brute force attacks in which an attacker uses a computer to try all the different possible keys. Key lengths on the order of 40 bits, for example, are considered insecure because they can be broken by brute force attacks in very short order by relatively inexpensive computers.

---

[2]According to an FAQ at the NIST web site, "The algorithm's developers have suggested the following pronunciation alternatives: 'Reign Dahl,' 'Rain Doll' and 'Rhine Dahl.'" The AES home page is http://csrc.nist.gov/encryption/aes/.

Single-DES has been brute-forced, as well; in general, 128-bit and longer keys are likely to be secure against such attacks for the immediate future.

Symmetric encryption algorithms can be vulnerable to other types of attacks. Most applications that use symmetric encryption for internet communications use session keys, meaning the key is used for only a single session data transmission (sometimes several keys are used for in one session). Loss of a session key thus compromises only the data that was sent during that session or portion of a session.

Other symmetric encryption algorithms that have been or are currently being used for internet applications include:

RC2/RC4: Commercial symmetric encryption algorithms developed and marketed by cryptography firm RSA.

CAST: Developed in Canada and used by Nortel's Entrust products, CAST supports up to 128-bit keys.

IDEA: The International Data Encryption Algorithm supports 128-bit keys; patented by Swiss firm Ascom, which granted permission for IDEA to be used for free non-commercial use in the seminal and open source encryption program Pretty Good Privacy (PGP) written by Philip Zimmermann and published for a time by Network Associates, Inc.

GOST: An algorithm reportedly developed by a Soviet security agency.

Blowfish: An algorithm developed by Bruce Schneier and released to the public domain.

Twofish: Bruce Schneier's submission to the AES competition.

Skipjack: An algorithm developed by the National Security Agency for use with the Clipper chip's escrowed key system.

26.3.2 PUBLIC KEY ENCRYPTION

Public key encryption, also called *asymmetric encryption*, uses pairs of keys: one, the *public key* is associated with the other, the *secret key*. The public key is intended to be made public. Any data encrypted with the public key can only be decrypted with the secret key—and any data encrypted with the secret key can be decrypted with the public key.

Anyone can get a public key and encrypt some data with it. That data can be decrypted only by the holder of the secret key. As long as an entity can keep its secret key a secret, other entities can be sure that any data encrypted with the public key will be accessible only to the holder of the associated secret key. The holder of the secret key can encrypt something using that secret key and make it available to another entity. That entity can verify the first entity as holding the secret key of a particular public key pair by decrypting the data with the public key.

Public key encryption tends to be computationally intensive and is most often used to encrypt session keys for network transmissions as well as for digital signatures.

The most commonly used type of public key encryption is the *RSA* algorithm developed by Ron Rivest, Adi Shamir, and Len Adleman. RSA defines a mechanism for choosing and generating the secret/public key pairs, as well as for the actual mathematical function to be used for encryption.

26.3.3   KEY MANAGEMENT

One of the most complex issues facing Internet security professionals is how to manage keys. This includes not only the actual distribution of keys through a key exchange protocol but also the negotiation of key length, lifetime, and cryptographic algorithms between communicating systems.

An open channel (an open communication medium over which transmissions can be overheard) like the global internet complicates the process of sharing a secret. This process is necessary when two entities need to share a key to be used for encryption. Some of the most important cryptographic algorithms relate to the process of sharing a key over an open channel securely, in a way that keeps the secret from anyone but the intended recipients.

Diffie-Hellman key exchange is an algorithm that allows entities to exchange enough information to derive a session encryption key. Alice (the customary entity name for the first participant in a cryptographic protocol) calculates a value using Bob's public value and her own secret value (Bob is the second participant in cryptographic protocols). Bob calculates his own value and sends it to Alice; they each then use their secret values to calculate their shared key. The mathematics are relatively simple (but outside the scope of this book); the bottom line is that Bob and Alice can send each other enough information to calculate their shared key but not enough for an attacker to be able to figure it out.

Diffie-Hellman is often called a public key algorithm, but it is not a public key *encryption* algorithm. Diffie-Hellman is used to calculate a key, but that key must be used with some other encryption algorithm. Diffie-Hellman can be used for authentication, though, and is also used by PGP.

Key exchange is integral to any Internet security architecture, and candidates for the IPsec security architecture include the *Internet Key Exchange* (*IKE*) protocol and the *Internet Security Association and Key Management Protocol* (*ISAKMP*).

ISAKMP is an application protocol, using UDP as its transport, that defines different types of messages that systems send to each other to negotiate the exchange of keys. The mechanisms and algorithms for doing the actual exchanges, however, are not defined in ISAKMP—it is a framework to be used by the specific mechanisms. The mechanisms, often based on Diffie-Hellman key exchange, have been defined in a number of different proposals over the years. These include:

Photuris: Based on Diffie-Hellman, *Photuris* adds the requirement that the requesting node send a *cookie*, a random number that is used as a sort of session identifier. The cookie is sent first, and the server acknowledges the request by returning the cookie. This reduces the risk from denial-of-service attacks made by attackers forging their source addresses. Photuris also requires all parties to sign their negotiated key to reduce the risk of a man-in-the-middle attack (in which an attacker pretends to be Bob to one system's Alice, while pretending to be Alice to the other system's Bob).

SKIP: Sun Microsystems' *Simple Key-management for Internet Protocols* (*SKIP*) is also based on Diffie-Hellman key exchange, but, rather than requiring parties to use random values to calculate their keys, SKIP calls for the use of a secret table that remains static. The parties look up secret values in this table and then transmit calculated values based on some secret value from the table.

OAKLEY: Although this mechanism shares some features with Photuris, it provides different modes of key exchange for situations where denial-of-service attacks are not of concern.

By defining a separate protocol, ISAKMP, for the generalized formats required to do key and Security Association exchanges, it can be used as a base to build specific key exchange protocols. The foundation protocol can be used for any security protocol, and does not have to be replaced if an existing key exchange protocol is replaced.

It should be noted that manual key management is an important option and in many cases the only option. This approach requires individuals to personally deliver keys and configure network devices to use them. Even after open standards have been firmly determined and implemented, particularly as commercial products, manual key management will continue to be an important choice.

As more research is done with IPsec, work on an IKE successor protocol (sometimes called *Son-of-IKE*) is ongoing, with IKEv2 one candidate prototocol that (as of 2002) is a work-in-progress.

26.3.4 SECURE HASHES

A hash is a digital summary of a chunk of data of any size. Simple types of hashes include check digits; secure hashes produce longer results (often 128 bits or longer). Good secure hashes are extremely difficult for attackers to reverse-engineer or subvert in other ways. Secure hashes can be used with keys or without, but their purpose is to provide a digital summary of a message that can be used to verify whether some data that has been received is the same as the data sent. The sender calculates the hash and includes that value with the data; the recipient calculates the hash on the data received. If the results match the attached hash value, the recipient can be confident in the data's integrity.

Commonly used hashes include the MD2, MD4, and MD5 message digest functions published by Network Associates. The *Secure Hash Algorithm* (*SHA*) is a digest function developed as a standard by NIST. Hashes may be used on their own or as part of digital signatures.

26.3.5   DIGITAL SIGNATURE

Public key encryption, as noted previously, relies on key pairs. Digital signatures rely on the property of public key encryption that allows data encrypted with an entity's secret key to be decrypted with the public key of the pair. The sender calculates a secure hash on the data to be signed, then encrypts the result using a secret key. The recipient calculates the same hash and then decrypts the encrypted value attached by the sender. If the two values match, the recipient knows that the owner of the public key was the entity that signed the message and that the message was not modified during transmission.

The RSA public key encryption algorithm can be used for digital signatures: The signing entity creates a hash of the data to be signed and then encrypts that hash with its own secret key. The certifying entity then calculates the same hash on the data being received, decrypts the signature using the signing entity's public key, and compares the two values. If the hash is the same as the decrypted signature, then the data is certified.

Digital signatures carry with them several implications:

- A signature that can be certified indicates that the message was received without any alteration from the time it was signed to the time it was received.
- If a signature cannot be certified, then the message was corrupted or tampered with in transit, the signature was calculated incorrectly, or the signature was corrupted or tampered with in transit. In any case, an uncertifiable signature does not necessarily imply any wrongdoing but does require that the message be resigned and resent in order to be accepted.
- If a signature is certified, it means that the entity associated with the public key was the *only* entity that could have signed it. In other words, the entity associated with the public key cannot deny having signed the message. This is called *nonrepudiation* and is an important feature of digital signatures.

There are other mechanisms for doing digital signatures, but RSA is probably the most widely used one and is implemented in the most popular internet products.

26.4   IPsec: The Protocols

IPsec is a security tunneling protocol, defining a mechanism that allows a node to encrypt and/or authenticate packets and encapsulate the secured packets (which may now be literally indecipherable, having been encrypted) into new packets. Figure 26–1 illustrates the basic idea behind IPsec and other security tunneling protocols.

IPsec depends on the use of *security gateways*, which encapsulate IP packets on behalf of their clients. In Figure 26–1, the security gateway labeled "X" serves, among others, hosts A', B', and C'; "Y" serves hosts A, B, and C. The PC off on the side has its own software security gateway. In this example, the tunnel from X to Y carries all secured traffic between the

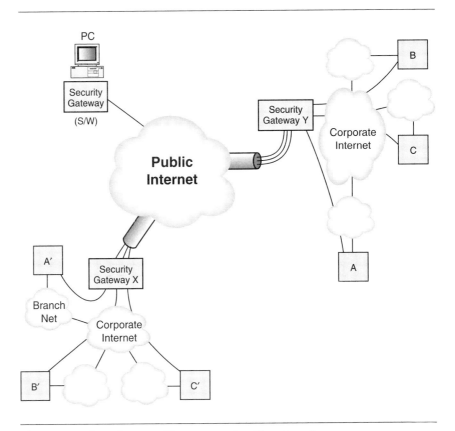

Figure 26–1: Security tunneling across a hostile network.

two pictured internets. In this case, each security gateway integrates all traffic for its local network, and encrypts and/or authenticates all of it between itself and the security gateway at the other end. If all traffic is being encrypted (a good bet), then any attacker sitting inside the public internet could intercept these packets but would get relatively little information from them. At best, the attacker would discover that there is a secure tunnel between X and Y, but she would likely learn only how much traffic was being sent between the two security gateways.

The security gateways create secure tunnels as shown in Figure 26–2, by accepting IP packets sent from one node (A) to another (B). A sends the

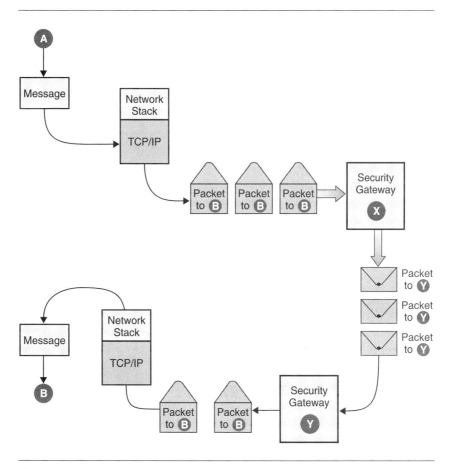

Figure 26–2: Using a secure tunnel.

packets off as if they were going to be delivered directly to B; the security gateway X then takes those packets (along with any others from the same network) and treats them as raw data to be sent to security gateway Y. The packets sent by A are shown as open envelopes to signify that they have not been encrypted while the packets sent from X are shown as sealed envelopes to indicate that they contain the encrypted packets sent from A.

The original IPsec specifications define security protocols for the Authentication Header (AH) and the Encapsulating Security Payload (ESP) IP options, as header options (for IPv4) or header extensions (for IPv6). As their names imply, AH provides an authentication mechanism while ESP provides an encryption ("encapsulated security") mechanism for privacy.

26.5   Internet Protocol and IPsec

IPsec provides security services for either IPv4 or IPv6, but the way it provides those services is slightly different in each. IPv4 uses header options: every IP packet contains 20 octets-worth of required fields, and any packet that has any "special" requirements can use up to 40 octets for those options. This tends to complicate packet processing, since routers must check the length of each packet it receives for forwarding—even though many of those options are related to end-to-end functions such as security, functions that routers are not concerned with otherwise.

IPv6 simplifies header processing: every IPv6 packet header is the same length, 40 octets, but any options can be accommodated in extension headers that follow the IPv6 header. IPsec services are provided through these extensions.

The ordering of IPsec headers, whether within IPv4 or IPv6, has significance. For example, it makes sense to encrypt a payload with the ESP header, and then use the Authentication Header to provide data integrity on the encrypted payload. In this case, the AH header appears first, followed by the ESP header and encrypted payload. Reversing the order, by doing data integrity first and then encrypting the whole lot, means that you can be sure of who originated the data, but not necessarily certain of who did the encryption.

26.5.1 SECURITY ASSOCIATIONS

The *Security Association* (*SA*) is a fundamental element of IPsec. RFC 2401 defines the SA as "a simplex 'connection' that affords security services to the traffic carried by it." This rather murky definition is clarified by a description; an SA consists of three things:

- a Security Parameter Index (SPI)
- an IP destination address
- a security protocol (AH or ESP) identifier

As a simplex connection, the SA associates a single destination with the SPI; thus, for typical IP traffic there will be two SAs: one in each direction that secure traffic flows (one each for source and destination host). SAs provide security services by using either AH or ESP, but not both (if a traffic stream uses both AH and ESP, it has two or more SAs).

The *SPI* is an identifier indicating the type of IP header the security association is being used for (AH or ESP). The SPI is a 32-bit value identifying the SA and differentiating it from other SAes linked to the same destination address. For secure communication between two systems, there would be two different security associations—one for each destination address.

Each security association includes more information related to the type of security negotiated for that connection, so systems must keep track of their SAs and what type of encryption or authentication algorithms, key lengths, and key lifetimes have been negotiated with the SA destination hosts.

26.5.2 USING SECURITY ASSOCIATIONS

As mentioned earlier, ISAKMP provides a generalized protocol for establishing SAes and managing cryptographic keys within an internet environment. The procedures and packet formats needed to establish, negotiate, modify, and delete SAs are defined within ISAKMP, which also defines payloads for exchanging key generation and authentication data. These formats provide a consistent framework for transferring this data, independent of how the key is generated or what type of encryption or authentication algorithms are being used.

ISAKMP was designed to provide a framework that can be used by any security protocols that use SAes, not just IPsec. To be useful for a particular security protocol, a *Domain of Interpretation (DOI)* must be defined. The DOI groups related protocols for the purpose of negotiating security associations—security protocols that share a DOI all choose protocol and cryptographic transforms from a common namespace. They also share key exchange protocol identifiers, as well as a common interpretation of payload data content.

While ISAKMP and the IPsec DOI provide a framework for authentication and key exchange, ISAKMP does not actually define how those functions are to be carried out. The IKE protocol, working within the framework defined by ISAKMP, does define a mechanism for hosts to perform these exchanges.

The sending host knows what kind of security to apply to the packet by looking in a *Security Policy Database (SPD)*. The sending host determines what policy is appropriate for the packet, depending on various selectors (e.g., destination IP address and/or transport layer ports), by looking in the SPD. The SPD indicates what the policy is for a particular packet: either the packet requires IPsec processing of some sort, in which case it is passed to the IPsec module for processing; or it does not, in which case it is simply passed along for normal IP processing.

Outbound packets must be checked against the SPD to see what kind (if any) of IPsec processing to apply. Inbound packets are checked against the SPD to see what kind of IPsec service should be present in those packets.

Another database, called the *Security Association Database (SAD)*, includes all security parameters associated with all active SAs. When an IPsec host wants to send a packet, it checks the appropriate selectors to see what the SAD says is the security policy for that destination/port/application. The SPD may reference a particular SA, so the host can look up the SA in the SAD to identify appropriate security parameters for that packet.

26.5.3   TUNNEL AND TRANSPORT MODE

IPsec defines two modes for exchanging secured data, *tunnel mode* and *transport mode*. IPsec transport mode protects upper-layer protocols, and is used between end nodes. This approach allows end-to-end security, because the host originating the packet is also securing it and the destination host is able to verify the security, either by decrypting the packet or certifying the authentication.

Tunnel mode IPsec protects the entire contents of the tunneled packets. The tunneled packets are accepted by a system acting as a security gateway, encapsulated inside a set of IPsec/IP headers, and forwarded to the other end of the tunnel, where the original packets are extracted (after being certified or decrypted) and then passed along to their ultimate destination.

The packets are only secured as long as they are "inside" the tunnel, although the originating and destination hosts could be sending secured packets themselves, so that the tunnel systems are encapsulating packets that have already been secured.

Transport mode is good for any two individual hosts that want to communicate securely; tunnel mode is the foundation of the *Virtual Private Network* (*VPN*). Tunnel mode is also required any time a *security gateway* (a device offering IPsec services to other systems) is involved at either end of an IPsec transmission. Two security gateways must always communicate by tunneling IP packets inside IPsec packets; the same goes for an individual host communicating with a security gateway. This occurs any time a mobile laptop user logs into a corporate VPN from the road, for example.

Tunneling, shown in Figure 26–3, allows two systems to set up SAes to enable secure communications over the internet. Network traffic originates on one system, is encrypted and/or signed, and is then sent to the destination system. On receipt, the datagram is decrypted or authenticated,

Figure 26–3: A pair of hosts using IPsec to communicate transparently, across the internet.

and the payload is passed along up the receiving system's network stack, where it is finally processed by the application using the data. This is a *transparent mode* use of security associations, because the two hosts could be communicating just as easily without security headers—and because the actual IP headers of the datagrams must be exposed to allow them to be routed across the internet.

An SA can also be used to tunnel secure IP through an internetwork. Figure 26–4 shows how this works. All IP packets from system A are forwarded to the security gateway X, which creates an IP tunnel through the Internet to security gateway Y, which unwraps the tunneled packets and forwards them. Security gateway Y might forward those packets to any of the hosts (B, C, or D) within its own local intranet, or it could forward them to an external host, like M. It all depends on where the originating host directs those packets. Whenever an SA destination node is a security gateway, it is by definition a tunneled association. In other words, tunneling can be done between two security gateways (as shown in Figure 26–4), or it can be done between a regular node and a security gateway. Thus, host M could create a tunneled connection with either security gateway, X or Y.

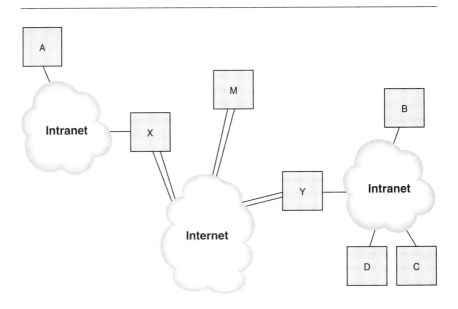

Figure 26–4: IP security tunneling.

It is tunneled by virtue of the fact that datagrams sent from M are passed first to the security gateway, which then forwards them appropriately after decrypting or authenticating.

26.5.4 ENCAPSULATING SECURITY PAYLOAD (ESP)

Specified in RFC 2406, "IP Encapsulating Security Payload (ESP)," the ESP header allows IP nodes to exchange datagrams whose payloads are encrypted. The ESP header is designed to provide several different services (some overlapping with the authentication header), including:

- Confidentiality of datagrams through encryption.
- Authentication of data origin through the use of public key encryption.
- *Antireplay services* through the same sequence number mechanism as provided by the authentication header.
- Limited traffic flow confidentiality through the use of security gateways.

The ESP header can be used in conjunction with an authentication header. In fact, unless the ESP header uses some mechanism for authentication, it is recommended that the authentication header be used with the ESP header.

The ESP header must follow any headers that need to be processed by nodes intermediate to the destination node—all data that follows the ESP header will be encrypted, with the encrypted payload beginning directly after the last ESP header field (see below).

ESP can be used in tunnel or transport mode, similar to the authentication header. In transport mode, the IP header and any hop-by-hop, routing, or fragmentation extension headers precede the authentication header (if present), followed by the ESP header. Any destination options headers can either precede or follow the ESP header, or even both; any headers that follow the ESP header are encrypted.

The result appears, in many respects, to simply be a regular IP datagram transmitted from source to destination, with an encrypted payload. This use of ESP in transport mode is appropriate in some cases, but it allows attackers to study traffic between the two nodes, noting which nodes are communicating, how much data they exchange, when they exchange it, and so forth. All this information may potentially provide the attacker with some information that helps defeat the communicating parties.

An alternative is to use a security gateway, much as described above for the authentication header. A security gateway can operate directly with a node or can link to another security gateway. A single node can use ESP in tunnel mode by encrypting all outbound packets and encapsulating them in a separate stream of IP datagrams that are sent to the security gateway. That gateway then can decrypt the traffic and resend the original datagrams to their destinations.

When tunneling, the ESP header encapsulates the entire tunneled IP datagram and is an extension to the IP header directing that datagram to a security gateway. It is also possible to combine ESP headers with authentication headers in several different ways; for example, the tunneled datagram may have a transport-mode authentication header.

The ESP header format is shown in below (taken from RFC 2406).

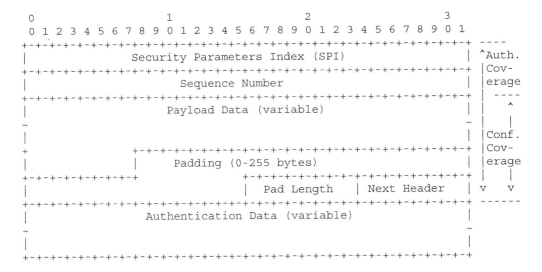

The ESP header includes the Next Header field, which appears near the end of the ESP header and indicates the presence (and identity) of any other headers (such as AH) that may follow. The rest of the ESP header consists of the following:

Security Parameters Index (SPI): This is the same 32-bit value referred to in the section on the authentication header. This value is used by the communicating nodes to refer to a security association, which can be used to determine how the data should be encrypted.

Sequence Number: This 32-bit value is set to zero to start and is incremented by one with each datagram sent. As described above for the authentication header, the sequence number can be used to protect against replay attacks, and a new security association must be set up before this value cycles through all 2^{32} values.

Payload Data: This is a variable length field and actually contains the encrypted portion of the datagram, along with any supplementary data necessary for the encryption algorithm (e.g., initialization data). The payload begins with an *initialization vector*, a value that must be sent in plaintext; encryption algorithms need this value to decrypt the protected data.

Padding: The encrypted portion of the header (the payload) must end on the appropriate boundary, so padding may be necessary.

Padding Length: This field indicates how much padding has been added to the payload data.

Next Header: This field operates as it normally does with other IPv6 extension headers; it just appears near the end of the header rather than at the beginning.

Authentication Data: This is an *Integrity Check Value* (*ICV*), calculated on the entire ESP header (except for the authentication data). This authentication calculation is optional. The ICV is discussed at greater length below.

26.5.5 AUTHENTICATION HEADER

The authentication header can be used to do the following:

- Provide strong integrity services for IP datagrams, which means the AH can be used to carry content verification data for the IP datagram.
- Provide strong authentication for IP datagrams, which means that the AH can be used to link an entity with the contents of the datagram.

- Provide nonrepudiation for IP datagrams, assuming that a public key digital signature algorithm is used for integrity services.
- Protect against replay attacks through the use of the sequence number field.

The authentication header can be used in tunnel mode or in transport mode, which means that it can be used to authenticate and protect simple, direct datagram transfers between two nodes, or it can be used to encapsulate an entire stream of datagrams that is sent to or from a security gateway.

AH is specified in RFC 2402, "IP Authentication Header," and the header is shown below (taken from RFC 2402):

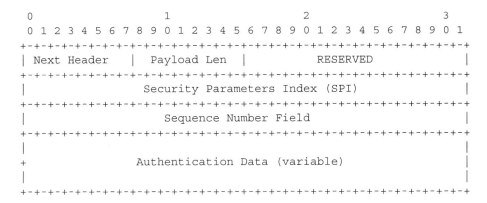

In transport mode, the authentication header protects the payload of the original IP datagram as well as the parts of the IP header that do not change from hop to hop (e.g., the hop limit field or routing headers). Figure 26–5 shows what happens to a transport-mode IP datagram as the authentication header is calculated and added to it (the destination options header may also appear before the authentication header). The destination IP address and extension headers are protected only insofar as they do not change from hop to hop.

When the authentication header is used in tunnel mode, however, it is used differently. Figure 26–6 shows the difference. The original destination IP address, along with the entire original IP datagram, is encapsulated into an entirely new IP datagram that is sent to the security gateway. Thus, the entire original IP datagram is fully protected, as are the portions of the encapsulating IP headers that don't change.

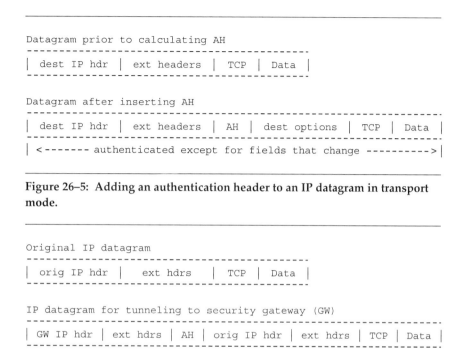

```
Datagram prior to calculating AH
---------------------------------------------
|  dest IP hdr  |  ext headers  |  TCP  |  Data  |
---------------------------------------------

Datagram after inserting AH
----------------------------------------------------------------
|  dest IP hdr  |  ext headers  |  AH  |  dest options  |  TCP  |  Data  |
----------------------------------------------------------------
| <------- authenticated except for fields that change ---------->|
```

Figure 26–5: Adding an authentication header to an IP datagram in transport mode.

```
Original IP datagram
---------------------------------------------
|  orig IP hdr  |    ext hdrs    |  TCP  |  Data  |
---------------------------------------------

IP datagram for tunneling to security gateway (GW)
----------------------------------------------------------------
|  GW IP hdr  |  ext hdrs  |  AH  |  orig IP hdr  |  ext hdrs  |  TCP  |  Data  |
----------------------------------------------------------------
```

Figure 26–6: Adding an authentication header to an IP datagram in tunnel mode.

AH header fields include:

Payload length: This eight-bit field indicates the entire length of the authentication header in units of 32-bit words, minus two. As originally defined, the authentication header consisted of 64-bits of header with the rest devoted to authentication data (see the following). Thus, the payload length field merely indicated the length (in 32-bit words) of the authentication data. With the addition of the sequence number field (see the following), this value now equals the length of the authentication data plus the length of the sequence number field.

Reserved: The next 16 bits are reserved for future use; at present, they must be set to all zeros.

Security Parameters Index (SPI): This 32-bit value is an arbitrary number. Together with the destination IP address and security protocol (in this case, AH to indicate the authentication header), the SPI uniquely identifies the security association to be used for the authentication header. An SPI value of zero is for local use only and should never be transmitted; values from 1 through 255 are reserved by the Internet Assigned Numbers Authority (IANA) for future use.

Sequence Number: This 32-bit value is a mandatory counter; it is also included by the sender, though it may not always be used by the recipient. Starting from zero, this counter is incremented with every datagram sent and is used to prevent replay attacks. When the recipient is using it for antireplay purposes, it will discard any datagrams that duplicate a sequence number that has already been received. This means that when the counter is ready to cycle through (when 2^{32} datagrams have been received), a new security association must be negotiated—otherwise, the receiving system will discard all datagrams once the counter is reset.

Authentication Data: This field contains the Integrity Check Value (ICV), which is the heart of the authentication header. The contents must be a multiple of 32 bits in length and may contain padding to attain that length. Calculation of this value is discussed in the next section.

26.5.6   CALCULATING THE INTEGRITY CHECK VALUE

The Authentication Data fields in the AH and ESP headers are variable-length fields, each of which contains an Integrity Check Value (ICV). The field is variable length to accommodate variations from ICV algorithms, and the length is specified by the selected function. This is an optional field: it is included only when an authentication service is in use for the SA that corresponds to the header, and information about the ICV function in use is maintained along with the rest of the SA data.

The ICV calculation is a bit tricky in that some of the data being authenticated may be modified en route, such as IP header hop counts. According to RFC 2402 the AH ICV is computed on the IP header fields that either don't change in transit or whose values on arrival can be predicted, the AH header itself (though the authentication data field is set to 0 for the calculation), and the upper level protocol data that is being authenticated (this is assumed to be unchanged in transit).

The ESP ICV, according to RFC 2406, is computed on the entire ESP packet, excluding the Authentication Data field. This includes the SPI, Sequence Number, Payload Data, Padding (if present), Pad Length, and Next Header; the last 4 fields will be in ciphertext form, since encryption is performed prior to authentication.

Suggested algorithms for ICV include:

> **Message Authentication Codes (MACs),** the result of which are then encrypted with an appropriate symmetric encryption algorithm (e.g., AES)
> **Secure hash functions,** such as MD5 or SHA-1 (an updated version of SHA).

To comply with the standard, implementations must support MD5 and SHA-1 keyed hashing, at least.

26.5.7   IPSEC HEADERS IN ACTION

IPsec security services are provided through the AH and ESP header in conjunction, of course, with appropriate and relevant key management protocols. The AH protocol is specified in RFC 2402, "IP Authentication Header;" ESP is specified in RFC 2406, "IP Encapsulating Security Payload (ESP)."

Either security header may be used by itself, or both may be used together in various combinations of transport or tunnel modes. When used together with AH encapsulating ESP, packet authentication can be checked prior to decrypting the ESP header payload. These headers can also be nested when using IPsec tunneling: an originating node can encrypt and digitally sign a packet, then send it to the local security gateway. That gateway may then re-encrypt and re-sign the packet as it sends it off to another security gateway.

The ESP and AH authentication services are slightly different: ESP authentication services are ordinarily provided only on the packet payload, while AH authenticates almost the entire packet including headers.

The Sequence Number field is mandatory for all AH and ESP headers and is used to provide anti-replay services. Every time a new packet is sent, the Sequence Number is increased by one (the first packet sent with a given SA will have a Sequence Number of 1).

When the receiving host elects to use the anti-replay service for a particular SA, the host checks the Sequence Number: if it receives a packet with a sequence number value that it has already received, that packet is discarded.

The authentication data field contains whatever data is required by the authentication mechanisms specified for that particular SA to authenticate the packet. The ICV may contain a keyed Message Authentication Code (MAC) based on a symmetric encryption algorithm (such as AES or Triple-DES) or a one-way hash function such as MD5 or SHA-1.

The most obvious difference between ESP and AH is that the ESP header's Next Header field appears at the end of the security payload. Of course, since the header may be encapsulating an encrypted payload, you don't need to know what next header to expect until after you've decrypted the payload—thus, the ESP Next Header field is placed after rather than before the payload.

ESP's authentication service covers only the payload itself, not the IP headers of its own packet as with the Authentication Header. And the confidentiality service covers only the payload itself; obviously, you can't encrypt the IP headers of the packet intended to deliver the payload and still expect any intermediate routers to be able to process the packet. Of course, if you're using tunneling, you can encrypt everything, but only everything in the tunneled packet itself.

26.6   Implementing and Deploying IPsec

IP layer security protects IP datagrams. It does not necessarily have to involve the user or any applications. This means users may be merrily using all of their applications without ever being aware that all their datagrams are being encrypted or authenticated before being sent out to the internet (of course, that situation will only occur as long as all the encrypted datagrams are properly decrypted by hosts at the other end).

As a result, one question that comes up is how to implement IPsec. RFC 2401 suggests several strategies for implementing IPsec in a host or in conjunction with a router or firewall:

Integrated implementation. Integrate IPsec into the native IP implemen-
    tation. This approach is probably the best, but also the most difficult,
    as it requires rewriting the native IP implementation to include
    support for IPsec. Integrating IPsec into the IP stack adds security
    natively and makes it an integral part of any IP implementation.
    However, it also requires that the entire stack be updated to reflect
    the changes.

"Bump-in-the-stack" (BITS). Implement IPsec "beneath" the IP stack and
    above the local network drivers. The IPsec implementation monitors
    IP traffic as it is sent or received over the local link, and IPsec functions
    are performed on the packets before passing them up or down the
    stack. This works reasonably well for individual hosts doing IPsec.

    This approach inserts special IPsec code into the network stack just
    below the existing IP network software and just above the local link
    software. In other words, this approach implements security through
    a piece of software that intercepts datagrams being passed from the
    existing IP stack to the local link layer interface. This software then
    does the necessary security processing for those datagrams and hands
    them off to the link layer. This approach can be used to upgrade sys-
    tems to IPsec support without requiring that their IP stack software
    be rewritten.

"Bump-in-the-wire" (BITW). Implement IPsec in a hardware crypto-
    graphic processor. The crypto processor gets its own IP address;
    when used for individual hosts, the bump-in-the-wire acts much like
    a BITS implementation, but when the same processor provides IPsec
    services to a router or firewall, it must behave as a security gateway—
    meaning that it must do IPsec security protocols in tunnel mode.

    This approach uses external cryptographic hardware to perform
    the security processing. The device is usually an IP device that acts
    as a sort of a router or, more accurately, security gateway for all IP
    datagrams from any system that sits behind it. When such a device is
    used for a single host, it works very much like the BITS approach, but
    implementation can be more complex when a single BITW device is
    used to screen more than one system.

These options differ more in terms of where they are appropriate than
in subjective terms. Applications that require high levels of security may

be better served with a hardware implementation. Applications run on systems for which new IPsec-compliant network stacks are not available may be better served by the BITS approach.

26.7   Chapter Summary

Network security is probably the subject of as many books and chapters within technical books as IP; this chapter provides a concise introduction to IP security issues and security goals, starting with the definition of the challenges facing security managers and the tools at their disposal. IPsec provides authentication services through the use of public key encryption, digital signature, and secure hashing tools; it provides privacy services through the use of public and secret key encryption as well.

On top of these cryptographic tools, however, IPsec requires additional protocols to handle the secure and verifiable distribution and management of encryption keys. IPsec combines these cryptographic and security protocols with IP, using security associations to link packets with hosts and a pair of optional IP security headers (ESP and AH) to transmit IP packets securely.

IPsec is often linked to the subject of the next chapter, IPv6, because while IPsec support in IPv4 is optional, it is mandatory for all IPv6-capable hosts. Although some cite "security" as a reason to prefer IPv6 over IPv4, as we'll see, there are better reasons to migrate to the next generation of IP.

27

Next Generation IP: IPv6

This chapter introduces the Internet Protocol version 6 (IPv6), the update to IPv4, starting with an overview of IPv6 features and functions and the new IPv6 protocol header and header extensions, an overview of the IPv6 address architecture, and a discussion of the transition from IPv4 to IPv6.

This chapter introduces IPv6, but is far from exhaustive. The interested reader is urged to read the relevant RFCs as well as *IPv6 Clearly Explained* (Morgan Kaufmann 2003) for more information about how IPv6 works.

27.1   Why IPv6?

With IPv4, IP addresses are unique and usually persistent identifiers of all nodes on IP networks. That view of IP addresses has been changing: it may not be necessary or efficient to allocate network and node addresses as we have been doing for the past 20 years. There is no question that the IPv4 address space is being depleted; this has been clear since the late 1980s, when work started on the IP Next Generation (IPng) project.

At first, the primary objective for the IPng working group was to come up with a way to extend the IP address space so that it could support more networks and more hosts. However, it soon became clear that any modification to IP to accommodate more hosts would require an update to every node's IP networking software, and if an upgrade of that magnitude was being undertaken, the reasoning went, why not do a true upgrade to IP? Fix not just the address space problem, but also the other problems, big and little, that have become apparent after 20 years of deployment. And while were at it, why not enhance the protocol as well?

It turns out that the address space squeeze was amenable to a variety of short-term fixes such as network address translation (NAT) and Classless InterDomain Routing (CIDR). However, the way IPv4 routing is done, combined with the growth of the number of discrete IP routes, has posed an even greater danger to the growth of the internet. Backbone routers must store all IP routes in order to forward datagrams anywhere in the internet. As the number of routes continues to grow, it becomes more and more difficult for routers to forward packets efficiently as they must look up routes on larger and larger routing tables.

The IPng working group published their first specifications for IPv6 as standards track RFCs in late 1995: RFC 1883 decribed the protocol itself, and RFC 1884 described the IPv6 address architecture. By the end of 1998 a second wave of revised specifications was published, describing draft standards for IPv6 and related protocols. Some networking vendors have been working on IPv6 implementations since the early 1990s, and commercial implementations are available from leading vendors like 3Com and Hitachi. As issues related to IPv4 address space and other shortcomings cause increasing problems and anxiety, IPv6 deployment will grow. By design, IPv6 can coexist with IPv4, so there is no need to mandate a cutover date when all systems on the internet must support the new protocol.

The internet protocol as we know it was designed during the late 1970s, when it seemed that a 32-bit address space—permitting an absolute maximum of 2^{32} (4,294,967,296) hosts—would be more than enough to address all the hosts connected to the Internet for the foreseeable future. For one thing, IP was still very much an experimental technology, of interest almost exclusively to academics and researchers. For another, the idea of ubiquitous networked personal computers was many years in the future.

IPv6 addresses are four times as long as IPv4 addresses, and at 128 bits provide an absolute maximum of $2^{128^{64}}$ individual hosts. This is very roughly 340 billion billion billion billion different hosts! Even if every human now living were to have a personal network, with a billion nodes on each network, the IPv6 address space is large enough to support (at least theoretically) roughly another 50 billion billion similarly wired planets.

27.1.1 WHATS NEW IN IPv6

IPv6 improves on IPv4 in five important areas:

Expanded addressing: Based on projections made as early as the late 1980s, the IPv4 address space would have been depleted by the early to mid 1990s without numerous stopgap measures such as network address translation (NAT) and Classless InterDomain Routing (CIDR). The IPv6 address space should be sufficient to accommodate all network growth for the foreseeable future.

Simplified header format: In practice, the IPv4 header was found to be more complicated than necessary and susceptible to improvement in ways that could improve routing efficiency as well as the overall performance of attached systems.

Improved extension and option support: Header extensions and options in IPv4 required treating datagrams as special cases, thus hampering the ability of routers to process those datagrams efficiently. A design goal of IPv6 was to improve the way header extensions and options are implemented so that they don't affect network and routing performance.

Flow labeling: Although IP is a connectionless, unreliable protocol, some applications suffer unless they can depend on the network to treat their data flows with some degree of predictability. Flow labeling provides a mechanism by which related packets can be treated as streams, improving the way IP works as a transport for real-time multimedia applications.

Authentication and privacy: In its original incarnation as a research project, IPv4 delegated security issues to higher layer protocols. From the start IPv6 was intended to incorporate security features to make it a desirable option for business and other types of users who need assurance that the information they send is received only by authorized entities, unchanged, and unseen by unauthorized entities.

The original IPng working group charter, approved by the Internet Architecture Board (IAB) in 1991, mandated most of these areas of concern.

27.1.2   IPv6 Addressing

The IPv4 address space is inefficient for most networks. Although with 32 bits, over four billion individual nodes could, in theory, be addressed, the way the address space is organized means that the actual number of nodes and networks possible is considerably lower. The 126 possible Class A networks use up almost half of the entire IPv4 address space; Class B networks use up one quarter, and Class C networks make up only one eighth of the space. Just increasing the number of bits in the address field goes a long way toward improving the situation, but is not sufficient to solve the problem for the long term.

IPv6 addresses are 128 bits long, but in addition to moving from a 32-bit address space to a 128-bit address space, the IPv6 addressing architecture makes some adjustments to the different types of addresses available to an IP host. IPv6 eliminates broadcast addresses but adds the concept of anycast addresses. Unicast addresses, specifying a single network interface, and multicast addresses, specifying an address to which one or more hosts may be listening, continue basically unchanged from their IPv4 incarnations. IPv6 addresses will be discussed in more detail later in this chapter.

27.1.3   Header Simplification

IPv6 headers contain eight fields, and all IPv6 headers are exactly 40 octets long. IPv4 headers contain at least 12 different fields and may be as short as 20 octets with no options or as long as 60 octets with options. By making all headers the same length, routers can process the datagrams more efficiently. Figure 27–1 shows the IPv6 header.

The IPv6 header is simplified partly because the protocol has been simplified. With all headers the same length, the header length field can be eliminated. Intermediate routers are not allowed to do packet fragmentation in IPv6 fragmentation is available only on an end-to-end basis as an option, so

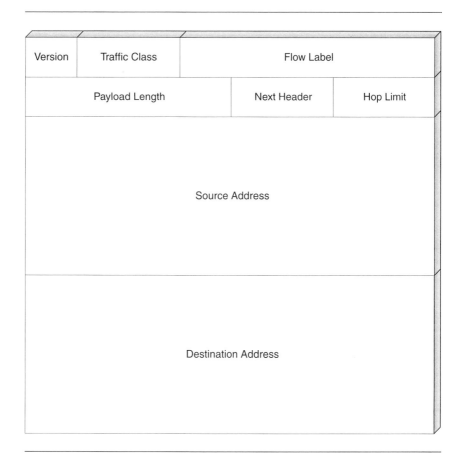

Version	Traffic Class	Flow Label	
Payload Length		Next Header	Hop Limit

Source Address

Destination Address

Figure 27–1: The IPv6 header fields are considerably simpler than the IPv4 header fields as shown in Figure 19–3.

all the header fields related to fragmentation have been removed from the IPv6 header. Finally, the IP header checksum has been removed from IPv6.

27.1.4 HEADER EXTENSION AND IPv6 OPTIONS

Unlike IPv4, in which options are appended as part of the IP header, IPv6 adds options in separate extension headers. This way routers not involved in processing the extension headers can ignore them and treat the datagram just like any other datagram.

As previously mentioned, IPv6 doesn't allow intermediate routers to fragment packets. Communicating nodes may decide they want to fragment packets on an end-to-end basis, in which case fragmentation information is carried in a fragmentation header extension. Routers don't bother with that header; they just process the datagram based on the IPv6 header. The source node does the fragmentation, putting fragmentation information into the header extension; that extension is processed only by the node at the receiving end.

Now consider a hop-by-hop option extension header specifying something that must be done by the router every time the packet is forwarded. This option requires that every node along the packets route process that extension header. Every router in the datagrams path has to process the hop-by-hop option as well as the main IPv6 header. The first such hop-by-hop option is defined for handling extra-large IP packets (jumbo payloads). Packets with jumbo payloads (over 65,535 octets) require special treatment because not all links will be capable of handling such large size transmission units, and routers want to avoid attempting to send them out on networks that cannot handle them. Thus, it is necessary for the option to be checked at every node the packet traverses.

27.1.5 FLOWS

In IPv4, all packets are treated roughly equally, which means each is handled on its own by intermediate routers. Routers do not keep track of packets sent between any two hosts so they can remember how to handle future packets. IPv6 implements the concept of the flow, which is, according to RFC 2460, a sequence of packets sent from a particular source to a particular (unicast or multicast) destination for which the source desires special handling by the intervening routers.

Routers keep track of flows by storing some flow information that persists from datagram to datagram within the flow. In this way the router can handle all datagrams in the flow similarly.

27.1.6 AUTHENTICATION AND PRIVACY

As already covered in the previous chapter, IPsec is a mandatory part of IPv6. Although IPv6 advocates often cite improved security as a benefit to the new protocol, the same security benefits are available to all IPv4 implementations as an option.

27.2   IPv6 Datagram Headers

The IPv6 protocol specifies the following fields for its header:

Version: A 4-bit value which for IPv6 must be equal to 6.

Traffic Class: This 8-bit value specifies what, if any, form of differentiated service is to be provided for the packet. Use of this field is defined separately from IPv6; see RFC 2474 for more about differentiated services. The default value for this field is all zeros.

Flow label: This 20-bit value identifies packets that belong to the same flow. A node can be the source for more than one simultaneous flow. The flow label and the address of the source node uniquely identify flows.

Payload length: This 16-bit field contains an integer value equal to the length of the packet payload in octets; that is, the number of octets contained in the packet after the end of the IPv6 header. IPv6 extensions are included as part of the payload for the purposes of calculating this field.

Next header: This field indicates what protocol is in use in the header immediately following the IPv6 packet. Similar to the IPv4 protocol field, the next header field may refer to a higher layer protocol like TCP or UDP, but it may also indicate an IPv6 extension header.

Hop limit: Every time a node forwards a packet, it decrements this eight-bit field by one. If the hop limit reaches zero, the packet is discarded. Unlike in IPv4, where the time-to-live field fulfills a similar purpose, sentiment is currently against putting a protocol-defined upper limit on packet lifetime for IPv6. This means that the function of timing-out old data should be accomplished in upper layer protocols.

Source address: This is the 128-bit address of the node originating the IPv6 packet.

Destination address: This is the 128-bit address of the intended recipient of the IPv6 packet. This address may be a unicast, multicast, or anycast address. If a routing extension is being used (which specifies a particular route that the packet must traverse), the destination address may be one of those intermediate nodes instead of the ultimate destination node.

It is instructive to compare the IPv4 header fields (in Figure 19–3) with the IPv6 header fields (in Figure 27–1). Although several of the fields are similar for both protocols, the only field entirely unchanged is the version field. The version field must remain the same for IPv6 to be backward compatible with IPv4. The next IPv4 field, header length, is irrelevant to IPv6 because all IPv6 headers are the same length; IPv4 requires this field because its headers can be as short as 20 octets and as long as 60 octets.

The IPv4 Type of Service (ToS) field is similar to the IPv6 traffic class field, but ToS is positioned later in the header than that field and it also has not found wide acceptance from implementers. The IPv4 datagram length field evolved into the payload length field in IPv6. The IPv6 payload length includes extension headers, whereas the IPv4 datagram length field specifies the length of the entire datagram including headers. Routers can calculate the length of the IPv4 datagram payload by subtracting the header length from the datagram length; this calculation is unnecessary in IPv6.

The datagram identification, flags, and fragment offset fields in the IPv4 header all pertain to datagram fragmentation, and are therefore dispensed with in the IPv6 header.

The IPv4 time to live (TTL) field has become the IPv6 hop limit field. The IPv4 TTL value is an upper bound, in seconds, of the lifetime of a packet within the Internet cloud. When the TTL value reaches zero the packet is discarded. IPv4 specifies that routers decrement this value by the number of seconds it took from receipt of a packet until the packet was forwarded, but in practice most routers simply decrement this value by one rather than attempting to measure the actual time spent in the router. The hop limit field in IPv6 makes official this approach to limiting the lifetime of the datagram by hop count.

The IPv4 protocol field identifies the next-higher layer protocol, usually a transport layer protocol. This function is retained in the IPv6 next header field, which refers to the protocol of the next header, whether that header is an IPv6 extension header or a higher layer network protocol like UDP or TCP.

The IPv4 checksum was deemed unnecessary to IPv6 and dispensed with. After all, many data link layer protocols (like Ethernet) apply checksums in some form or another, TCP and UDP both use their own checksums, and more serious integrity checks are available through the IP security architecture headers.

Finally, the 32-bit IPv4 destination and source address fields have been expanded to 128 bits to accommodate IPv6 addresses.

27.3   IPv6 Options

IPv4 options, as described in Chapter 7, change the shape of the IP headers. This means that optioned packets must be treated as special cases by routers, which are usually optimized to handle standard datagrams. As a result, datagrams with options tend to be delivered more slowly not so much because they require special processing as because they tend to be shunted off to the side to be handled when the router is not busy forwarding normal packets. IPv6 extension headers should drastically reduce, if not eliminate, this kind of performance hit on packets that use options. Except for hop-by-hop options, which by definition must be processed by each forwarding router, options on IPv6 packets are hidden from intermediate routers and thus can have no affect on how the packets are forwarded. One of the benefits of IPv6 is that it simplifies the process of defining new options. So far, the following are the first options defined for IPv6 extension headers.

Hop-by-hop options header: This header always appears immediately after the main IPv6 header and contains optional data that every node on the packets path must examine. So far, two hop-by-hop options have been specified: the Jumbo payload option and the router alert option. The Jumbo payload option identifies the payload of the packet as being longer than 65,535 octets (including the hop-by-hop option header). If a router cannot forward the packet, it returns an ICMPv6 error message. The router alert option notifies routers that information inside the IPv6 datagram is intended to be viewed and processed by an intermediate router even though the datagram is addressed to some other node (e.g., control datagrams that contain information pertaining to bandwidth reservation protocols).

Routing header: This header causes the packet to visit specific nodes, specified in the header, on its route to its destination. The initial destination address of the IPv6 header is not the same as the ultimate destination of the packet, but rather the first address in the list contained in the routing header. When that node receives the packet, it processes the IPv6 header and the routing header and resends the packet to the second address listed in the routing header. This process continues until the packet reaches its ultimate destination.

Fragment header: The fragment header contains all the information about IP fragments that formerly would be stored in the main IPv4 header fields. This extension includes fields for a fragment offset, a More Fragments flag, and an identification field; it is used to allow a source node to fragment a packet too large for the path MTU between the source and the destination.

Destination options header: This header stands in for the IPv4 options field. At present, the only destination options specified are padding options to fill out the header on a 64-bit boundary if the (future) options require it. The destination options header is meant to carry information intended to be examined by the destination node.

Authentication header (AH): This header provides a mechanism for calculating a cryptographic checksum on some parts of the IPv6 header, extension headers, and payload.

Encapsulating Security Payload (ESP) header: This header will always be the last, unencrypted header of any packet. It indicates the rest of the payload is encrypted, and provides enough information for the authorized destination node to decrypt it.

27.4   IPv6 Addressing

The IPv6 addressing architecture is described in RFC 2373. There are several facets of IPv6 addressing that are important: the structure of the 128-bit IPv6 address representation, address architecture, address space structure, and the different types of IPv6 addresses: unicast, multicast, and anycast. Each of these is covered in this section.

27.4.1 IPv6 Address Representation

As explained in Chapter 2, IPv4 addresses are usually represented as a dot-delimited four-part series of values ranging from 0 to 255 (hexadecimal values of 00 through FF). IPv6 addresses, four times as long as IPv4 addresses, are not so easy to represent. The basic representation of an IPv6 address is of the form:

```
X:X:X:X:X:X:X:X
```

where X is a four-digit (16 bit) hexadecimal integer. Note that instead of being dot-delimited, IPv6 addresses are colon-delimited, for clarity. For example, the following are valid IPv6 addresses:

```
CDCD:910A:2222:5498:8475:1111:3900:2020

1030:0:0:0:C9B4:FF12:48AA:1A2B

2000:0:0:0:0:0:0:1
```

These are hexadecimal integers; decimal equivalents could also be used.

Some conventions have been designated to simplify IPv6 address representation. A series of zeros in an address can be collapsed, with a double-colon replacing the zeros. The last address shown in the preceding example would be represented as:

```
2000::1
```

In mixed IPv4/IPv6 environments, where some IPv6 addresses may encapsulate IPv4 addresses, those addresses can be represented in the form:

```
X:X:X:X:X:X:d.d.d.d
```

In these cases, the colon-delimited values are 16-bit integers (standard for IPv6 addresses), and the dot-delimited values are 8-bit integers (standard for IPv4 addresses). For example, the following is a valid IPv6 address, encapsulating an IPv4 address:

```
0:0:0:0:0:0:10.0.0.1
```

27.4.2   IPv6 Address Architecture

The IPv6 addressing model is similar to the IPv4 model: each address consists of two parts. The most significant bits of the address (those bits starting at the left of the address) represent the network to which the node is attached. The least significant bits of the address (those bits starting at the right of the address) represent the unique node connected to the network.

As in IPv4, the network portion of the IPv6 address is aggregatable. This is another way of saying that subnets are considered to be part of the parent network, and that to nodes outside of a subnetted network, all datagrams addressed anywhere within that network are forwarded to a single point. Consider a Class B network that has been subnetted. Routers inside that network need to be aware of routes for subnets, but routers outside that network need to know only one route for that network.

IPv4 network classes were a good idea, but the implementation turned out to be too rigid to accommodate the kind of growth in personal computers as well as networks that we've experienced since 1980. IPv6 addresses are designed to avoid the problems of running out of network node address space within networks as well as the problem of running out of organizational network addresses. At the same time, IPv6 addresses are all aggregatable, thus solving the problem of IP backbone routing.

A backbone router stores a single route for all nodes on a Class B network, no matter that there may be dozens or hundreds of subnets that are routed locally inside that network. IPv6 addresses are all aggregatable in a similar way.

IPv6 addresses are divided into two parts: the high-order 64 bits identify the network address, the low-order 64 bits identify the node. Each node address includes an interface identifier based on the IEEE EUI-64 format for interface identifiers. This format builds on existing MAC addresses to

```
| 3 |  13   | 8 |    24     |    16    |         64 bits          |
+--+-----+---+---------+---------+--------------------------+
|FP| TLA  |RES|   NLA    |   SLA    |       Interface ID       |
|  |  ID  |   |    ID    |    ID    |                          |
+--+-----+---+---------+---------+--------------------------+
```

Figure 27–2: The format for IPv6 global aggregatable unicast addresses, from RFC 2373.

create 64-bit interface identifiers that can be unique across a local or global scope.[1]

With 64-bit interface identifiers, as many as 2^{64} unique physical interfaces (about 18 billion billion) can be addressed on any given network. With 64-bit network addresses, the same number of different networks is possible.

So far, all IPv6 network addresses are specified to be aggregatable, either by network service provider or by some other basis. Whatever entity provides the network address block is also responsible for maintaining the network route. IPv6 unicast addresses take the form shown in Figure 27–2, and the fields designated within the address are described next.

The IPv6 unicast address is broken down into these fields:

FP: The format prefix is the 3-bit prefix to the IPv6 address that identifies where it belongs in the IPv6 address space (as shown in the IPv6 address map in Figure 27–3).

TLA ID: The top-level aggregation identifier contains the highest-level routing information of the address. This is the grossest level of routing information in the internetwork, and at 13 bits there can be no more than 8,192 different top-level routes.

The next 8 bits are reserved for future use. They may ultimately be used to expand the top-level or next-level aggregation ID fields.

NLA ID: The next-level aggregation identifier is 24 bits long, and is intended to be used by organizations that control top-level

---

[1]This IEEE standard is available at: standards.ieee.org/db/oui/tutorials/EUI64.html.

```
Allocation                           Prefix         Fraction of
                                     (binary)       Address Space
-----------------------------------  -------------  -------------
Reserved                             0000 0000      1/256
Unassigned                           0000 0001      1/256

Reserved for NSAP Allocation         0000 001       1/128
Reserved for IPX Allocation          0000 010       1/128

Unassigned                           0000 011       1/128
Unassigned                           0000 1         1/32
Unassigned                           0001           1/16

Aggregatable Global Unicast Addresses 001           1/8
Unassigned                           010            1/8
Unassigned                           011            1/8
Unassigned                           100            1/8
Unassigned                           110            1/8
Unassigned                                          1/8
                                     1110
Unassigned                           1111 0         1/16
Unassigned                           1111 10        1/32
Unassigned                           1111 110       1/64
Unassigned                           1111 1110 0    1/128
Unassigned                                          1/512
                                     1111 1110 10
Link-local Unicast Addresses         1111 1110 11   1/1024
Site-local Unicast Addresses                        1/1024

Multicast Addresses                  1111 1111      1/256
```

Figure 27–3: The allocation IPv6 addresses, from RFC 2373.

aggregation IDs to organize that address space. In other words, those organizations (probably to include large Internet service providers and others providing public network access) can carve that 24-bit field into their own addressing hierarchy. Such an entity might break itself down into 16 top-level routes (internal to the entity) by taking 4 bits for those routes and leave itself 20 bits of address space to allocate to other entities (likely to be smaller-scale, more local service providers). Those entities, in their turn, could also subdivide the space they are allocated in the same way, if there is enough room.

SLA ID: The site-level aggregation identifier is the address space given to organizations for their internal network structure. With 16 bits available, each organization can create its own internal hierarchical network structure using subnets in the same way they are used in IPv4. As many as 65,535 different subnets are available using all 16 bits as a flat address space. Using the first eight bits for higher-level routing within the organization would allow 255 high-level subnets, each of which has as many as 255 sub-subnets.

Interface ID: This 64-bit field contains a 64-bit value based on the IEEE EUI-64 interface ID discussed earlier.

Consider a host originating a packet outside the destinations top-level aggregation entity. The host forwards the packet to its local router, which examines the destination address. It immediately recognizes a foreign top-level aggregation entity, so it can forward that packet to the route designated for all packets sent to that entity. It works similarly to postal services: consider a letter originating in Australia with a destination in the United States. The sender drops the letter off at a post office in Adelaide, where it is sorted because it is addressed to the United States, it will probably be put in a sack with other letters intended for that part of the world. The local postal authorities don't worry too much about the rest of the address.

Datagrams that originate within the same top-level aggregation entity (or letters that originate within the same country) get forwarded based on what the next-level aggregation entity is. A letter originating in Zurich with a destination in Berne does not leave Switzerland.

With aggregation, no router—not even a backbone router—needs to know every route on the internet. Each router needs to know detailed routes only within its own aggregation entity; outside the entity, the router needs to know only default routes to each other aggregation entity at the same level. Backbone routers can manage with no more than 8,192 routes; reports in 1998 have put the number of routes some backbone routers were storing at over 130,000. Although the 24-bit section of the address devoted to the next-level aggregation entity might seem to permit over 16 million (2^{24}) routes, in practice that section will almost certainly be subject to its own aggregation, as mentioned earlier.

27.4.3   IPv6 Address Space Structure

Figure 27–3 shows how the IPv6 address space is allocated. A similar break-down for IPv4 would be considerably simpler and would tell the story of inefficient address allocation. Fully one half of all IPv4 addresses are Class A addresses and largely underused. One fourth are Class B, and only one eighth are Class C addresses. Class D (multicast) addresses take up one sixteenth of the address space, and the rest is either reserved or unassigned.

By contrast, only one eighth of the IPv6 address space is allocated to aggregatable unicast addresses; the vast majority of the IPv6 address space is left unassigned. Of course, this approach leaves plenty of slack in the event that the internet and IP continue their rapid growth for the next 20 years. The new address space can accommodate all foreseen and perhaps even any imaginable growth for the foreseeable future.

Two important allocations are for link-local and site-local unicast addresses. In IPv4, the private network allocations used for network address translation (NAT) give organizations an option for setting up networks with whatever type of network address they want datagrams sent on those networks are not supposed to be forwarded outside the private network. These addresses were added more as an after thought, however, than as part of the original design of IPv4.

In IPv6, link-local and site-local unicast addresses are designed to function almost like private network addresses. However, there are some big differences. Link-local addresses are intended to stay on the physical network link they are not to be forwarded off the link. Site-local addresses can be forwarded throughout the organizational site but not out to the public internet.

Unlike NAT addresses, all IPv6 networks and nodes support link-local and site-local addressing. You could use the site-local address range to enumerate an entire organizational network, but one important purpose of these addresses is to help nodes that haven't yet been configured for their correct IP network address to locate various services on the link or site level.

27.4.4   IPv6 Address Types

IPv6 supports three types of addressing: unicast, multicast, and anycast. Unicast and multicast work much the same as they do in IPv4; broadcasts are not supported in IPv6. The unicast address is defined as an identifier for a single network interface. When a datagram is addressed to that unicast address, it is delivered to the interface identified by that address.

A multicast address is defined as an identifier for a set of one or more interfaces. When a datagram is sent to a multicast address, it is delivered to all the interfaces associated with that address.

An anycast address is, like a multicast address, defined as an identifier for a set of one or more interfaces. Unlike multicast, datagrams sent to an anycast address are delivered to only one of the interfaces identified by that address. The datagram is supposed to be delivered to the nearest interface, as defined by a measure of the distance of the receiving node from the sender.

An important use of anycast addresses is for stateless autoconfiguration. Standard anycast addresses are defined for functional categories like domain name servers and time servers. When a node needs one of these services, it can send out an anycast datagram, and it will get a response from the closest server rather than from all servers within earshot of the node.

27.5   Migrating to IPv6

It was IPv4's success that made an upgrade necessary, which means that there is a significant installed base of users to upgrade. Keeping the transition orderly was a major objective of the entire IPng program, and there are no plans for a cutover date when IPv6 would be turned on and IPv4 turned off.

The strategy chosen for the upgrade is to deploy the IPv6 protocol stack in parallel with IPv4. In other words, hosts that upgrade to IPv6 will continue to exist as IPv4 hosts at the same time. An experimental IPv6 backbone, or 6bone, has been set up to handle IPv6 internet traffic in parallel with the regular Internet. Such hosts will continue to have 32-bit IPv4 addresses but will add 128-bit IPv6 addresses. By 1999, hundreds of networks were linked to the 6bone.

The transition can be achieved through two approaches: protocol tunneling or IPv4/IPv6 dual stack.

27.5.1   PROTOCOL TUNNELING

One strategy that will help facilitate the growth of the IPv6 internet is protocol tunneling. Hosts on IPv6 intranets can interoperate fine on their own network, but if the intranets are connected to the internet only through an IPv4 route, they cannot link to other IPv6 hosts via IPv6. The answer is to allow tunneling: the IPv6 packets are encapsulated within IPv4 packets and forwarded across the internet to a router that can strip off the IPv4 headers and forward the IPv6 packets to their destination.

Likewise, hosts can operate on IPv4 intranets and be connected to the IPv6 internet through a router. Data from those hosts could be encapsulated within IPv6 packets by the router and forwarded across the IPv6 internet to a router that would strip off the IPv6 headers and forward the IPv4 packets to their destination.

Another possibility that is neither encouraged nor discouraged by the authors of the IPv6 protocol is the use of protocol translators. These take IPv6 packets and convert them to IPv4 packets, and vice versa.

The IPv6 tunneling approach makes it possible for isolated IPv6 islands to interoperate with each other across seas of IPv4 networks.

27.5.2   IPv4/IPv6 Dual Stack

Any node can run both IPv4 and IPv6 network stacks simultaneously. In this way, the node can send and receive both IPv4 and IPv6 packets. This approach makes possible heterogenous networks where both IPv4 and IPv6 coexist on the same network infrastructure. This makes it possible to deploy IPv6 on an organizational network without losing IPv4 connectivity for the nodes implementing IPv6.

27.6   Chapter Summary and References

In this chapter, we introduced the issues that made IPv6 necessary as well as the goals set for the next generation of the internet protocol. We looked first at why IPv6 was necessary, followed by an overview of the new features and functions available in IPv6.

We discussed the IPv6 protocol header fields, contrasting them with the IPv4 header fields. A discussion the IPv6 network addressing, including an overview of the IPv6 network address space, the architecture of IPv6 addresses, the address space allocation, and IPv6 address types including anycast, multicast, and unicast followed. We finished up with an introduction to the transition strategies used to migrate IPv4 populations to IPv6.

In Part VI, we look at some aspects of the practical side of networking with TCP/IP, starting with a look at the evolution of the FTP protocol and FTP implementations over the past decades.

Part Six

Practical Internetworking

28

The Evolution of File Transfer Protocol

Although the protocol-oriented details of FTP have already been covered in Chapter 12, there is a difference between the FTP protocol commands and ftp[1] application commands. Some of the protocol commands are similar to the application commands; for example, there is the RMD protocol command for removing a directory which matches the typical ftp application command `rmdir`.

The evolution of FTP implementations over the years has mirrored the evolution of many other types of end-user application. This brief look at the way FTP protocol commands and responses have been mapped onto end-user applications over the years should prove instructive to anyone interested in using network application protocols or building network

---

[1] In this chapter, "FTP" refers to the File Transfer Protocol, while "ftp" refers to a software implementation of FTP. File transfer programs that support FTP have traditionally been named "ftp." Fortunately, the confusion has been lessened since the acquisition of the company named "FTP Software" by NetManage, Inc.

applications using existing protocols. For reference while reading this chapter, FTP commands, ftp commands, and FTP response codes can be found in Chapter 12 and Appendix B.

28.1   Protocol and Applications Commands

One can imagine a very early version of ftp that accepted raw FTP protocol commands, although by the mid-1980s most versions of ftp had added some "user friendly" features such as slightly more intuitive commands, or new features. Consider the simple process of opening an FTP session. Using the raw protocol commands, several steps would be necessary:

1. Open a TCP session on port 21.
2. Wait for a positive response (reply code 220 "Server ready").
3. Send the USER command with a username.
4. Wait for a positive or intermediate response (if positive, the session requires no passphrase; in almost all cases, an intermediate reply of 331 "User name okay, need password" will follow).
5. Send the PASS command with a passphrase.
6. Wait for a positive response (230 "User logged in, proceed").
7. Send any other initialization commands (e.g., SYST to retrieve system information from the server) and wait for results.

Most command line ftp implementations allow you to open a session just by starting up the ftp program with a destination server name:

```
ftp ftp.example.net
```

All the required protocol commands are then exchanged automatically. Another way to get the same result would be to open ftp on the local host, and then (from an ftp command line) enter the open command:

```
ftp> open ftp.example.net
```

In either case, there is no need for the user to explicitly send every protocol command. Similarly, most FTP implementations include a "multiple get" command, usually called mget, for retrieving more than one file at a time.

Mget generally allows the use of wildcards to specify filenames to be downloaded:

```
ftp> mget *.txt
```

This command will retrieve all files in the current working directory that end with the extension .txt even though there is no corresponding FTP protocol command for retrieving more than one file at a time. FTP does provide a directory listing command that lists only file names in the current or specified directory: LIST. The output from LIST can be used as the basis for further sequences of operations, such as multiple file retrieval.

The mget command may use data already retrieved from the server (e.g., if the user has already requested a directory listing of the desired directory) to determine what files to request for download, one by one. If the data is not already available, the ftp client program will send a directory listing command on its own, specifying any desired wildcards, and use the results to send individual RETR commands to the server.

Likewise, FTP specifies a pair of commands to be used for renaming files; RNFR ("rename from," sent with the file's current name) and RNTO ("rename to," and sent with the new file name). Most versions of ftp collapse the two protocol commands into a single command, rename.

As has been discussed elsewhere, FTP provides specification for a protocol that allows end users, wherever they may be, to manipulate files on an FTP host. The goal for FTP was to reduce the complexity of managing files on any networked host—in effect, to make moving files to and/or from a remote host equivalent to moving files to and/or from any filesystem within the local host.

Thus, it should not be surprising that ftp programs written for systems running MS-DOS would use commands similar to MS-DOS commands such as dir and those written for *nix would use the ls command for the same function: listing directory contents of the current directory. If you could copy, rename, or delete files on your local host filesystem, doing the same functions on an FTP server from an FTP client would not likely be any more difficult.

28.2   Ease and/or Simplicity

Most internet development, including the design and testing of application protocols, began on *nix systems. As demand for TCP/IP applications grew in the mid-1980s, software publishers ported the network applications from *nix platforms to the MS-DOS platform with little or no change to the user interface. As a result, what would be fairly intuitive for a *nix user could baffle an MS-DOS user.

At about the same time, interest in graphical user interface (GUI) and "user friendliness" was increasing as personal computers were everywhere. Apple's Macintosh OS was followed by Microsoft's early forays with Windows, and other software vendors responded to customer demands. GUIs have long been viewed as easy to use for many reasons, largely because they free the casual user from having to learn often cryptic commands and keystroke combinations: accessing resources is as simple as pointing and clicking with the mouse, or choosing options from menus. Even nongraphical applications proclaimed their "user friendliness" based on their use of menus and submenus: casual users can read the options offered from each menu and then choose the one they need.

Unfortunately, many of the early versions of GUI/user friendly applications (in all areas, not just network applications) suffered from one or two serious problems. Menu-driven applications are user friendly only insofar as all the menu items are accurately and completely described for the user in terms that the user can comprehend. Cryptic commands attached to menu options are no easier to use than a command line interface with a list of valid commands.

Another common, and flawed, approach was to take applications already equipped with text-based menu interfaces and translate them, unchanged, into a GUI operating system (OS)-enabled application. Instead of unappealing text menus, the new application opens with a nice OS-compliant window and nifty looking pulldown menus—but the underlying application remains unchanged.

Meanwhile, programmers faced another challenge as they implemented FTP on new platforms: what exactly should the ftp program *do*? Was the goal to produce a version of ftp running on DOS (or Windows, MacOS, etc.) that behaved to the user in the same way that the original *nix versions do? Or should the new OS-based version of ftp adopt a user interface to the file transfer functions more in harmony with the OS?

In either case, any implementation would have to interoperate with any other implementation. A Macintosh version of an ftp client would have to be able to exchange files with an IBM MVS version of an ftp server. Interoperability between computers is clearly an absolute requirement—but the need for interoperability (or compatibility) between the users of different computers is less clear.

One reason to stick with cryptic commands and a text-based interface when implementing FTP on new platforms is to make the program easier to use for anyone who already knows how to use a version of ftp on another platform. To be more honest, however, one might suggest that early PC versions of ftp used the same (or almost the same) set of user commands (and interface) as that found on *nix systems mostly because the people who wanted to use ftp on a PC were already using ftp on some other system—most likely a *nix or similar system—and it would be easier to replicate that experience on the PC.

Only as the population of ftp users expanded to include users most comfortable with a mass market, user-friendly PC OS, did software publishers begin to modify their approach to Windows and Macintosh network file transfer applications. The change in approach meant acceptance of an approach to implementing FTP that emphasized the adaptation of the protocol to each platform rather than imposing a single approach to the protocol for all platforms. The resulting applications may not have maintained a uniform user interface, but they maintained the original philosophy of turning the network into an extension of the local system. If you can manage files locally, the local FTP implementation should make seamless the process of managing files remotely.

28.3 Mapping Protocols to Applications

Implementers must be able to map functions to protocol elements if they hope to make FTP (or any other application protocol, for that matter) seamless and transparent to the user. Protocol commands and responses are the elements that must be mapped to OS functions. Some FTP elements are more easily mapped than others.

Consider FTP response codes and their accompanying human-readable text. Many of these would simply confuse the typical user, while others carry useful information. The implementer must consider which responses are relevant and which are not; even then, decisions must be made as to how the information in those responses should be delivered to the user. Some GUI ftp clients offer users the option of displaying protocol interactions in a text window: when a file is copied, client commands (USER, PASS, RETR) appear in the window, accompanied by the server's responses (220 Server ready).

The requests and responses will always be important to the client and server software, but may not be relevant to the user. For example, users usually don't need to see responses indicating that a session has been initiated, or intermediate success messages during the transfer of many files. GUI clients may display progress with a progress bar or by having file icons appear in their destination window. Even the use of progress bars requires the use of protocol features: with a command line interface, a user may not check the size (or any other attributes) of files being downloaded, especially when many files are being transferred. A GUI version of ftp can provide this information by requesting a detailed directory listing for each file to be downloaded, and then calculate and display progress graphically to the user.

Similarly, FTP offers a small set of commands for managing files, just enough for a client to maneuver through a directory tree, copy files to and from that tree, and add or delete directories. Although there is no FTP protocol command for transferring more than one file at a time, the implementations make it possible for end users to believe that their local ftp client is capable of such transfers.

More to the point, application developers were far more likely to implement the mget and mput commands in newer GUI versions without changing them substantially. These versions allowed users to specify a wildcard template to indicate which files are to be transferred, but only with later versions would GUI-style selection of unrelated files be supported.

28.4   Command Line to Graphical User Interface

The evolution of FTP implementations from command line tools intended for use by system administrators and network engineers, to easy-to-use file management utilities took more than a decade to occur. The applications that use FTP have continued to evolve, just as the forms and functions of internet applications continue to evolve.

In less than a decade, the web grew from an academic experiment to a staple of daily home and work life for hundreds of millions of people and millions of businesses. Not only are there web server programs available for virtually any device capable of being networked, but one would be hard-pressed to find a commercial computer sold anywhere that did not incorporate hypertext transfer protocol (HTTP) client and server support. At the same time, FTP continues to carry a respectable share of internet traffic for a number of reasons:

1. It has always been used for certain functions, as long as anyone can remember.
2. Internet hosts are required to support it, per RFC 1123, "Requirements for Internet Hosts—Application and Support."
3. FTP client and server software is built on a foundation of over 30 years experience with FTP and related predecessor protocols, resulting in FTP implementations that might be considered more robust, secure, or reliable than HTTP servers.
4. Older hosts may not support HTTP.
5. Long-time FTP services may have become so institutionalized that removing them would cause failures of systems that rely on them for downloading information around the world.
6. Maintenance, backup, and administration of FTP servers and FTP sites may be less onerous than those same tasks for HTTP servers and sites.

At the same time, the end-user interface continues to improve as implementers learn to treat FTP not so much as its own special application but as a service that can be accessed by other applications. For example, web browsers can access files stored on FTP servers without burdening the user with logging in. The user may encounter a directory structure, but maneuvering is as simple as clicking on a file or directory name and letting the browser figure out what to do next. When properly configured, the browser will automatically download the file and open it in an appropriate application.

FTP may not be the best of all possible application protocols: the use of two separate channels for transfers and control provides an interesting approach that was in some ways ahead of its time yet at the same time significantly flawed. However, FTP works adequately and its ubiquity ensures survival for the foreseeable future.

28.5   Chapter Summary

As a product becomes easier to use, more people are willing to try it out. This applies to network application protocols as much as it does to auto-mobiles, video cassette recorders (VCRs), and mobile telephones. FTP, as one of the first application protocols designed for an interoperable inter-network, started out as a set of basic file management protocol commands; implementers have used those commands to create FTP implementations that have grown increasingly easy to use.

Early on, FTP programs required the use of commands that mirrored com-mand line file management on the host system; if you could manipulate files on that host, you could also manipulate files on that host from a remote host. Implementers were relatively slow to build appropriate GUIs for FTP, merely translating commands to pulldown menus at first. However, by the late 1990s, GUI FTP programs were available that could be easily, and transparently, used by non-expert users.

Most products change and improve over the years: automobiles no longer include a hand-cranked starter, mobile telephone service prices spiral downward as service billing grows simpler. FTP has not only become easier to use, but has also been modified to make it work more smoothly: hosts need not permit inbound connections from servers for downloads, for example. Likewise, some artifacts of less than great product features, such as the VCR's continuously flashing unset clock and FTP's support for proxy file transfers (see section 11.3), take longer to fix or replace.

Although many, if not most, of the applications for which FTP was impor-tant in 1983 are now performed with more modern protocols, newer tech-nologies rarely eradicate older ones entirely; just as the radio and motion picture industries were not destroyed by the introduction of television, they were forced to adapt to an environment in which people turned to newer technologies to meet their needs for entertainment and information.

The next chapter discusses some of the issues involved in planning and deploying IP networks.

29

Planning Internet Protocol Networks

With modern operating systems and hardware, building an internet protocol (IP) network can be as easy as putting together a few personal computers and a router/firewall and hooking them all together with a network hub or switch. The task is too insignificant, as in the case of most small office/home office (SOHO) networks, to take up an entire chapter; yet at the same time it is far too broad, as in the case of building an enterprise network, to even begin to cover in a single chapter.

Yet this chapter looks at some of the issues related to planning and/or building a smallish IP network that may not be covered in other books or articles. Well-planned networks support all sorts of organizational change, whether it be growth, reorganization, contraction, or anything else; they are easier to administer and manage; they are capable of enhancing an organization's effectiveness and efficiency. Poorly planned networks can become extremely costly in terms of both time and money.

Rather than summarizing the principles of network planning, this chapter provides some suggestions and tips—things to keep in mind when designing a network.

29.1   Problem Statement

In today's modern world, where all operating systems are TCP/IP capable right out of the box, building a small, functional, IP network requires little (if any) skill. The most difficult aspect of SOHO networking may be assembling the components and getting them plugged together properly.

As recently as 1995, setting up such a simple network could require considerable expense and expertise, with tasks that might include:

- Purchasing and installing network interface cards on every system to be networked.
- Purchasing and installing a local area network (LAN) hub.
- Purchasing and installing internet devices including router, firewall, and others.
- Purchasing and installing TCP/IP network protocol stack software on all hosts.
- Configuring and troubleshooting each host network configuration; this includes locating appropriate drivers for the network card, properly configuring network cards for use with software (operating system as well as TCP/IP stack), properly configuring IP options on host.

The expense of the hardware and software, combined with the difficulty of getting it all properly installed and configured, were considerable. Most of these difficulties have been eliminated or minimized:

- New computers are now typically delivered with Ethernet network interface cards; add-on cards for desktops can be had for as little as under $10, while even laptops can be outfitted with PCMCIA cards for under $40.
- Small hubs and switches, even for high-speed (100 Mbps) Ethernet, are widely available for under $100 (or less). Reasonably priced wireless network interfaces are also available; prices are higher than for wired cards, but costs for wiring are saved.

- Easily configured and inexpensive internet appliances are widely available, providing one or more functions including router, firewall, network address translation (NAT), virtual private network (VPN), web/mail/file/application server, web cache, DNS server, and DHCP server.
- Starting with Windows 95, Microsoft's operating systems all bundle support for TCP/IP. Apple's MacOS and OS X, all *nix systems, and any other commercial or open source OSes now all support TCP/IP as well.
- Newer hardware standards (including PCI and USB) allow plug-and-play installation of new hardware. Drivers may be necessary, but most operating systems automate the process of installation and configuration. Incorporation of TCP/IP support in current OSes means no need to use third-party drivers to configure the interface between the network interface and the protocol stack.

Although it is possible to put together a small TCP/IP network with little or no experience, building even a small network that is reliable, robust, secure, efficient, and fulfills all network requirements can still be challenging. System administration, router configuration, backbone design, and many other key topics are well-documented in a wide range of books and courses; some are vendor-specific, others are vendor-neutral, but the vast majority offer something of value to the network professional. Yet not all networks are designed by network professionals, and not all network design documentation is appropriate for novice network managers. Some of the aspects of network design discussed here include:

- What does "network architecture" really mean?
- What components are necessary for a stable, robust, and secure network?
- For which ongoing network tasks must resources be allocated?
- What services should a TCP/IP network offer to its users?
- What about security?

29.2 Network Architecture

The shape of a network can be considered the outward manifestation of the network's architecture. However, that shape goes much farther than

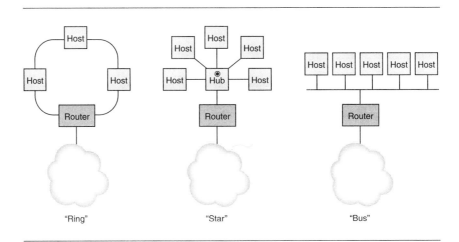

"Ring"   "Star"   "Bus"

Figure 29–1: Ring, star, and bus network architectures.

merely defining whether hosts are linked through a ring, star, or bus architecture (Figure 29–1). These characterizations have lost much of their relevance as existing technologies change and new ones appear. For example, most Ethernet networks in 1988 were based on a bus design, with hosts all connected directly to a single cable that would physically run the length of the area being networked. By 1998, most Ethernet networks used cables to link all nodes to a hub or switch, often with each of those links providing a dedicated Ethernet link between node and switch (rather than the shared Ethernet bus of 1988).

The networks shown in Figure 29–1 all share one attribute: a router, which connects them to some other network. Small and stable networks without any links to other networks are quite simple to setup (some OSes support plug-and-play local networking): each node need only be configured with a unique IP address, and the desired network services set up.

However, internet-connected networks of any size require some degree of architecture design. For example, a simple SOHO network might consist of only two linked internal nodes, both of which are to be given access to the global internet. As shown in Figure 29–2, there is no discernable architecture here; many blanks must be filled in before a network can be implemented. Some of the issues to be resolved include:

- How are the two nodes to be connected to each other? The assumption is that both nodes will be connected to the

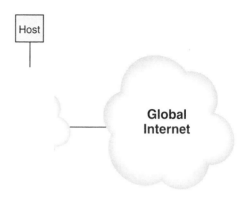

th internet link.

ght be through an Ethernet switch, or over
a two-node network could conceivably be
a direct serial connection—or through some
agement of switches and hubs or even over

odes on the LAN connected to the inter-
o provide direct connections for each node,
to connect through separate links (with a
phone line or through separate broadband
oroach might be acceptable if neither node
e internet at the same time, or if only one
des is ever connected for any significant
f only one node is ever used at any given

is to connect one of the nodes to the inter-
nnection, and then have that host act as a
the second host. This approach might be
teway host is always up and running and if
issues related to it being connected directly

is to add a dedicated gateway/router to
the network. All three devices (the two hosts and the router)
connect to the same LAN, with only the router connected to

the internet. Other variations on this approach, which is well suited to any situation—especially those in which security is an issue—are covered later in the section on security.

• How is internet connectivity provided? Closely related to, but slightly different from the previous bullet, the issue of how to connect to the internet includes the choice of internet service provider (ISP) as well as the choice of internet service. How much inbound and outbound bandwidth is needed?

Except for the most basic dialup internet access service, these questions should be answered before shopping for an ISP. Likewise, security issues should be examined early in the process (see section 31.6). Service providers may not always be clear about their security offerings—or lack thereof.

• How much bandwidth can the ISP provide? Are there special services offered from within the intranet that need to be available to outsiders? Are there special services (mail, web hosting, mailing lists, application serving) that cannot be provided internally, and if so, does the ISP offer those services? Where will the router be situated, and who is responsible for maintaining it?

Some organizations prefer to work with a single vendor for all their networking/internet needs, although more often some services are provided in-house and/or from vendors other than their ISP. Hiring a single vendor to provide all services may reduce costs through special deals as well as reduce the overhead of dealing with multiple vendors—but it presents a degree of risk by relying on a single vendor for all network function.

Bringing some or all of the work in-house requires a serious commitment from management to provide the resources to keep the network running, even if key employees become unavailable. When done properly, in-house network support allows management more control over the network as well as corporate data. Spreading the functions around, between in-house groups and multiple vendors, may be the best compromise: it eliminates single points of failure, allows the organization to keep sensitive tasks in-house and to maintain relationships with different vendors, important in the event that the services of any one vendor are no longer acceptable or available.

• How are network addresses assigned? Is there a need for a routable network address or can a private network address be used? Will the ISP provide a stable network address or do they require configuration with DHCP? Are there any limitations on inbound traffic to internet servers set up on the attached network? Who is responsible for maintaining DNS listings?

In any case, network address space should be managed carefully to allow for growth or change; if a routable network address is to be used, chances are it will be small—in which case even more care must be taken. Understanding the basics of routing and IP will help in deciding when subnets should be used on a single local link, and when they are unnecessary even when the intranet consists of two or more local networks.

Although the task of providing of DHCP and DNS services is not necessarily onerous, it is an issue to be aware of. Similarly, it pays to be aware of any extra charges for peak or unexpected traffic demand.

•   How do ISP and customer guarantee performance? What kinds of contracts or other agreements must be signed? What kind of terms can you set for maintaining adequate service from the ISP? Is there a standard service level agreement (SLA)? Again, these issues should be discussed internally before meeting with potential ISPs; and they should be discussed with the vendor before signing any service agreement.

All networks need an architecture, whether simple or complex, and even in the simplest network there will be options. The simplest LAN is one in which one or more nodes are connected to a single transport layer medium, such as the one shown in Figure 29–3, with hosts all linked through an Ethernet switch. As will become apparent, security issues often (but not always) trump performance issues—certainly, a sluggish car with excellent brakes will be appropriate for some applications while a rocket-powered car with no brakes will be appropriate for others. Performance, cost, and security must all be balanced appropriately for each network.

In the simple intranet, the first architectural decision, to use an Ethernet switch instead of a hub, affects performance: every host connected to the switch gets the full bandwidth of its own Ethernet. Collisions are eliminated[1] between switch and host, and the switch takes care of passing

---

[1] At least for full-duplex LANs, where the host-to-switch link is separate from the switch-to-host link; in half-duplex LANs, collisions will be significantly reduced.

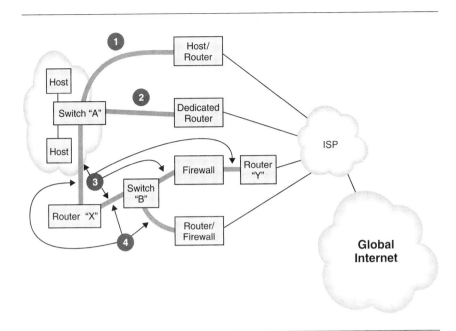

Figure 29–3: Different approaches to firewall/switch/router placement.

frames from node to node. Adding an internet connection immediately increases complexity, as the issue of what to do with that link is raised. Figure 29–3 shows some of the possibilities.

The simplest option is to add (or use an existing) host on the LAN to act as a router. Add the necessary equipment at the premises to allow a single host to connect to the internet through the ISP, add or modify software on that host to allow it to route packets to and from the internet, and the other hosts on the Ethernet will be connected. A host/router (in which the host acts either as an end-use workstation or a network server) will likely provide adequate performance for smaller networks. However, routing performance may be affected depending on the type and configuration of the system. Routing in SOHO intranets is not a processor-intensive task, but if the host must handle significant amounts of local traffic in addition to routing packets, its local link interface can become saturated and cause problems.

The next level of complexity, adding a dedicated router, is architecturally indistinguishable from turning a host into a host/router, but it should improve performance as well as provide the potential for better security than if the system has other functions. An attacker targeting a dual-purpose host/router can focus on both router and host vulnerabilities; gaining root access to the host often means gaining control over everything including the router side. Not only do simple systems allow improved security, but they also make it possible to improve performance. Designers can optimize hardware and software for systems that do only one task, such as routing packets.

Either of these approaches work best for small networks to be integrated within organizational networks where security services are not required and where costs are to be minimized, but most organizational networks require greater attention to security as well as being more sensitive to performance issues. SOHO networks can function perfectly adequately with internet routing performed by an old 80386 PC, but larger organizations with high-speed internet connectivity and many users must spend more for reliable and secure networking.

The third and fourth approaches shown in Figure 29–3 are also architecturally quite similar but not quite identical. In both cases, Router "X" is added to connect two physical networks, the production network connected to Switch "A" and the *bastion network*[2] connected to Switch "B." Bastion-connected nodes include the router, firewall, and any other systems that must be accessible to the outside such as web, ftp, and internet mail servers.

The main difference between (3) and (4) in Figure 29–3 is the separation of the firewall and router. Each approach has benefits. Combining routing and firewall protection in one system reduces maintenance, operating, and administrative costs as well as initial costs for hardware and software. Another truism of security is that the chain is only as strong as its weakest link, a chain with fewer but stronger links will be preferable to a chain with more links. Network architects must weigh the benefits and risks of deploying separate dedicated firewall and router against using a single combination device.

---

[2]A *bastion network* serves as a buffer zone between an intranet and the internet, for placement of insecure servers, firewalls, and other security systems. The rationale for bastion networks is to deny a direct path in from external routers or firewalls to intruders. Attackers would have to crack the router/firewall and then pass through the internal router as well as any intrusion detection systems, *honeypots* or *honeynets* (decoy systems or networks designed to attract attackers away from production systems and networks).

29.3   Network Components

As can be seen, the architect must balance cost, performance, and security in the design of any network. Each network component brings its own attributes: a particular network medium may be expensive or inexpensive, relatively secure or insecure, fast or slow. Decisions about the components with which to build a network depend on balancing the requirements of the organization with the attributes of the components—and the combinations of components being used.

This section introduces some of the categories of network components and how they fit into modern networks.

29.3.1   NETWORK MEDIA

The network medium (as discussed in Chapter 2) offers a physical means by which signals move from one network node to another. The sending node injects the signal into the medium, and the receiving node plucks the signal out of the medium.

For most organizations, the medium of choice continues to be some form of cabling capable of carrying Ethernet segments. Since the 1980s, the Ethernet cable of choice has evolved from coaxial (similar to that used by cable television providers) to CAT 5 (Category 5, a standard specified by the Electronics Industries Association) unshielded twisted pair (UTP) cable very similar in appearance to standard telephone cable, though terminated with broader RJ-45 plugs (allowing access to eight pairs of individual wires) rather than the RJ-11 or RJ-8 plugs used for standard telephone connections. CAT 5 designates the technical specifications of the cable. The latest specification for UTP wiring is CAT 5E, an enhanced version of the CAT 5 specification, modified to support Gigabit Ethernet.

Network architects may have to decide what medium to use for a new network. Some of the variables that must be balanced include:

- Cost of medium. The actual cable and network interface devices that will have to be purchased. The cost of the network interface devices, including network interface cards for networked nodes and network hubs or switches, must also be considered as part of the medium chosen. Thus, although wireless networking requires no cabling, the medium requires purchase of wireless hubs as well as wireless network cards for all connected nodes.

- Cost of installation. The potentially prohibitive cost of retro-fitting CAT 5 cable in a historic building might easily drive an architect to opt for wireless on a basis of cost. Planning a network often requires planning for future change: how much more expensive will it be to install CAT 6 cable, which is (currently) unnecessary for most users but might at some future date be required? How much of a site should be cabled?

- Performance. An organization that uses very high bandwidth applications within the network (such as video-conferencing) may find CAT 6 cabling worth the added expense to buy and install. Most networks work well within the bounds of 100 Mbps or even gigabit Ethernet; there are very few computers that can saturate such a big data pipe (or cope with that much inbound data), so CAT 6 or optical cabling to the desk is rarely needed.

  Often a network designer will choose more than one medium for different parts of a network. For example, a high-capacity, high-performance medium like optical fiber may be specified for an organizational backbone or for linking nodes within a bastion network, where premium performance is required. Such diversification would be overkill for a network with a fractional T-3[3] internet connection, however.

- Security. Wireless media allow interception of raw network data by attackers, wired media make such interception less likely.

- Adaptability and useful life. Changing media for all or part of a network presents a considerable challenge, so network designers may attempt to design the future into their networks. Essentially, this means watching the industry and choosing a medium that can be expected to capture and dominate an appropriate section of the market for a significant length of time. Clairvoyance is a helpful skill for this task, as it requires accurate predictions in a notoriously surprising industry.

These variables can be applied to any component of the network, as can maintenance costs, interoperability with existing systems, and

---

[3]In North America, a standard form in which connectivity can be purchased in 1.544 Mbps units.

anything else that can affect the overall network cost, performance, or security.

29.3.2 ROUTING, ADDRESSING, AND MIDDLEBOXES

By now, the concept of routing should be familiar to the reader. As noted earlier in this chapter, the network architect makes decisions about where routers should be placed within the architecture, as well as how they work. A *middlebox* is "any intermediary device performing functions other than the normal, standard functions of an IP router on the datagram path between a source host and destination host."[4] The implication is that these devices modify packets at the IP layer (or higher) without the knowledge of the source or destination nodes. Typically, firewalls and NATs are the two most common middlebox devices. The network architect decides on the placement of all these devices, at least within the network being designed.

An internet-linked network will have at least one device that acts as a router: there must always be a system to connect the inside with the outside. That router acts as the *edge device* for the network, relaying data from inside to destinations outside. In the networks run by and linking ISPs (or very large non-ISP networks), BGP (see Chapter 24) is used to link ISPs (and private networks that have multiple connections to the global internet) together through backbones, with most ISP customers using internal routing protocols (see Chapter 23) to allow them to link their organizational networks with the internet (via their ISP).

Very large organizations may require their own internal backbones, with external routers running BGP at each site; smaller networks can usually function with one or a handful of routers running basic routing protocols. As was shown in Figure 29–3, router placement is never entirely trivial, even in the simplest network.

Middleboxes present another challenge. Widely used for many years in the form of NATs and firewalls, the middlebox category includes other devices such as load balancers, application gateways, web caching servers, content/application distribution systems, and at least a dozen more—but the characterization of these systems as middleboxes only began when Lixia Zhang made a presentation at the UCLA Computer Science Department's Sprint Research Symposium in March, 2000. By 2002, the middlebox

---

[4]RFC 3234, "Middleboxes: Taxonomy and Issues."

communications working group (MIDCOM) had already begun work on describing the suitability of various internet protocols for use with middleboxes and how those protocols could be used for communication with and between middleboxes. Though this working group is limited to the firewall/NAT subset of middleboxes, the group's work will likely be useful for other categories.

29.3.3 SECURITY DEVICES

Network security tasks may be active or passive. For example, VPN devices and most modern firewalls actively participate in the processing of in- and out-bound packets; intrusion detection systems and network/system security scanners evaluate system/network states or contents of network data and then report on their findings without modifying anything. The passive systems usually leave the remediation to humans, while the active systems perform a particular task related to security without human intervention.

These systems are more or less effective depending on whether or not they are positioned correctly within a network. As with most network design decisions, the correct position will be determined by circumstances: what is correct for one site will be incorrect for another. For example, a sensitive internal network might require its own independent VPN for communications within the organization, as well as its own internal intrusion detection systems. Intrusion detection monitoring stations may not be necessary in a small and concentrated network within which there is plentiful bandwidth, but monitoring stations may be called for in situations where networks encompass many sites and bandwidth between those sites is at a premium.

When systems are performing an active function on data passing from one domain to another, such as with packet filtering (firewalls) or securing sensitive traffic (VPNs), the network design should ensure that all traffic crossing domain boundaries is routed through those systems. Passive monitoring systems should be positioned within the network to access the entire network.

29.4 Network Maintenance and Administration

Although it is possible to build a network with no moving parts, failure to properly administer and maintain a network is as surely an invitation to disaster as failure to properly service a motor vehicle. Businesses and other organizations increasingly rely on reliable networking as a part of mission-critical functions.

Organizations often neglect to budget for ongoing support, or underestimate the amount of resources needed to provide that support. Considering the degree to which network availability, information security, and productivity all depend on reliable and robust networking, cutting corners on network support can be a very costly mistake. Even the smallest organization will benefit from assigning the task of network management to a specific individual (as well as providing a backup plan for when that individual is unavailable), and allocate the appropriate resources (including budget items for software, hardware, training, and tools, as well as personnel costs).

Some of the ongoing tasks associated with network management and administration include:

Evaluation. Most network devices record performance information including data about the volume, origin and destination, and type of traffic as well as network errors, during the time the systems are running. Some entity (whether a person or a system) should monitor, collect, and analyze this information, along with any other performance data that may be required to evaluate how well the network is working. With this information in hand, the network manager should be able to determine the degree to which an ISP is meeting (or falling short) of service level agreements (SLAs). Other uses of this information include tracking down potential legal liabilities in the form of inappropriate use of the internet, avoiding network outages as a result of growth in demand outstripping the ability of the network to cope with increased traffic, and opportunities for improving performance through reorganization.

Maintenance. System bugs or security vulnerabilities are bound to crop up on even the simplest solid-state internet appliance. Although it is not possible to predict where or when these problems crop up, network administrators should monitor vendor and network security web sites and mailing lists for reports of any vulnerabilities or bugs in the systems they administer. Most vendors release fixes to these flaws fairly quickly, but the most vigilant netadmins will remove compromised systems from service immediately when a flaw has been reported (replacing them with systems about which the netadmin is more confident). The majority of successful system and network attacks launched over the internet depend on vulnerabilities that have been reported *and fixed by the vendor*. They succeed only when someone fails to load the patches.

Authentication. An important facet of security, authentication is the task of identifying an entity for the purpose of allowing it access to a system. Entity, rather than person, because a system or a process may initiate contact with a network resource. The scope of this task, coupled with authorization, may be very limited in a smaller organization but can quickly become a huge task as the number of systems and users increases.

Authorization. Once an entity has been authenticated, the next task is to determine what resources that entity is permitted to access. Authenticated users may be authorized to access any system or network resource (although such unlimited access is at best unwise) or restricted from accessing any system or resource on a network (terminated employees may find their network access restricted in this way). Although authorization and authentication for specific systems may both be administered by departments rather than by centralized network support groups, *single sign-on* (SSO) systems are often deployed to centralize the task of administering and managing user accounts.

Planning. Any organizational change is likely to precipitate changes to the organization's network requirements. Netadmins must be involved early in the planning of such changes; even in the absence of such changes, they must actively plan for changes in requirements related to new applications or other technologies as well as changes in the business uses of the network.

Staffing. Every network should be maintained by experienced and trusted netadmins, whether hired as full- or part-time employees or brought in as consultants. Given the degree to which a netadmin has access to an organization's data, thorough background checks should be a part of any hiring process for staff as well as employees.

Support. Proper network function demands that one or more experts be available for resolving network issues. Network services such as mail, web, file/printer sharing, and even automated backup and configuration, must also be supported and maintained. In well-managed networks, netadmins will either support or assist in the support of all these systems, even if all they do is to monitor and act as an emergency support service.

Ongoing network tasks may include everything from installing cables to managing data communications services. The complexity and cost of providing these services will increase as the network grows. The best netadmins are the ones who are best able to manage that growth within their budgets.

29.5   Offering Services

Networks only make sense when services are provided over them (even if those services are peer-to-peer applications in which there are no servers). Netadmins must be mindful of the services to be offered—and the services that are to be explicitly excluded. As with any other network entities, netadmins should be aware of every authorized service on the network as well as the contact information of the person or group responsible for it.

Organizations commonly field some or all of the following services for use by their staff and others:

Web. Most organizations maintain a web presence of some sort, even if only a single page with basic contact information. Web services may be provided by internal network support staff, by external consultant or service providers, or by the same groups that develop web content from within sales, marketing, public relations, or other departments.

Mail. Internet mail services are typically managed centrally, often using organizational standards for client and server software. Products such as Microsoft Outlook may add proprietary features to basic internet standard mail protocols. Netadmins may be called upon to manage an organization's mail server architecture centrally, with servers placed remotely at remote or branch offices. Netadmins should be knowledgeable about the differences in system requirements for deploying different mail protocols. For example, IMAP offers the greatest flexibility for a mobile workforce but also requires close monitoring to remove unsolicited commercial mail (also known as *spam*) as well as avoiding scalability problems as the mail stores grow.

FTP. Organizations often use FTP servers for both internal and external file exchanges. Anonymous servers may be set up to distribute software or to accept contributions from individuals. These services may be offered on their own or in conjunction with more sophisticated groupware applications.

Telnet/Secure Shell Protocol (SSH). Legacy applications running on mainframes may still be accessed over the internet only through terminal sessions. Wherever possible, such services should incorporate security on top of the basic Telnet specification, with SSH or TLS/SSL (Chapter 16) or with Telnet security extensions.

LAN. Traditional networks offer services such as file and printer sharing through proprietary software such as Microsoft's Windows networking or Novell's NetWare; Samba is an open source networking application similar to Windows. LAN services may be administered locally or centrally, but may be considered departmental resources.

Dial-in. Netadmins serving a mobile user population may offer "dial-in" services for remote network access. Remote users may use telephone lines and modems to dial in to a remote access server (RAS), or they may be able to access network services remotely through a standard local internet connection. When connecting through a public IP network, many organizations require the use of data encryption and/or authentication with virtual private network services. Netadmins offering dial-in services should make every effort (including monitoring in-bound data calls routed directly to individual computers) to prevent unauthorized use of corporate systems.

Intranet/extranet. Web services may be offered internally to an organization's employees as well as externally to corporate partners and/or customers. Restrictions on the use of these systems can be implemented based on user logins or other criteria.

Backup. Centralized backup services provide a significant benefit for end users as well as system administrators managing departmental mainframes. Before offering network backup, however, managers must consider the impact on network traffic and bandwidth, available archival storage, backup technologies and strategies, and protocols for backup techniques, retrieval, and off-site storage.

Configuration/Upgrades. In an effort to reduce total cost of ownership, network managers may wish to offer configuration support by offering software upgrades as well as centrally specified system configuration services over the network. Benefits include the potential for improved support on individual systems and better compliance with required system updates and standards. On the down-side, this kind of centralized access to corporate systems offers an attractive target to attackers seeking to compromise individual systems or entire networks. Also, local system administrators may be taken by surprise by changes in the absence of appropriate and timely notifications.

Security. Network managers should be very clear about what security services are to be offered, and what should be the responsibility of individual system users and administrators. Security is increasingly a core feature of internet protocols and applications. In most organizations security services are mandated centrally; some or all responsibility for system administration and support may be delegated to remote sites. In general, organizations take on responsibility for their own network security either by doing it themselves or hiring outside consultants to provide it; ISPs and other service providers typically do not provide any security services to consumers of internet connectivity.

The degree to which security concerns drive much corporate networking activity cannot be understated. Providing for the continued integrity of a network is as important as providing for uninterrupted electrical power or telephone service. The next section introduces some of the network security issues that the network administrator should be prepared to deal with.

29.6   What About Security?

The degree to which a network is secure depends upon the combination of its systems, services, and attributes of the network's components. Users often see security as little more than the rules concerning the appropriate use of passphrases: how frequently they must be changed, passphrase lengths and composition requirements, and so on. Defined more broadly network security addresses anything that might cause a network resource to be unavailable or unusable in any form. Security tasks may be as disparate as providing for emergency power supplies to managing server backups to implementing secure web commerce:

Uninterrupted Power Availability. Small uninterruptable power supplies (UPSes) provide enough backup power to allow PCs to be gracefully shut down in the event of a power failure. Data center and network managers must provide more powerful UPSes capable of powering much larger systems for longer periods of time, to allow the sometimes lengthier power-down processes. Backup power systems should be tested periodically to ensure they work properly.

System/Data/Network Backup. Netadmins must provide for backup of all network systems, including custom system configurations such as those for firewalls and routers, which may be time-consuming to reproduce. Netadmins should keep older versions of system software so they can reverse upgrades for servers, routers, and other devices in the event that the newer versions prove unusable (due to security or other flaws).

Security Updates. Netadmins must monitor system software upgrades, revisions, and patches and evaluate when to install them (and be prepared to revert to less current versions if the upgrade proves inappropriate). Automated tools and services may be available to check daily (or more frequently) for news of vulnerabilities and availability of fixes.

Data Encryption. Data privacy is most often provided through encryption, although not always completely effectively. Data can be encrypted before it is stored to disk if it must be kept private from anyone with access to the system. Data can be encrypted prior to being sent out onto the internet to prevent interception by eavesdroppers. Data can be encrypted by applications prior to being passed down the protocol stack. Maintaining privacy over a public network involves a complex set of tasks in addition to those related to encrypting data: there are algorithms and protocols for the secure exchange of encryption keys, and for proving identity, and for sharing secrets. There are also well-known and hard-to-thwart attacks against encrypted data. The netadmin should understand how encryption, public key cryptography, and digital signatures work; what applications use them;

and under what circumstances they can be defeated or compromised. It does little good to encrypt data transmitted over the internet if it is stored to disk in plain text on an unsecured system.

Data Integrity. Network data integrity relies on the use of strong and secure data hashes as well as use of public key cryptography. The goal is to detect and discard (and / or log) any attempts to modify data in flight. Secure hashes provide a far more reliable mechanism for detecting changes than that offered by protocol checksums. Digital signatures can be used both to prevent data tampering and to link data to the holder of a specific private key—the data can be linked to a specific entity only if we trust that no attacker has stolen the key.

Authentication/Authorization. Already discussed earlier in this chapter, these tasks often fall on the netadmin.

Intrusion Detection. Although computerized systems can help, humans do best at discerning patterns of benign internet activity and those of attacks. No single tool is sufficient for this task, and many organizations are choosing to contract with security service providers to monitor their network activity for malicious intruders. Netadmins are often key participants in the process of setting up intrusion detection systems as well as determining where they must be placed and maintaining them; when outside contractors are brought in, the netadmin may be called upon to assist in setting requirements, choosing vendors from whom to request proposals, and evaluate those proposals.

Intrusion detection systems of any kind are literally worthless unless an organization has a formal *incident response* process set up (see next item).

Incident Response. Although it is important to know that an intrusion or attack is taking place, without a set of procedures for responding to those events, the knowledge may be of little worth. Following one's first instinct, to disconnect or power off the system or network being compromised, is often not the best response to an attack. Formal incident response protocols may include attempting to identify the intruder, attempting to identify the attack type and vulnerability used in the attack, gathering *forensic evidence* (evidence of sufficient quality to be used in legal proceedings) to be used in the event of legal action, identifying the systems and networks that have been compromised, isolating systems and networks that appear to be uncompromised, determining the degree to which systems/networks have been compromised, remediating (fixing) the damage, and plugging the holes.

Computer security intrusion response teams (*CSIRTs*) consist of network, system, and other administrators and managers as well as technical, legal, and executive members, many of whom will also help in formulating incident response protocols. Network architects must be aware of the need for such teams and make sure that funding and staff are allocated to the task.

Interdepartmental Coordination. Whenever employees terminates employment, their authorization to access corporate systems also terminates. Netadmins should coordinate termination of former employees' network access with corporate personnel departments. See also Continuity, below. Likewise, netadmins often coordinate responses to network attacks, especially when incident response protocols require action by members of different departments (see items on intrusion detection and incident response, above).

Disaster Response/Planning. Netadmins don't have primary responsibility for an organization's disaster response and contingency planning processes, but they should be involved in such planning and should initiate their own programs in the absence of organization-wide efforts. Network emergencies may occur independently of any more general emergencies, as when a key service provider loses connectivity.

Network Continuity. No network can be considered secure without up-to-date plans for continuity. For example, who terminates a network administrator's access to sensitive organizational systems when the netadmin quits or is fired? Who responds to emergencies that occur while the netadmin is on vacation? Who takes charge during an emergency when the netadmin is injured or dies?

System and network security are critical aspects of any organization's information technology mission. The corporate investment in systems goes far beyond the cost of hardware, software, support services, custom programming, maintenance and any other cost of owning and running those systems. To an almost frightening extent, an organization's business exists on and operates through the mediation of computers. Failure to protect the systems could result in the failure of the entire organization. Given that there is no way to ensure perfect security for any system or network (short of encasing it in concrete and submerging it in the ocean depths, after first removing all data), the wise network administrator will adopt a policy of constant vigilance to minimize the potential threat and the potential damage.

Godel, Escher, Bach: An Eternal Golden Braid, by Douglas R. Hofstadter (1979) remains a must-read book for anyone who works with computers and particularly for anyone interested in system and network security. Among many other things, Hofstadter proves the impossibility of creating a formal system (i.e., a computer) with perfect security.

29.7   Chapter Summary

Network design and management, like so many other topics covered in this book, can only be introduced in a single chapter: anyone seeking comprehensive and detailed help designing and deploying a TCP/IP network of any complexity should seek further help, whether from a consultant, technical education, the web, or other more specialized books.

In this chapter we only introduce some of the challenges that must be met by the network designer, including choosing a network architecture and desiging the network, assembling the network components, allocating resources for network support and maintenance, choosing network services to offer to users, and how to approach security issues.

Security issues are raised in almost every RFC published by the IETF, as they are in almost every published network protocol. The next chapter takes a look at some of the more general issues related to internet security.

30

Internet Security

It seems that since the late 1990s, a staple of the news media has been the scary internet story, in which journalists and broadcasters breathlessly report on the endless and sometimes seemingly futile war waged on computer criminals of one type or another. These dastards impose their will on individuals by ensnaring them in fraudulent schemes, enticing children into corrupt behaviors, and illegally assuming honest citizens' identities and using their credit cards without permission. These same villains deface web sites; steal computer, network, and telephone service; pirate software; abuse copyrights of all kinds; and otherwise bedevil corporations as well as government agencies.

These are all serious problems, but reporters tend to exaggerate the importance of the internet as the cause of these problems, just as they do almost any new technology that is value-neutral but that can be used for both good and evil. New technologies enable new techniques for committing crimes, and criminals avail themselves of those technologies if they can.

The telephone prompted similar outcries in its early days, as a useful tool for perpetrating frauds as well as for crimes against people. Despite its long history, telephone-related crime shows no signs of abating. Likewise the automobile provided an excellent means of escaping the scene of a crime and still serves that purpose.

Certainly, the internet is a new technology that can be used in the commission of crime. It is hardly unique in being used this way, but the degree to which the internet facilitates harm done without the knowledge of the victim may be greater than any other technology; more frightening is the degree to which harmful acts may be automated and repeated over the internet.

That security is a key element of the TCP/IP internet can be attested to by the degree to which security-oriented protocols such as IPsec, secure shell protocol (SSH), transport layer security (TLS), and secure sockets layer (SSL) have been created and deployed. All new RFCs must include a section that discusses security implications raised by the specification, protocol, or topic of the RFC. Software vendors routinely disavow all liabilities associated with the use of their software, and the networking and computing trade presses report almost daily new vulnerabilities, flaws, and security exploits (instances where attackers have successfully created an attack technique).

Throughout this book we've discussed security issues as they relate to the TCP/IP protocols. In this chapter, we will take a brief look at internet security issues and see how they relate to the protocols—and how they don't. We'll begin with a brief and informal discussion of security issues, followed by a discussion of the more prominent internet security threats and solutions that may have relatively little to do with technology.

Hundreds of books about security are available, including some very good ones and some not so good ones; rather than attempt to comprehensively introduce security here, we will take a less formal look at some of the issues and paradoxes inherent in the common approaches to network security.

30.1   Security Concepts

Security is about keeping safe the people and things you care about. For an individual, that may mean doing a number of things:

- Securing the home. Activities might include making sure all the locks are strong, the doors are reinforced. Making windows burglar-unfriendly, lighting the exterior at night, perhaps even hiring a security service.

- Securing personal safety. Activities might include installing fire extinguishers and smoke detectors throughout the house, learning self-defense, teaching one's children how to be safe, avoiding dangerous situations, and so on.

- Securing personal health. Activities include prophylactic medical treatments (flu shots, annual medical and dental examinations, exercise, healthy diet) as well as education and use of safety devices (seatbelts, helmets, knee/elbow pads).

- Securing financial health. Activities include the purchase of health insurance as well as life insurance and homeowners (or renters) insurance. Maintenance of balanced investing programs, retirement investment, prudent spending and careful investments; keeping an up-to-date will.

Notice that all of these activities are related to security, but they are also spread all over the map: there is no single store you can go to for "one-stop solutions for personal security." You may have the strongest locks on your doors, but if your children don't know that they should never allow a stranger in the house, they are not safe. If your children know better than to invite a stranger in, and your locks are strong, but you leave your back door unlocked, you are not safe. And if you take every precaution but your house burns down anyway, you are not safe unless you have sufficient insurance.

Anyone who expects internet security protocols to offer a single-source solution to every security problem are deluded. Network security depends on the people who use it, as well as on the immutable laws of computing and the laws of nature.

30.2 The Human Factor

Organizations likewise must secure their people (employees) and things (assets). There is no single solution, and there is certainly no technology that can make a corporation or its network entirely safe. Putting aside the problems of securing physical assets and human resources, organizations need to protect their digital assets in a number of ways. Corporate networks are vulnerable in a number of ways:

- Denial of service (DoS). An attacker may deny legitimate users access to a resource by actively attempting to overloading a system or network. In this case, the purpose of the attack may actually be to deny access to the resource, or it may be to put the resource into a state in which it can be subverted, or it may even be to cover a more subtle attack.

- Information theft. The attacker attempts to gain access to some proprietary or otherwise sensitive information held by the organization. It may be insider information, or a private database, or exchanges of internet mail, or resumes, or the corporate compensation schedule. When any sensitive data passes from one system to another across a network, there will be at least a moment when it may be vulnerable to interception.

- Information damage. Web site vandals may have a political axe to grind, or simply take the same joy as urban taggers defacing subway cars. Attacks may be obvious (as with web site deface-ments) or they may be subtle, as when a disgruntled employee executes a small program that periodically extracts $0.50 from a few random accounts.

- Malicious software. Virii, worms, trojan horse programs, back-door programs, all can be considered *malware*. Individuals with assorted motivations may release these programs intending to damage a specific victim, or just become famous, but a suc-cessful piece of malware will invariably cause damage and/or result in denials of service.

The security technologies available to reduce vulnerability to these attacks can only reduce vulnerability—they cannot eliminate vulnerability. In general, the technologies aim to provide security through the following goals:

Authentication: Ensures that an entity attempting to access resources is who it claims to be.

Authorization: Controls what resources an entity may access.

Data integrity: Ensures that data has not been modified or damaged.

Privacy: Keeps sensitive data accessible only to entities that can be authenticated as having proper authorization.

If all the entities involved in network security were purely mechanical, rather than human, network security might be a less difficult problem.

Security is as much an issue of human factors as anything else. One can approach perfect certainty that all entities accessing a network resource are properly authenticated (by submitting valid user ID and passphrase, token, and even biometric data), as well as properly authorized to access a resource (by comparing the ID with resource permissions)—but all that security is worthless if the person who is accessing the resource is a spy.

Network security protocols can protect data in flight, from the moment it is entered into a computer or other system to the time it arrives at its destination, but no protocol can prevent the *social engineering*, or extracting of information from a victim by a clever attacker. Time and again, attackers gain access to other people's systems by simply asking for it. A common ploy is for the attacker to pose as a system support technician and request that the victim log into his system to "check on something" so that the attacker can extract authentication data (perhaps through a previously installed trojan horse program, or perhaps simply by *shoulder surfing*, or looking over the user's shoulder while she enters passphrase and ID).

Although it is possible to implement security schemes that are intractably difficult to break through the means of technology, those same schemes invariably are subject to attack through extortion and bribery.

30.3 Laws of Computing

If one allows that computing and networking systems are mechanisms, then the art and science of building and maintaining those systems should be considered a form of engineering. A structure can be destroyed by a bomb, a delicate instrument may be rendered useless by sand in an escapement, a mechanism may be affected adversely by excessive magnetic fields; computers are also sensitive in this sense, because they can be vulnerable in many different ways.

First, as physical entities, networks and their components are subject to theft, fire, flood, or tinkering (whether by hired attackers or by curious children, the effect may be the same). Achieving system security frequently means adding physical security measures as well as designing, testing, and maintaining a catastrophe response program.

Other aspects of the systems also present vulnerabilities: how secure is the software running on the systems? How secure is the configuration? How secure are the passphrases selected by system users? Although easily guessed passphrases can be screened out by the system, and frequent changes mandated by system policies, it can be difficult to prevent users from writing down those passphrases (how else to remember them, if they are hard to guess?).

Configuration and implementation vulnerabilities may be more difficult to deal with. Busy system administrators may install their own backdoor software to facilitate remote systems support while at the same time opening up those systems to outside attackers. Or those same admins may add a "secret" administrator account to all the systems they manage, or even configure those systems to accept without question logins from the administrator's PC.

Purposeful security lapses like these can be reduced or even prevented with education and corporate policy, but configuring and implementing the complex software used for internet mail services and the DNS is another matter. Accepting default values for many systems may mean leaving a door wide open for attackers; improperly configuring systems can also leave a network vulnerable.

Implementation presents another source of vulnerability. The strongest encryption algorithm in the world will not prevent intruders from decrypting messages that have been encrypted by software that does not implement the algorithm properly. Early versions of the Netscape web browser implementing encryption were vulnerable not because of any flaw in the encryption algorithm but because the program chose keys that were based on the system clock. As a result, attackers could narrow down their brute-force searches of the keyspace sufficiently to consistently read encrypted data almost as fast as it could be encrypted. The situation is parallel to building the world's most impenetrable vault and then leaving the key somewhere in the vault's antechamber.

Other implementation problems arise from an absence of good programming practices in much of the industry. Frequent and intense reviews of software code generally reveal flaws and vulnerabilities, usually related to poor error-checking. *Buffer overflow* attacks are made possible when software checking of data input is not done. The *Ping of Death* attack relies on the ability to send a ping with a too-large payload to a host that doesn't check payload length against the allowed maximum, with disastrous results.

30.4 Laws of Nature

Godel's Theorem proves, among other things, that no formal system can completely describe itself without going outside the system. The details are available in Douglas Hofstadter's *Godel, Escher, Bach: An Eternal Golden Braid*, required reading for anyone who depends on computers for their livelihood.

In metaphysical terms, Godel's Theorem demonstrates that for every Superman, there will be some Kryptonite. For every software program (that does anything interesting) there will be some input that causes the software to break. For every method of securing a system, there will be some attack that can succeed in breaking in.

The task of security in networks is similar to the task of security in national defense: every measure has a counter-measure, and every counter-measure has a counter-counter-measure (and so on, infinitely). Country A develops a shield that protects its borders against conventional weapons, so Country B develops new types of weapons that can penetrate the shield. Country A then develops a thicker shield, causing Country B to develop stronger weapons (or perhaps a new delivery system that bypasses the shield). For those without time or patience to read Hofstadter's book, Dr. Seuss presents a more concise version in *The Butter Battle Book*.

Perfect security is impossible, although perfection can be approached as long as you are willing to expend the resources to cover up every crack and every loophole in the system. Unfortunately, every patch on the original system may close some vulnerability but it likely opens up some new vulnerability.

Ultimately, the issue of network security must be understood as nothing more than another aspect of "security" in general. There are risks, and there are ways to reduce those risks—but there is no way to eliminate them entirely. Sensible managers understand that and do what they can to reduce risk to a sensible level rather than throw endless resources into a futile effort to create perfection.

30.5   Chapter Summary

Security can be enhanced through the use of technologies, but it can never be provided entirely by those technologies—not as long as there are non-technological systems (i.e., people) involved. Despite the fact that the TCP/IP protocol suite and application protocols that run on top of it are all openly specified and easily intercepted and interpreted, and despite the open nature of the security protocols and algorithms themselves, security on the internet remains a realistic goal. As long as one is willing to use the appropriate tools, and use them appropriately, these open protocols can be used in a reasonably secure way.

We explored some of the challenges that must be faced when attempting to secure networks, the most obvious being the potential for subversion of networks and other systems through social engineering. In the next chapter, we look at the simple network management protocol to see how a single application can be used to manage the widest imaginable diversity of systems.

31

Simple Network Management Protocol

Network management covers a lot of ground: anything from workstation configuration and assignment of internet protocol (IP) addresses through network design, architecture, and topologies can be considered within the scope of the network manager. Network management functions can be broadly considered as falling into one of the following categories:

- Providing network service without interruption
- Resolving network service interruptions
- Avoiding network service interruptions or degradation
- Deploying and maintaining network systems, hardware and software

The principles of network management are reasonably uniform, whether the network being managed is a high-speed Ethernet running TCP/IP, a token-ring network running Novell NetWare, a DECnet network, or an AppleTalk network. However, when managing an individual network, the manager has the benefit of a uniform network medium over which network management tools can operate at the data link layer.

Managing an internet poses some special problems, though the internetwork manager still has to be able to provide consistent, reliable, and efficient network services with minimal interruption, and to be capable of handling increasing or changing network demands.

Any protocol or mechanism for managing internetworks must allow network devices and systems of virtually any type to communicate statistics and status information to network management stations, with minimal impact on the networks being monitored, and independent of the underlying network transmission medium. Network management workstations need to be able to request management information from remote managed nodes, and they must be able to make changes in the way the remote node handles network traffic without knowing anything about the particular node itself.

31.1   Managing Networks with SNMP

The standard TCP/IP network management protocol, simple network management protocol (SNMP), provides a simple and elegant framework in which internetwork management tools can be designed. Vendors design SNMP support in their network devices like routers, bridges, and network servers, so those devices can be monitored and managed from network management stations. These network management stations implement SNMP with a user interface, usually a graphical one, that makes management tasks simple. The SNMP protocol itself is not always easy to describe, particularly since it uses formal constructs and tools from the discipline of computer science to define a set of tools usable across a wide range of systems and devices.

Internetwork management, through SNMP implementations, relies largely on the ability of the protocol to monitor network statistics, modify network routing tables, and change the status of network links and devices. The framework in which all this information is gathered and stored is called a Management Information Base (MIB). This is a hierarchical representation of data that offers a standard representation of information across all network and vendor boundaries.

Other tools in the internetwork managers toolbox, some discussed earlier, relate to management issues on a smaller scale. For example, ping and traceroute (Chapter 20) are both excellent diagnostic tools for troubleshooting connectivity problems. Even the use of some standard TCP/IP application, like FTP or telnet, can offer insight into connectivity problems. Likewise, use of the loopback interface (Chapter 19) can help pinpoint problems as well. To these can be added the network traffic analyzer, a device that connects to a network and collects network traffic flowing on the wire. By carefully filtering out unwanted types of traffic, it is possible to diagnose network problems and verify that hosts are sending and receiving properly.

Netstat is another program often included with TCP/IP application suites to provide information about the host and its TCP/IP connections. A brief description of netstat and its output follows the sections on SNMP.

31.2   Simple Network Management Protocol

The whole idea behind the SNMP is to specify a mechanism for network management that is complete, yet simple. Essentially, information is exchanged between agents, which are the devices on the network being managed, and managers, which are devices on the network through which the management is done. The terms agent and manager are operative when discussing network management rather than client and server—just as a client can also be a server, so an agent can also be a manager. Since clients and servers may also be, at times, agents and managers, the more general terms are usually avoided when discussing network management.

Items of interest to the manager include things like the current status of a network interface on a router, the volume of traffic being passed by a router, how many datagrams have been dropped recently, or how many error messages have been received by a router. The network manager may want to disable a network link, reroute traffic around a downed router, or even reboot a router or gateway.

There are a lot of possible transactions between the manager and the agent, and they may vary widely with the different possible types of devices that can be agents. Attempting to implement all the different commands that a manager could possibly send to an agent would be very difficult, particularly for new devices. Instead of attempting to re-create every possible command, SNMP simplifies matters by forcing different commands to be expressed as values that are stored in the devices memory. For example, instead of including a down link command to close a network link on a router, SNMP agents maintain a variable in memory that indicates whether a link is up or down stored along with information about each of the routers network links. To down any given link, a manager simply sends the value corresponding to down into the link status variable.

Possible transactions between agent and manager are limited to a handful: the manager can request information (get and get-next) from the agent or it can modify information (set) on the agent. Under certain specific circumstances, the agent will notify the manager of a change in status (trap) on the agent.

Some of the data to be retrieved or changed are stored as simple variables, like error message counters, but other information is stored in tables, like interface data that includes hardware addresses, IP addresses, hardware type, and more, for each network interface.

By keeping the implementation of the protocol fairly simple through limited commands, the barriers to implementing SNMP on a device are kept low, which also means that it can be implemented widely, thus making it more useful.

Another implementation issue for any network management protocol is whether to have agents be active and transmit updates about their status on a regular basis or have them be passive and polled periodically by the manager to check on their status. Each has its own drawback. When agents are passive, major problems may not be detected in a timely way if the manager doesn't check frequently enough, and undue load on the network may result if the manager checks too frequently. On the other hand, forcing agents to report status changes puts pressure on the network devices computing resources and can stress the network further when a problem occurs.

SNMP permits the use of traps from agents to signal changes to managers, but the model encourages the use of a single trap to be sent when an important event occurs and relies on the manager to request further relevant information from the agent.

Reliability is another issue for network management. It might seem that a reliable protocol like TCP should be specified to make sure that management information gets passed reliably between agent and manager. However, UDP is the TCP/IP protocol used for SNMP, for reasons that go beyond the fact that most SNMP exchanges are request/response pairs. One of the most important functions for network management is to resolve problems that occur with transmitting or routing network traffic. Network management information is more important at times of network failure or reduction in service than at any other time, which also happens to be the time that reliable protocols like TCP are more likely to fail to connect. These are also the times when any extra load on the network is least welcome. Finally, it should be recalled that a protocol may be reliable, but if the link over which it is being sent has been severed, no data will get through.

31.3   SNMP Commands

Five different messages are possible with SNMP. Three cover transactions initiated by a manager (read and write an individual variable on an agent; read a group of variables on an agent), the fourth defines the response from the agent to any of these requests from a manager, and the fifth defines the reporting of an extraordinary event (a trap) by the agent to the manager. Table 31–1 shows these commands; SNMP agents listen to UDP port 161 for requests from SNMP managers, and the SNMP manager listens to UDP port 162 for traps from agents.

By encoding device status within variables, rather than implementing network management commands, SNMP makes it possible to manage many different types of devices with a minimum command set.

By using two separate ports for SNMP, one for sending management requests and one for sending agent traps, network devices can function as both an agent (reporting traps and processing requests from managers) and as a manager (making requests of and receiving traps from agents) without confusion.

31.4   Structure of Management Information

The methods for representing managed information objects—the data items that network management is concerned with, like network traffic

Command	Description
get-request	Retrieve the value of a specified variable on the agent
get-next-request	Retrieve the value of a specified variable on the agent after the one indicated in the request, used for traversing tables where there are multiple "rows" of information; for example, when getting information about a router's network interfaces
set-request	Change the value of a specified variable
get-response	Respond to manager requests with the value of the item being queried
trap	Notify the manager of a change in status or some event on the agent

Table 31–1: SNMP commands.

counters and interface addresses—are relatively complicated and strictly defined by sets of formal rules. A basic understanding of how managed information is stored is useful, but few people other than those responsible for designing SNMP management software need more than that.

The Structure of Management Information (SMI) is a framework within which management information can be named and referenced authoritatively. One way to think about the SMI and MIBs is to imagine that TCP/IP networks are simply vastly distributed databases, containing nothing but network management information stored in network devices like routers and servers. These bits of the database may be stored in various different forms at the different network devices, but using a standard schema for organizing the data means the devices that store the data know they are required to report that data in a particular form when asked for it, and to store it locally in a form that they can interpret according to this standard.

Object identifiers for management information are organized like the Domain Name System, with an unnamed root parenting three nodes: itu(0), iso(1), and joint-iso-itu(2). Each node has a name and a number: the name is for people; the number is used by computers for simplicity of computing. These top nodes represent the partitioning of the management information space and allocation of a section for joint use by the International Telegraph and International Telecommunications Union (ITU) and the International Organization for Standardization (ISO).

Beneath iso(1) are four more nodes used by the ISO to assign standards, for use by OSI (Open Systems Interconnection, an effort underwritten by ISO in support of open network standards) registration authorities, member organizations of ISO, and other organizations that ISO identifies. TCP/IP management information falls under the last category, and it is listed under the Department of Defense (DOD). As shown in Figure 31–1, the MIB (version 2) is listed as a node six layers down in this structure. (Figures 22–1 and 22–2 show some of the relevant nodes in this framework for simplicity.)

The use of this system ensures that each managed item can be uniquely identified as well as related to its parent nodes, just as the Domain Name System (DNS) does for domain and host names. Also like DNS, items in this framework have no inherent way to determine whether or not an identifier is a leaf node (a node actually referring to an item of management information rather than containing other nodes).

The labels are generally used to make the management object identifiers easier to deal with for people, whereas computers use the numbers, which are easier for them to deal with. So, the representation of the MIB itself within this framework is, more formally,

```
iso.org.dod.internet.mgmt.mib
```

and can be expressed for use by computer as

```
1.3.6.1.2.1
```

Figure 31–2 shows the main groups in the MIB. Other structures for managing network information that aren't listed in the MIB can be listed under other nodes; for instance, vendors can set up product specific information bases under the hierarchy represented by

```
iso.org.dod.internet.private.enterprises
```

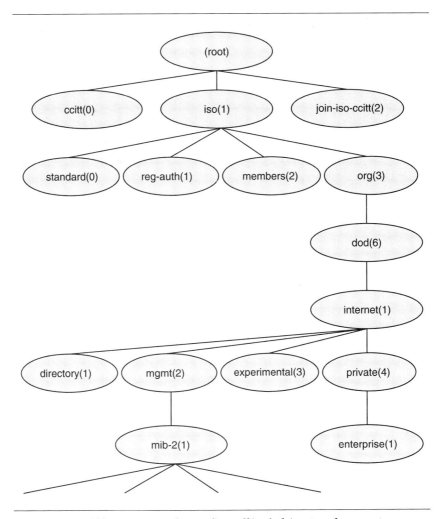

Figure 31–1: Different approaches to firewall/switch/router placement.

Each item of management information within this framework can be very specifically identified and therefore requested by a manager. Not all managed nodes will be able to, or even want to, maintain all the defined information items, but whatever they keep track of can be requested by a manager by specifying the item number. The next section looks at the MIB itself.

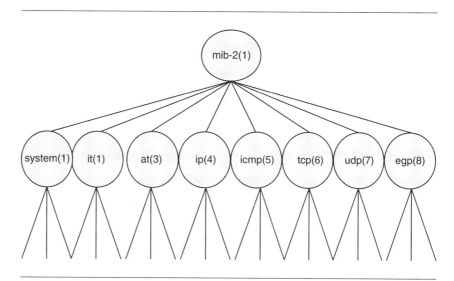

Figure 31–2: Different approaches to firewall/switch/router placement.

31.5 Management Information Base

Several basic categories of managed information are listed beneath mib-2(1) in the SMI. They correspond to various different categories of information relevant to TCP/IP networking. Not discussed here are the Transmission Group, where management information for devices relating to network medium protocols like Ethernet, IEEE 802, and other network hardware is stored, and a special group used for managed information relating to the first version of SNMP. Table 31–2 shows the main groups and the types of information they contain.

Network information may be maintained as single units of information; a counter, for example, indicating the number of user datagram protocols sent out by the device. Other types of information require a tabular approach: a router will have at least two network interfaces (and often more) to manage. Tables are used to represent this type of information; for instance, in the IP address translation table, each network interface gets a single row in the table, including values for network interface number, a hardware address, and an IP address for each interface.

MIB Group	Description
system (1)	Information about the device itself, including a description, what network services it provides, the contact person, the location, and the name of the device
it (2)	"Interfaces" group: basic information about the network interfaces on the device, including hardware address and statistics on transmissions sent and received on the interface
at (3)	"Address translation" group: information that relates the hardware addresses of the device's network interfaces with their IP addresses (this group is currently "deprecated," meaning that with the shift from the first to the second version of SNMP, the functions this group fulfills have been shifted to the IP group)
ip (4)	IP specific information including statistics about IP datagrams sent and received, and tables that include IP addresses and associated hardware interfaces, IP routing and forwarding information
icmp (5)	Tracks ICMP messages sent and received and statistics on the different types of ICMP messages generated and received
tcp (6)	Tracks TCP statistics, including the volume of TCP segments sent, received, and retransmitted; error messages and types; and a table that tracks current TCP connections (which ports and interfaces are in use, connecting to which remote IP address and port)
udp (7)	Tracks UDP statistics, as well as current UDP ports being used
egp (8)	Used on routers using the Exterior Gateway Protocol

Table 31–2: Management Information Base groups used for TCP/IP network management.

As an example, the first object in the IP group is ipForwarding. There are two valid options: if the value is 1 then the system is configured to forward IP datagrams, to act as a router; if the value is 2 the system is not forwarding datagrams (is not acting as a router). Not all variables can be modified by a manager, but this one can be, which means that a network manager can effectively take a router out of service by changing this variable from 1 to 2, or put a router in service by changing this value from 2 to 1.

Another similar example is the ifAdminStatus column within the ifTable in the interface group. Each network interface has a row of various entries in this table, and the ifAdminStatus object can be changed to change the status of any particular interface: the interface can be up, down, or testing.

By and large, however, MIB objects can't be reset by a manager when they contain network statistics. For example, within the ifTable are other columns like ifInOctets and ifOutOctets, which reflect (respectively) the total number of octets received and transmitted over each network interface.

Network devices keep track of all these variables and more, and make them available to managers upon request. The network management stations collect this information from the different agents (usually routers and other critical network devices) and build a picture of where network traffic is being passed. With this information, the network administrator is able (in theory) to avoid or fix problems due to down systems or interfaces and to improve network performance in some cases.

31.6   Remote Network Monitoring

In larger internetworks, some value can derive from configuring network devices to gather network management information remotely, including setting up packet filters for gathering network traffic and analyzing results. A separate MIB has been defined for this function, the Remote Network Monitoring (RMON) MIB. Remote network monitors can be used to gather data link layer network data, which is inaccessible to remote network managers connected across an internetwork: routers screen out all that information when they forward IP datagrams.

31.7   Simple Network Management Protocol v2

The first version of the SNMP proved to be a little too simple for some. A handful of major problems and shortcomings flawed SNMPv1, so a second version called SNMPv2 was first issued in 1993 and updated with various flavors in 1996.

31.7.1 SIMPLE NETWORK MANAGEMENT PROTOCOL v1 PROBLEMS

Authentication in SNMP is trivial, based as it is on a simple, unencrypted community name. This field is included with all SNMP messages, and if the agent's community name is the same as the community name sent out from a manager, then the agent will respond. This presents security issues, to say the least. Anyone can monitor a TCP/IP network and sniff out SNMP packets, determine a valid community name, and perform any SNMP management function available, including bringing the network to its knees. In fact, the default community name for many devices, public, is sufficiently often left unchanged so that a criminal could easily bypass network monitoring and perform management functions.

SNMPv1 can generate very high network traffic overhead. Getting a single piece of network information from a managed device is relatively easy, but getting complete routing tables, network statistics, or even just interface status from routers requires a seemingly endless procession of get-next requests. Monitoring agents on remote sections of an intranet can also generate a lot of traffic as messages may need to be relayed across many routers. Even the most basic network management tools can generate huge volumes of traffic from simple maintenance functions and can adversely impact network function during peak periods.

Another cause of high network management traffic is the need for network management nodes to send and receive SNMP requests and responses across large intranets. There is no way for network manager nodes to share management information: each manager must gather information independently. This can mean additional traffic, either from having multiple network management workstations monitoring the same TCP/IP intranet, or from a single management workstation monitoring a large intranet.

31.7.2 SIMPLE NETWORK MANAGEMENT PROTOCOL v2 SOLUTIONS

SNMPv2 adds two new commands, *GetBulkRequest* and *Inform*, to address the problem of high traffic overhead.

The GetBulkRequest command allows an SNMP manager workstation to get the entire contents of a part of the MIB, like a routing table, with a single command rather than with a continuing stream of get-next requests. The result is that instead of dozens of requests and responses, the manager workstation can send a single request and the agent device can send a single response.

The Inform command allows remote network manager workstations to notify other network manager workstations of the status of network agents that they are monitoring, thus reducing the amount of network traffic while monitoring a large intranet.

SNMPv2 does not address the security issue quite as comprehensively or completely. There are at present three flavors of SNMPv2, each offering a slightly different approach to security. Community-based SNMPv2, or SNMPv2c, uses the same trivial authentication scheme as SNMPv1. SNMPv2u, or the User-Based Security Model for SNMP, adds authentication, whereas more complete security is provided by the SNMPv2* approach. Because a general consensus on what approach is most useful, it is widely believed that this issue will be dealt with more adequately by IETF workgroups in the future.

31.8 Chapter Summary

At the same time simple and complex, the Simple Network Management Protocol (SNMP) provides a mechanism by which virtually any device can be managed from virtually any other device.

SNMP's small set of requests and replies, when combined with the Structure of Management Information (SMI) and a Management Information Base (MIB), allow network managers to extract information about network interfaces as well as to reconfigure those interfaces.

This brief introduction should not be taken as a comprehensive overview of SNMP and network management but rather as yet another example of a useful application that can be used over IP networks. For more detailed coverage of these protocols, see the relevant RFCs.

Part Seven

Appendices

Appendices include information that is particularly relevant, but doesn't always fit into the rest of the book. Appendices included with this volume include:

- Appendix A: Internet and Other Network Organizations. This appendix provides an overview to the organizations and groups that develop, maintain, and manage the deployment of the protocols discussed in this book.
- Appendix B: Selected Protocol Summaries. This appendix includes quick introductions to various internet protocols that have not been discussed at length in this text, including the basic header structures and protocol command summaries.

Internet and Network
Protocol Organizations

Although many of the examples presented in this book have been fanciful and impractical, the internet is based on real networks and using real protocols, from those included in the TCP/IP suite to many others defined by other bodies for different purposes. This appendix presents an overview to the organizations behind the protocols.

The global internet is more of an anarchy or even a conspiracy than an organization. There are organizations that develop internet protocols, and there are organizations that administer the internet address and name spaces, and there are independent organizations developing protocols related to internet protocols. The Internet Society (ISOC) and its affiliated organizations are responsible for the development and support of internet protocols while the regional internet registries (RIRs) and the Internet Corporation for Assigned Names and Numbers (ICANN) administer internet addresses and domain names. Network protocol development that relates to internet protocols is being done by organizations ranging from the

International Telecommunications Union (ITU) and the Institute of Electrical and Electronics Engineers (IEEE) to the World Wide Web Consortium (W3C) and the ATM Forum.

A.1   Internet Protocol Development Groups

ISOC, which bills itself as a professional society for the internet, provides an organizational umbrella under which internet protocol development occurs. ISOC entities are described below:

- The Internet Engineering Task Force (IETF) is not really an organization. Anyone who wants to "join" the IETF merely has to show up on the appropriate working group mail list and make useful contributions. Most discussion is done through those lists, although IETF meetings are held three times each year for resolving issues that require more direct contact. There are no dues, membership applications, or any other formal or administrative requirements. IETF work revolves around the scores of working groups, each dedicated to a specific issue, problem, application, or protocol. Workgroups (and individuals) may publish their results (protocol specifications or other documentation of their area) as works-in-progress called *Internet-Drafts* (*I-Ds*).
- The Internet Engineering Steering Group (IESG) is composed of IETF area directors and the IETF chair. The IESG approves working group results and other actions; once an I-D is approved, it can become a Request for Comments (RFC) document. The IESG also determines whether a specification should be on the Standards track. Full internet standard specification are considered complete and mature and required for full IP-compliance. Draft standards have gone through considerable use and testing and are largely complete, though there may still be some issues to be resolved. Proposed standards have been implemented and may even be in wide use, but there may still be significant issues to be resolved before the spec can be advanced.
- The Internet Architecture Board (IAB) consists of a dozen chosen IETF leaders plus the IETF chair. These 13 provide oversight to the rest of internet standards organizations, including the IETF and the IESG, as well as acting as liaison to other

standards bodies. The IAB is also responsible for publishing RFCs and other documents; this function is performed by the RFC Editor.

- The RFC Editor, a position originally held by the late Jon Postel, is responsible for making sure all RFCs are published correctly and in a timely fashion. The standards track documents described above usually require careful editing and checking to make sure they fulfill all requirements; in addition to the standards track documents, other types of RFC include the Informational, which may document a proprietary protocol or describe some activity or process; the Experimental, which describes a protocol that has yet to be proven in any significant use; and Historical, which were once on the standards track but which have become obsolete. Certain RFCs are also published in several separate series, including the STD (Internet Standards), BCP (Best Current Practices), and FYI (For Your Information) series. Each document in these series gets a static series number, but the documents come from the RFC series. RFC numbers are never recycled, so when a document is revised it gets a new RFC number and (if it is part of one of the series) the new RFC is published under the same series number.

There are other bodies, including the Internet Research Task Force (IRTF), the Internet Research Steering Group (IRSG), and others that tend to be less visible, less active, and generally lower profile than these four. The research-oriented groups tend to work more closely with universities and research labs on the future directions for internet protocols.

Table A–1 lists URLs for these organizations, where additional information and news can be found.

A.2 Name and Address Administration Groups

Internet addresses will be discussed at greater length in Chapter 14, and internet domain names will be discussed in Chapter 9, but this section discusses how these addresses and names are allocated and administered. One other related (but less well-known) function, administering internet assigned numbers, will also be covered here.

Organization	URL
Internet Society (ISOC)	www.isoc.org
Internet Engineering Task Force (IETF)	www.ietf.org
Internet Engineering Steering Group (IESG)	www.ietf.org/iesg.html
Internet Architecture Board (IAB)	www.iab.org
RFC Editor	www.rfc-editor.org
Internet Research Task Force (IRTF)	www.irtf.org

Table A–1: Internet standards development organizations.

Originally, the Internet Assigned Numbers Authority (IANA) had authority over these functions,[1] but since Jon Postel's death in 1998, ICANN has taken on reponsibility for them. ICANN has three supporting organizations that serve as advisory bodies to ICANN:

- The Address Supporting Organization (ASO) provides support for the three RIRs.
- The Domain Name Supporting Organization (DNSO) oversees the domain name registrars and provides technical and administrative guidance in areas such as intellectual property issues related to domain names.
- The Protocol Supporting Organization (PSO) advises ICANN on issues related to assignment of parameters, such as protocol version numbers or protocol-related constants, for internet protocols.

The RIRs are independent of ICANN and accept members (usually from their own regions). Each RIR administers its own ranges of network addresses, which can be assigned to RIR members (mostly ISPs and very large organizations) as well as non-members. Addresses are allocated in blocks, and fees are assessed based on the number of addresses within allocated blocks. The three RIRs are:

- American Registry for Internet Numbers (ARIN) serving North and South America as well as the Caribbean and sub-Saharan Africa.

---

[1] See RFC 1594, "Domain Name System Structure and Delegation."

- Asia Pacific Networking Information Center (APNIC) serving Asian and Pacific nations.
- Réseaux IP Européens-Network Coordination Centre (RIPE-NCC) serving Europe, Middle East, and parts of Africa.

The RIRs provide IP network address registration services to all regions around the globe, but domain name registration is handled by domain name registrars. Originally, all name registration services were provided by US-based Network Solutions, Inc., but a large part of the justification for creating ICANN revolved around the potential for expanding the registrar community. As of early 2002, there are already a few dozen registrar members of the DNSO, and the original handful of top-level three-letter domains (.com, .net, .org, .gov, .mil, .int) and the two-letter ISO international country codes are already being augmented by new domains including .aero, .biz, .coop, .info, .museum, and .name (more about those domains in Chapter 9).

Finally, there is the matter of assigned numbers. Protocols frequently use more or less arbitrary codes as parameters. For example, IP packets begin with a four-bit value that indicates which version of IP is being used (see Chapter 20 for more details), while transport layer protocols use *well-known ports* (see Chapter 16 for more details). The IANA, operating under ICANN, records all valid values of all these (and other) protocol parameters, or else maintains links with other organizations that may have responsibility for maintaining such values.

Table A–2 lists URLs for these organizations, where considerably more information is available.

A.3   Related Protocol Development Groups

There are many communication and networking protocols that are crucial to the current and future function of the internet, but they are not developed within the internet protocol process. Instead, other organizations, some of them in existence long before the internet was ever thought of, support their development. Notable among these groups are those included in Table A–3.

Organization	URL
Internet Corporation for Assigned Names and Numbers (ICANN)	www.icann.org
Address Supporting Organization (ASO)	www.aso.icann.org
Domain Name Supporting Organization (DNSO)	www.dnso.icann.org
Protocol Supporting Organization (PSO)	www.pso.icann.org
American Registry for Internet Numbers (ARIN)	www.arin.net
Asia Pacific Networking Information Center (APNIC)	www.apnic.net
Réseaux IP Européens-Network Coordination Centre (RIPE-NCC)	www.ripe.net
Internet Assigned Numbers Authority (IANA)	www.iana.org

Table A–2: Internet address, name, and protocol parameter organizations.

Organization	Protocols	URL
Institute of Electrical and Electronics Engineers (IEEE)	Ethernet, wireless, and other 802-series protocols	www.ieee.org
International Telecommunication Union (ITU)	Standards for telecommunications networks	www.itu.int
World Wide Web Consortium (W3C)	Web protocols, including HTML and XML	www.w3c.org
ATM Forum	Asynchronous Transfer Mode (ATM) protocols	www.atmforum.org

Table A–3: Non-ISOC/ICANN affiliated organizations involved in internet-related protocol development.

Selected Protocol
Summaries

This appendix includes some of the protocol information related to key TCP/IP protocols, including protocol commands, extensions, reply codes, and header structures.

B.1   Domain Name System

The DNS standard (STD 13) is documented in RFCs 1034 and 1035 and updated or supplemented by the following RFCs:

RFC3090: DNS Security Extension Clarification on Zone Status

RFC3110: RSA/SHA-1 SIGs and RSA KEYs in the Domain Name System (DNS)

RFC3130: Notes from the State-of-the-Technology: DNSSEC

RFC3152: BCP0049 Delegation of IP6.ARPA

RFC3172 (BCP 0052): Management Guidelines & Operational Requirements for the Address and Routing Parameter Area Domain (arpa)RFC3197 Applicability Statement for DNS MIB Extensions

RFC3225: Indicating Resolver Support of DNSSEC

RFC3226: DNSSEC and IPv6 A6 Aware Server/Resolver Message Size Requirements

Valid DNS resource record types include:

TYPE: value and meaning

A 1 a host address [RFC1035]

NS 2 an authoritative name server [RFC1035]

MD 3 a mail destination (Obsolete—use MX) [RFC1035]

MF 4 a mail forwarder (Obsolete—use MX) [RFC1035]

CNAME 5 the canonical name for an alias [RFC1035]

SOA 6 marks the start of a zone of authority [RFC1035]

MB 7 a mailbox domain name (EXPERIMENTAL) [RFC1035]

MG 8 a mail group member (EXPERIMENTAL) [RFC1035]

MR 9 a mail rename domain name (EXPERIMENTAL) [RFC1035]

NULL 10 a null RR (EXPERIMENTAL) [RFC1035]

WKS 11 a well-known service description [RFC1035]

PTR 12 a domain name pointer [RFC1035]

HINFO 13 host information [RFC1035]

MINFO 14 mailbox or mail list information [RFC1035]

MX 15 mail exchange [RFC1035]

TXT 16 text strings [RFC1035]

RP 17 for Responsible Person [RFC1183]

AFSDB 18 for AFS Data Base location [RFC1183]

X25 19 for X.25 PSDN address [RFC1183]

ISDN 20 for ISDN address [RFC1183]

RT 21 for Route Through [RFC1183]

NSAP 22 for NSAP address, NSAP style A record [RFC1706]

NSAP-PTR 23

SIG 24 for security signature [RFC2535]

KEY 25 for security key [RFC2535]

PX 26 X.400 mail mapping information [RFC2163]

GPOS 27 Geographical Position [RFC1712]

AAAA 28 IP6 Address [Thomson]

LOC 29 Location Information [Vixie]

NXT 30 Next Domain [RFC2535]

EID 31 Endpoint Identifier [Patton]

NIMLOC 32 Nimrod Locator [Patton]

SRV 33 Server Selection [RFC2782]

ATMA 34 ATM Address [Dobrowski]

NAPTR 35 Naming Authority Pointer [RFC2168, RFC2915]

KX 36 Key Exchanger [RFC2230]

CERT 37 CERT [RFC2538]

A6 38 A6 [RFC2874]

DNAME 39 DNAME [RFC2672]

SINK 40 SINK [Eastlake]

OPT 41 OPT [RFC2671]

APL 42 APL [RFC3123]

UINFO 100 [IANA-Reserved]

UID 101 [IANA-Reserved]

GID 102 [IANA-Reserved]

UNSPEC 103 [IANA-Reserved]

TKEY 249 Transaction Key [RFC2930]

TSIG 250 Transaction Signature [RFC2845]

IXFR 251 incremental transfer [RFC1995]

AXFR 252 transfer of an entire zone [RFC1035]

MAILB 253 mailbox-related RRs (MB, MG or MR) [RFC1035]

MAILA 254 mail agent RRs (Obsolete—see MX) [RFC1035]

* 255 A request for all records [RFC1035]

Note: In RFC 1002, two types are defined (NB, 32, NetBIOS general Name Service and NBSTAT, 33, NetBIOS NODE STATUS). It is not clear that these are in use, though if so their assignment does conflict with those above.

B.1.1 DOMAIN NAME SYSTEM MESSAGE HEADER AND FIELDS

DNS message header fields are show in Figure B–1 and described below.

Header Fields (from RFC 1035):

ID A 16-bit identifier assigned by the program that generates any kind of query. This identifier is copied by the corresponding reply and can be used by the requester to match up replies to outstanding queries.

QR A one-bit field that specifies whether this message is a query (0) or a response (1).

OPCODE A four-bit field that specifies kind of query in this message (see table below for list of valid values). This value is set by the

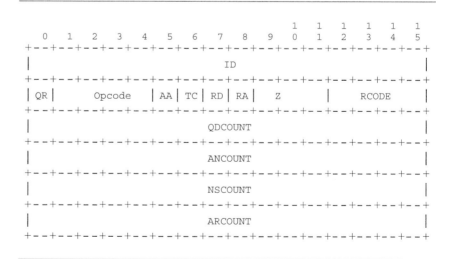

Figure B–1: DNS message header format (from RFC 1035).

originator of a query and copied into the response. Current values are available at the IANA DNS parameters page (http://www.iana.org/assignments/dns-parameters):

AA Authoritative Answer - this bit is valid in responses, and specifies that the responding name server is an authority for the domain name in question section. (Note that the contents of the answer section may have multiple owner names because of aliases. The AA bit corresponds to the name that matches the query name, or the first owner name in the answer section.)

TC TrunCation - specifies that this message was truncated due to length greater than that permitted on the transmission channel.

RD Recursion Desired - this bit may be set in a query and is copied into the response. If RD is set, it directs the name server to pursue the query recursively. Recursive query support is optional.

RA Recursion Available - this is set or cleared in a response, and denotes whether recursive query support is available in the name server.

Z Reserved for future use. Must be zero in all queries and responses.

RCODE Response code - this 4-bit field is set as part of responses (see IANA for current values)

QDCOUNT an unsigned 16-bit integer specifying the number of entries in the question section.

ANCOUNT an unsigned 16-bit integer specifying the number of resource records in the answer section.

NSCOUNT an unsigned 16-bit integer specifying the number of name server resource records in the authority records section.

ARCOUNT an unsigned 16-bit integer specifying the number of resource records in the additional records section.

Valid opcode values for DNS are listed in Table B–1.

OpCode	Name
0	Query
1	IQuery
2	Status
3	reserved
4	Notify
5	Update
6-15	available for assignment

Table B–1: Opcode values (from IANA).

B.2 Simple Mail Transfer Protocol Details

RFC 2821 defines valid reply code values based on the scheme reproduced here:

`First Digit:`

1yz Positive Preliminary reply The command has been accepted, but the requested action is being held in abeyance, pending confirmation of the information in this reply. The SMTP client should send another command specifying whether to continue or abort the action. Note: unextended SMTP does not have any commands that allow this type of reply, and so does not have continue or abort commands.

2yz Positive Completion reply The requested action has been successfully completed. A new request may be initiated.

3yz Positive Intermediate reply The command has been accepted, but the requested action is being held in abeyance, pending receipt of further information. The SMTP client should send another command specifying this information. This reply is used in command sequence groups (i.e., in DATA).

4yz Transient Negative Completion reply
The command was not accepted, and the requested action did not occur. However, the error condition is temporary and the action may be requested again. The sender should return to the beginning of the command sequence (if any). It is difficult to assign a meaning to ``transient'' when two different sites (receiver- and sender-SMTP agents) must agree on the interpretation. Each reply in this category might have a different time value, but the SMTP client is encouraged to try again. A rule of thumb to determine whether a reply fits into the 4yz or the 5yz category (see below) is that replies are 4yz if they can be successful if repeated without any change in command form or in properties of the sender or receiver (that is, the command is repeated identically and the receiver does not put up a new implementation.)

5yz Permanent Negative Completion reply
The command was not accepted and the requested action did not occur. The SMTP client is discouraged from repeating the exact request

(in the same sequence). Even some ''permanent'' error conditions can be corrected, so the human user may want to direct the SMTP client to reinitiate the command sequence by direct action at some point in the future (e.g., after the spelling has been changed, or the user has altered the account status).

Second Digit:

x0z Syntax: These replies refer to syntax errors, syntactically correct commands that do not fit any functional category, and unimplemented or superfluous commands.

x1z Information: These are replies to requests for information, such as status or help.

x2z Connections: These are replies referring to the transmission channel.

x3z Unspecified.

x4z Unspecified.

x5z Mail system: These replies indicate the status of the receiver mail system vis-a-vis the requested transfer or other mail system action.

Third Digit:

The third digit provides finer-grained information about each reply, and each is associated with a recommended message string in RFC 2821. However, those messages may be modified if needed.

B.3   Post Office Protocol v3

The Post Office Protocol (POP), defined in RFC 1939, describes a mechanism by which users can retrieve mail on demand from mail servers. POP
makes it possible for users to receive their mail on personal computers
that are frequently powered off; SMTP services require the receiving host
to be online at all times. This command summary is taken from RFC 1939,
Section 9.

```
POP3 Command Summary


Minimal POP3 Commands:

USER name     valid in the AUTHORIZATION state
PASS string
QUIT
STAT          valid in the TRANSACTION state
LIST [msg]
RETR msg
DELE msg
NOOP
RSET
QUIT


Optional POP3 Commands:

APOP name digest valid in the AUTHORIZATION state
TOP msg n valid in the TRANSACTION state
UIDL [msg]


POP3 Replies:

+OK
-ERR
```

Note that with the exception of the STAT, LIST, and UIDL commands, the reply given by the POP3 server to any command is significant only to ``+OK'' and ``-ERR''. Any text occurring after this reply may be ignored by the client.

B.4   Telnet Protocol

Values for basic telnet options, taken from IANA web site (http://www.iana.org/assignments/telnet-options); more authentication and encryption related options are available and listed there as well.

```
Options Name References

------- ---------------------- ----------

0 Binary Transmission [RFC856]

1 Echo [RFC857]

2 Reconnection [NIC50005]

3 Suppress Go Ahead [RFC858]

4 Approx Message Size Negotiation [ETHERNET]

5 Status [RFC859]

6 Timing Mark [RFC860]

7 Remote Controlled Trans and Echo [RFC726]

8 Output Line Width [NIC50005]

9 Output Page Size [NIC50005]

10 Output Carriage-Return Disposition [RFC652]

11 Output Horizontal Tab Stops [RFC653]

12 Output Horizontal Tab Disposition [RFC654]

13 Output Formfeed Disposition [RFC655]

14 Output Vertical Tabstops [RFC656]

15 Output Vertical Tab Disposition [RFC657]

16 Output Linefeed Disposition [RFC658]
```

17 Extended ASCII [RFC698]

18 Logout [RFC727]

19 Byte Macro [RFC735]

20 Data Entry Terminal [RFC1043,RFC732]

21 SUPDUP [RFC736,RFC734]

22 SUPDUP Output [RFC749]

23 Send Location [RFC779]

24 Terminal Type [RFC1091]

25 End of Record [RFC885]

26 TACACS User Identification [RFC927]

27 Output Marking [RFC933]

28 Terminal Location Number [RFC946]

29 Telnet 3270 Regime [RFC1041]

30 X.3 PAD [RFC1053]

31 Negotiate About Window Size [RFC1073]

32 Terminal Speed [RFC1079]

33 Remote Flow Control [RFC1372]

34 Linemode [RFC1184]

35 X Display Location [RFC1096]

36 Environment Option [RFC1408]

37 Authentication Option [RFC2941]

38 Encryption Option [RFC2946]

39 New Environment Option [RFC1572]

40 TN3270E [RFC1647]

41 XAUTH [Earhart]

42 CHARSET [RFC2066]

43 Telnet Remote Serial Port (RSP) [Barnes]

44 Com Port Control Option [RFC2217]

45 Telnet Suppress Local Echo [Atmar]

46 Telnet Start TLS [Boe]

```
47 KERMIT [RFC2840]

48 SEND-URL [Croft]

49 FORWARD_X [Altman]

50-137 Unassigned [IANA]

138 TELOPT PRAGMA LOGON [McGregory]

139 TELOPT SSPI LOGON [McGregory]

140 TELOPT PRAGMA HEARTBEAT [McGregory]

255 Extended-Options-List [RFC861]
```

B.5   File Transfer Protocol

Reply codes defined in RFC 959 include:

```
110 Restart marker reply. In this case, the text
is exact and not left to the particular
implementation; it must read: MARK yyyy = mmmm
Where yyyy is User-process data stream marker,
and mmmm server's equivalent marker (note the
spaces between markers and ''='').

120 Service ready in nnn minutes.

125 Data connection already open; transfer
starting.

150 File status okay; about to open data
connection.

200 Command okay.

202 Command not implemented, superfluous at
this site.

211 System status, or system help reply.

212 Directory status.
```

213 File status.

214 Help message. On how to use the server or the
meaning of a particular non-standard command.
This reply is useful only to the human user.

215 NAME system type. Where NAME is an official
system name from the list in the Assigned Numbers
document.

220 Service ready for new user.

221 Service closing control connection. Logged
out if appropriate.

225 Data connection open; no transfer in
progress.

226 Closing data connection. Requested file
action successful (for example, file transfer or
file abort).

227 Entering Passive Mode (h1,h2,h3,h4,p1,p2).

230 User logged in, proceed.

250 Requested file action okay, completed.

257 ``PATHNAME'' created.

331 User name okay, need password.

332 Need account for login.

350 Requested file action pending further
information.

421 Service not available, closing control
connection. This may be a reply to any command
if the service knows it must shut down.

425 Can't open data connection.

426 Connection closed; transfer aborted.

450 Requested file action not taken. File unavailable (e.g., file busy).

451 Requested action aborted: local error in processing.

452 Requested action not taken. Insufficient storage space in system.

500 Syntax error, command unrecognized. This may include errors such as command line too long.

501 Syntax error in parameters or arguments.

502 Command not implemented.

503 Bad sequence of commands.

504 Command not implemented for that parameter.

530 Not logged in.

532 Need account for storing files.

550 Requested action not taken. File unavailable (e.g., file not found, no access).

551 Requested action aborted: page type unknown.

552 Requested file action aborted. Exceeded storage allocation (for current directory or dataset).

553 Requested action not taken. File name not allowed.

B.6   Valid Schemes for Uniform Resource Identifiers

Uniform resource identifiers (URIs) identify web resources uniquely. Most web pages are HTTP resources, identified as such by the "http://" string.

Other valid schemes are listed here, taken from the IANA web site, last updated April 5, 2002.

Scheme Name	Description	Reference
ftp	File Transfer Protocol	[RFC1738]
http	Hypertext Transfer Protocol	[RFC2068]
gopher	The Gopher Protocol	[RFC1738]
mailto	Electronic mail address	[RFC2368]
news	USENET news	[RFC1738]
nntp	USENET news using NNTP access	[RFC1738]
telnet	Reference to interactive sessions	[RFC1738]
wais	Wide Area Information Servers	[RFC1738]
file	Host-specific file names	[RFC1738]
prospero	Prospero Directory Service	[RFC1738]
z39.50s	Z39.50 Session	[RFC2056]
z39.50r	Z39.50 Retrieval	[RFC2056]
cid	content identifier	[RFC2392]
mid	message identifier	[RFC2392]
vemmi	versatile multimedia interface	[RFC2122]
service	service location	[RFC2609]
imap	internet message access protocol	[RFC2192]
nfs	network file system protocol	[RFC2224]

Scheme Name	Description	Reference
acap	application configuration access Protocol	[RFC2244]
rtsp	real-time streaming protocol	[RFC2326]
tip	Transaction Internet Protocol	[RFC2371]
pop	Post Office Protocol v3	[RFC2384]
data	data	[RFC2397]
dav	dav	[RFC2518]
opaquelocktoken	opaquelocktoken	[RFC2518]
sip	session initiation protocol	[RFC2543]
tel	telephone	[RFC2806]
fax	fax	[RFC2806]
modem	modem	[RFC2806]
ldap	Lightweight Directory Access Protocol	[RFC2255]
https	Hypertext Transfer Protocol Secure	[RFC2818]
soap.beep	soap.beep	[RFCSOAP]
soap.beeps	soap.beeps	[RFCSOAP]

Reserved URI Scheme Names:

afs	Andrew File System global file names	
tn3270	Interactive 3270 emulation sessions	
mailserver	Access to data available from mail servers	

B.7   Internet Message Access Protocol

Proprietary e-mail products, designed to be implemented on an organizational LAN and served from a single organizational server, offer some useful functions and features to the end users. Storing all messages on a central server means that those messages can be backed up centrally and made accessible at a later date. It also means that users can access their mailbox from any network-connected system, not just from their own "home" system. SMTP and POP simply don't offer these amenities to users, so the Internet Message Access Protocol (IMAP) was developed.

IMAP, specified in RFC 2060, "INTERNET MESSAGE ACCESS PROTOCOL-VERSION 4rev1," defines a protocol that allows users to access and manipulate their messages stored on a remote server. By design, it allows users to read, delete, file into folders, and otherwise manipulate messages stored on a server as if they were stored on the user's own local system.

B.8   Network News Transport Protocol

Network News Transport Protocol (NNTP), as well as Calendaring and Scheduling (iCAL) and Workgroup Integration protocols, provide important collaborative tools for Internet users as well as corporate users. Calendaring and scheduling tools have long been a part of the workgroup software toolkit, but these tools have not been a traditional part of most TCP/IP application suites. That is changing, as the iCalendar and related protocols have been published as proposed Internet standards late in 1998. iCalendar, defined in RFC 2445, specifies a special MIME content type/subtype called text/calendar and specifies how that MIME type is used to carry calendar and scheduling information across network transports.

iCalendar specifies how the text/calendar MIME enclosure can be used to carry information necessary to perform calendaring and scheduling activities like setting up appointments, checking for free time, notifying participants of upcoming meetings, notifying participants of cancellation of a scheduled meeting, and other related functions.

Published as proposed standards at about the same time as iCalendar are the iTIP (RFC 2446) and iMIP (RFC 2447) protocols. iTIP, which stands for iCalendar Transport-Independent Interoperability Protocol, defines a protocol for using iCalendar data with any calendaring or scheduling system. iMIP, which stands for iCalendar Message-Based Interoperability Protocol, specifies how iCalendar and iTIP data is to be bound into internet e-mail messages for delivery. Together, these three protocols make it possible for software developers to permit users of personal productivity tools like PDA organizers as well as more sophisticated proprietary workgroup tools to interoperate with each other, independent of the proprietary products each is using.

Index